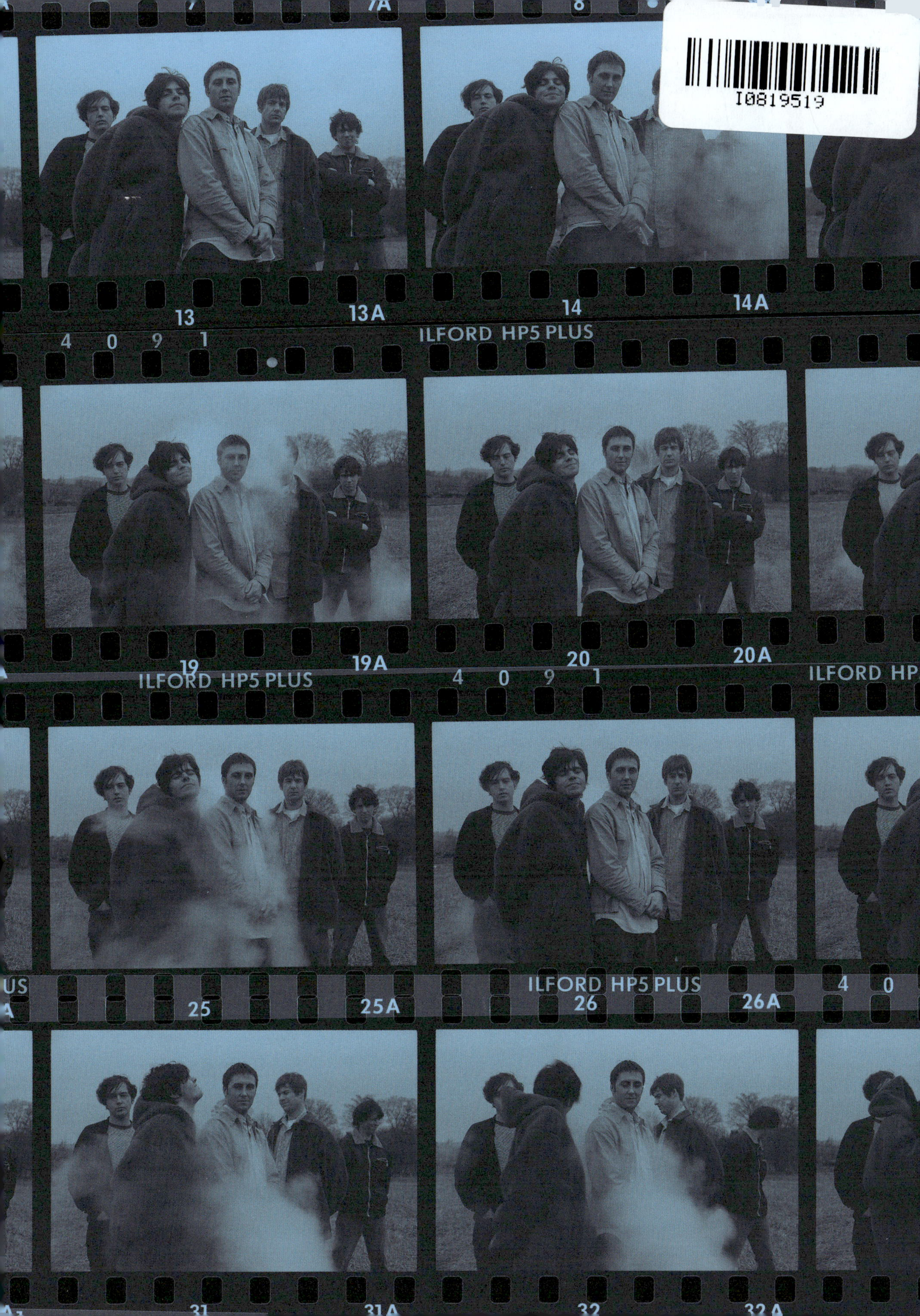

7A
8
I0819519
13
13A
14
14A
4 0 9 1
ILFORD HP5 PLUS
19
19A
20
20A
ILFORD HP5 PLUS
4 0 9 1
ILFORD HP
US
25
25A
ILFORD HP5 PLUS
26
26A
4 0
31
31A
32
32A

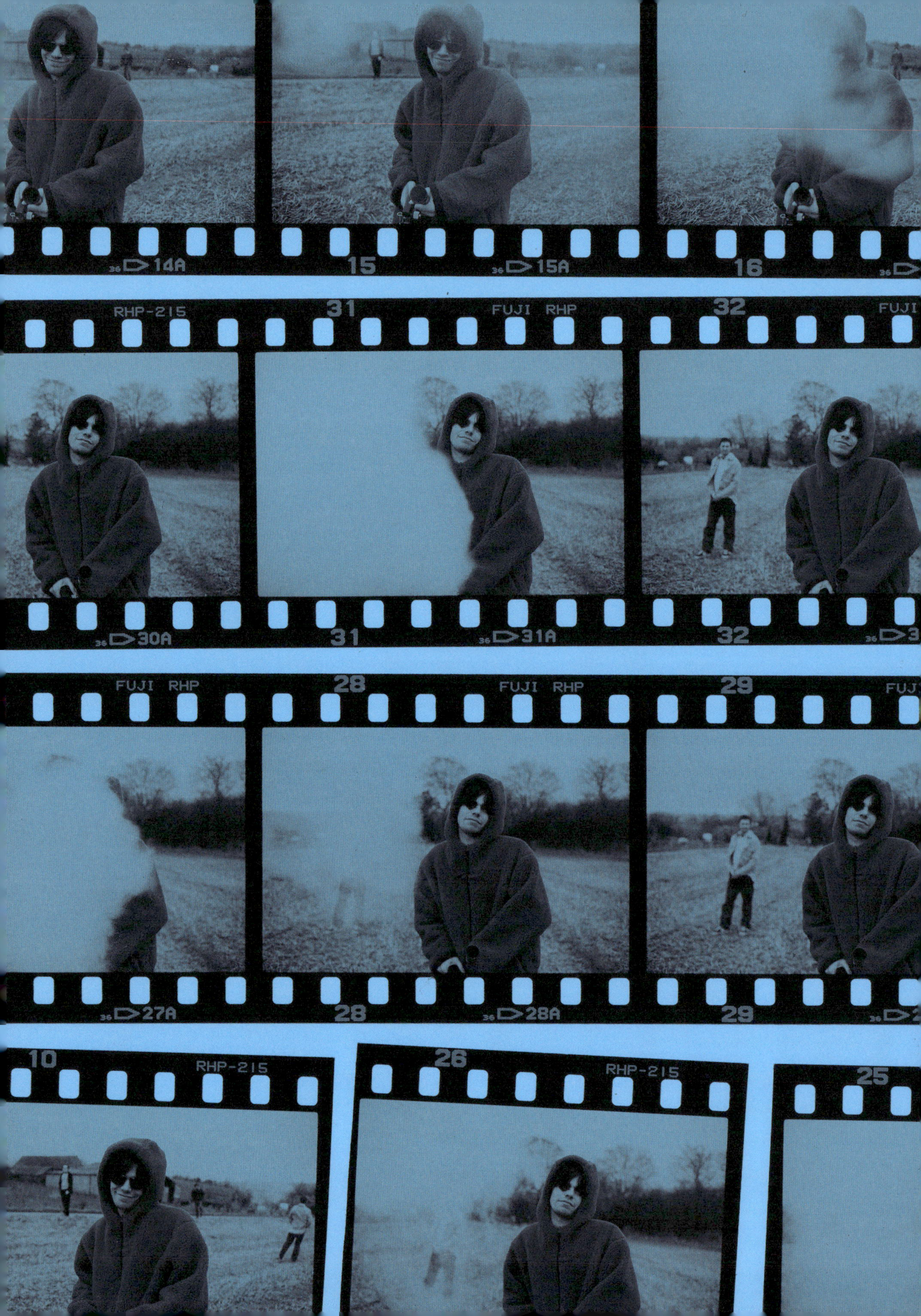
14A
15
15A
16
RHP-215
31
FUJI RHP
32
FUJI
30A
31
31A
32
FUJI RHP
28
FUJI RHP
29
27A
28
28A
29
10
RHP-215
26
RHP-215
25

How High

A Portrait of The Charlatans

Tim Burgess and Tom Sheehan

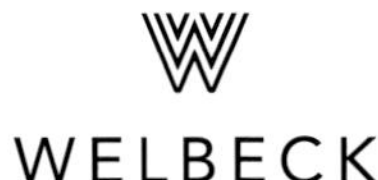
WELBECK

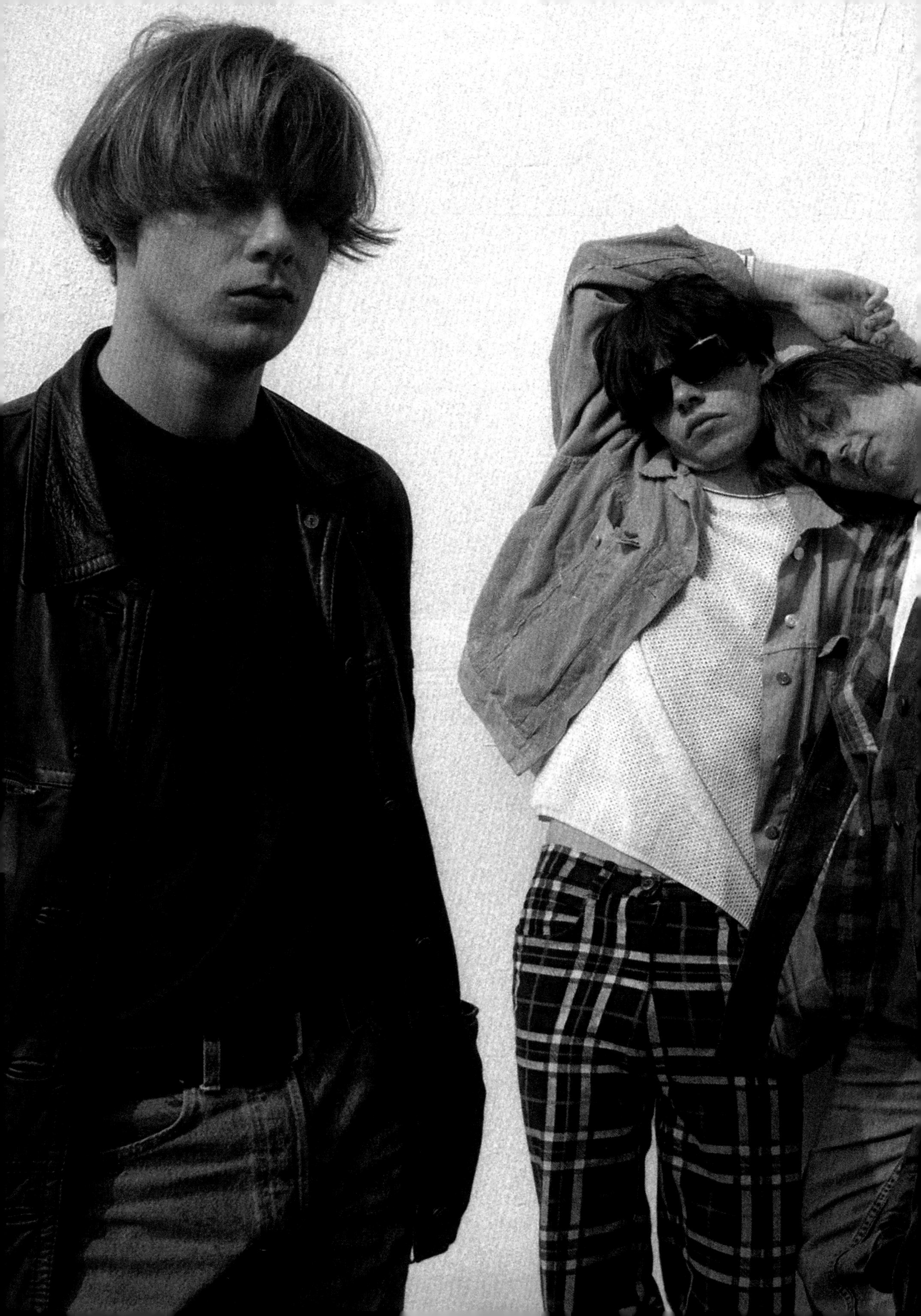

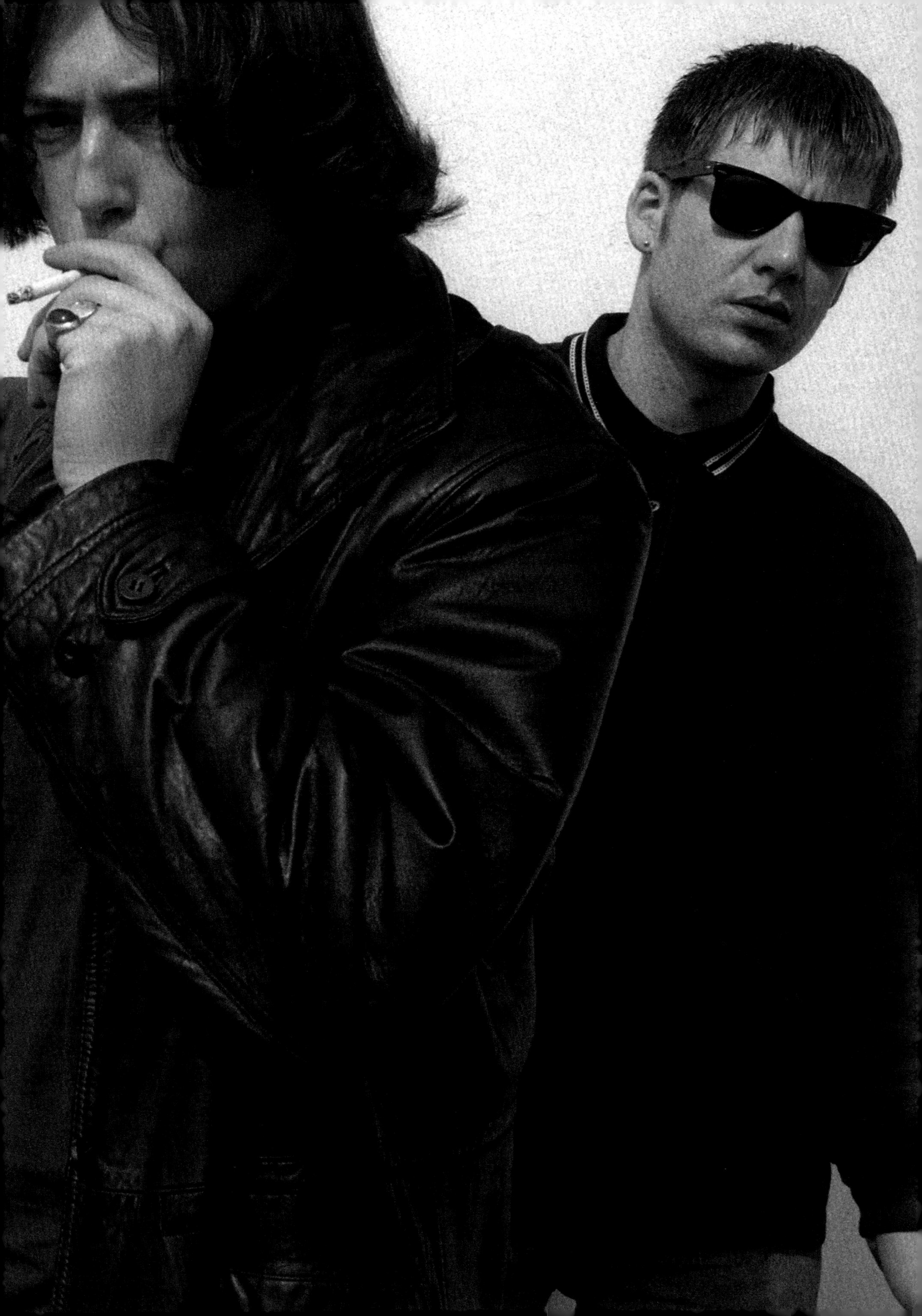

Photographs
Tom Sheehan

Words
Tim Burgess

For
Jamie, Alex and Florrie X

With thanks to:
Tim Burgess,
Carl Glover,
Joe Cottington,
Adam Powell

TS 2025

For
Morgan

With thanks to:
Martin Blunt,
Mark Collins,
Tony Rogers,
Ally Dawkins,
Nick Fraser,
Tom Sheehan

TB 2025

In Memory of Jon Brookes and Rob Collins

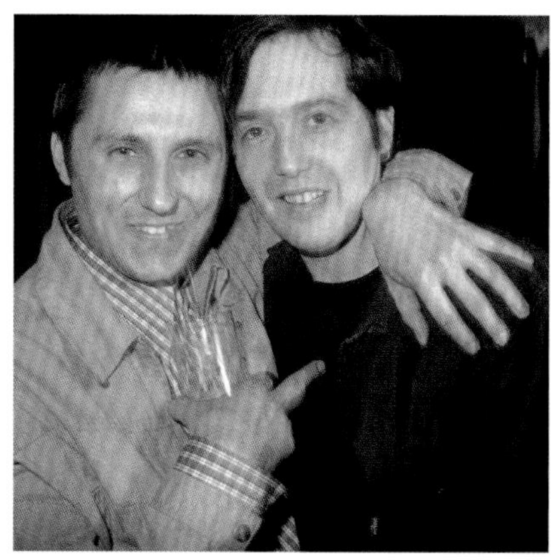

Contents

Introduction by Tom Sheehan

The first thing I noticed about The Charlatans was their name. I knew The Charlatans as the band who were, to all intents and purposes, the first psychedelic group in San Francisco in the 1960s. But here was an editorial piece in the *Melody Maker*, a little half page showing a solo picture of Tim on some non-league-looking football terrace. And I thought, interesting name, but that band needs some decent pictures taken.

A few months went by and, lo and behold, I get asked to go down to Bristol to shoot them, before and during a gig at the Bierkeller there. As was often the case with new, young bands like that, there was a bit of bravado. They were from the North, I was a cockney, I'm from the gutter press, they were throwing the gauntlet down to me a little bit, so I needed to find my way in. I wanted to bring out the lead singer in some way, but I got pushback from them, "no, no, we're a group, we only do group shots".

On the train down I'd spotted a scrapyard, so I took the band there and gave the guy on the gate £10 for a beer, went in and took some pictures. Then we went back to my hotel room, cleared all of the furniture out of the way and did some shots there. There was one shot of the group with their eyes closed, which I explained was in homage to The Band's fourth album, *Cahoots*, which had Richard Avedon's portrait of the five of them with their eyes closed on the back cover. I asked Tim to "open his minces" to complete the shot, which he just about understood after the twelfth explanation. ("Minces, mince pies, eyes.")

I think it was that homage that set the scene for us working together. A love of music, it's a shorthand that helps to create an understanding. Tim and I would talk about the records we loved, he would lay stuff on me and I'd lay stuff on him and it cemented a kind of mutual respect.

I watched the band live at the gig at the Bierkeller that night and it was absolutely astonishing, sweat dripping off the ceiling, the lot.

One of our other early encounters was a trip to LA in 1991. It's always important when shooting a band to highlight the lead singer somehow, but I was still struggling to get a shot of Tim on his own, and the only way I could do it was to ambush him. We were in a taxi driving down Sunset. I knew the Sunset Grill was coming up, so I said to Tim, "Have you ever heard the Eagles' song, 'Sunset Grill'?" Mentioning the Eagles at that time was probably a hanging offence – though I maintain they made some great songs – but thankfully it got Tim's interest, and he was happy to stop the car and jump out for a few shots.

One of those shots made the *Melody Maker* cover and I remember when I showed it to the rest of the band a month or so later, they thought it was great, Martin said he couldn't believe how good Tim looked. And that was it, after that they were happy to leave the photoshoots to Tim and it was the devil's own job to get them together again. So much for "we only do group shots". I think it helped that the rest of the band wanted to avoid the early starts often required for a shoot.

We started working together quite a bit after that and I think the band began to realize that I wasn't the enemy, that I was honest in what I wanted to do, I was never going to stitch them up. I was spending lots of my time with them at Monnow Valley Studio, staying for three or four days at a time while they were recording. For *The Charlatans* album we had an idea to create a montage of images for the inside, so I'd go down and shoot lots of different moments and environments to build up a portfolio of different images we could use. I used to do small prints and Polaroids, and we had a "Wall of Shame" in the studio where we'd stick dodgy Polaroids and news cuttings and all sorts of nonsense. My days there weren't structured in the way that the band's days were – at least loosely, they were there to record an album, so they had to focus. But my time was spent looking for opportunities, to pull someone aside here or go in and take some pictures there, just keep it relaxed and spontaneous.

I've been lucky enough to have long working relationships with some incredible bands and artists, including The Cure, Radiohead, Manic Street Preachers and Paul Weller. But it's with The Charlatans that I probably have the biggest body of work, partly because of that freedom, that lack of formal structure and the variety of the shots it gave us.

I look back at these photographs with a lot of fondness and a lot of happiness. We achieved a lot together, and a friendship grew with the band and particularly Tim. I love Tim's enthusiasm for music, he has a thirst for it that's insatiable, and I find that really endearing. I can't take music that way, I can't process it and turn it into something new, but Tim really can, he'll lift something, play with it and make it his own. His double solo album, *Typical Music*, is four sides of brilliant music, and I can see where he's taken different influences and used them to make something of his own. And he brings that creativity back to The Charlatans and enriches what they do.

Tim and I certainly spent a lot of time on the blower down the years, talking absolute tosh about records. We still do, and long may it continue.

Tom Sheehan

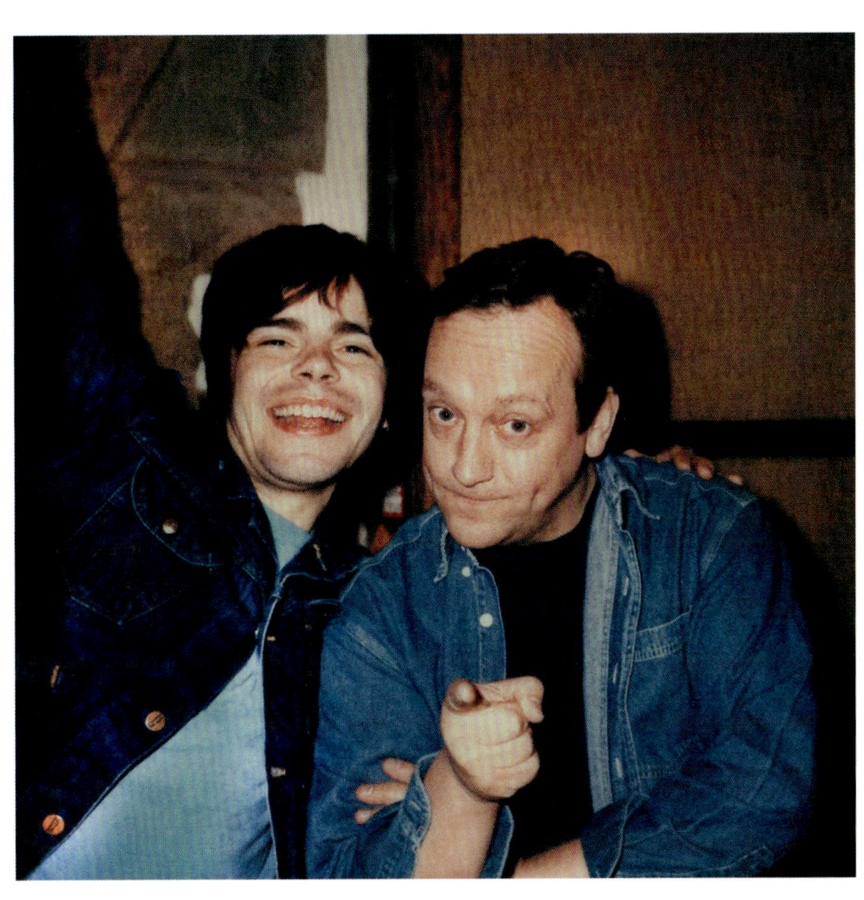

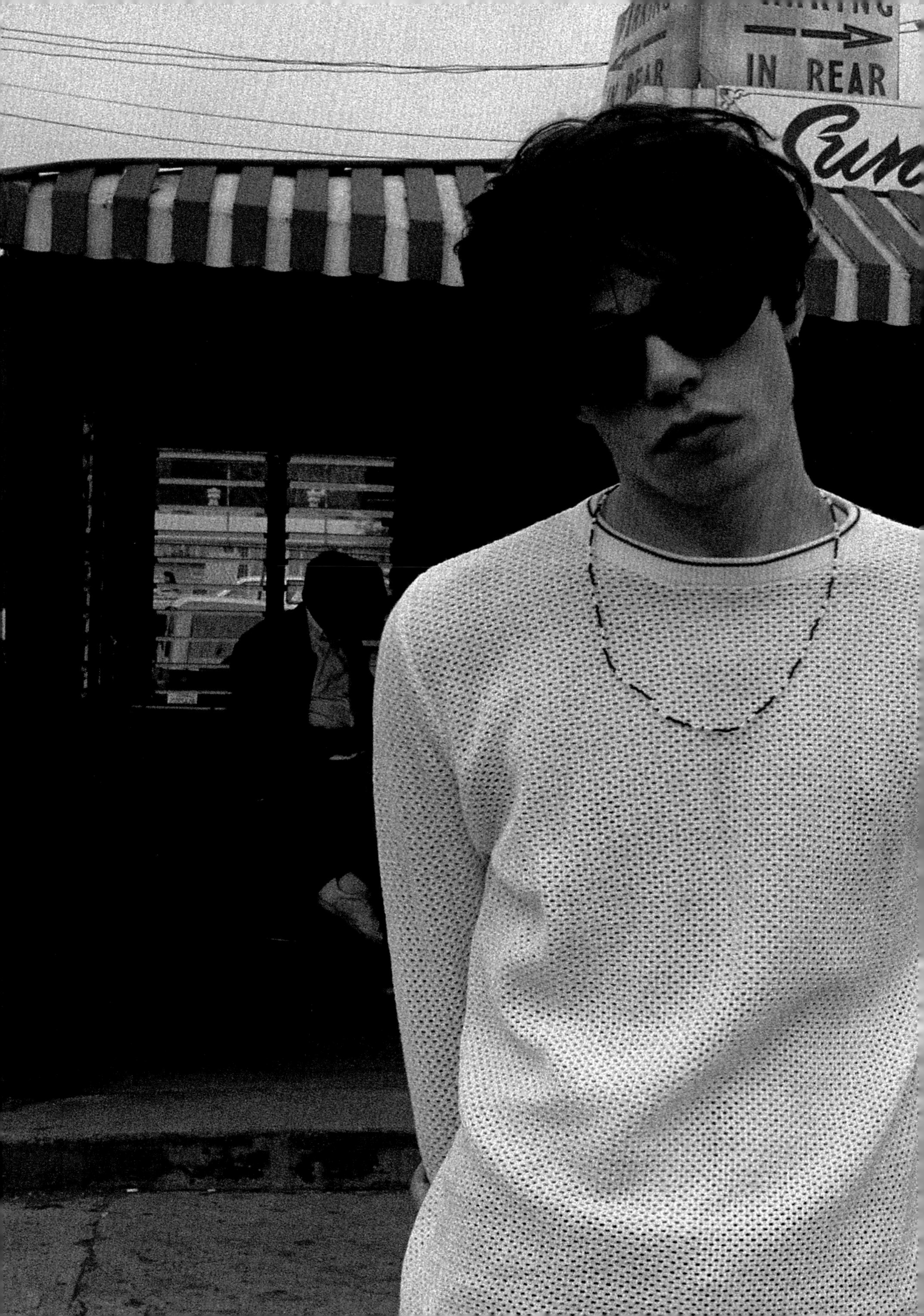
IN REAR

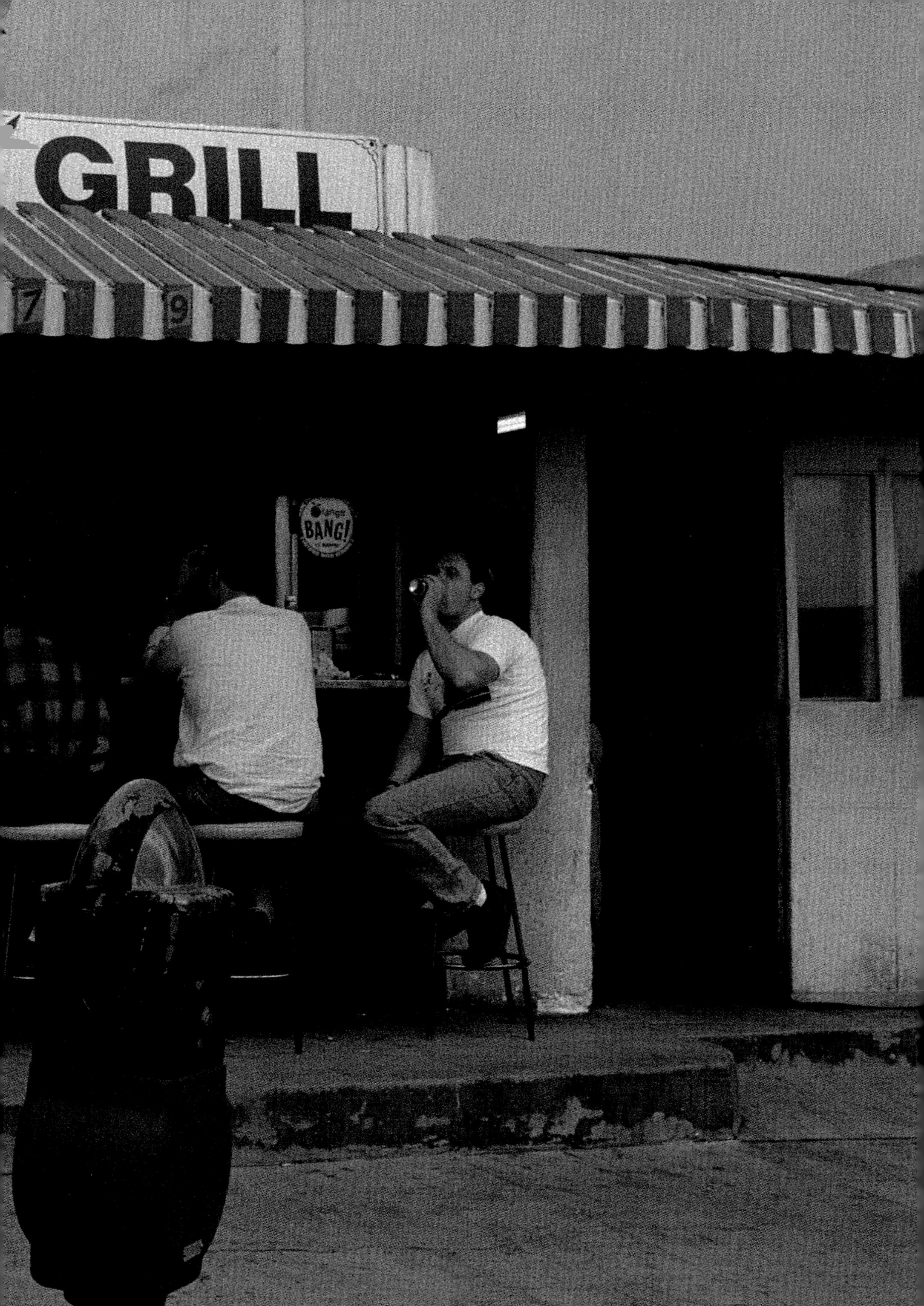
GRILL
BANG!

Introduction by Tim Burgess

They say a picture is worth a thousand words, yet here is me writing thousands of words in a book of pictures.

Best that we begin at the beginning.

As a band, The Charlatans felt untouchable live. A mixture of the hubris of youth and the fact that we simply were.

We were playing, writing and recording as much as we could in the early months of 1990. We'd do any gigs that would have us; jumping in the van, playing a show, then heading back in the early hours for a bleary day's work in the jobs we wanted to leave.

Recording was a nocturnal affair, to make the most of lower rates at local studios. Writing was an as-and-when occurrence. Breaks at work, over the phone – after 6pm due to parental demands for off-peak pricing, Wednesday evenings and Sunday afternoons in Wednesbury, in the Midlands.

It felt like we were part of the zeitgeist. There was a groundswell of like-minded haircuts and attitudes, and the northwest was the epicentre of a cultural earthquake. To us, the visuals were as important as the sound, both onstage while we played and off. Lava lamps and oil wheels heightened the feeling into a holistic experience for audience and band alike.

It was the beginning of it all, and, with the exception of being photographed by our roadie Derek Phillip, we were very new to the art of having our pictures taken.

When we released our first single, "Indian Rope", most of the pictures I remember seeing were either Derek's or photographs that fans brought along with them to the next gig. Then, for a spell post "The Only One I Know", our second single, I barely remember a photograph being taken by anyone else but Tom Sheehan.

I first encountered Tom in a hotel foyer in Bristol and we became fast friends. On that day, the rest of The Charlatans and I jumped into a van and headed down to a local scrapyard for a feature in the *Melody Maker* and our first full band shoot for a national publication. We loved the photos and we took Tom's details.

Tom's knowledge of mid- to late-60s psychedelic bands played a big part in our friendship. The Byrds, Jefferson Airplane, Love and Buffalo Springfield we all agreed on, but Tom's suggested listening of Boz Scaggs and Grateful Dead gave us something new to explore.

Tom had a very strong view of what looked right in a photograph. His mastery of cockney rhyming slang was often lost on us, but we picked up on what he meant by his general enthusiasm or otherwise. The chemistry worked so well that we created a great body of work together, much of which you're just about to see.

Lots of the photographs in this book have never been shown before, and going through them with Tom took us all back and reconnected us with times gone by. Some amazing memories and a lasting friendship.

Tom captured the times – the lows and many highs – and shared them all with us, documenting, encouraging and capturing a real, authentic timeline of fantastic pictures. He captured so many front covers, so many live shots and fly-on-the-wall moments. In the gatefold sleeve of our fourth album, *The Charlatans*, there are 99 pictures taken by Tom. (The hundredth is by Martin, a picture of his dog, MaGoo.)

We became a gang together, the six of us. Our songs were climbing the charts, we were travelling the world and Tom was documenting it all.

The live shots really capture where the band was at in those early days, pre-*Some Friendly*, our debut album, and right in the thick of the mania that came with "The Only One I Know". More than that, they also signposted to where we were heading.

In the early days of The Charlatans, there was a policy that I wasn't necessarily aware of. A silent pact ushered in whereby the singer was not photographed on his own for fear that he might be perceived as a pop star.

As with many policies, late nights, a heavy schedule and life in general conspired to bring about changes. Lie-ins after gigs, the potential of early-morning flash bulbs and the realization that our new lives were going to be around for a while made the lure of the photoshoot much less appealing to everybody else. So Tom and I became somewhat of a double act. I couldn't get out of it because no singer and no band meant no pictures at all and, anyway, I really enjoyed it. Being a pop star, talking music, going to record shops, having your photograph taken and being on the cover of magazines had been a dream of mine since I was a kid.

Everything moved fairly fast, but we were taking it in our stride. *Melody Maker*, *NME*, *Smash Hits*, *Top of the Pops*, LA, A Gathering of the Tribes, KROQ, we ticked them all off. Martin and I even did a feature for *Number One* magazine.

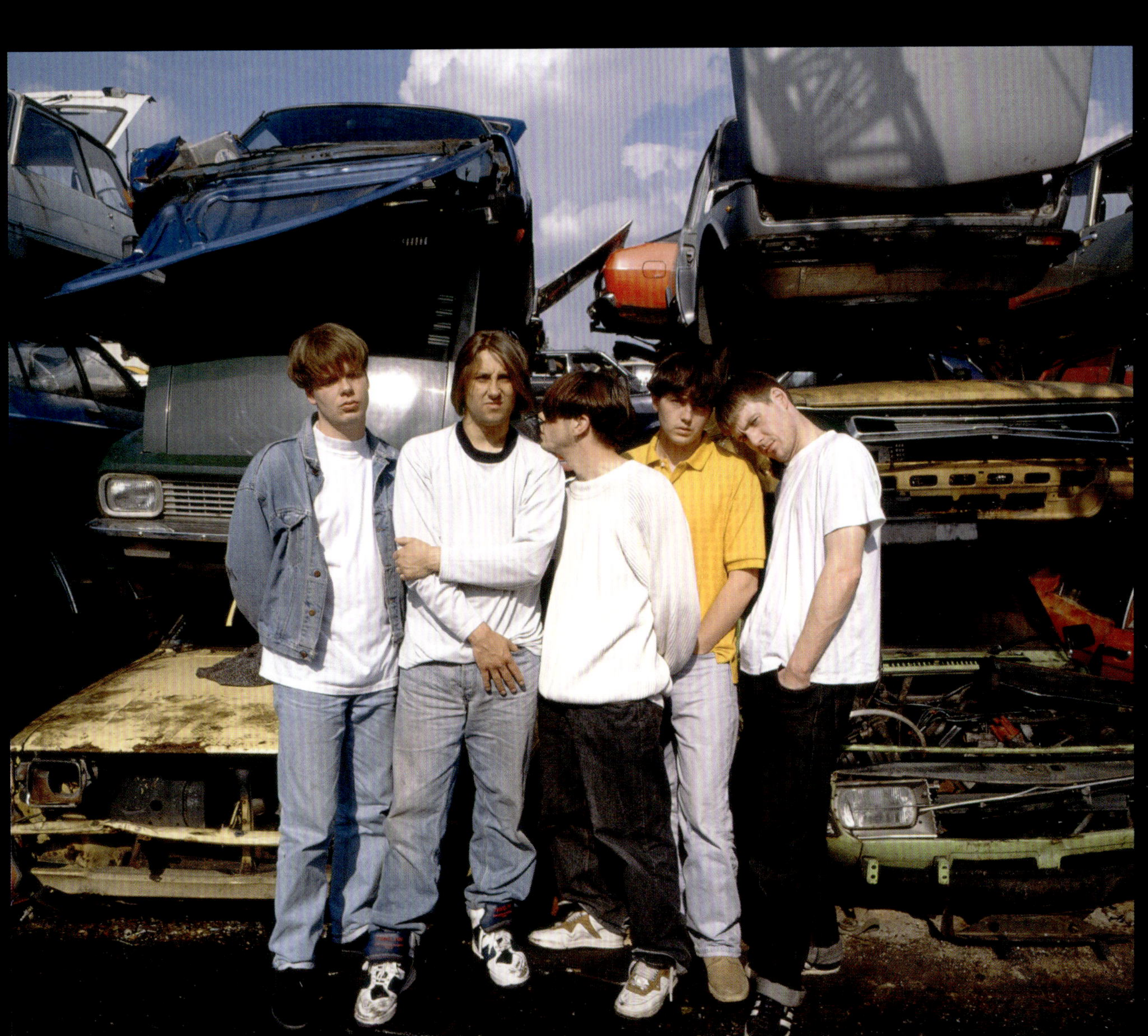

But we were still battling with the basics of photoshoots, like the five of us all having both eyes open at the same time. Top tips were learnt swiftly. Foremost of those was "never get your hair cut the night before a photo session". This was adhered to only after I had committed that cardinal sin. Don't wear sunglasses indoors. ("You're not Lou Reed. He can, you can't. Them's the rules.") Never drink, go to a party or stay up late beforehand. This last one was never done by all of us at the same time. But we decided three out of five would be seen as a success.

Whenever Tom was taking our picture he would always have a portable stereo and the best music. We were fairly self-conscious, although it might not have seemed it, and the sterile backdrop of a studio in Clerkenwell wasn't the best inspiration for throwing shapes or moody demeanours.

One of my favourite photographs ever happened outside the Sunset Grill in Los Angeles. It was late and we were heading to KROQ's studios. The band were staying at the Hyatt Hotel (in the legendary building previously known as Riot House, on the Sunset Strip) and I stayed with a friend at the Chateau Marmont.

When we met halfway at the Sunset Grill before piling into the car to the radio station, Tom offered to come along with me and a journalist called Ted Mico, but could we rattle off "a few frames" as he called them, before we "hightail it", as he would say in his cockney hip speak. I was in my best *Head*-era Micky Dolenz state of mind, complete with beads and Airtex, mesh, white, long-sleeved top. I was ready.

Tom's feel for the right moment was vindicated by the fact that one of the pictures was used for the following week's front cover of *Melody Maker*.

The backdrops of our shoots together were many and varied, from the glamour of the Capital Records headquarters, the majesty of the Empire State Building, the down-at-heel Joshua Tree Hotel and the eternally grim Britannia Hotel on Portland Street in Manchester.

Throughout the years we talked a lot with Tom, whether while waiting for the light to change or the mood to take us, and just because he was great company. Subjects varied from our favourite Bob Dylan albums to his on-the-road hijinks with the likes of Ozzy Osbourne and Public Enemy, through to stories that can't be repeated for fear of him breaking non-disclosure agreements with past "clients". There was no afternoon that couldn't be improved by a couple of hours in a backstreet bar talking about music. I loved hearing tales of his home life and adventures with his kids back home in Croydon.

The natural next step was for us to talk about cover artwork for records. Kim Peters did our early sleeves and still works with us to this day on video footage and live shows. In 1994 we started working with Tom on sleeve designs. "Crashin' In", released on Boxing Day that same year, was the first record cover we worked on together. The end result was a brilliant shot capturing The Charlatans on a street corner outside Rob Collins' house in Bloxwich, inspired by a Beastie Boys' portrait that we all loved. The only other person in the image was a shadowy old bloke in a white mac shambling by. Fast-forward a few years and we were in Northwich for the cover of our compilation album, *Melting Pot*. The final version we settled on had the same old man checking in on us, something that wasn't noticed until months after the album came out. In another quirk of fate, our future keyboard player Tony Rogers lived on the same street as Rob, but at the time he didn't know any of us.

In three years, we spent 19 unforgettable months in Monmouth, only leaving to go out on tour, then returning as soon as we could. In that time we recorded *Up To Our Hips*, our eponymous fourth album, and *Tellin' Stories*. Steve Hillage told us we should head straight back into the studio once Rob Collins had served his sentence in early 1994 [he served 4 of 8 months] – the exact piece of advice we needed.

Mark and I had written one song together out of ten for *Up To Our Hips*. We wrote ten out of twelve for *The Charlatans* album, after conceptualizing what we were going to do on a pair of lilos in Costa del Sol. Tom documented some of the writing sessions, which took place in my flat in Chalk Farm, London, and listened keenly to skeletal demos of "Bullet Comes", "Just When You're Thinkin' Things Over" and "Tell Everyone".

Tom took the front cover image. Anyone looking at this image will probably assume that it's a composite, but it's not. It was our difficult second number one album and it showed we were here to stay, which may not have been news to our fans but it was something that we were getting used to. The photograph is a classic, capturing the band in our new-found notoriety. Rob was on fire during the making of *The Charlatans*. To me, looking back now, his aura was fractured when he spent time in prison, and afterwards he seemed to get more distant. Sadly, I can see it quite clearly in this photograph.

According to either tradition or urban myth, some cultures believe that a photograph takes a piece of the soul of the subject. That might be partially true, but it only borrows it. It hands it back when you look at the pictures years later. You suddenly know in an instant the version of you that existed then.

Looking back at Tom Sheehan's photographs is akin to hopping into a time machine and meeting all the different versions of me over the past 35 years or so. Some are a nervous kid thrust into the limelight. I tried to seem cockier and more confident, especially at a photoshoot, but the real me is always in there somewhere. Whatever state I happened to be in.

Tim Burgess

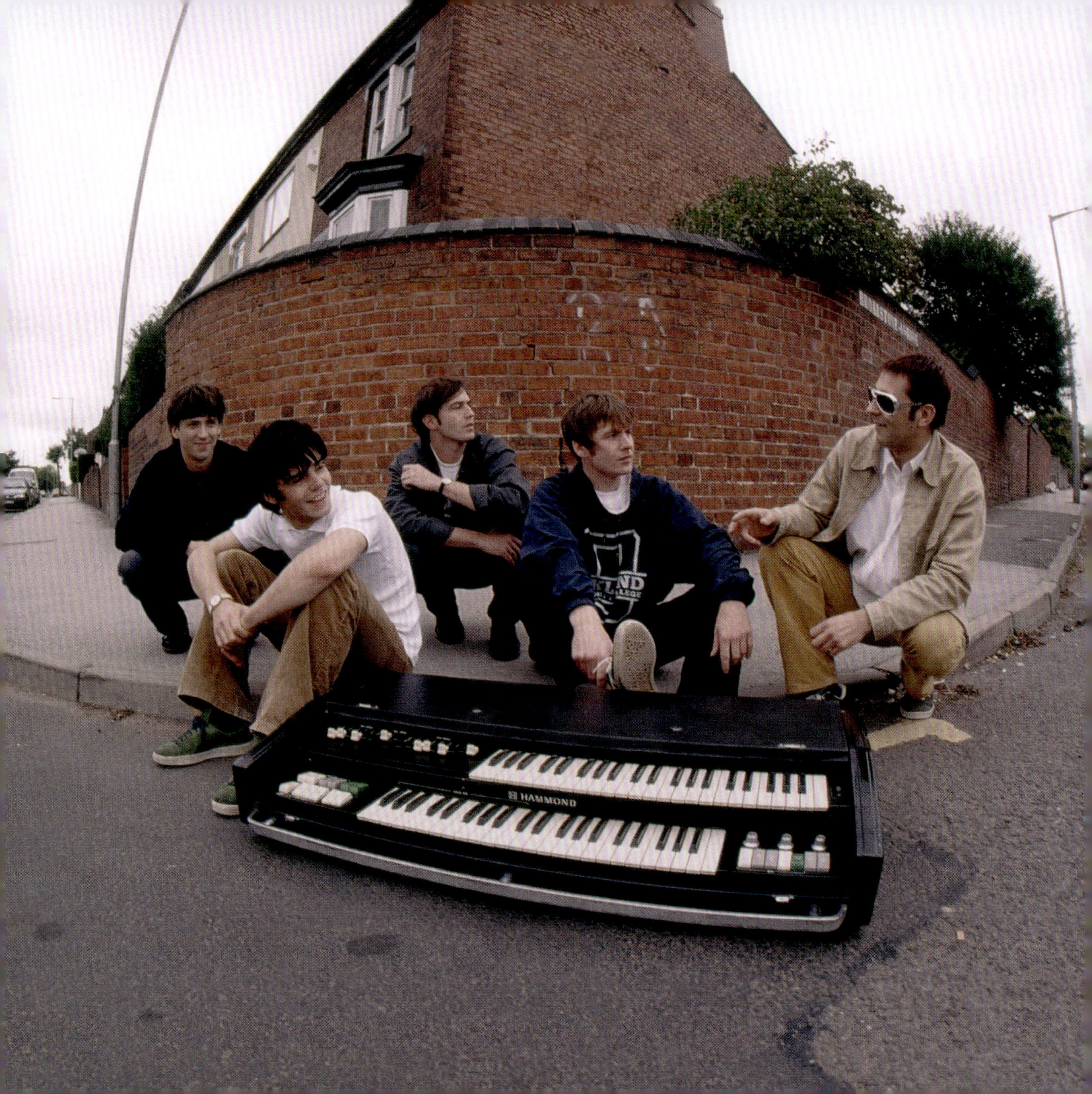
HAMMOND

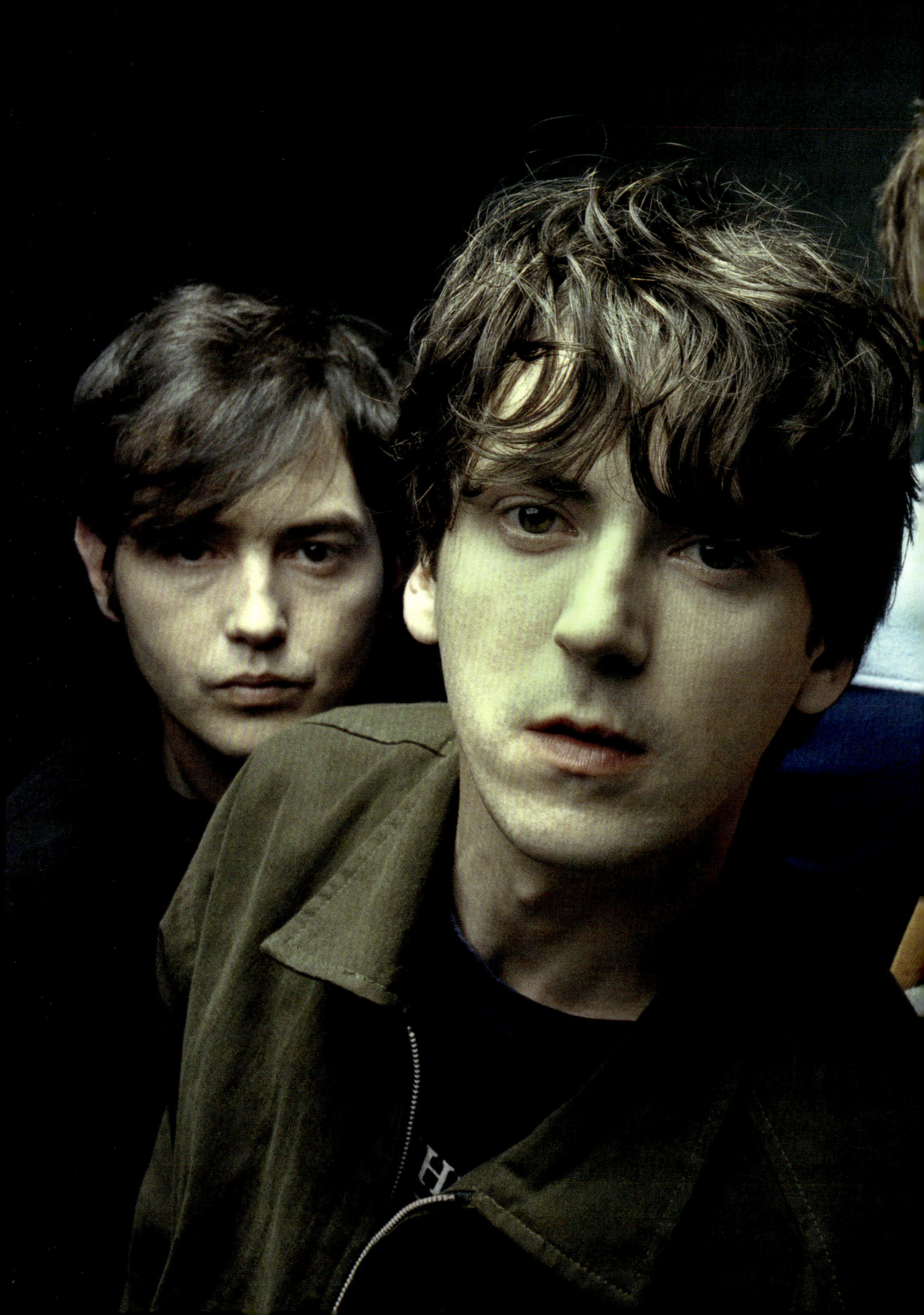

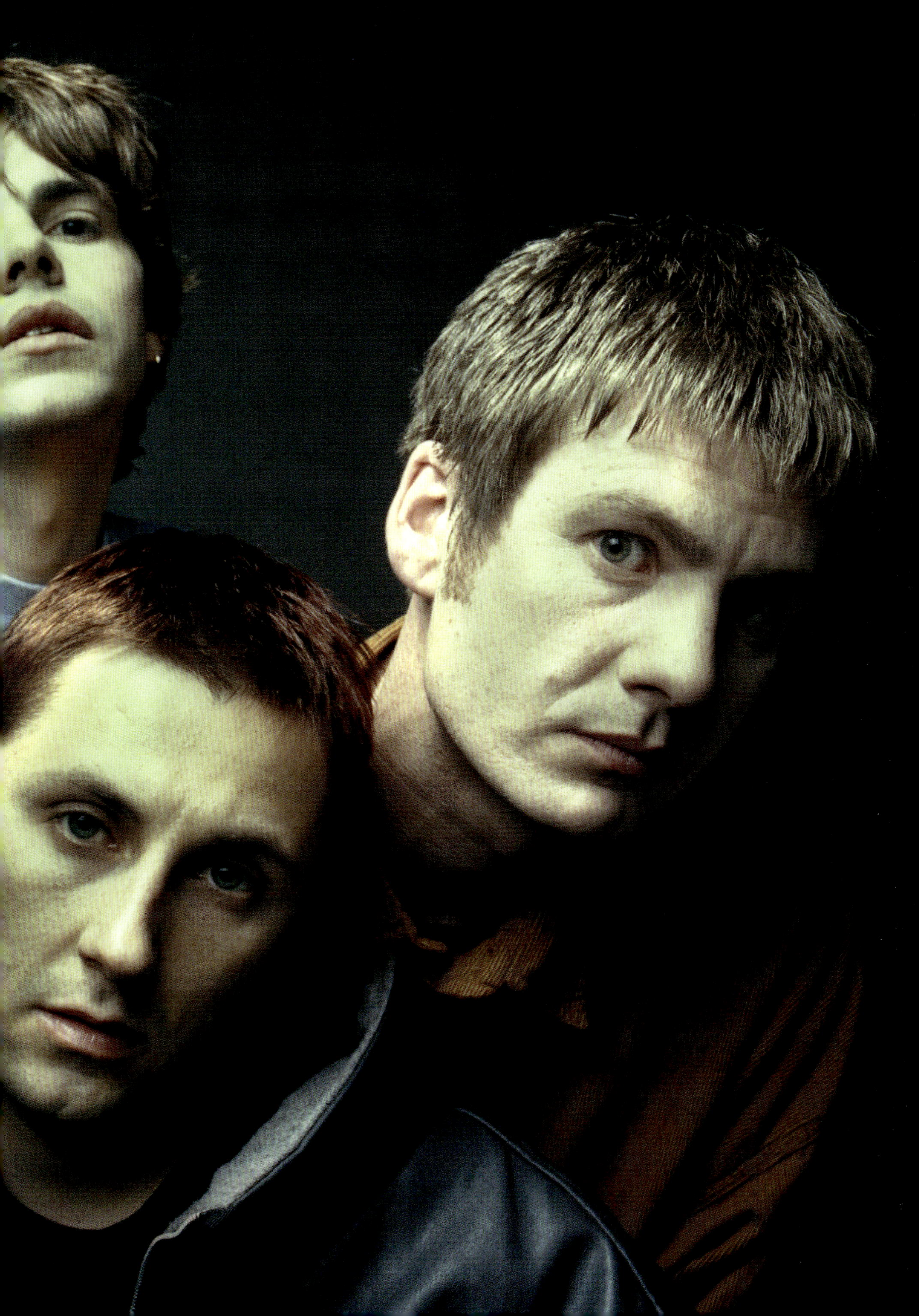

The first shoot that was organized by Tom was in Bristol, on the day of our gig at the Bierkeller on 30 May 1990, my 23rd birthday. Times were changing fast for us. Up until then we had been getting in touch with people asking them to play our records, interview us and take our photos, but now actual magazines and music weeklies were contacting us. We'd played at Northwich Memorial Hall earlier that month and "The Only One I Know" was out and starting to make waves worldwide.

Times were hugely exciting, but there was also a fear that everything could implode and we'd end up in the *Where Are They Now?* features in those same magazines that were celebrating us just a couple of years later. We wanted to enjoy every moment, but in the back of our minds we were figuring out what we were going to do to be around for the longest time possible.

Lots of people think that at this stage bands are dreaming of five-star hotels and heart-shaped swimming pools, but it's closer to the truth that our dreams were not having to go back to our regular jobs. I left ICI in Runcorn in the January of that year. My boss kindly let me know that they would keep my job open "just in case" I needed it. At the time I took this to be a generous gesture, but writing it now I am thinking that he didn't believe we stood a chance of "making it big" – and why would we? Northwich had a tenuous grip on the history of rock 'n' roll thus far. The Beatles had played at the Memorial Hall, as had The Cure, The Rolling Stones and others, but the venue's place in the pages of music folklore pretty much ended there. But the petrochemicals sales world's loss was music's gain (citation needed).

Our influence had spread from a few friends to our ever-growing audience, and the measures of this became slightly surreal. Sutton's, the barbershop I frequented, started reporting an uptick in kids coming in asking for a "Tim Burgess" – or just bringing in a photo of me. "As many boys as there are girls," was my favourite quote from Dean, who cut my hair and was now "taking bookings".

So, we arrived in Bristol to meet Tom with a certain swagger and new-found confidence. Looking back now, I think we were cocky and drunk. Tom was a well-seasoned pro, probably in his 40s, so to us he seemed to be an elder statesman from another generation. He brought with him cockney rhyming slang, a love of Dylan and bands like The Beau Brummels and Delaney & Bonnie. He loved what he'd heard of our music, we'd seen his name next to photos of Dinosaur Jr., Madonna and Siouxsie, so that was good enough for us.

Tom had arrived in Bristol the day before and he led us to a scrapyard that he'd already scoped out. As we were to discover, outside of studios and on stage at venues, scrapyards would become a regular haunt, as they were a favourite setting of photographers at the time. We took the approach that photos would feature all five band members, which sometimes went against what magazines had requested from the photographer, but we stood our ground. Tom has always joked that there was a moment in time a couple of years later, especially for early morning shoots, when it was agreed that "everyone didn't have to be there".

From morning to soundcheck to the actual gig, we split our time between an interview with the *Melody Maker* journalist and shoots with Tom at the venue, his hotel room and at the scrapyard among the mothballed Skodas, Saabs and Allegros.

If you're in any doubt that this was 1990, my Travel Fox trainers carbon-date the shoot accurately.

Bands in the 80s had gone for outlandish clothes from piratical to baroque, Edwardian and everything in between, but we played gigs and had photoshoots in whatever we happened to be wearing at the time. Jon Brookes and Martin Blunt wore white T-shirts, I had my school cricket jumper on, Jon Baker rocked the "Tennessee Tuxedo", aka double denim, and Rob went for desert boots and a canary-yellow polo shirt.

The five of us could never sync up our eyes-open/eyes-shut status, but I had the advantage via my fringe of it not being obvious whether my eyes were open or closed. In the session at Tom's hotel – The Holiday Inn – it looks like we were experimenting with band members consciously having their eyes closed.

Later that night Tom got in amongst the audience at our sold-out Bierkeller gig, took photos on stage and became an important new team member of our soon-to-be-legendary after-show parties – aka a pack of cigarettes and a six-pack of warm lager in the dressing room.

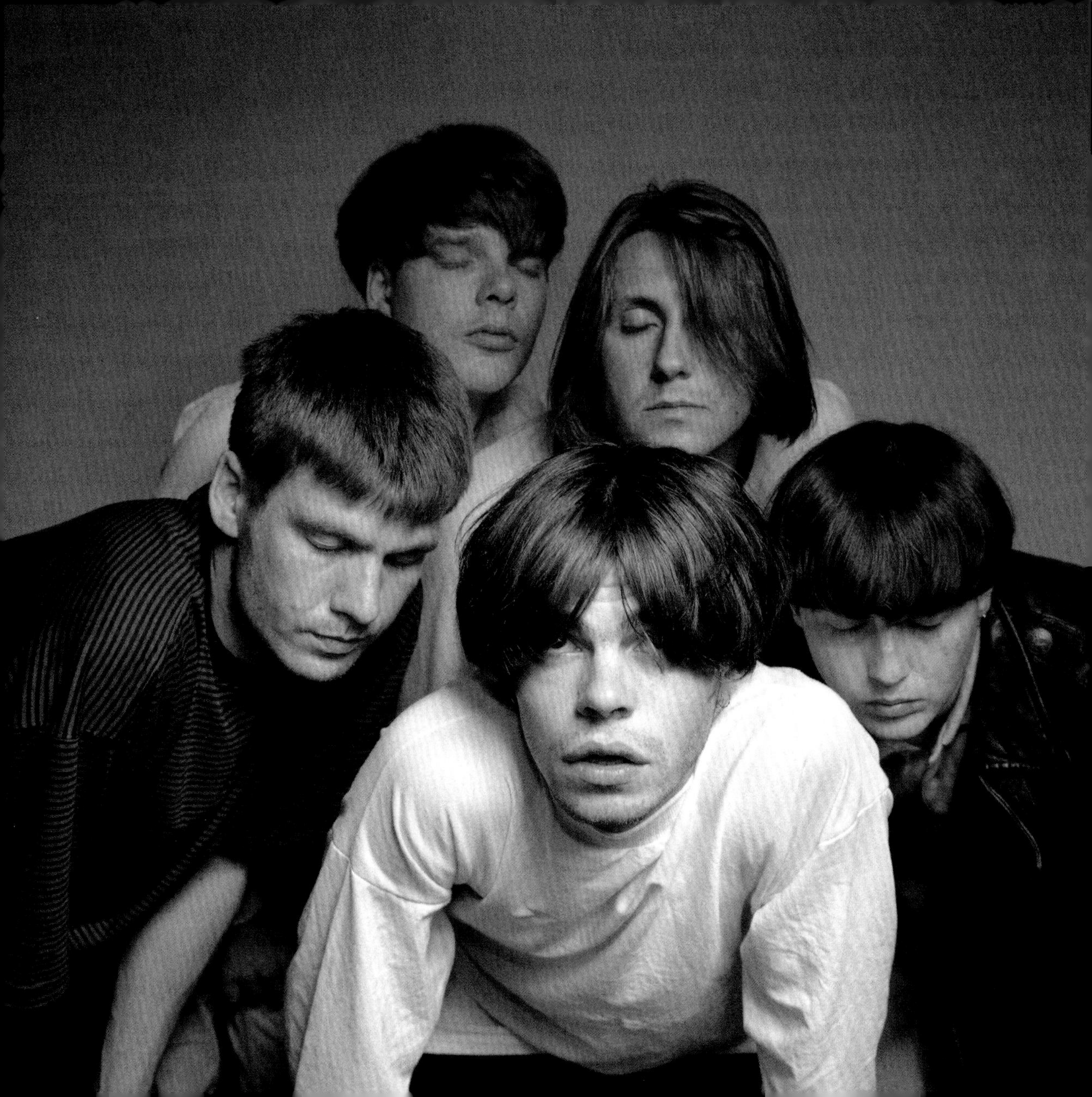

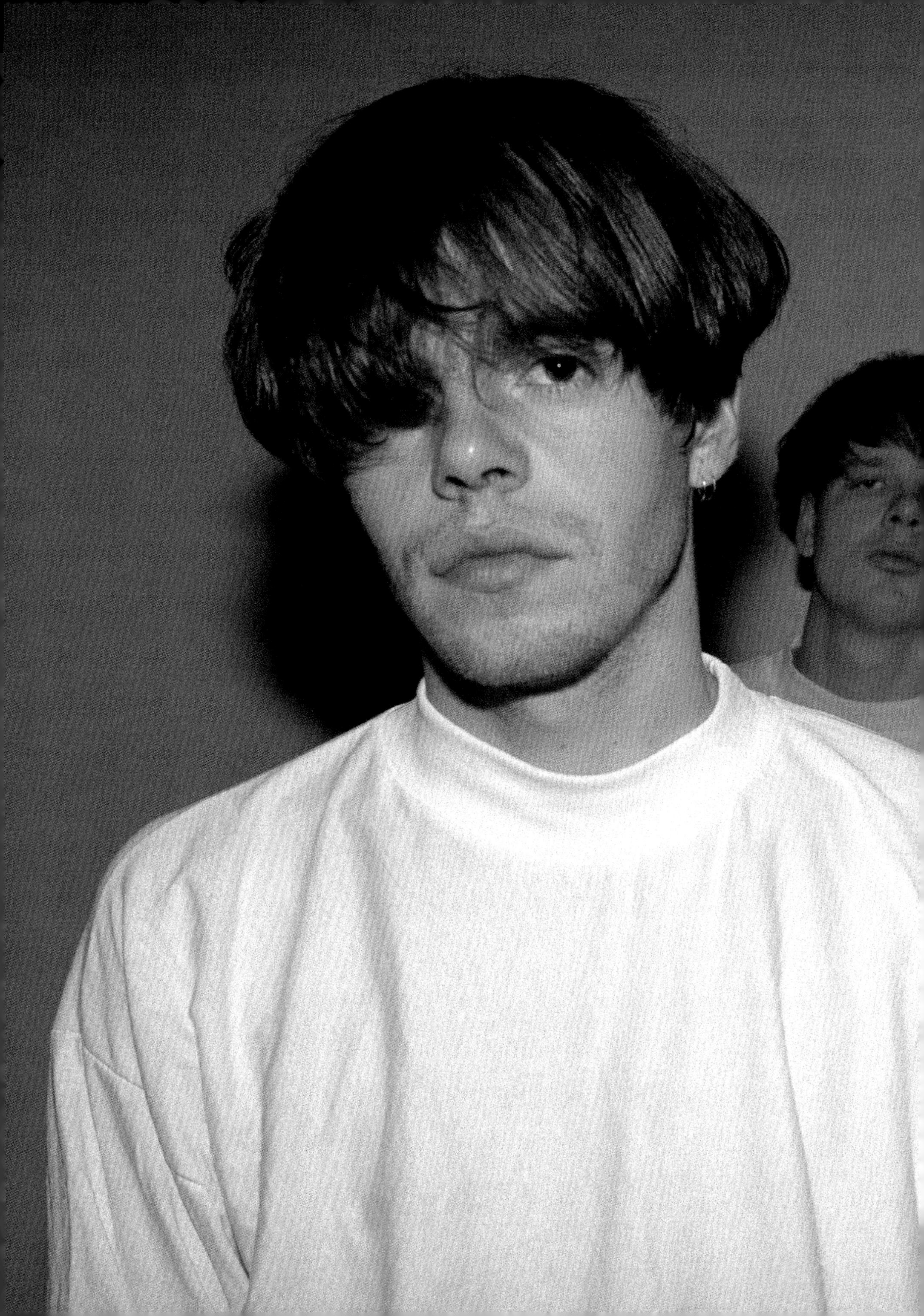

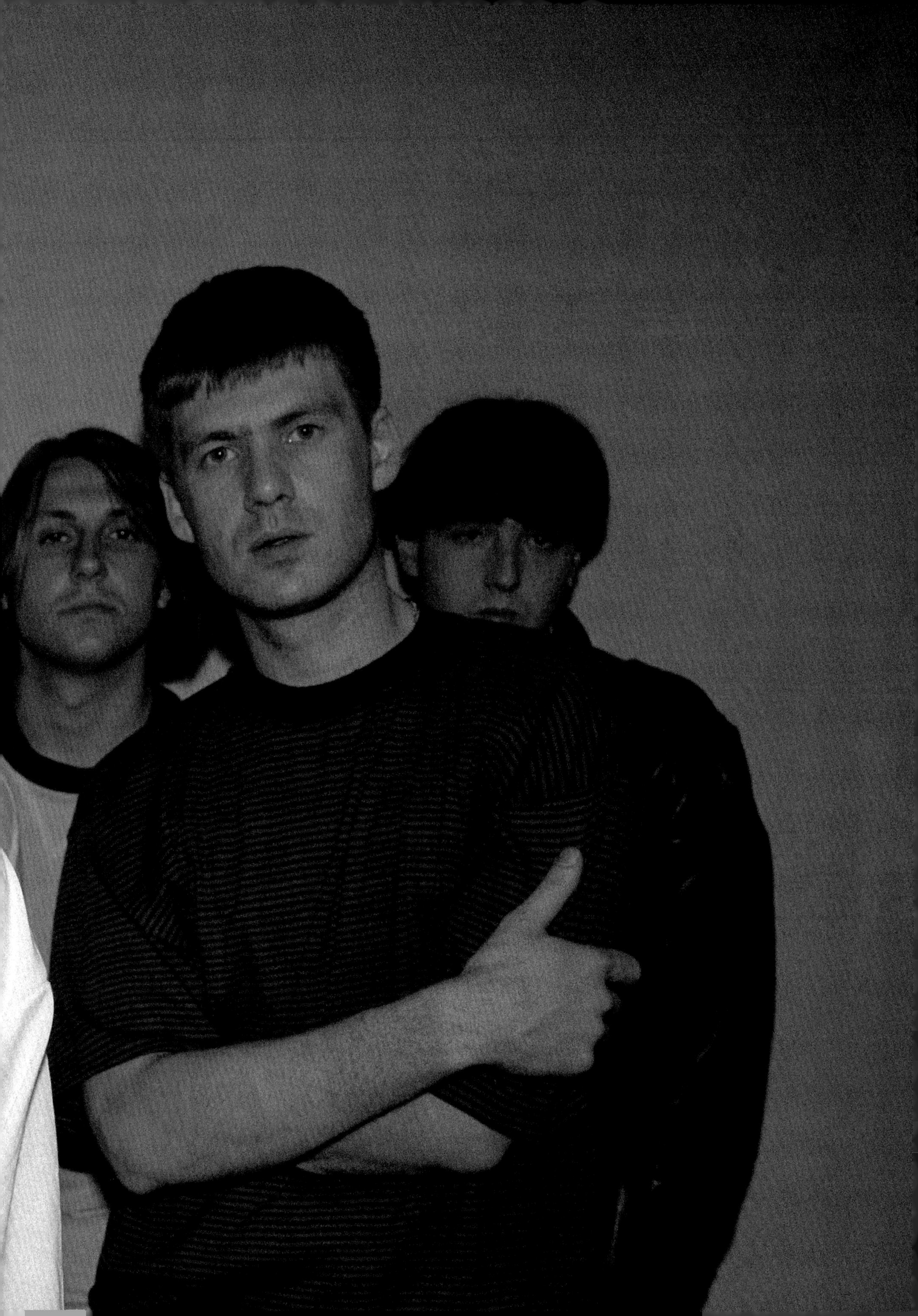

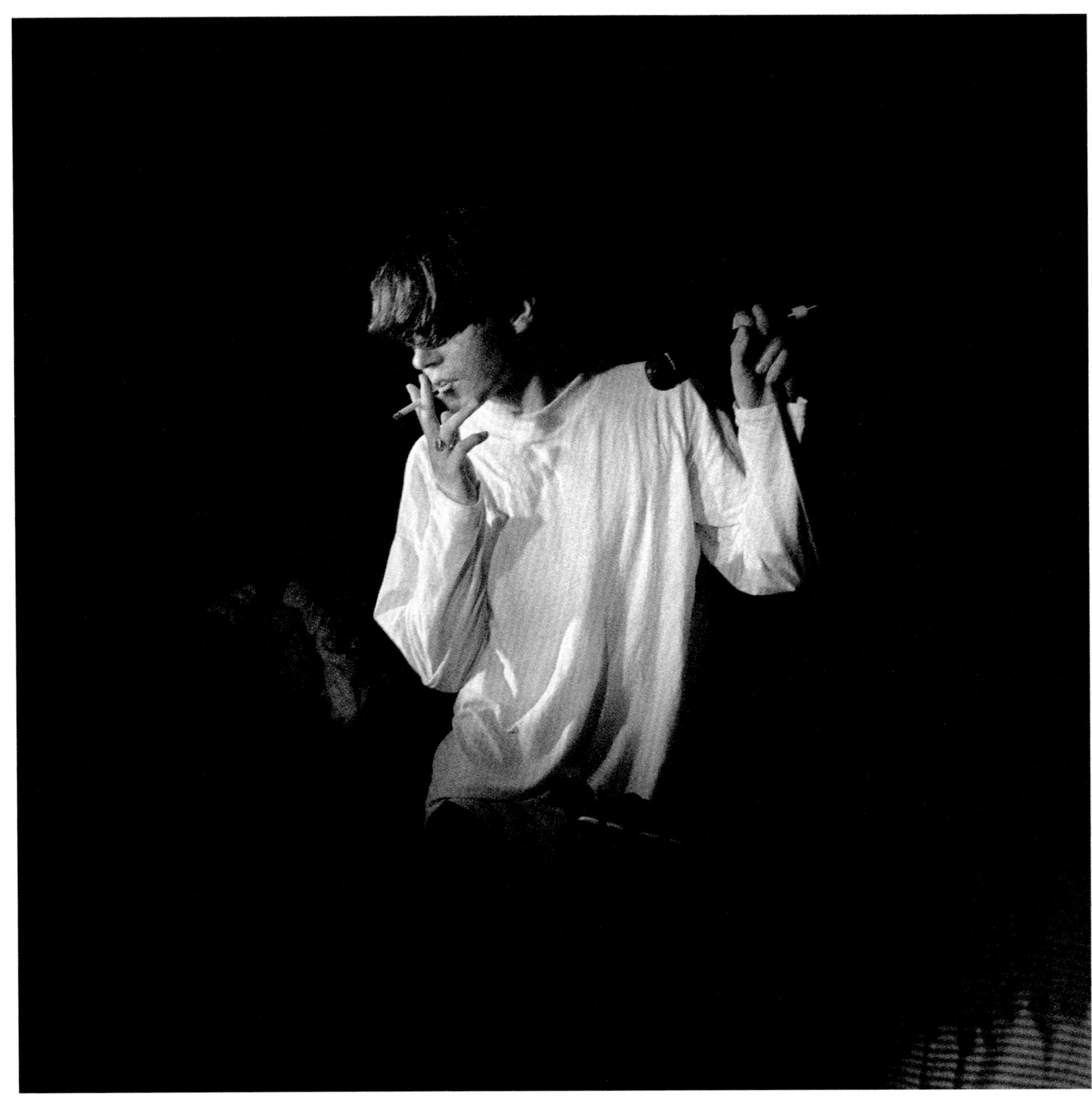

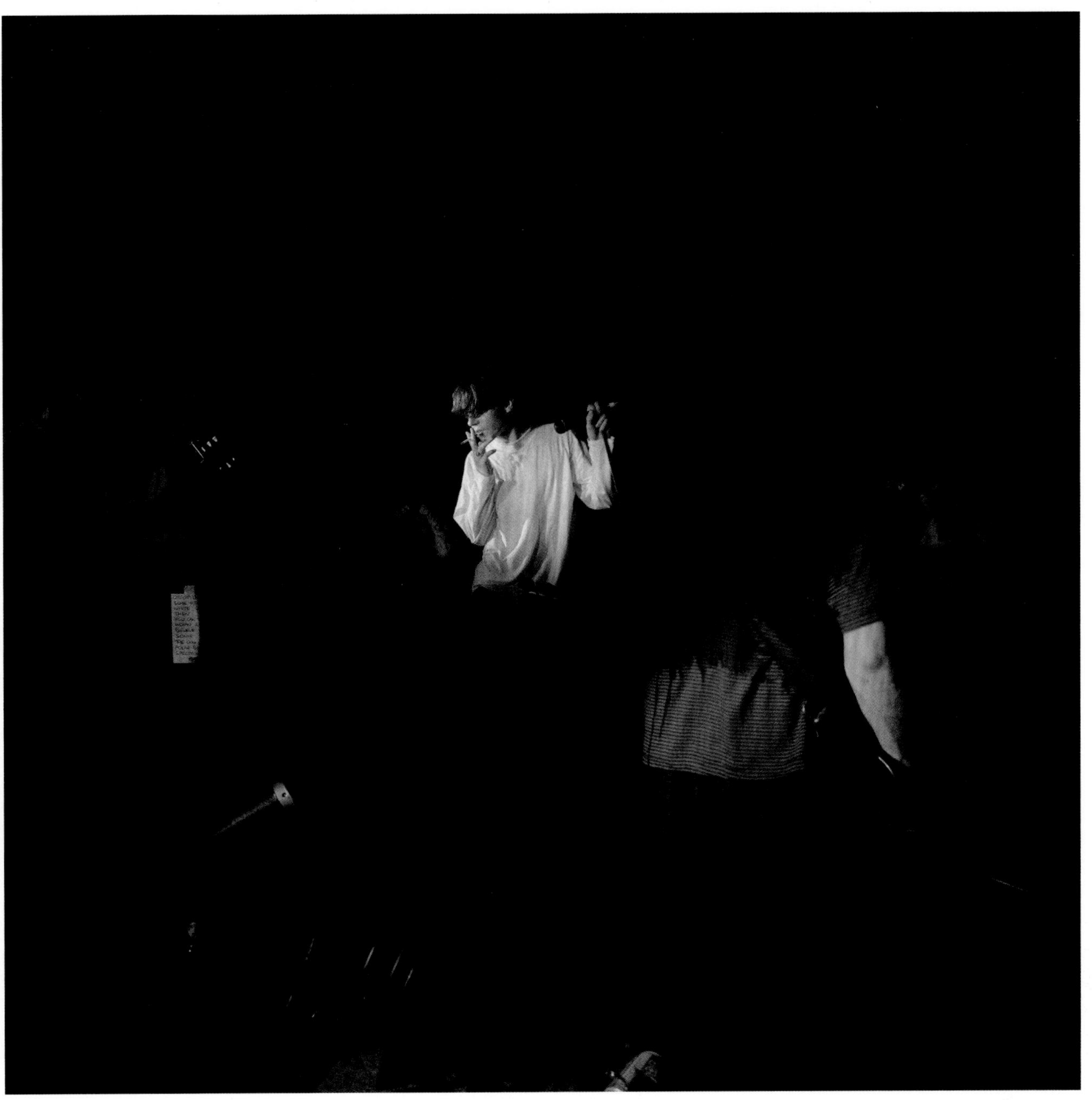

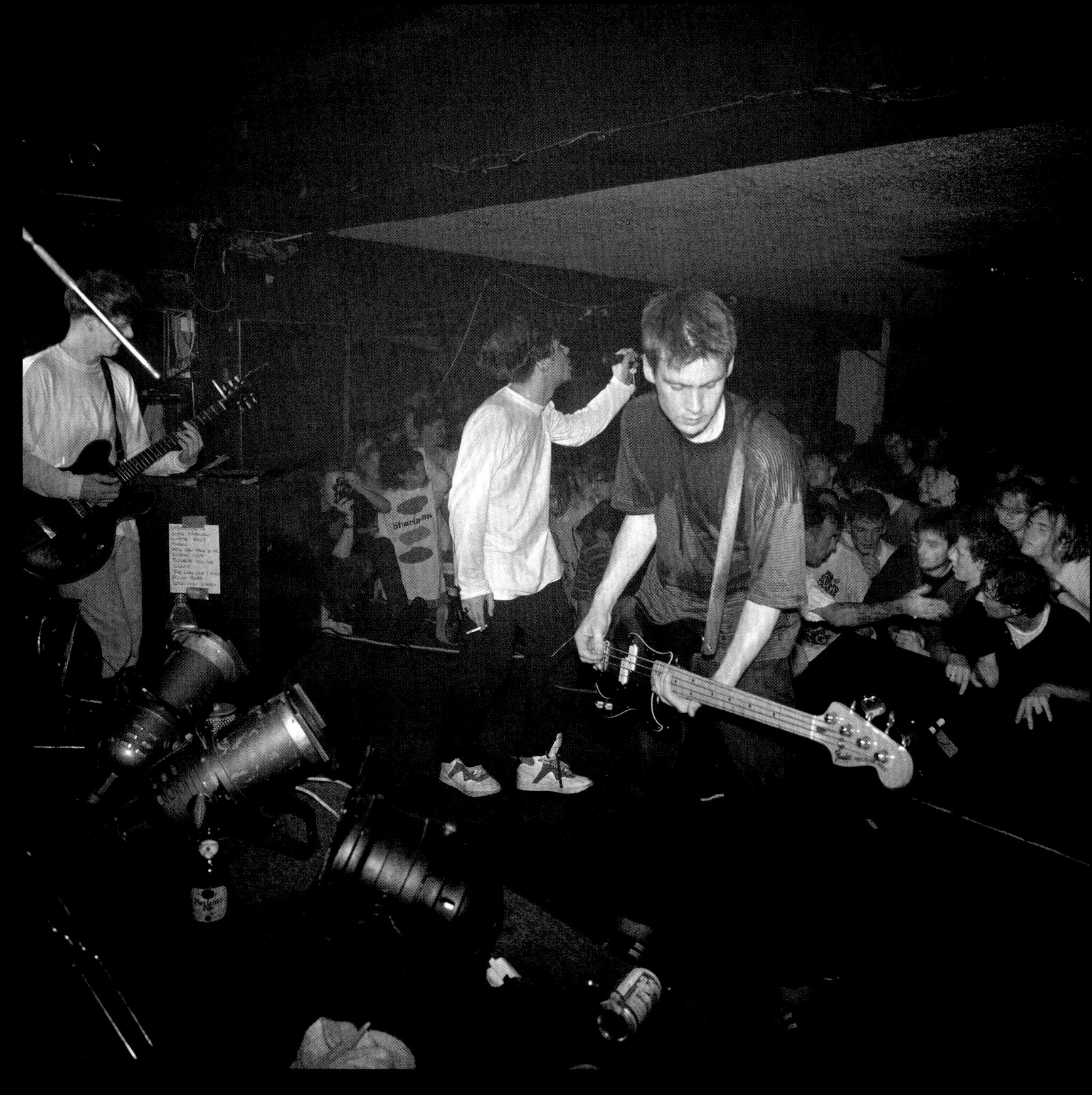

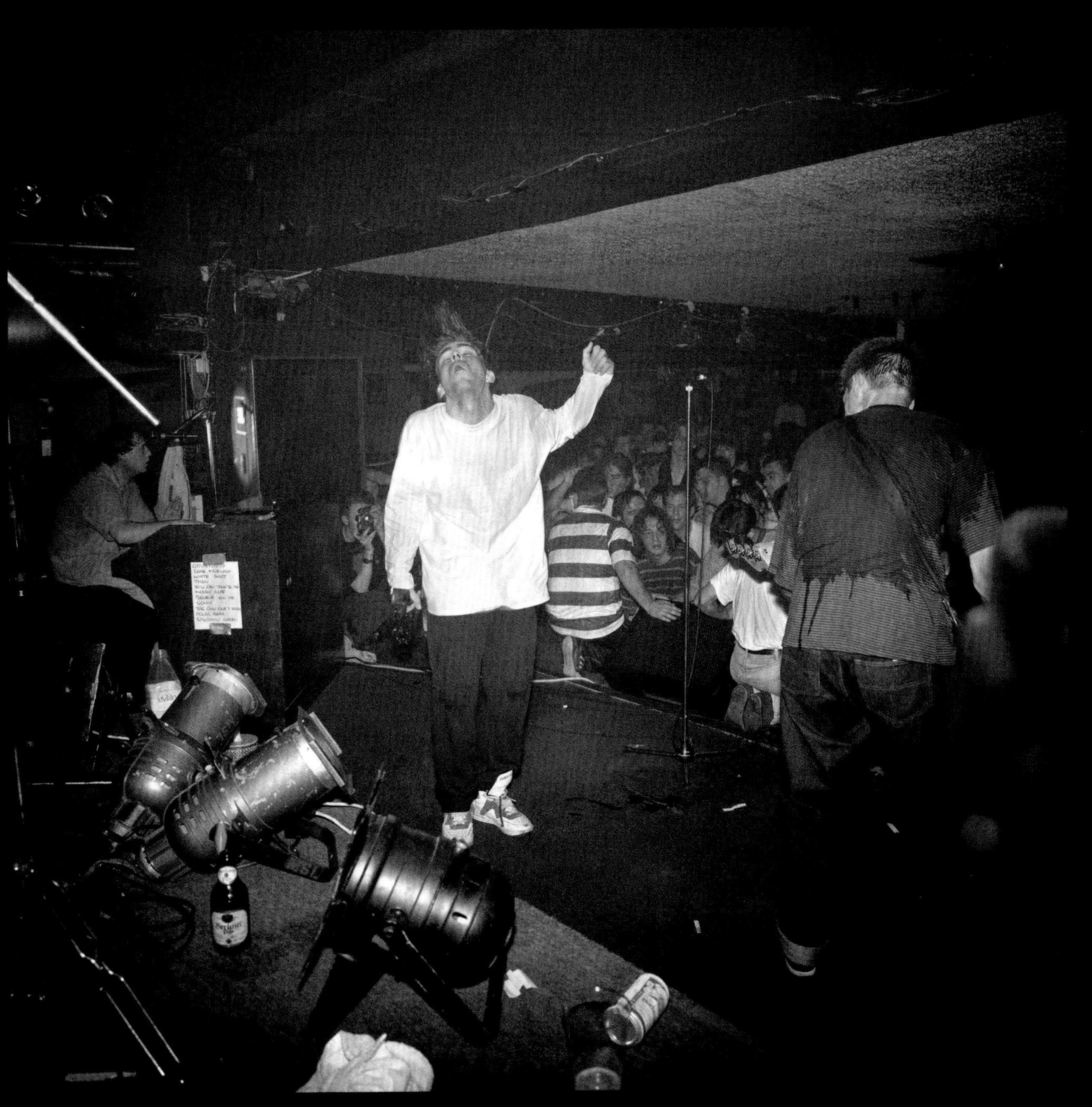

It was all glam back in those days. Another early encounter with Tom was in Clerkenwell, just up the road from Camden, for a shoot for a magazine which more than likely doesn't exist anymore and I can't for the life of me remember the name of, as worldwide there were dozens of magazines and we seemed to be asked to be in all of them.

This time we were in an actual, real studio, set up with lights and everything. No Austin Allegros or angry dogs on chains, this was the big time – or, given that it was in Clerkenwell, the medium time. I had a new haircut, which, according to our manager, was "a haircut that had gone too far". Thinking back, I could have sworn he mentioned the biblical story of Samson, the guy who lost his powers after a trip to the barbers, but maybe he wasn't that dramatic.

I felt comfortable with Tom and he gave us a little more direction in the studio. Back in the scrapyard days it was more "look at me", "look over there", "look down" and I always remember him telling us to "keep yer mince pies open".

This time we were encouraged to bring a selection of clothes and we were given guidance as to what worked best in photographs. We got a budget from our manager and went to the King's Road on a clothes-shopping trip for the first time in our lives. It was like the movie montage scenes of a wide-eyed young band on the up and up, and Tom was with us every step of the way. I even remember a shoot where Ian T. Tilton (who famously took legendary shots of Nirvana and The Stone Roses) was taking photos of us while Tom was taking photographs of us. It was like a photographic baggy version of an Escher drawing.

Spending time looking at these pictures now, I see five young men stepping into a world they didn't know, being guided by a Jedi. Tom would set up the lights, play some music (The Beau Brummels, Boz Scaggs, New Riders of the Purple Sage), which was all new to us but was music he loved from when he was a kid. He wanted to influence us and get across how utterly cool he was. I'd ask him what almost every track was and he'd gleefully tell me all about the artist, the background of the song and how it came to be in his life. I would mention my love of Gram Parsons and he would tell me all about Lowell George. It was like, "I'll see your country rock favourite and raise you a lesser-known, more obscure artist in the same vein".

I devoured this new-found knowledge and Tom would bring me mix tapes when we met. There was no better way to communicate a new friendship, at least in the male world of repressed emotions, than handing someone a carefully curated cassette. Tom was one of the few people who wrote to Rob while he was in prison, and his communications would often include a C90. I'm guessing prison authorities would have had to listen to these and I am hoping that Tom's choices and influences would have been picked up by whoever had to scan the audio for cryptic escape advice.

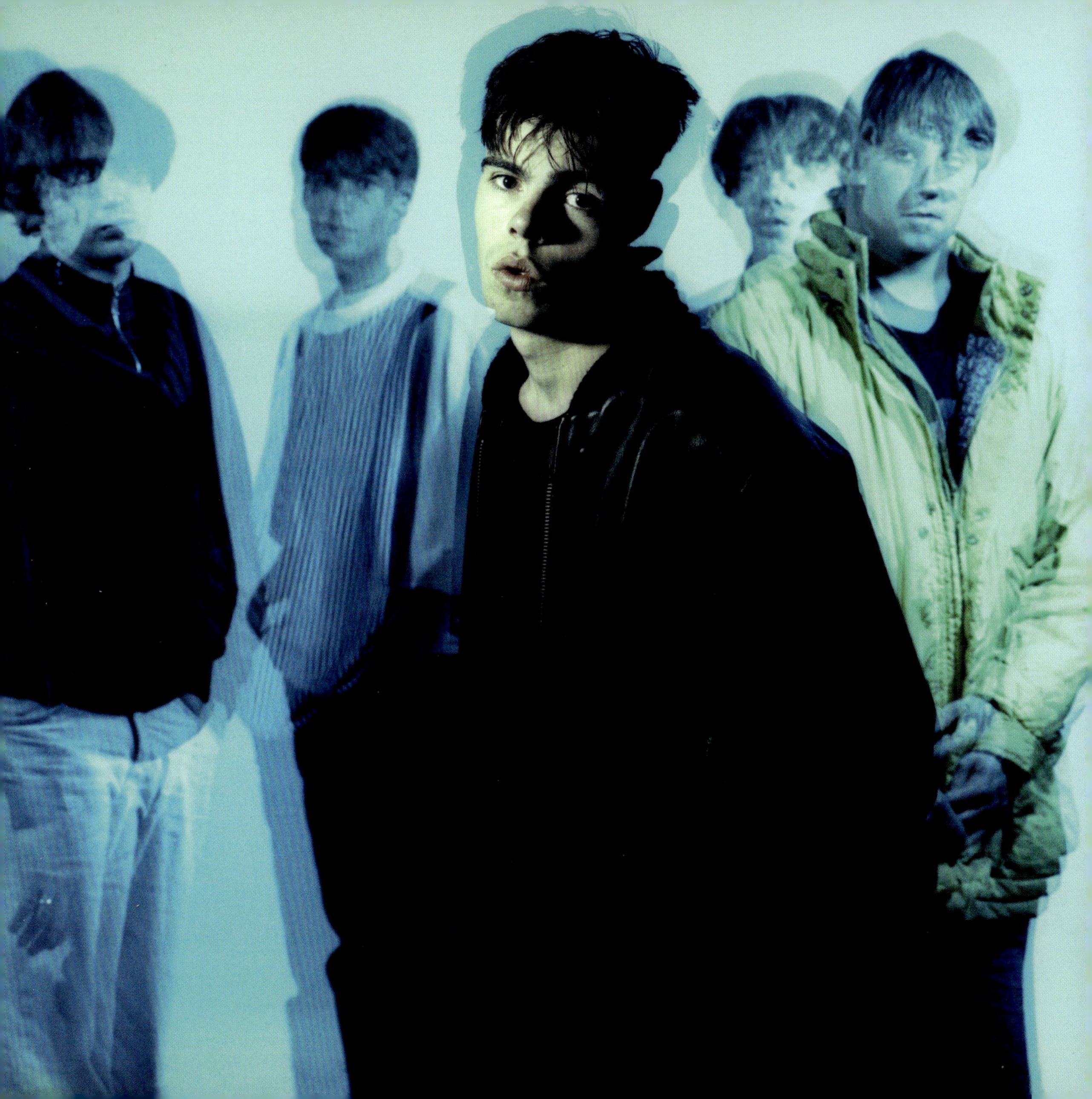

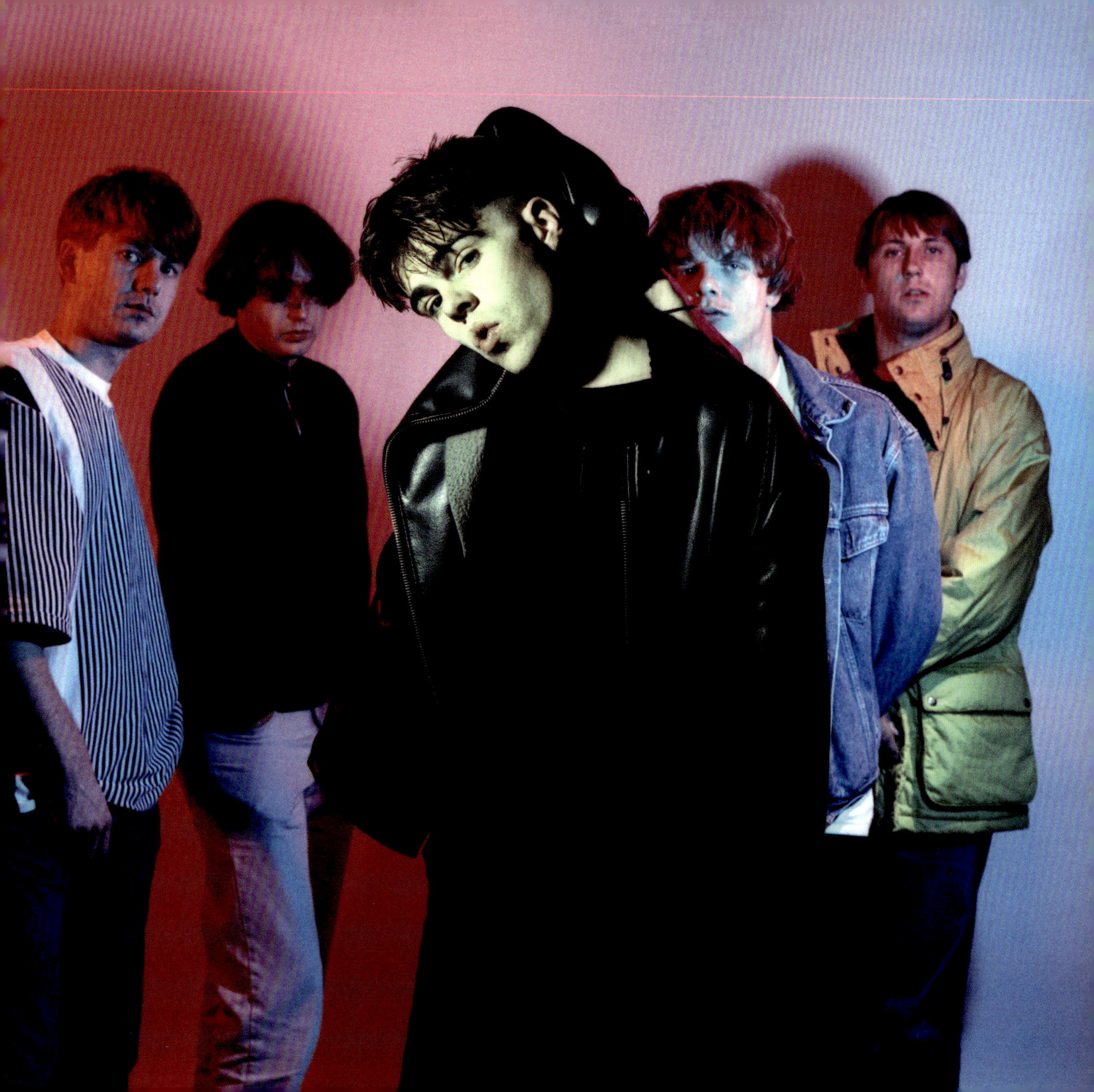

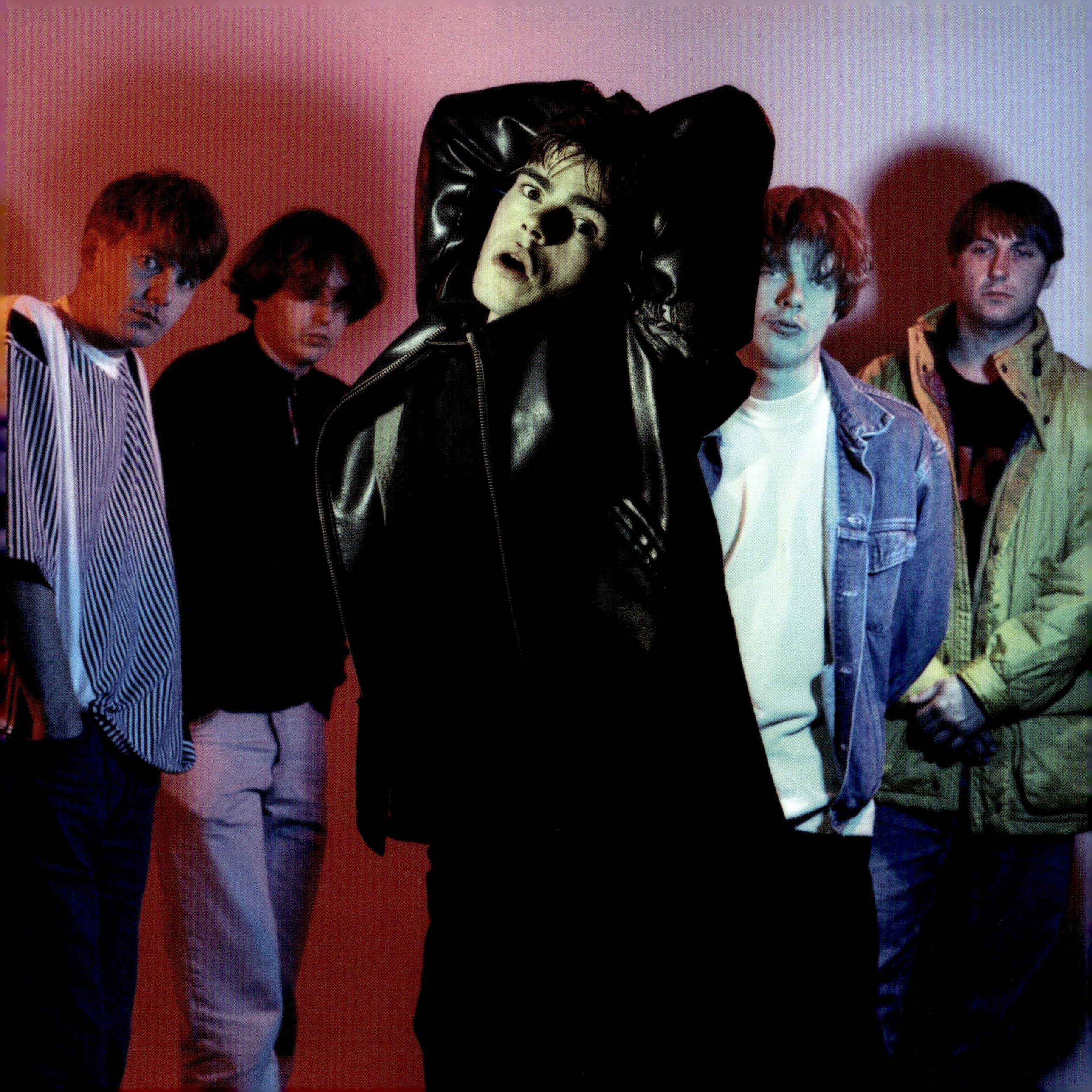

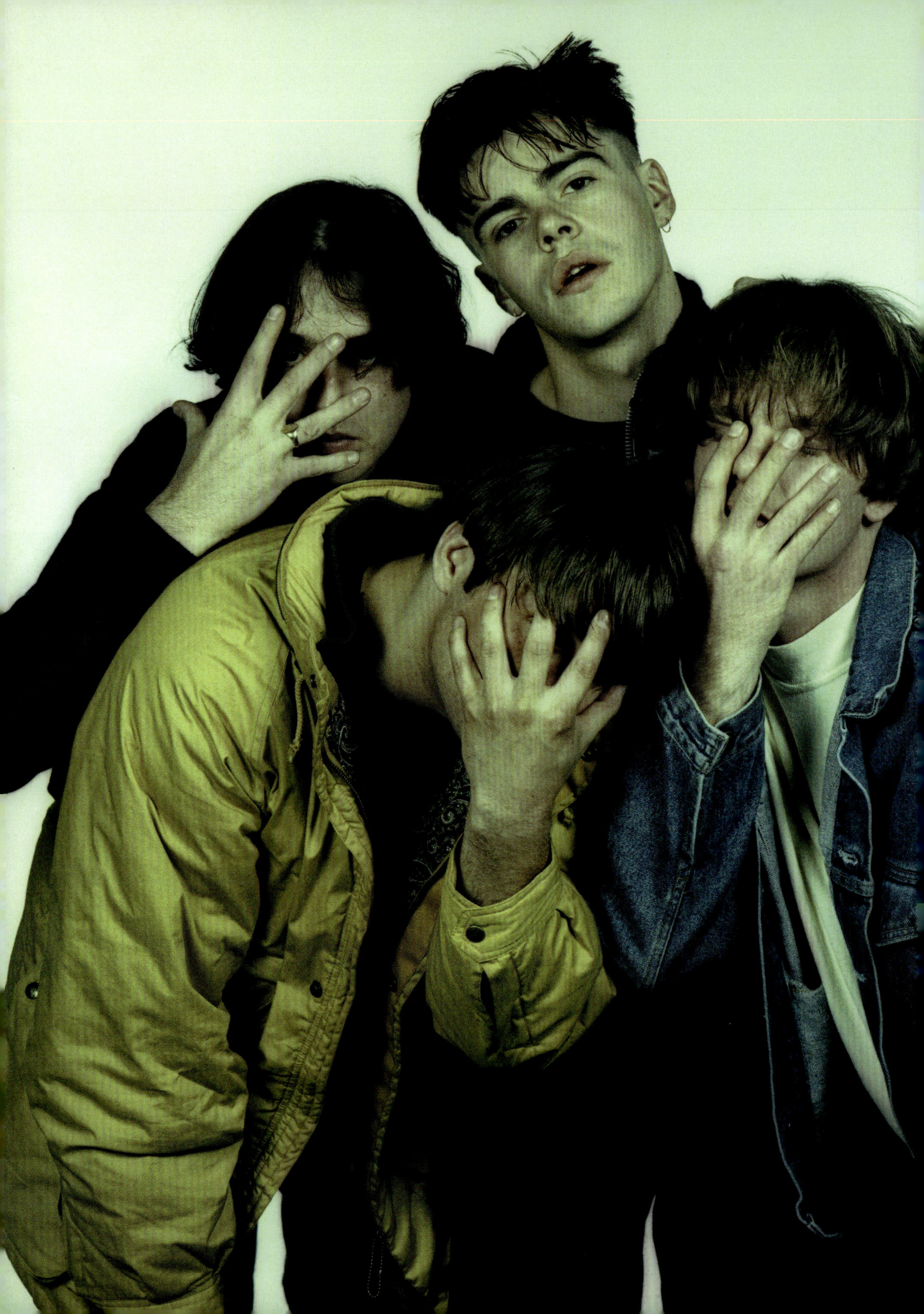

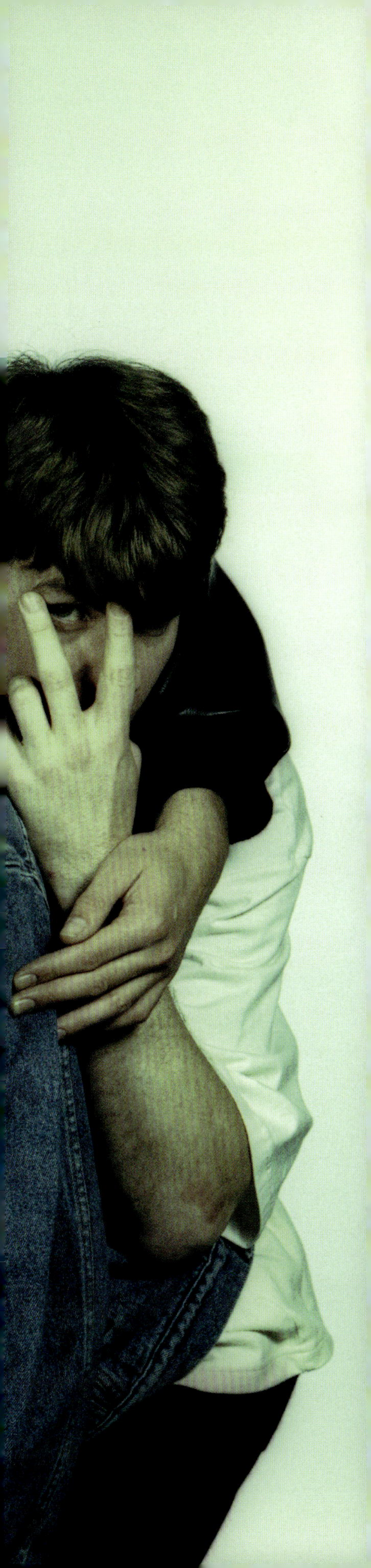

The next time we met Tom was geographically and metaphorically a world away from Clerkenwell, in Orange County, California. We were there after an invitation from Ian Astbury of The Cult to play at his A Gathering of the Tribes festival – widely recognized as the forerunner to Lollapalooza, which featured Soundgarden, Iggy Pop, Public Enemy, The Mission and Joan Baez, among others.

On the trip we played at The Horseshoe Tavern in Toronto, The Marquee in New York and A Gathering of the Tribes in San Francisco, before Tom joined us the next day at the Los Angeles version of the festival, in Orange County. Admittedly, he was there to photograph Ice-T, who was further up the bill.

It was two days before our debut album was released and we were making the most of every opportunity, as we presumed this would be our one shot at greatness before heading back to our regular jobs. I was a huge fan of The Mission and got to spend some time with Wayne Hussey that day, which was a real thrill – and happily I can say that we remain friends to this day.

When it was The Charlatans' turn to play, I noticed Tom in the pit, so I gave him a wave and he gave me a smile and a thumbs up. We were playing to our biggest audience to date – around 20,000 – so it was great to see a familiar face, and I realized then that we had a really good connection.

In true 90s' style, bottles of Jack Daniel's were thrown by people on the line-up who shall remain nameless, with the added bonus of Ice-T stepping in to prevent a brawl between stage crew and other members of the line-up, who shall also remain nameless but could also be said to be in The Charlatans. It's been slightly lost in the mists of time, but a band might have unknowingly slightly overrun, which might have enraged those tasked with ensuring everything was on time.

We've never knowingly or unknowingly played longer than our allotted time since that day.

Tom:
I didn't know The Charlatans were on the bill at A Gathering of the Tribes. I was there to shoot someone else entirely and was idly taking pictures of whoever was on. And then Tim appears, picking me out of the crowd and giving me the Vs.

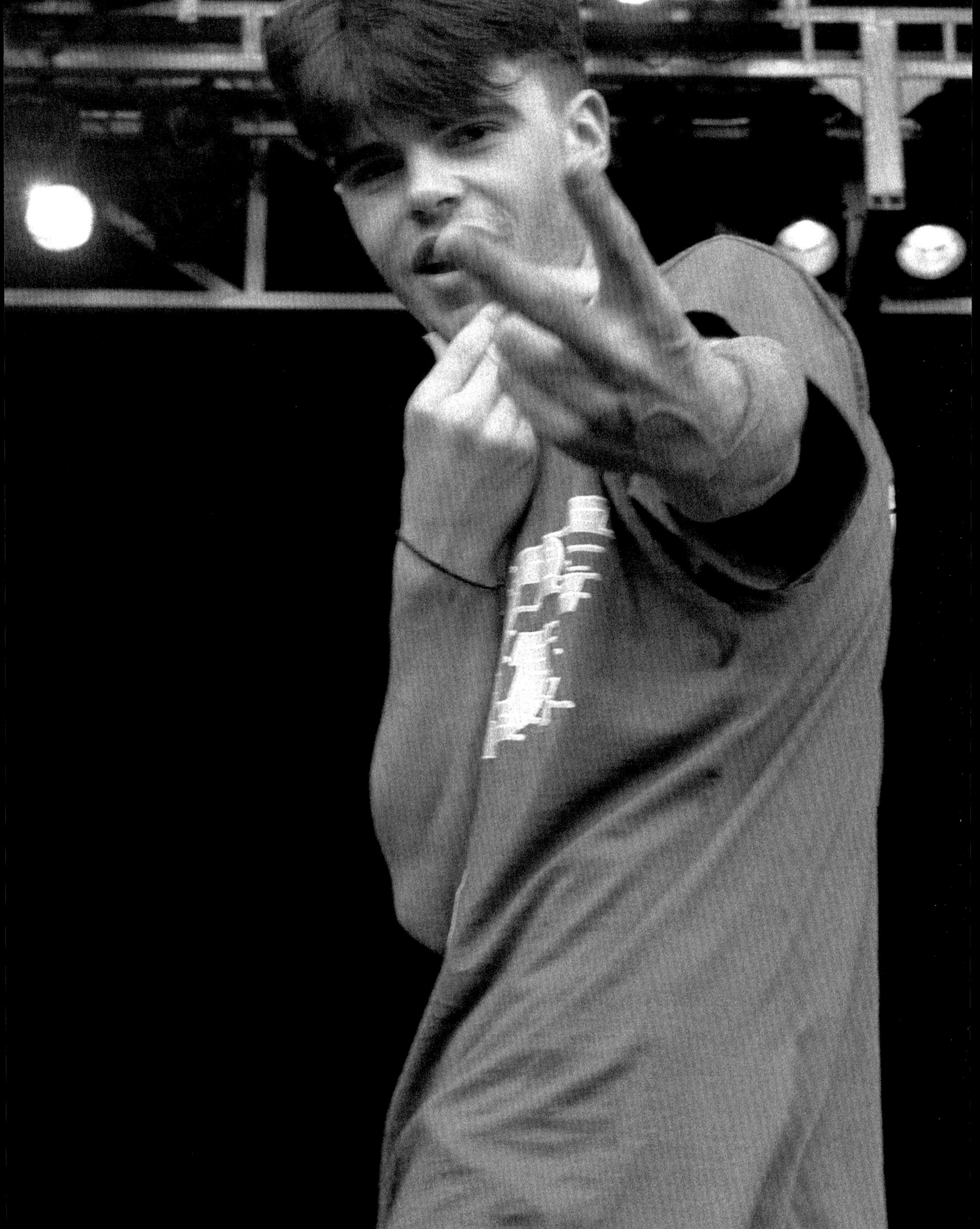

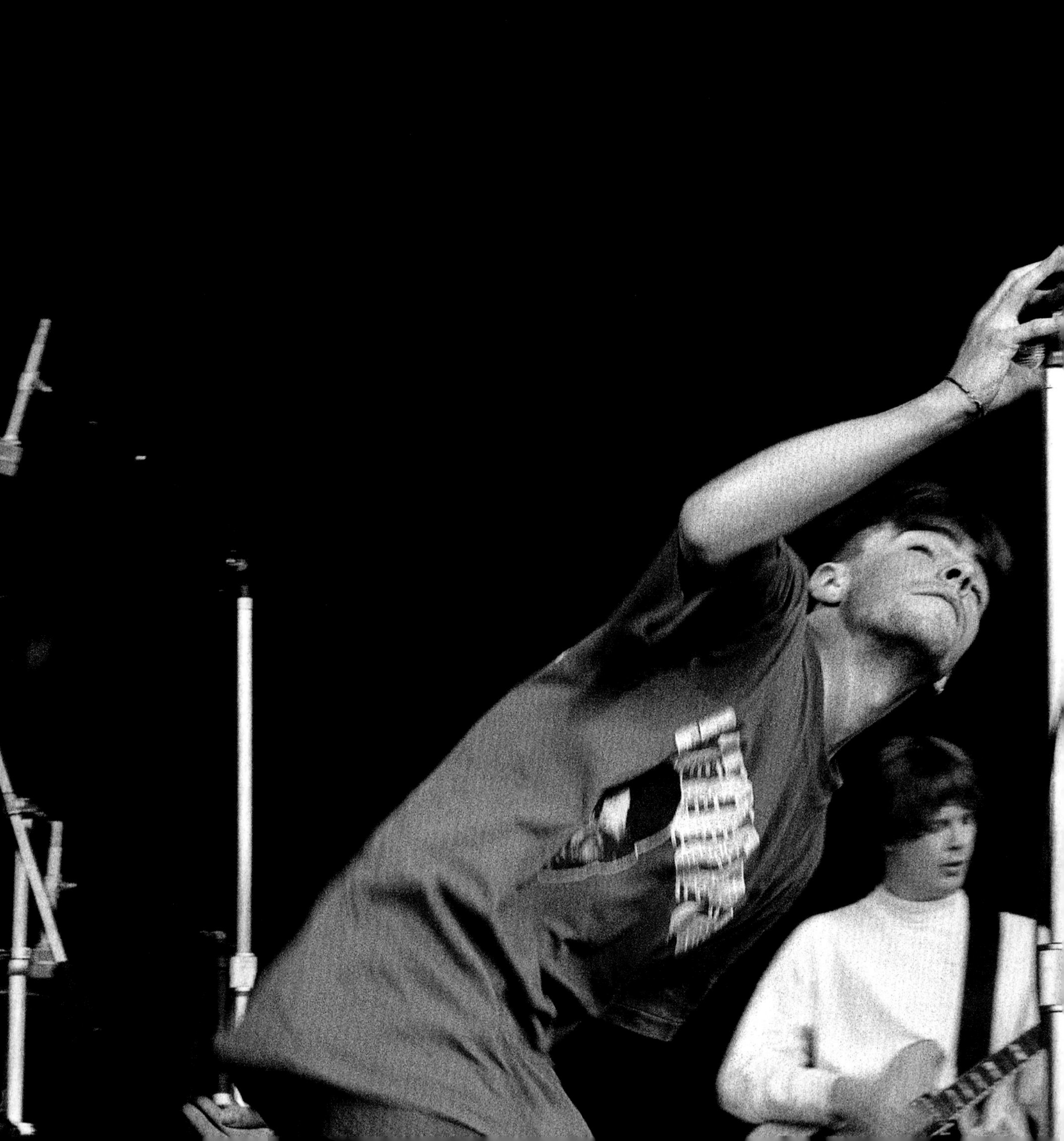

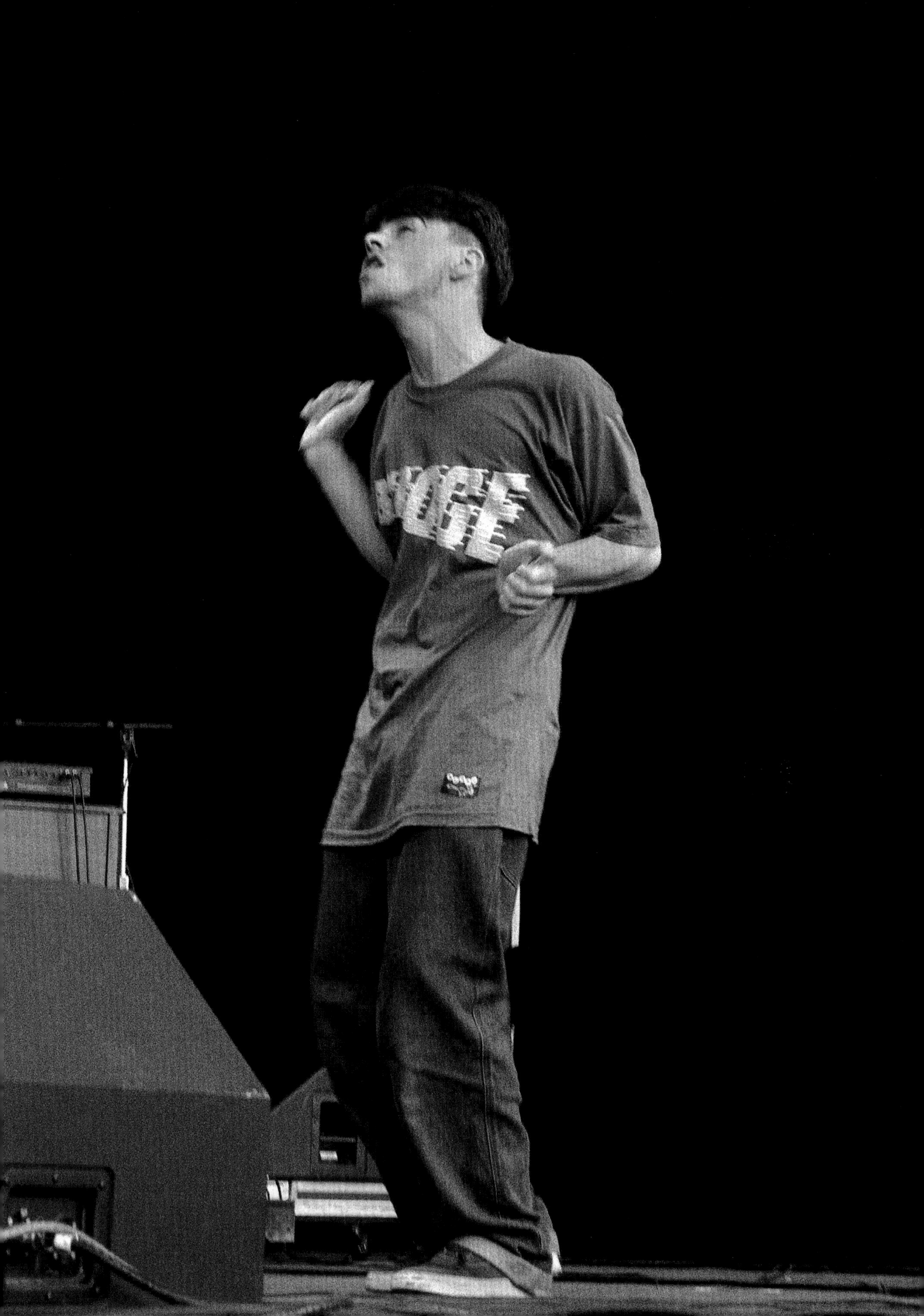

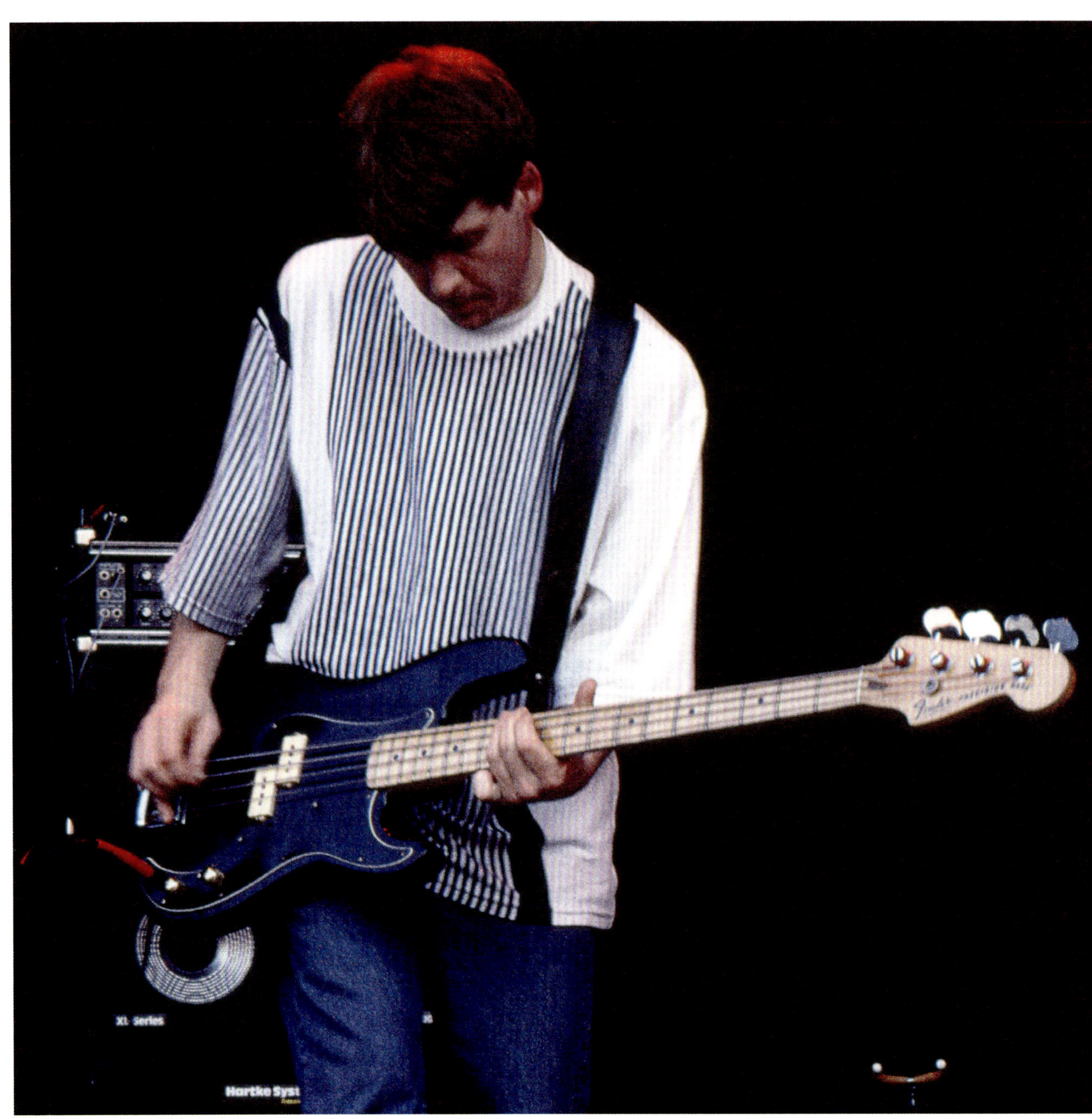
XL Series

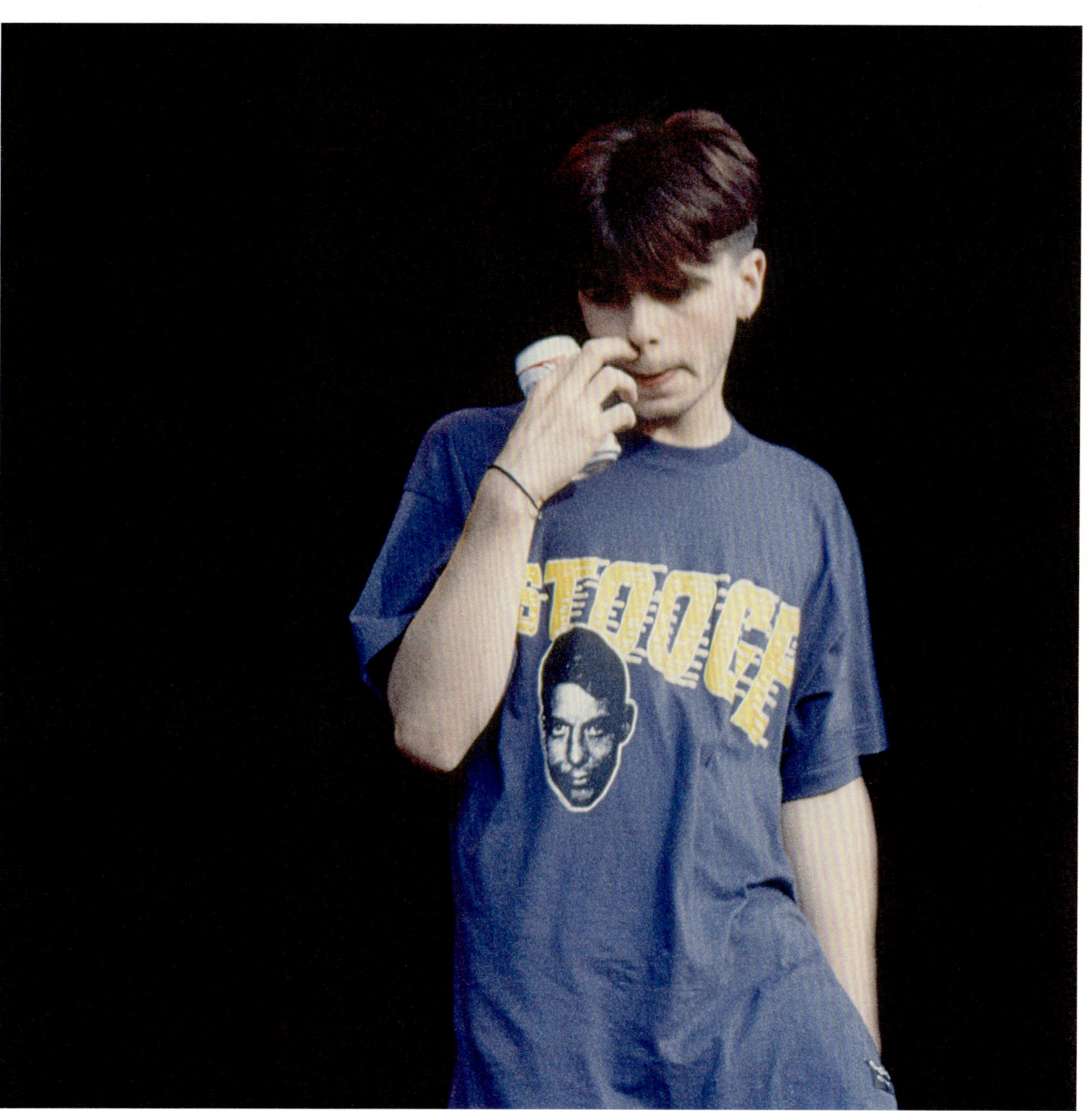

We next paired up a few months later for a planned *Melody Maker* front cover – we had been on the cover already, but that one had been unplanned and a nice surprise. This time it was promised and "guaranteed".

The band was staying at the Hyatt Hotel, aka The Riot on Sunset – aka another sign that we were part of the big time, or at least were approaching the driveway to the big time. I had an appointment for an interview at KROQ, which was a short ride away.

Tom always had an eye out for a backdrop, and as we were waiting for the cab his eyes were scanning for a suitable spot. What he wanted was a "classic" LA cover shot. Opposite us was the Sunset Grill, and I noticed a look in his eyes.

We had developed an understanding to get candid photos quickly. He would always be carrying a giant bag of cameras, lenses, film, flashes and those reflector things that they stick under your chin. But on this occasion we had to be quick due to the imminent arrival of the taxi and the fact that we were already late for the interview. He "rattled off a few frames" (an expression he often used), which always put me at ease – it seemed to suggest that it wasn't important and we could get them quickly, but I came to realize that it was more often because he had been struck by some inspiration and didn't want to lose any of the informality and relaxed feel that we had.

To date-stamp these pictures there is a billboard nearby for the newly released Doors movie by Oliver Stone. So rather than it being a picture of me in front of Jim Morrison, it's actually a picture of me in front of Val Kilmer – 1991 with the spirit of 1971.

We were playing a show at the Ackerman Grand Ballroom, but Tom didn't seem inspired by the surroundings, so he asked if we could head out the following morning, before our bus was due to leave for San Francisco, as he had some ideas in mind. Five band members meant a cat-herding operation for Tom, as it didn't take much to distract us in California. From the cars to the characters and the movie settings, we were giddy and happy living life.

Next door to the hotel was The Comedy Store, a tattoo parlour and a car rental place. All ideal backdrops in Tom's world. Rob had a three-quarter-length leather jacket and I was dressed in my version of Micky Dolenz meets Johnny Rotten.

This might have made us stand out anywhere else, but in Los Angeles everyone just gets on with it as there are pictures being taken and movies being filmed on every other street corner.

Tom:
This is a great sequence. It was round the back of The Comedy Store in LA, just before the band headed off at the end of our time together there. I got them all to sit on a slope and told them to slowly walk towards me, and Tim to stay there until the end. It felt very LA, in a car park, a tattoo studio just opposite. There was an advertising hoarding just above us, saying, "Don't go to bed until you've scored". Make of that what you will.

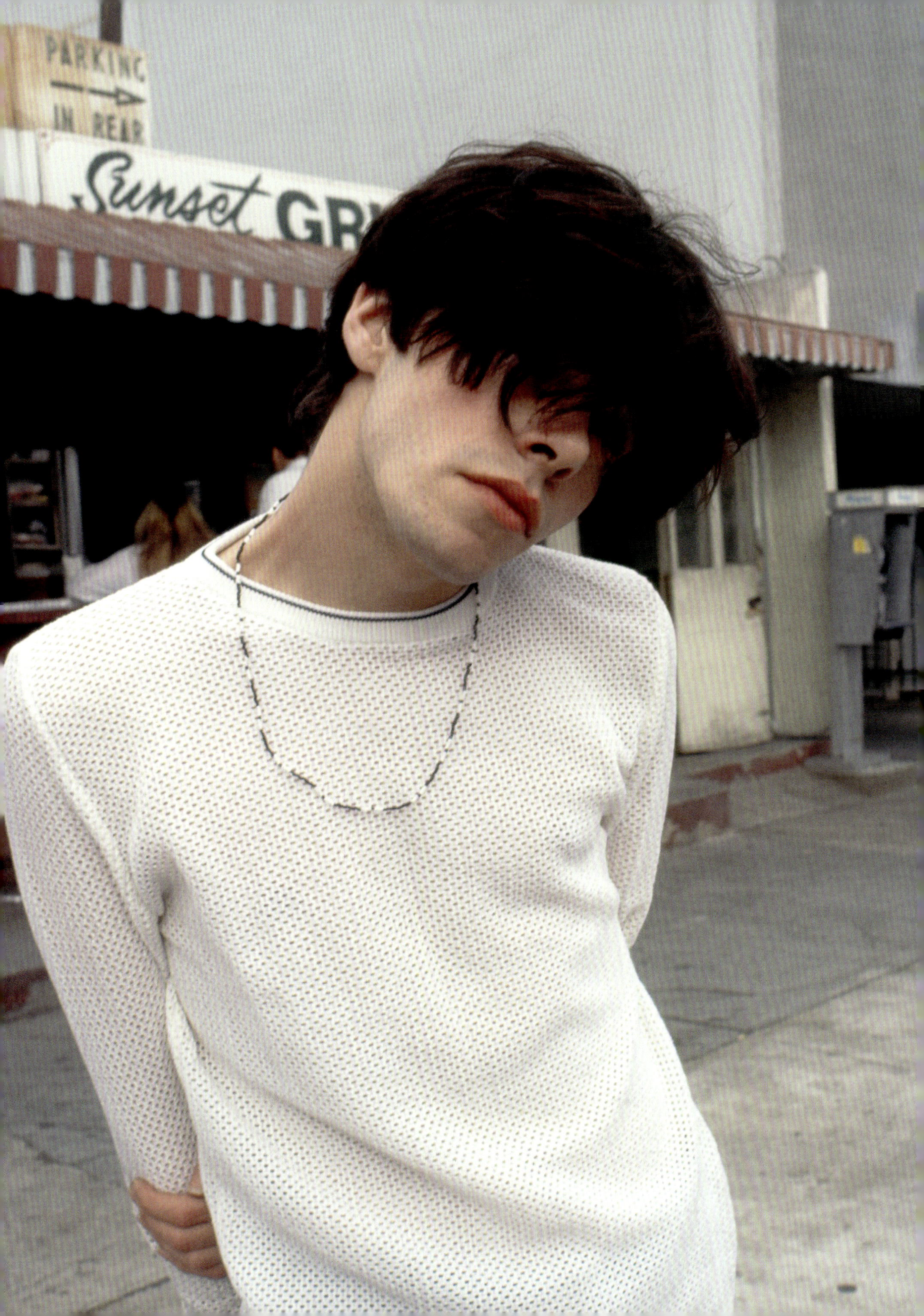
PARKING
IN REAR
Sunset

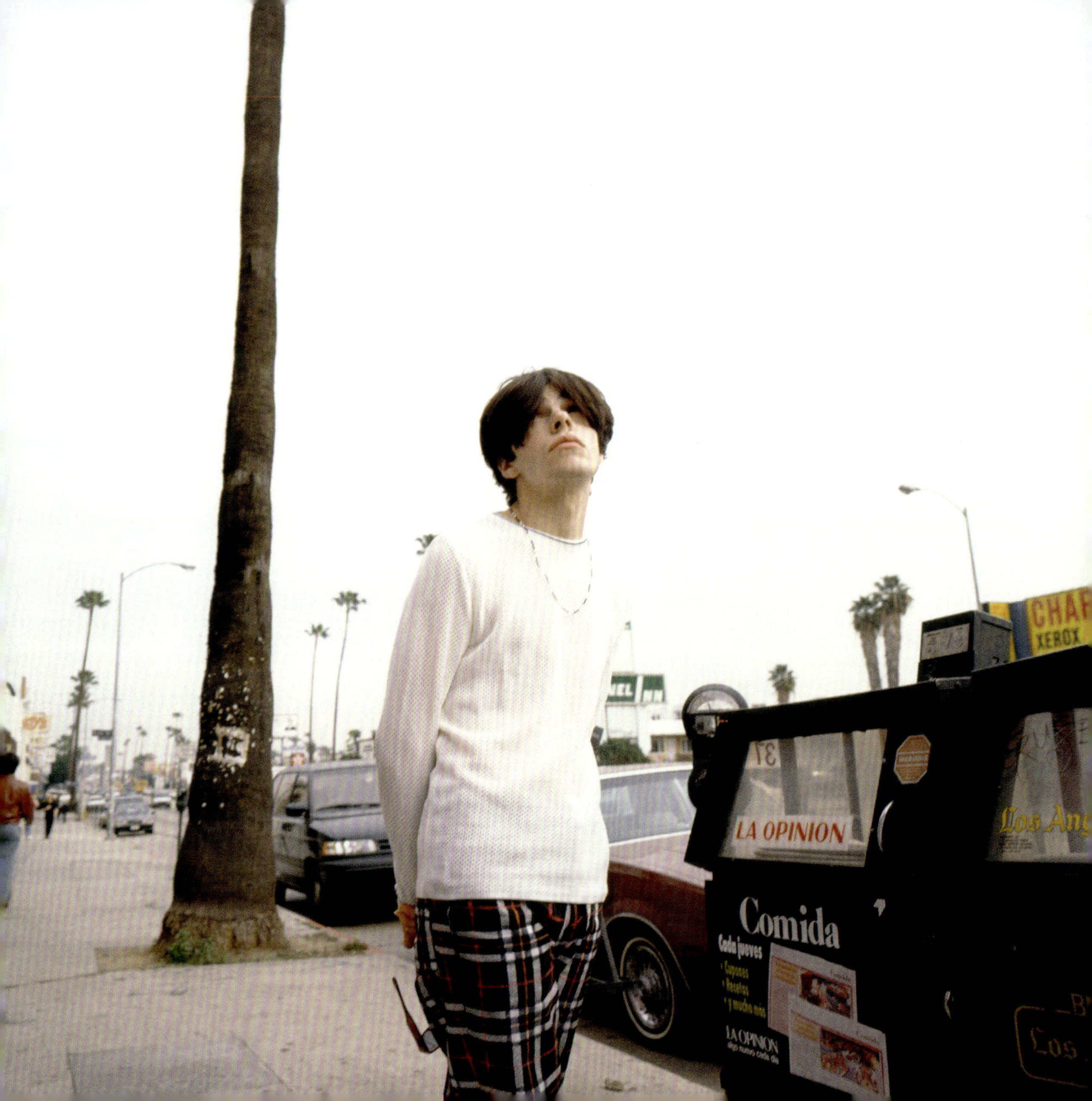
XEROX
LA OPINION
Comida
Cada jueves
• Cupones
• Recetas
• y mucho más
LA OPINION
algo nuevo cada día

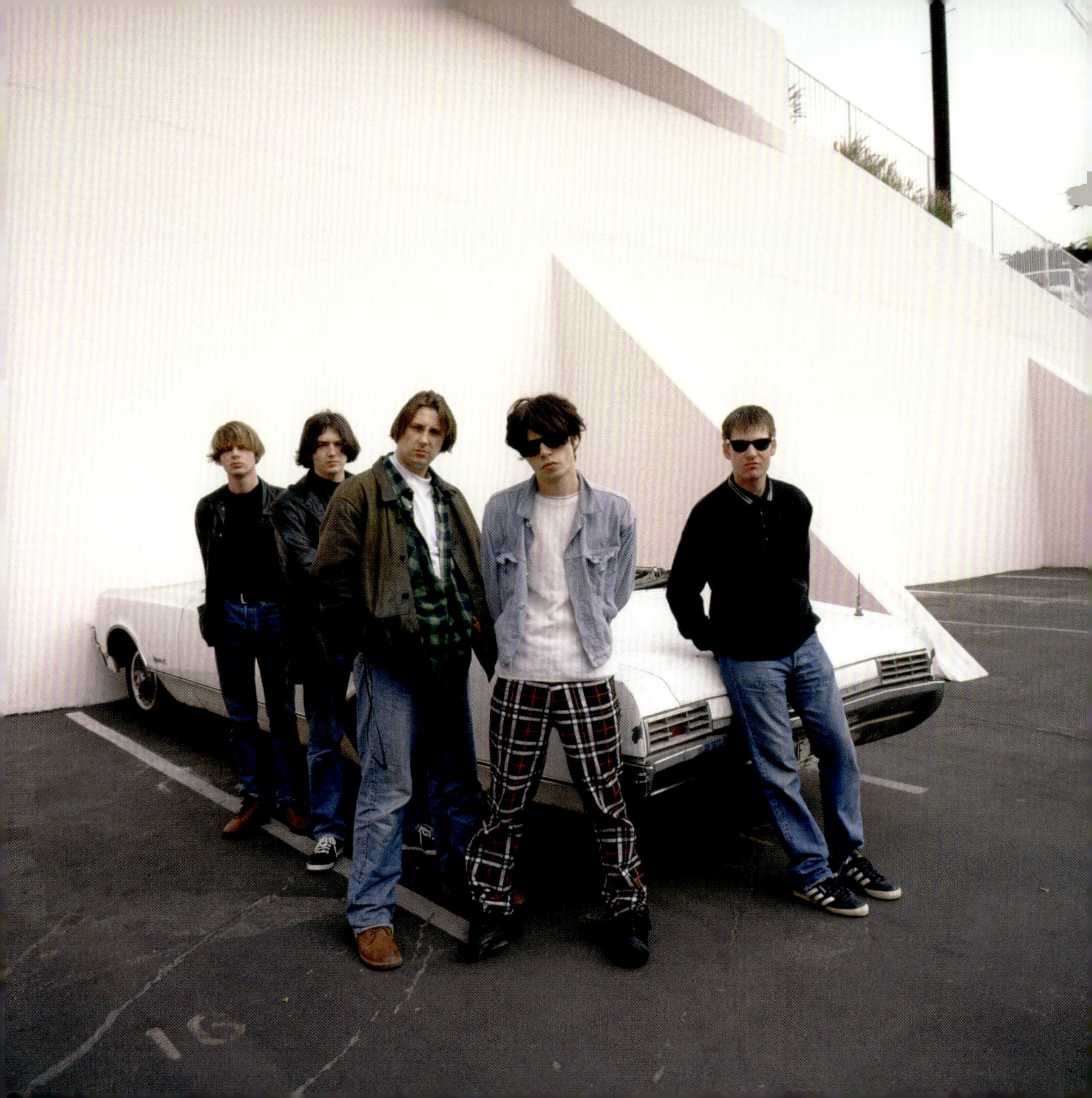
16

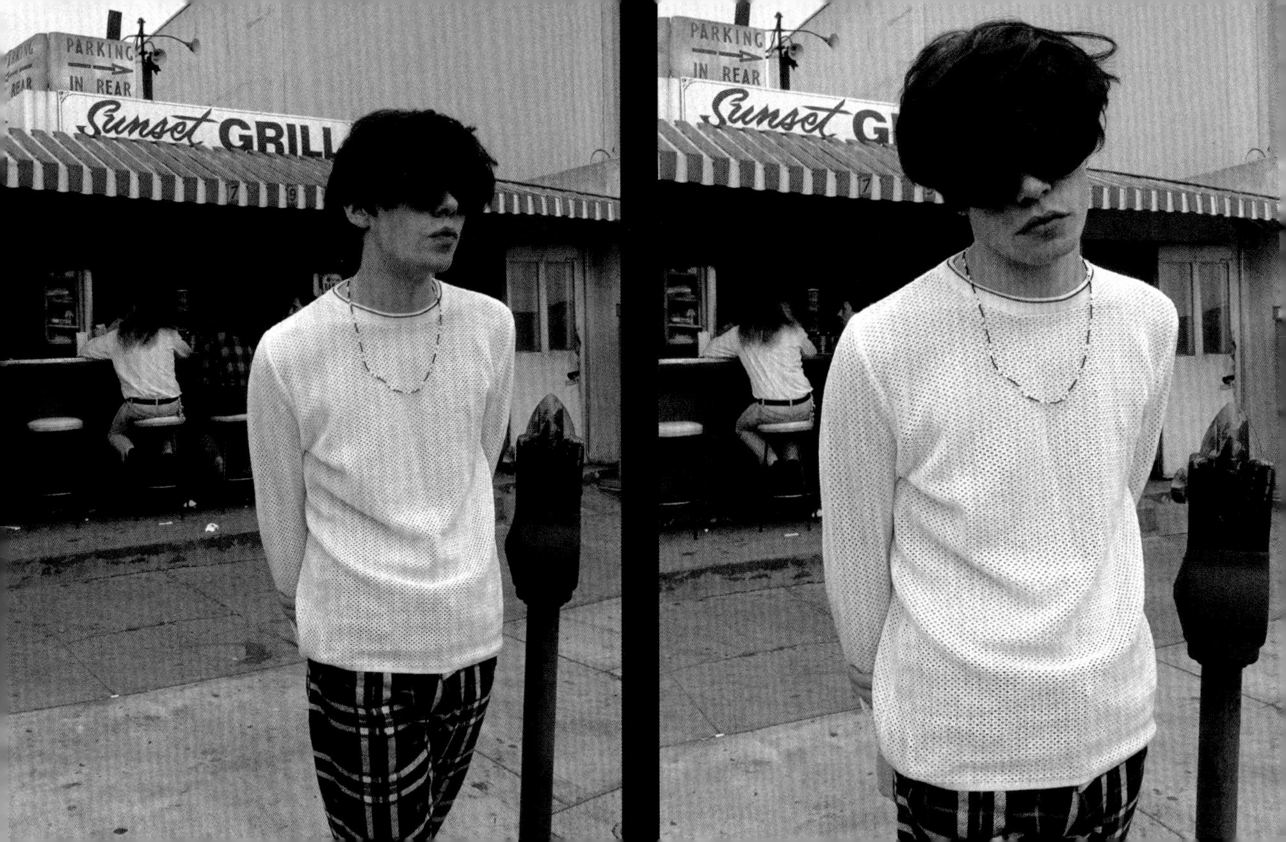
PARKING
IN REAR
Sunset GRILL
PARKING
IN REAR
Sunset

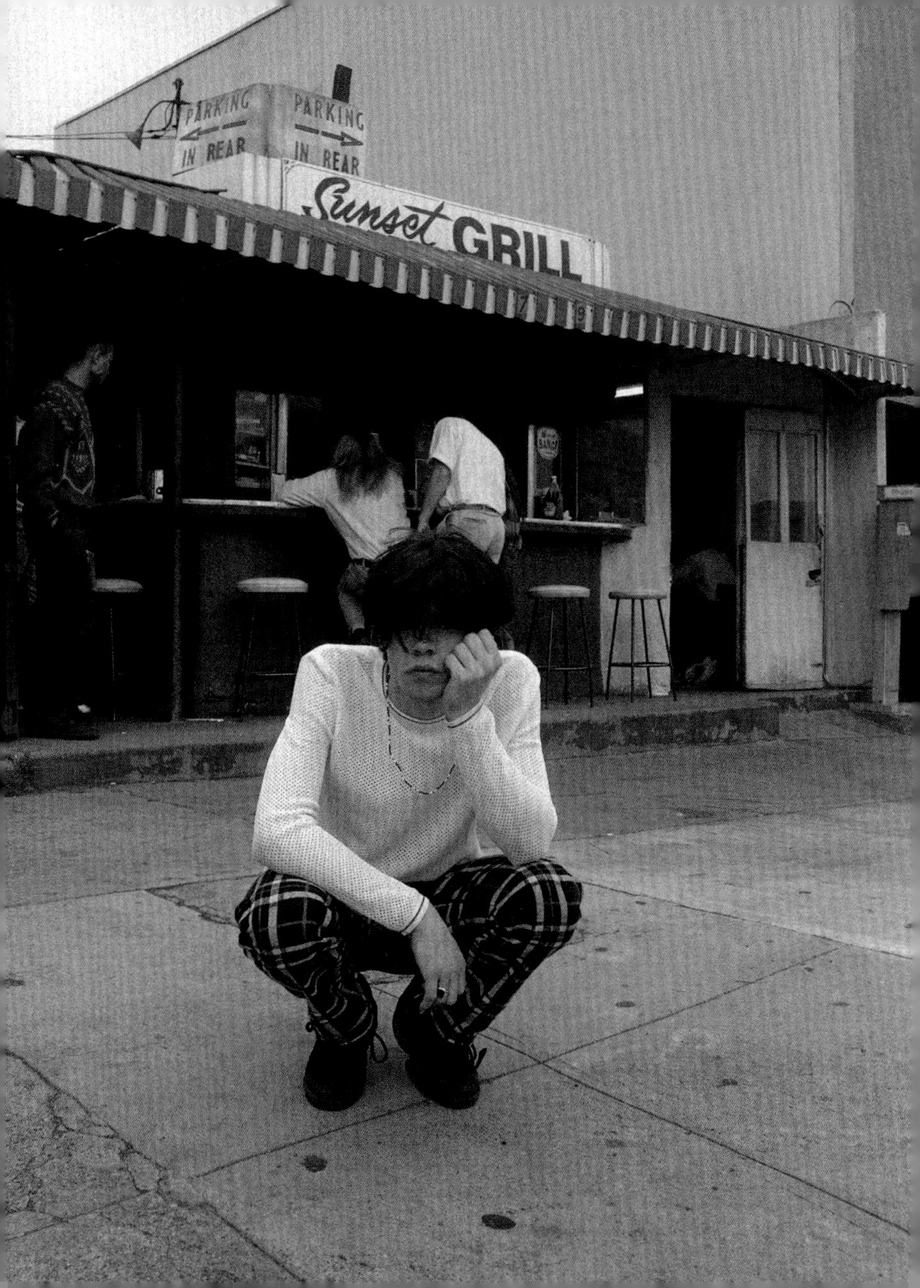
PARKING IN REAR
PARKING IN REAR
Sunset GRILL

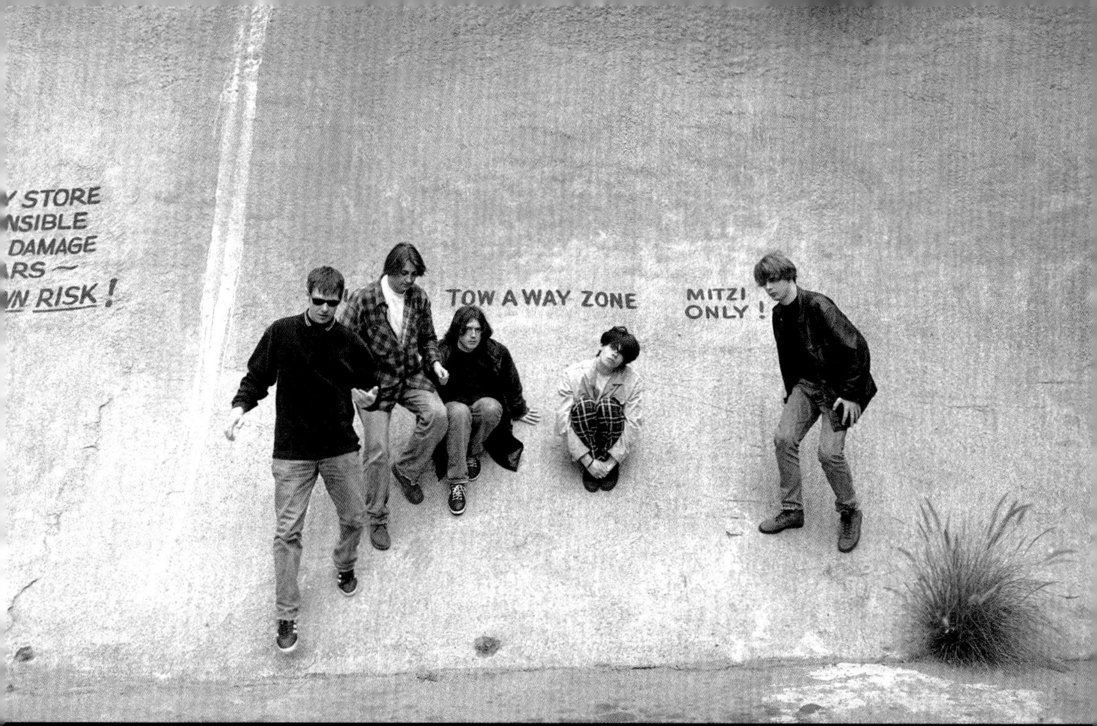

Y STORE
NSIBLE
DAMAGE
ARS ~
WN RISK !
TOW A WAY ZONE
MITZI
ONLY !

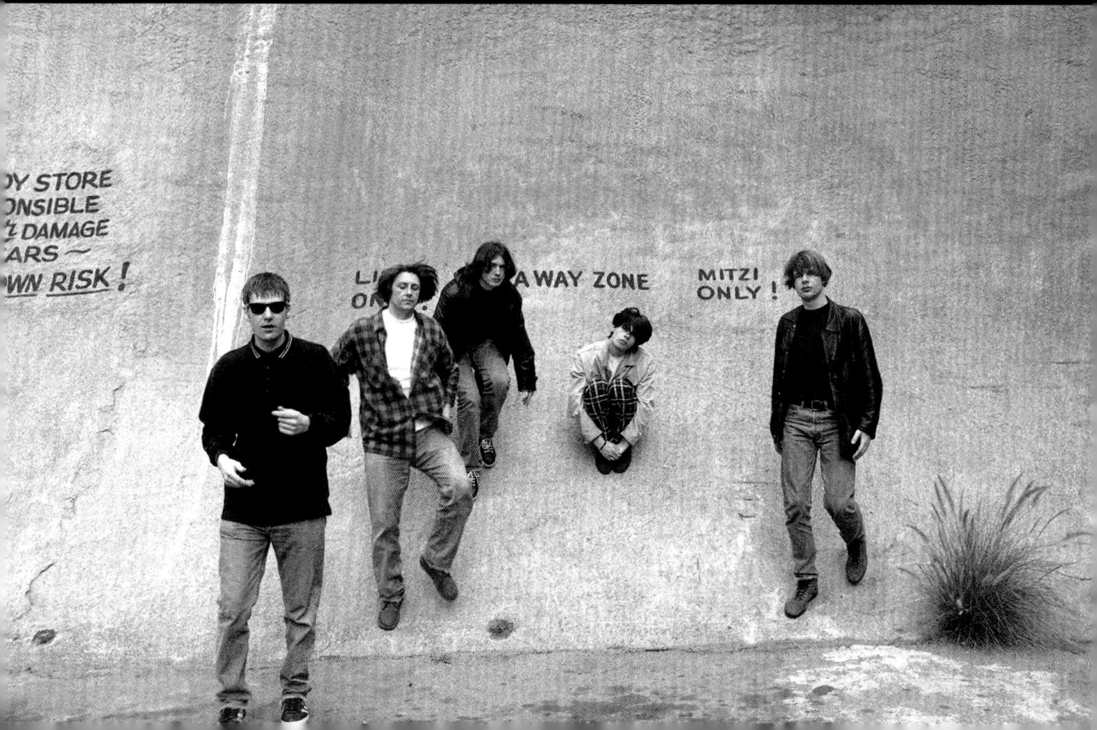

DY STORE
ONSIBLE
DAMAGE
ARS ~
WN RISK !
LI
ON
AWAY ZONE
MITZI
ONLY !

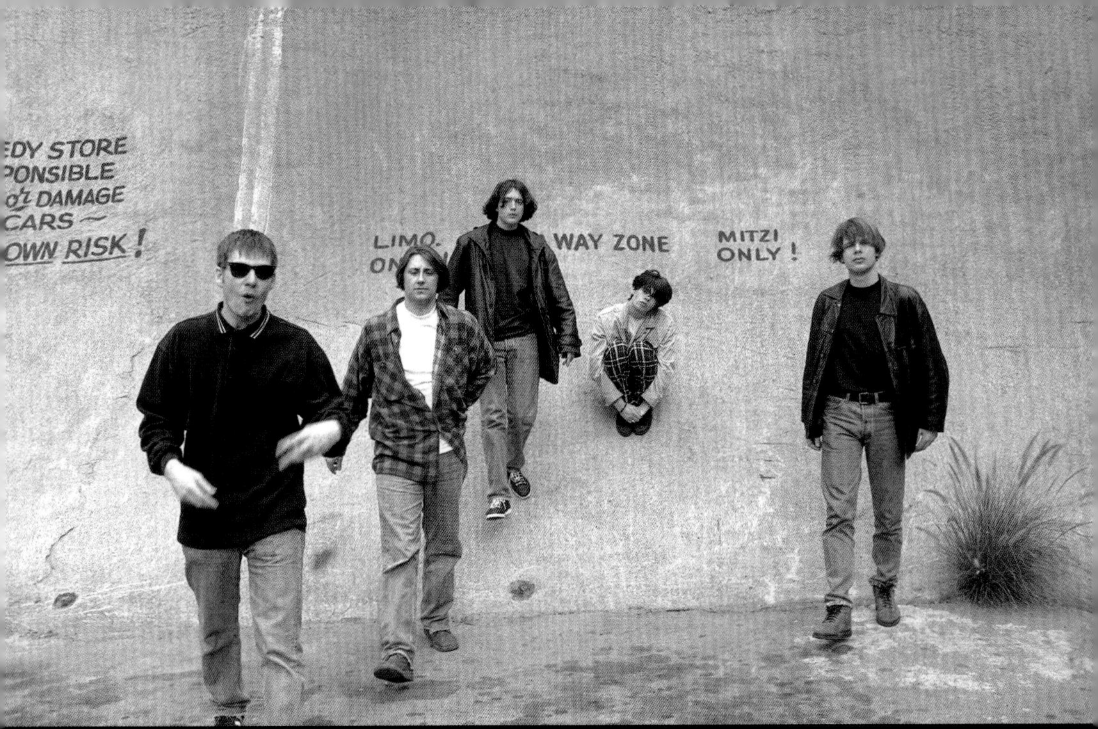

EDY STORE
PONSIBLE
or DAMAGE
CARS ~
OWN RISK !
LIMO.
ON
AWAY ZONE
MITZI
ONLY !
Y STORE 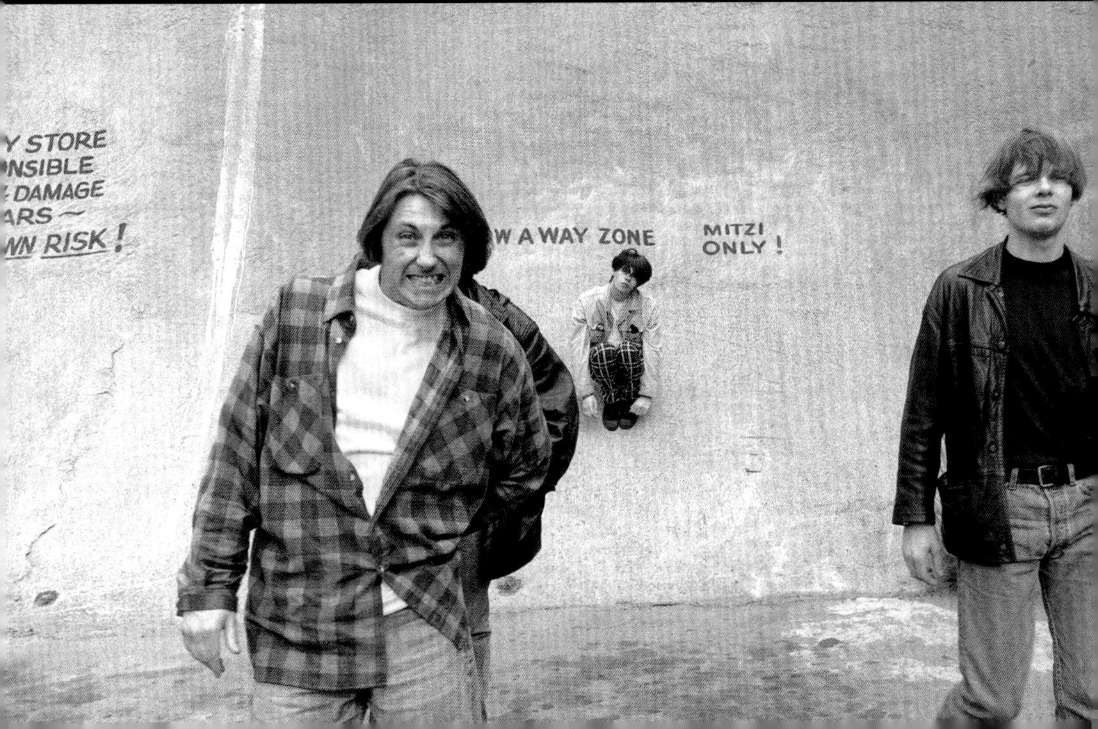
NSIBLE
DAMAGE
ARS ~
WN RISK !
W A WAY ZONE
MITZI
ONLY !

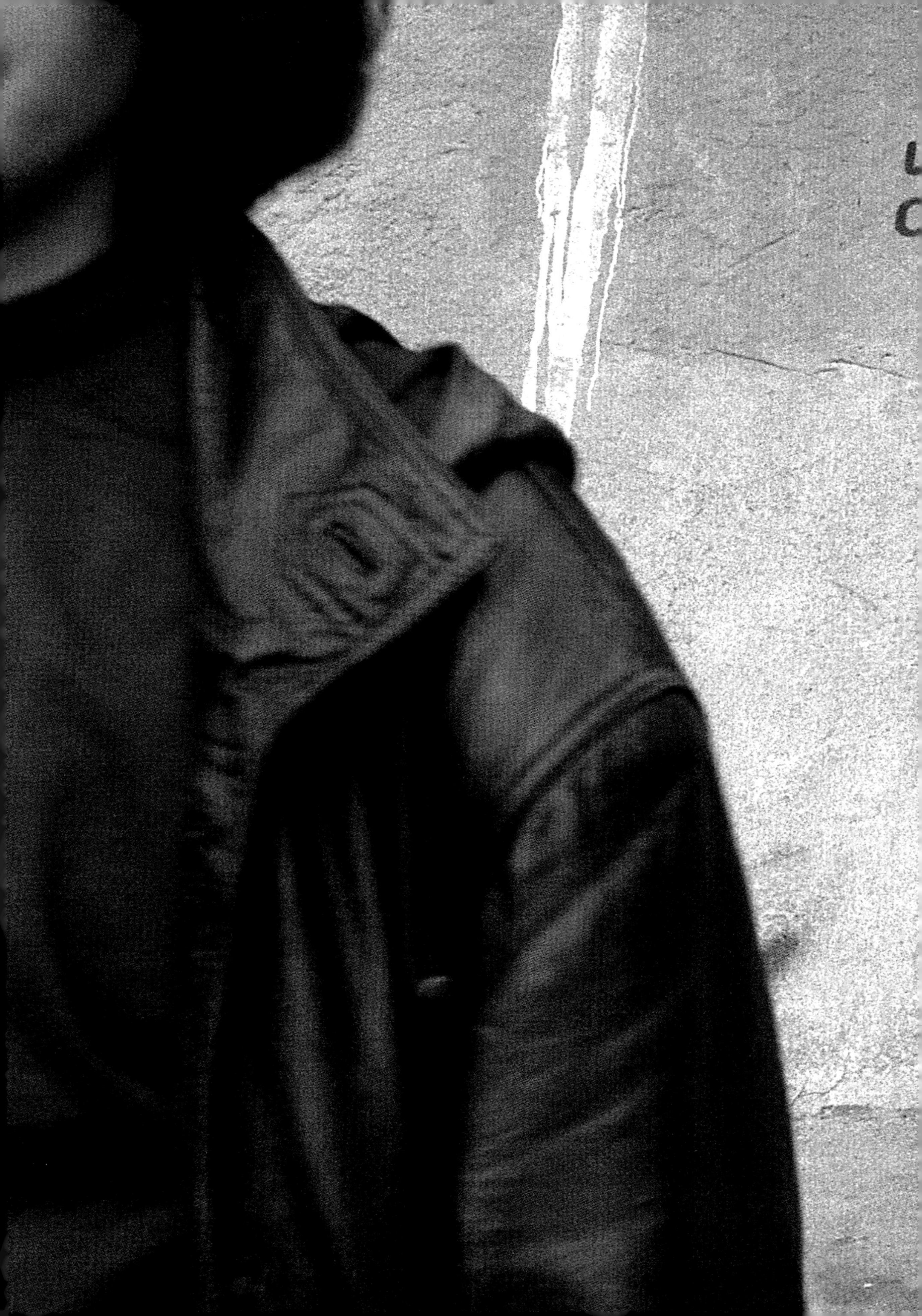

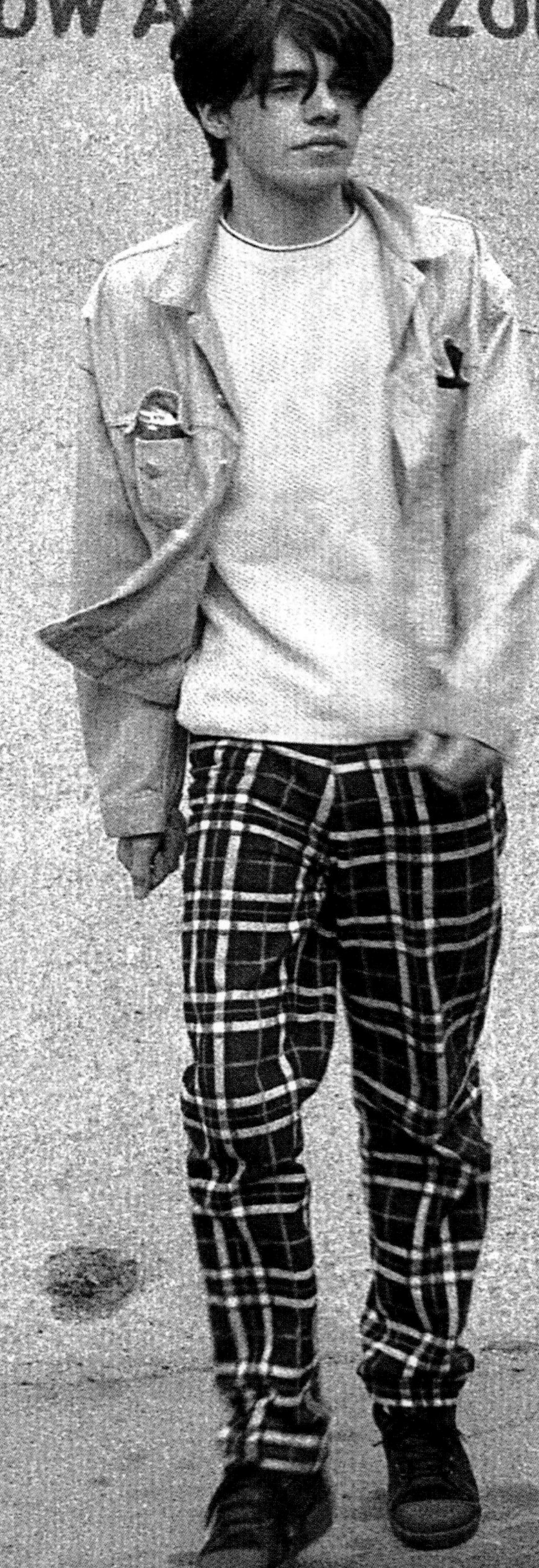
TOW A
ZONE
MITZI
ONLY !

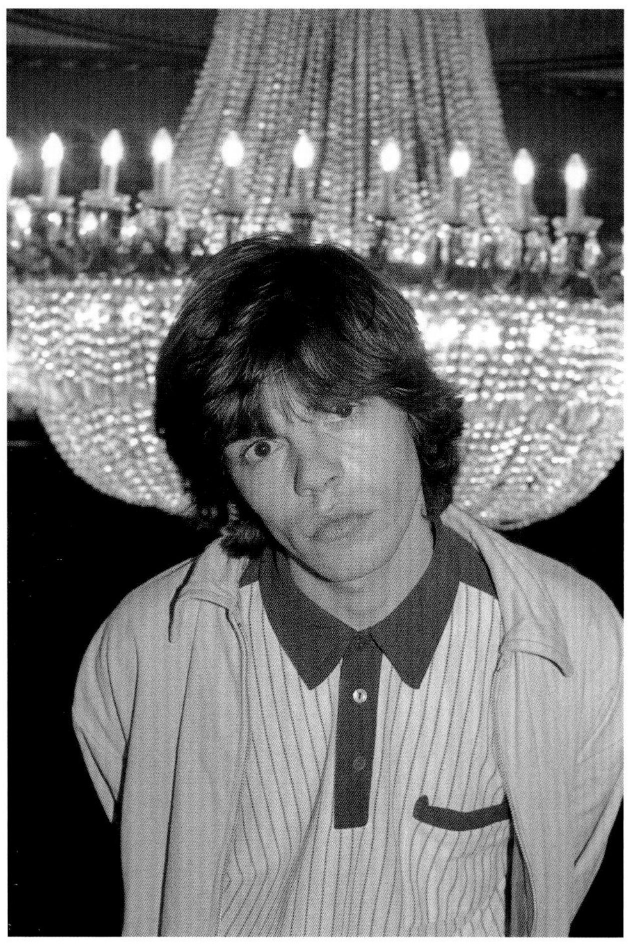

A well-known hotel in the history of Manchester music, much more infamous for its down-at-heel demeanour and rock-bottom value, especially the rooms that didn't have windows. It's like New York's Hotel Chelsea in the 1970s but without the notoriety and with fewer deaths. The shot with my hand over my face is one of my favourite pictures that Tom took of me, possibly down to the fact that you can't really see my face.

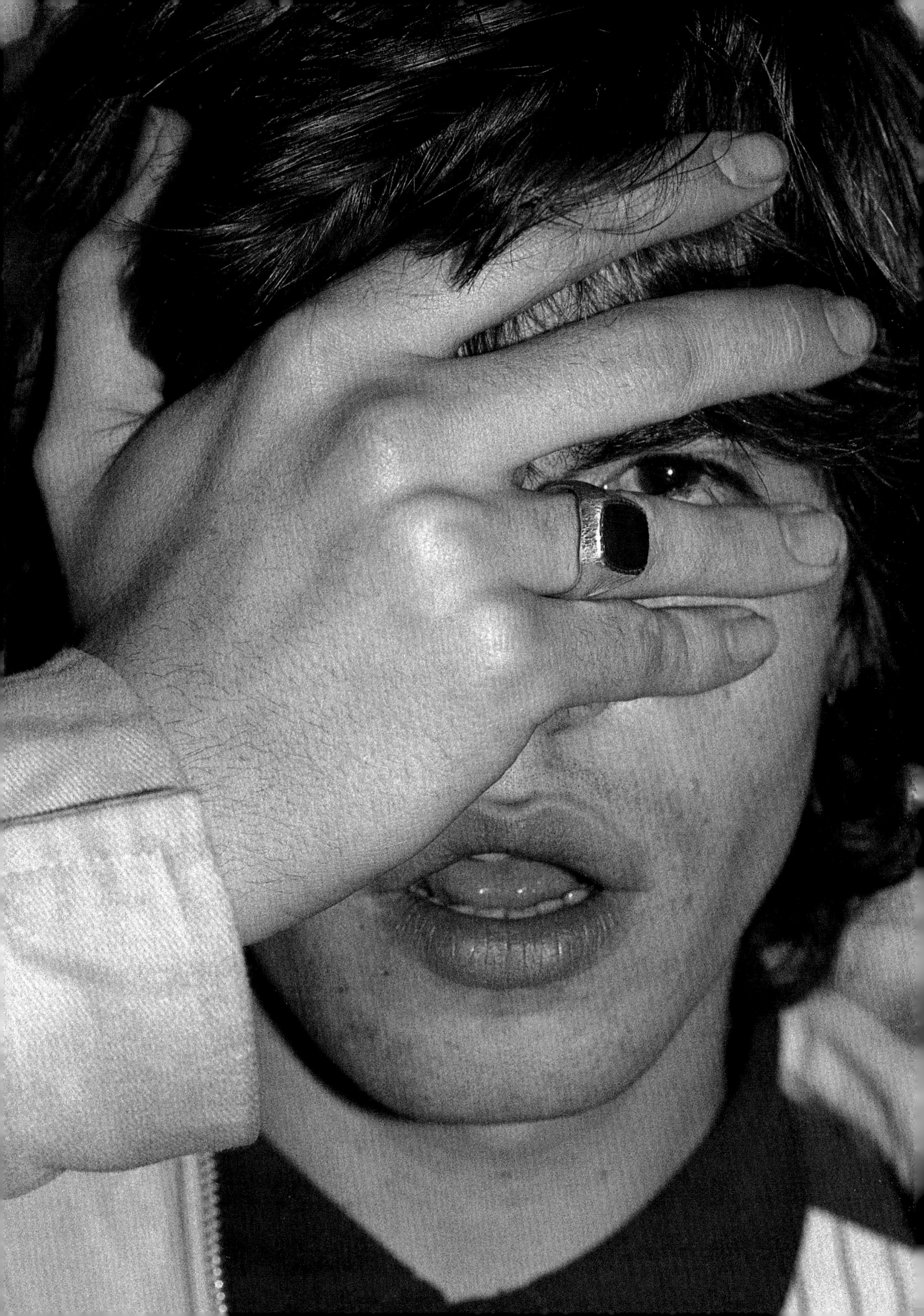

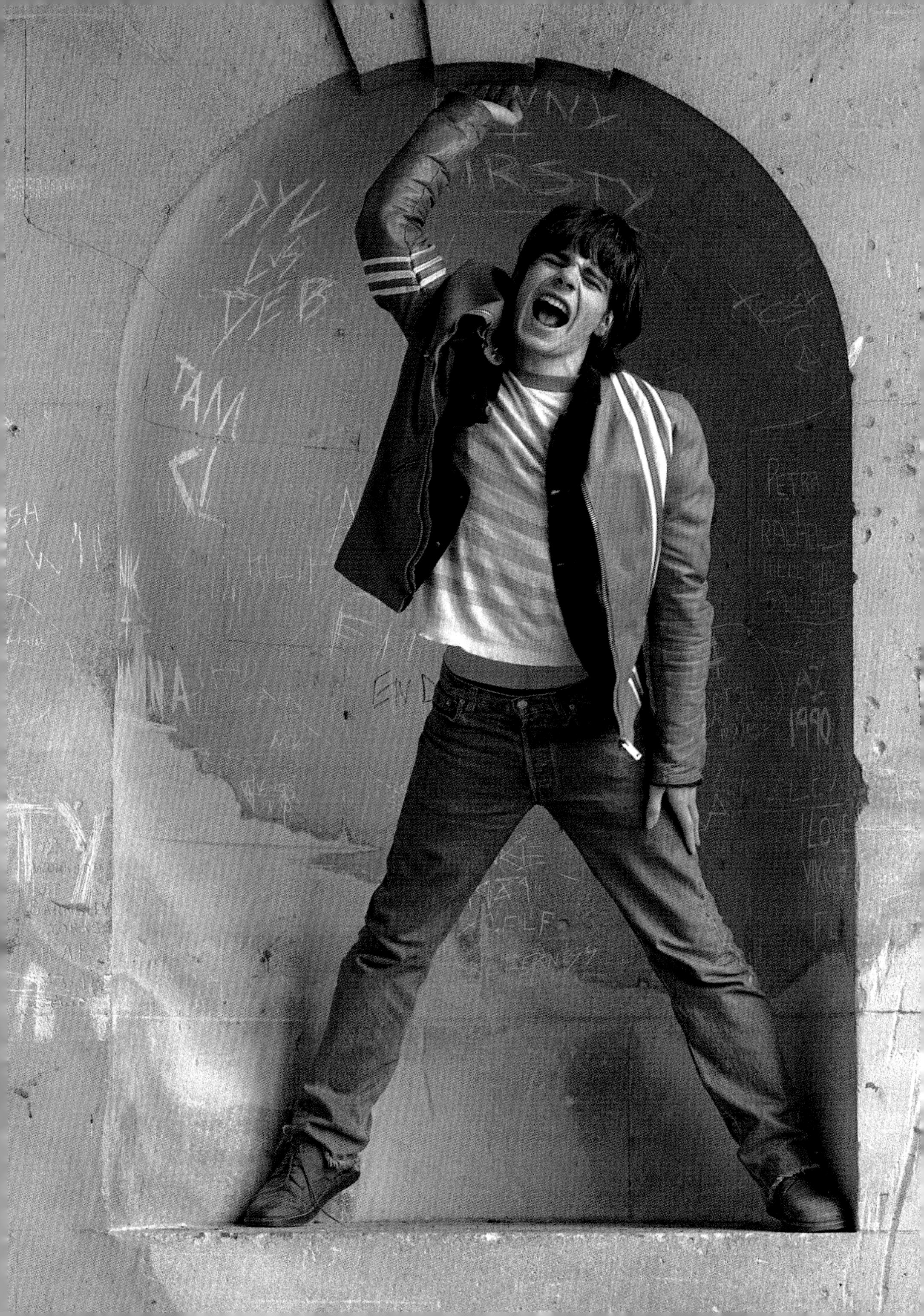
DEB
TAM
PETRA
1990

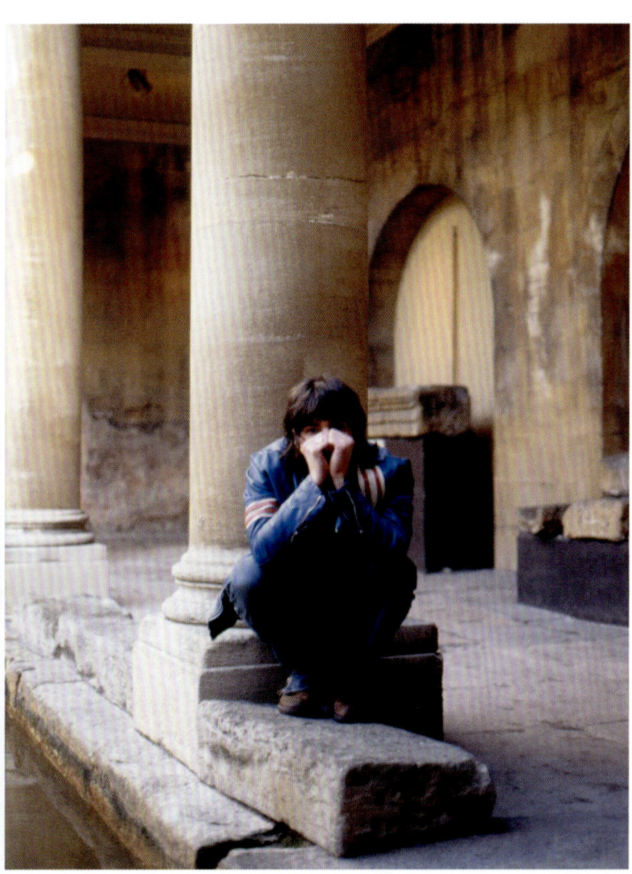

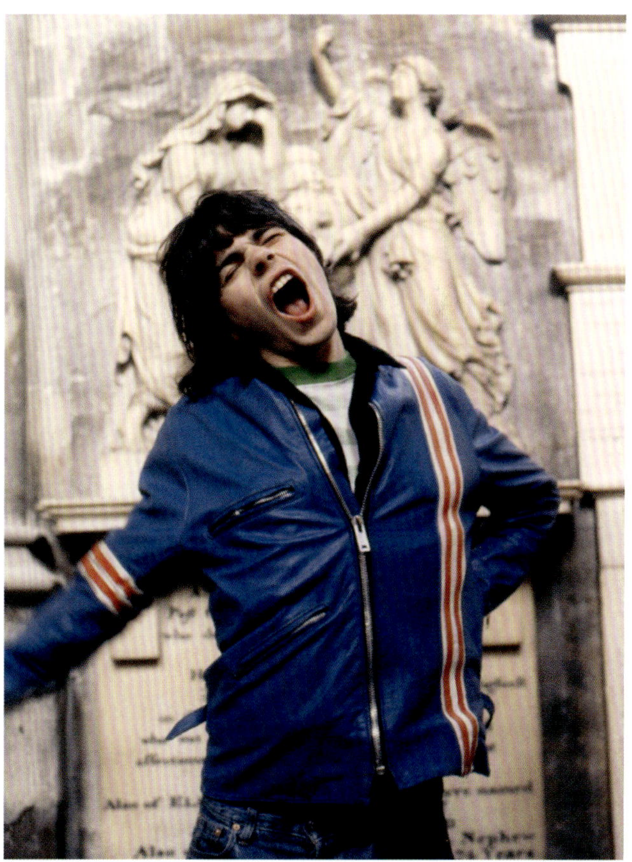

The shot standing in the Roman archway was accompanied by a soundtrack of a tour guide shouting, “Oi kid, get down from there”, and as cocky as I looked when it was taken, it was followed by a profuse apology and a promise that it wouldn’t happen again. These were all taken for a *Melody Maker* feature being written by the Stud Brothers, aka Ben Marshall and Dominic Wills, so the four of us passed the time enjoying Bloody Marys on the train and a few drinks by the river while they conducted the interview.

Tom:
This was a feature that we just invented, really. We needed something with the band for *Melody Maker*, I think they had a single out, and someone suggested we have a day out in Bath, because, why not? So we met at Paddington, cracked open a few drinks on the way down, wandered around, went to the pub, came back, cracked open a few on the way back, and went for a curry. All in a day’s work.

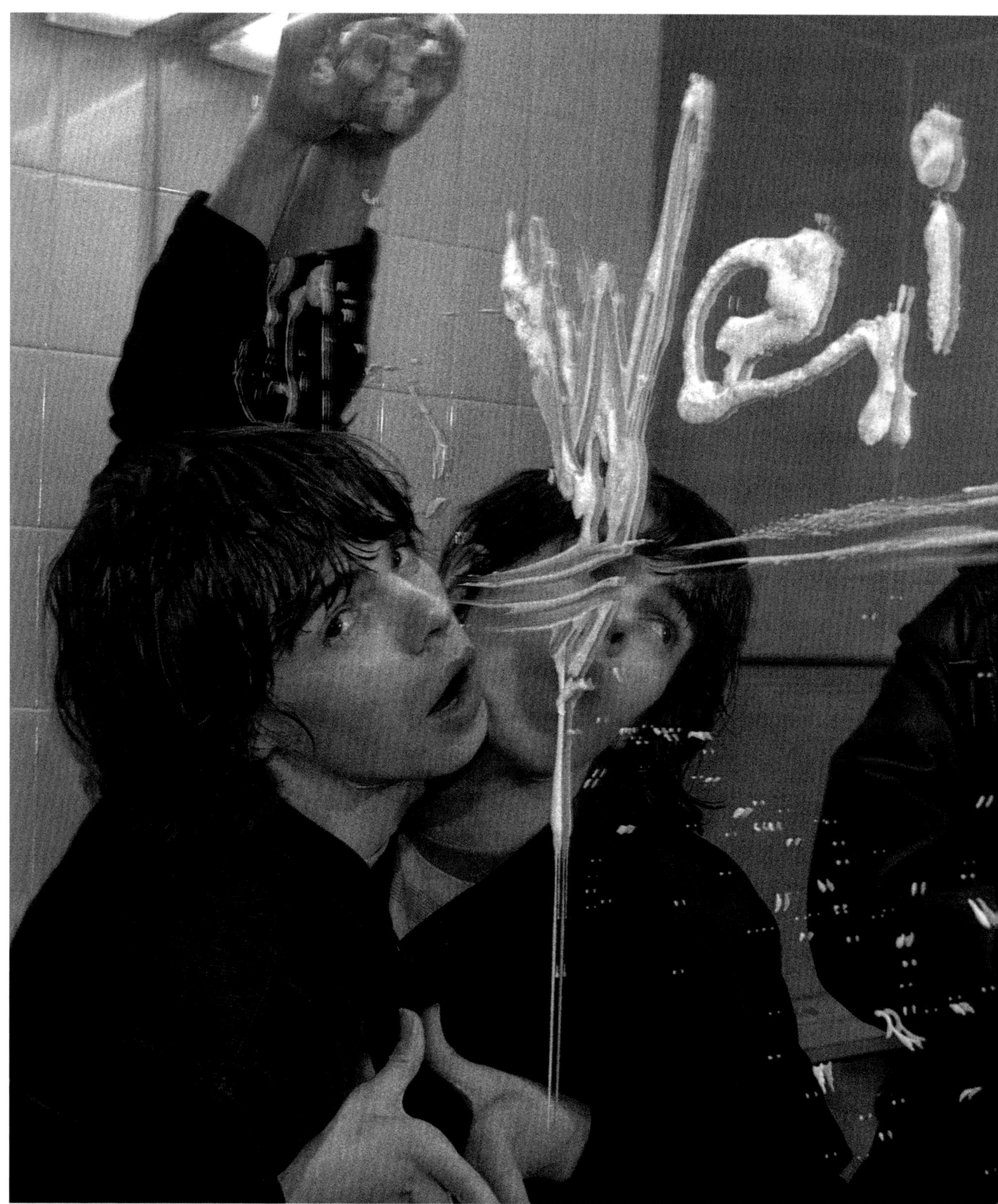
Wei

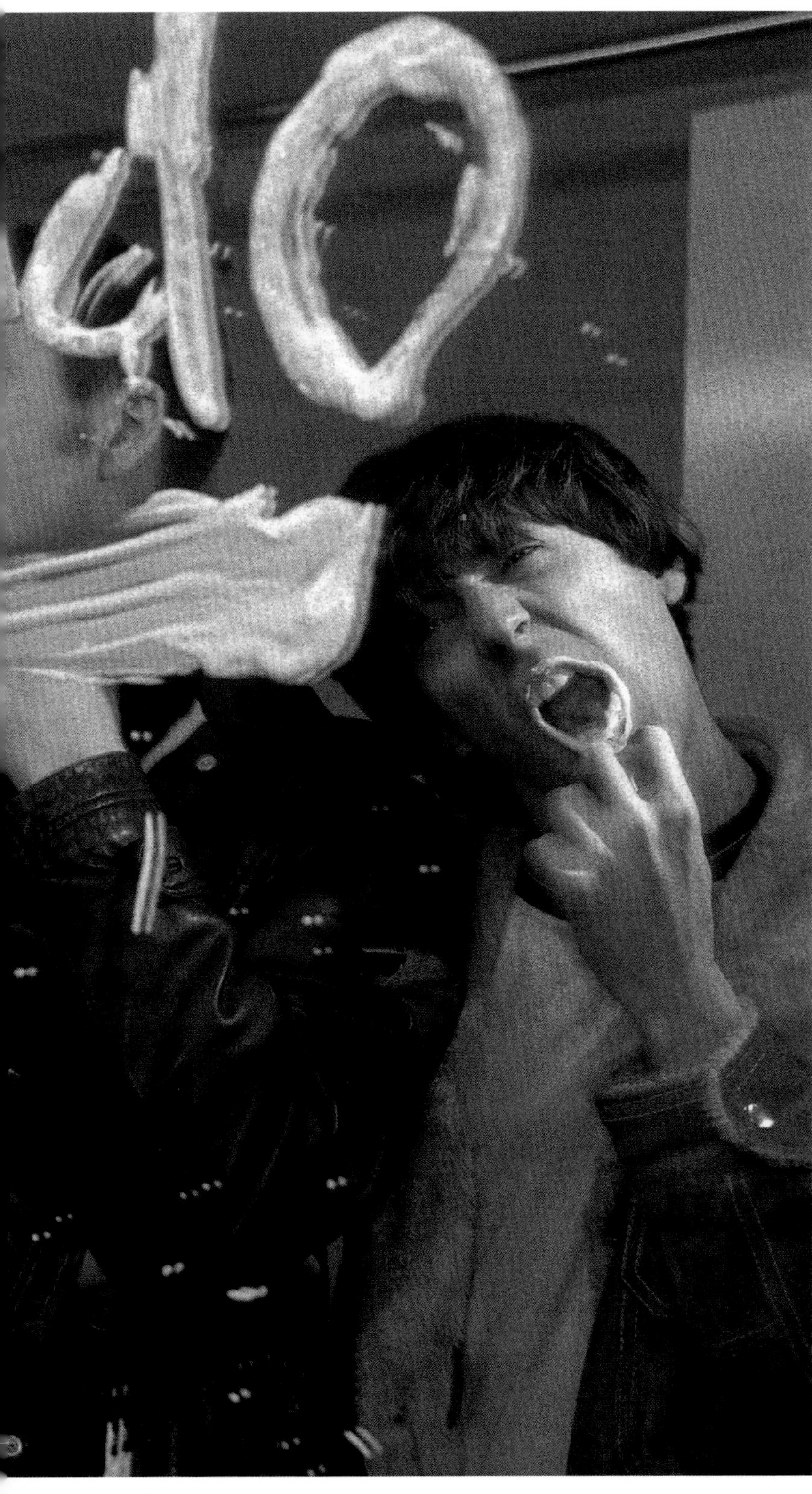

This was taken at a hotel in London. We had ten minutes and a can of shaving foam. Some sessions took months to plan, with props and stylists, etc., but this remains one of my favourites, the first pictures Mark had taken with us.

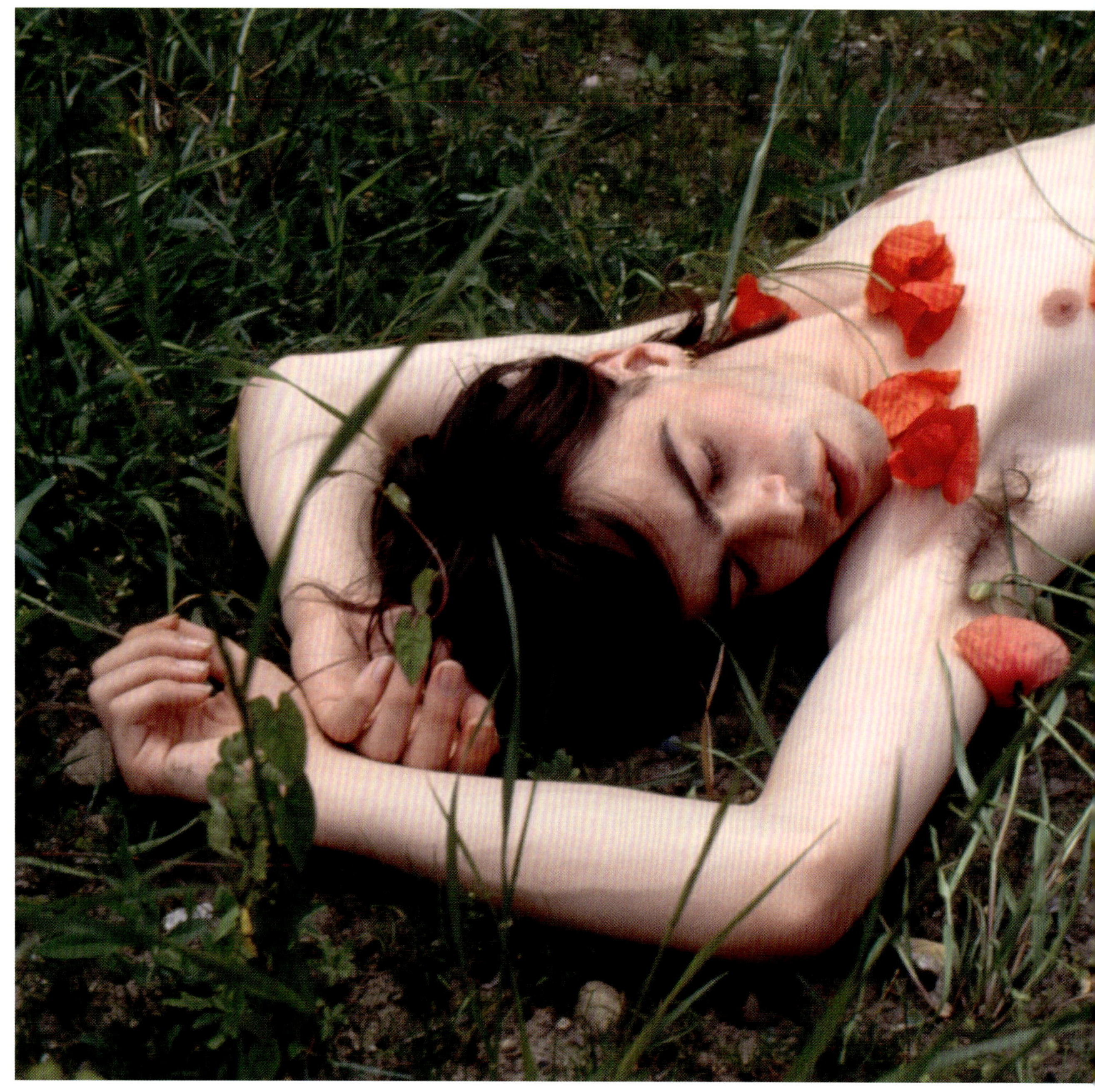

Most of the time, I am not only wearing a T–shirt/top I am often sporting a jacket/coat/rainwear. For the record, this was Tom's idea and I simply went along with it. Looking at these pictures now it seems like Morrissey might've been the inspiration, but at the time Tom mentioned a host of 70s' pop pin-ups, including David Cassidy, and who was I to argue? It was definitely a departure from the usual alleyways, scrapyards and party scenes that made up 90s' magazine content. I like these pictures as they show a different side of me. I aways wanted to be a pop star anyway, in amongst my desired roles as beat poet, sage and all-round hero.

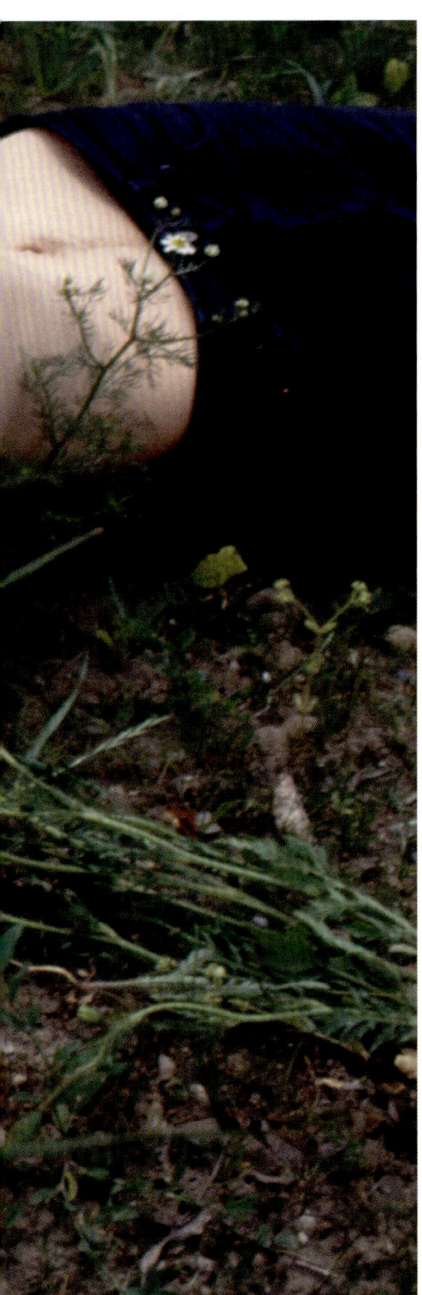

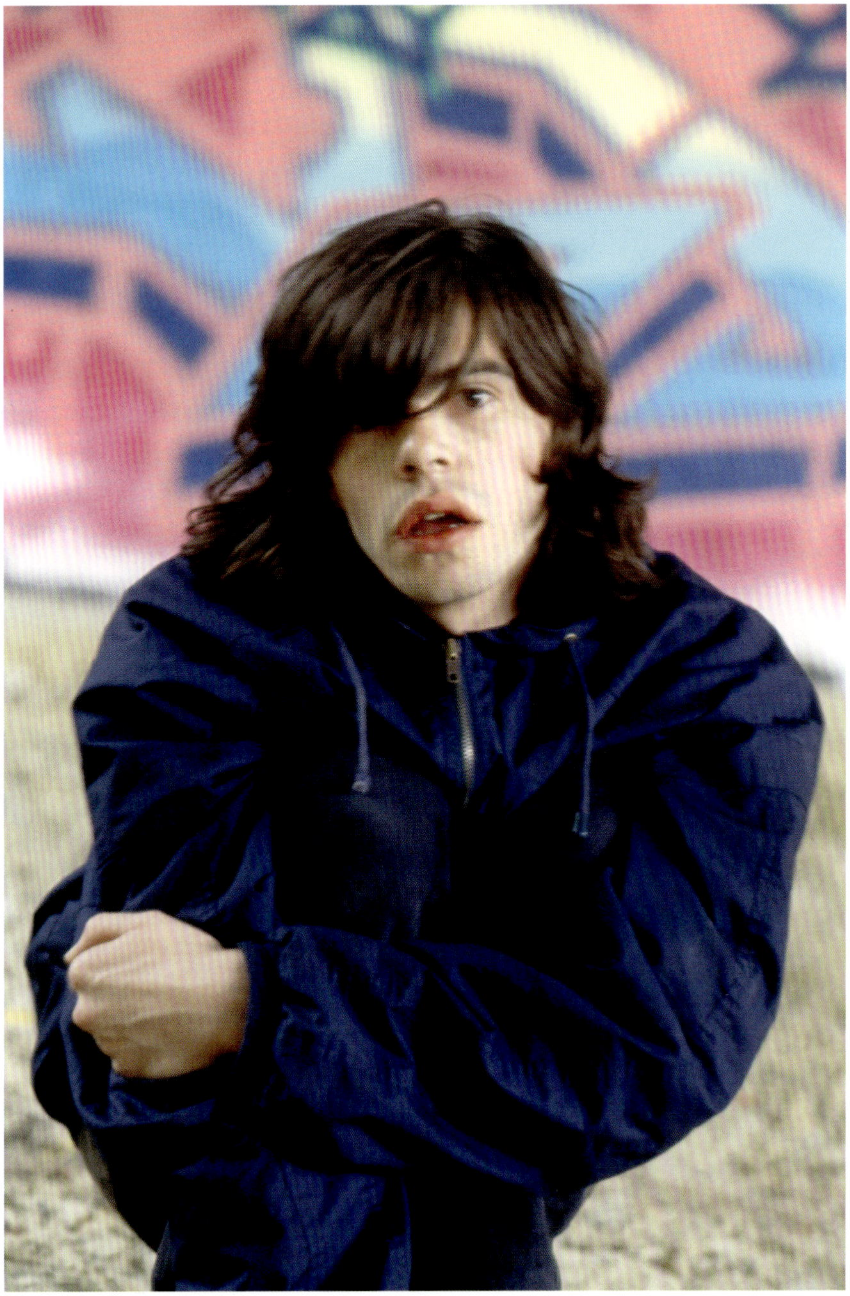

The eternal conundrum with photos was that we would always want the pictures to include all band members. But often magazines would ask for pictures of just me. After a few months of attempting to wrangle all concerned to get up for early morning shoots, I am pretty convinced that everyone became okay with it sometimes just being me having to get up and attempt to make myself look human. Tom and I were always early risers, and we'd go scouting for locations after leaving the safety of the tour bus. I remember we found this graffiti underneath a flyover – I am thinking Hamburg, but don't hold me to that. It's not necessarily my memory that's bad but straight after a tour days, gigs and events are scrambled in your brain to give a fake sequence, like a movie of what happened rather than actually what happened.

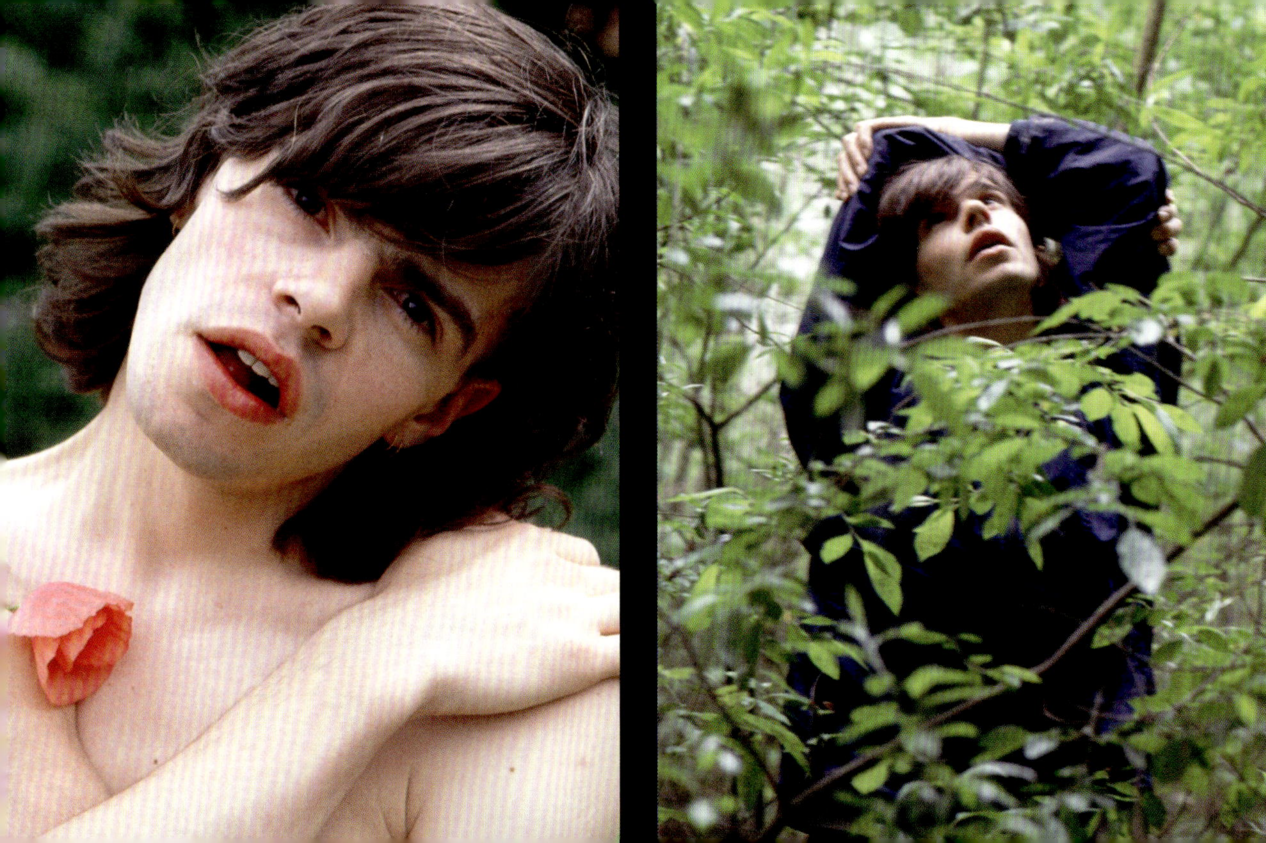

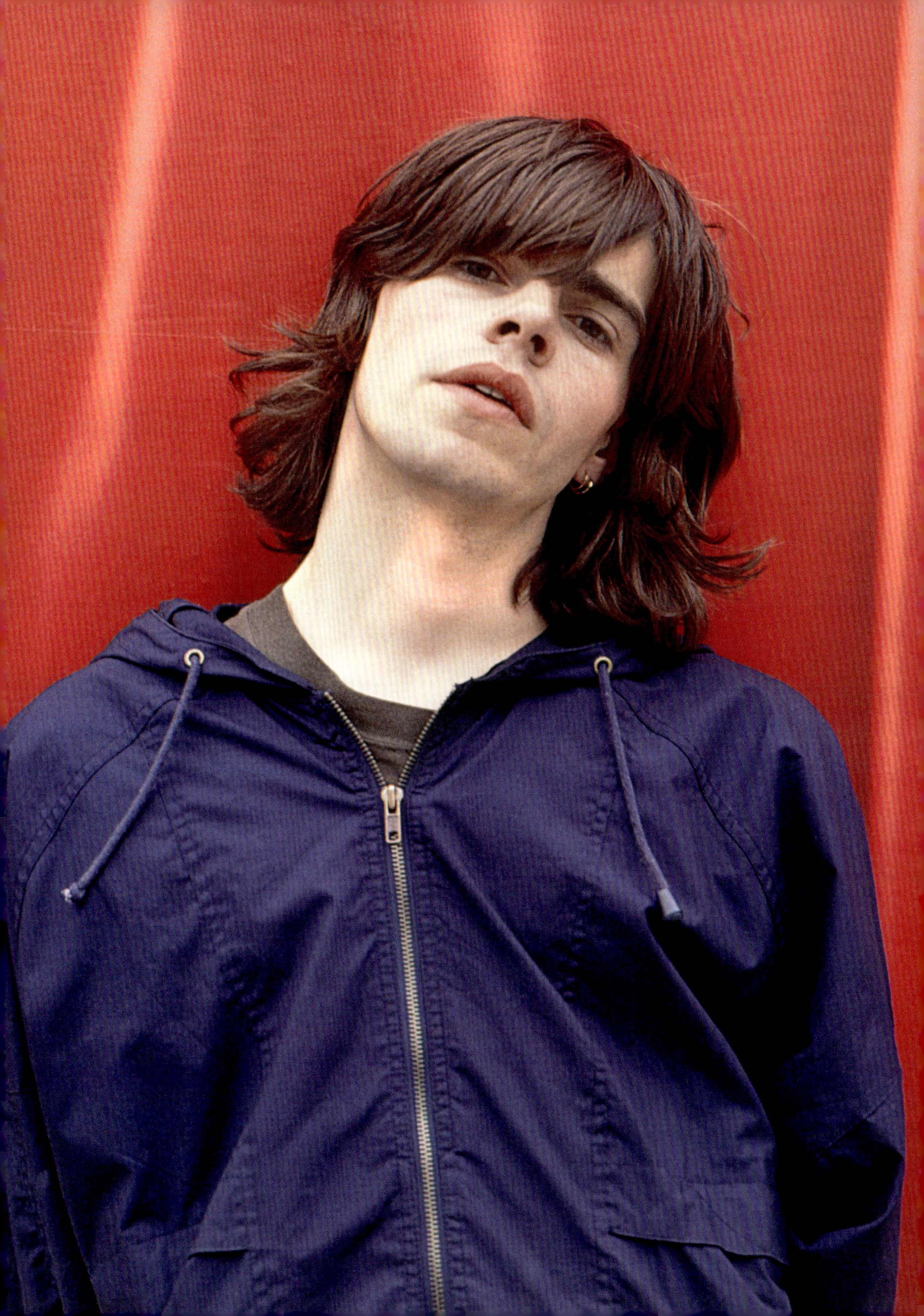

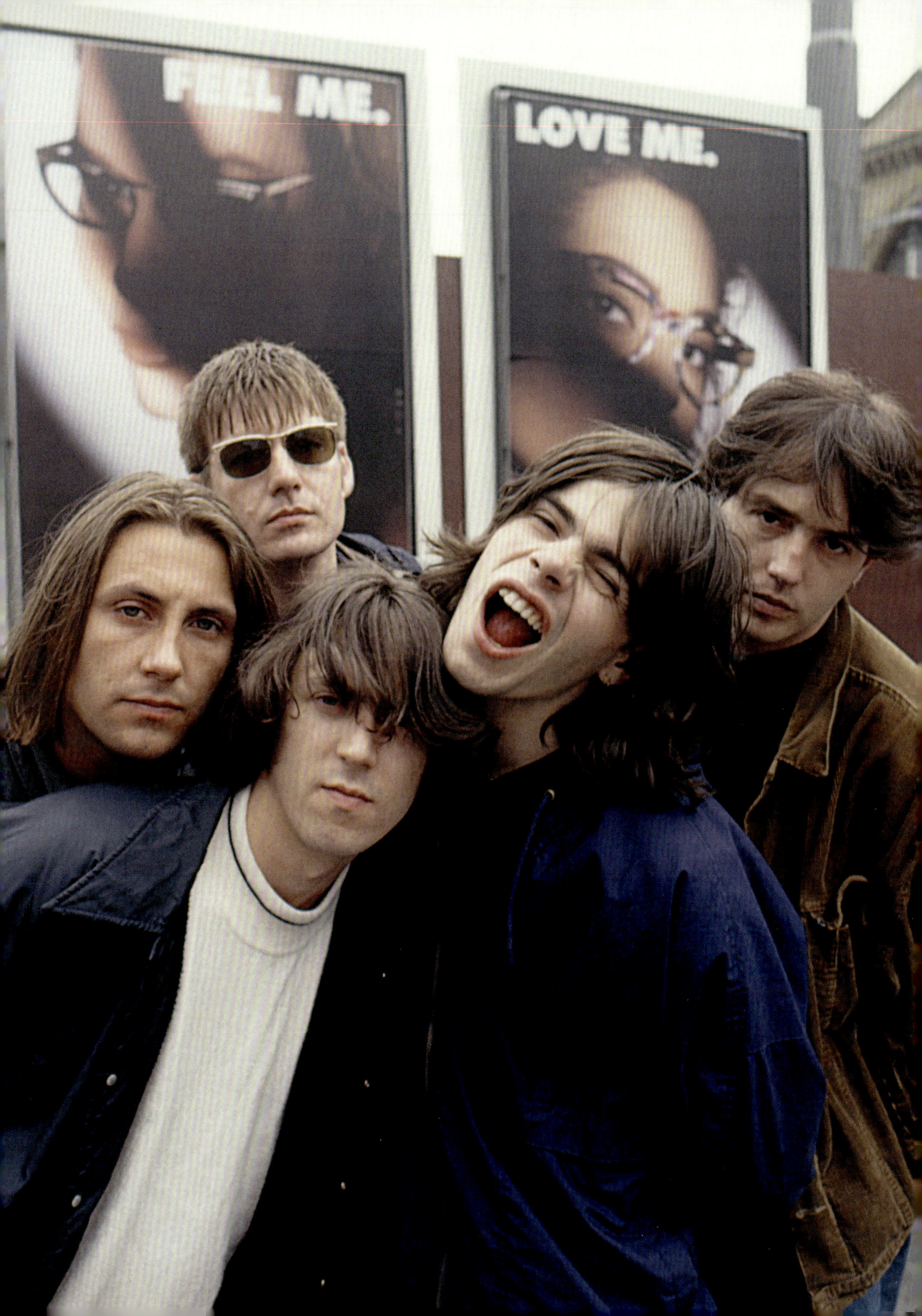
FEEL ME.
LOVE ME.

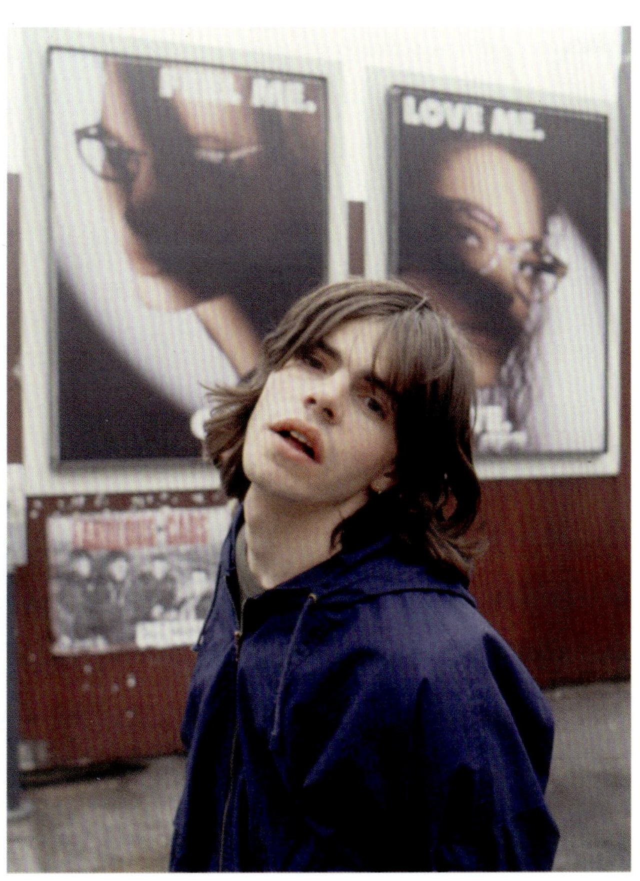

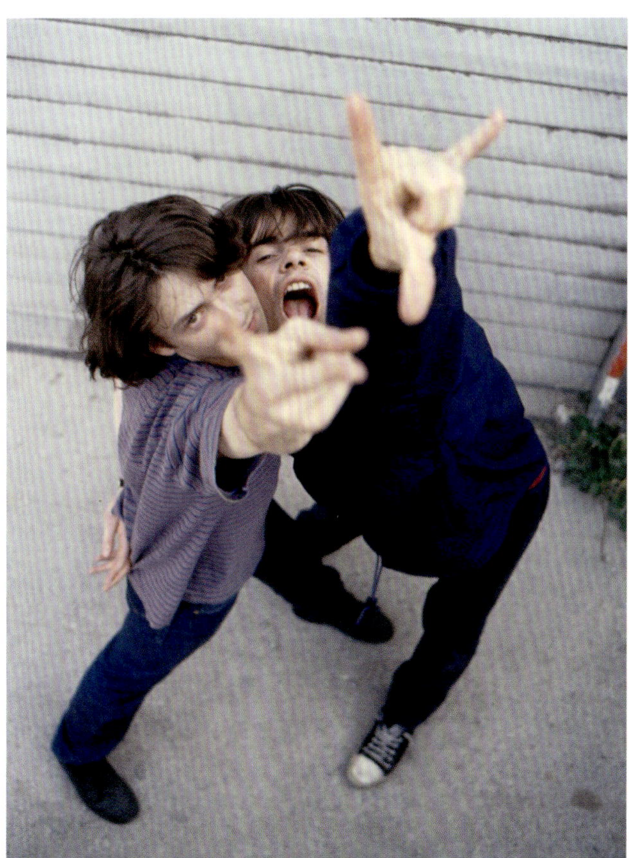

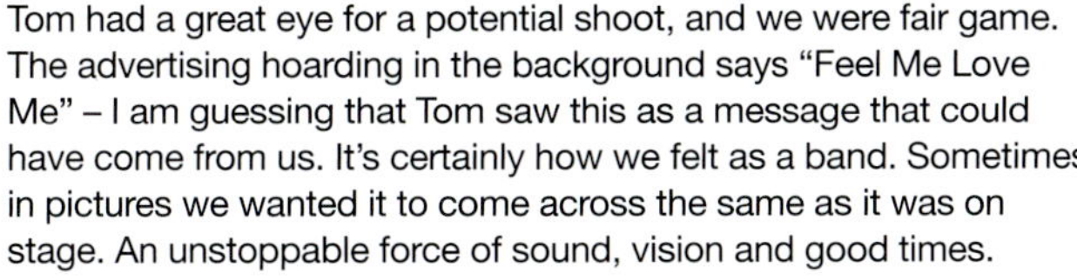
Tom had a great eye for a potential shoot, and we were fair game. The advertising hoarding in the background says "Feel Me Love Me" – I am guessing that Tom saw this as a message that could have come from us. It's certainly how we felt as a band. Sometimes in pictures we wanted it to come across the same as it was on stage. An unstoppable force of sound, vision and good times.

Within the band there was always an ever-changing dynamic of friendships, with an overriding element that we always loved each other – a feeling that we were siblings rather than work colleagues. Rob and I didn't have brothers, so it was an even greater feeling for us to be a part of what we had. I love this photo of Mark and me. Being in the band meant we got closer than lots of friends would have had the opportunity to do, and we have these photos to treasure and remind us of that.

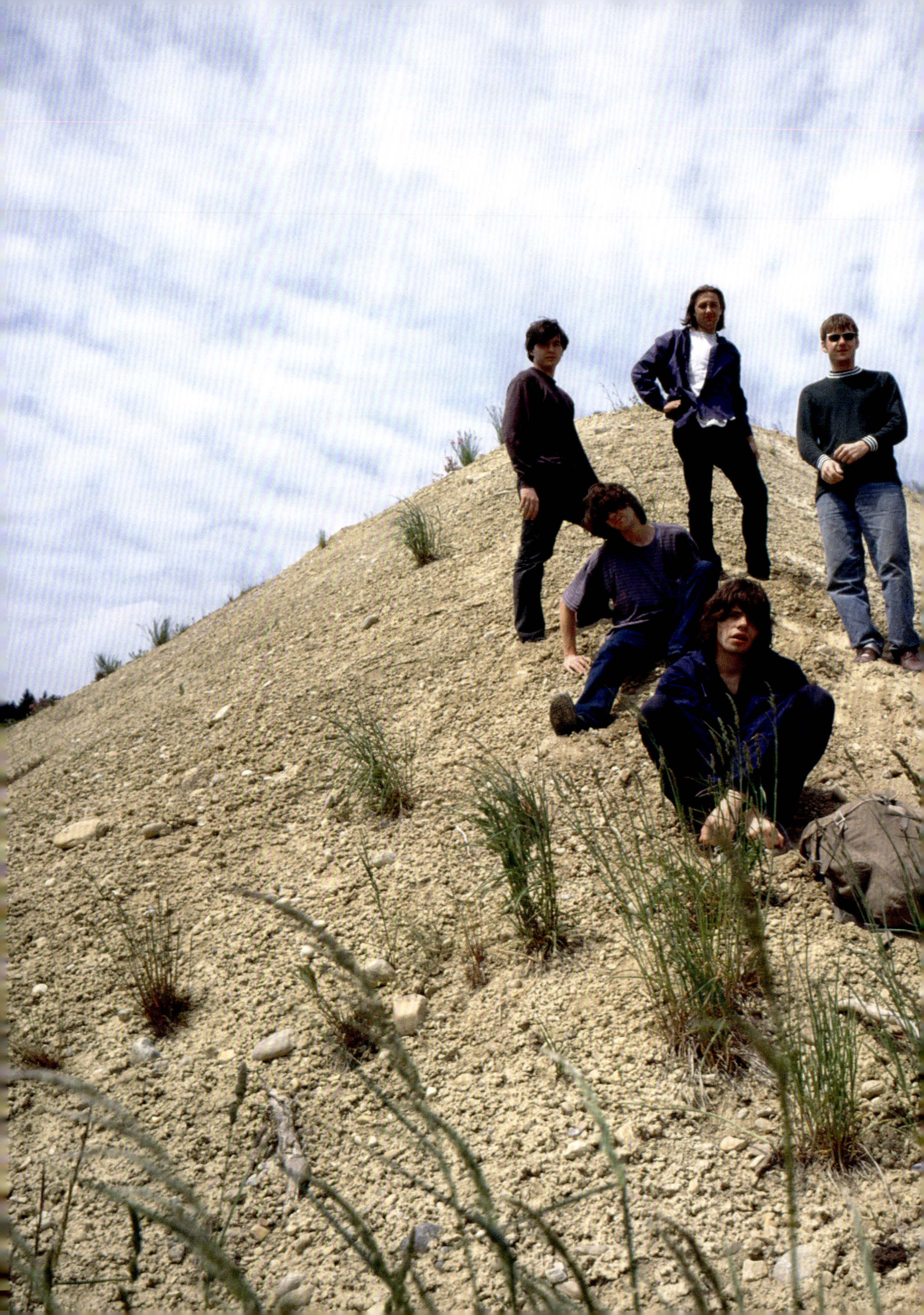

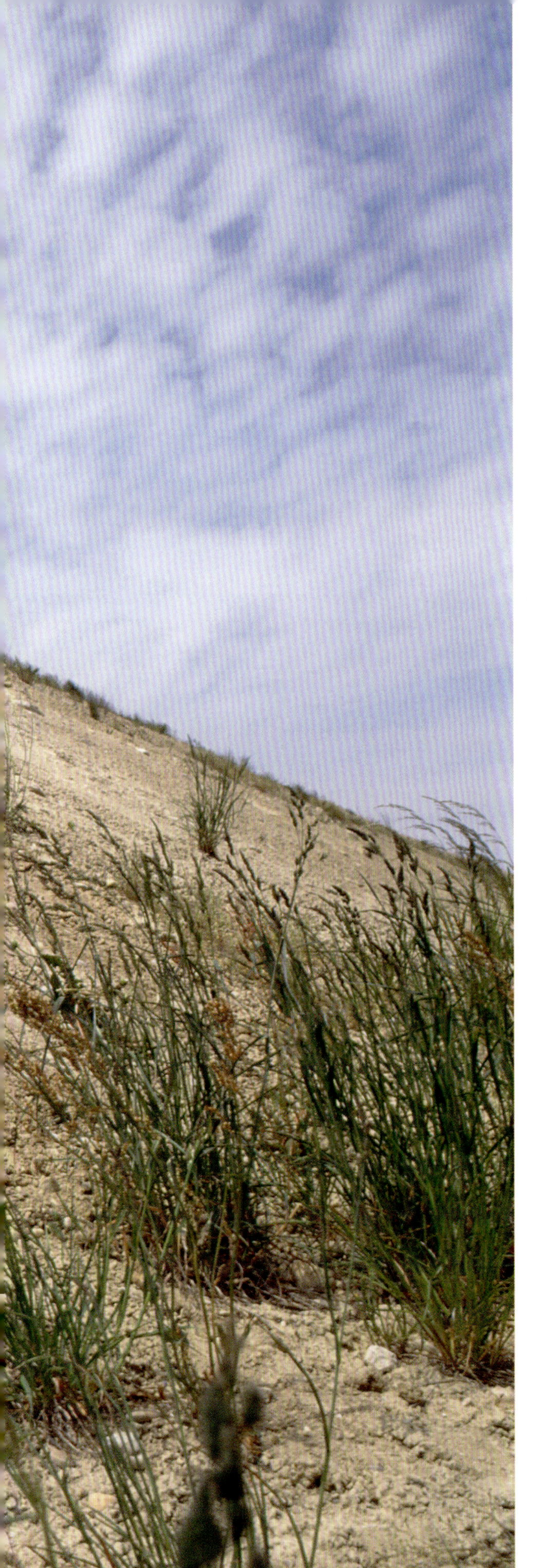

Another one where the backdrop inspired the pictures. I'm guessing there was a shout of "pull over!" from Tom as we sped to our next show. The call would go out to anyone in their bunk on the tour bus, then within 30 minutes we'd all be back where we started, picking up our card games, beer bottles and conversations, with Tom peering out the window looking for an abandoned gas station, a burnt-out car or similar when we'd hear the shout to pull over again.

The only thing that I took with me for the pictures was the rucksack that I'd borrowed from my dad. He'd used it all over Europe, climbing any peaks and mountains that he came across, including the Matterhorn. I didn't have many reminders of home with me and I know my dad was really proud of the miles covered by his faithful bag so, for both practical and spiritual reasons, I asked him if I could take it on tour with me, given that my dad's mountain-climbing days were coming to an end. It accompanied me around the world over the next few years until a broken strap brought about an enforced retirement.

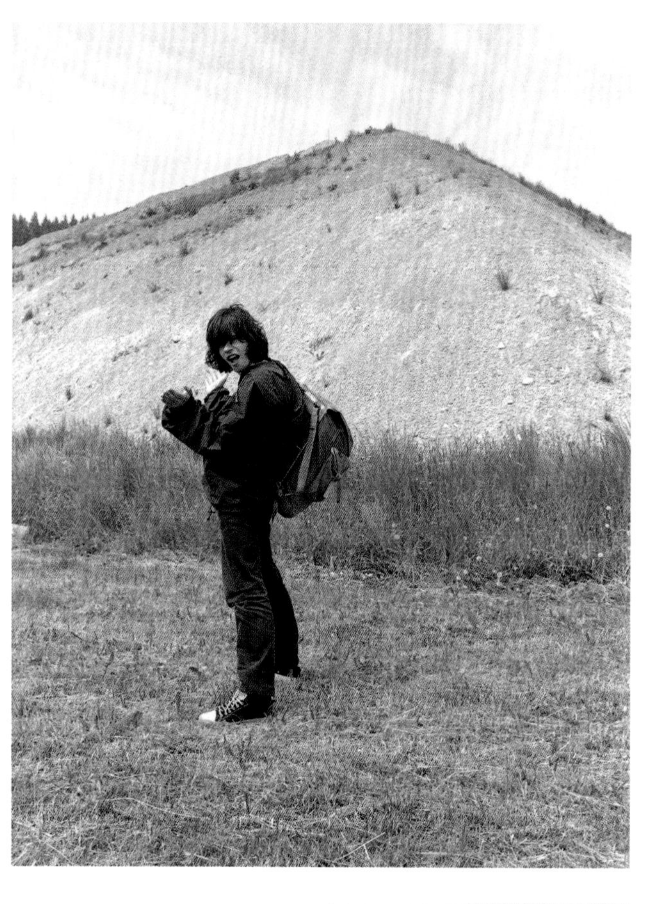

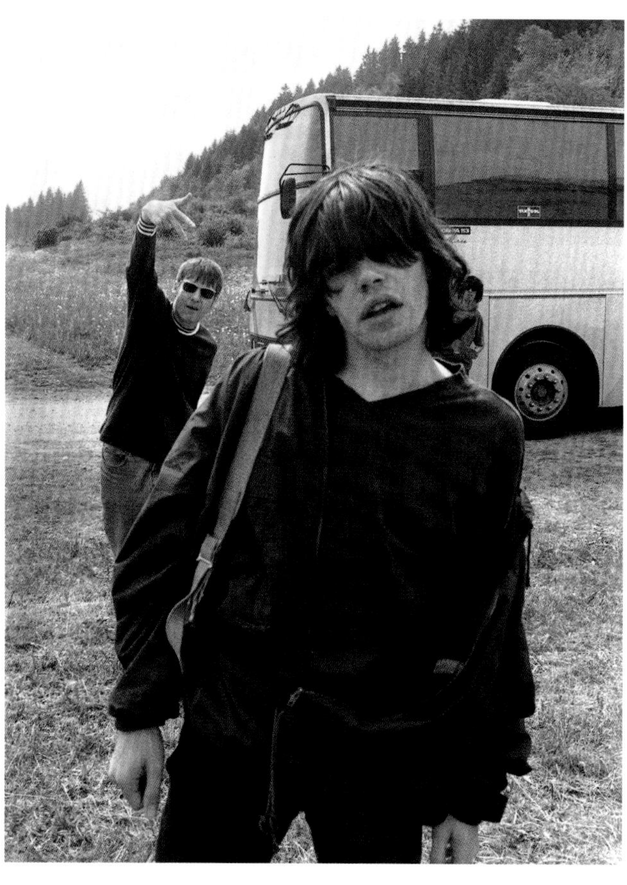

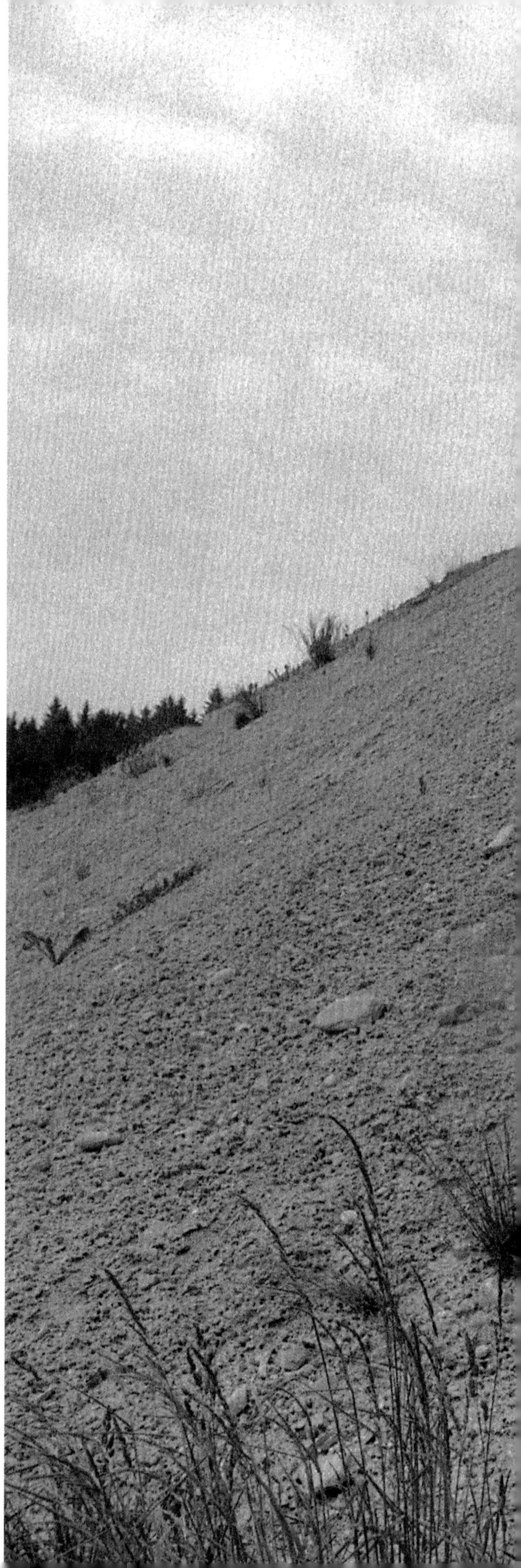

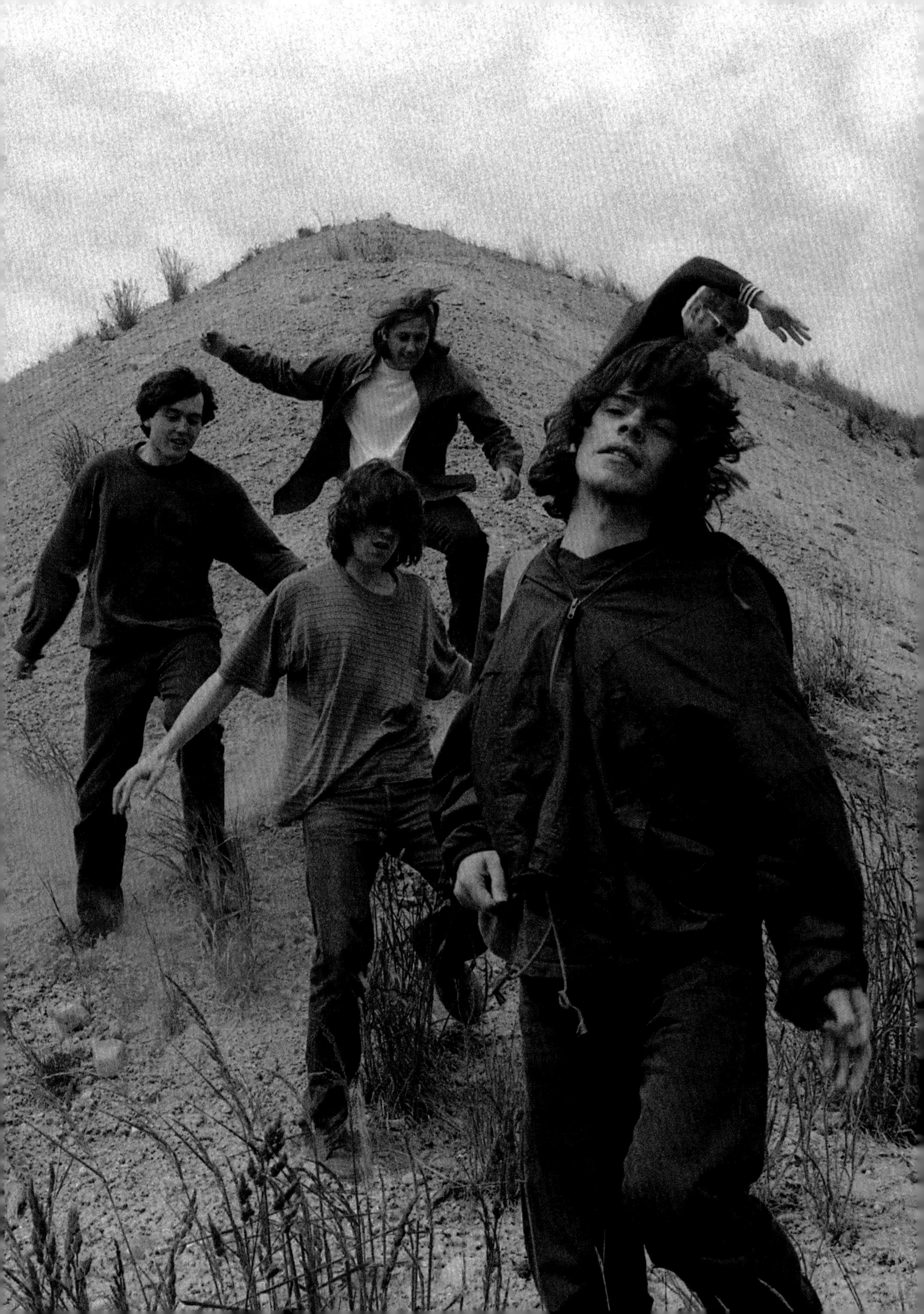

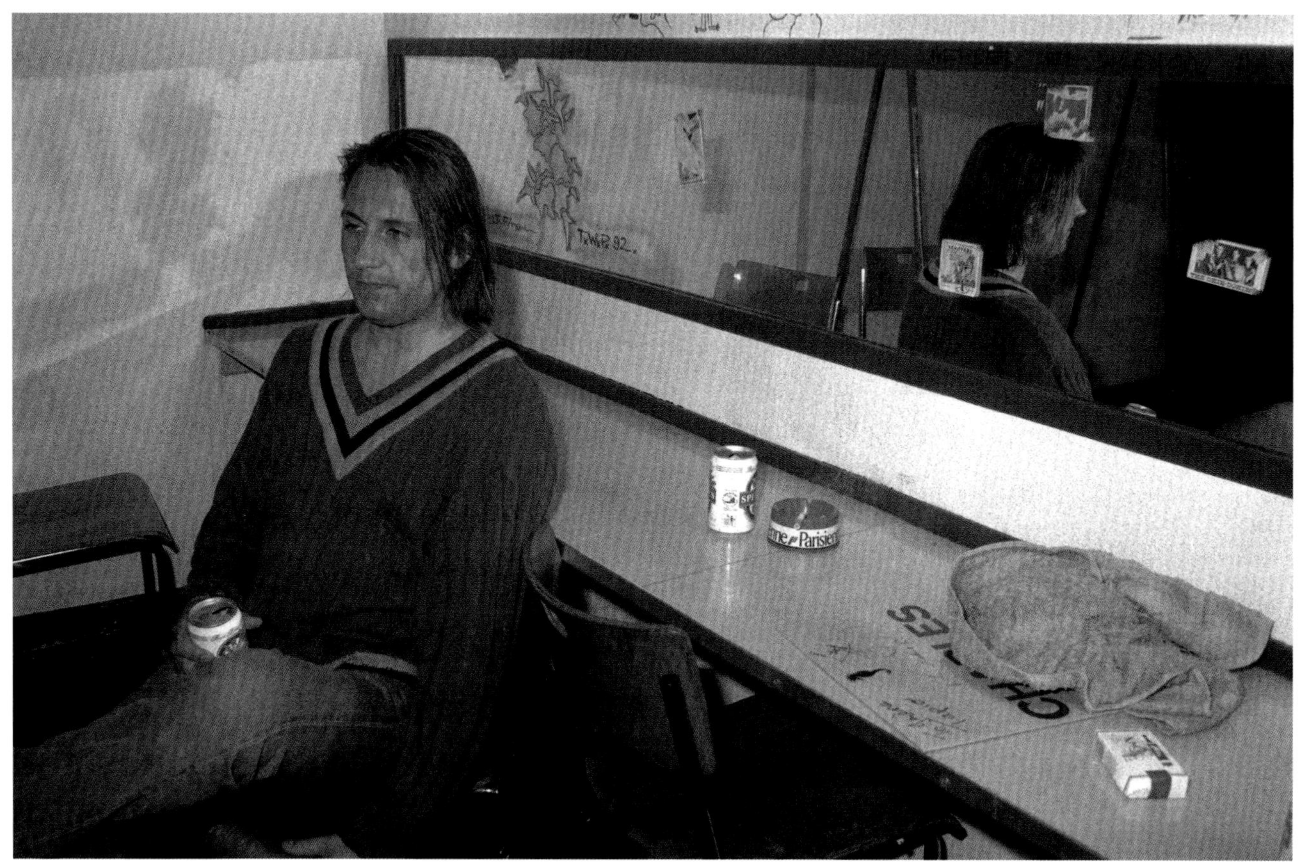

The thing about being the singer in a band is that so many pictures are just of me and it can get to the point where you're fed up of looking at them – there aren't so many of the other band members just on their own, which is what makes me love this one of Jon.

This captures a feeling in the dressing room after a show. We'd be absolutely drained, when everyone probably thought we'd be bouncing around having a party. Just the five of us spending time after a set was always something special. Jim, our security guy then and now, would always tell people that we needed 20 minutes for a band meeting. I'm assuming label people thought this was a post-show drug frenzy, but it was our own moment before sharing it with friends, family and those with backstage passes.

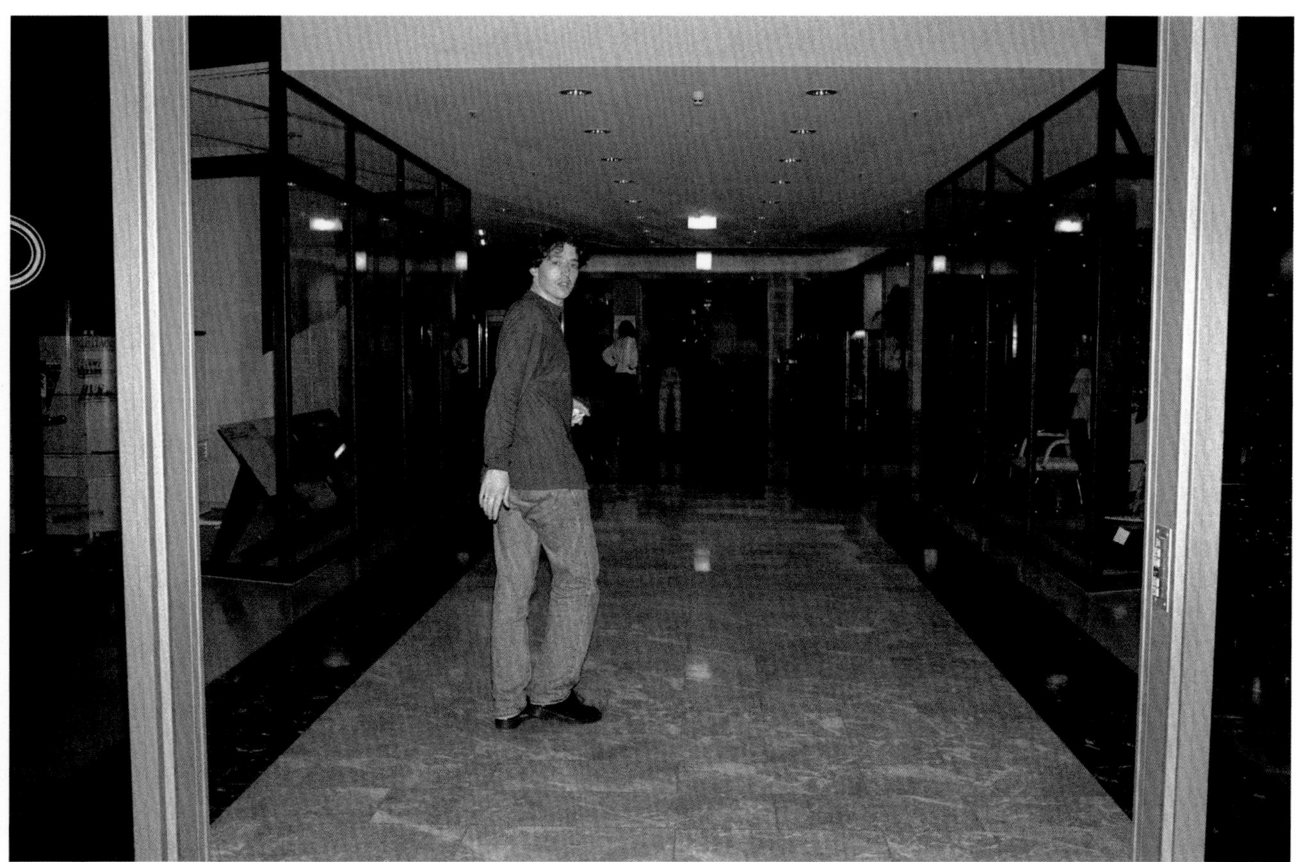

Candid shots like this are among my favourites. No planning, just taken in the moment. It could literally be from my mind's eye as we were walking into a hotel before a soundcheck. The poignancy of this picture is increased when thinking what was to happen to Rob in the upcoming months and years.

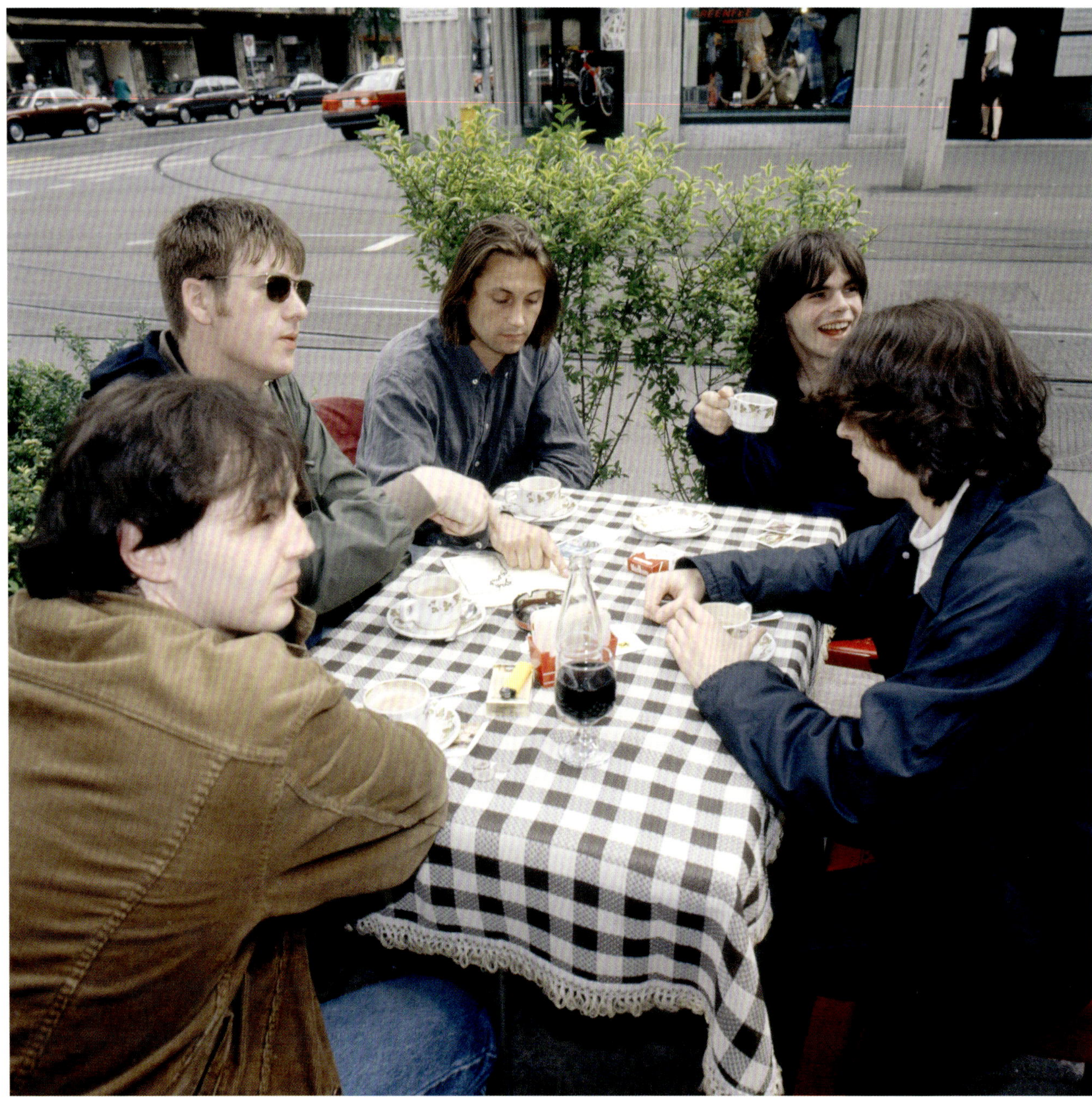

Sometimes we wanted to show candid moments with the band, but there would have to be an element of 'set-up' – us lot actually sitting round a table in a café might not have the room needed to get a decent picture, or it would just be us lot actually eating without the intrusion of a camera. This is a good example of an organized session that appears to be just a moment in time. Tom would have taken time placing the cups, wine and arranging the tablecloth, also asking permission from the café owner, usually even before anyone from the band arrived. Directions would be given on who should be drinking what, a call of action for some general chit-chat. I doubt there was anything in my cup on these. We'd be on our way after 15 minutes, before any kind of drudgery had set in.

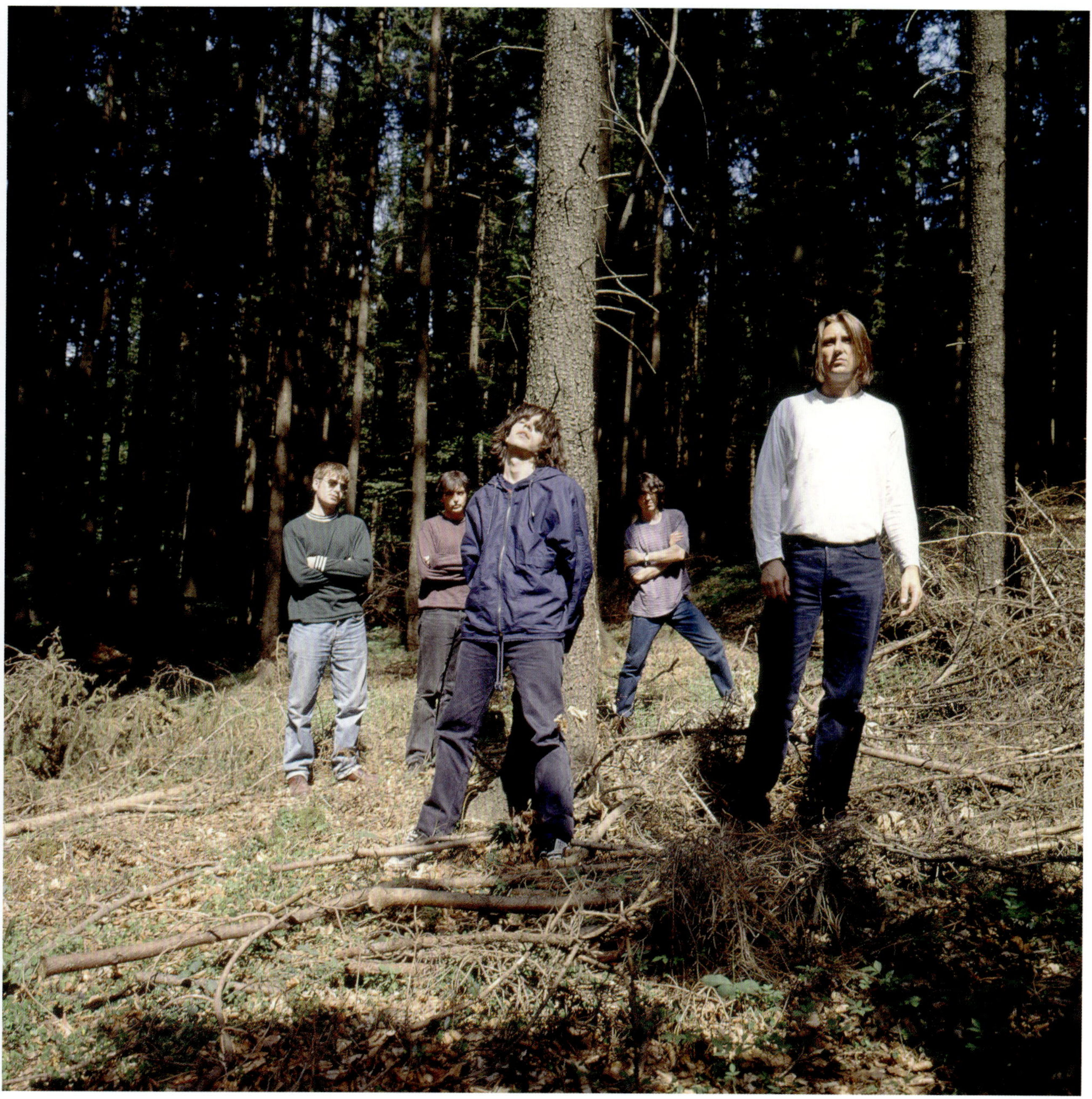

By now if we were playing a run of dates we'd always give Tom a shout, and though weekly music papers didn't have huge budgets back then, even the thought of air fares being covered seems like something from an era long since gone.

We had been out on a European tour for about three weeks when Tom joined us in Turin on 27 May 1992, as we headed to Switzerland and Germany, where I celebrated my 25th birthday in Munich with a gig at Nachtwerk.

In Europe, scrapyards gave way to pine forests, car ferries and, by the looks of it, afternoon tea somewhere in Germany.

These are the most memorable photographs we have ever worked on with Tom. We were all in our mid-twenties, we were doing what we had dreamed of and we had all the time in the world. The most amazing part is that it seemed like it might never come to an end.

Mark had replaced Jon Baker, and the next chapter of The Charlatans was about to be written. Mark and I gravitated towards each other in terms of songwriting and we felt we were honing our craft. We were getting used to our new lives. If we weren't on the road we were in the studio, and Tom was always welcome to document our adventures.

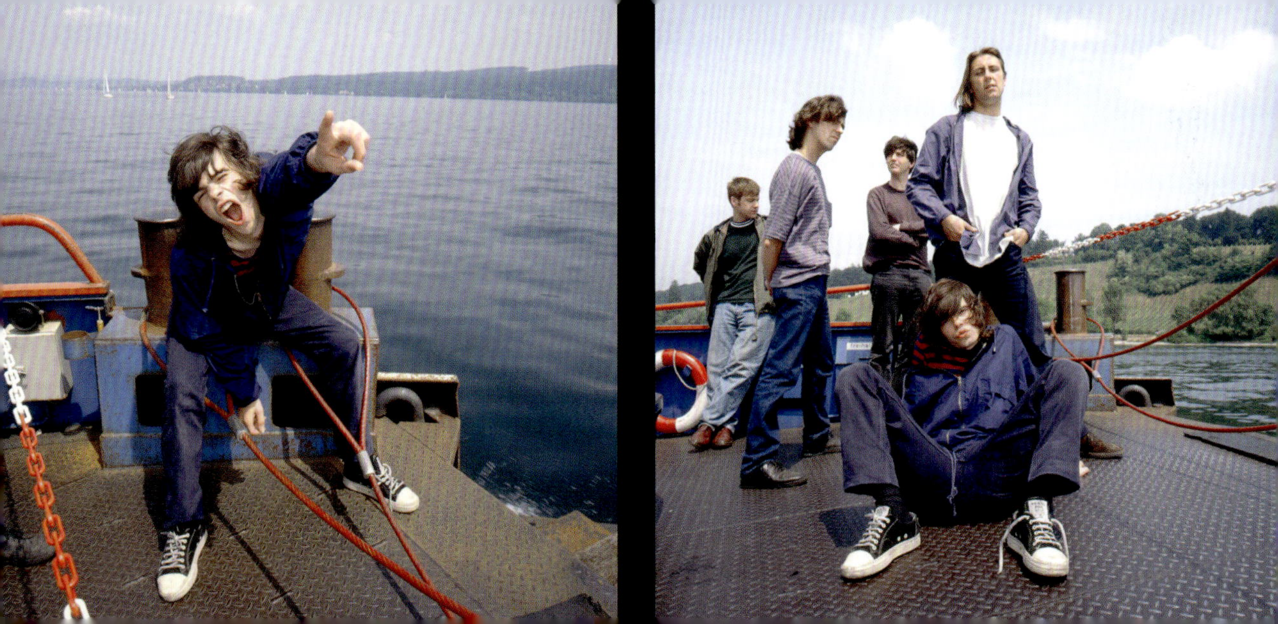

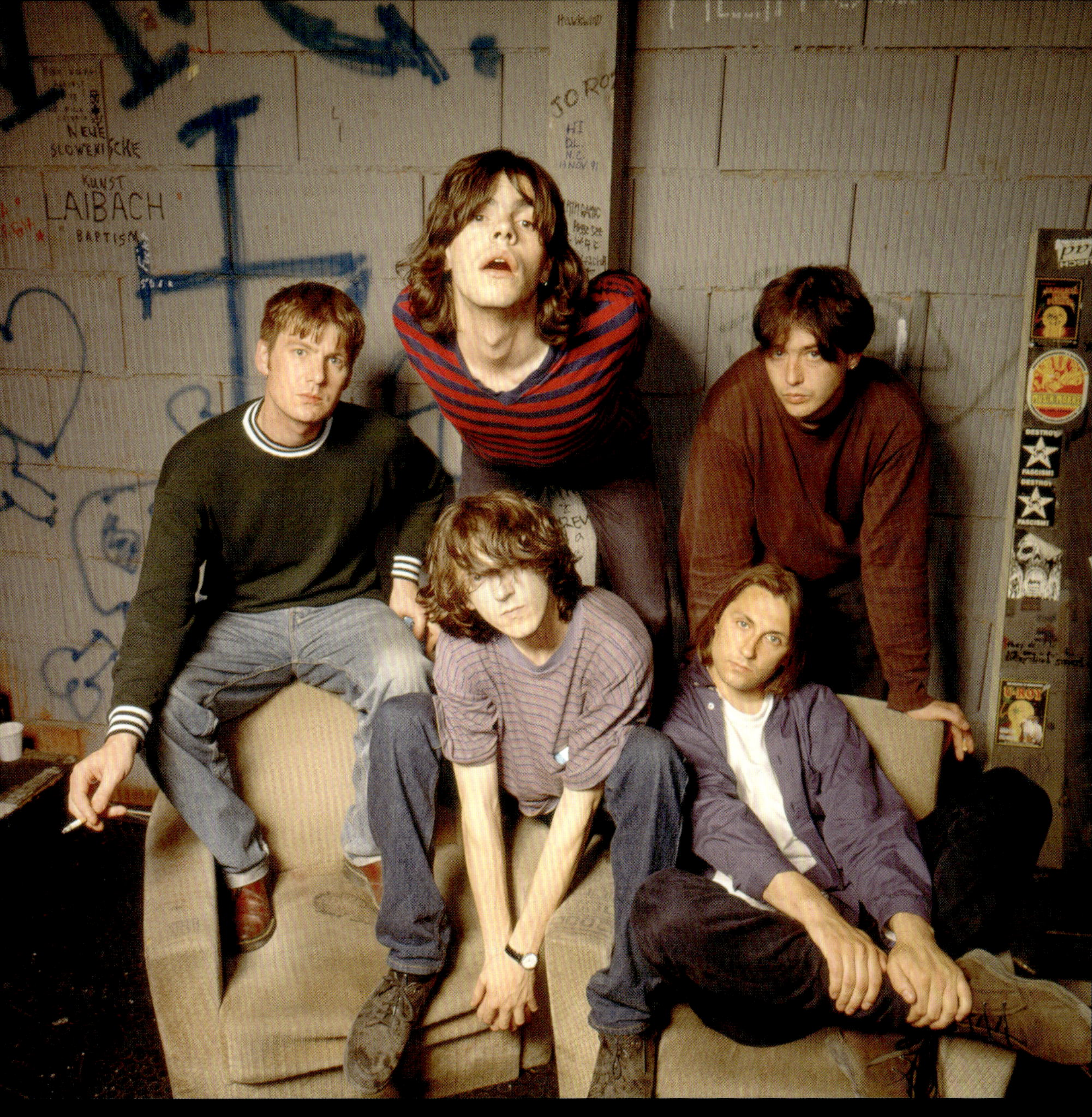
NEUE
SLOWENISCHE
KUNST
LAIBACH
BAPTISM

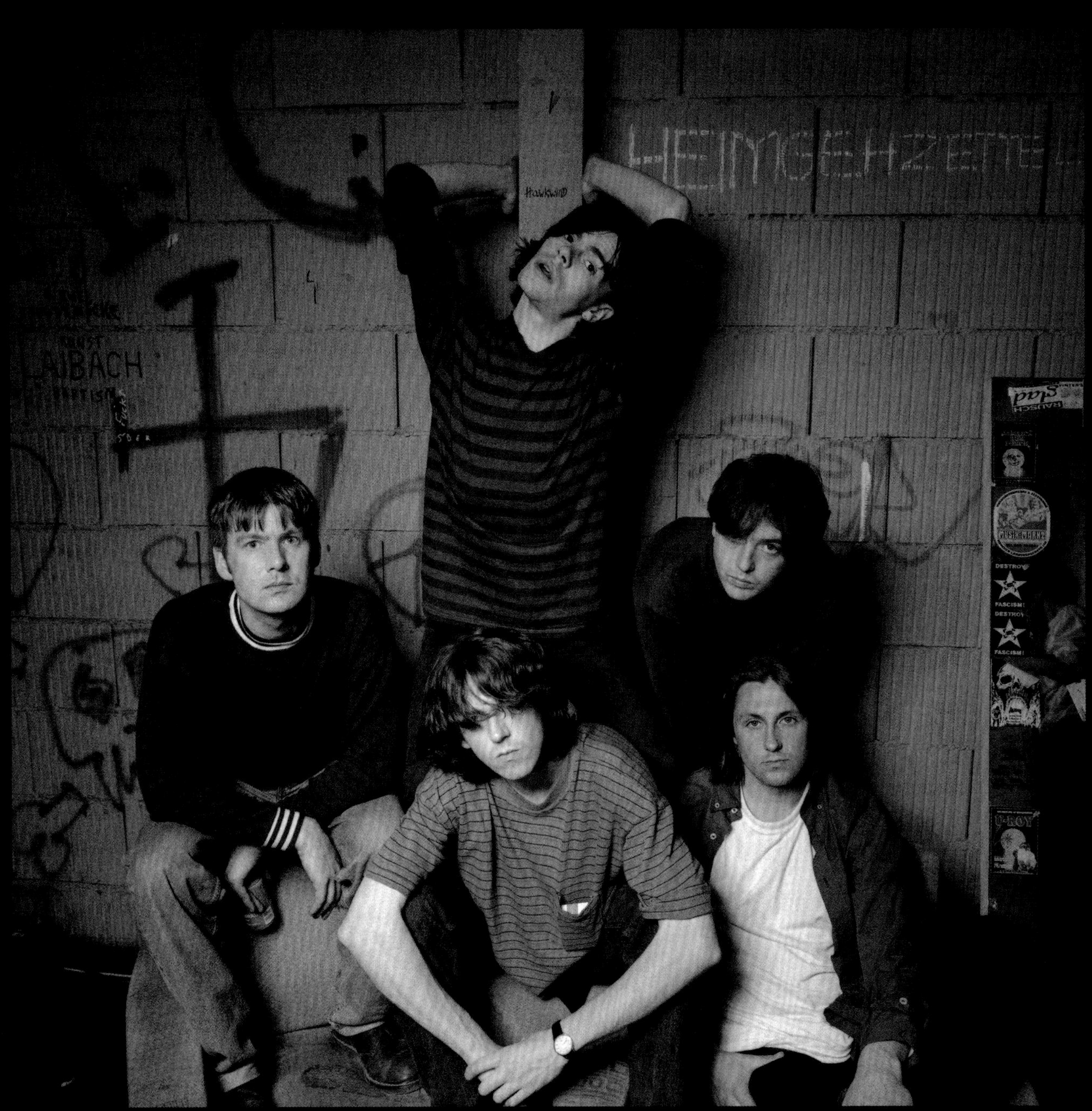
LAIBACH
DESTROY
FASCISM!
DESTROY
FASCISM!

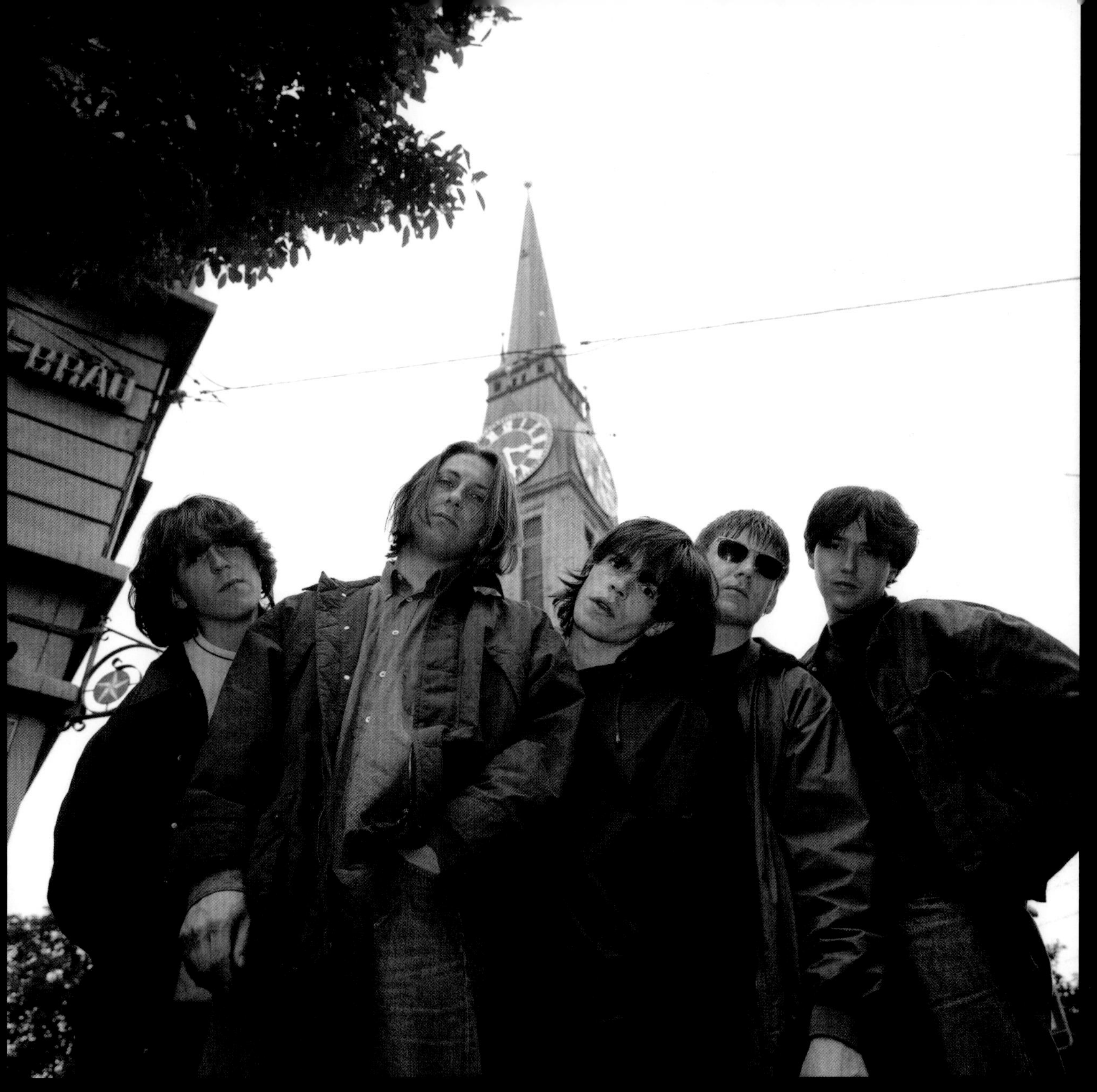
BRÄU

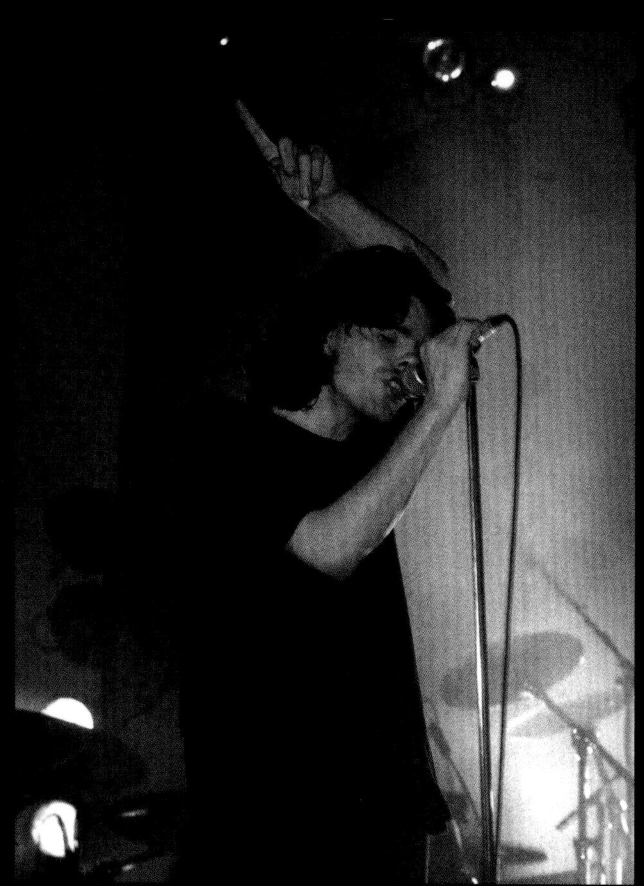

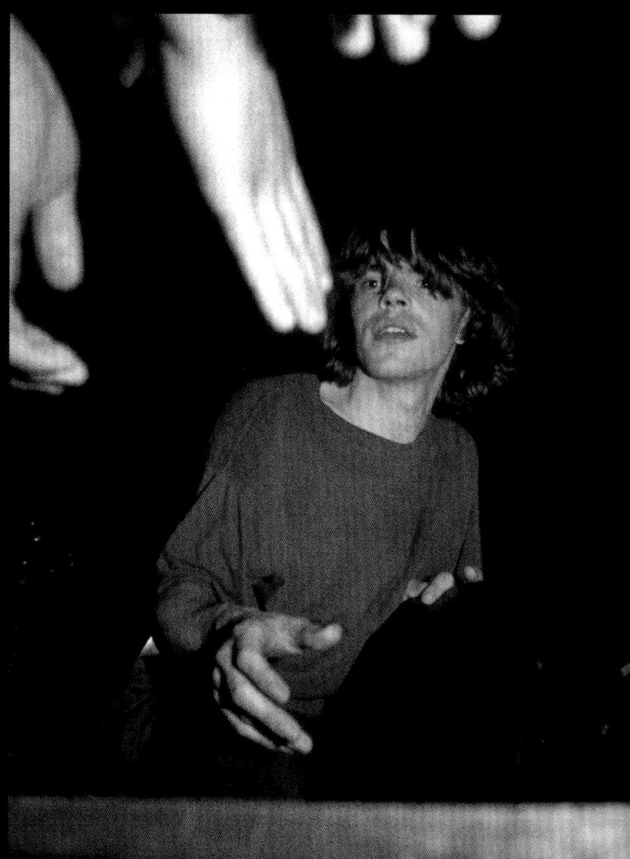

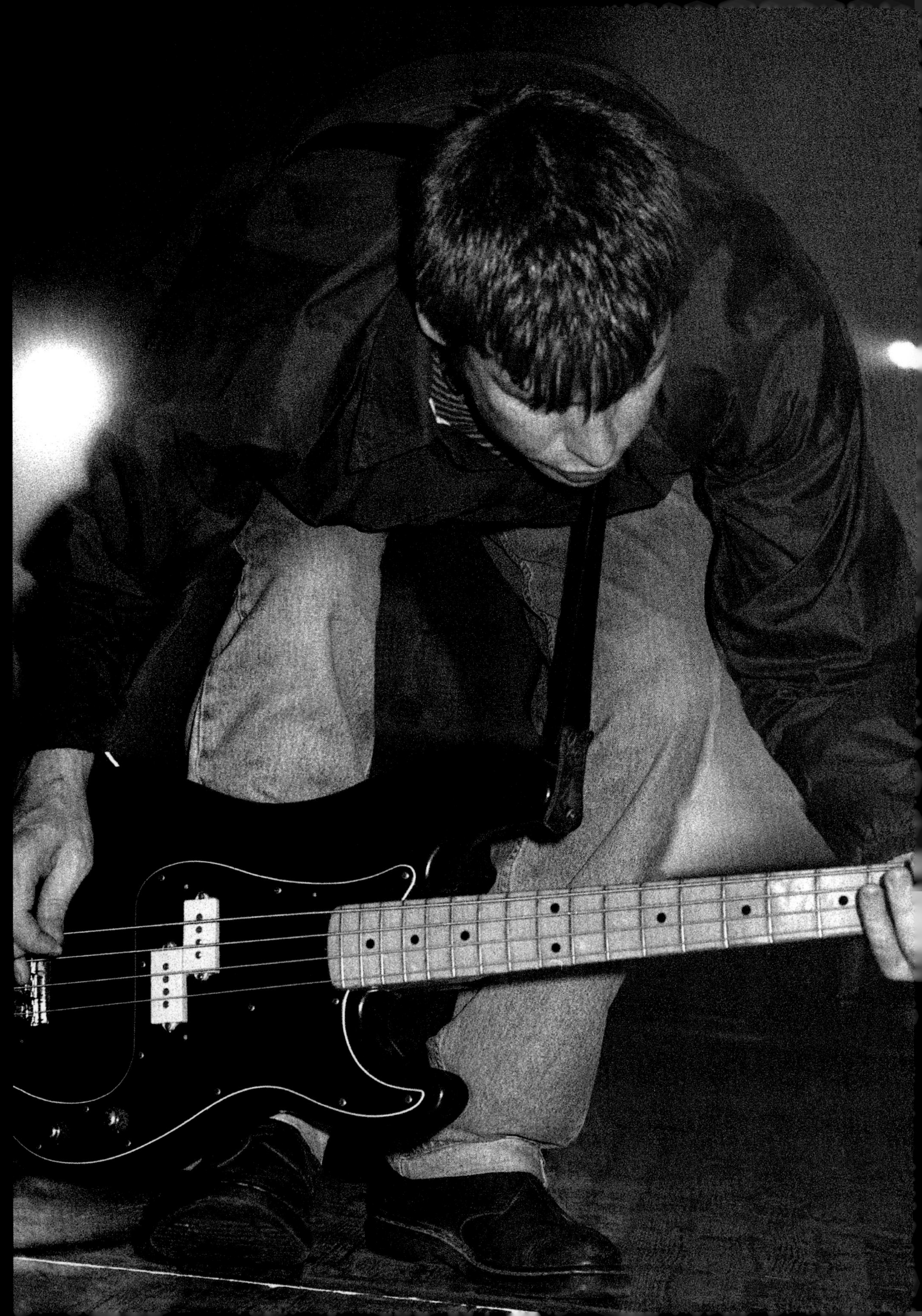

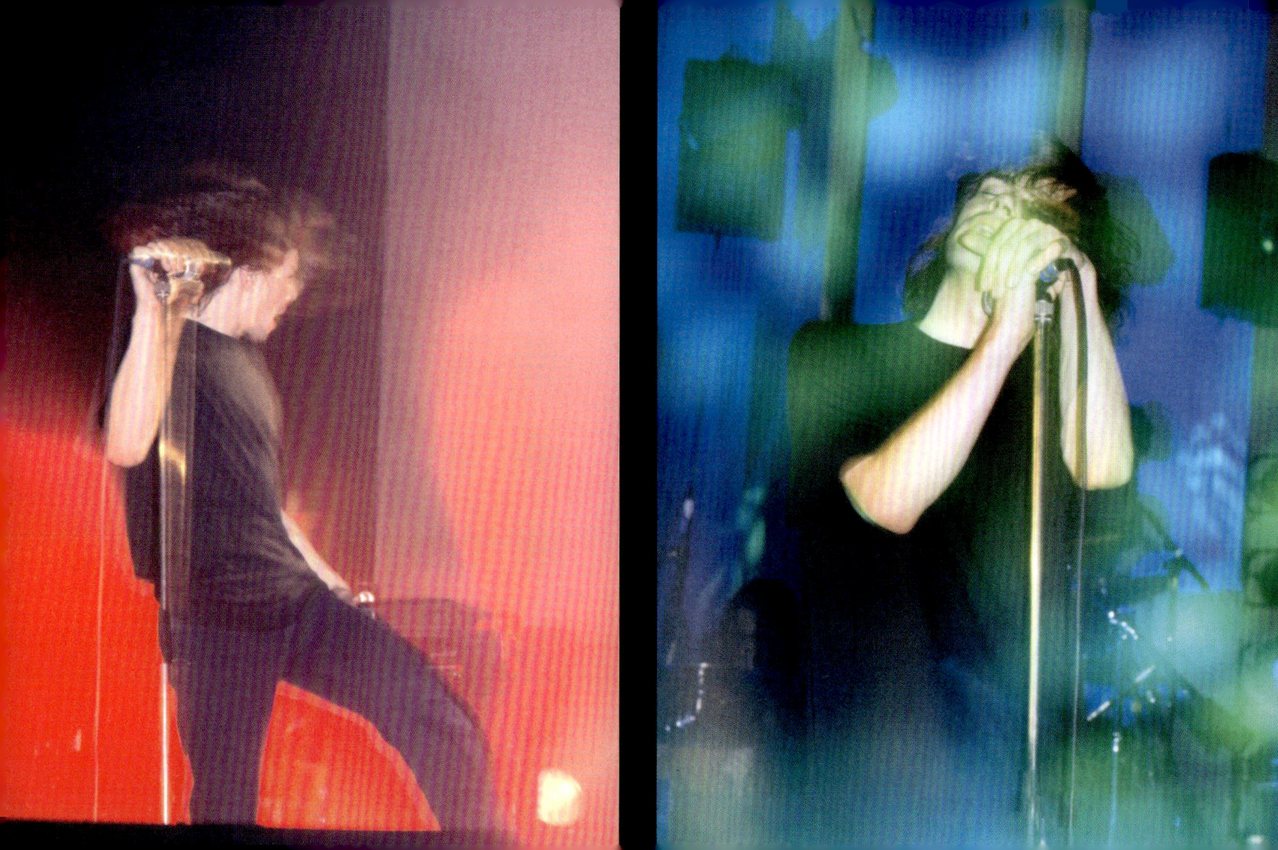

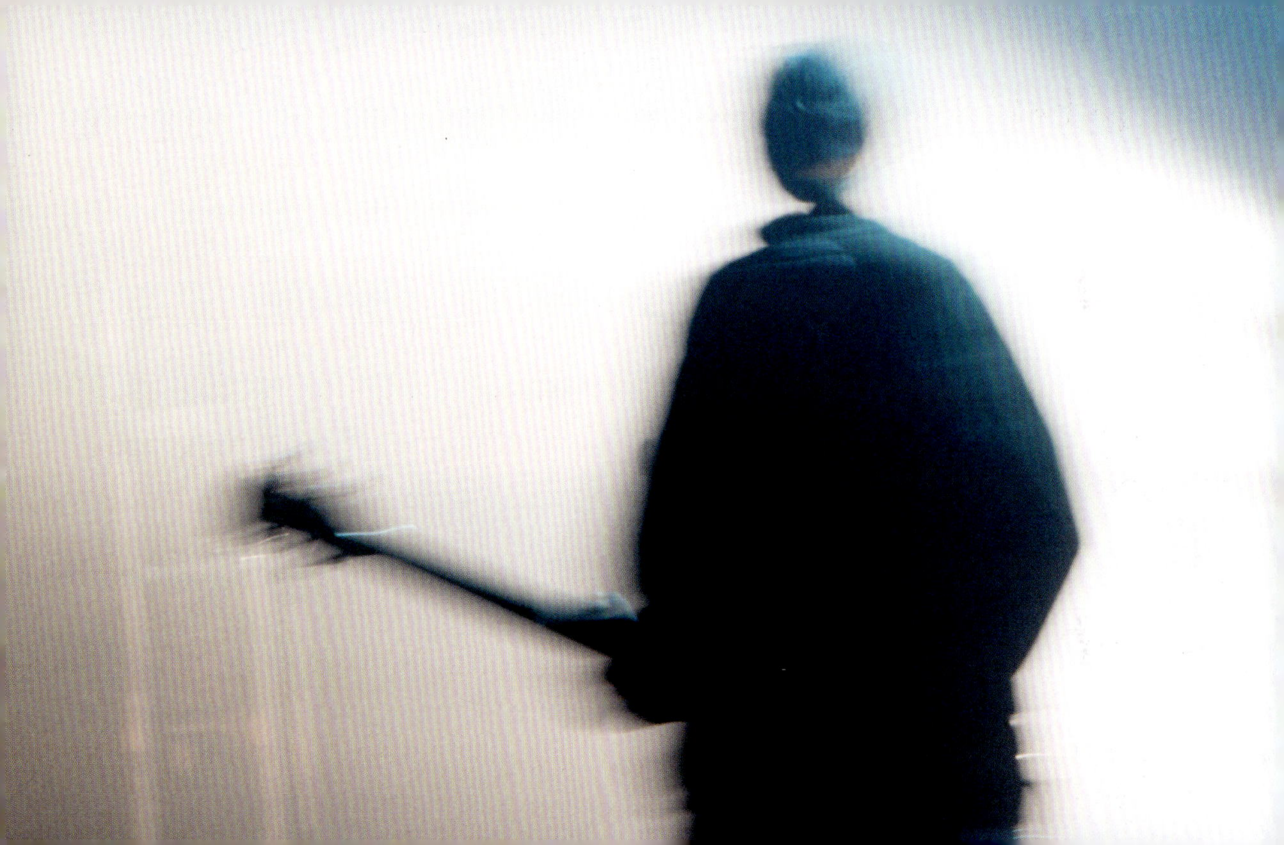

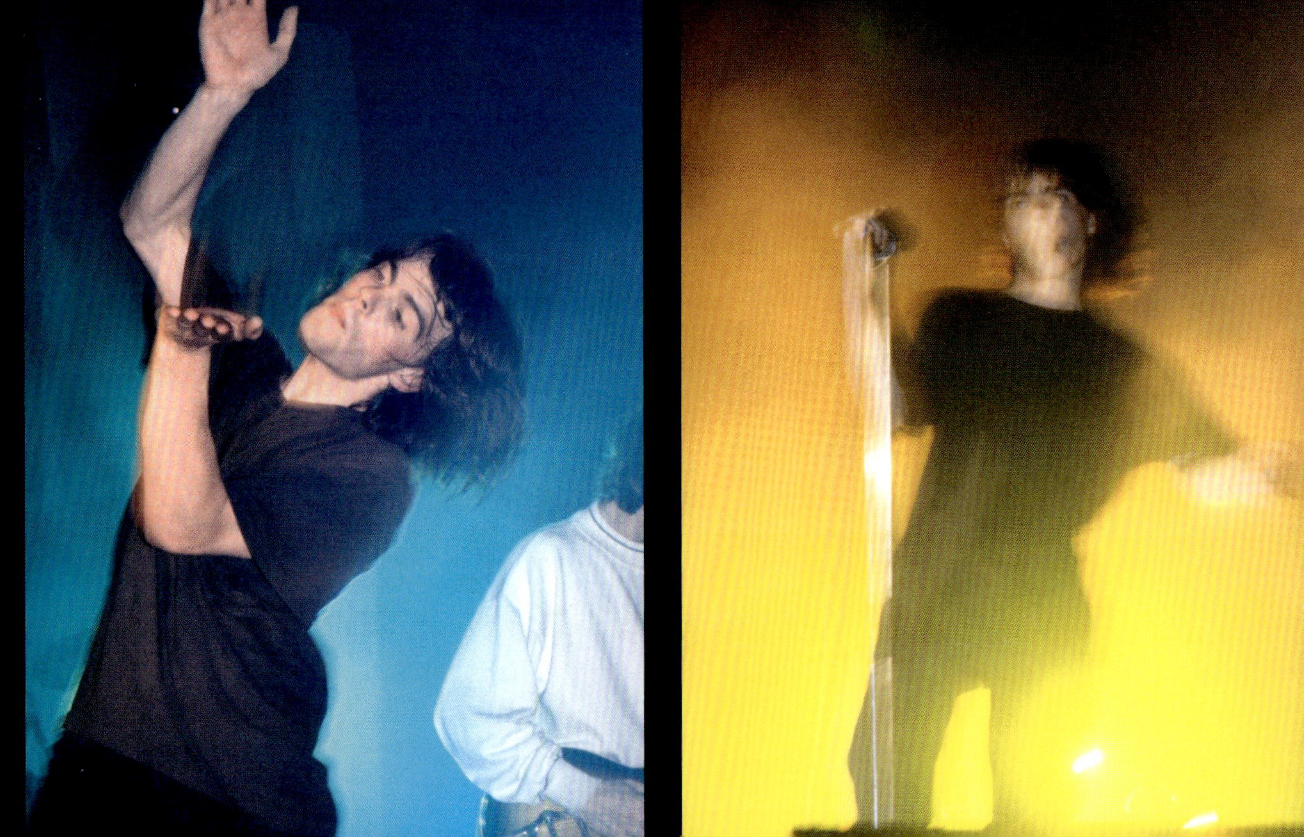

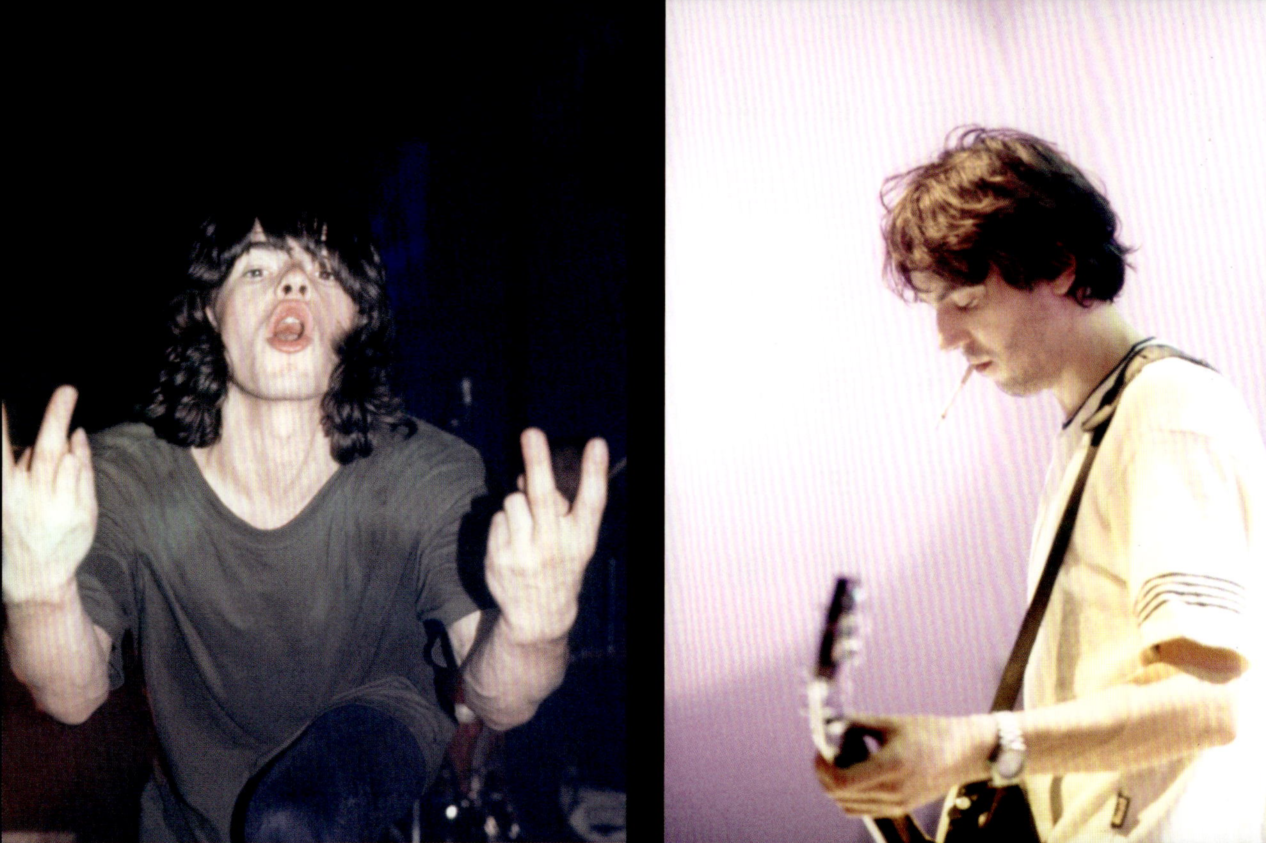

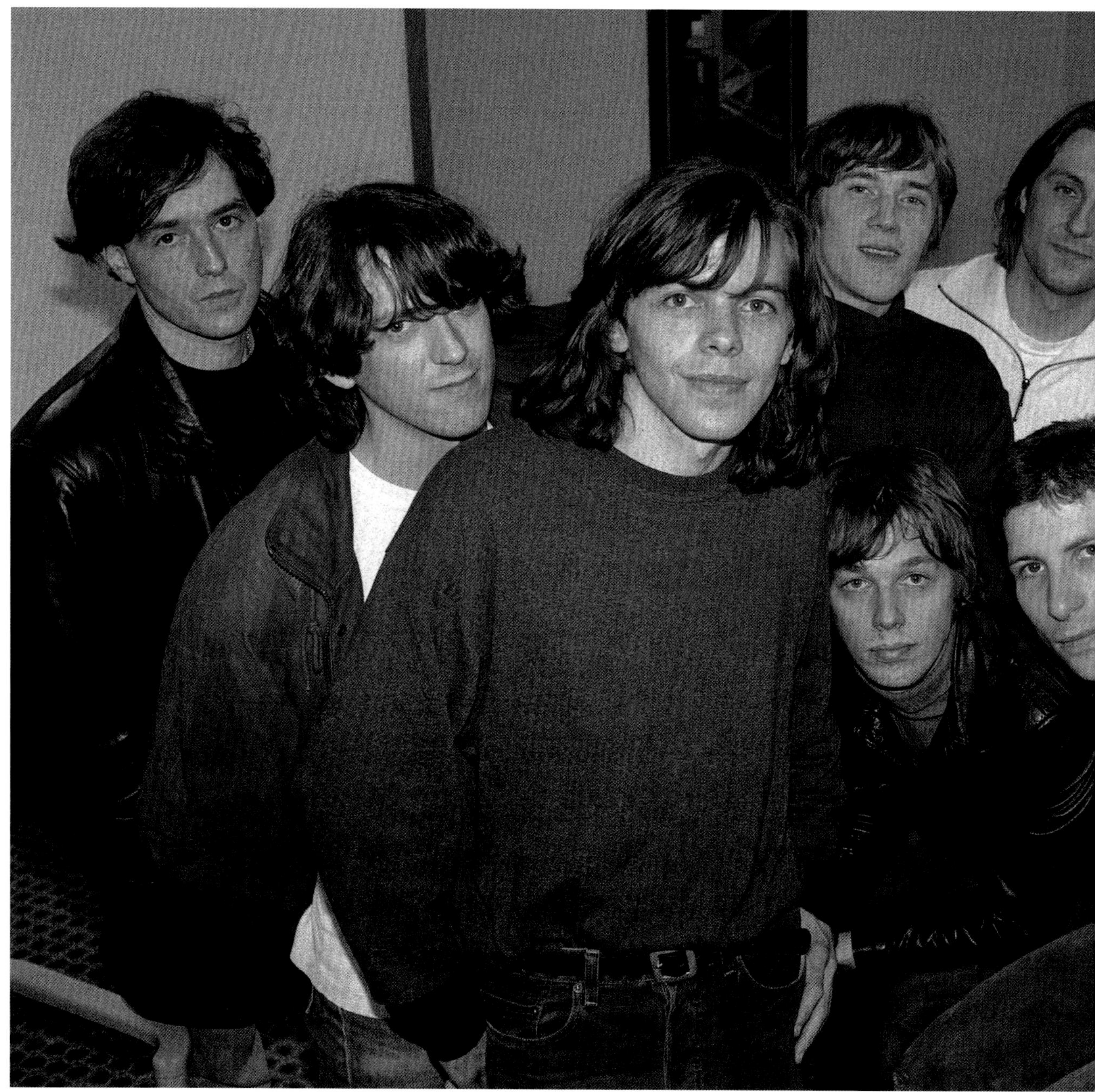

We were building up to what we felt was a moment in time. We'd forged a friendship with Ride and talk arose of us doing a couple of big gigs together. One in the north, where The Charlatans would headline, and one in the south, where Ride would top the bill. Andy Bell came up with the name Daytripper for the event, and everything started to come together.

We were playing songs for the first time that were recorded during the *Up To Our Hips* sessions: "Subterranean", "Withdrawn", "Out". They ended up as B-sides and one of them didn't see the light of day until the 30th-year anniversary editions – and I've just realized that "Withdrawn", which at the time was called "Everybody Get Stoned", and "Subterranean" were only ever played live at those two Daytripper gigs.

Ride were on a high after releasing *Nowhere* and *Going Blank Again*, both of which feature heavily on peoples' lists of seminal albums. Both bands had lots in common, with geographical differences taken into account. Shoegaze and Baggy intertwined and became other things, but one thing we did share was lots of fans and a song called "Polar Bear". Tom came down to the Brighton gig (with us playing first), so he witnessed the lighting of the blue touchpaper.

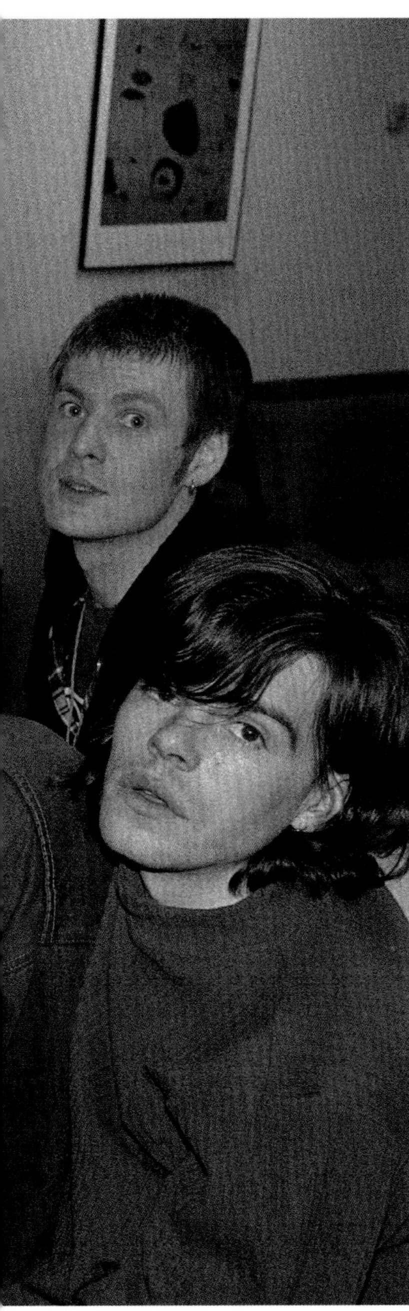

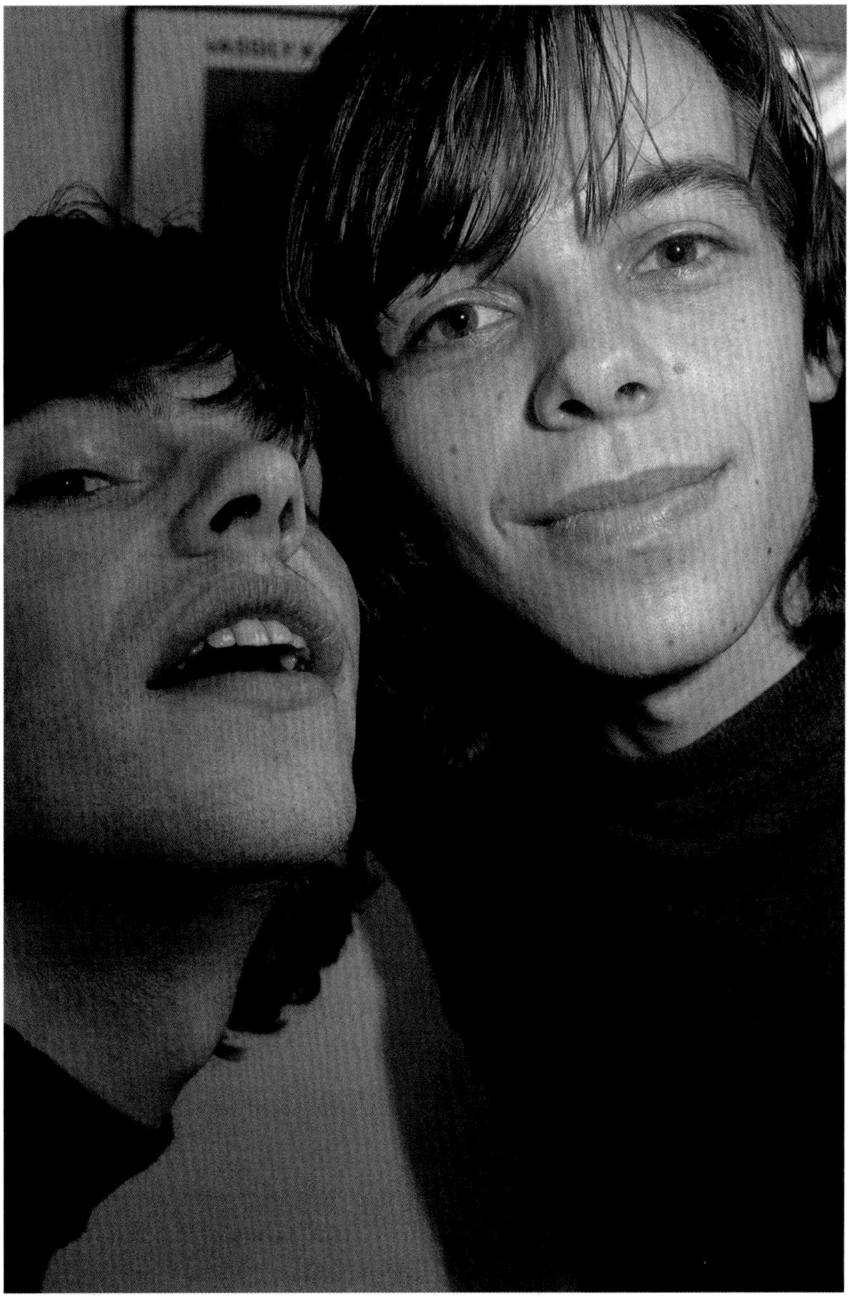

As the two lead singers, we were in demand as the faces of the Daytripper shows. This photo was taken backstage before the Brighton leg. We loved watching Ride over the two nights, and we sealed a friendship that endures to this day.

In 2022 and 2023 we got together for two North American tours. We played *Between 10th and 11th* in full and they played their debut album, *Nowhere*. I'm guessing nobody would have imagined when this picture was being taken that 30 years later both bands would be on the road again for double-header gigs.

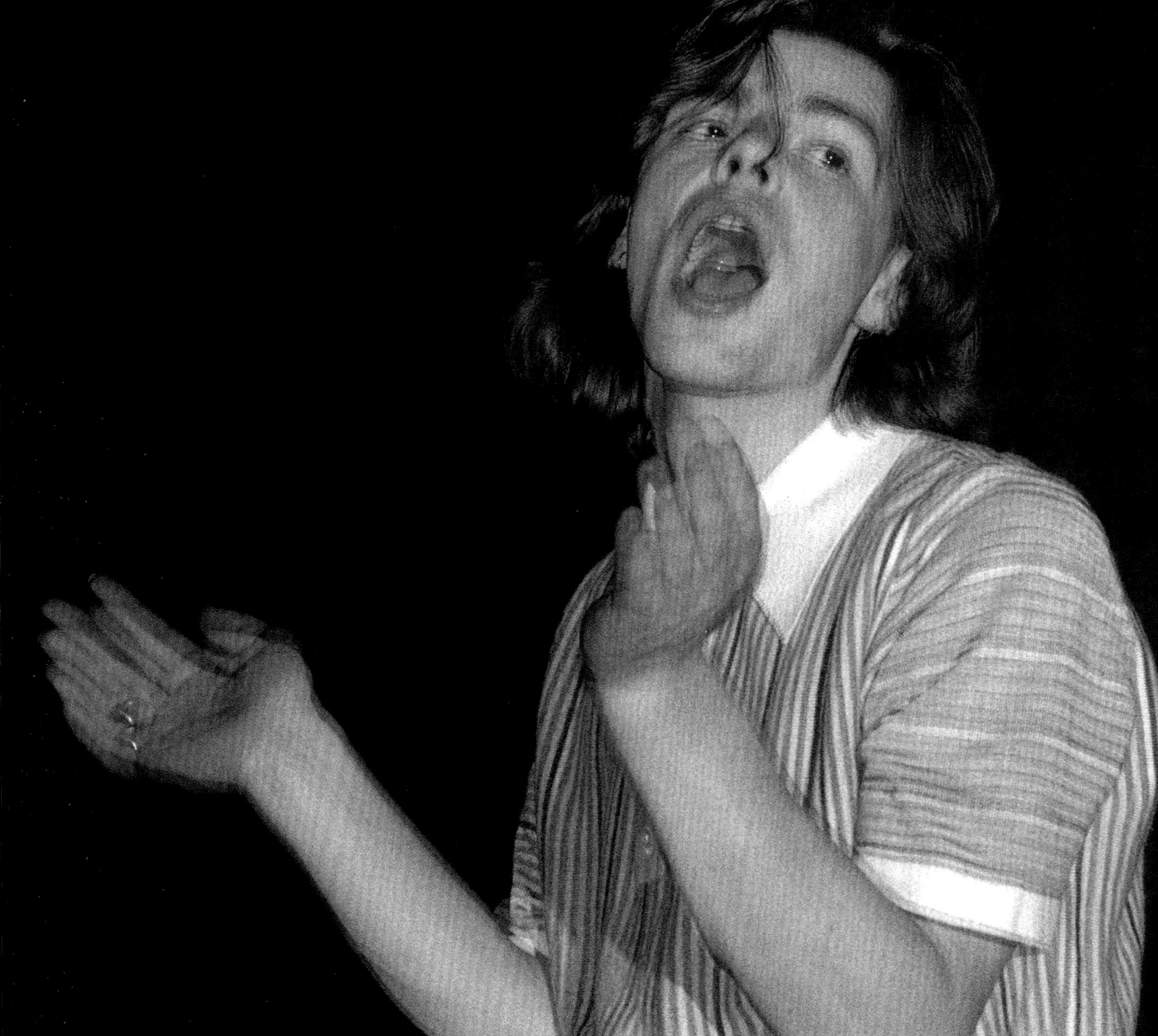

The Mick Jagger years.

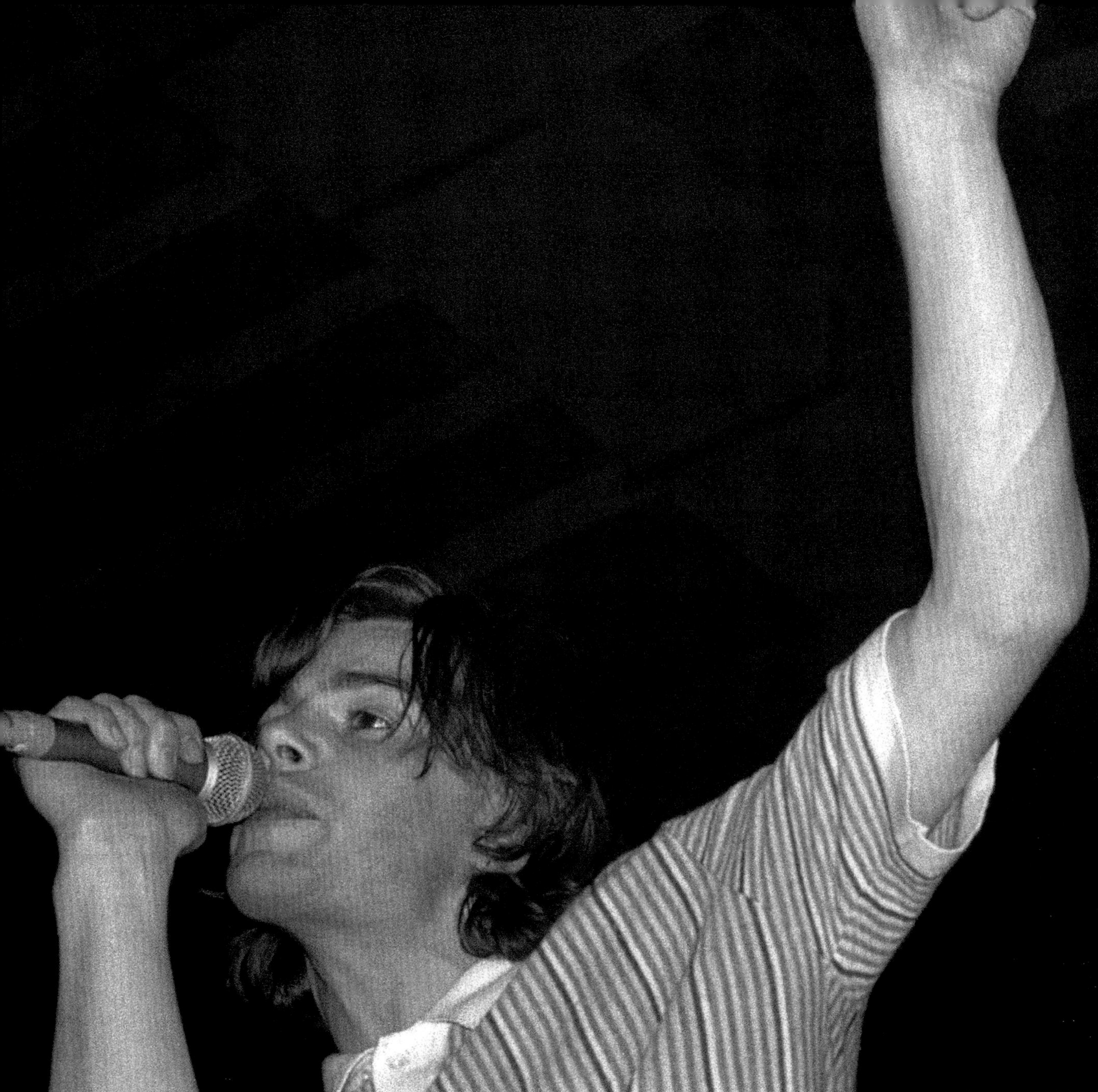

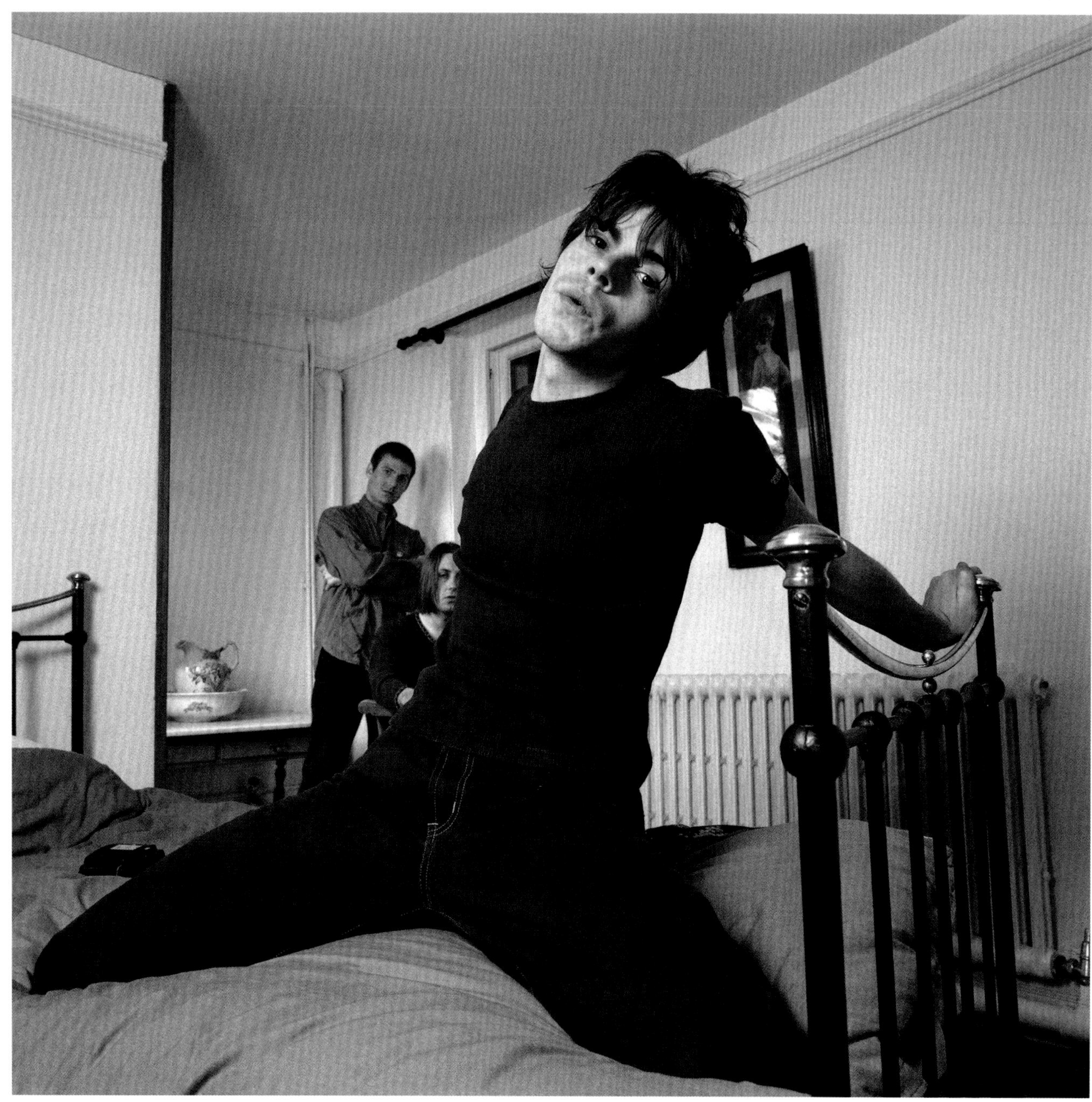

In late 1993 we went to Monnow Valley Studio in South Wales to complete the recordings for *Up To Our Hips*. Rob was in prison and he'd told us to get on with it rather than wait for him, so we recruited John Collins, Mark's brother, to help us out, as he was a decent pianist and knew his way around a Hammond organ. It was an odd atmosphere and the first time we'd felt weakened and vulnerable – but this did bring out strengths in us, and in Rob. We'd finished six tracks before he was sentenced, and he had laid down guide tracks for the others. Being a man down we were unable to do shots with the whole band, so Tom would get one or two of us, and even other people in the background. We had a book of photos by 1960s' photographer Lewis Morley, which I seem to remember being part of the inspiration.

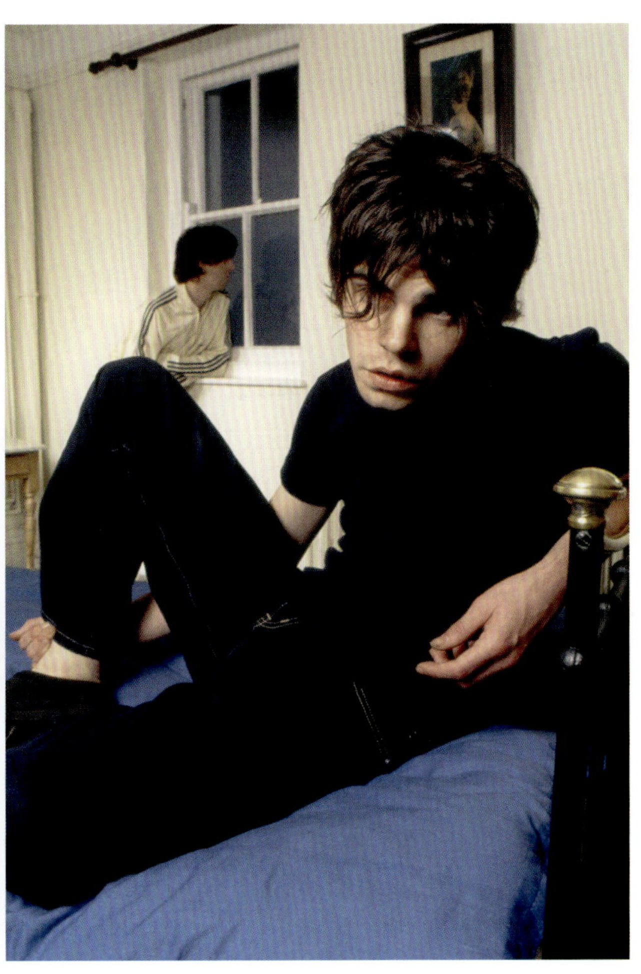

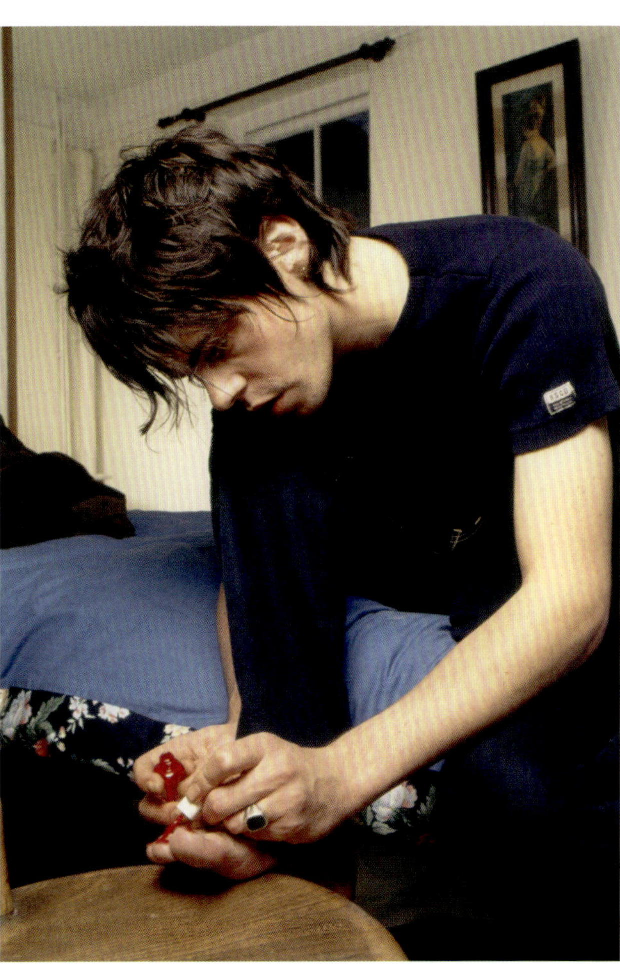

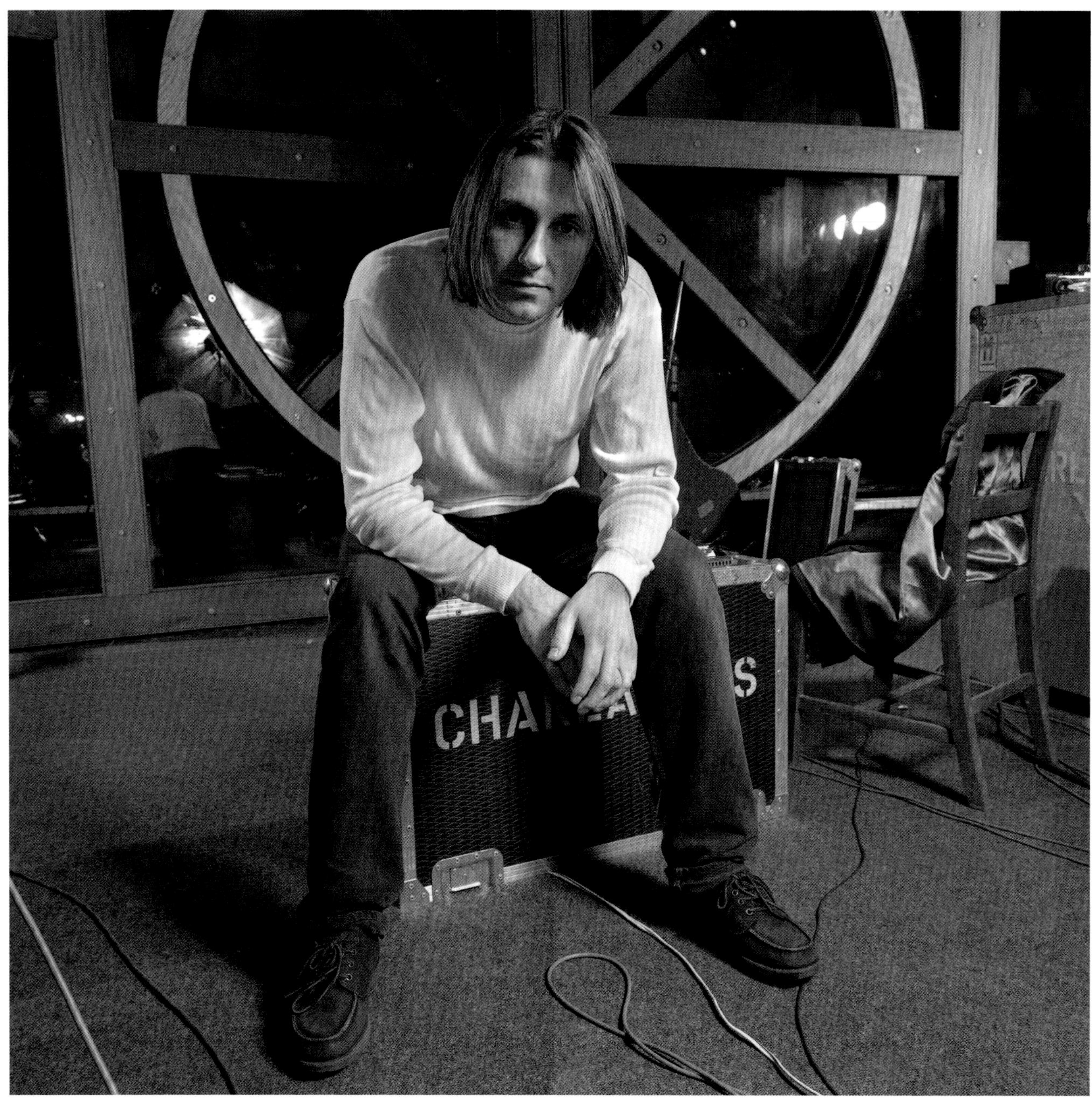

This backdrop became slightly more famous a year or so later as the front cover of “Supersonic” by Oasis.

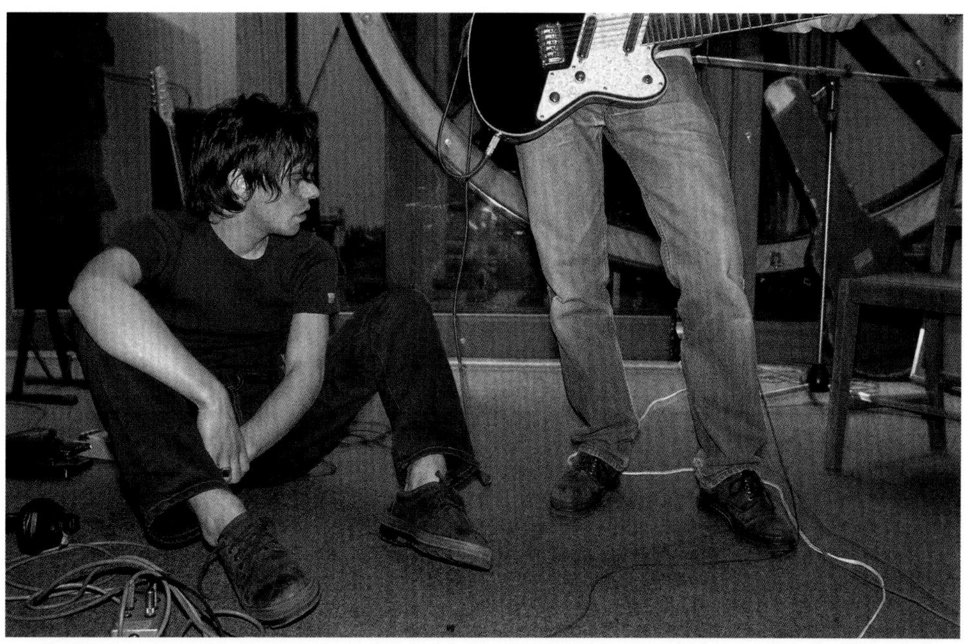

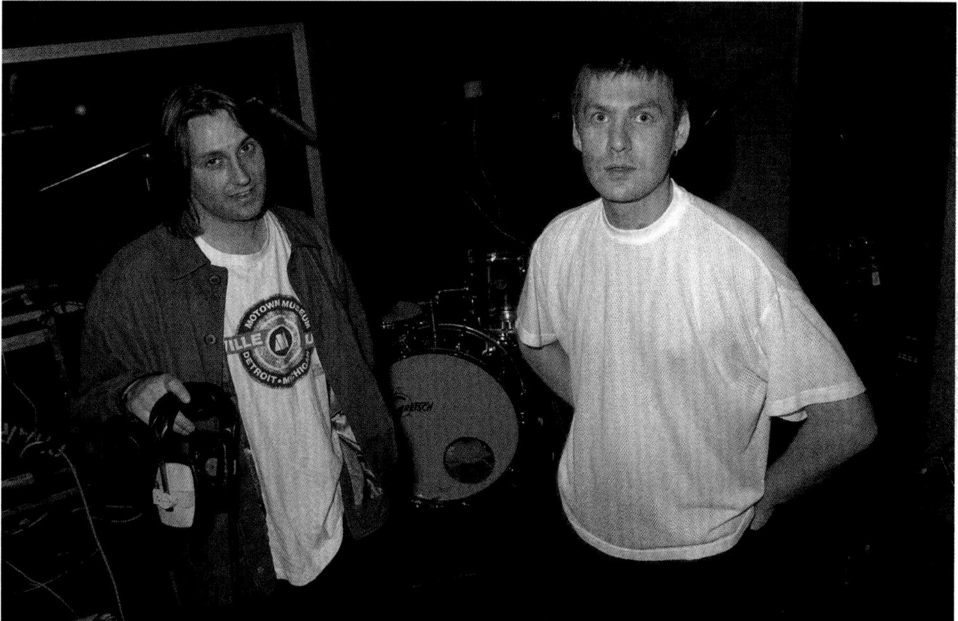

While we are in the studio the whole context of the world changes, as the focus becomes about the smallest detail. I love this picture of Martin as it shows him practising in between takes – his headphones are off, which means we're not recording and my guess is that the tape is being rewound, giving him a couple of minutes to work things out.

When we go into a recording studio we are generally about 60 per cent prepared and the rest is worked out at the time, which we've found suits us best.

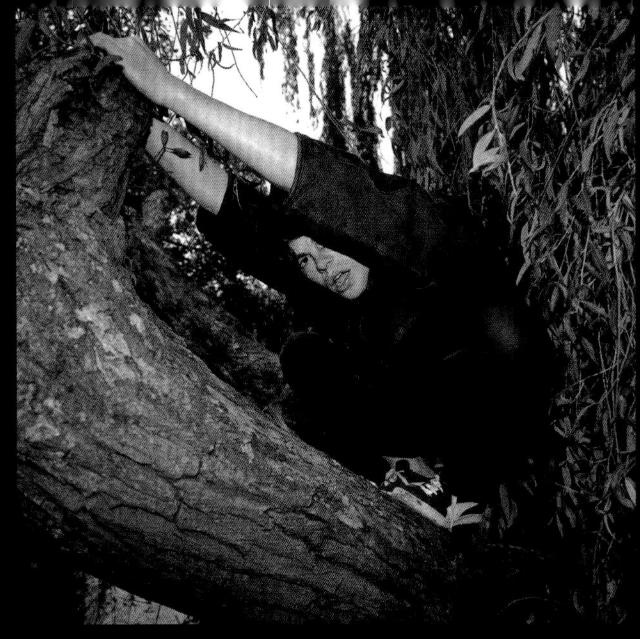
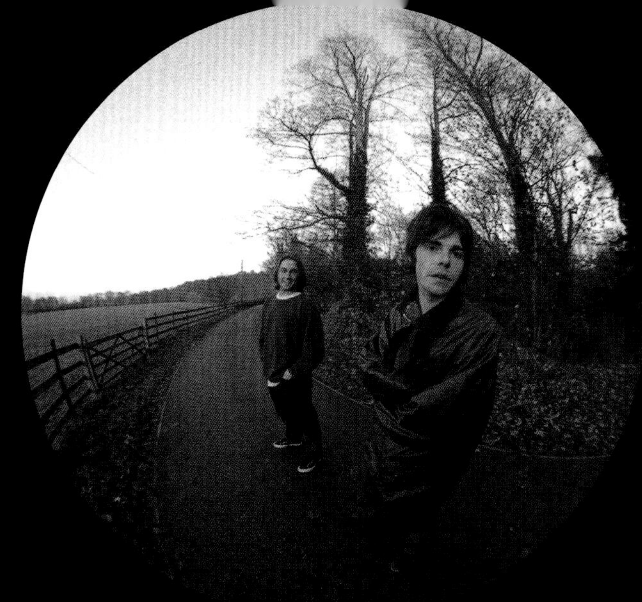

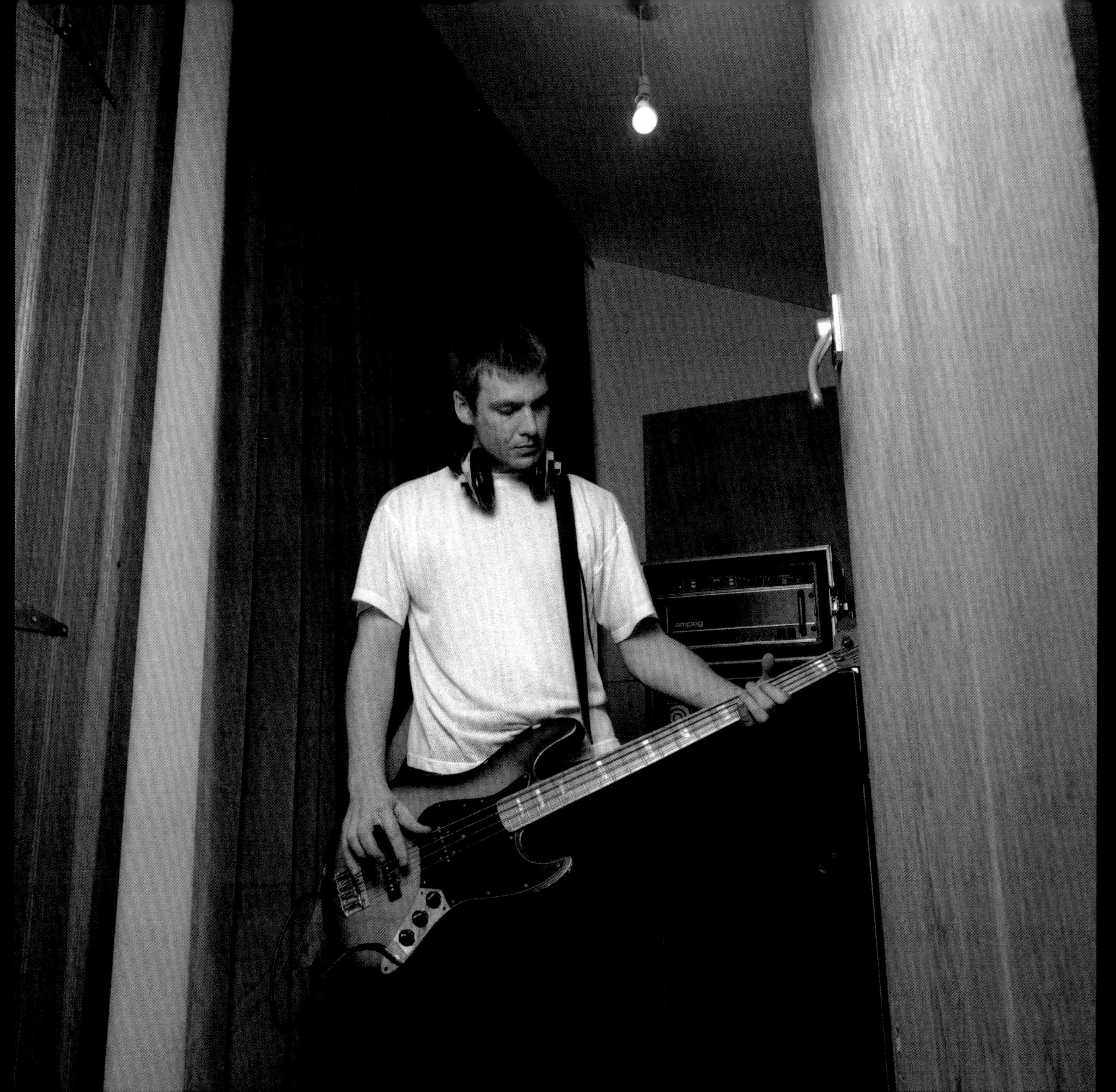
ampeg

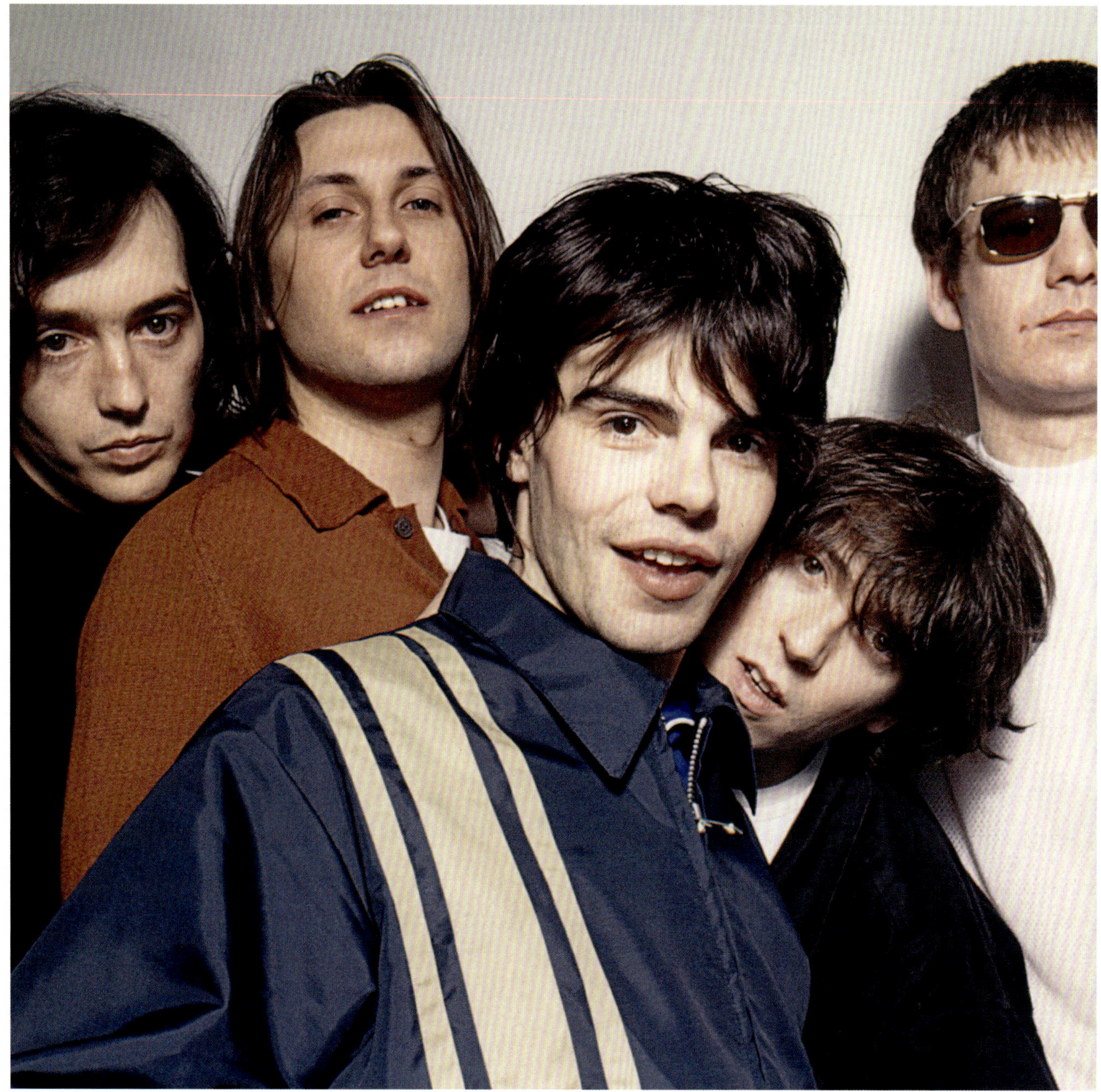

We went to Amsterdam for a few days of press. The band, management, Tom and even Pete Mitchell, the radio DJ, all stayed in a four-star hotel, with label people and various music execs dropping by. If ever you need an illustration of how much more money was around in the 1990s, this is it. If we also need an illustration of stuff that bands were paying for but didn't realize, then also this.

Melkweg is one of my favourite places to play in Europe. The cultural experience of Amsterdam meant hundreds of our fans would fly out or even travel by coach. That meant when we were taking in the city, people would be shouting out from bars, bringing stuff to our hotel to sign – the full rock-star experience.

This photo was taken in a room at the American Hotel. We used to pride ourselves on taking up the minimal amount of a frame, and our goofiness and camaraderie would come across because of this. The jacket lived on a coat hanger at the studio for the following twenty years, making trips out occasionally for *Top of the Pops* or a tour until our Different Day event in Manchester in May 2017. We took over Oldham Street in the Northern Quarter and various other shops and disused buildings. The jacket was part of a bunch of stuff that was sold in the Oxfam shop, along with drum skins and other bits of pieces.

I recall the dressing room after the gig, and seeing Saint Etienne, Mick Jones, members of Cypress Hill and Primal Scream. It's where I met Martin Duffy for the first time. He went on to become a great friend and joined The Charlatans after Rob died, before we recruited Tony. I have treasured memories of when he joined my solo band in 2012 and he's a much-missed part of my world.

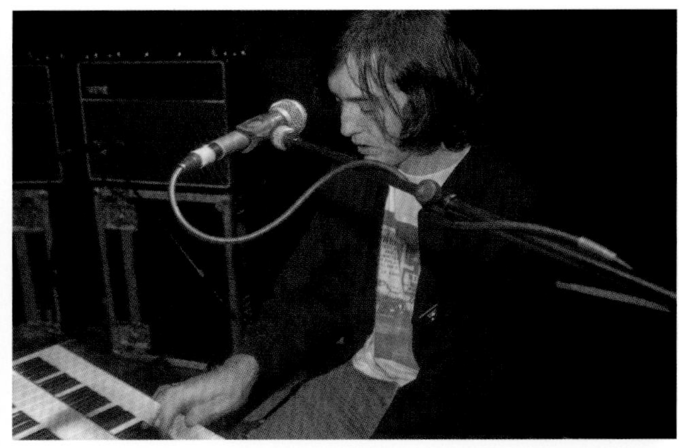

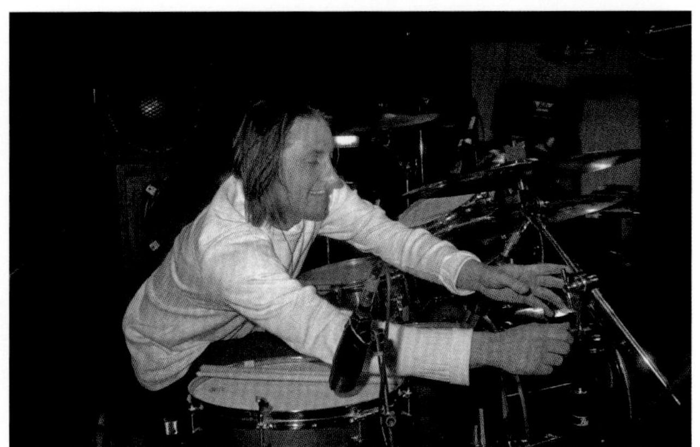

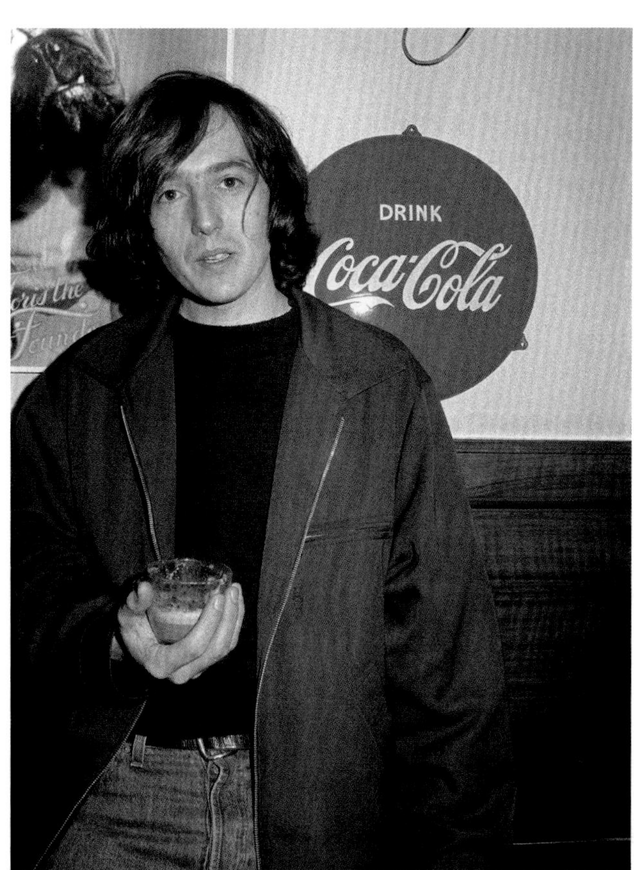
DRINK
Coca-Cola

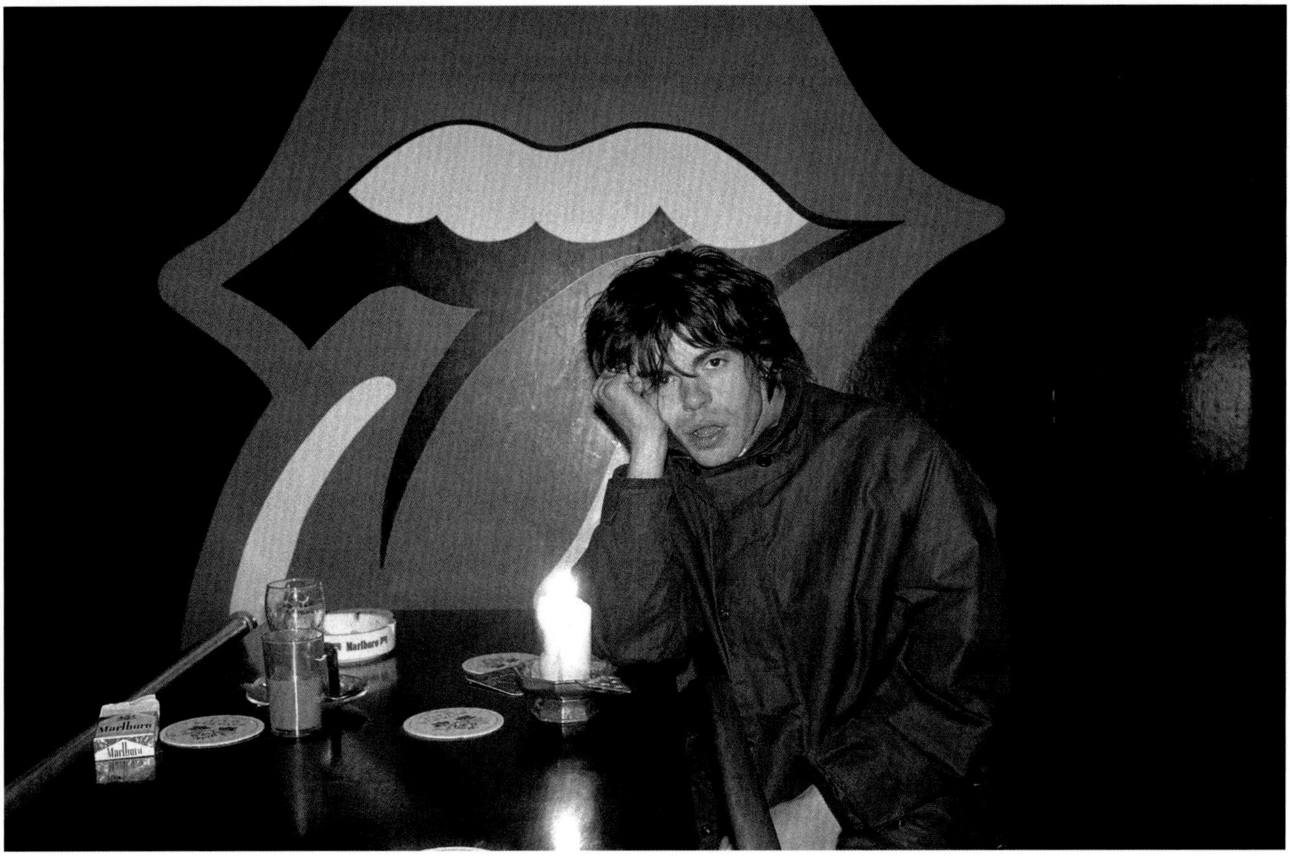

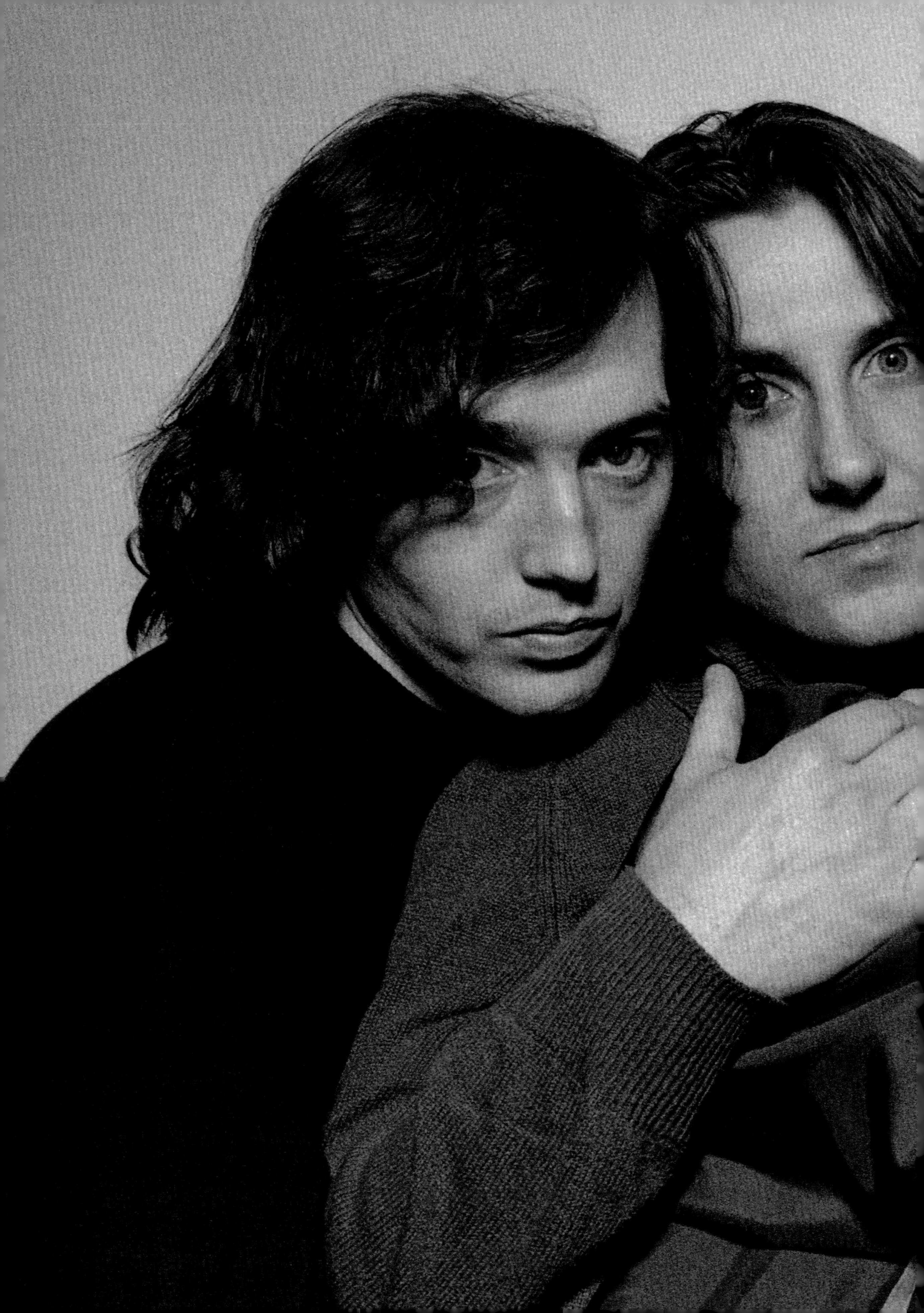

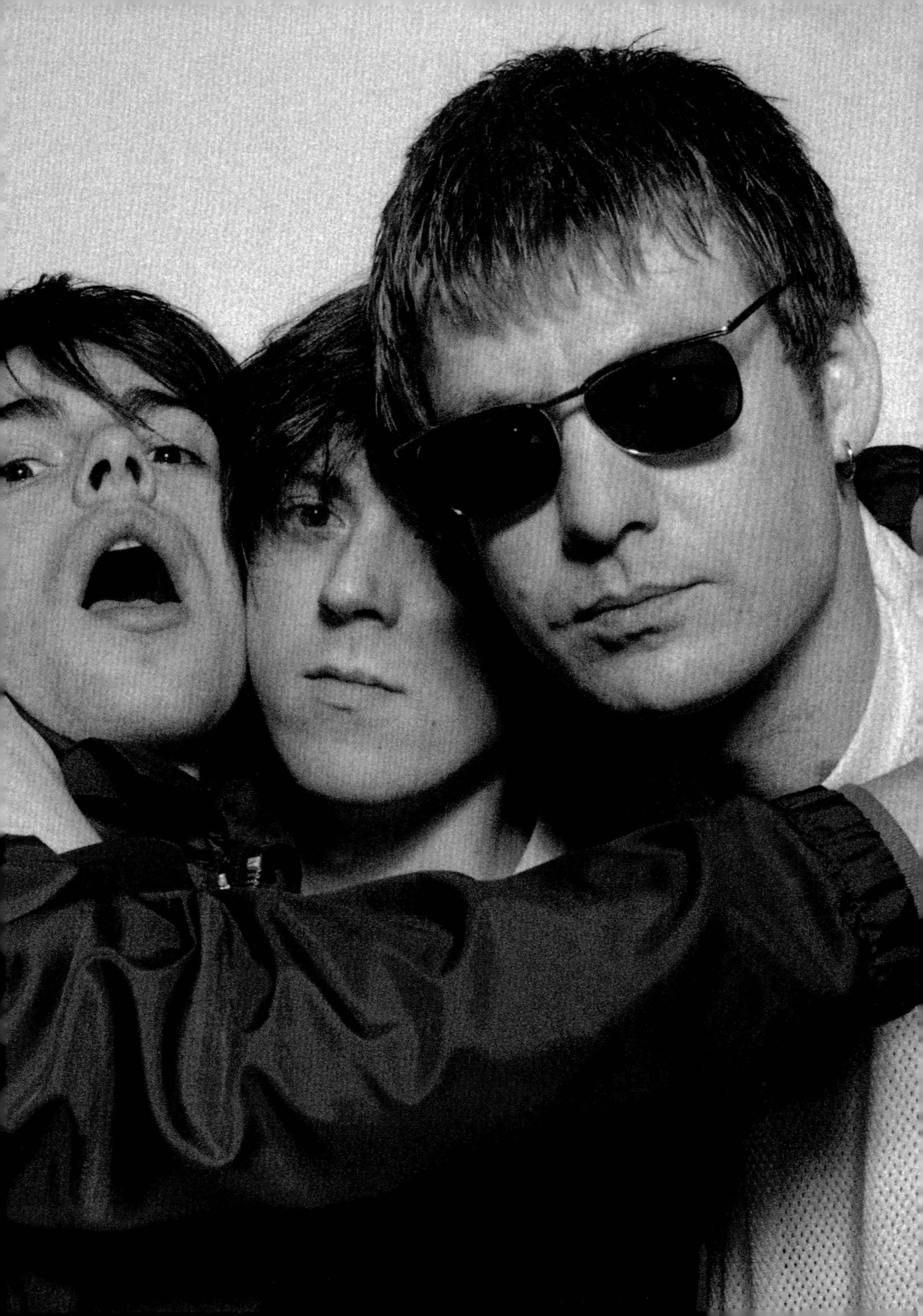

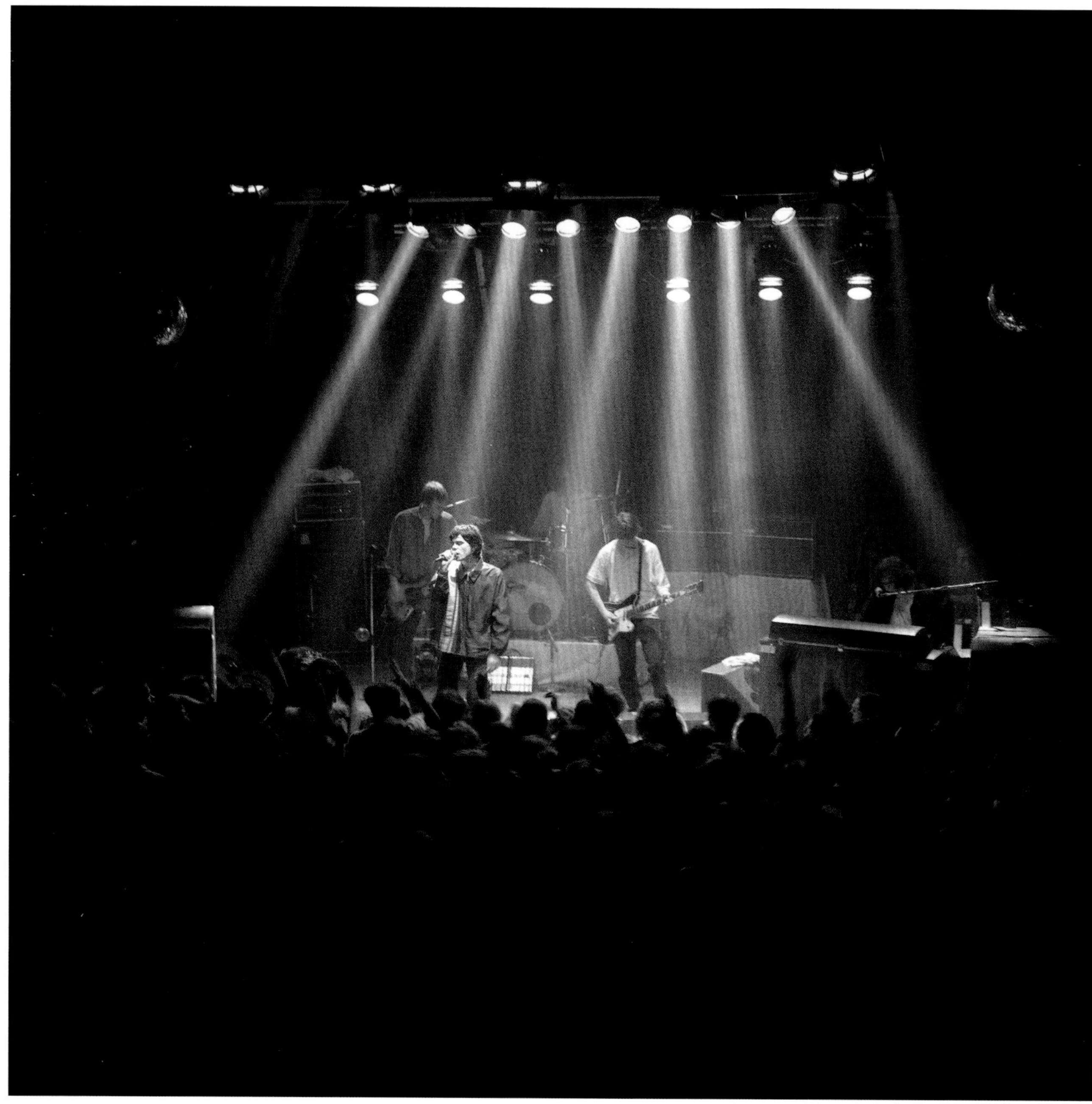

You can see that the guitar that Mark is playing is a Charvel Surfcaster 12-string.

I would see Tom in the oddest places while we were playing, but he got some fantastic shots and he really captures the connection between band and audience here.

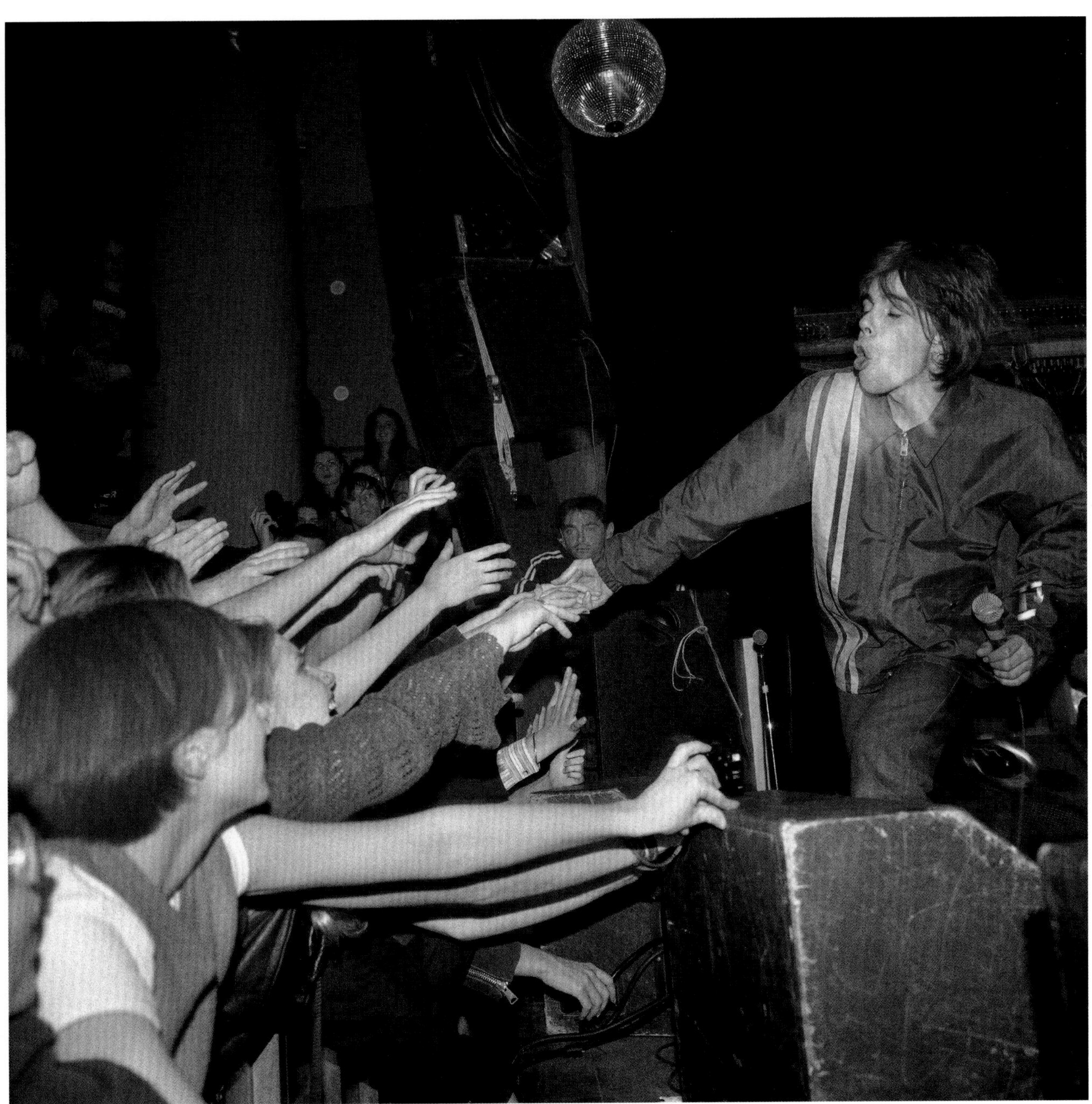

I really love this photo; it appeals to the music fan in me. The point of view is that you're in the crowd. I am definitely thinking I want to shake that hand, but I am hoping they don't pull me off the stage. It was sometimes funny to see Tom in a crowd and I would always be excited to see the shots I'd been watching him take.

Tom:
Live, when the band are on, they're on, big time. Rob was the driving force of the band on stage. He was a quiet man, a hilarious man, but he made The Charlatans with his sound on the organ, so powerful and with such melody. Mark's guitar was brilliant, he brought a real vitality. The drumming is great and Martin's bass is underrated, for sure. I've seen them so many times now but I'll never forget the first time I saw the band live, in Bristol. Now, though, they've got a catalogue of incredible singles, you can recognize them instantly, from the first chord.

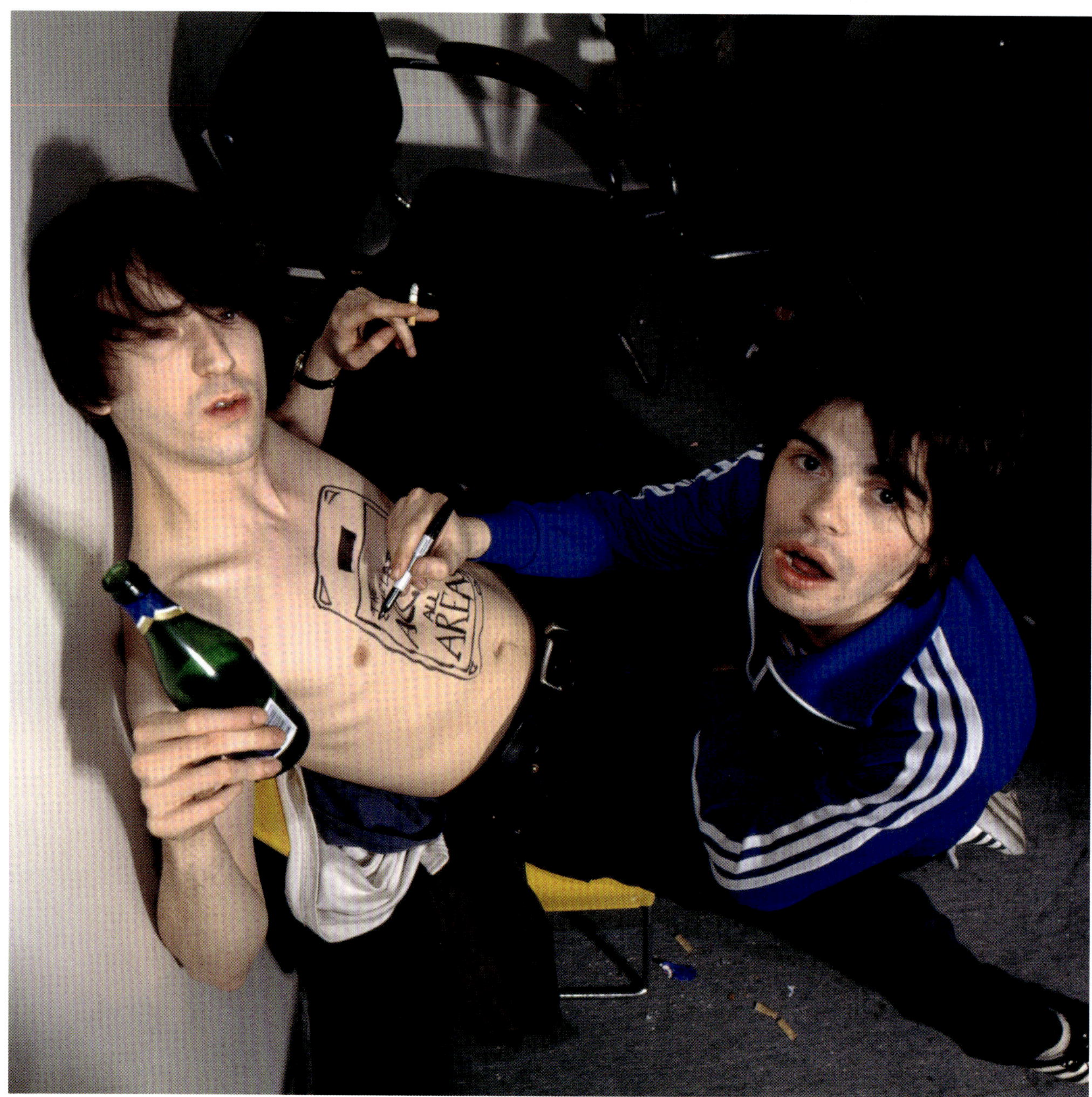

Sometimes ideas are better than actual photos, and this is a case in point. Mark was notorious for losing his pass that would get him in and around a venue. I had the bright idea of giving him a semi-permanent version, drawn on his chest. Gig days are 90 per cent sitting around and 10 per cent actually doing something, so clowning around helped pass the time.

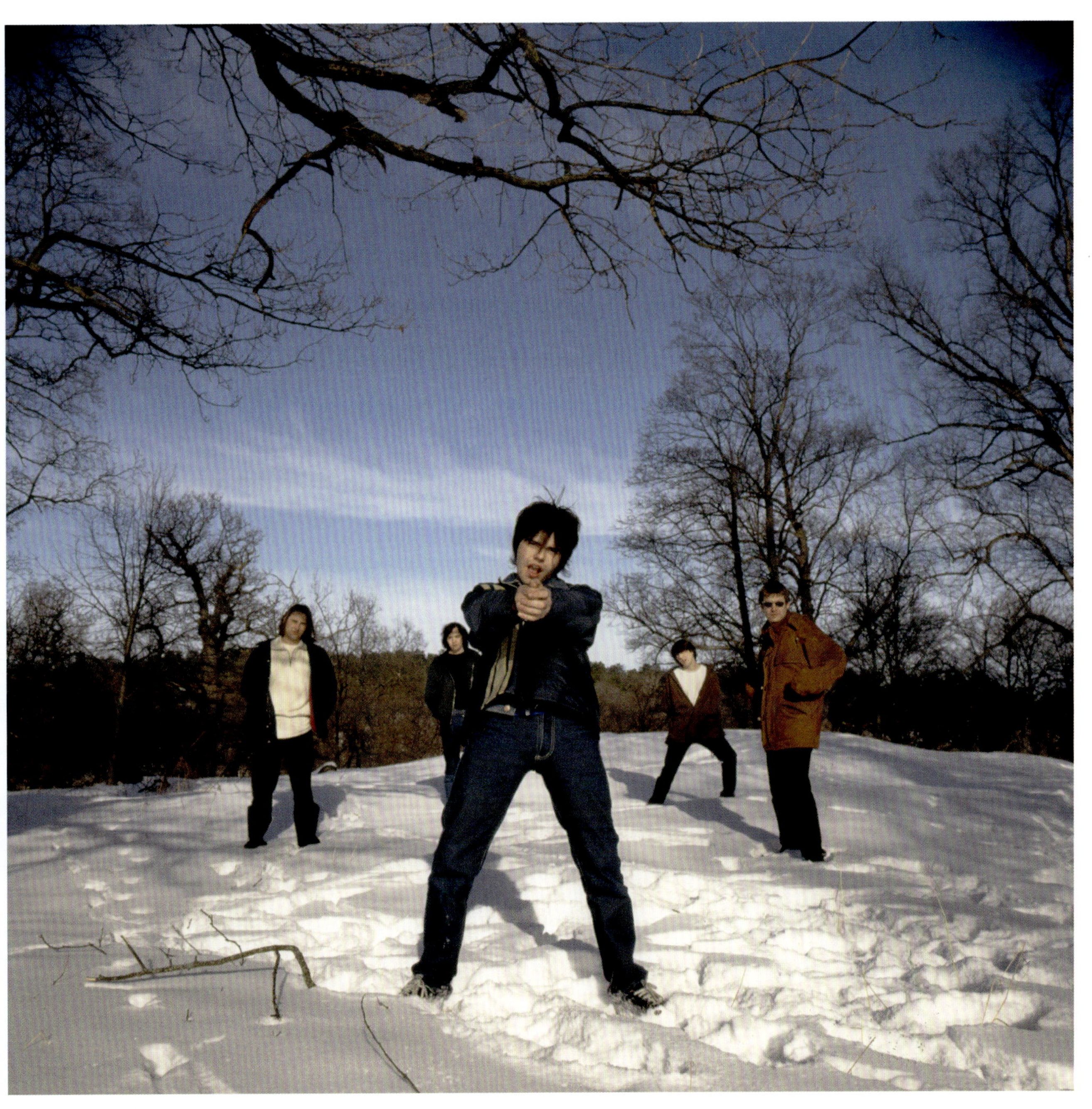

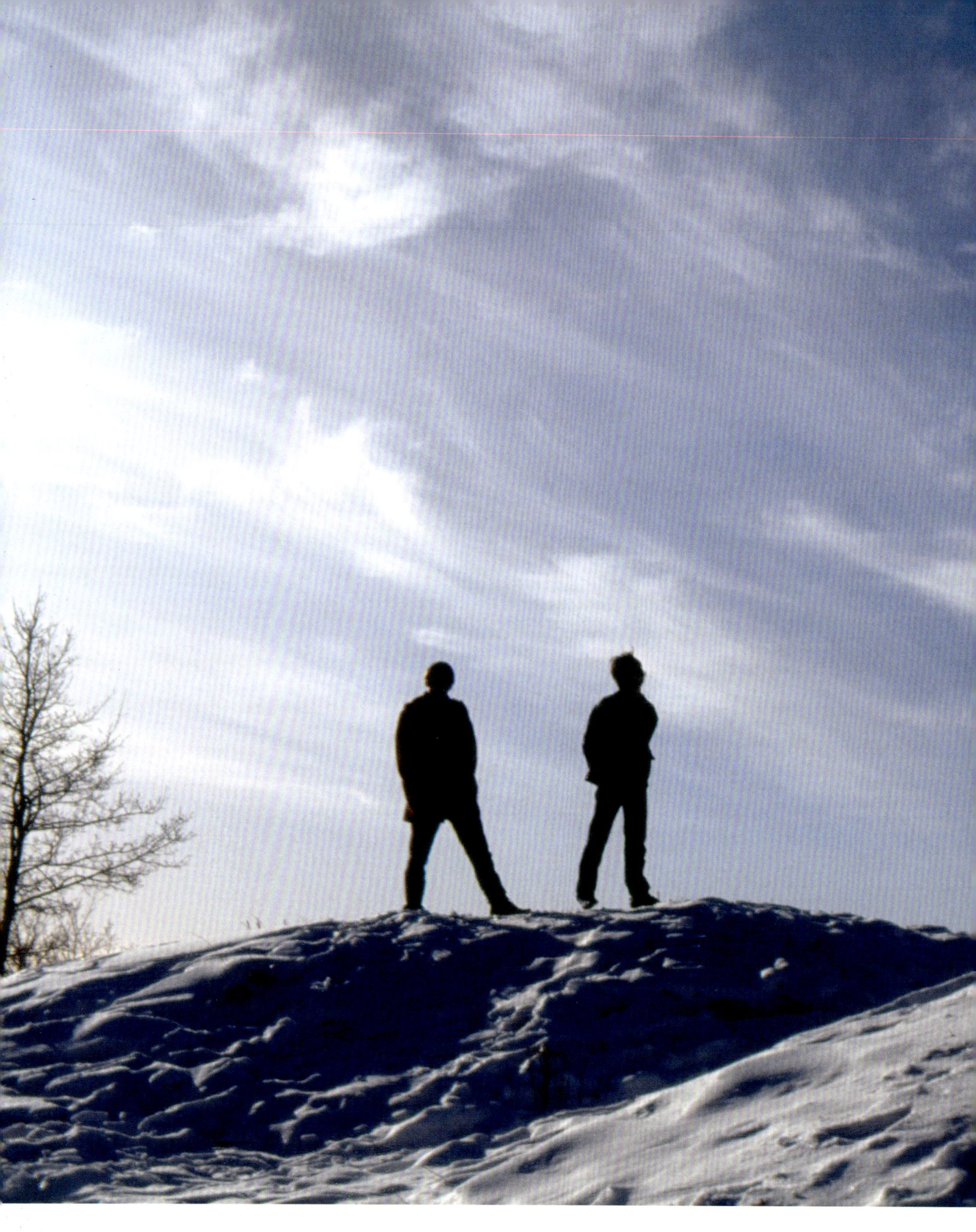

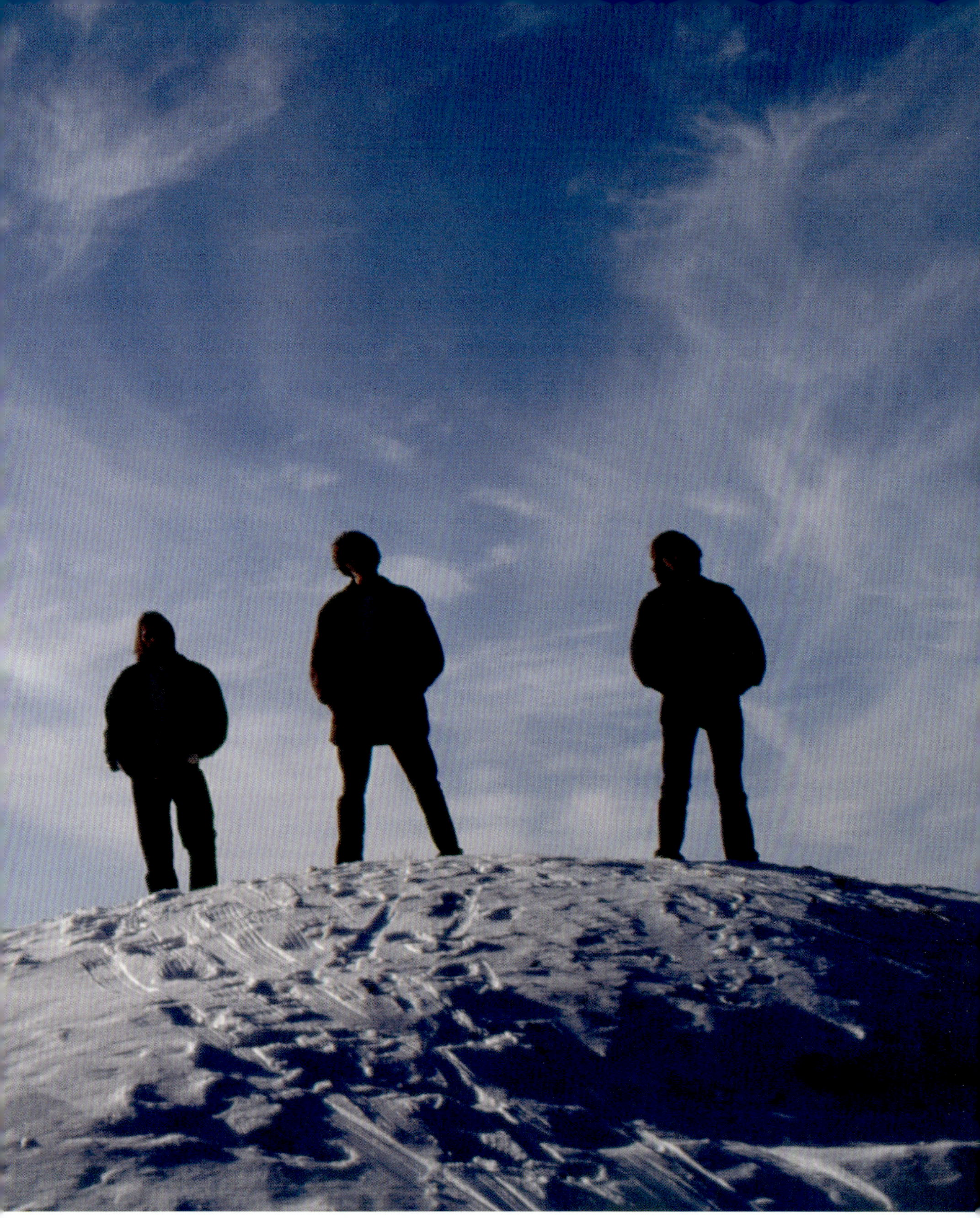

We were all big fans of the record covers that Brian Griffin did with Echo and the Bunnymen, so we would always jump at the chance of a group shot atop a snowy mountain beneath a vast sky.

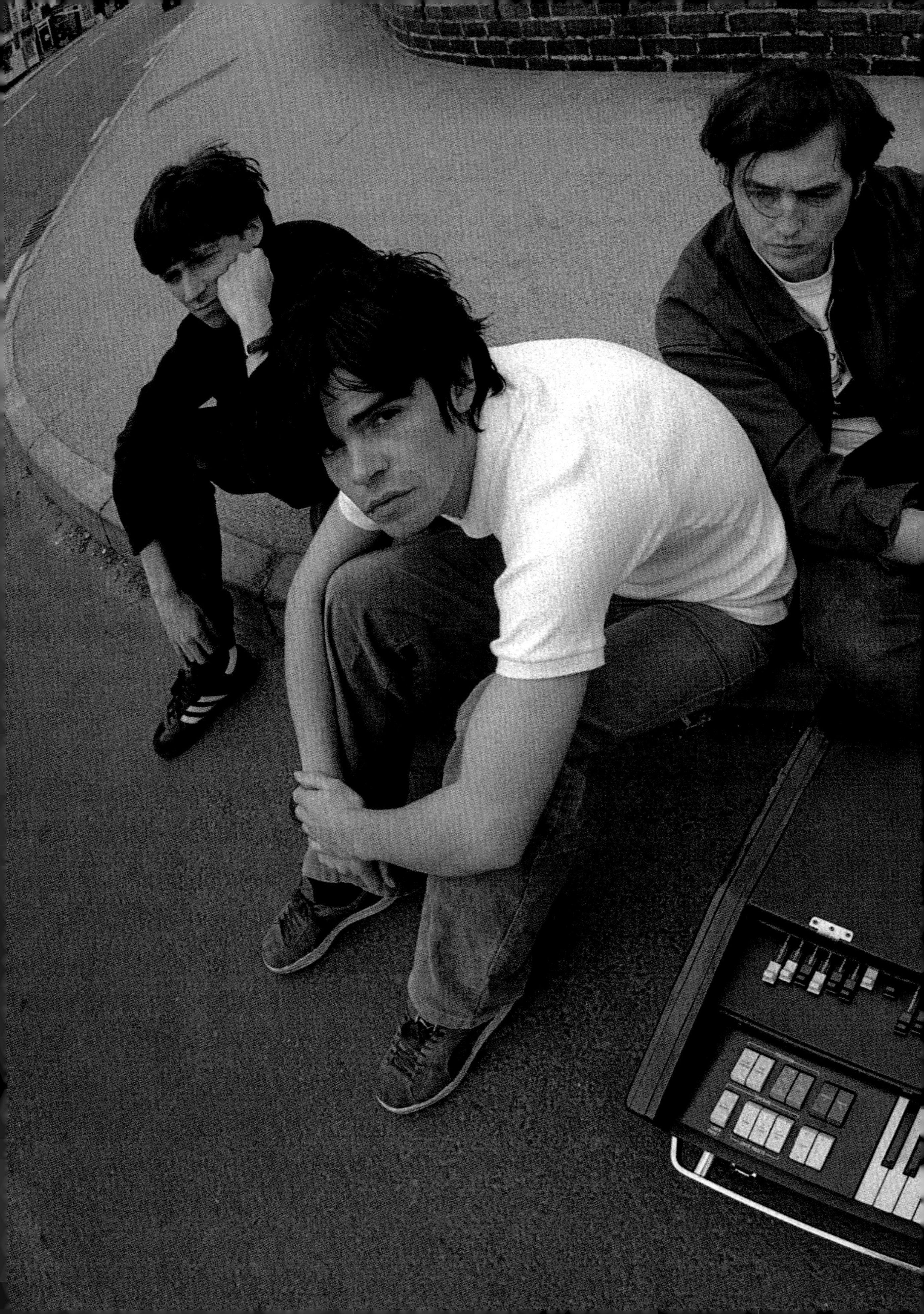

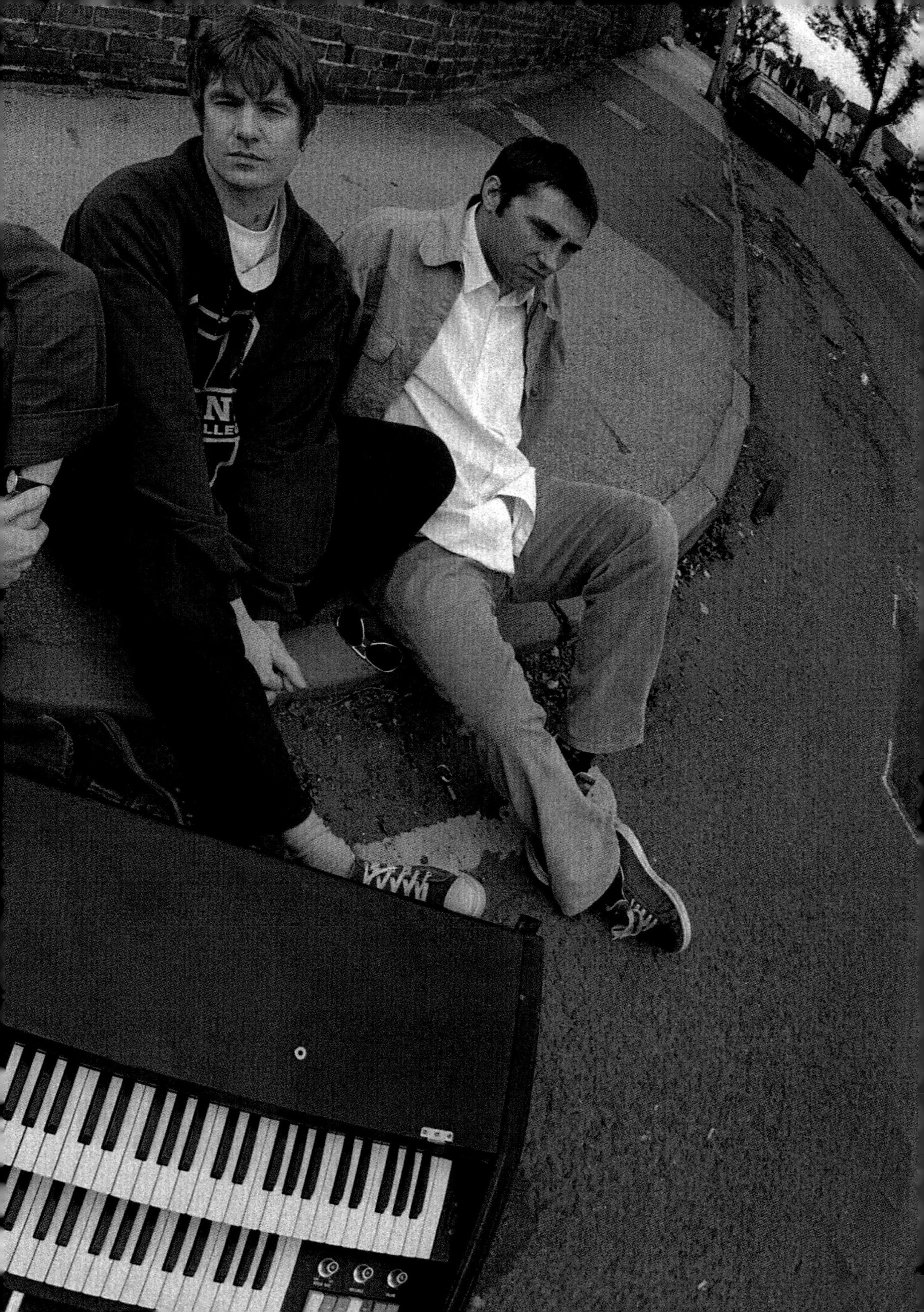

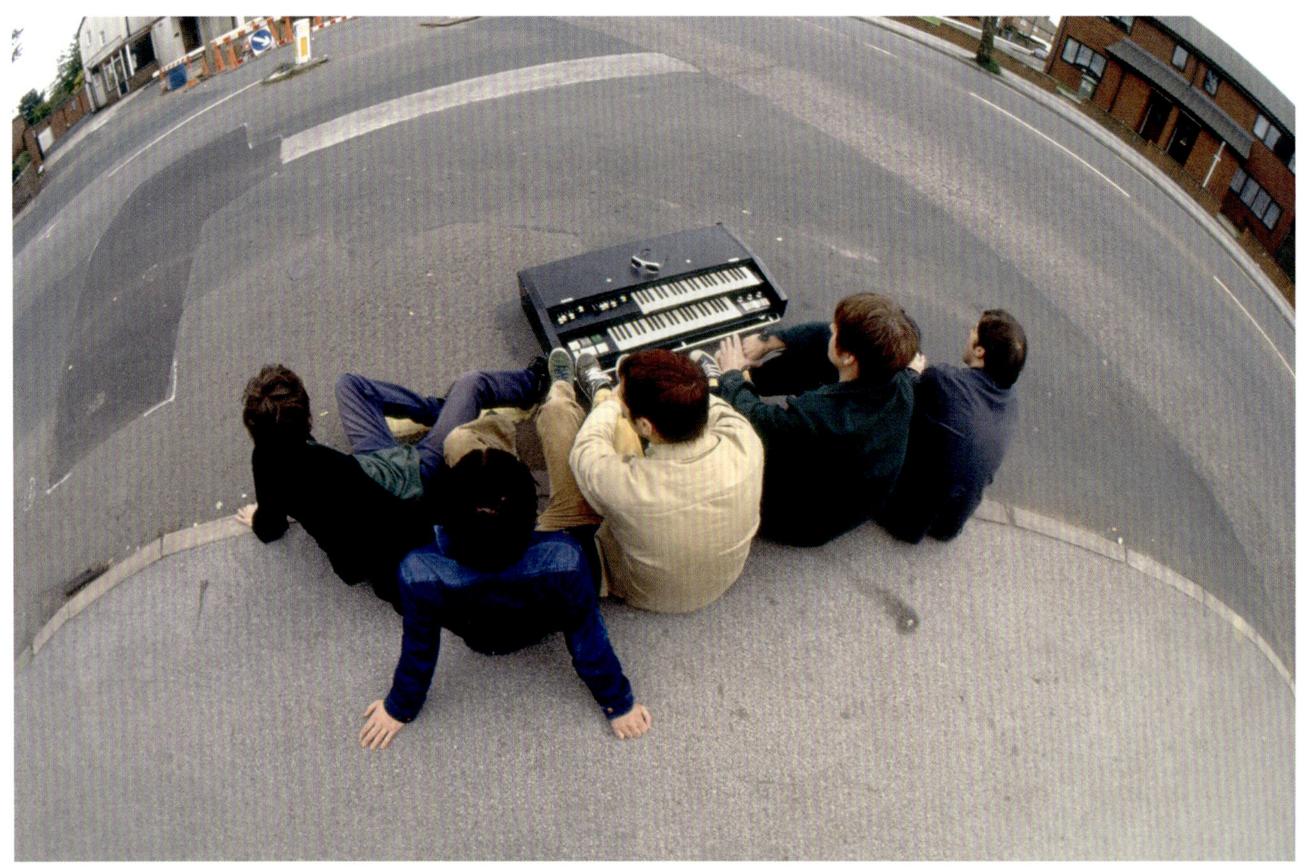

We'd ticked off a lot of firsts with Tom, and next up was his debut record sleeve with us. "Crashin' In" was released on Boxing Day 1994. Rob was just out of prison and living in Bloxwich, so it was decided we would do the shoot on his actual street, as it was to feature his Hammond X5 organ. After years of carrying it up and down the stairs for gigs, we were relieved that the location was a mere 20 yards from where it spent its days.

We were all big fans of the Beastie Boys and decided that the sleeve was to be a West Midlands-based homage to the photo on the cover of *Check Your Head*.

Another of Tom's sleeves was for our *Melting Pot* compilation, and, years after they'd both been released, someone pointed out that the only other person on the sleeve apart from the band seemed to be the same guy that nobody had noticed at the time, an older man wearing a white mac, which gave rise to all kinds of ghostly theories.

Tom:
Tim and I used to talk about records that we liked, but also about record covers, the visual side of things. This one was a nod to a Beastie Boys' album. It's like a musician lifting a guitar riff or a drum solo – of course you're lifting it from somewhere else, but it's meant as a homage, you'd never deny that you took the original inspiration from somewhere else. It's meant as a sign of respect.

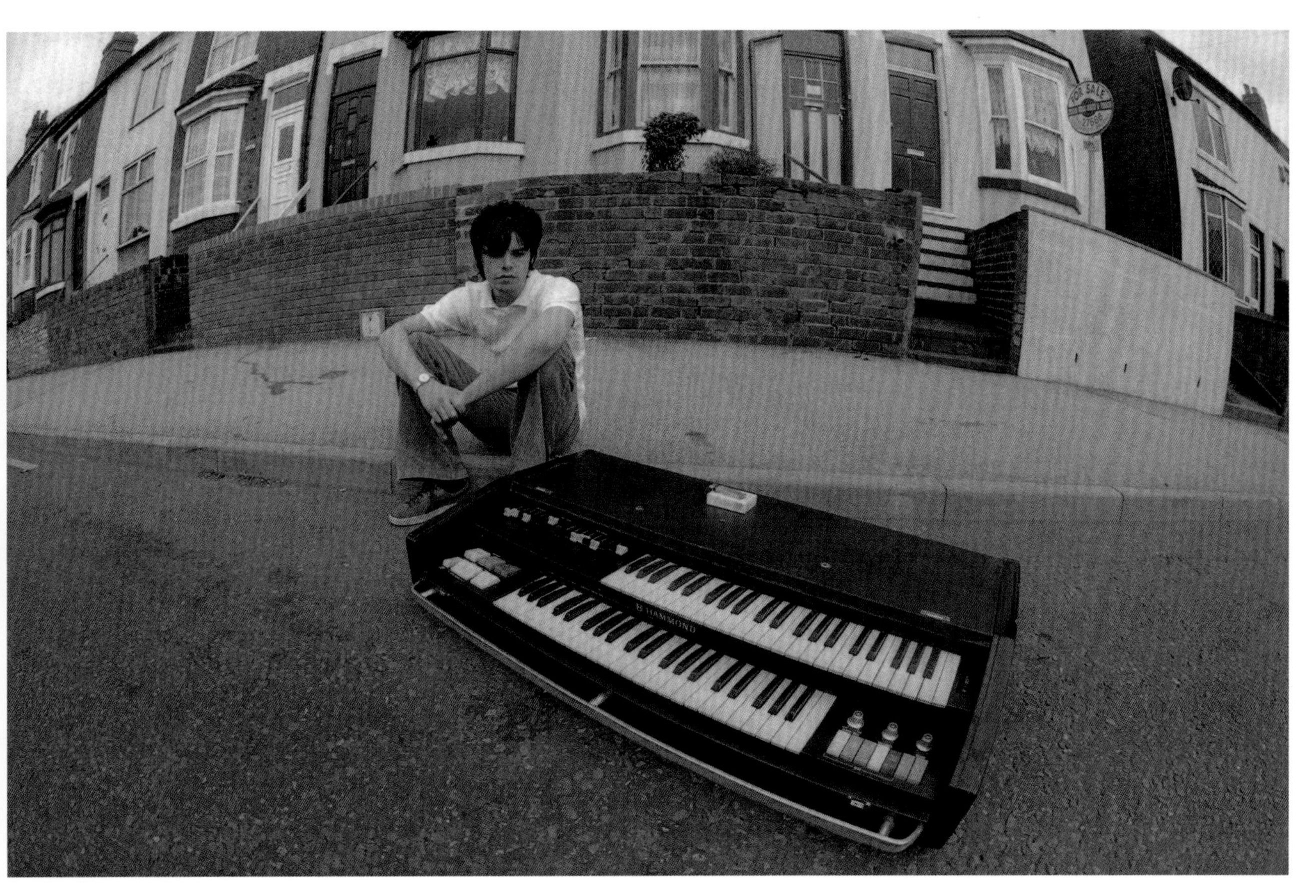
FOR SALE
HAMMOND

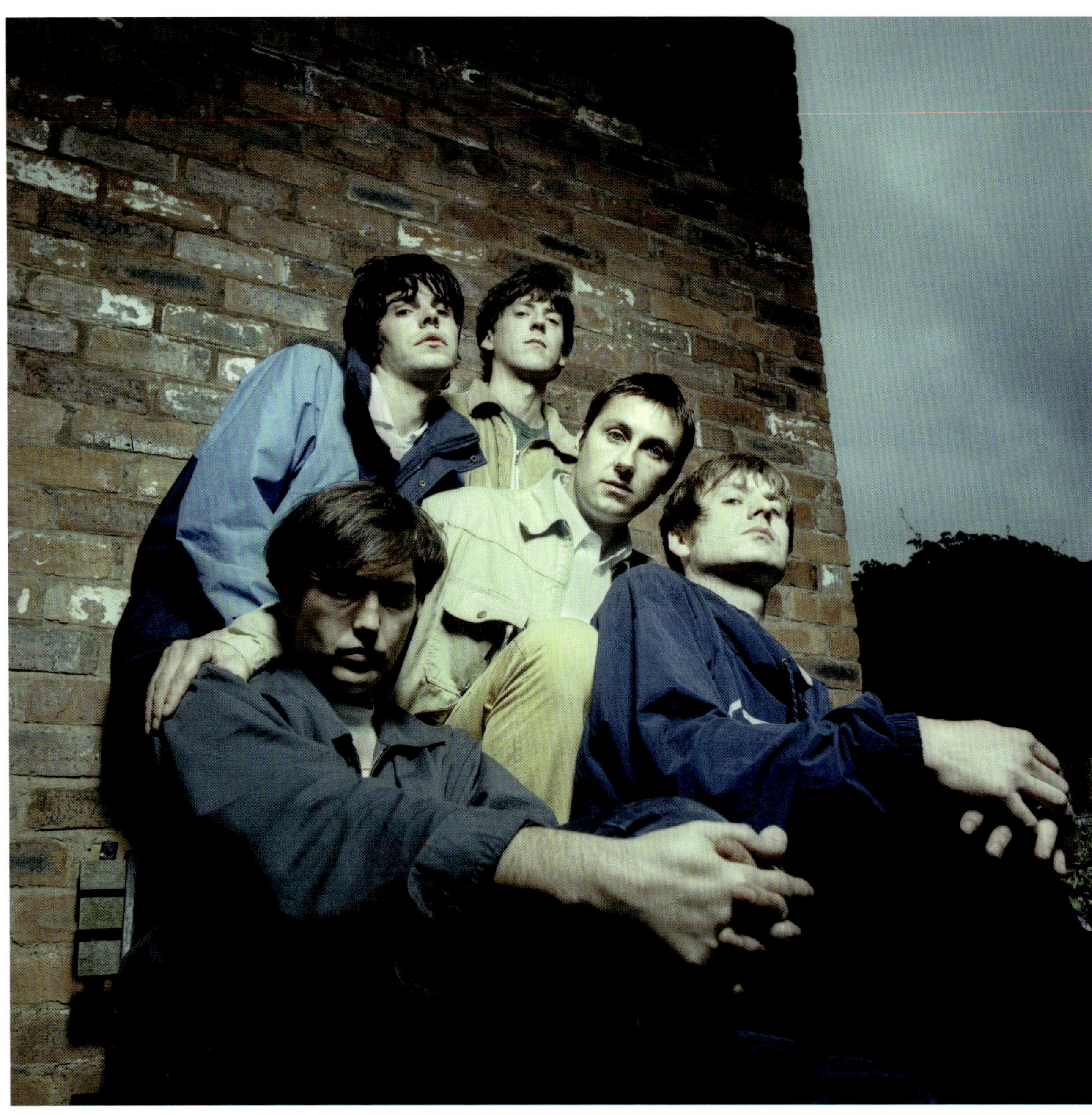

We assembled at Rob's house to shoot the cover of "Crashin' In", the location suggested by Tom. The picture eventually used on the sleeve was taken round the front, but this shot was from round the back, in Rob's garden. Inspired by the back cover of "Free Your Mind" by Funkadelic, it made it into the final shortlist of three images to be used as the front cover.

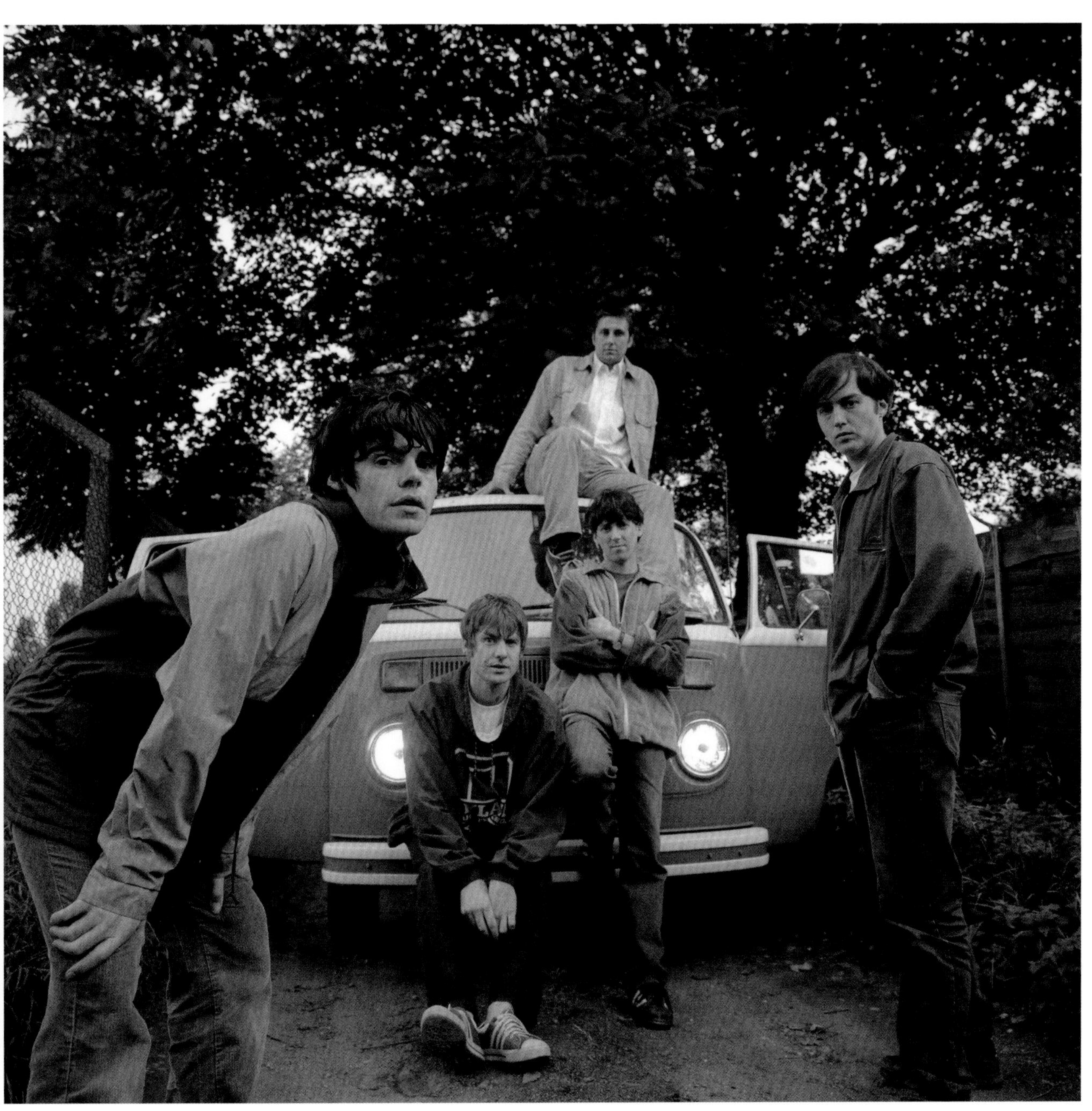

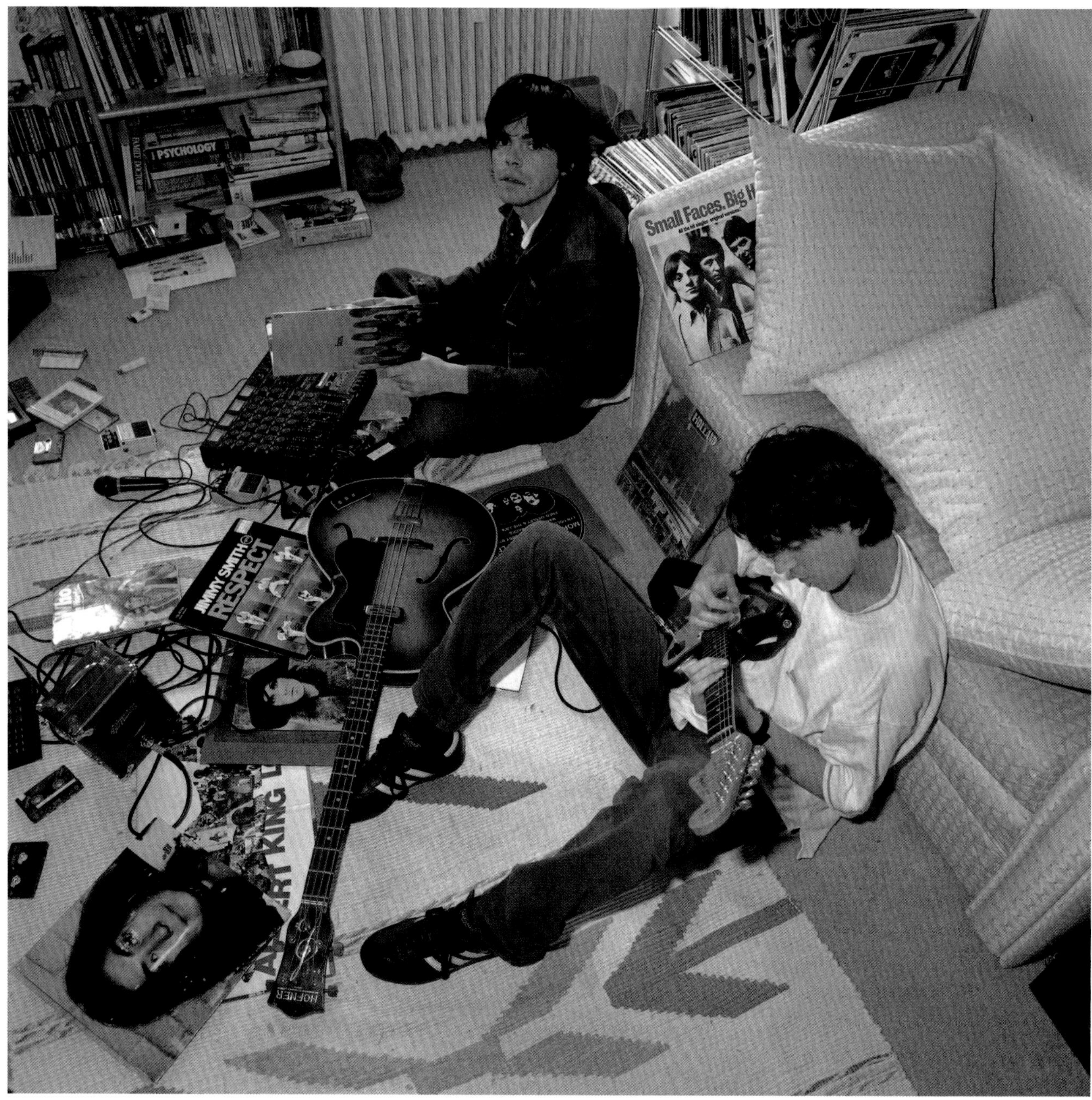

Mark and I had reached a rich vein of form in terms of our songwriting. Obviously, he was new to the band, so we were catching up on lost time.

In terms of practicalities, I had a flat in Chalk Farm, North London, and Mark would travel down from Manchester for three or four days at a time. He'd have the sofa bed in the lounge and we'd get started around 10am. We'd listen to records and wait for the inspiration, a guitar each, with books and paper strewn across the floor.

Tom loved the idea of seeing into the writing process, so we planned one day for him to come and listen to our efforts so far and capture the spirit of our endeavours, breaking off in the afternoon for a pint of Guinness at The Engine Rooms up near The Roundhouse.

I remember seeing photographs of Joe Strummer lying on the floor, pen in hand, surrounded by freshly written lyric sheets, and I could feel the buzz of "London Calling" or "The Magnificent Seven" in its earliest form.

At the Chalk Farm flat we wrote the basic outlines to "Bullet Comes", "Back Room Window", "Just When You're Thinkin' Things Over", "Tell Everyone" and "Here Comes A Soul Saver". Visitors included *NME* journalists, Liam Gallagher, The Chemical Brothers, Beth Orton and various characters from the pages of the music weeklies. It really felt like we'd made it.

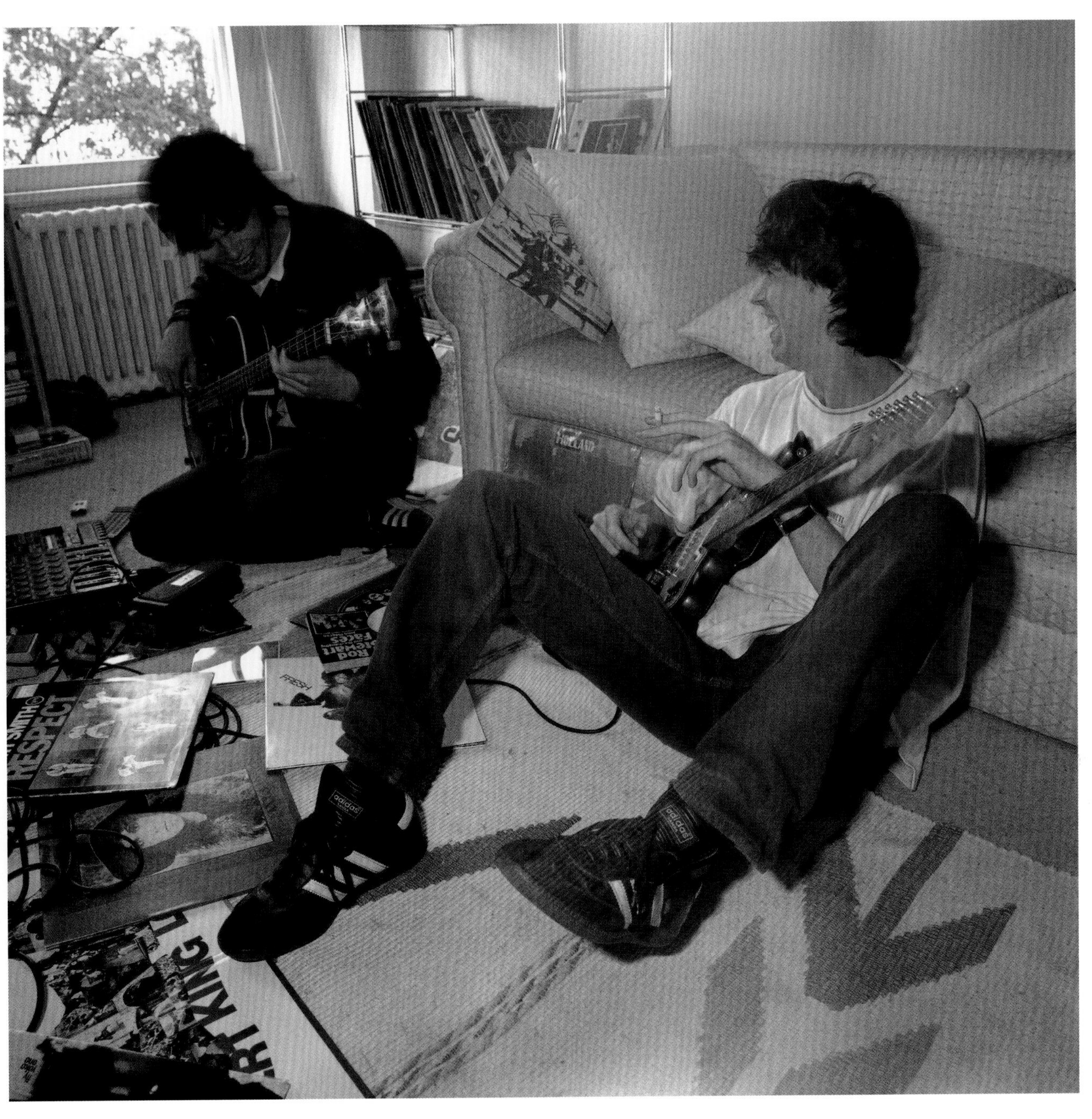
SMITH
RESPECT
FRESH
adidas

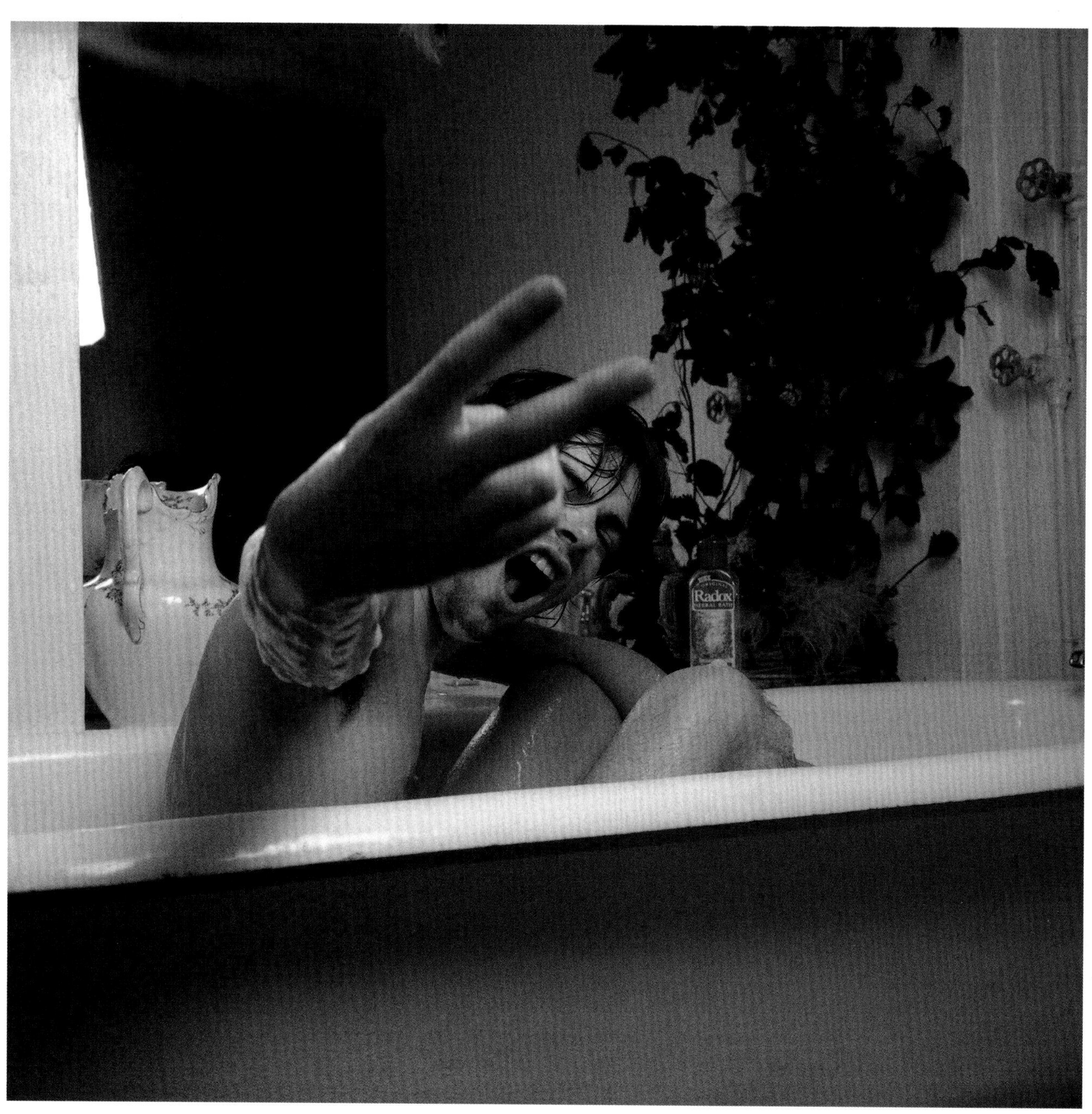
Radox

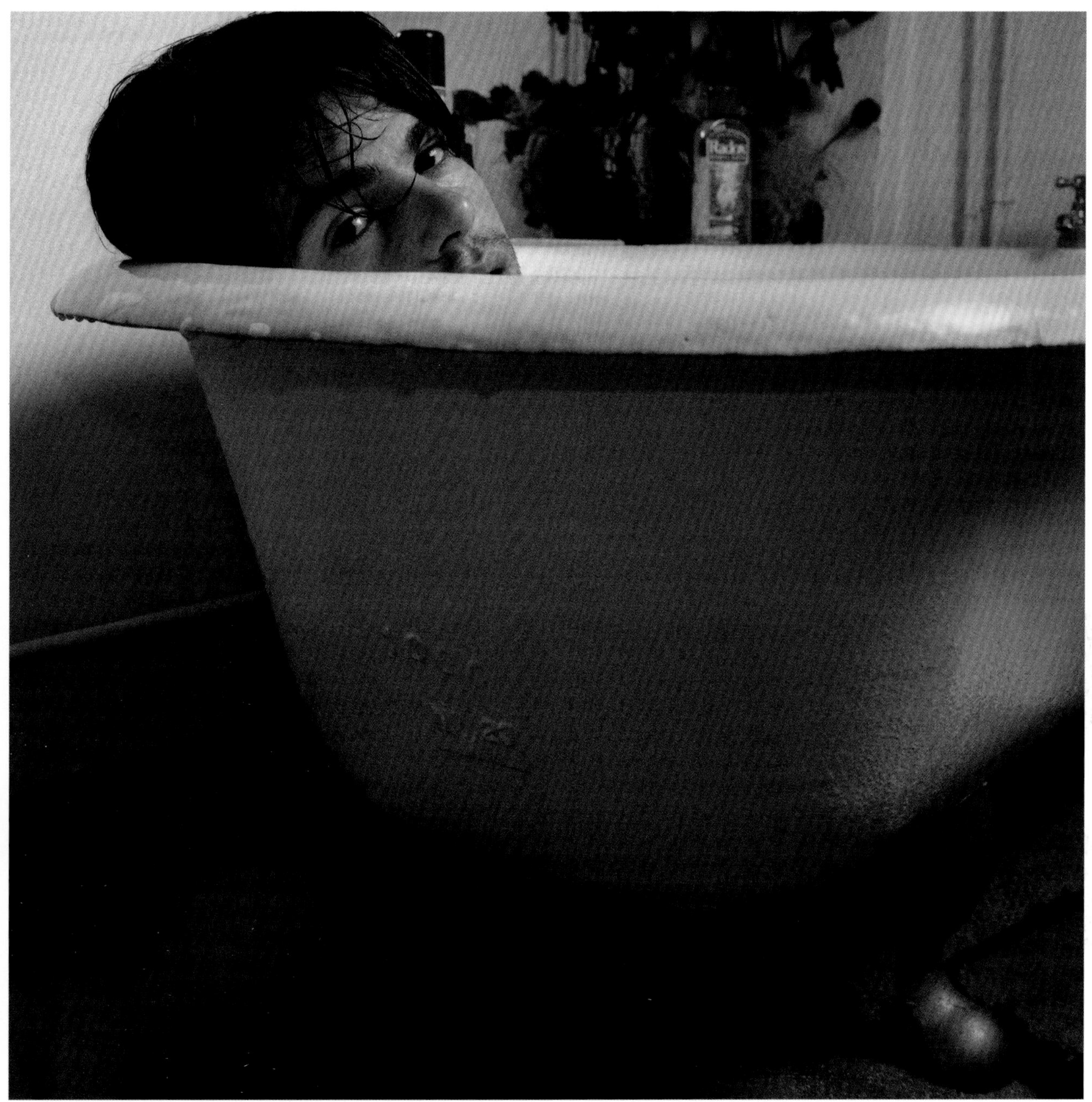

The whole band were at Monnow Valley recording our eponymous album, a time when we were in every magazine and on every music show in town. It was a fun look at there being nowhere to hide and no privacy, something I had actually pursued.

We had just recorded "Just When You're Thinkin' Things Over". It seemed to come to us quite easily and we were on a real high. Rob was back with us after his time away and Steve Hillage had recommended that we get straight back into the studio. It was sage advice.

I've always found having a bath is a great time and place to think – and the acoustics are often brilliant. The bathrooms at Monnow Valley were fairly grand and if I was stuck for lyrics that's where I would head, Radox in hand.

I have always been a big fan of baths. To me, showers were the preserve of games lessons on a freezing-cold football pitch and waking up hungover and having to be somewhere. Lots of my life at that time was hectic and done in the public eye, so time in the bath was all mine, with the world on the other side of a locked door – unless of course it was a photoshoot in the bath. I've just noticed that this one includes a photo of Adam Ant. Not sure why it's there but I like it.

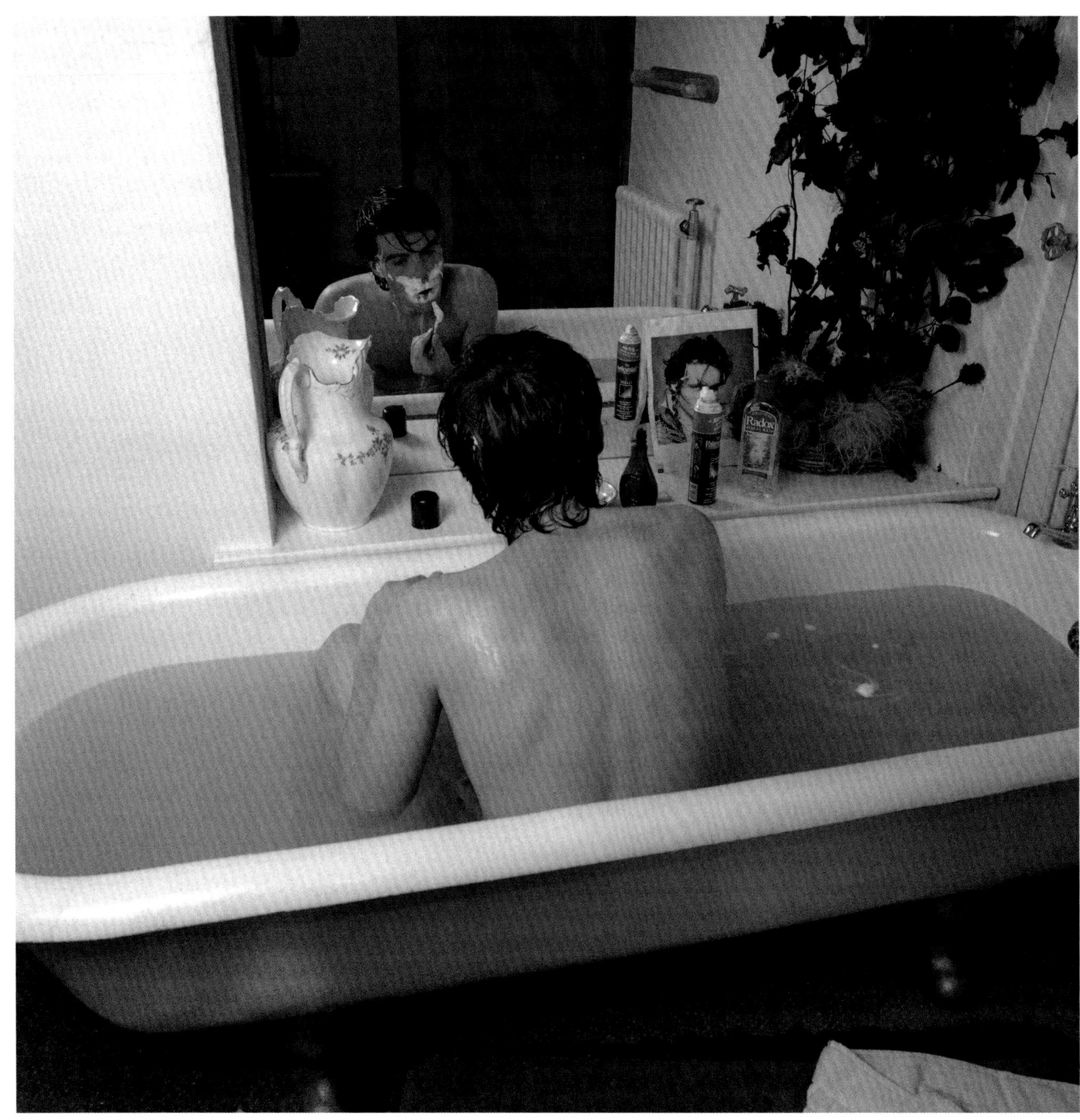

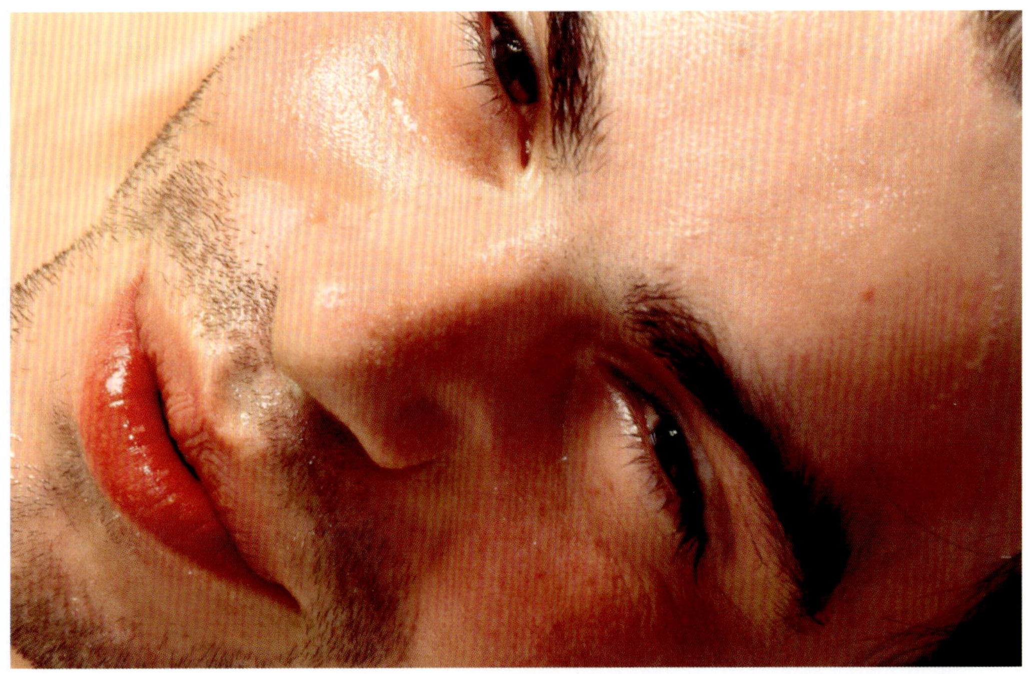

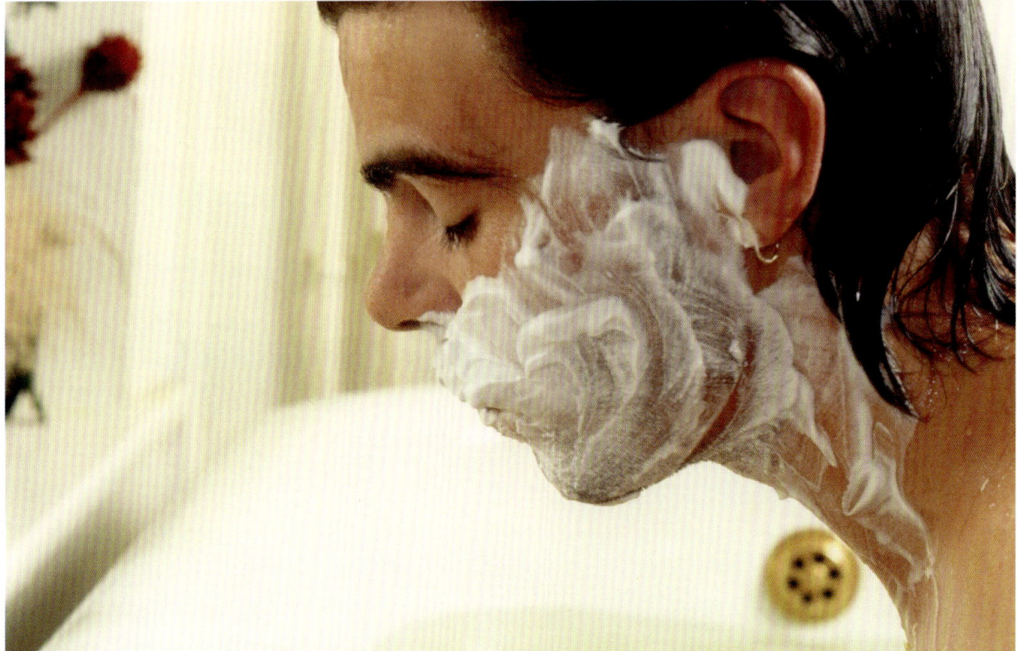

Tom:
I remember when I first took these Tim saying, 'Tommy, you can't use that, I look like a newborn baby!' So of course I said okay, and set it to one side. What happens years later when we come to do this book? He expressly asks for this bloody picture.

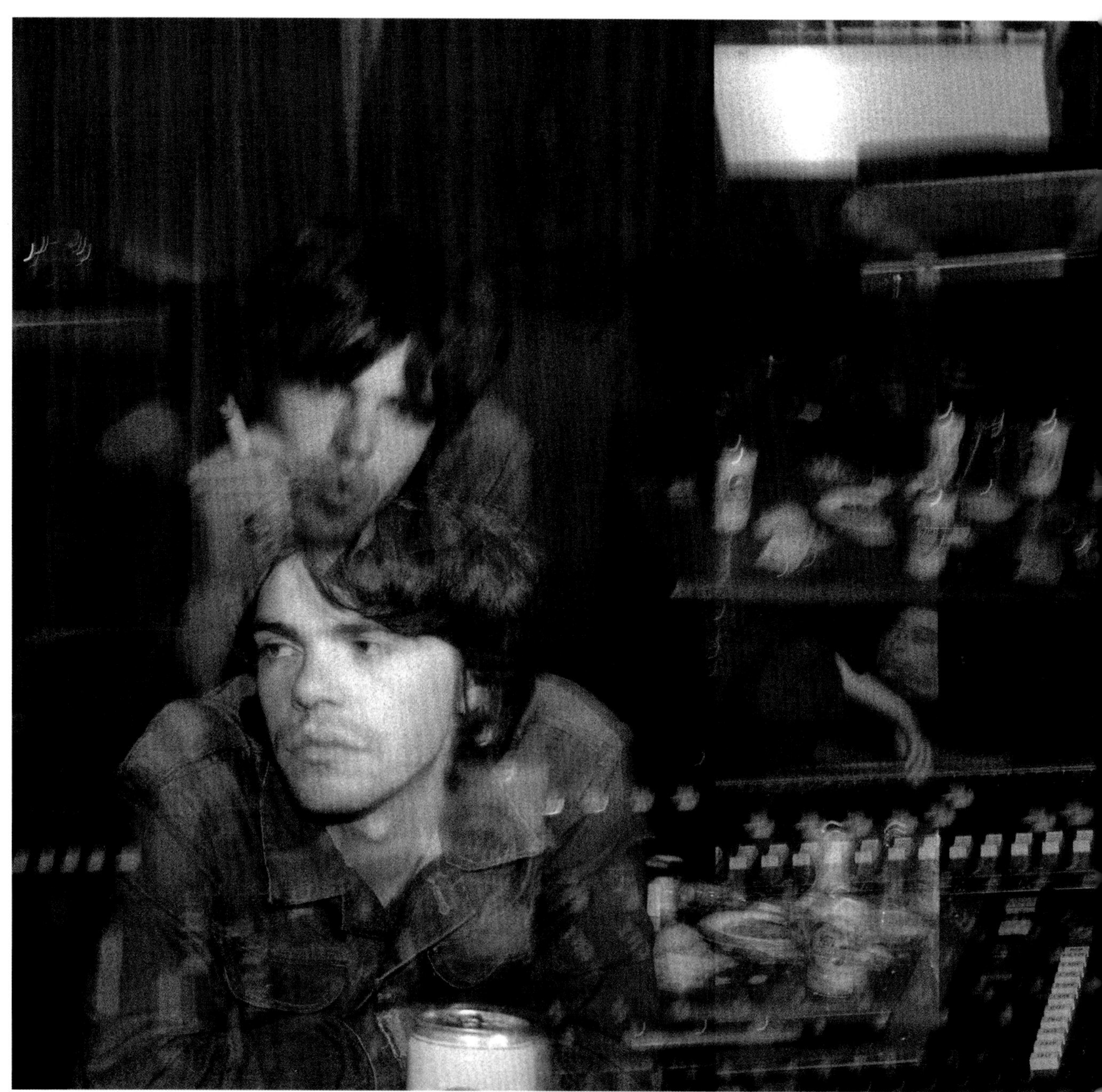

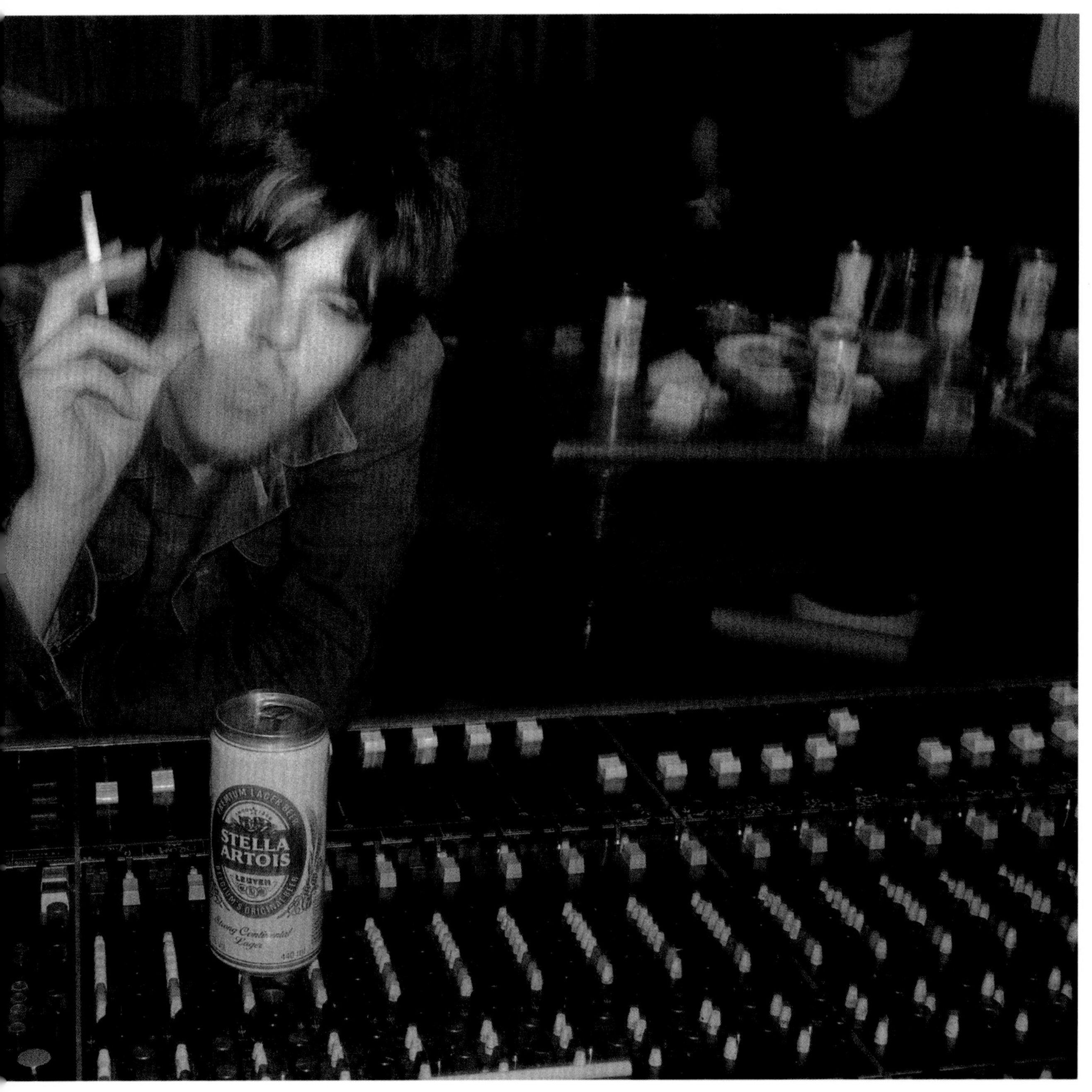
PREMIUM LAGER BEER
STELLA
ARTOIS
LEUVEN

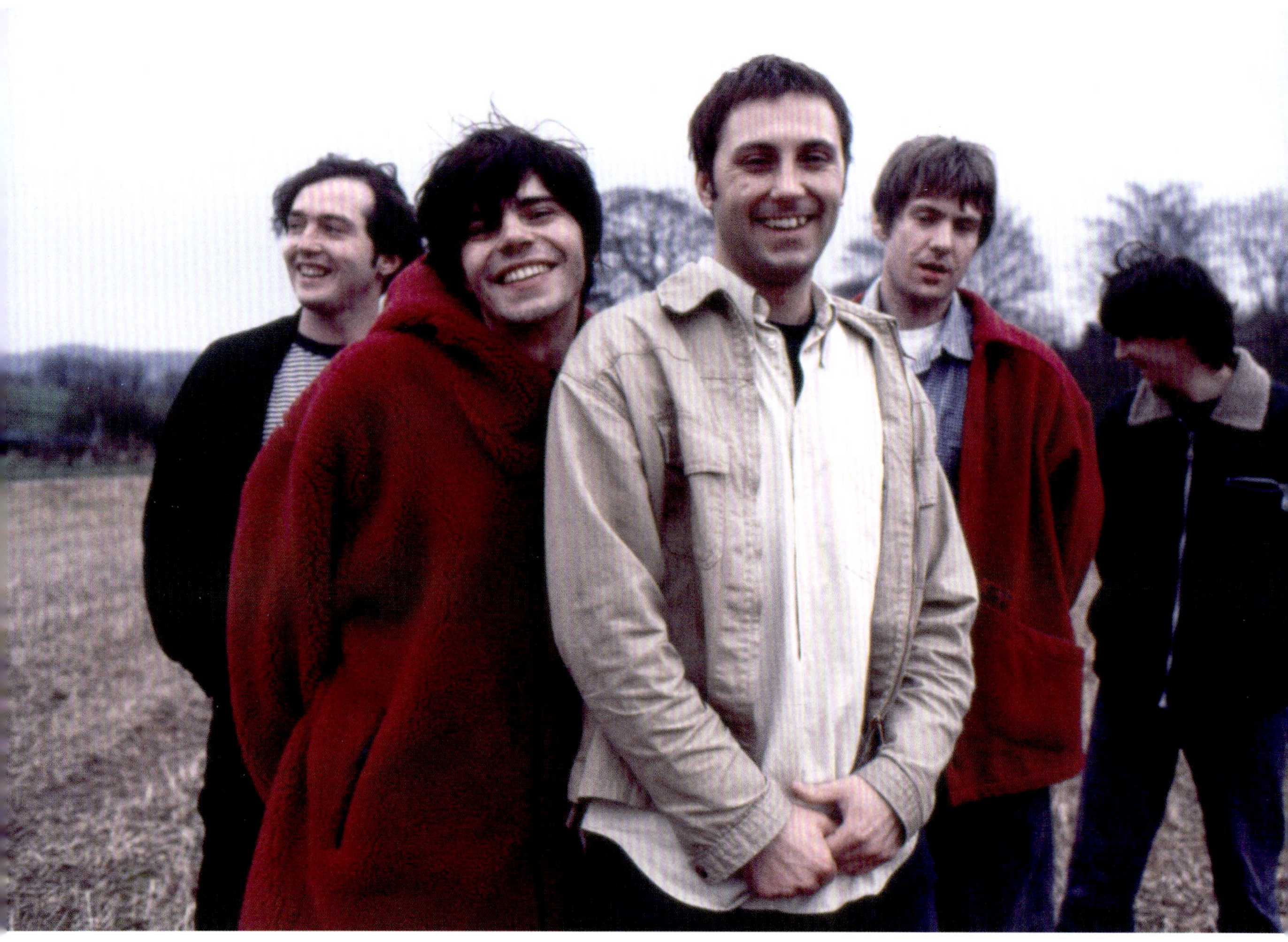

We definitely wanted to present ourselves as serious and moody, in the spirit of the bands we loved the most. The majority of us smiling in a picture is a rarity, which makes me love this one all the more. Tom was always making wisecracks and telling jokes and it looks like this one hit home. I'm guessing we wouldn't have okayed it for a magazine, but it's so good to see it now.

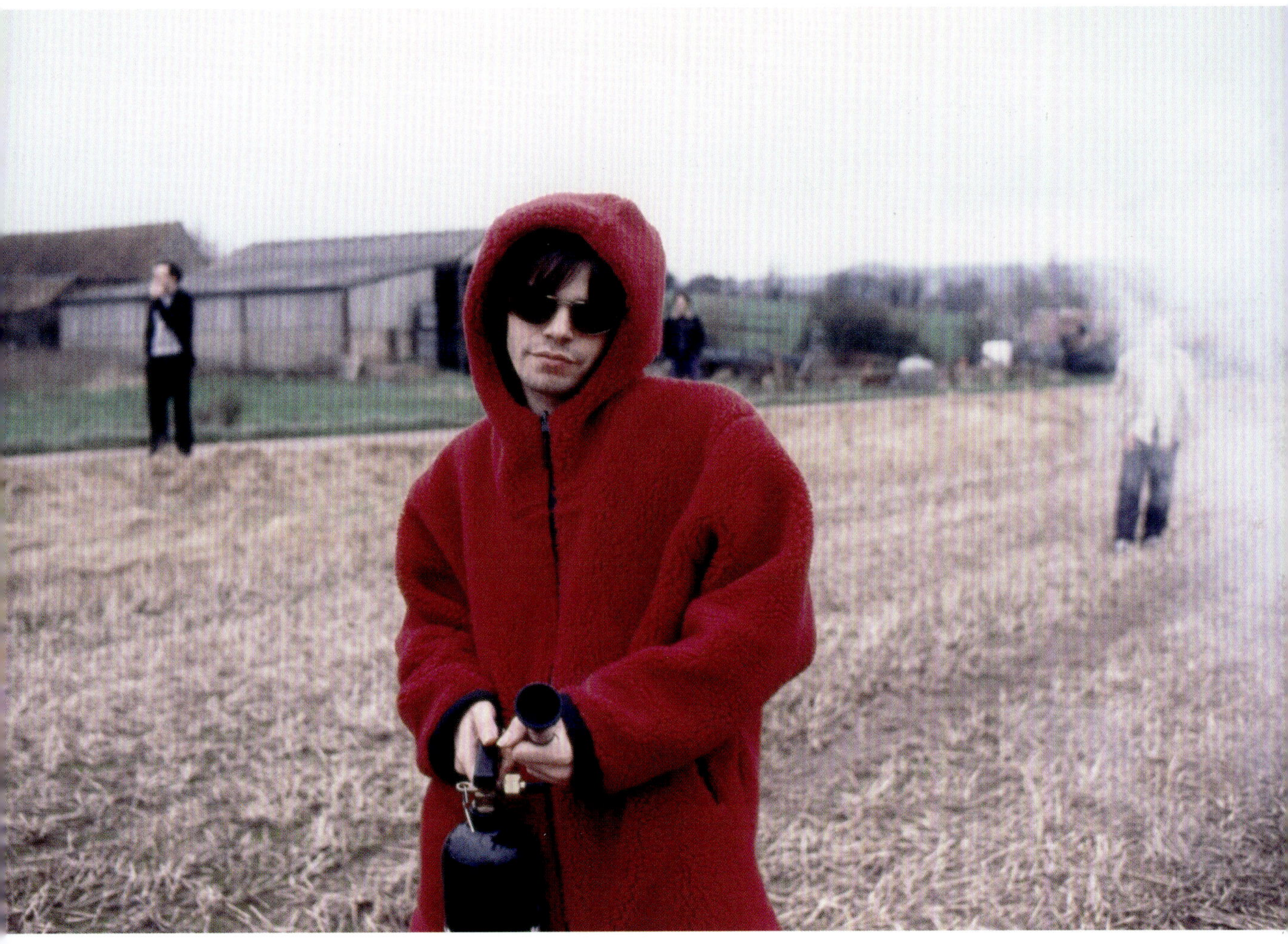

Tom:
Tim got his wrist slapped for this one, setting off a fire extinguisher in Monnow Valley. You can see it just blowing away on the right of frame. I told him to shoot off to one side so he didn't absolutely cover me in foam, and then we fired off a whole roll to get the shots. But Kingsley, one of the brothers who ran the studio, gave him a telling off, albeit in a jocular way.

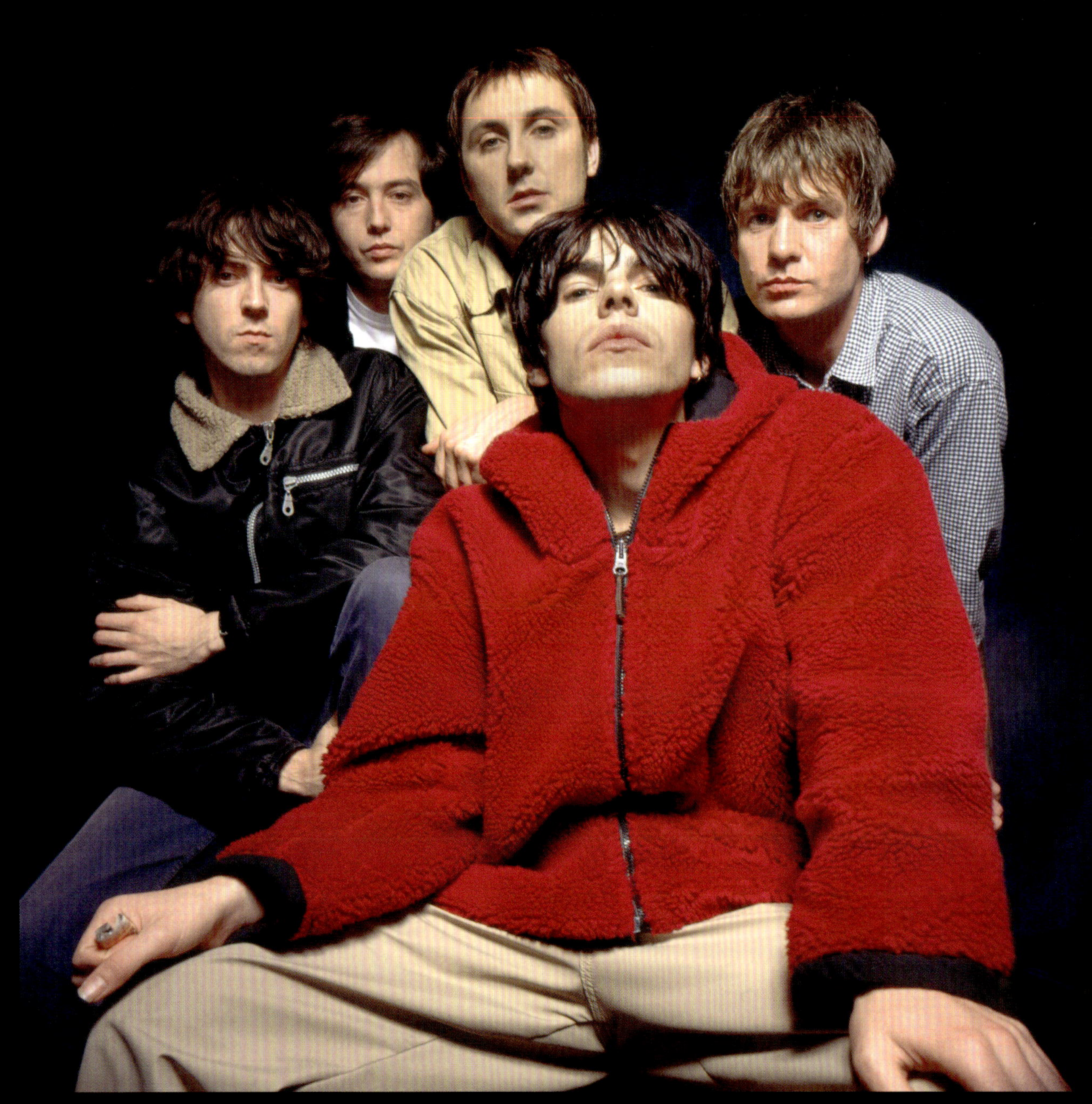

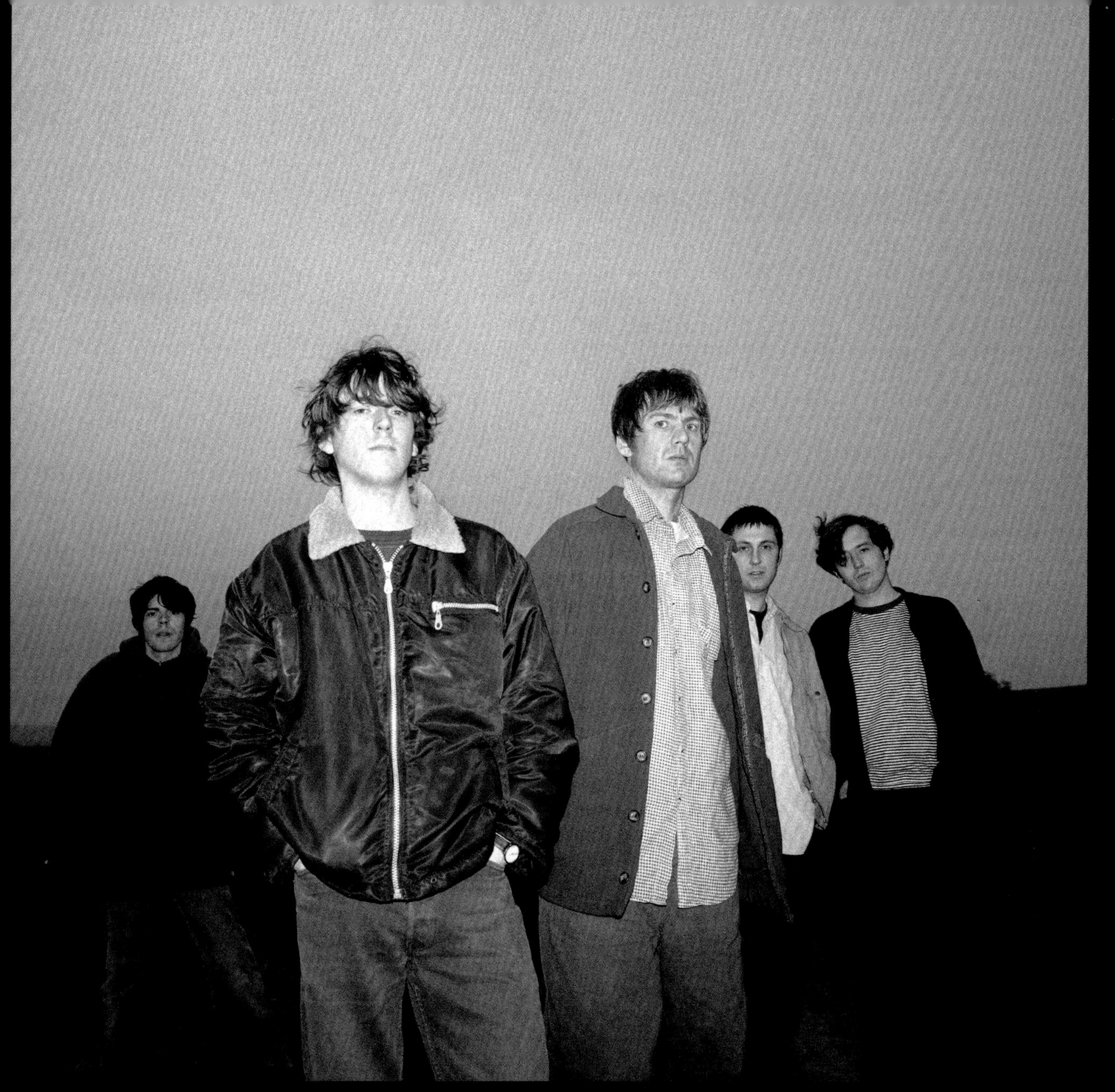

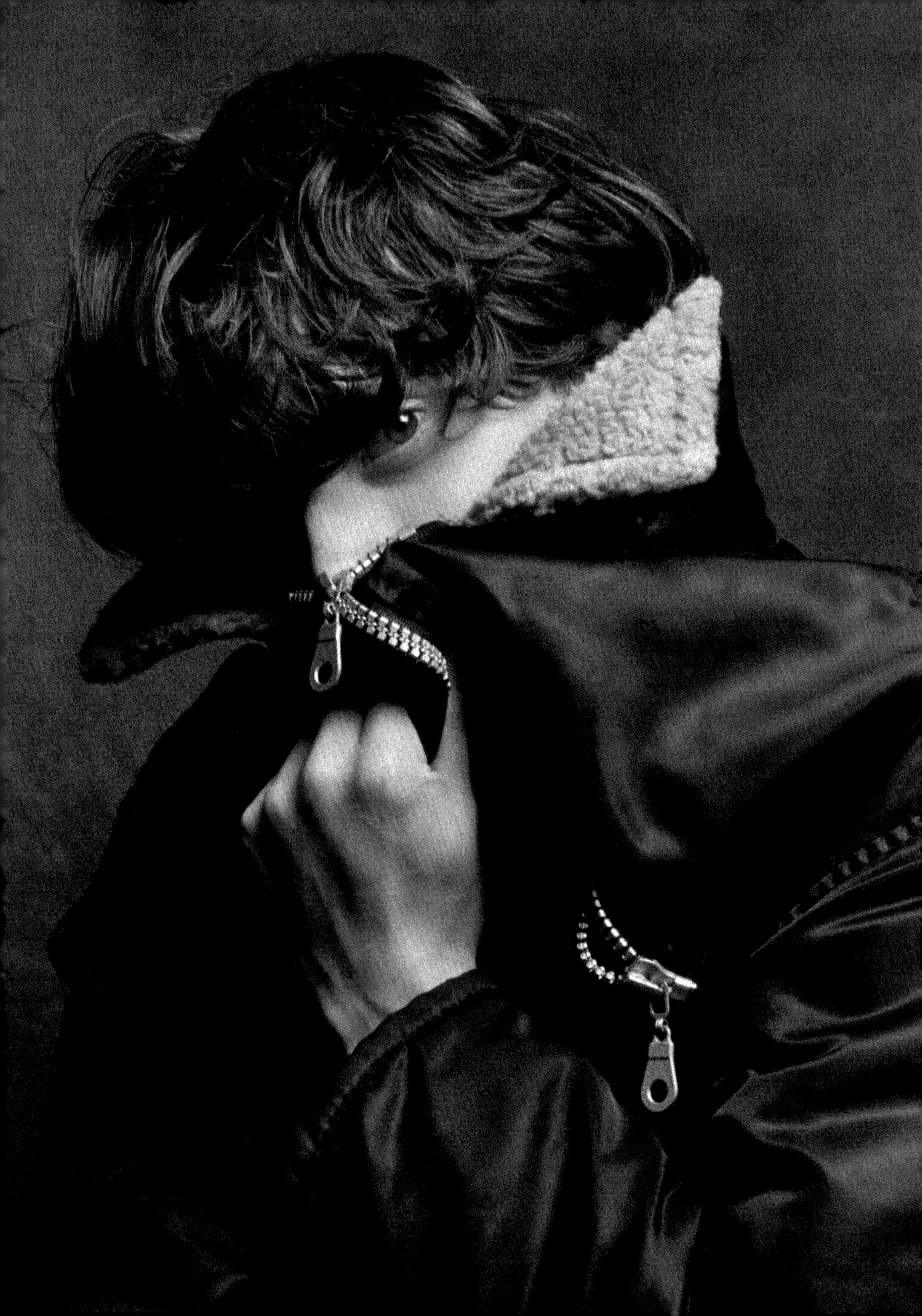

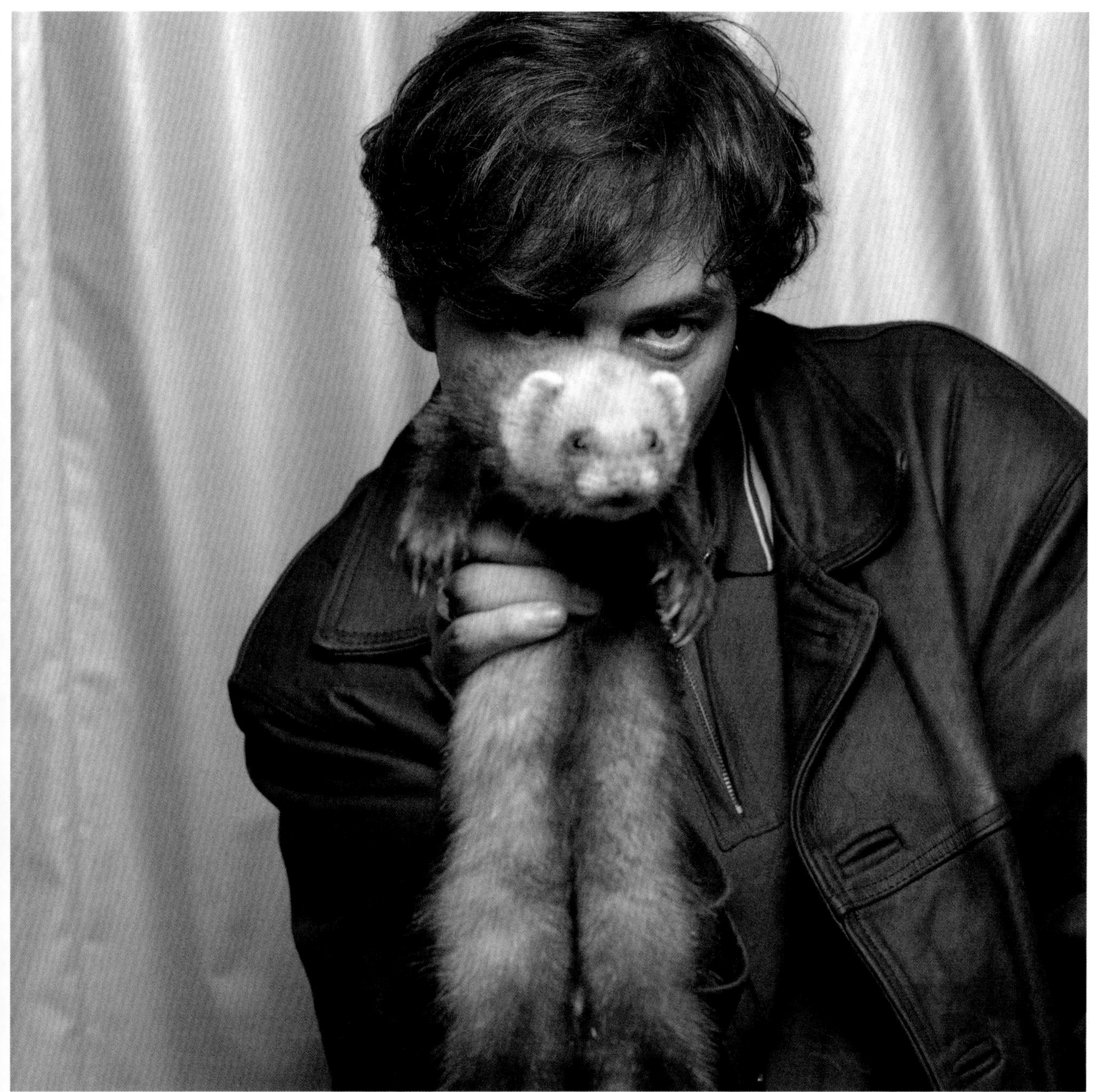

While we were recording *The Charlatans* we fully integrated to our surroundings. We'd spend time in local pubs, clubs, playing pool and waiting for inspiration. One afternoon Rob came back from The Griffin, in Monmouth, with two new acquaintances. The less interesting of the two took human form and his glamorous sidekick was a ferret. Rob was of the mind that we all needed to meet the ferret. It kind of captures the oddness and bizarre nature of our time spent recording.

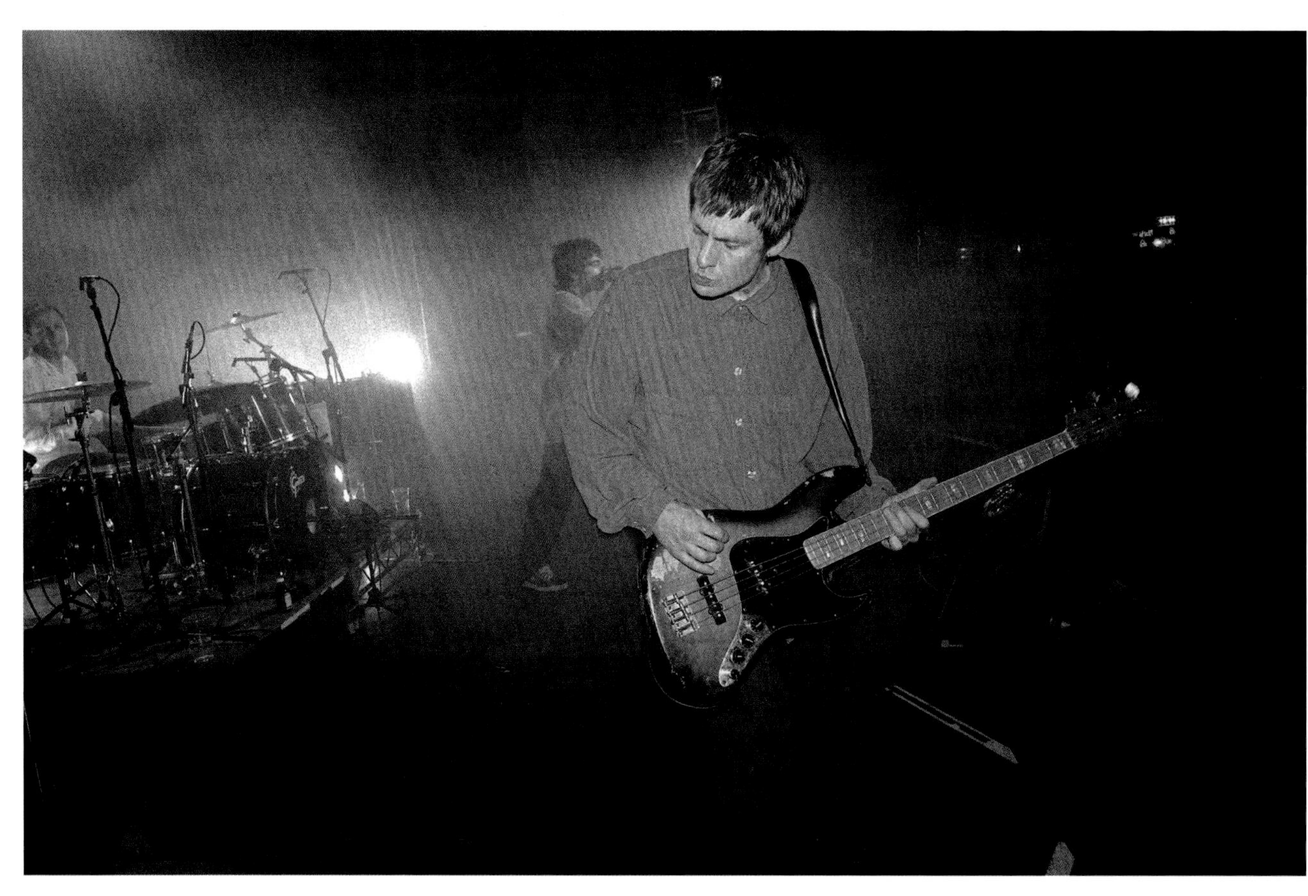

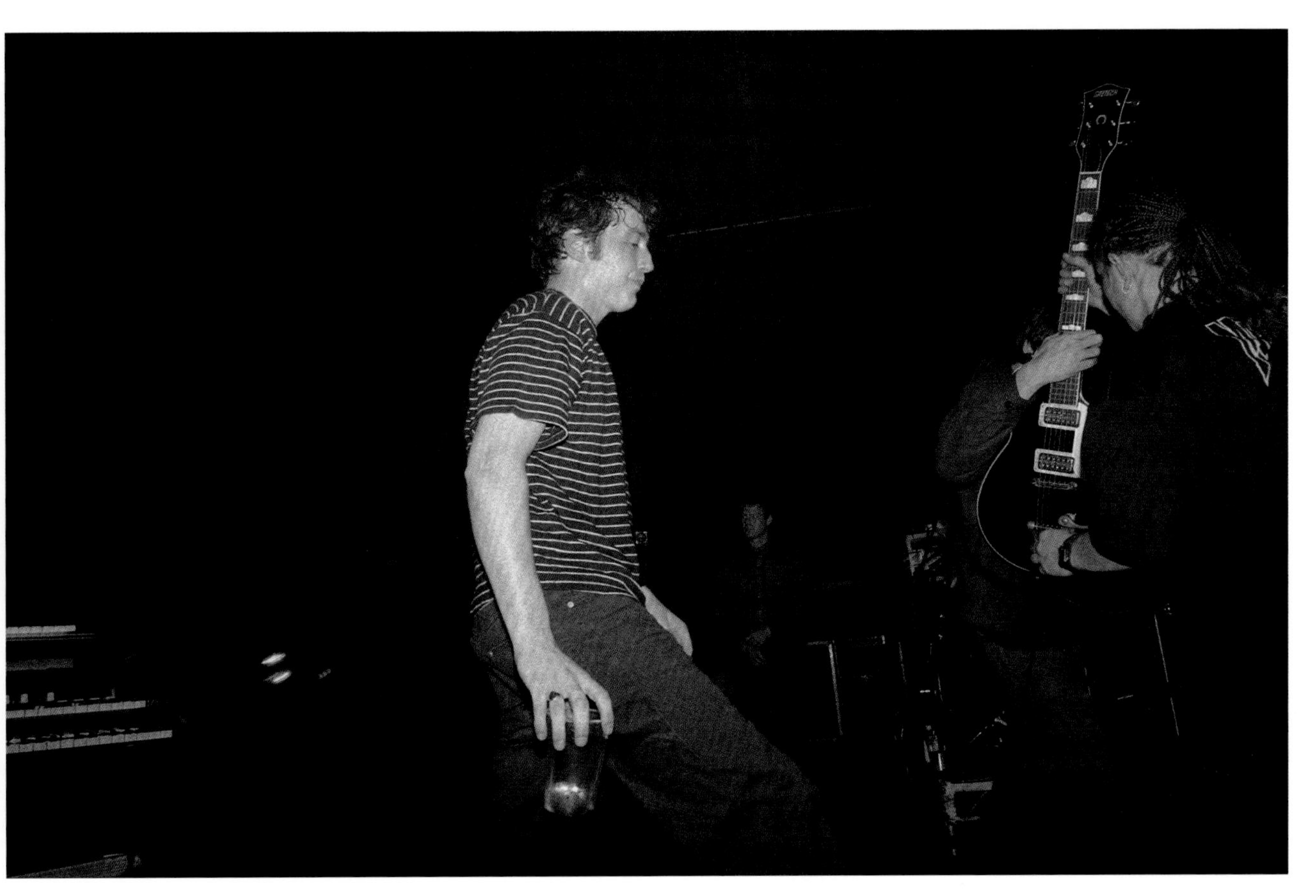

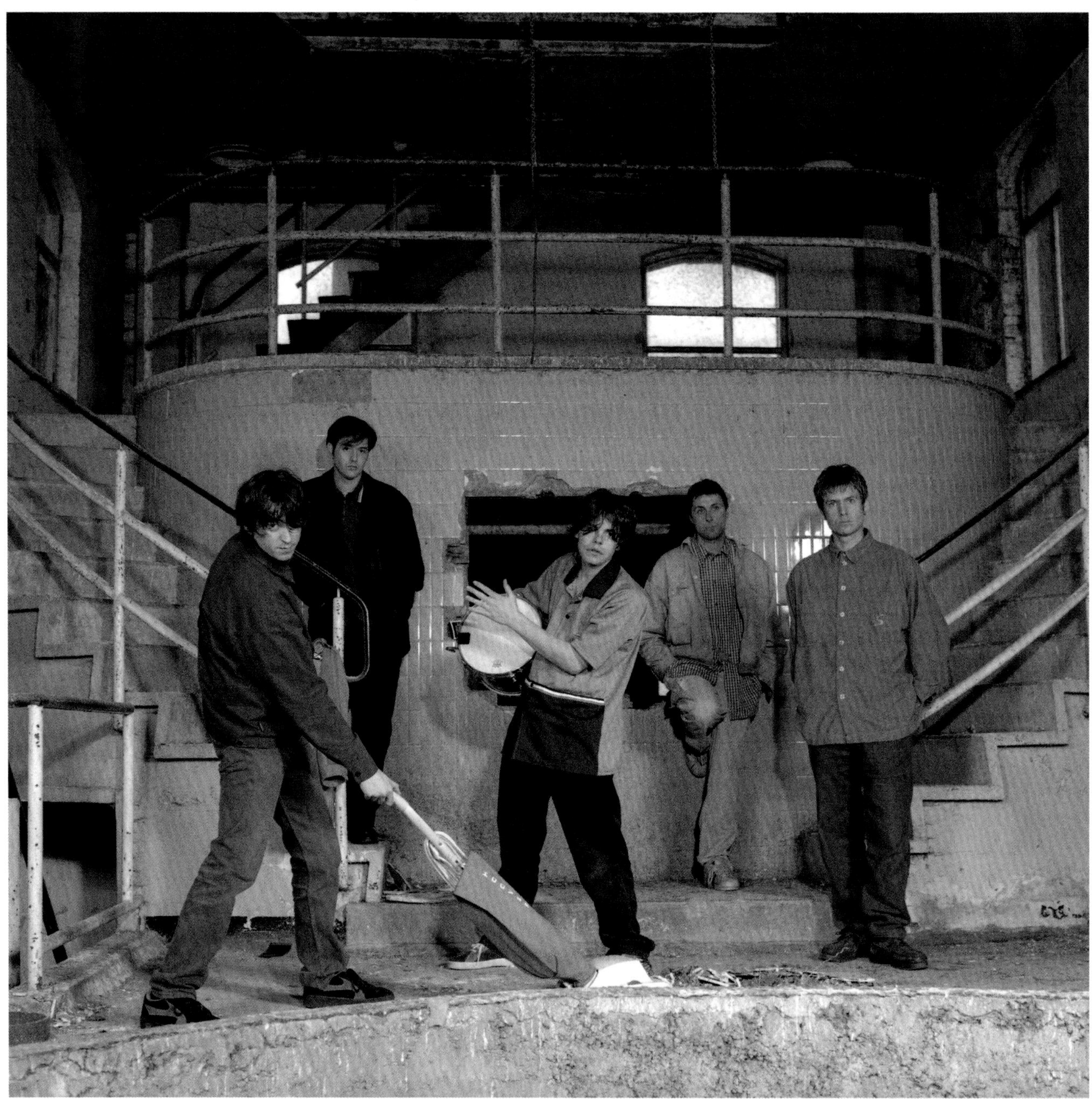

Taken in our rehearsal room. Nowadays photos are much more of a common occurrence, with everyone having phones in their pockets, but we wouldn't generally take pictures in our rehearsal room, so there just aren't that many around.

We probably spent more time there than we did with our own families. It was an old warehouse taking up a couple of storeys, with other bands coming and going. It had a communal smoking room with a TV and a coffee machine. We were mostly in our own world and possibly came across as aloof to our fellow residents, but it was a hugely creative space for us.

This shot is a good example of why we didn't stage photoshoots there, but sometimes, like with recordings, it's a case of try anything and see what comes of it. If it's used you feel elated, and if it's not you just move on.

The fact that I've not seen this in 30 years takes me right back to the rehearsal room in Stone, where some of our best songs were written. "One To Another", "Toothache", "Crashin' In" and "Thank You" were all worked out there. Tony did his audition there, too – we'd asked him to learn "Weirdo", which we considered our most difficult song, and by the end we knew we had found our new keyboard player.

I'm not sure what we were doing here but I'm getting heavy "I Want to Break Free" vibes from Mark.

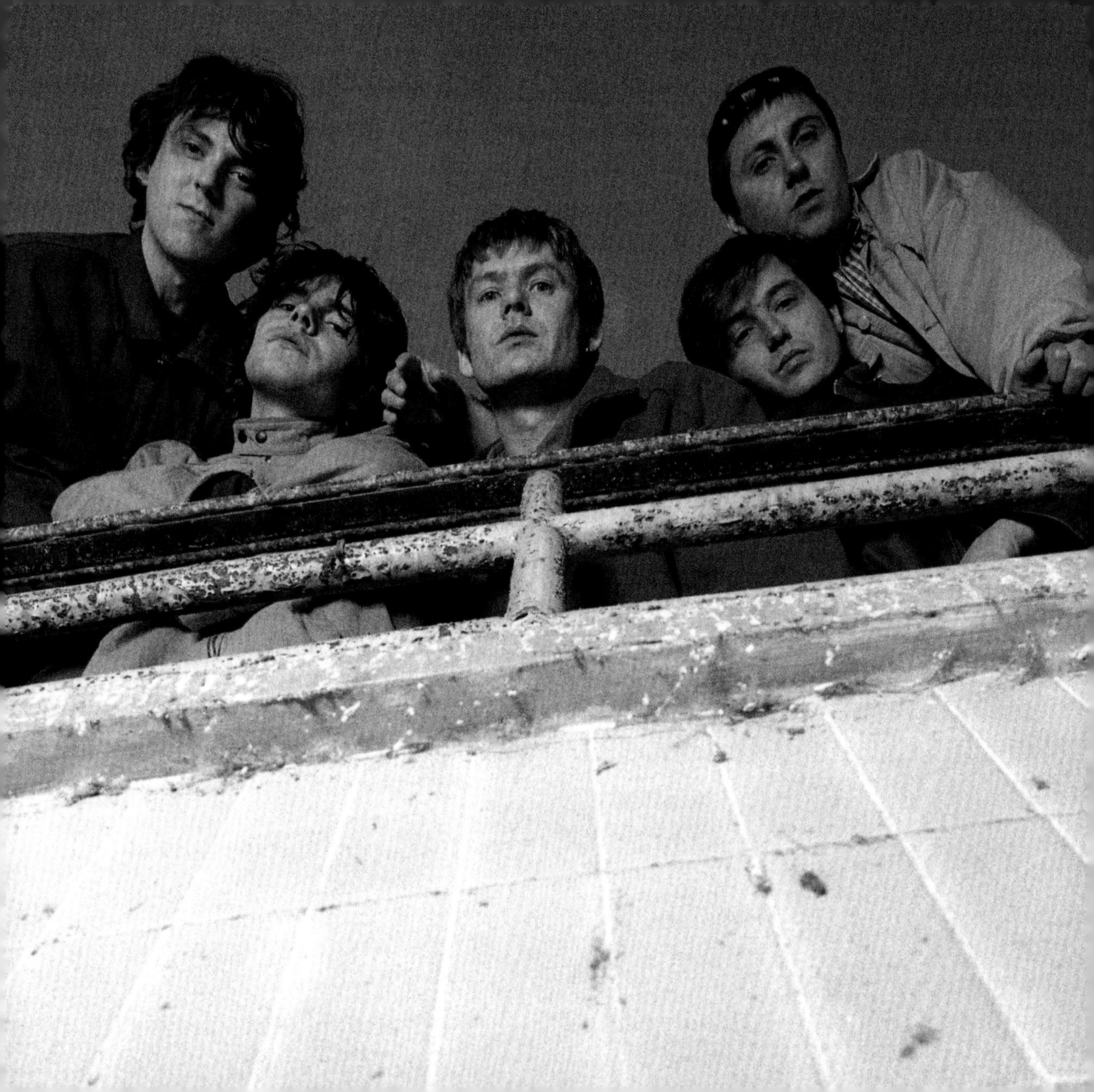

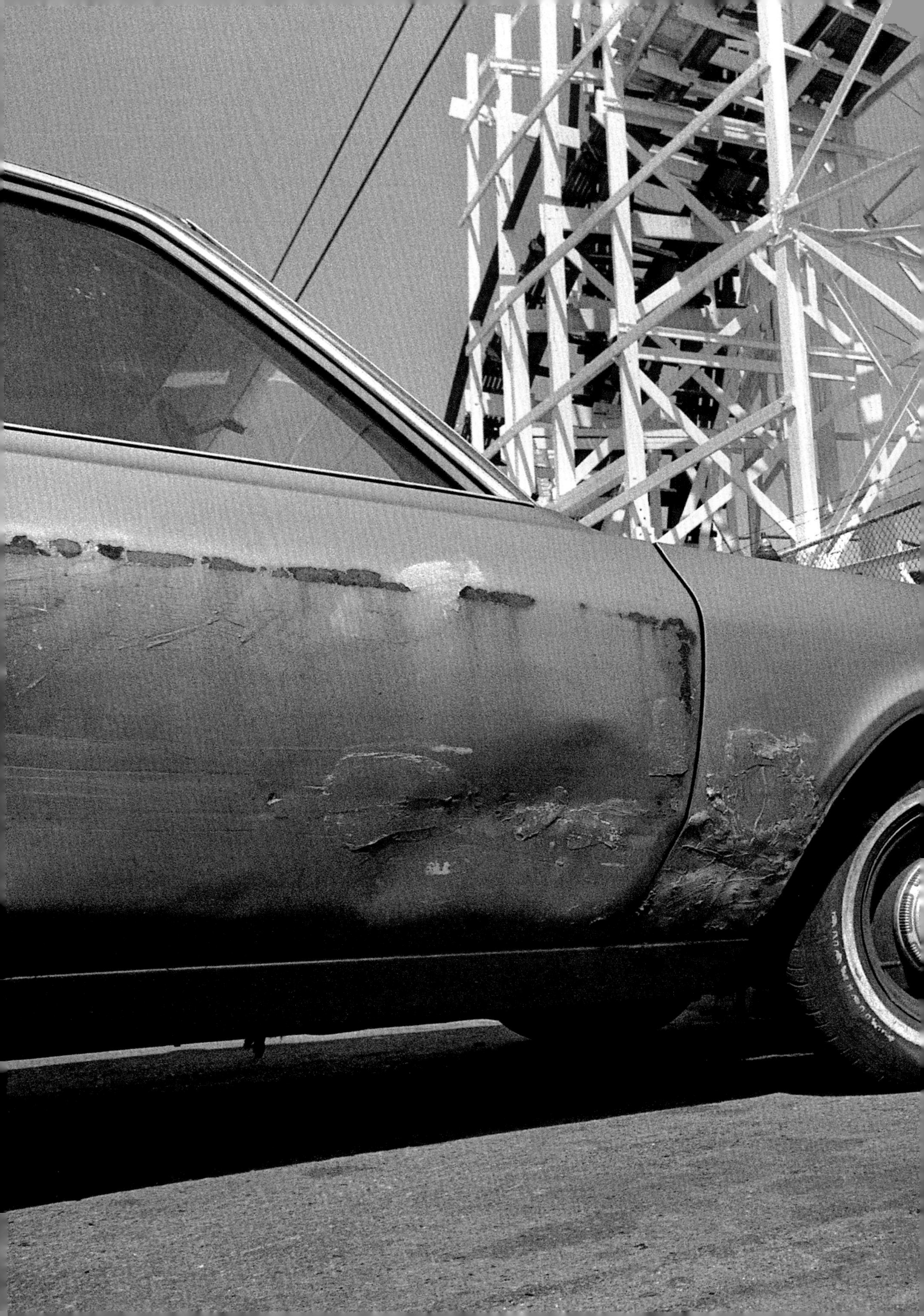

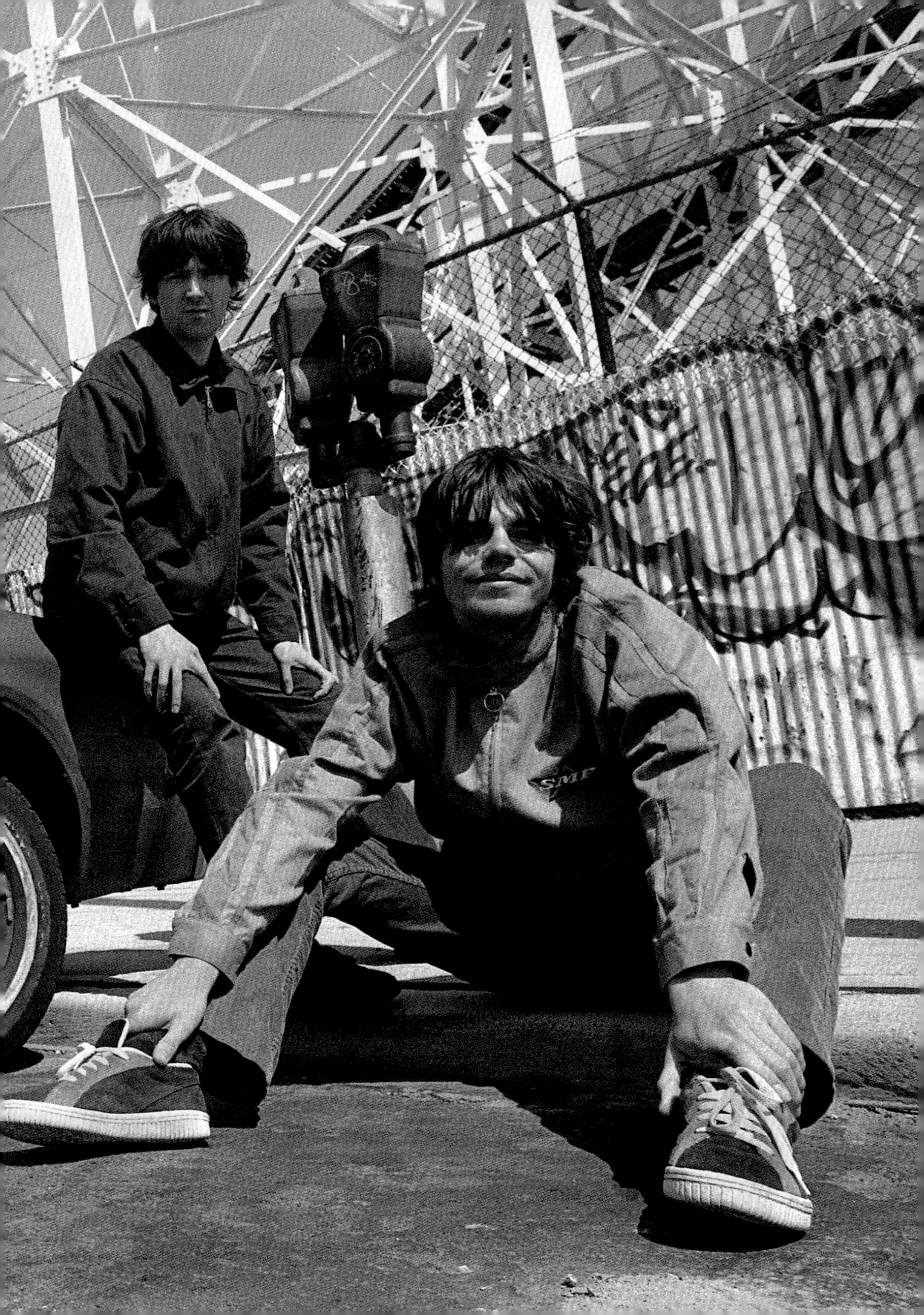

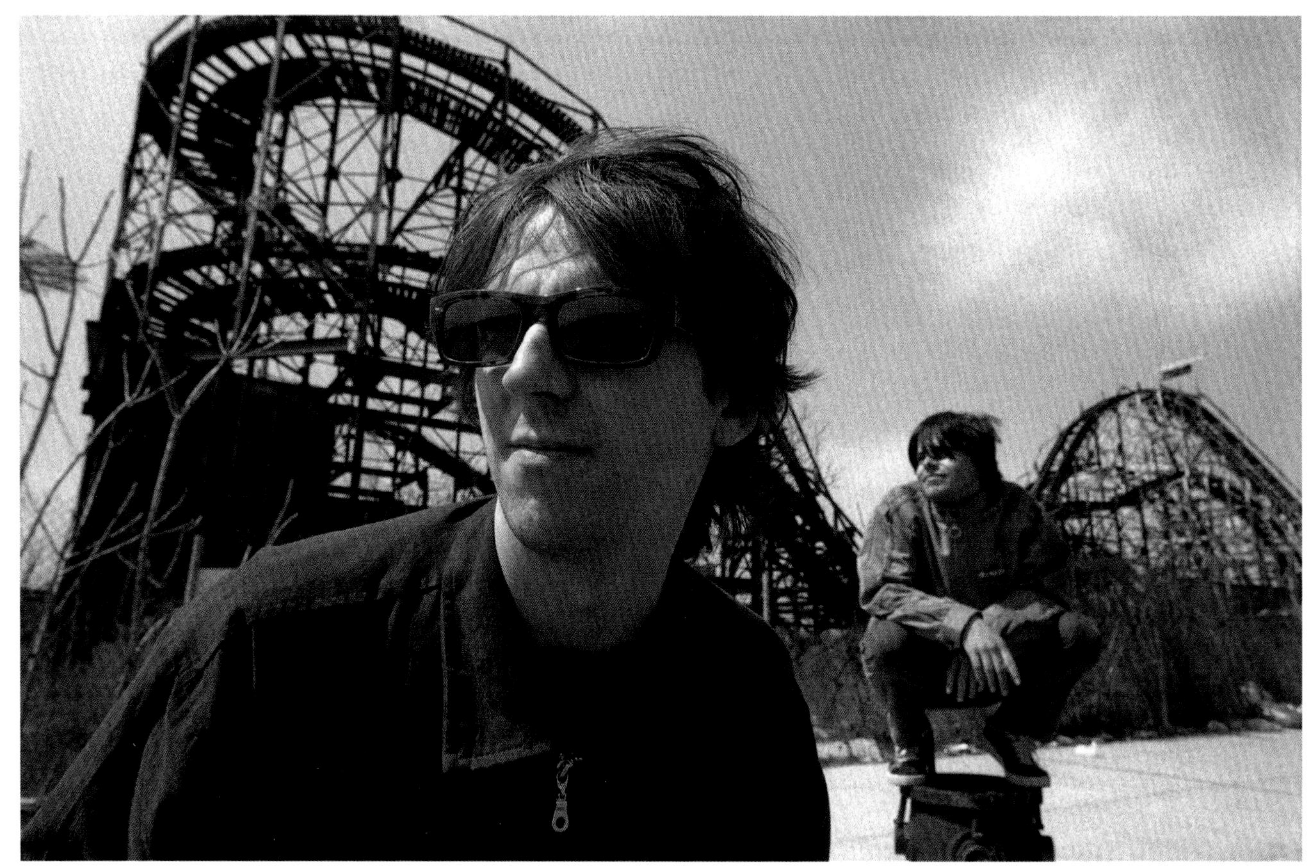

Some cities make the most natural backdrops, and we were always excited when we found out we were going to New York. Coney Island was visually rich with some great locations. I can't imagine a much better image for an allegory of life in the music industry than a huge, rusting, broken rollercoaster. I'd seen pictures of Debbie Harry taken by Bob Gruen, and The Ramones were the soundtrack in my head. Much more than Manhattan or Brooklyn, Coney Island seemed to suggest a fractured romance I associated with Lou Reed, *The Warriors* and *The French Connection*. In some ways it was a reminder of our first encounter with Tom in the scrapyard.

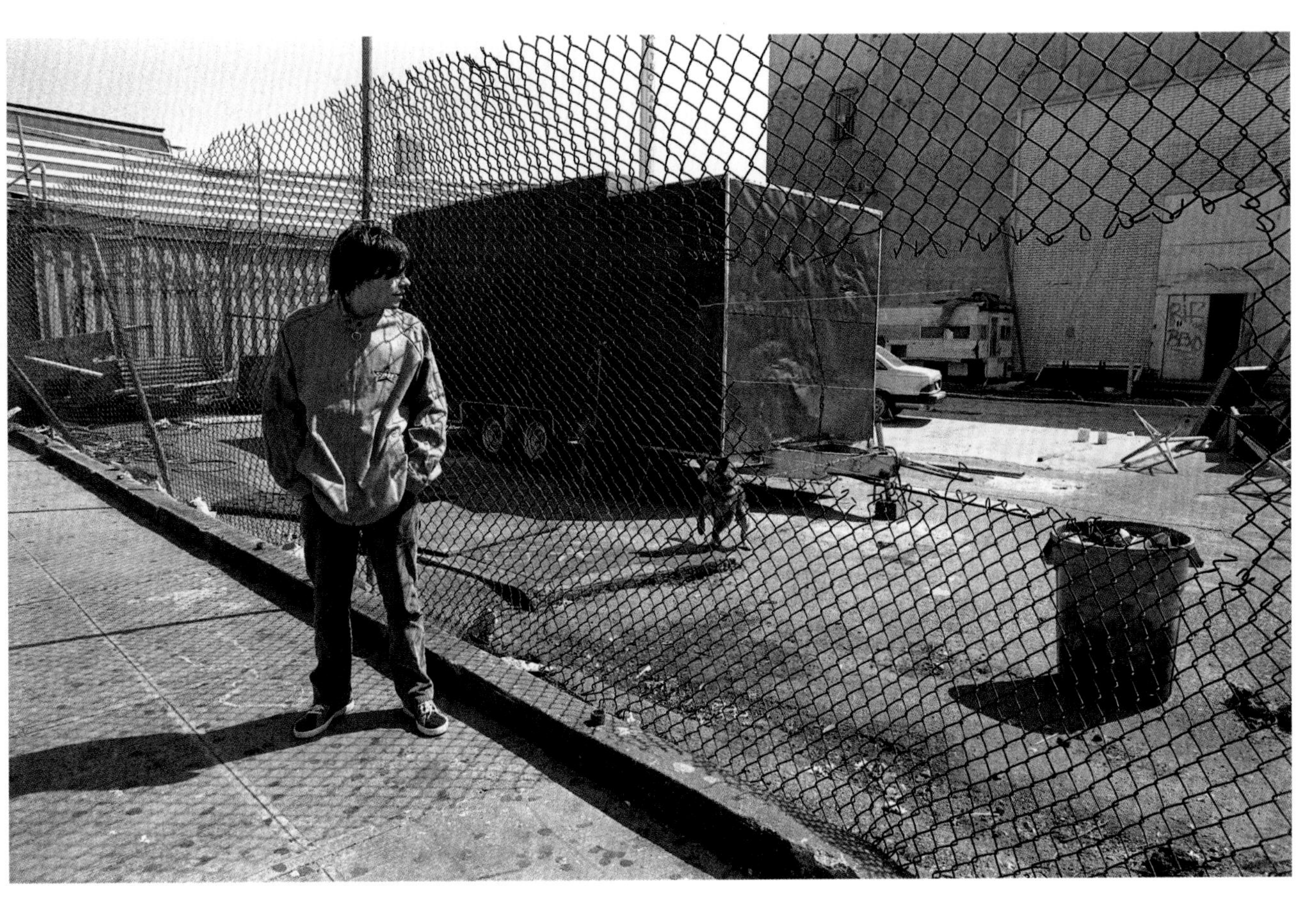

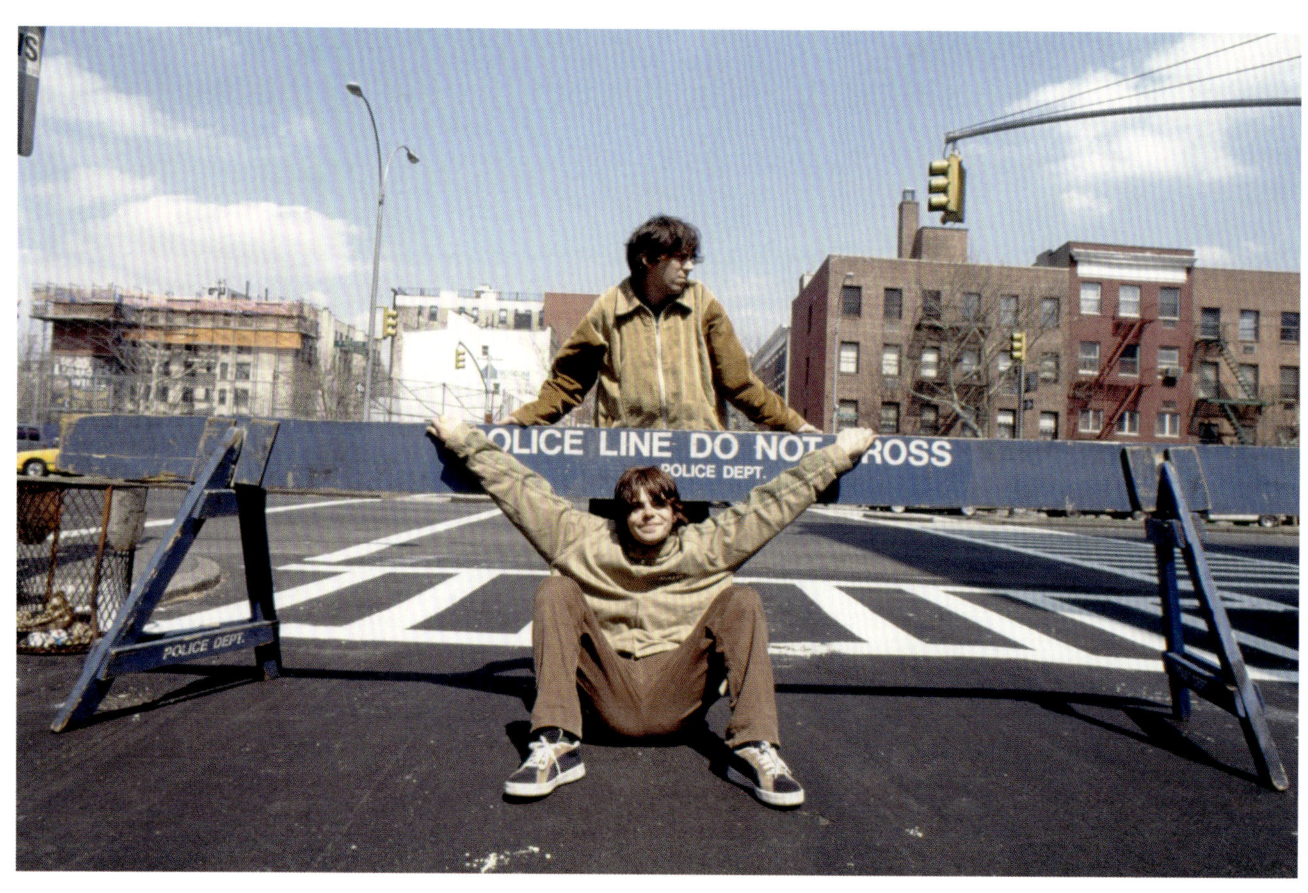
OLICE LINE DO NOT ROSS
POLICE DEPT.
POLICE DEPT.

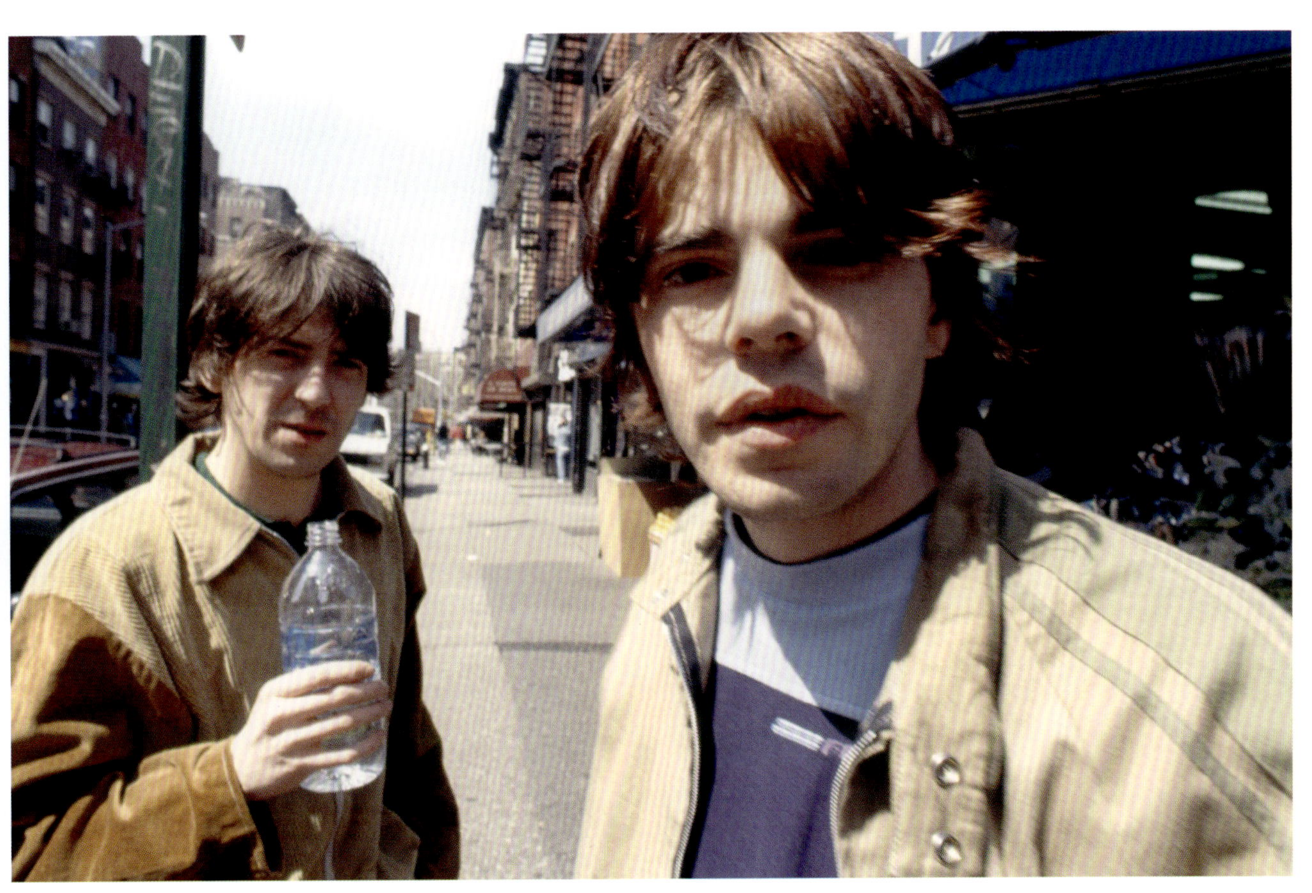

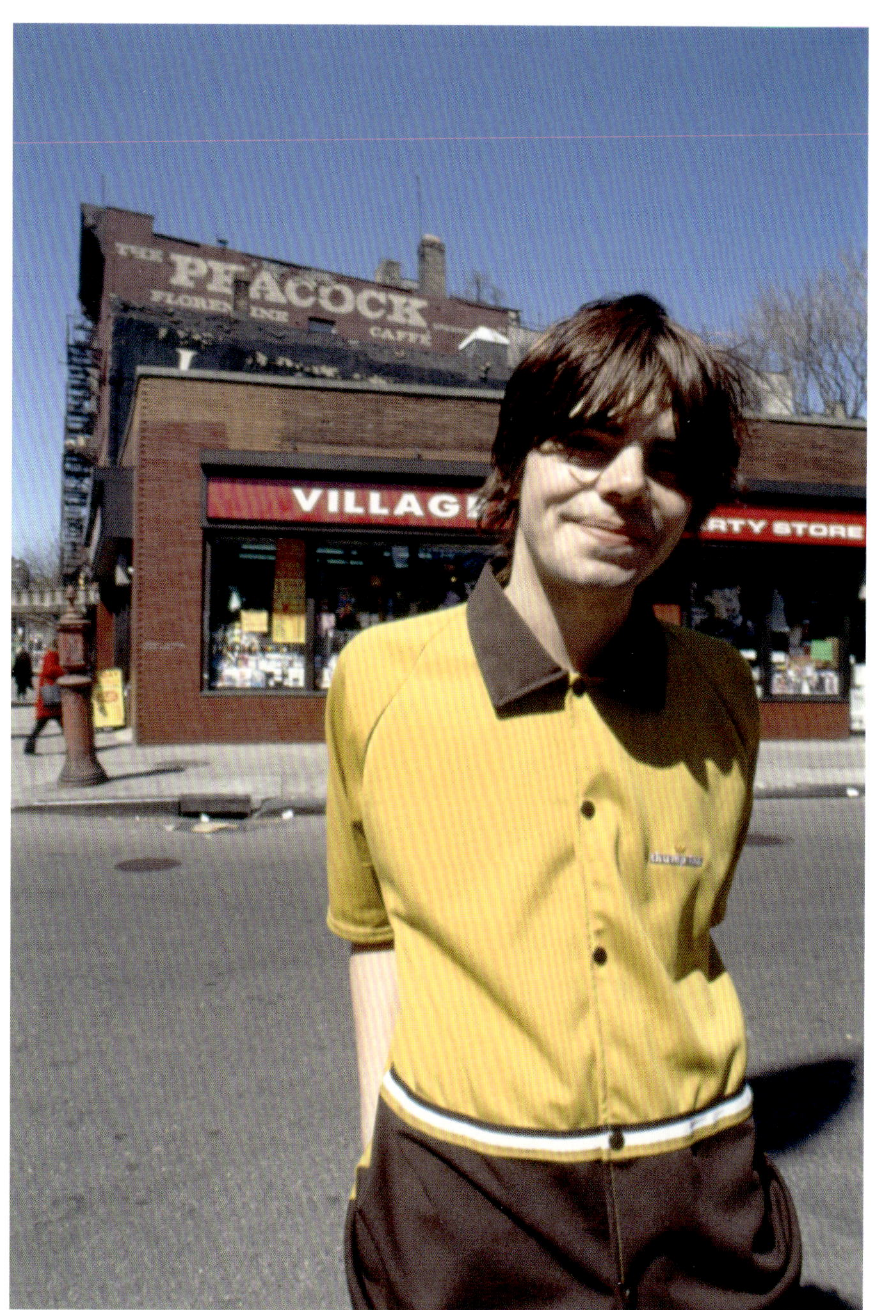
THE PEACOCK
FLORENTINE
CAFFE
VILLAG
RTY STORE

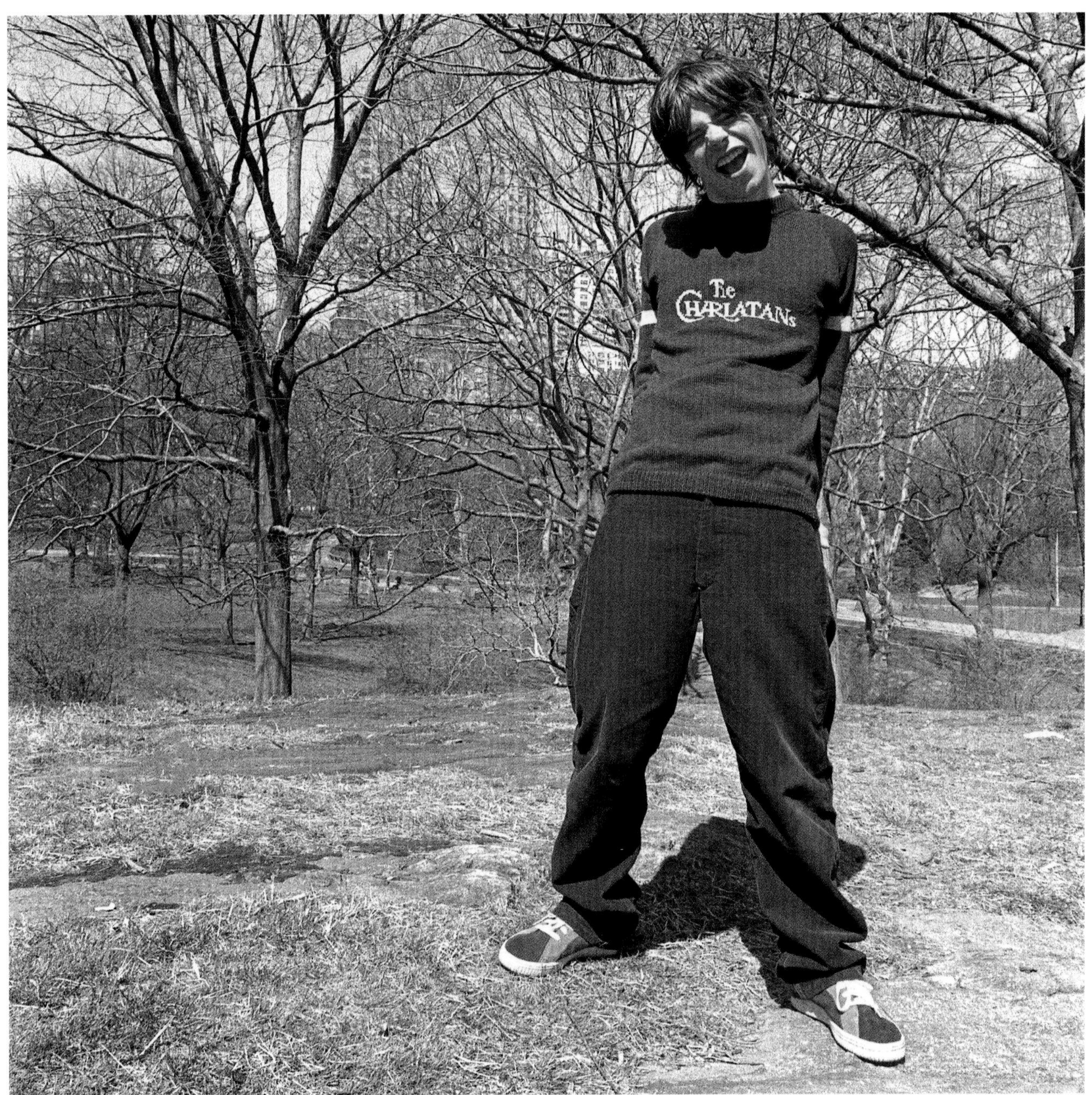

The Charlatans jumper that I am wearing was originally knitted in *drumroll* 1968. Lots of people in America will be aware of The Charlatans, who were from San Francisco and around in the 1960s – they led to us being known as The Charlatans UK across the Atlantic. We were totally unaware of them, but once they were in touch we did our level best to smooth things over and we all became friends of a sort. Who were The Charlatans and who were the charlatan Charlatans?

We were both happy being custodians of the name, them from 1964 to 1969 and us from 1989 to the present day. I have seen reissues of theirs under the name of The Amazing Charlatans, so I'm now guessing we keep the shortened version.

But back to the photo. This was Tom's jumper, knitted when I was one year old. We unearthed it at our studio and included it at our North By Northwich exhibition in 2018, where my then five-year-old son proudly wore it to one of our shows. The fact that Tom was a few years older than us had a kind of "older brother's record collection" feel to it, in that he'd been buying albums since the early 60s and wanted to impart his musical wisdom to us. When Rob was in prison, Tom would send him Grateful Dead bootlegs. I'd remarked how kind and considerate this was, but Tom pointed out that he'd tried to get Rob to listen previously, to no avail. But this time Rob had no excuse, there was literally no escape. Rob wrote to Tom thanking him for his kindness – and though it could have happened under better circumstances, Rob had finally become a Grateful Dead fan.

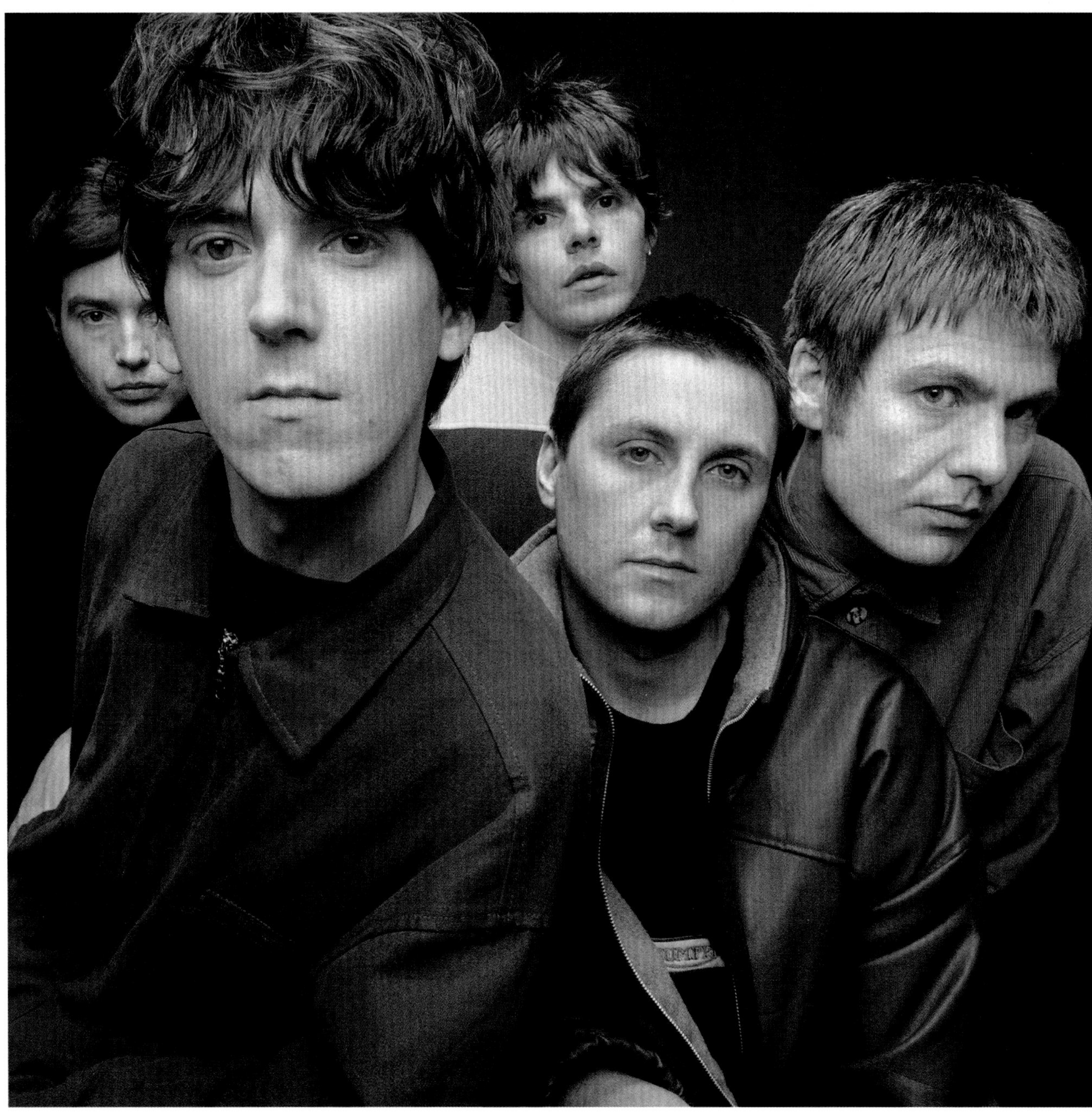

This entire shoot took a few hours in Holborn Studios. Tom was ready with what he wanted for the album. Me not being at the front was a stipulation. So many of the shots could have been the final version, and these days it'd be a composite of the best one of each of us. We were looking at Polaroids as we went and by the time we left we knew we had it.

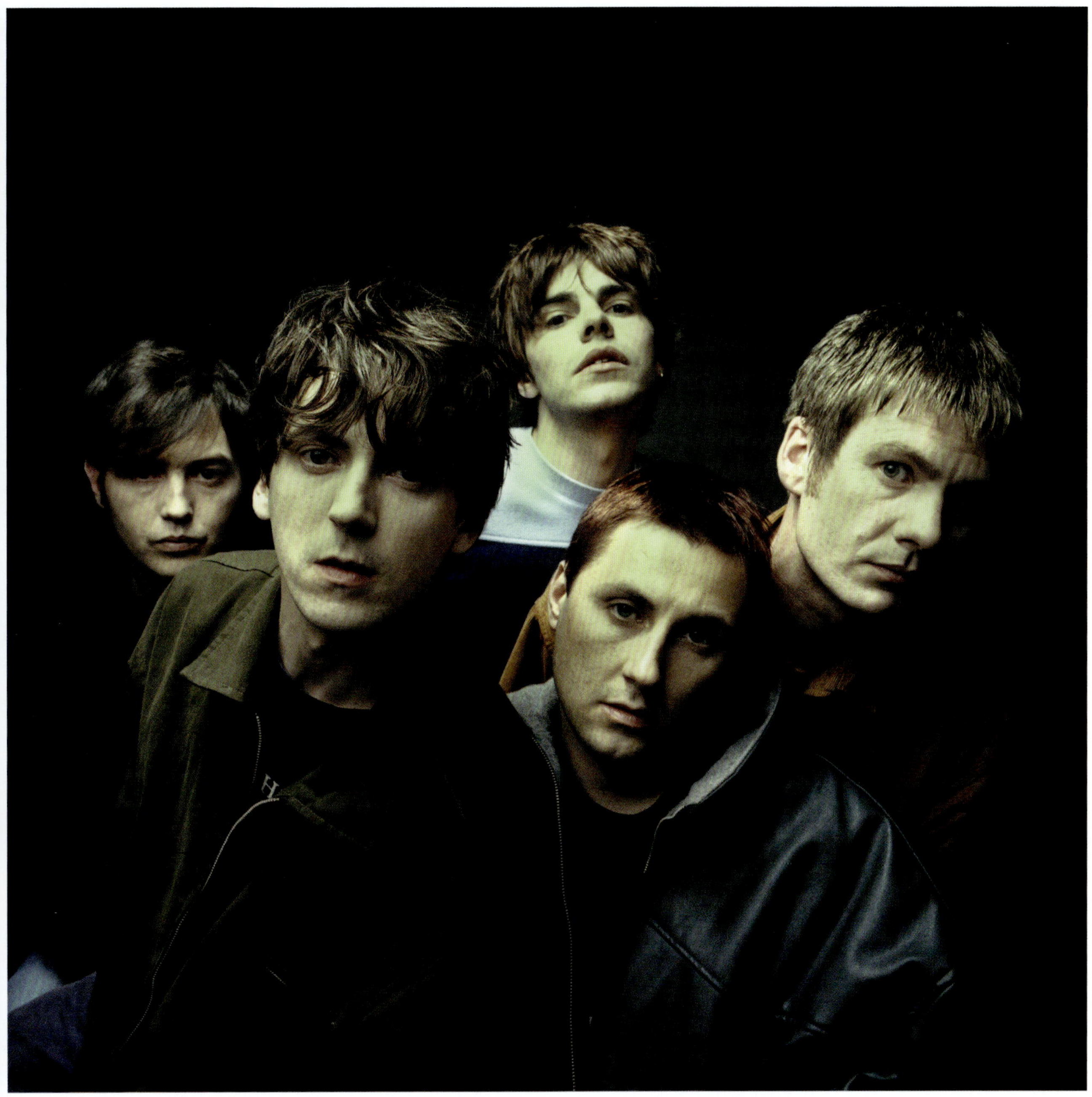

This is the frame just before or just after the one that was used on the sleeve of our eponymous album.

We always had discussions about album covers and the fact that we had never used a recognizable picture with all our faces on the cover of the record. We used *Out Of Our Heads* by The Rolling Stones as a template – not the video for "Bohemian Rhapsody", as some people have suggested. I was always shoved to the front of the group shots, so I was happy to stand at the back for this one. We gathered at a rented studio in Holborn and the whole thing was done in a couple of hours.

Our plan was always to have the track listing on the front like some of our favourite 60s' records, *A Christmas Gift For You*, *The Beach Boys Today*!, Bob Dylan's *The Freewheelin'*, *Parsley, Sage, Rosemary and Thyme* by Simon & Garfunkel and all the *Top of the Pops* compilation albums.

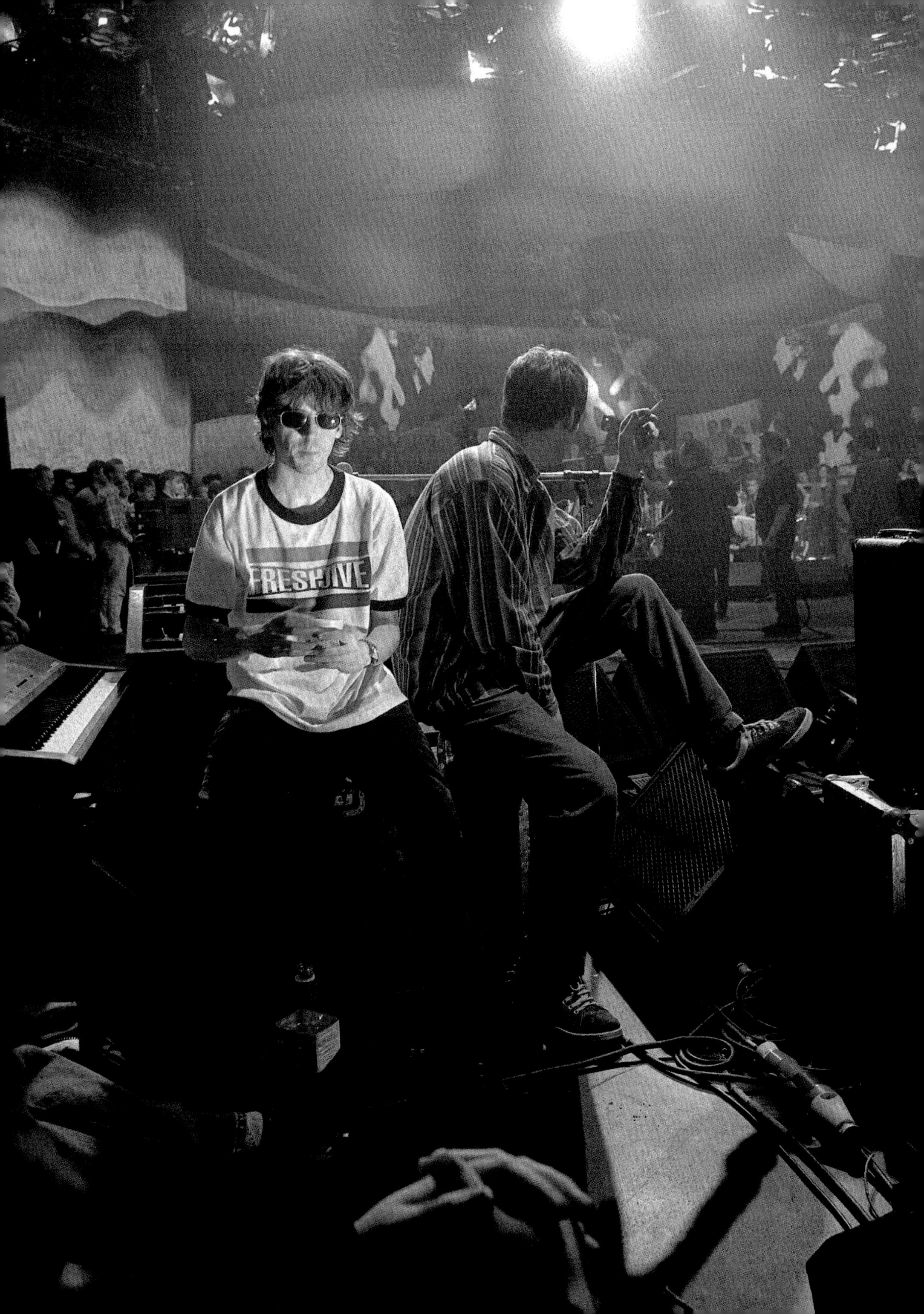
FRESHJIVE

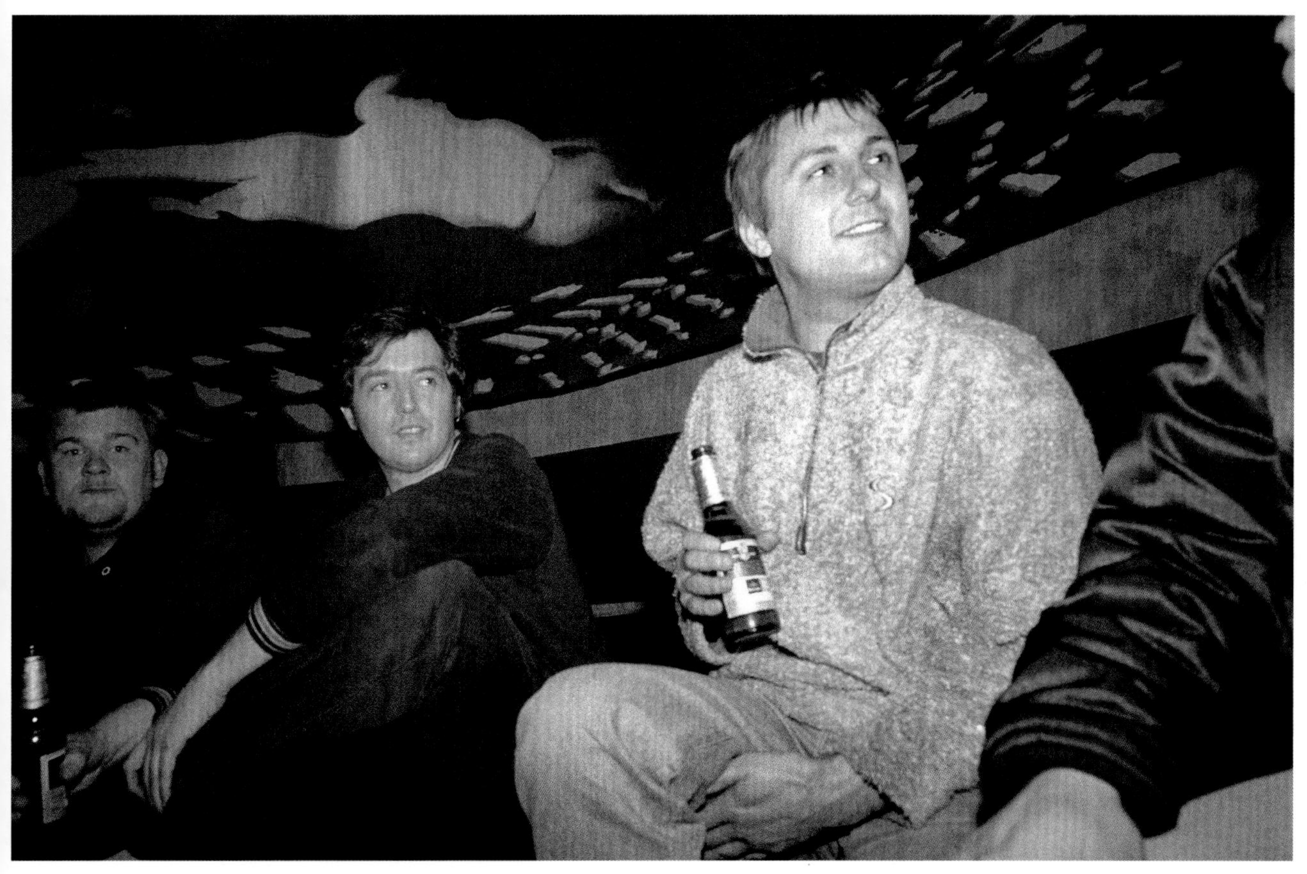

A trip to film an episode of *Later... with Jools Holland* always meant a lottery of who you would be appearing alongside. For this episode we played "Just Lookin'" and "Just When You're Thinkin' Things Over", and we had a photograph taken with our fellow guests, Van Morrison and Tori Amos. Van was his legendary grumpy self, but we wouldn't have wanted it any other way. Me and Tori got on well.

Gigs are often done in isolation, just our band in whichever venue, often too caught up in our own thing to appreciate the support act. But Jools Holland is a full evening spent with fellow musicians, playing just a couple of songs each, so you get a real party spirit and a chance to spend time with like-minded people. It was great to have Tom on hand to document the goings-on.

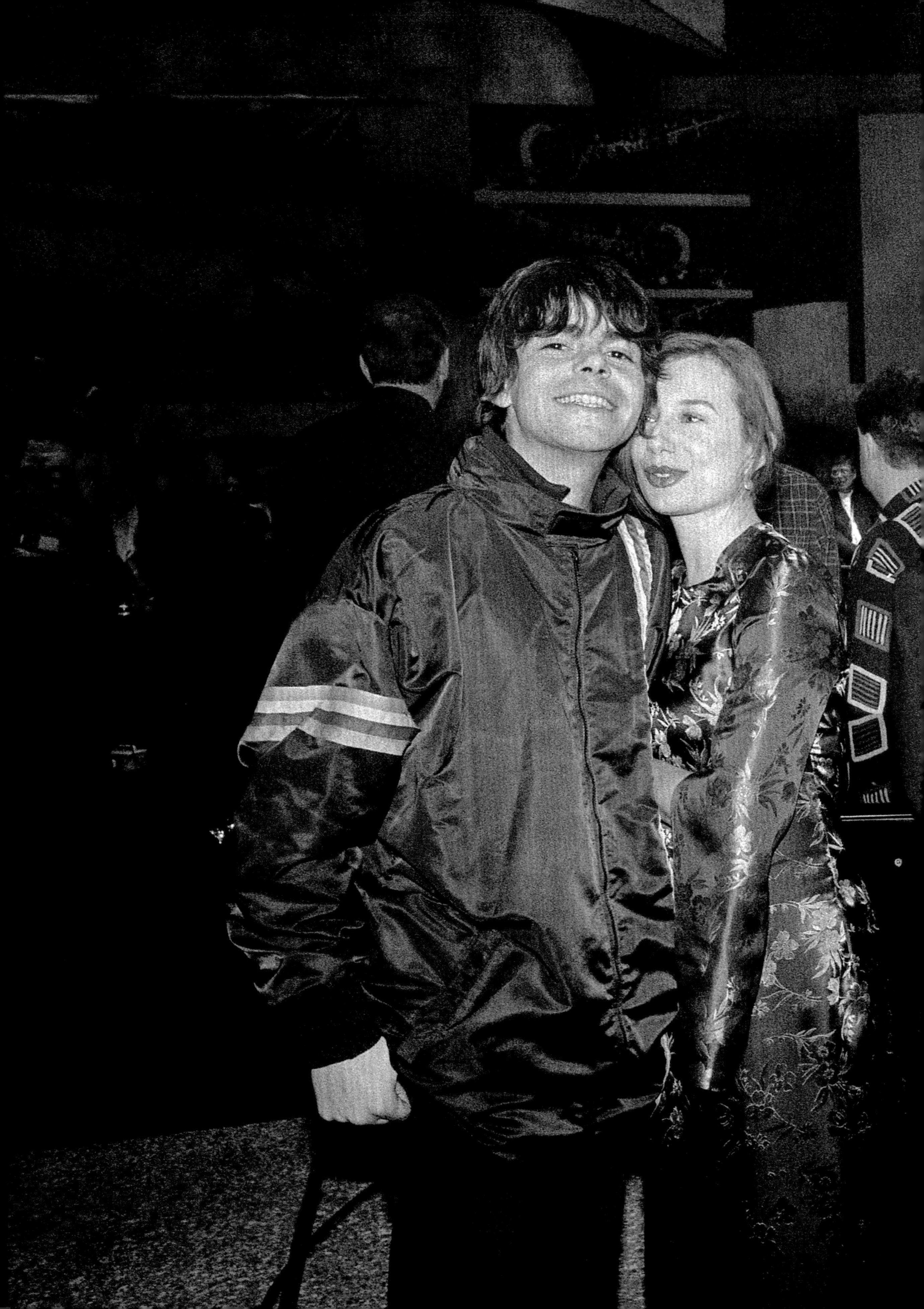

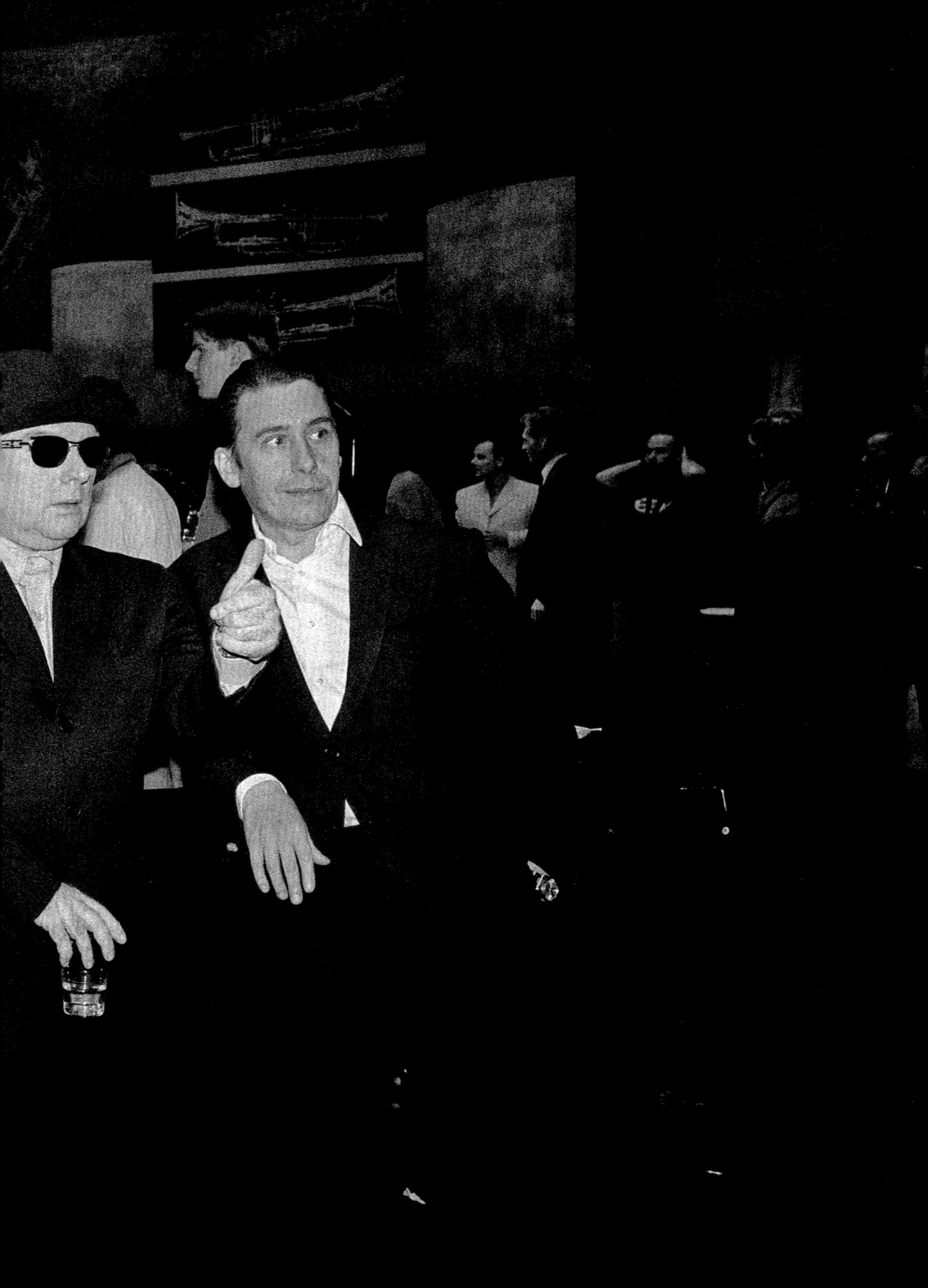

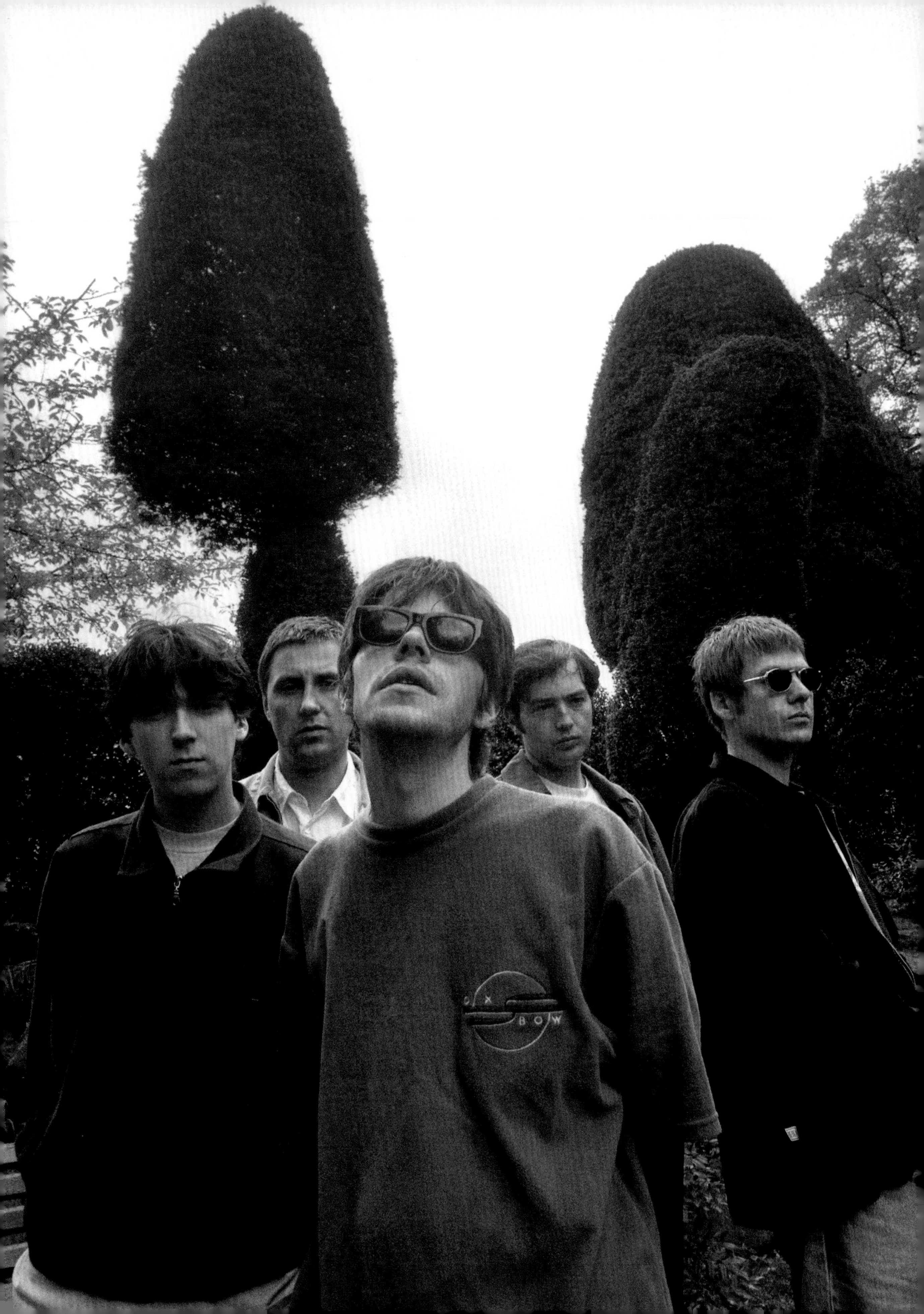
OX
BOW

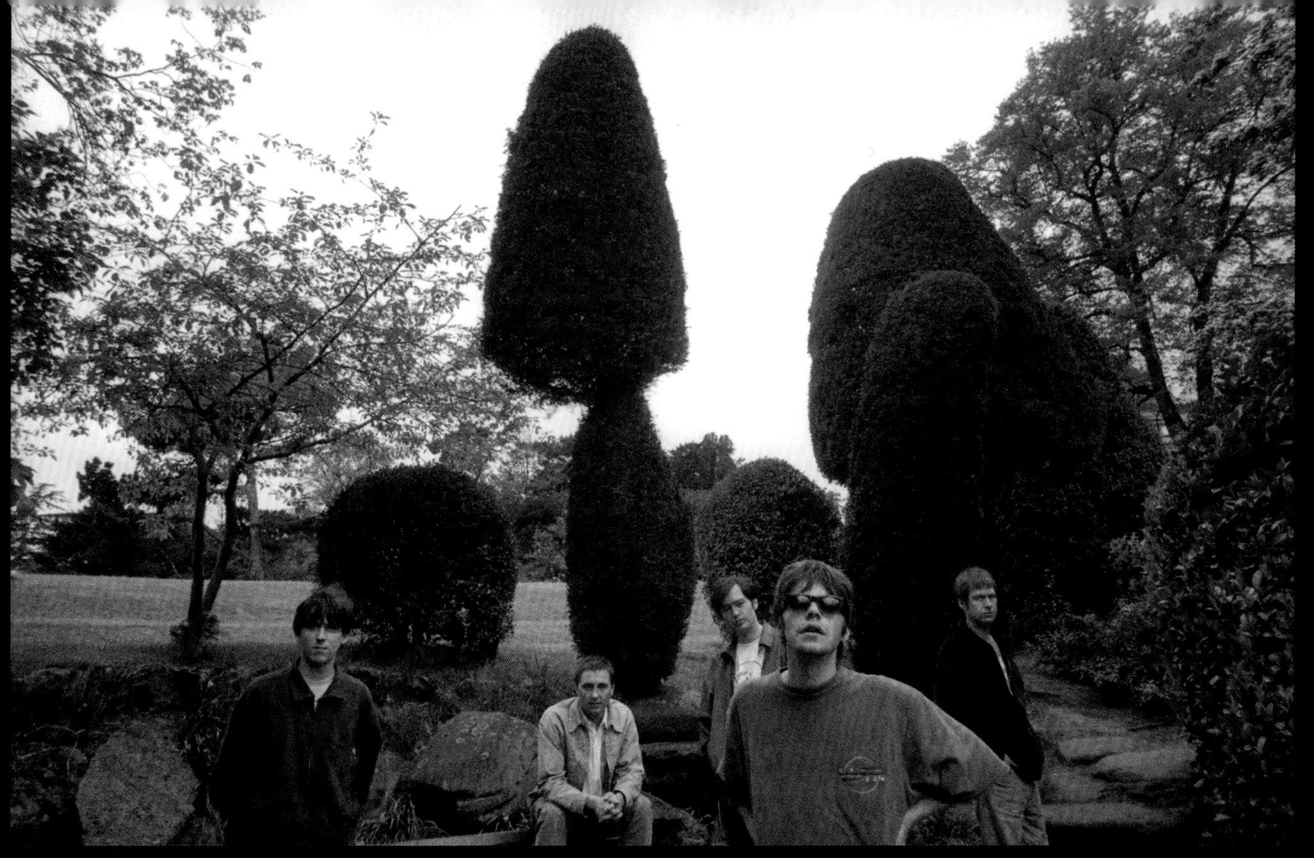

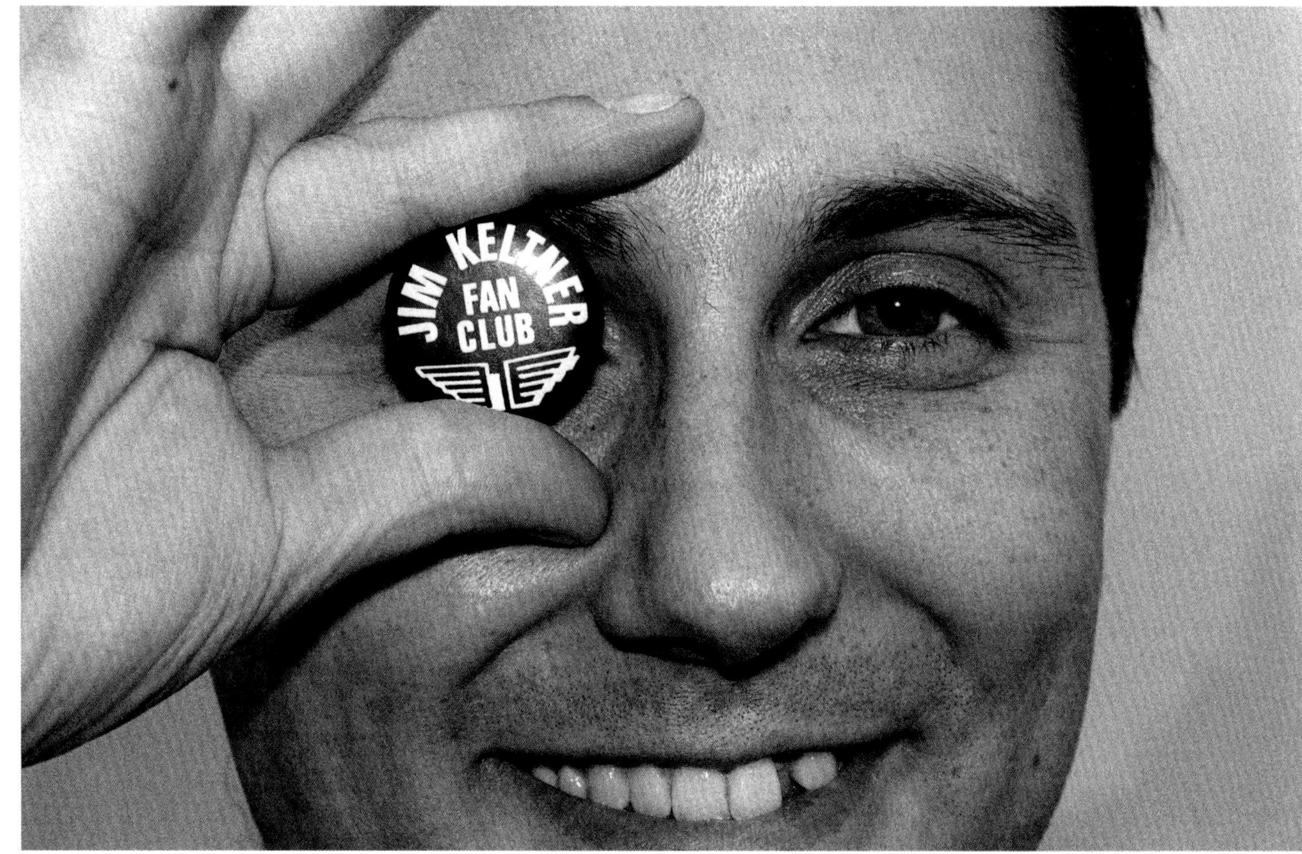

Tom gave Jon this badge. Both of them were big fans of Jim Keltner, one of the most brilliant drummers in recorded-music history. He played drums for Sérgio Mendes, Bob Dylan, Joni Mitchell, Carly Simon, Leonard Cohen, Dolly Parton, Nilsson, Lalo Schifrin, John Lennon, Barbra Streisand and even Ringo Starr & his All-Starr Band.*

This photograph was taken in 1995, and five years later we were in a studio in Los Angeles with Jim as he recorded "Love to You". Danny Saber was producing *Wonderland* and knew Jim through a friend of a friend. He asked Jon if he minded if Jim called round and we all got on really well. This culminated in Jim and Jon playing together on "A Man Needs to Be Told".

*I used Google to confirm this list and also to see if The Charlatans were deemed worthy of being mentioned, and we were.

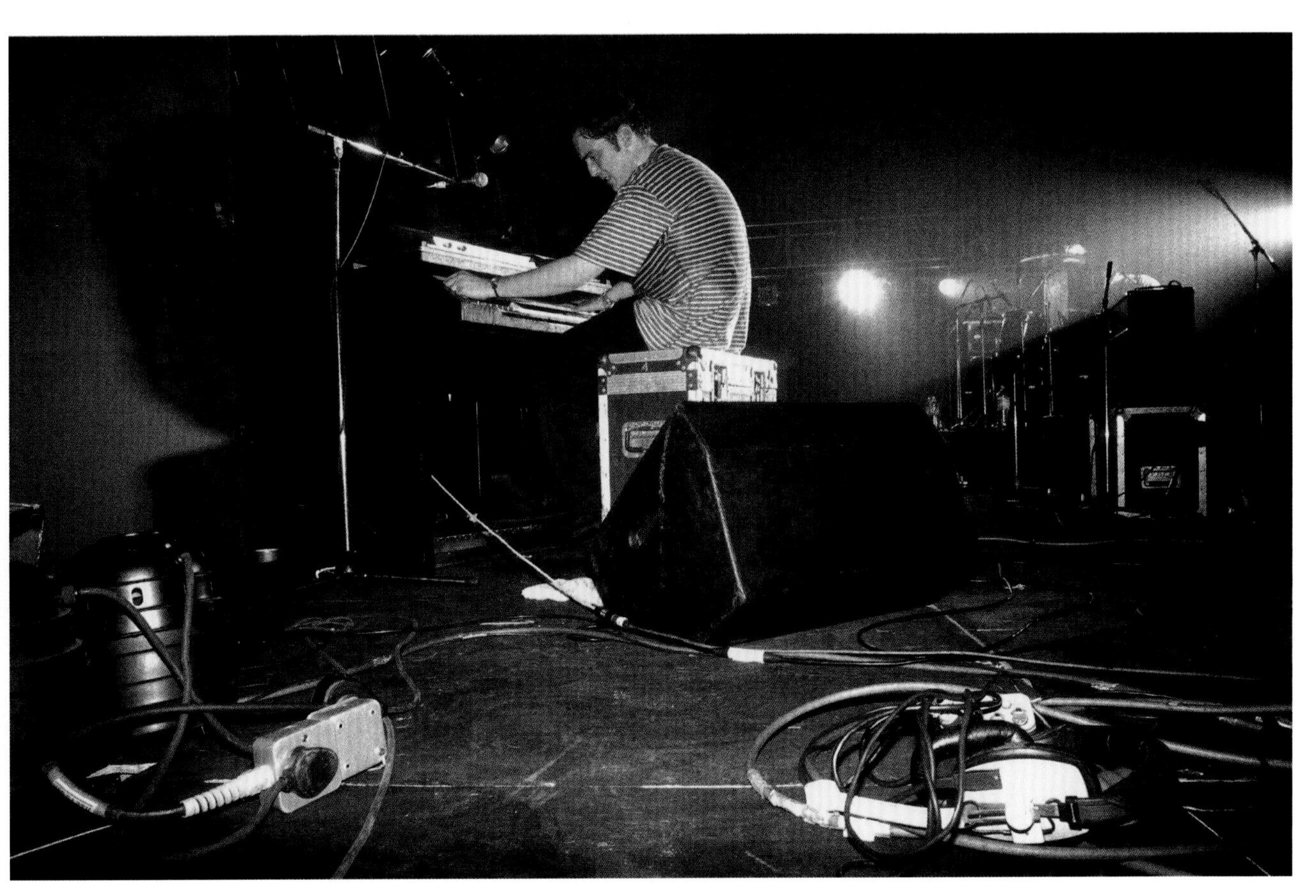

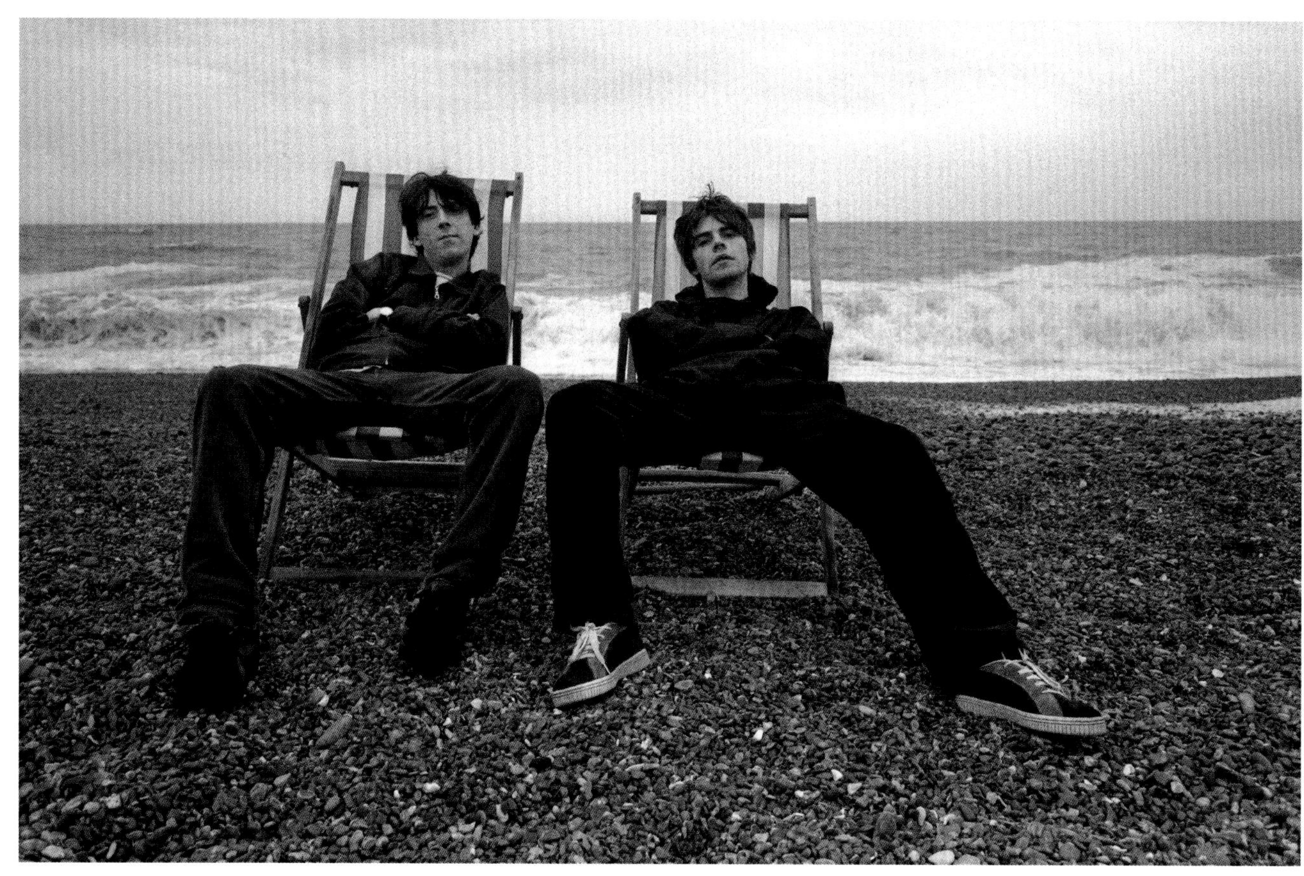

Ubiquitous deckchairs and skimming-stones shots. I don't remember what these photos were used for, or even if they ever saw the light of day. We may all live in front of a camera these days, but not everybody did in the 1990s. We certainly did, though, and these candid shots send me right back to those days.

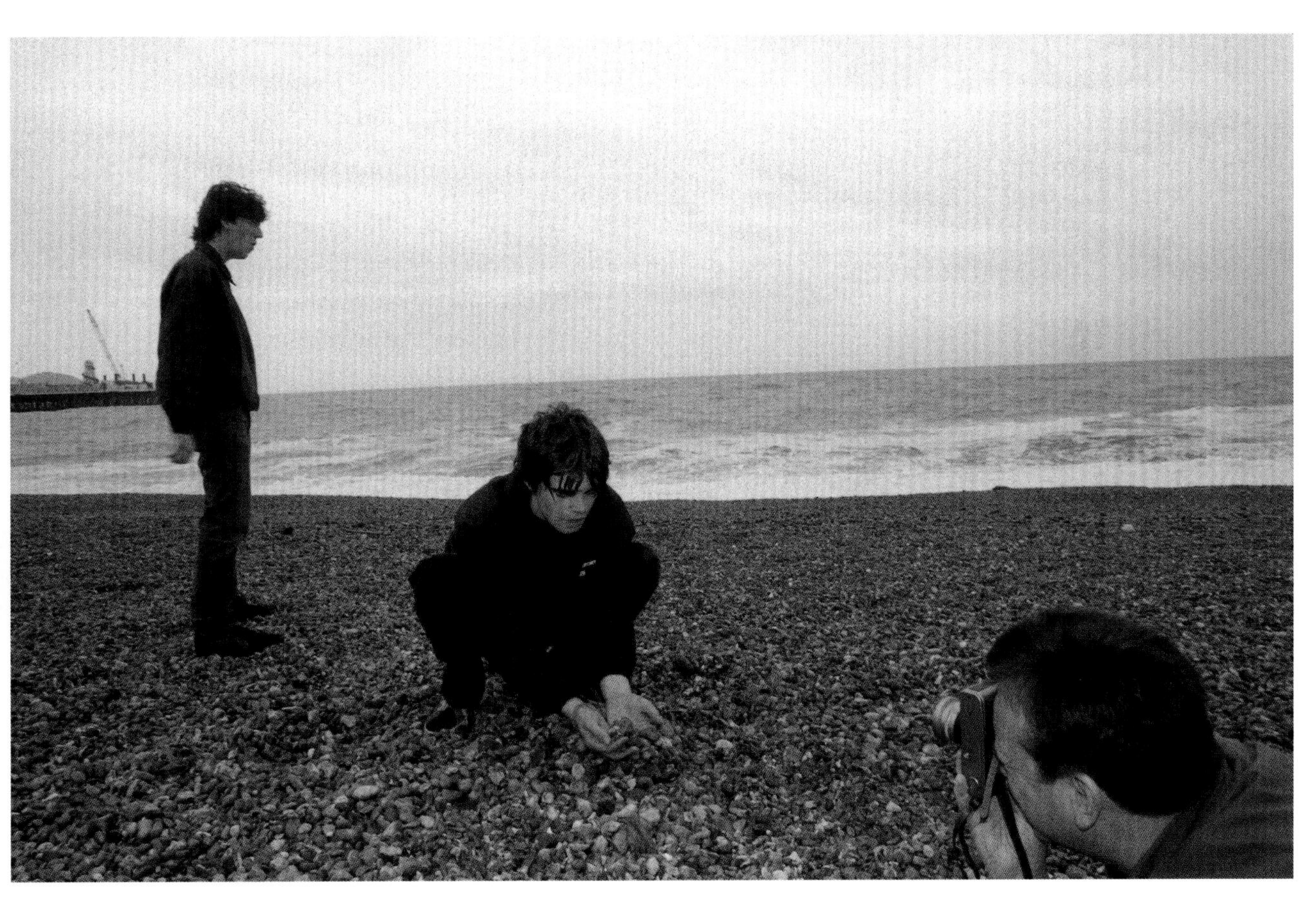

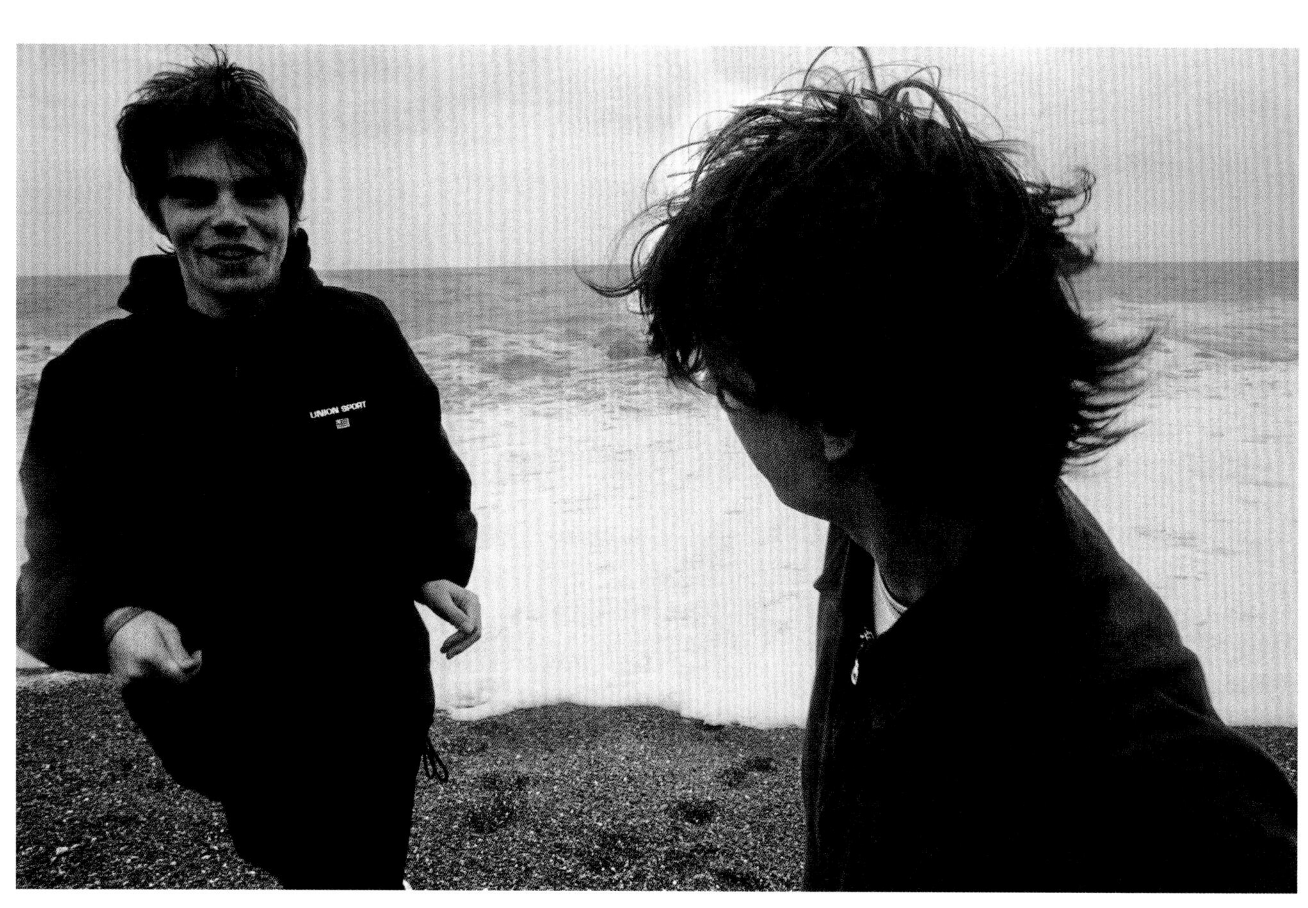
UNION SPORT

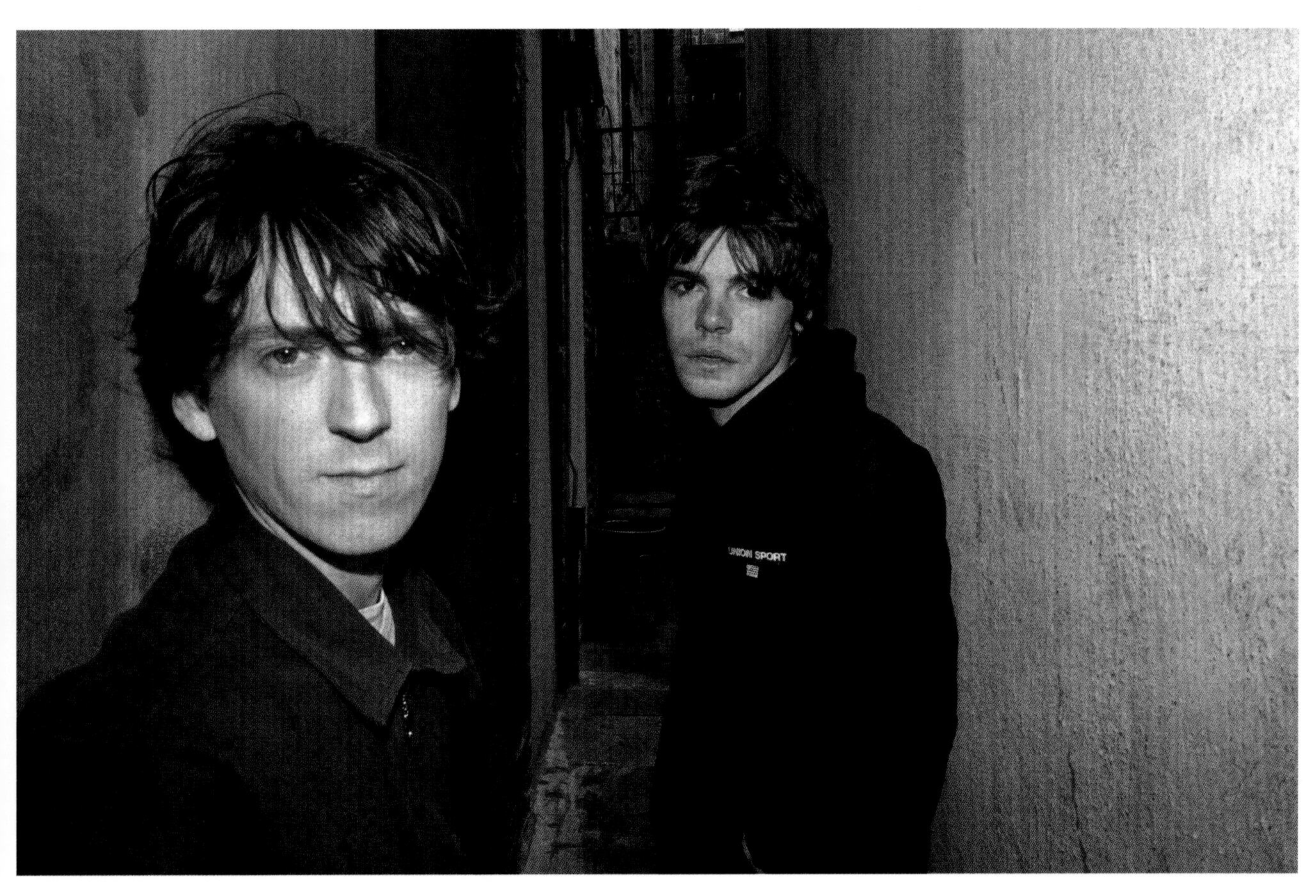

When in Brighton it is necessary to take the obligatory photograph in the alleyway made famous in *Quadrophenia*.

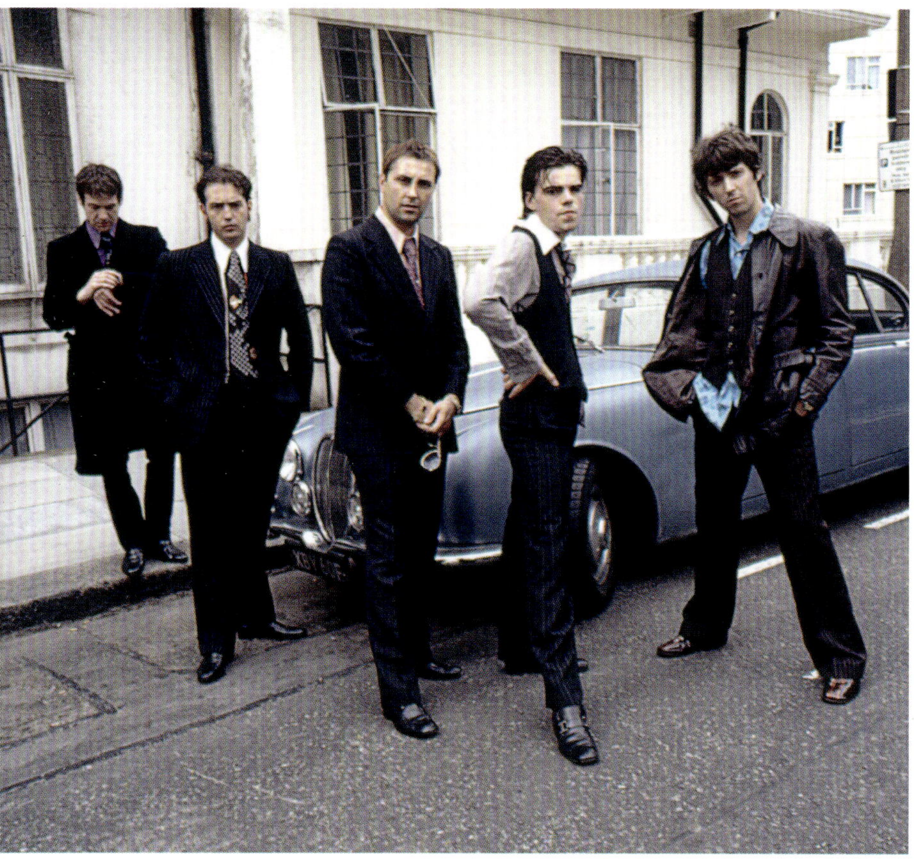

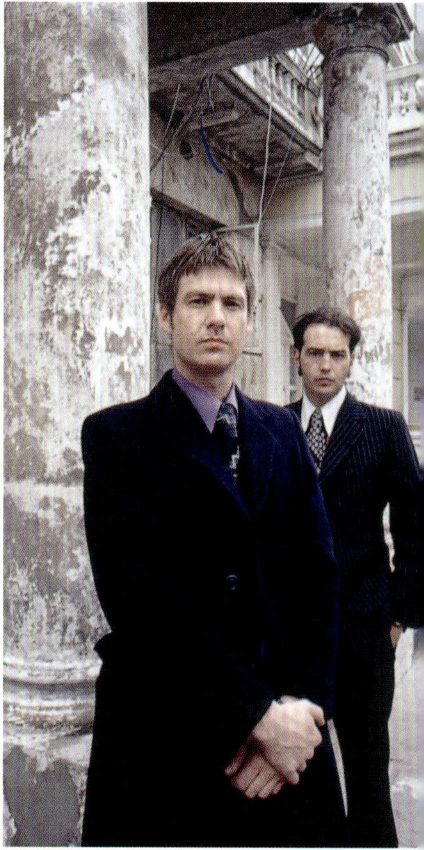

Before being in a band the idea of filming a video was like a holy grail. The suggestion of a record label funding a camera crew, storyboarding, finding a location, etc., was a big sign that they felt the band was worth investing In. (Spoiler alert, it's always recouped later from the band, but that's another story.)

By the time of "Just When You're Thinkin' Things Over", the novelty had worn off a little, but I'd still get excited heading to the set. This one was filmed in an old hotel in Lancaster Gate, London. One of my favourite people, Lindy Heymann, was directing. We'd been measured up for suits and they were waiting for us when we got there. The video was inspired by *Performance*, Nic Roeg's 1970 British crime drama, with an added hint of Scorsese's *Mean Streets*. Mark got thoroughly into his character, based on Al Pacino in *Dog Day Afternoon*.

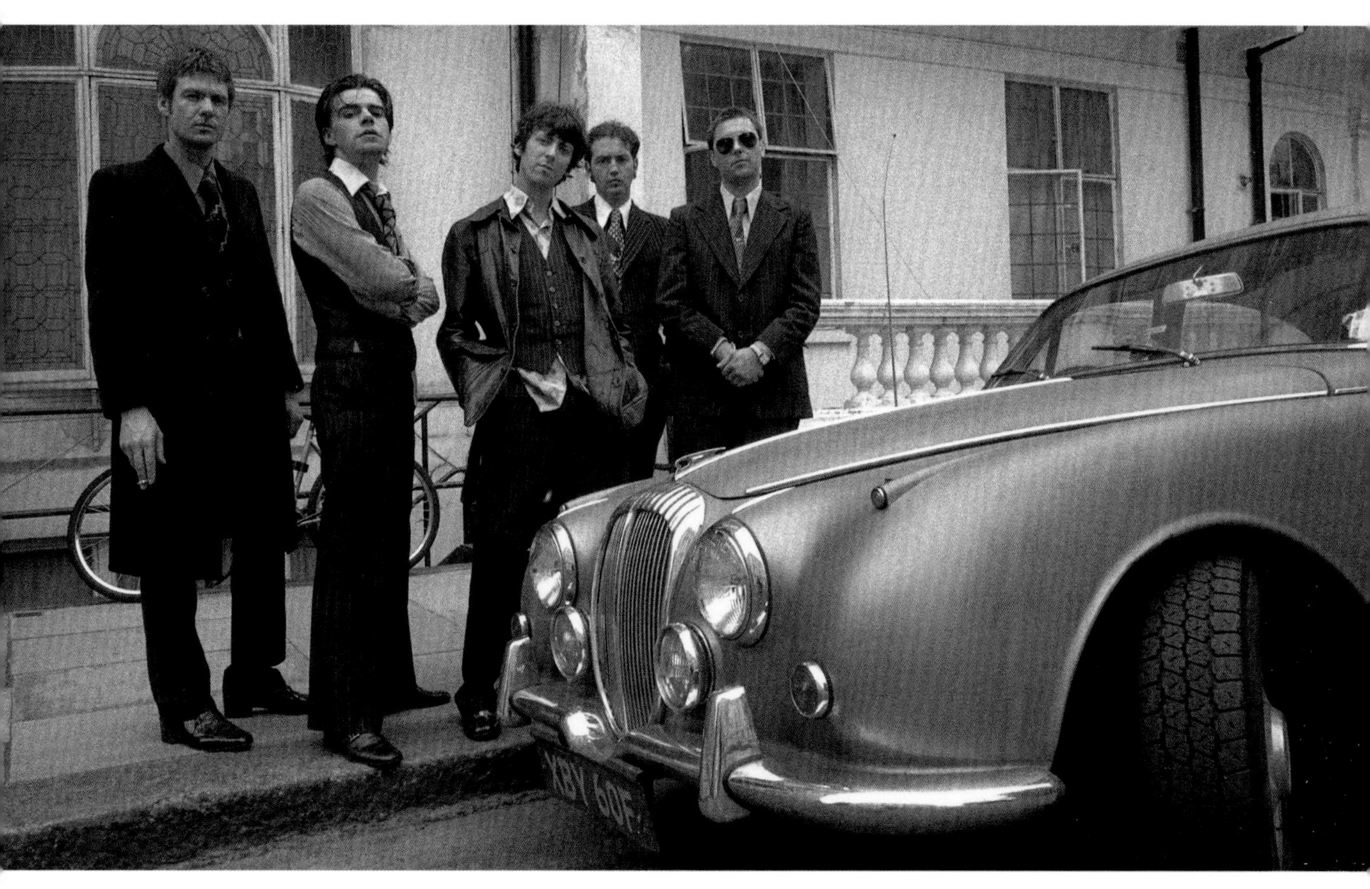
XBY 60E

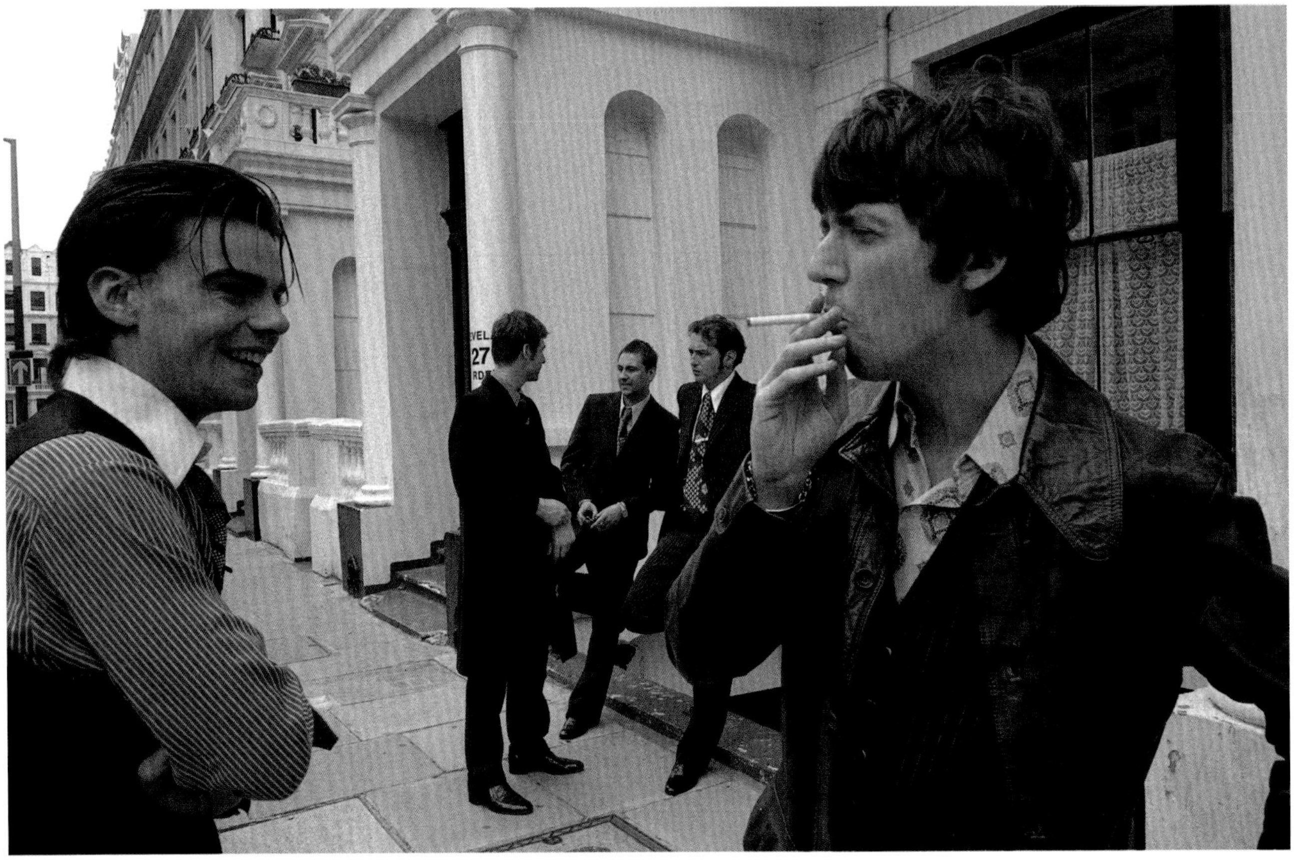

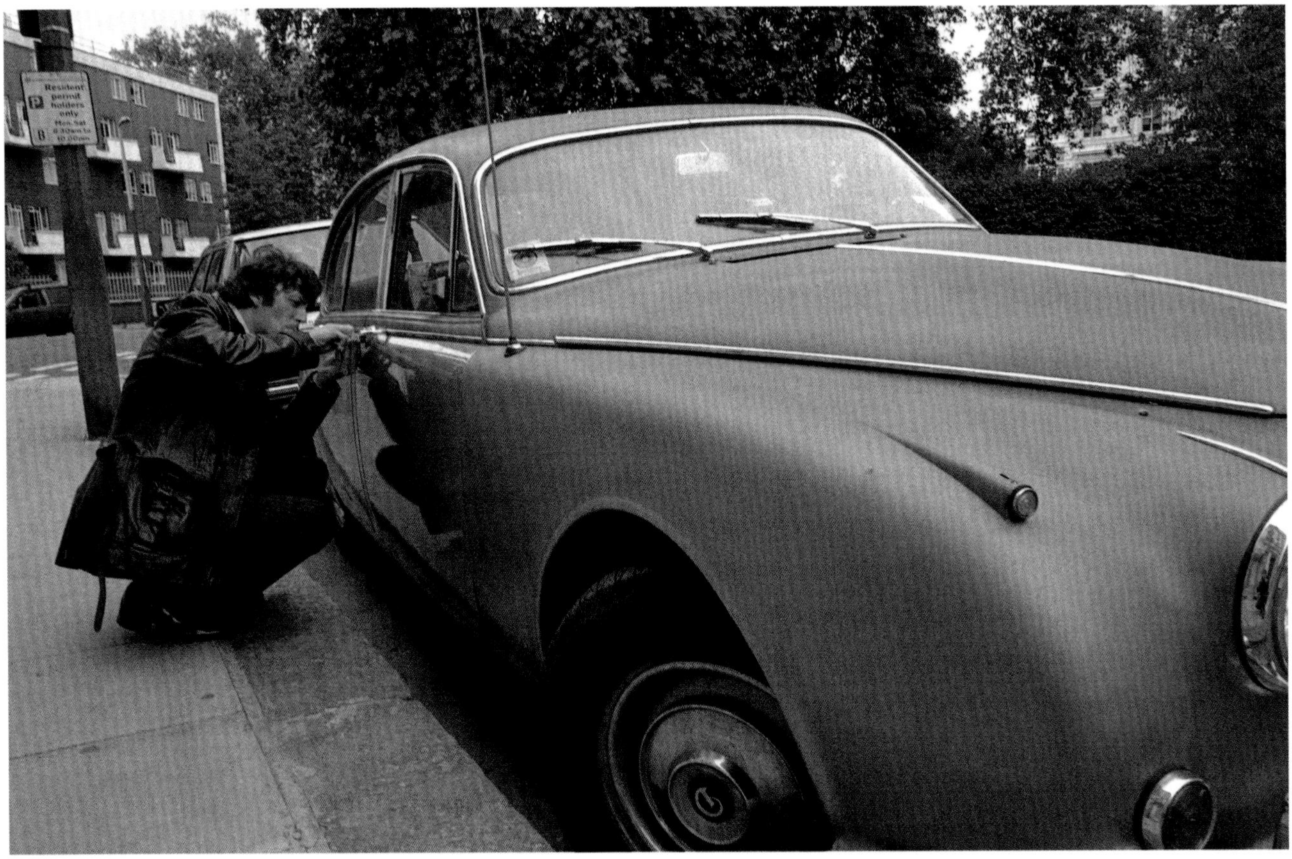
Resident permit holders only

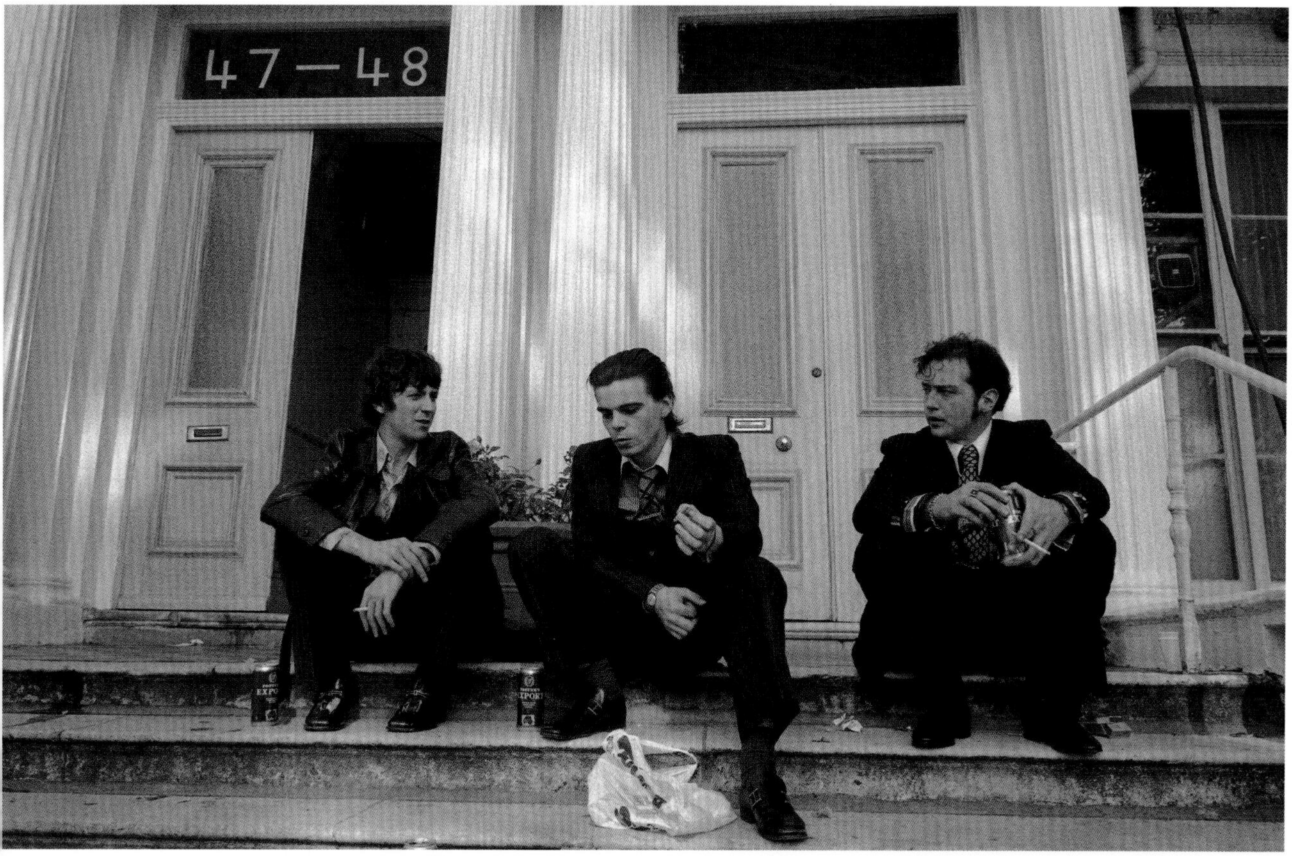

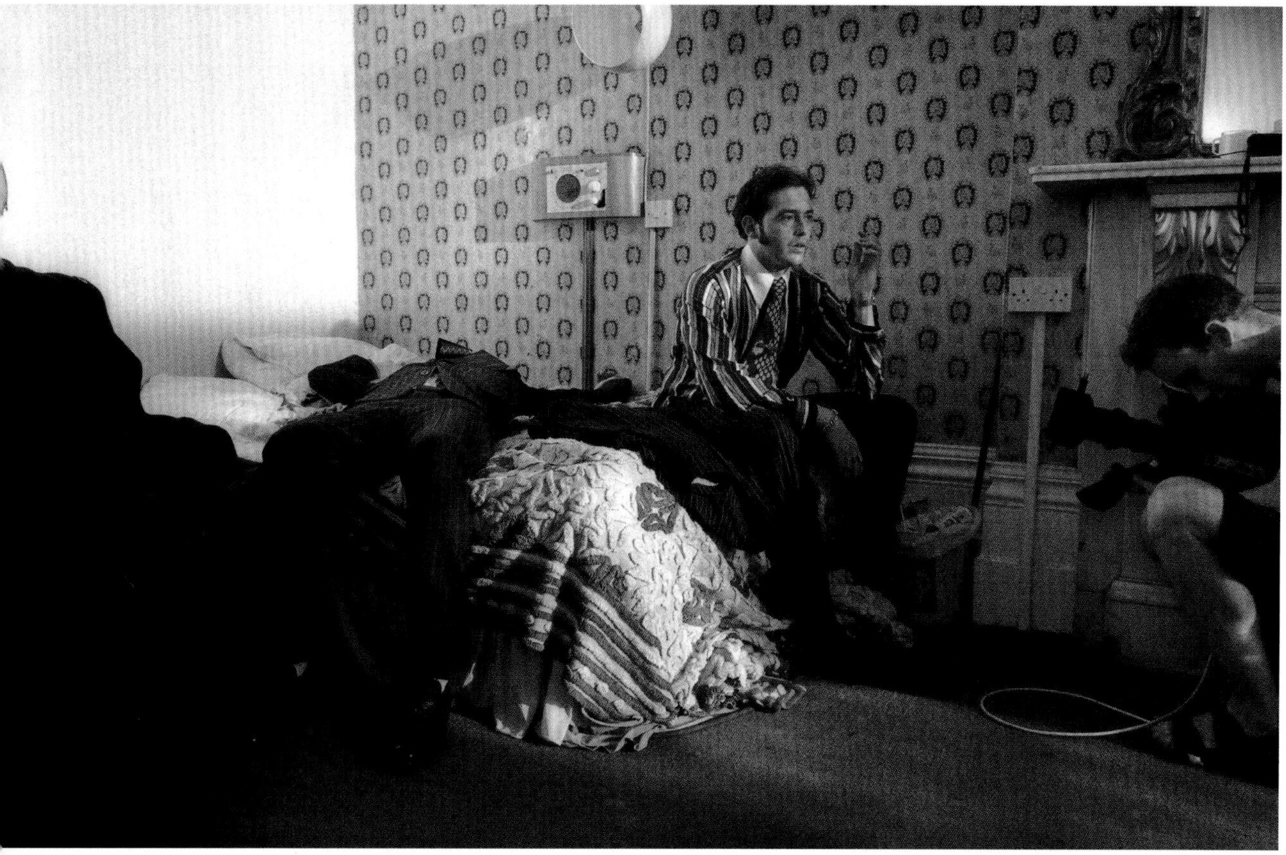

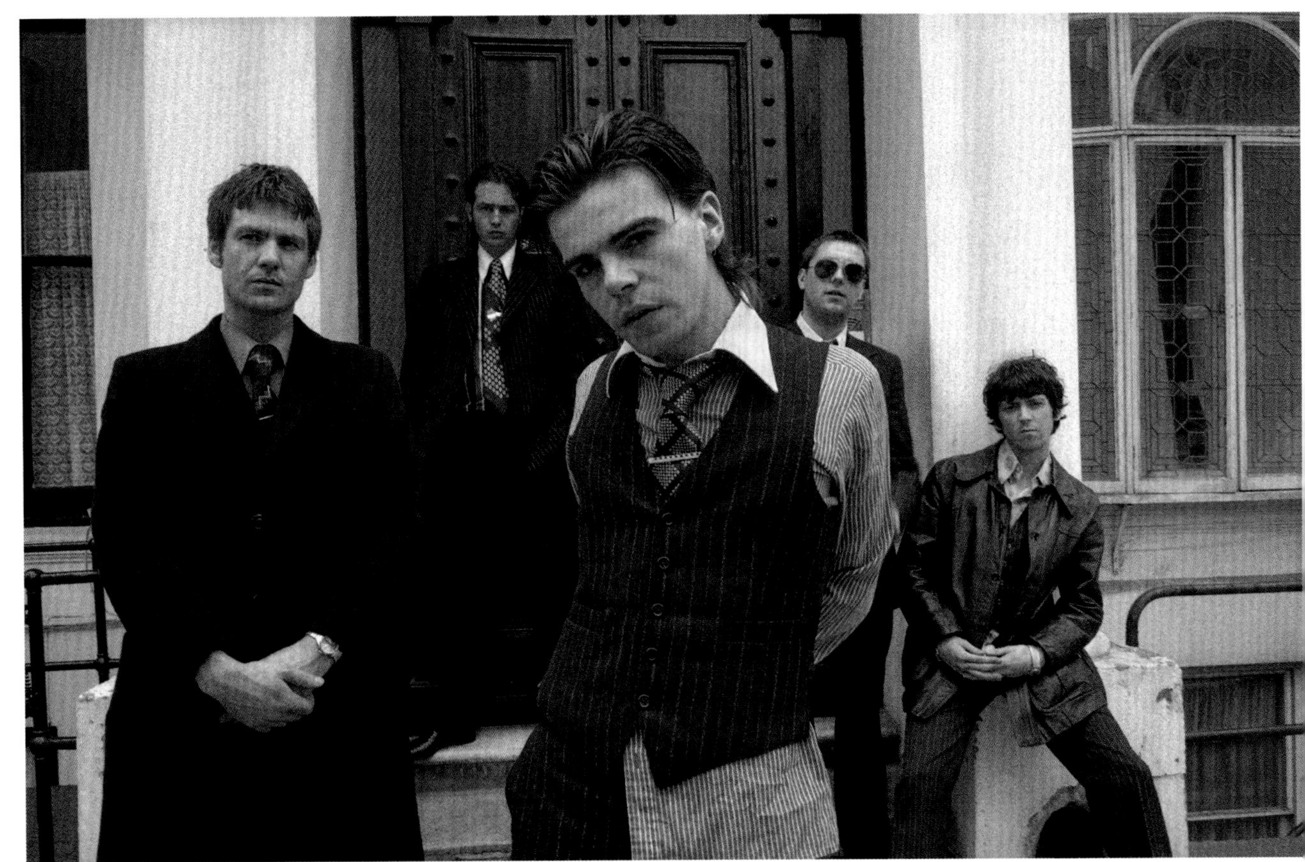

Opposite page: This image was used as the front cover of "You're So Pretty – We're So Pretty".

I guess this was our brush with method acting, but it made for an enjoyable time. The day flew by, which is not always the case when making videos. Whether with photoshoots, performances or videos, we generally just did things in the clothes we were standing up in. This all changed when we started working with Lindy.

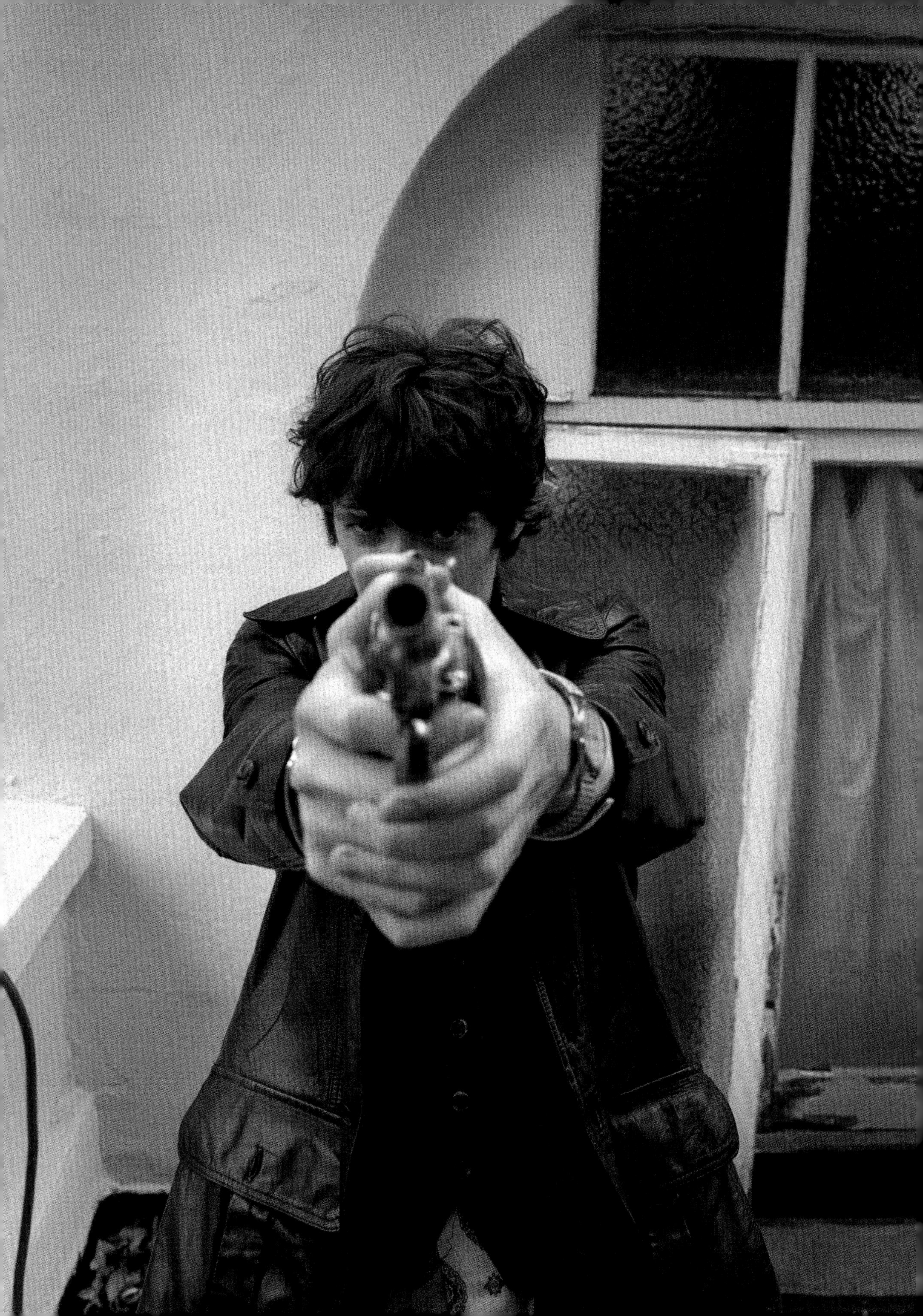

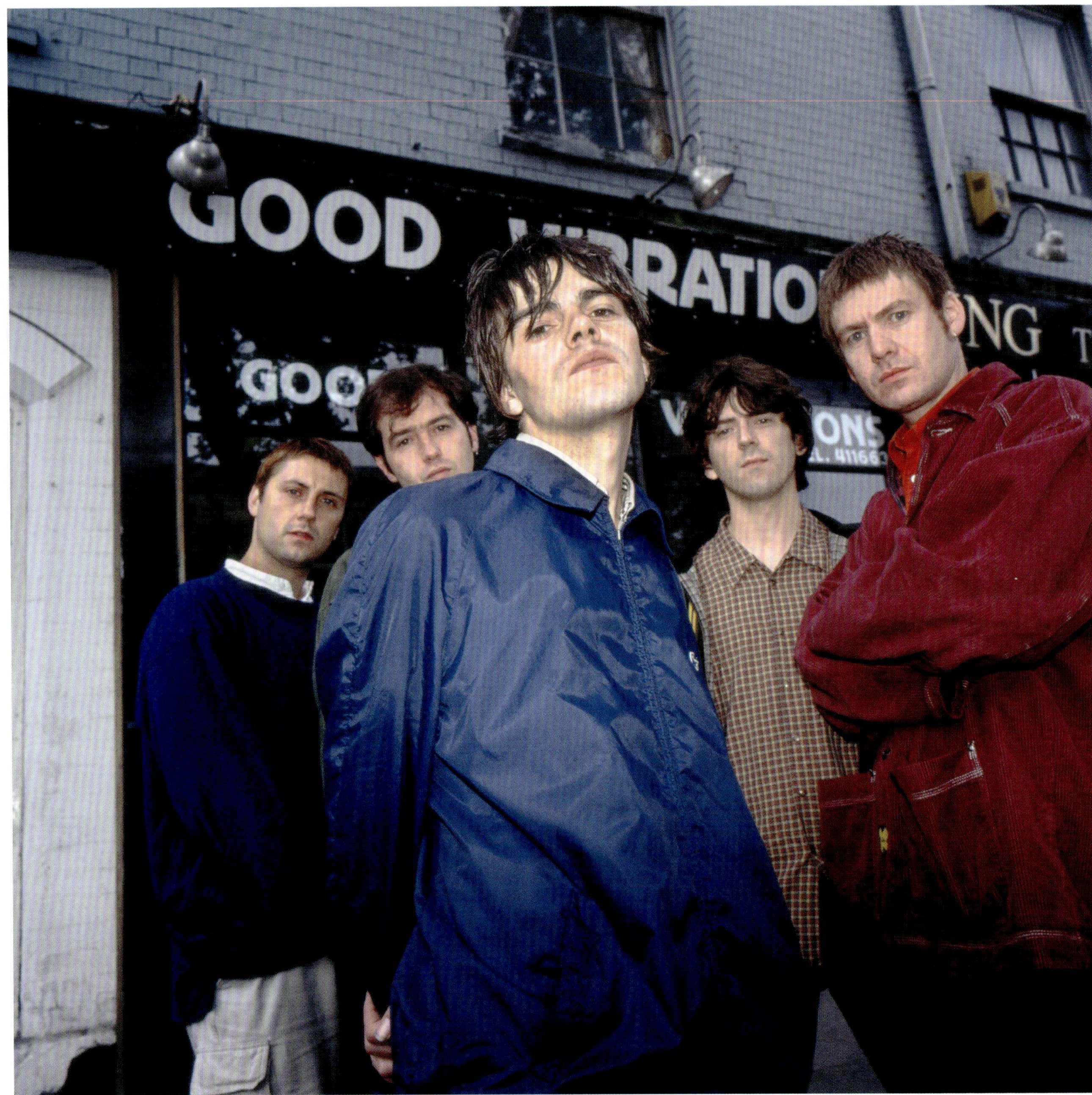

This was taken outside Good Vibrations in Nottingham, where we were recording in a studio round the corner. War Child had got in touch and asked if we could contribute to an album they were putting together. I suggested "Time For Livin'" by Sly and the Family Stone and that we do it with The Chemical Brothers. When we were in a location Tom would always know where the record shops were, and crate-digging with him became an enjoyable offshoot when we weren't doing photos. If my memory serves correctly, the Lacoste jacket was a gift from Wags (Paris Angels/Black Grape), who joined us on that day as well as for performances on *Top of the Pops* and a few gigs.

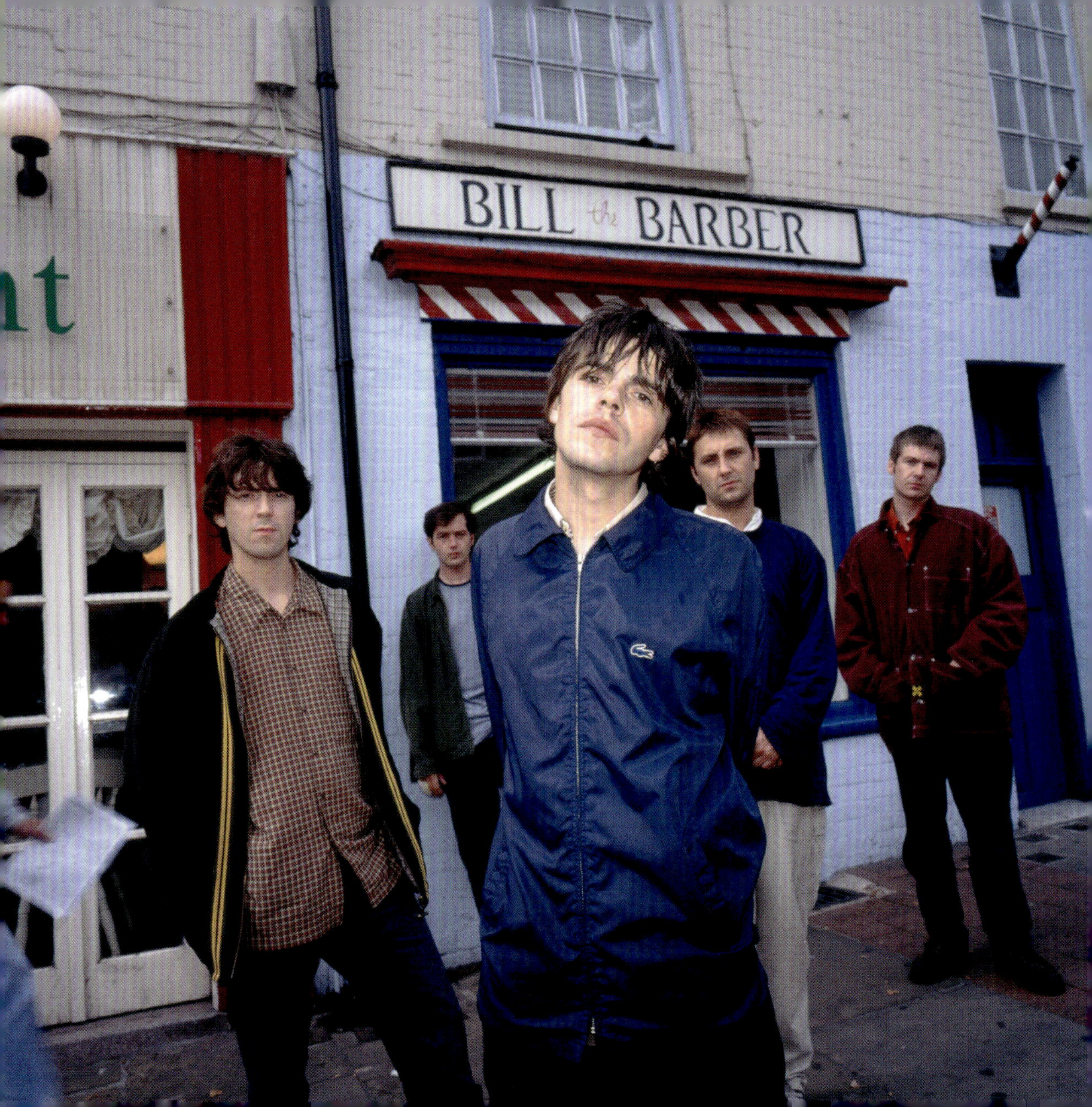
BILL the BARBER

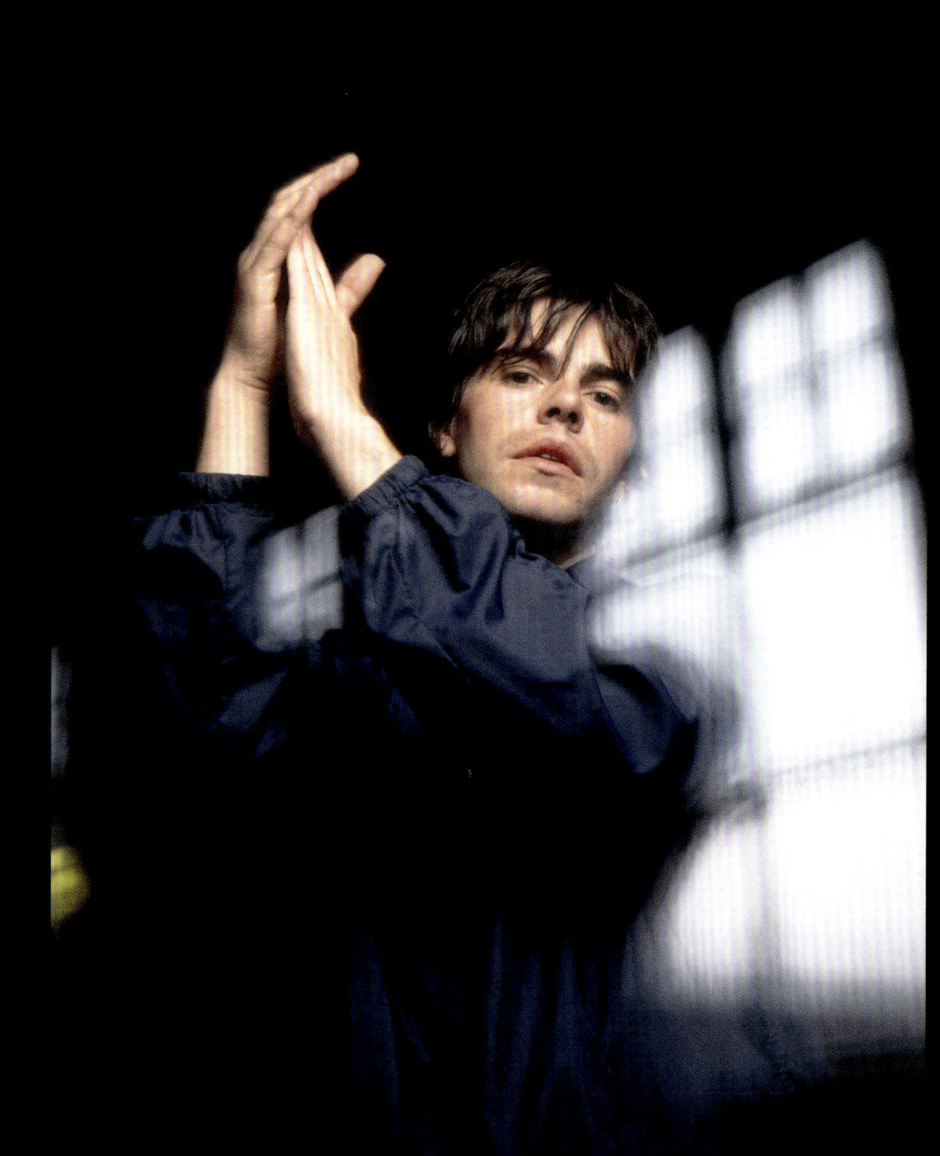

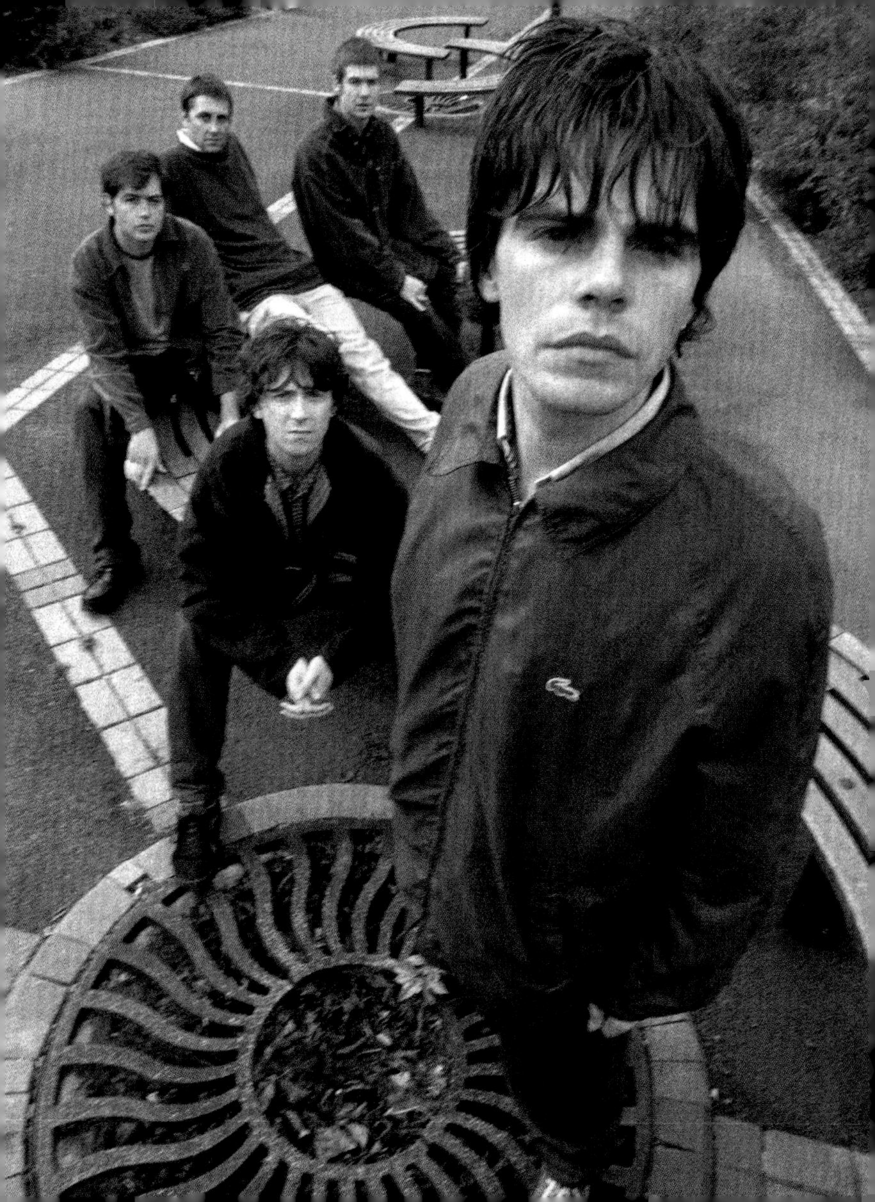

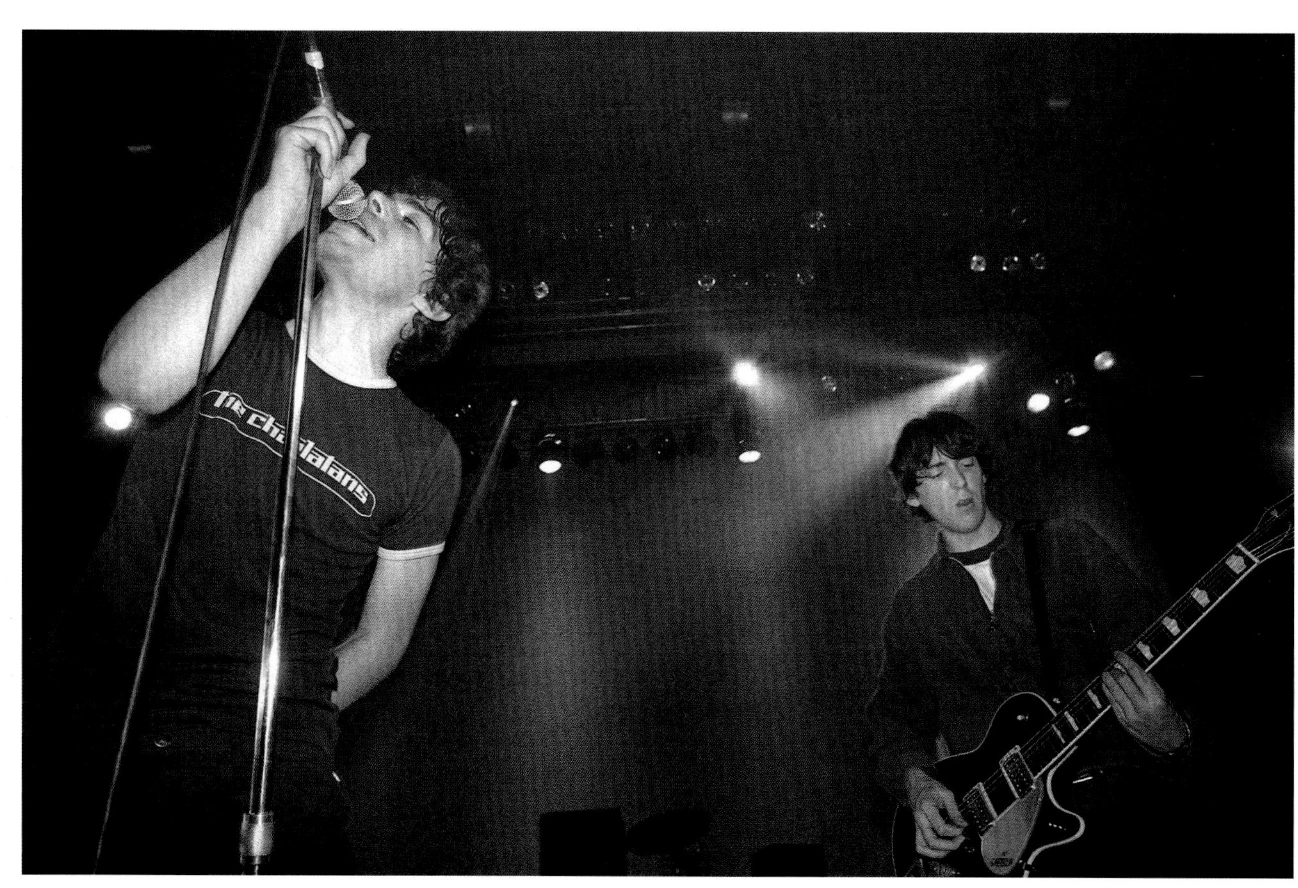

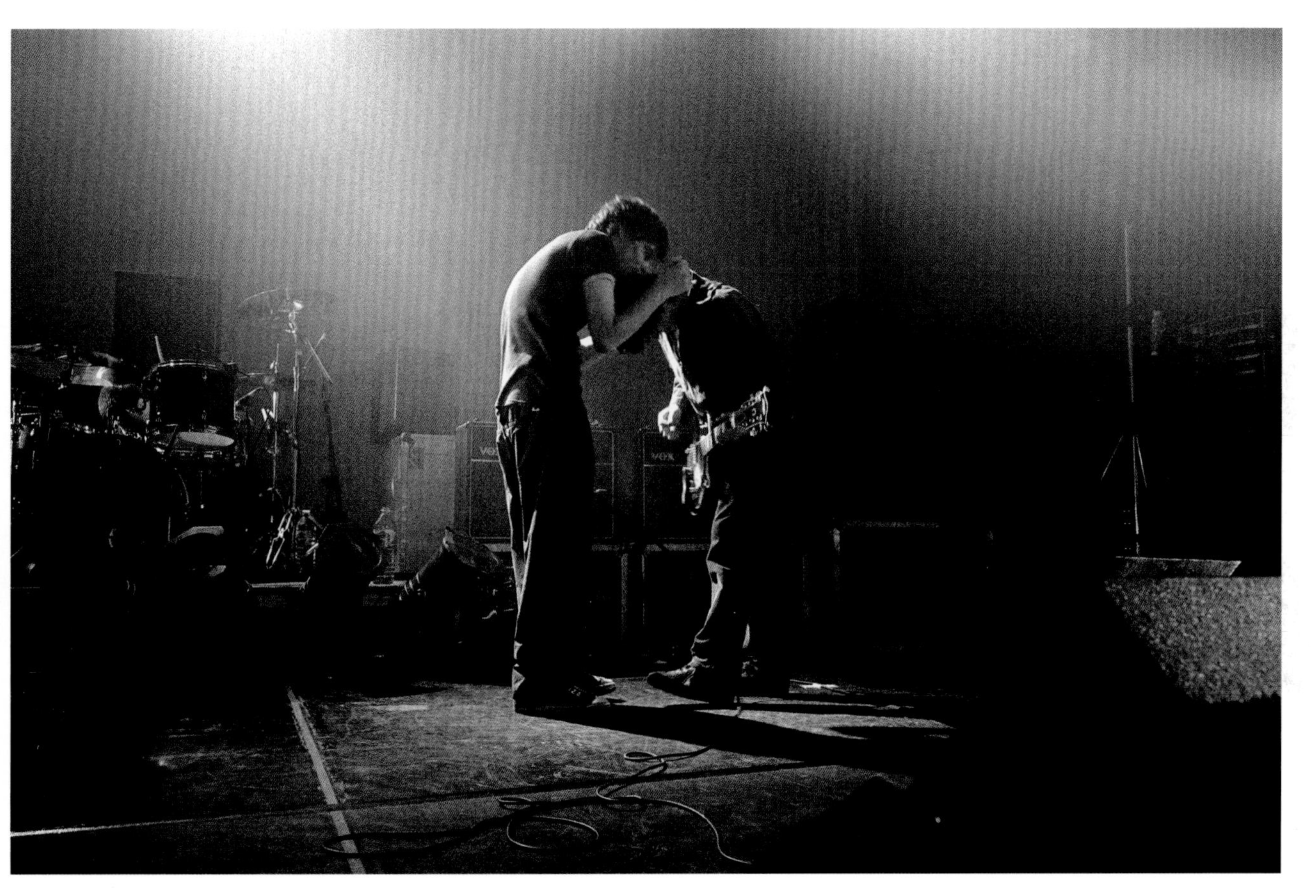

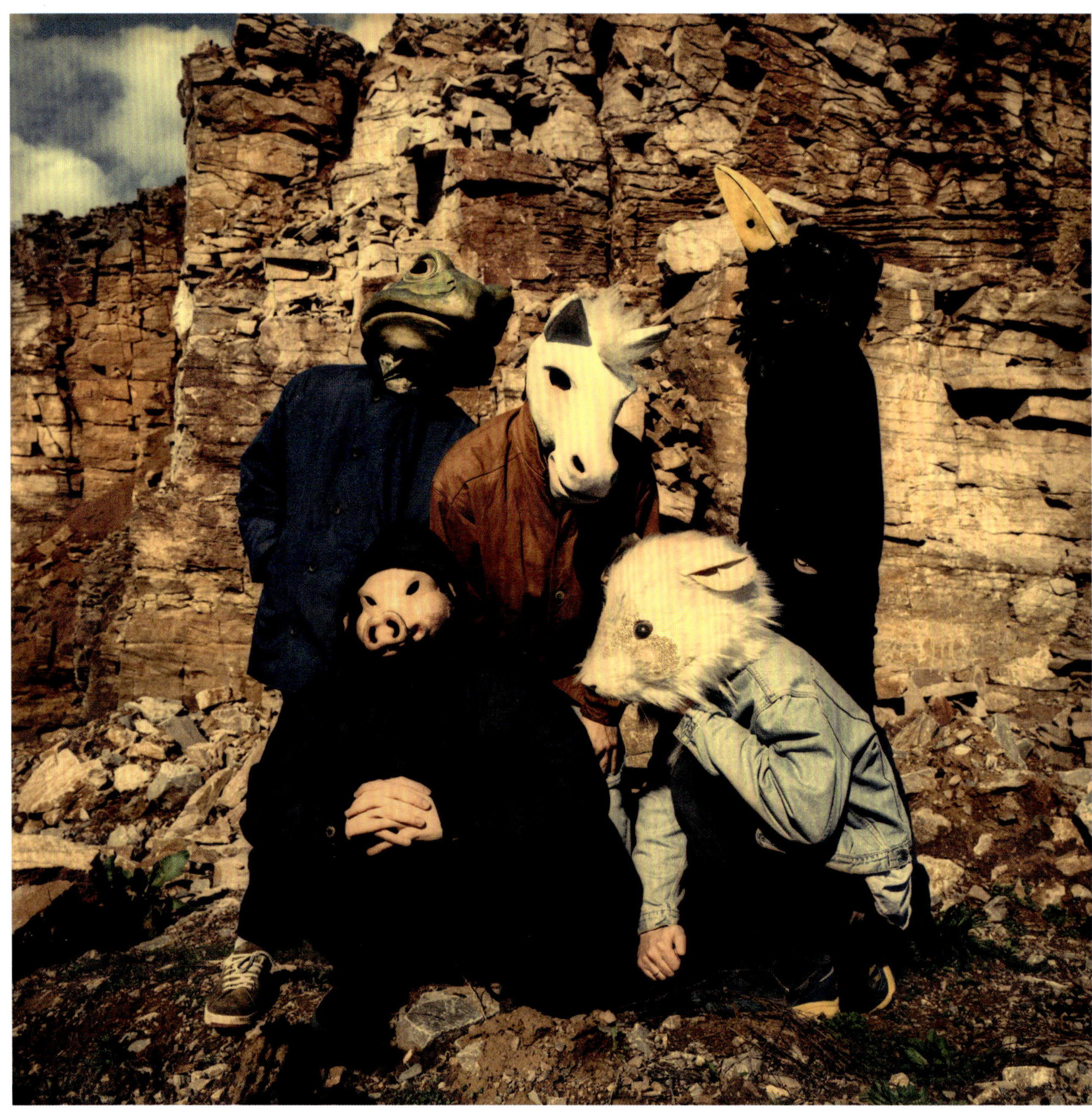

By this stage we were getting sick of the sight of our own faces. We had the bright idea of wearing masks and thought it would bring an otherworldly folk-horror atmosphere. This was a shoot for the cover of "One To Another" – the pig's head was the only thing that actually made it onto the real cover. When this was sent to our label it was dismissed as 'a bit too *Tales of the Riverbank*'. For those unfamiliar with 1970s' kids' TV, it was a live-action show featuring real animals and their inevitably unpredictable, unscripted adventures.

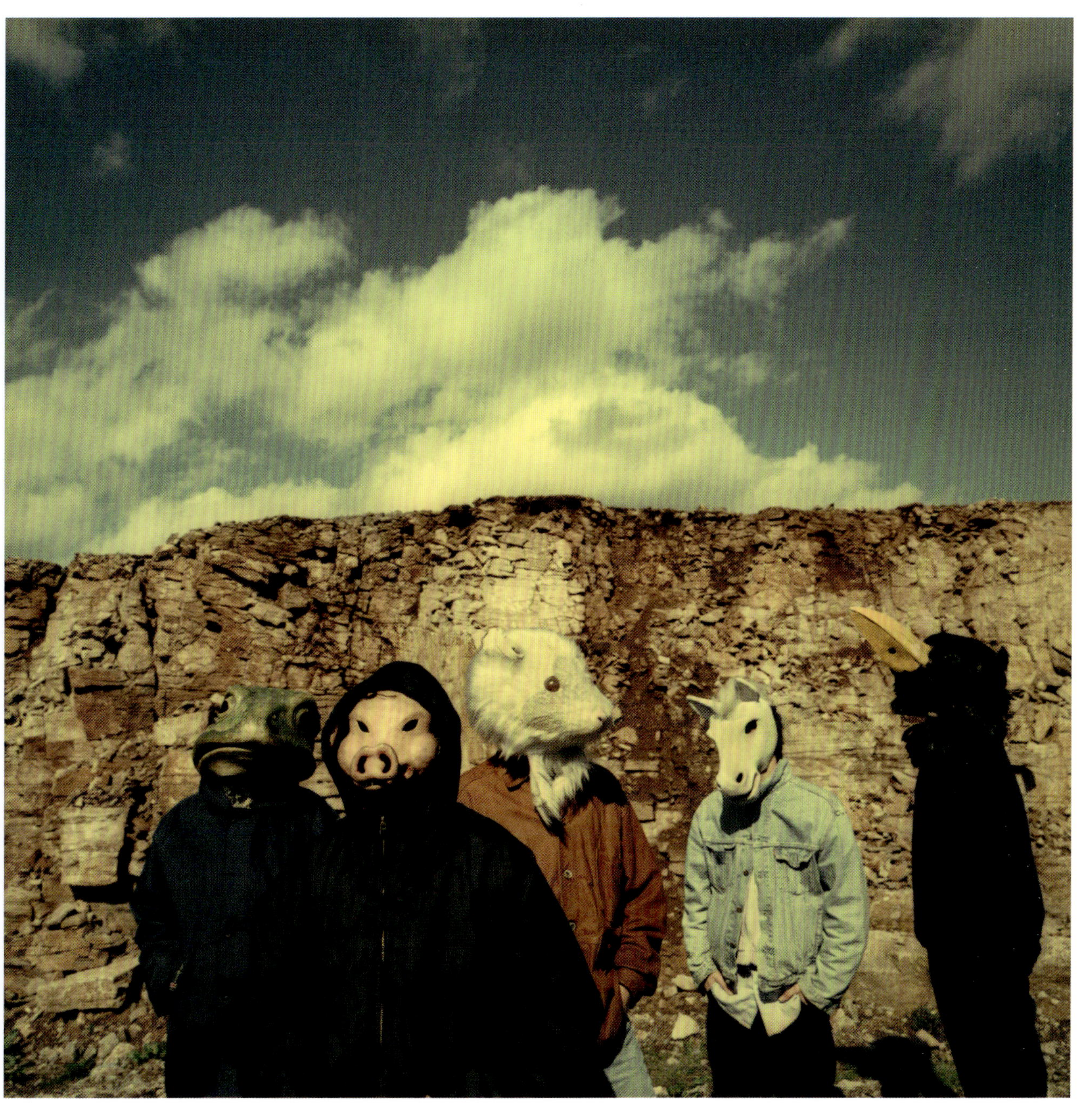

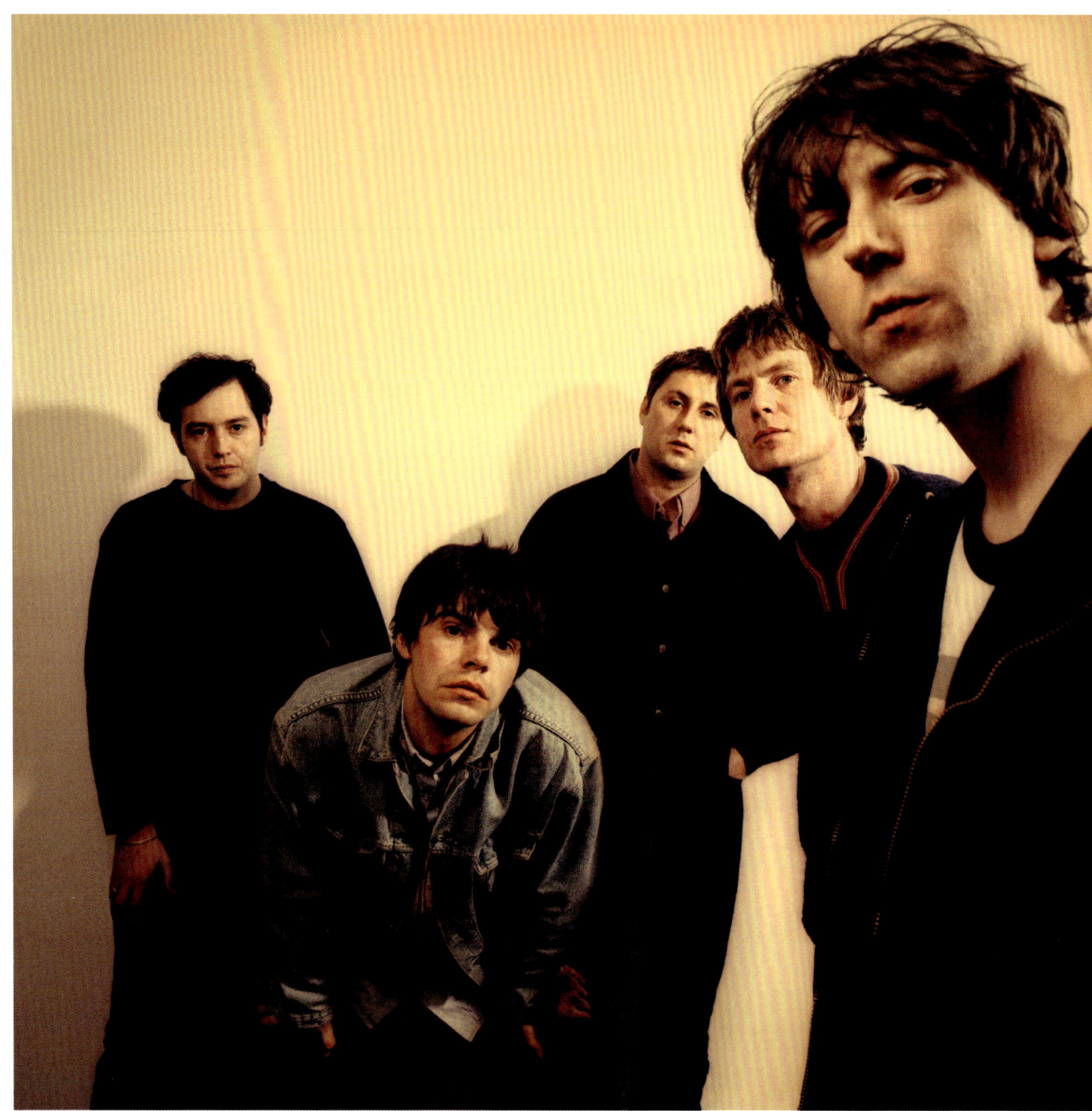

I've noticed in these later pictures that Rob looks detached. He'd come out of prison as a different person. With the recording of *Tellin' Stories* he brought in his own engineer, as he wanted to work on his own through the night.

This is probably the last photograph taken of Rob.

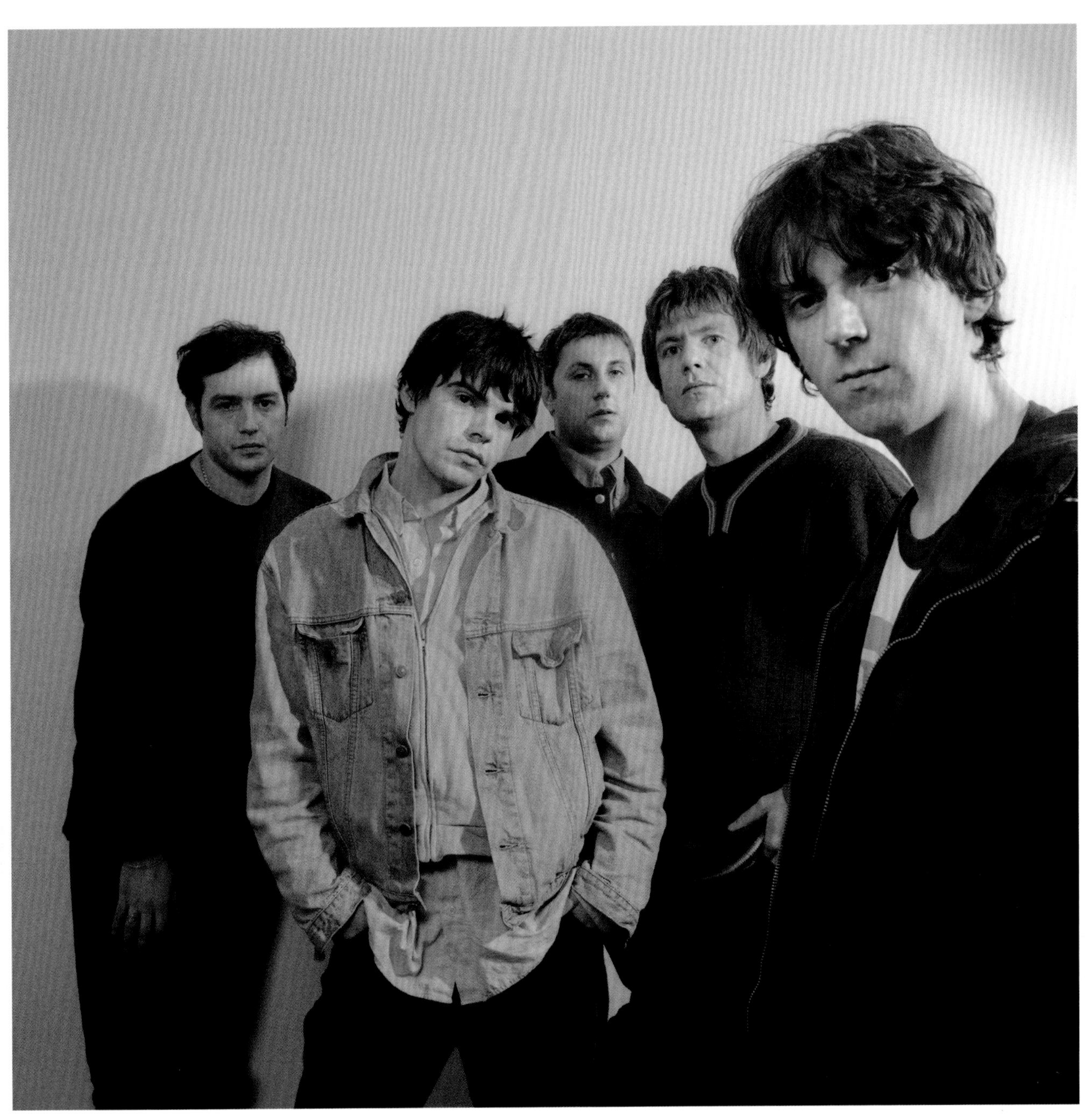

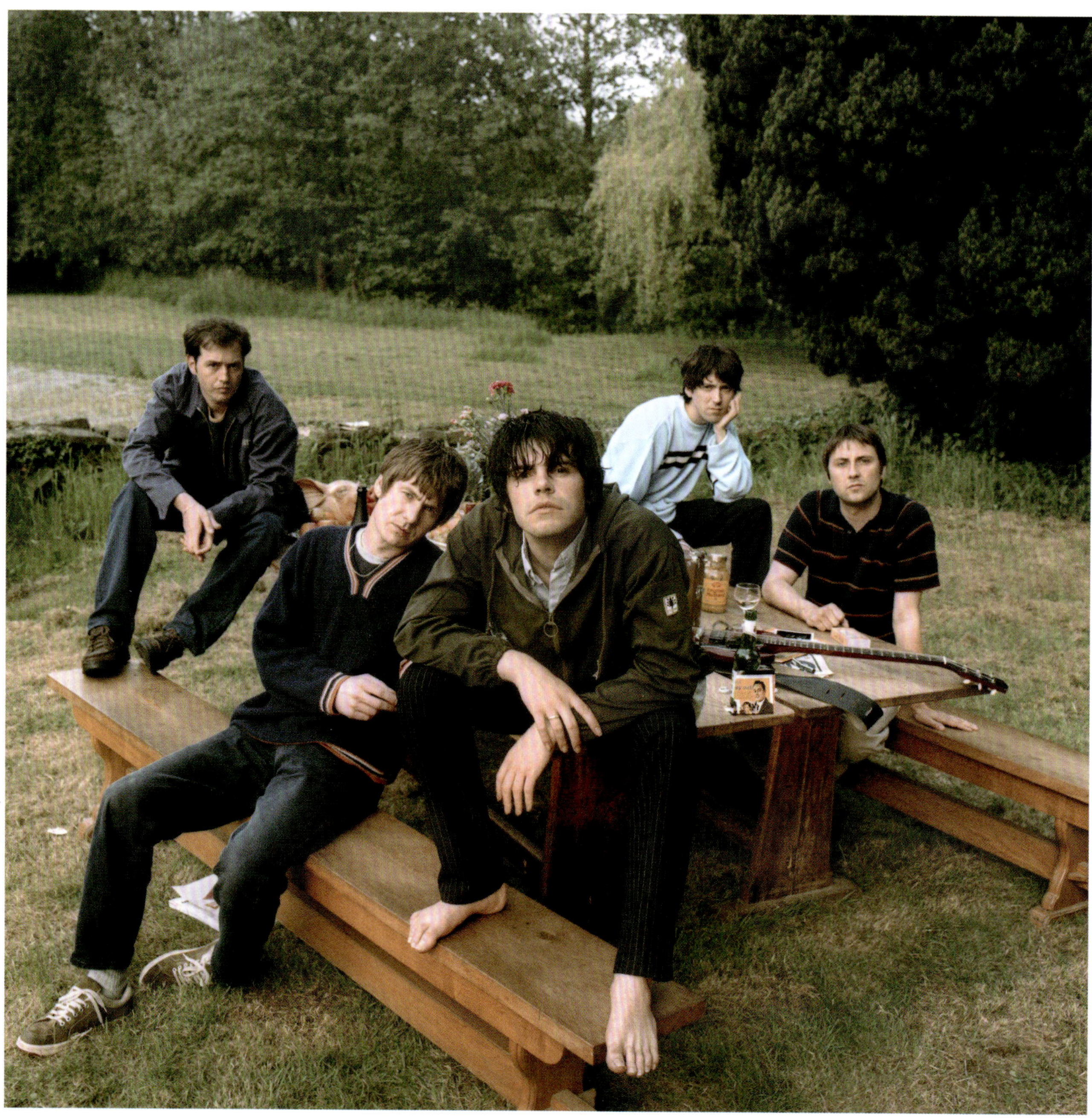

The sleeve for "One To Another". This was taken a few weeks before Rob died. Sadly, by the time the record was released he was no longer with us.

Tom:

We had an idea to do a Rolling Stones' *Beggars Banquet* piece, a picnic out in the garden with loads of props on the table. We went into Monmouth to try to find a pig's head at the butchers – we were waylaid for a while in the pub, so I remember it smelled a bit funky by the time we got it back – then swung by the supermarket to get some lobsters and all kinds of other tasty morsels. We had some fun with the set-up, though a lot of it was wasted, as of course with five people in a band you always have one of them getting in the way of what's on the table. But that's how we liked to work; plans were made, things were sketched out, but nothing was bolted down. My theory has always been to keep things loose and see how things take shape when you do it, a lot like a musician working on something in the studio. As we shot, it started getting dark, so we parked a few cars on the grass and beamed their headlights at the table to buy a bit more time. It was a fun shoot – and we barbecued the lobsters for dinner that night

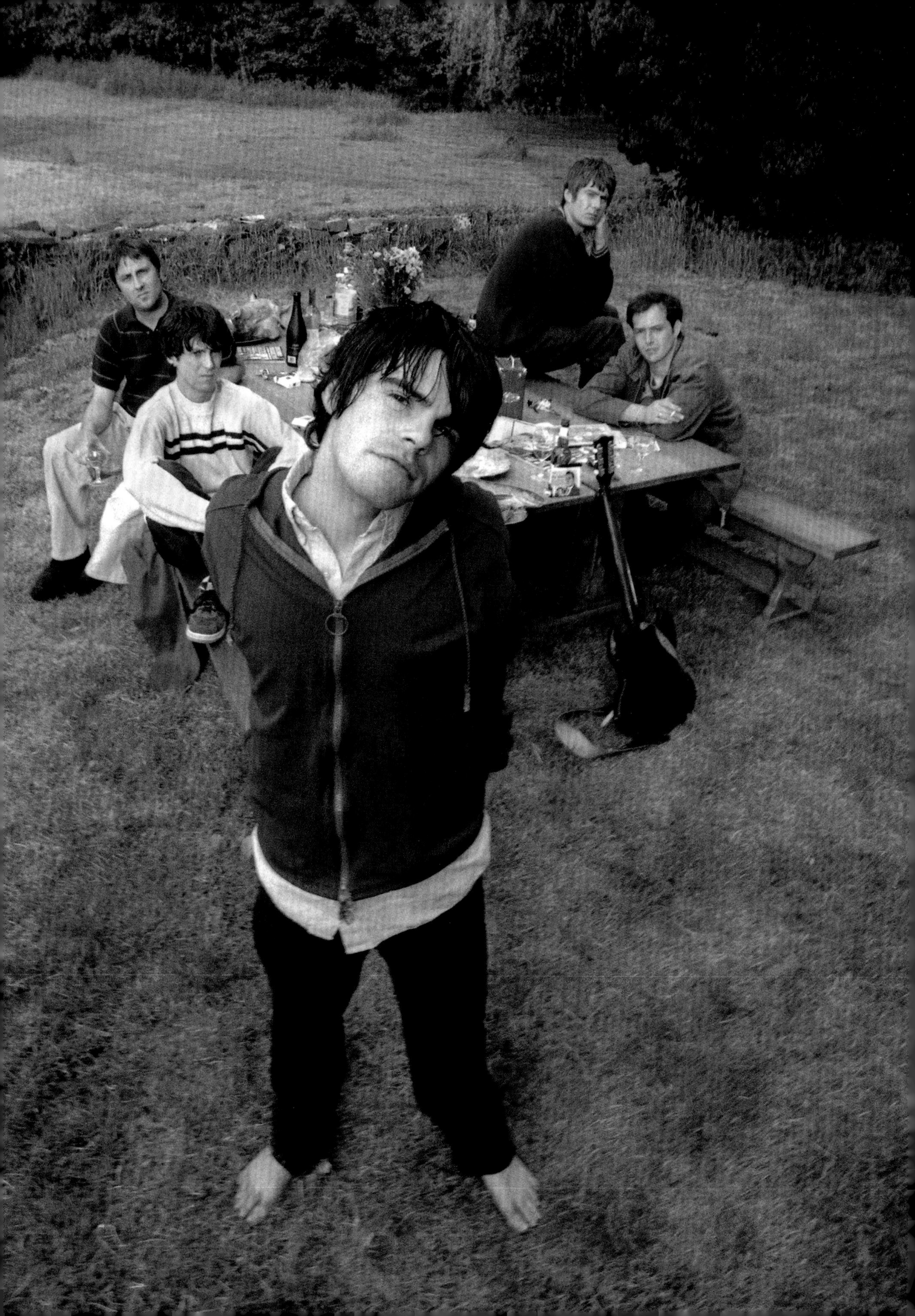

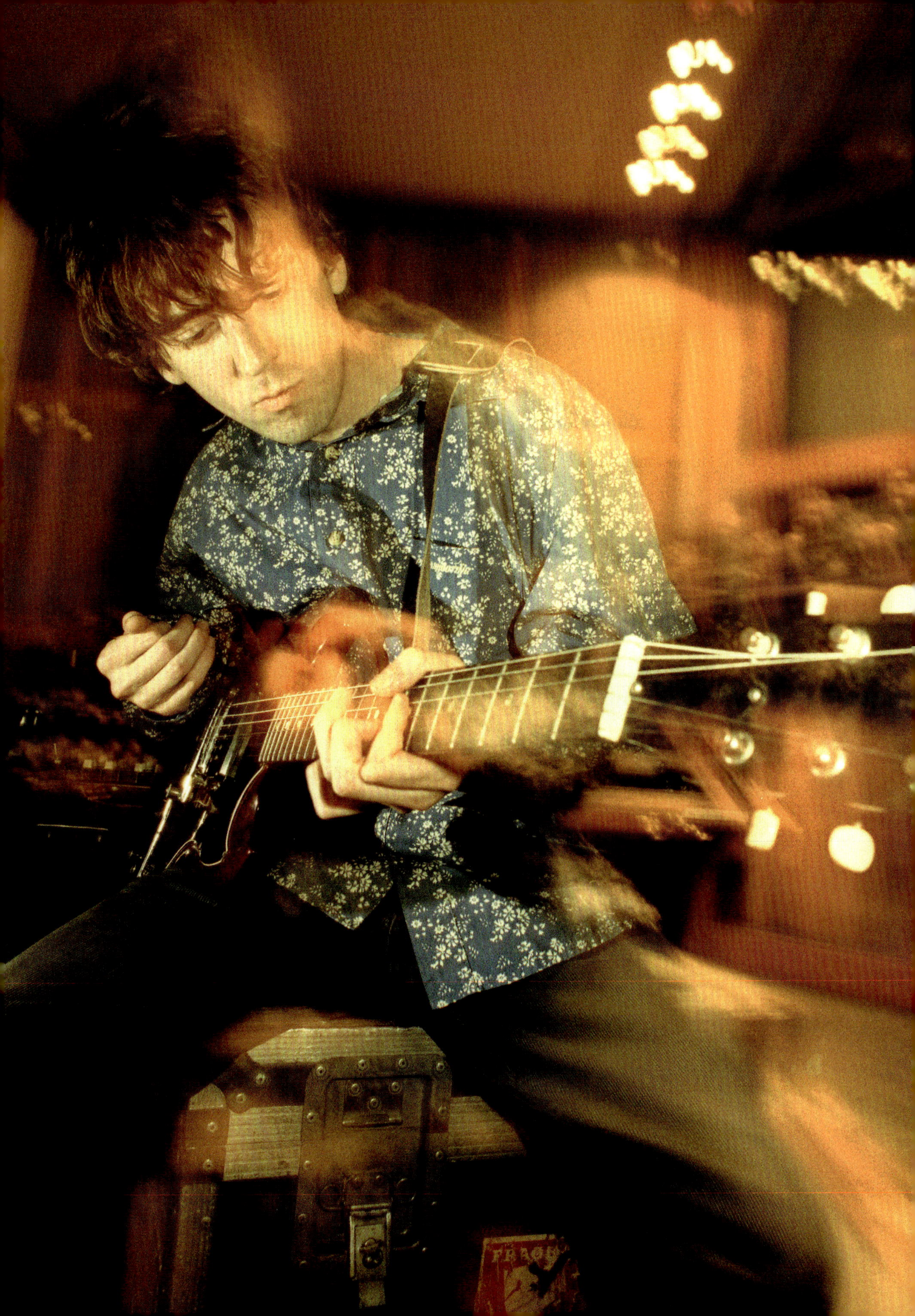

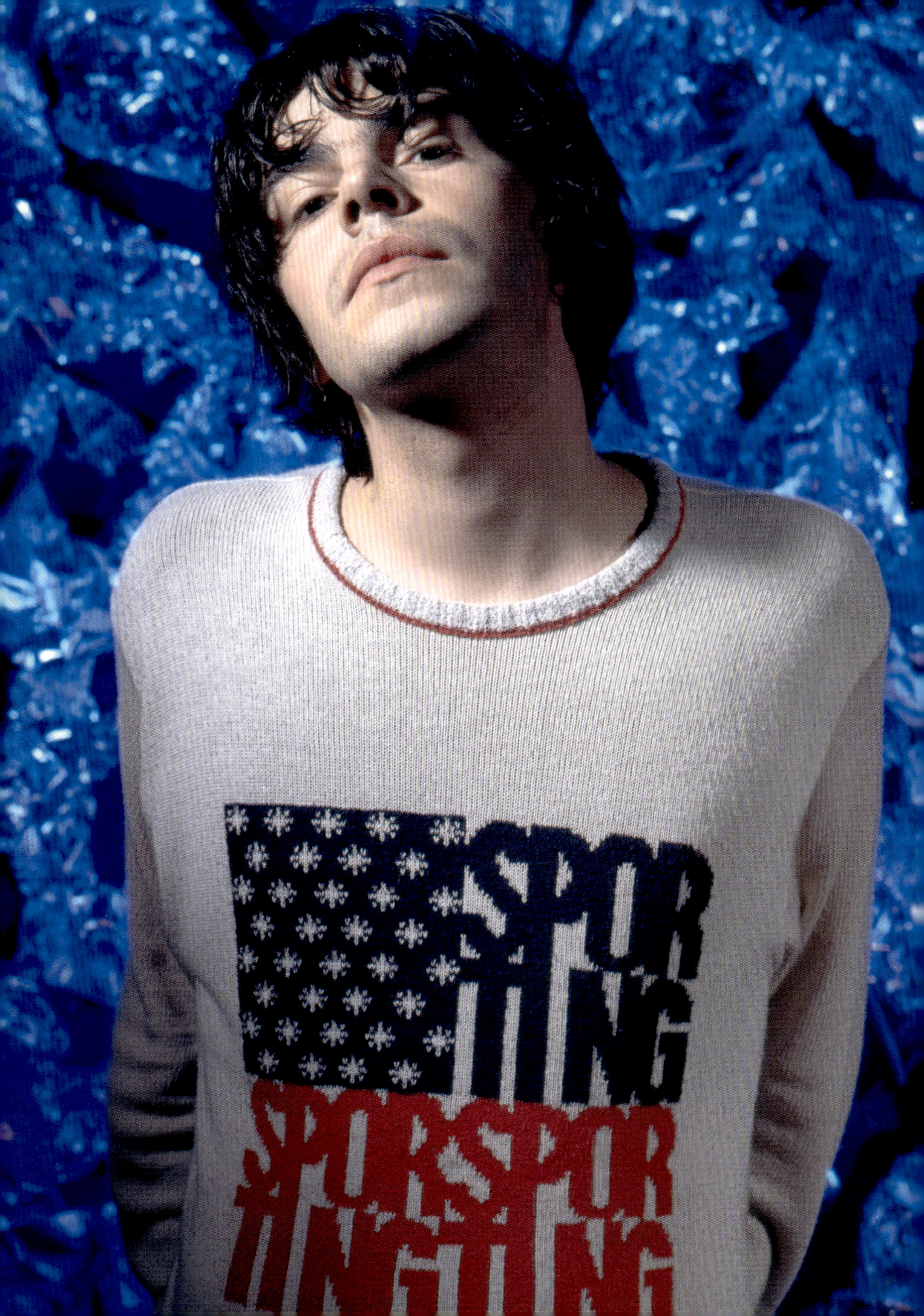
SPOR
TING
SPORSPOR
TINGTING

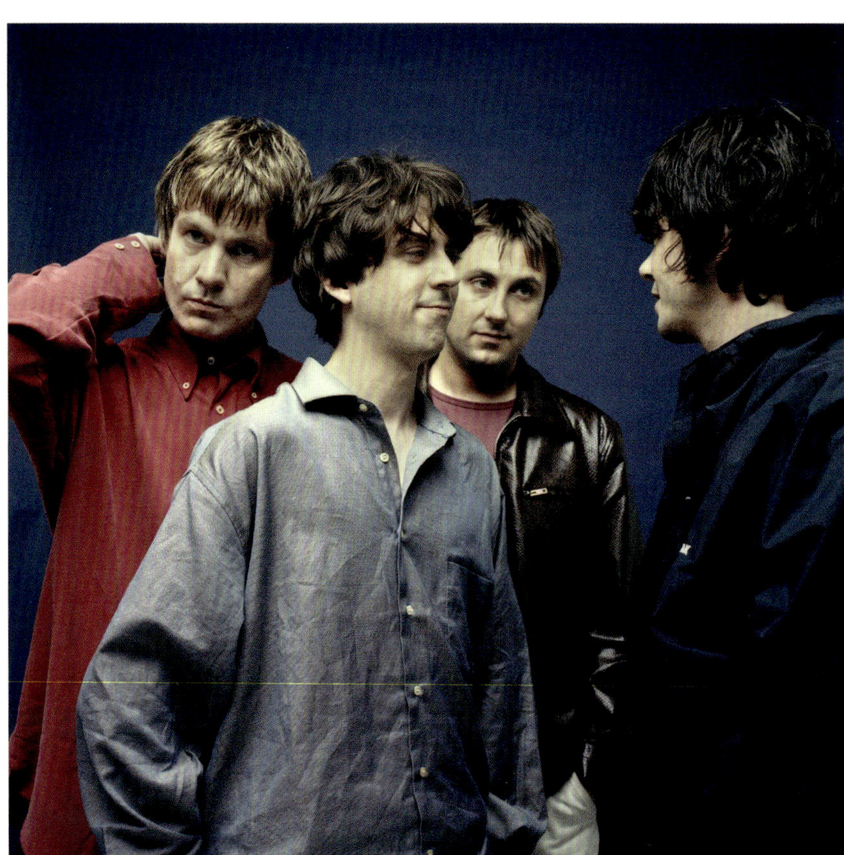

Left: The first photo taken after Rob had died. We had an album to finish and our future to contemplate. We even had to decide whether we had a future at all.

Right: Tom brought a framed photograph of Rob to the first photoshoot where it would just be the four of us. It was a few weeks after his funeral, and we were tentatively taking our next steps.

Tom had taken a photograph of Rob and had it framed so as not to forget his friend and to keep his memory alive. He took it with him everywhere over the next few years, and he would share pictures with us of Rob on his "travels" to Tokyo, New York and Rome.

The more that time passes by, the more I treasure this picture.

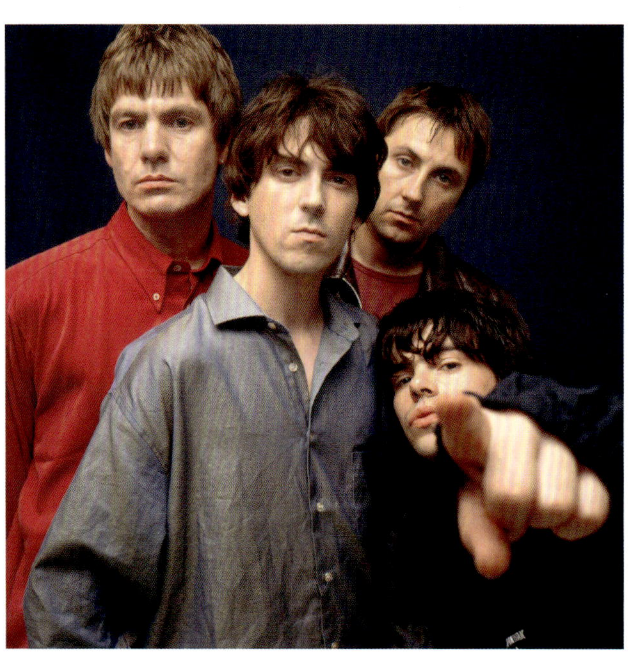

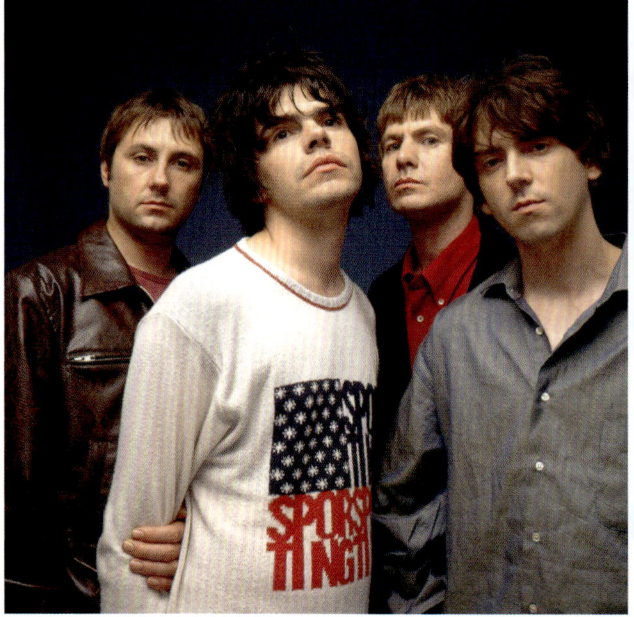

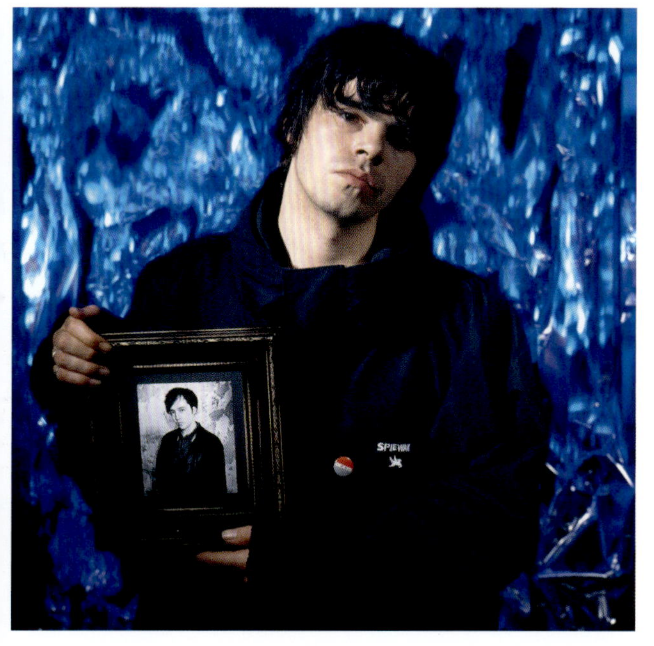

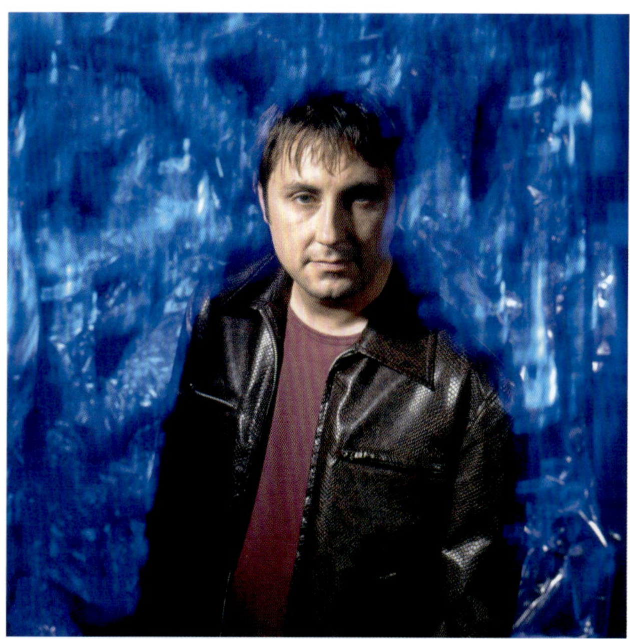

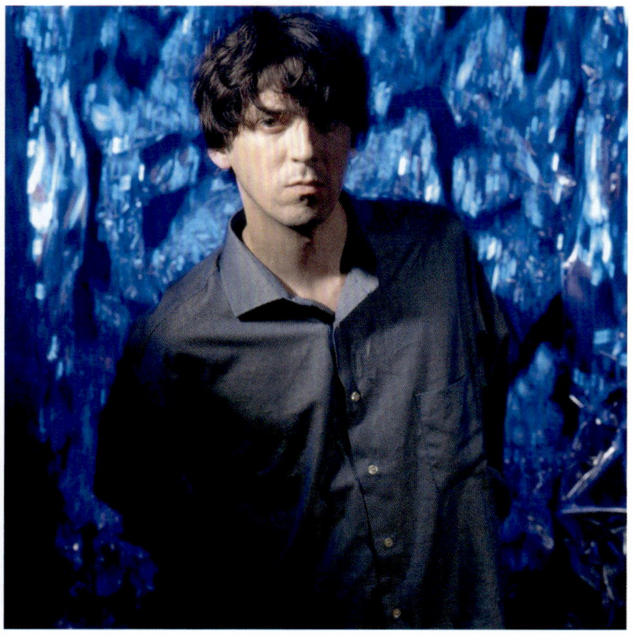

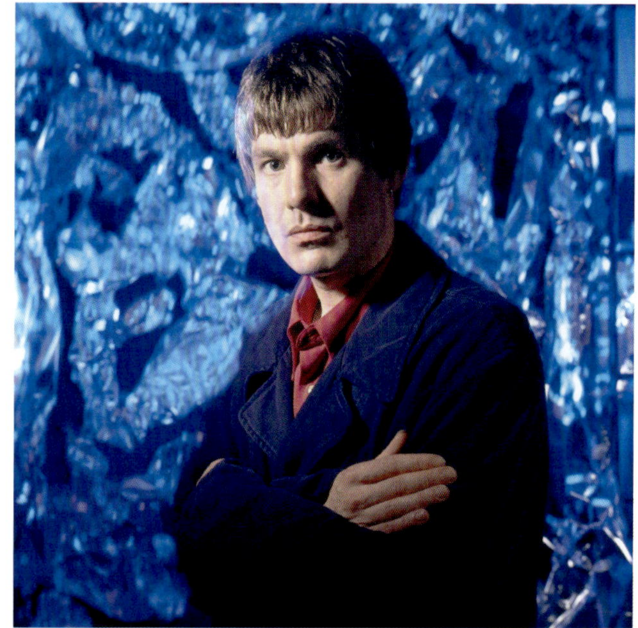

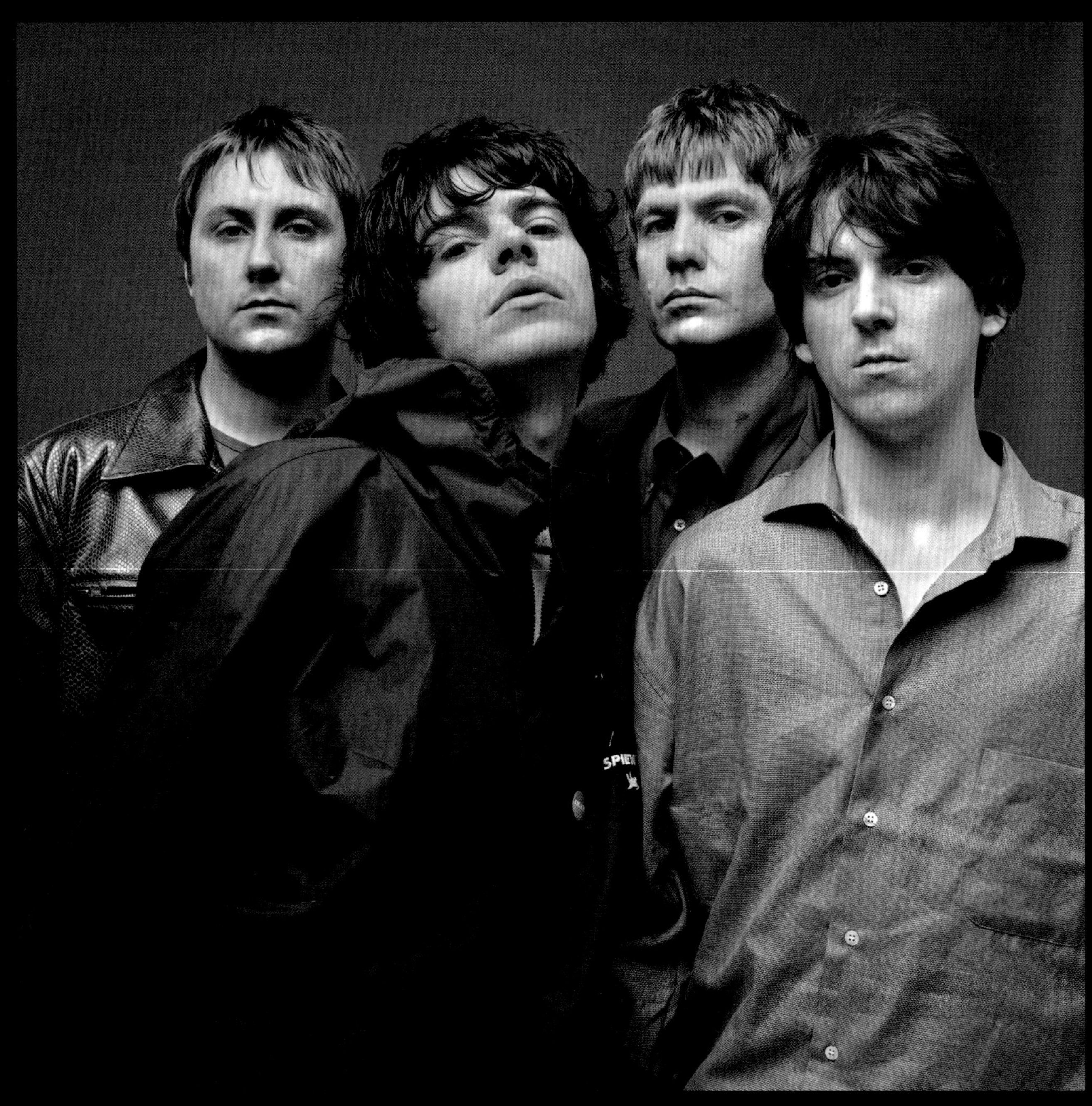

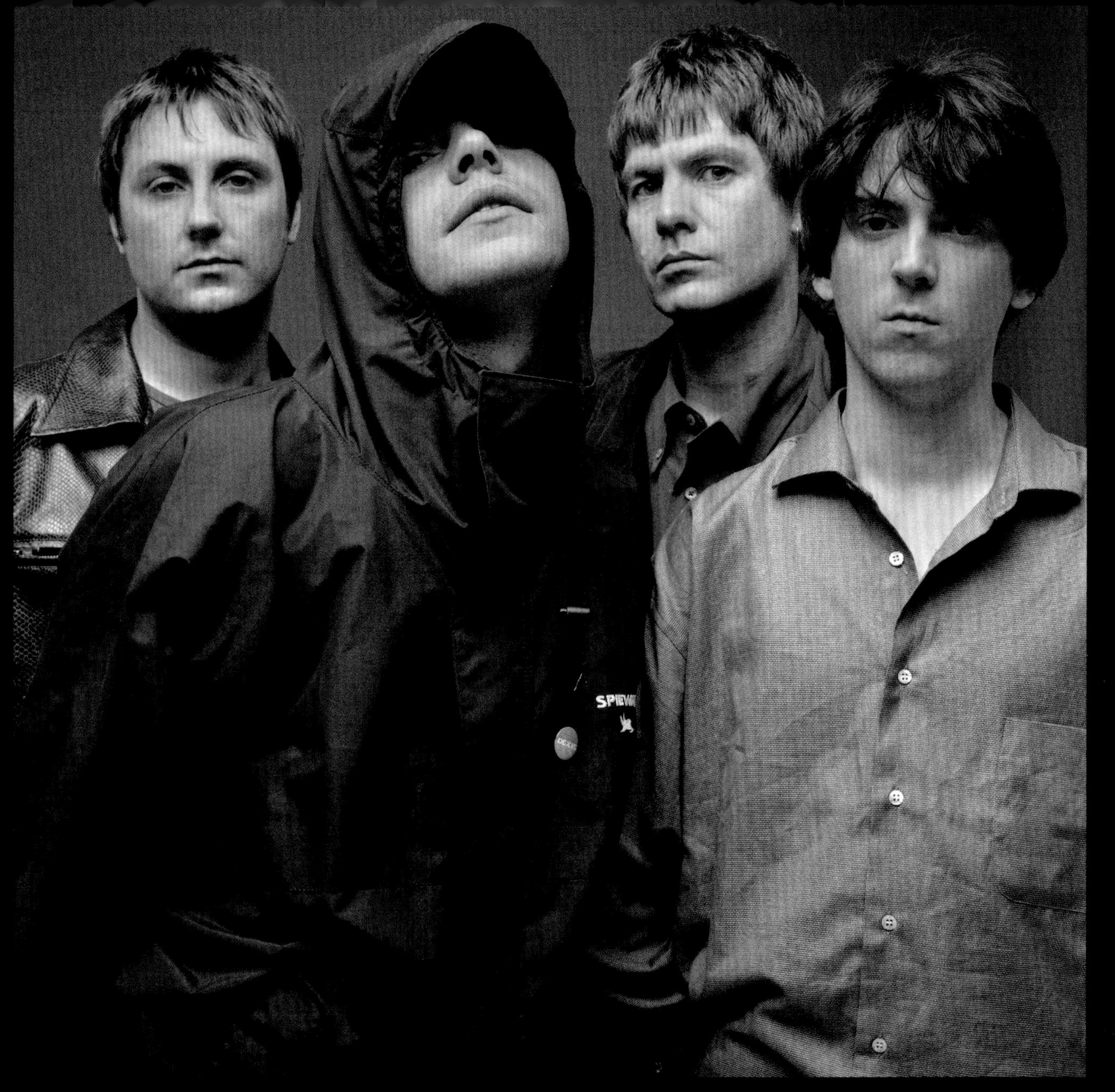

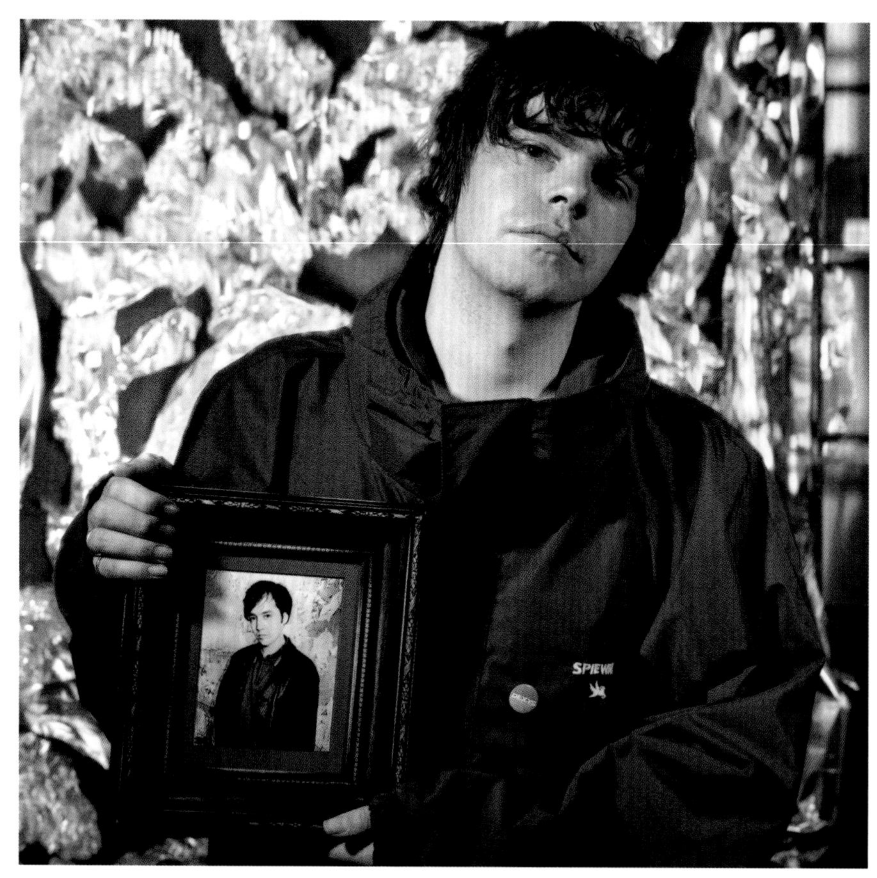

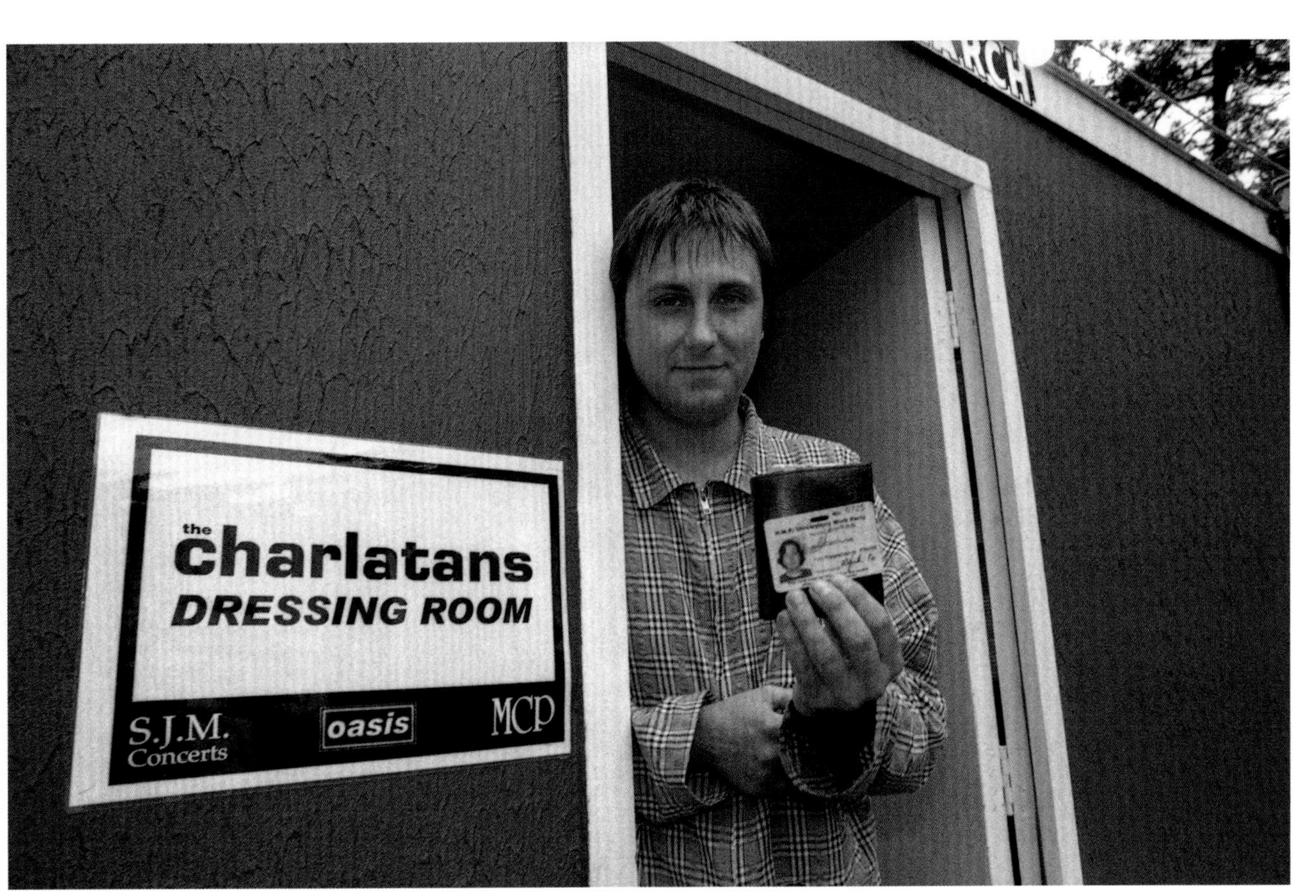
the
charlatans
DRESSING ROOM
S.J.M.
Concerts
oasis
MCP

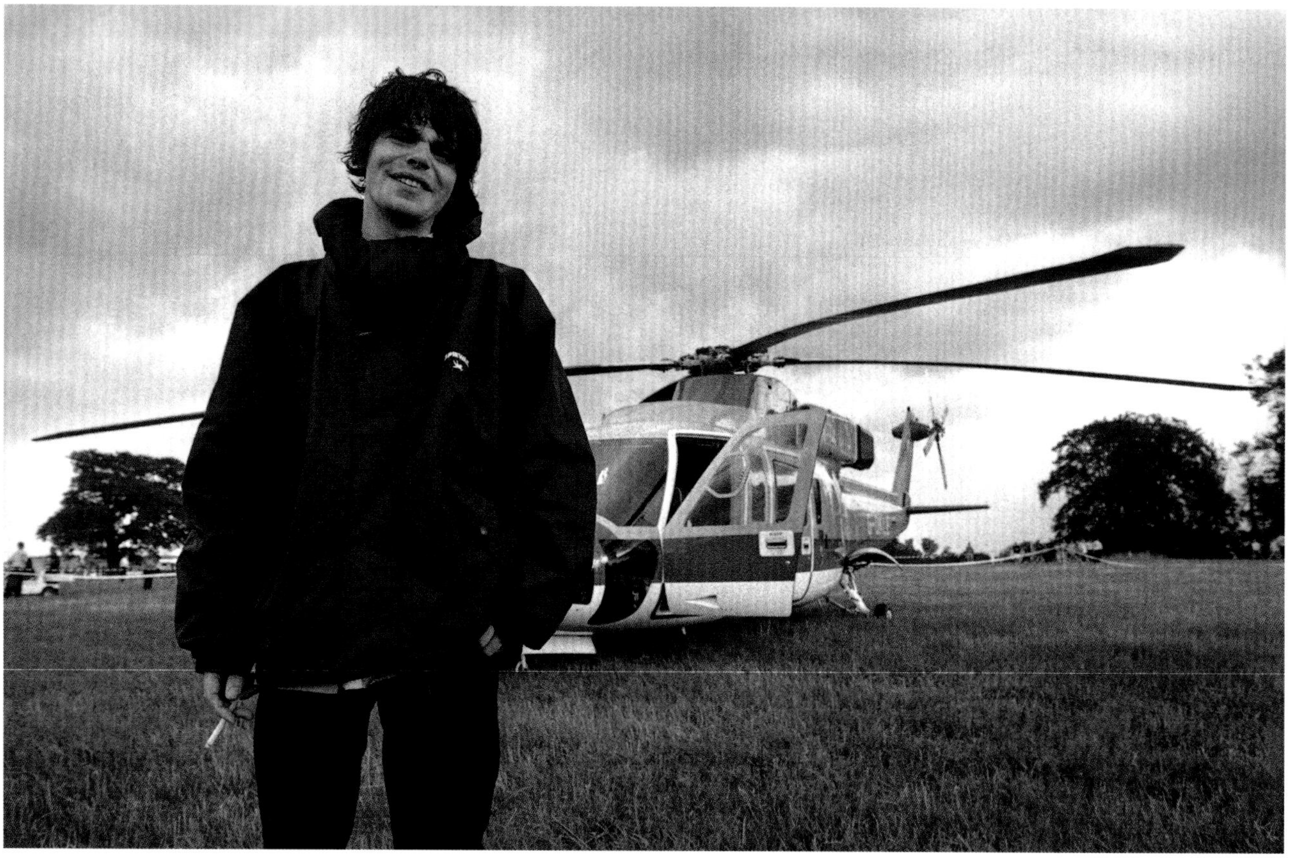

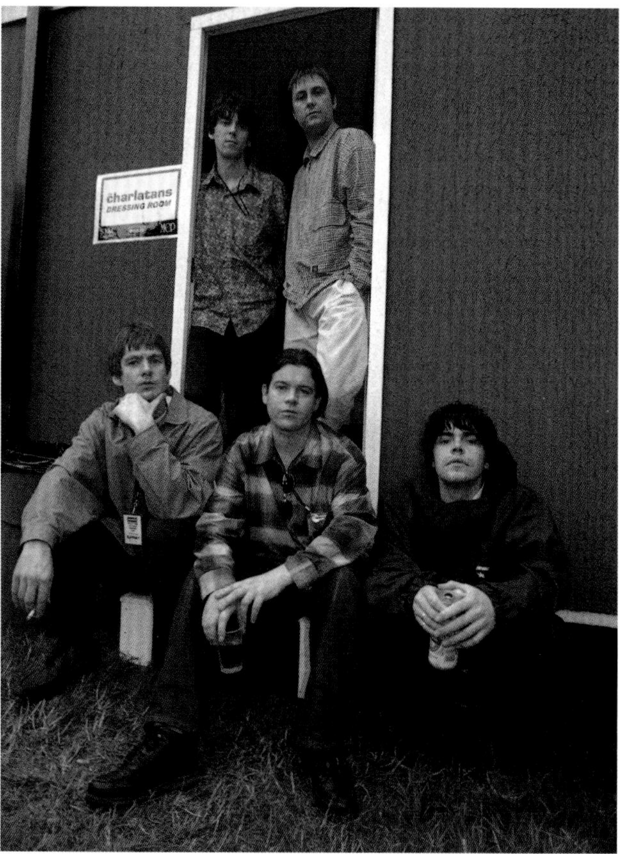

Knebworth was unlike anything we'd ever played, including Roskilde, Glastonbury, etc. At those we'd usually head from the hotel to the site in a people carrier, but the promoter foresaw the potential traffic issues, so of course we had to travel by helicopter.

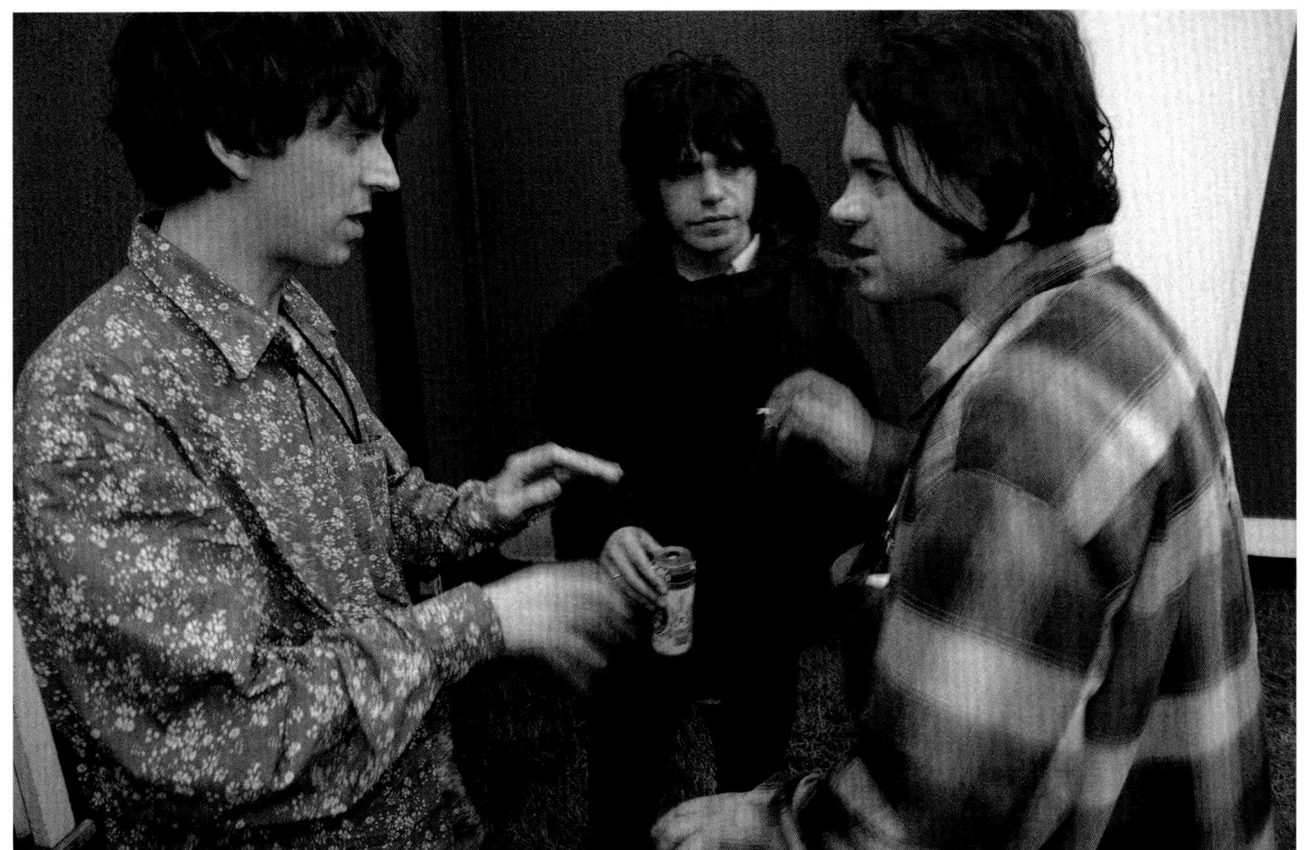

I've stared at this photograph for so long now, never having seen it at the time it was taken. It captures the day incredibly well. At any show in the previous six years we'd have all been confident in what we were going to do. Rob wasn't around anymore and Martin Duffy had kindly offered to play keyboards in order to save the gig. But he did more than that – he saved The Charlatans.

The end might not have been hugely dramatic, but not playing that gig might have led to us not playing the next gig. *Tellin' Stories* would have come out, but we could easily have been convinced that it was over for us.

In the moment this photograph was taken you can feel what is happening. Mark is talking about a keyboard part and showing it with his hands. It had been two years since we saw Martin Duffy, in Amsterdam. One of the side effects of us and our friends finding success was that one or other of us would be away, and between touring and recording it would be up to a year or two between seeing people like Mani or Duffy. Even when we did it could be in the crazy set up of a festival in Japan.

It looks to me like it's to do with timing or rhythm, "...and that's where you come in", or maybe "this one has to be punctuated as fast as you can". Duffy was taking absolutely everything in, but we have to remember he was getting "advice" from three other members of the band. We'd rehearsed as much as we could, but this was literally moments before we walked up the ramp onto the stage.

Knebworth was just over two weeks after Rob had died; that will give you some kind of insight into our physical and emotional states. Nothing seemed real.

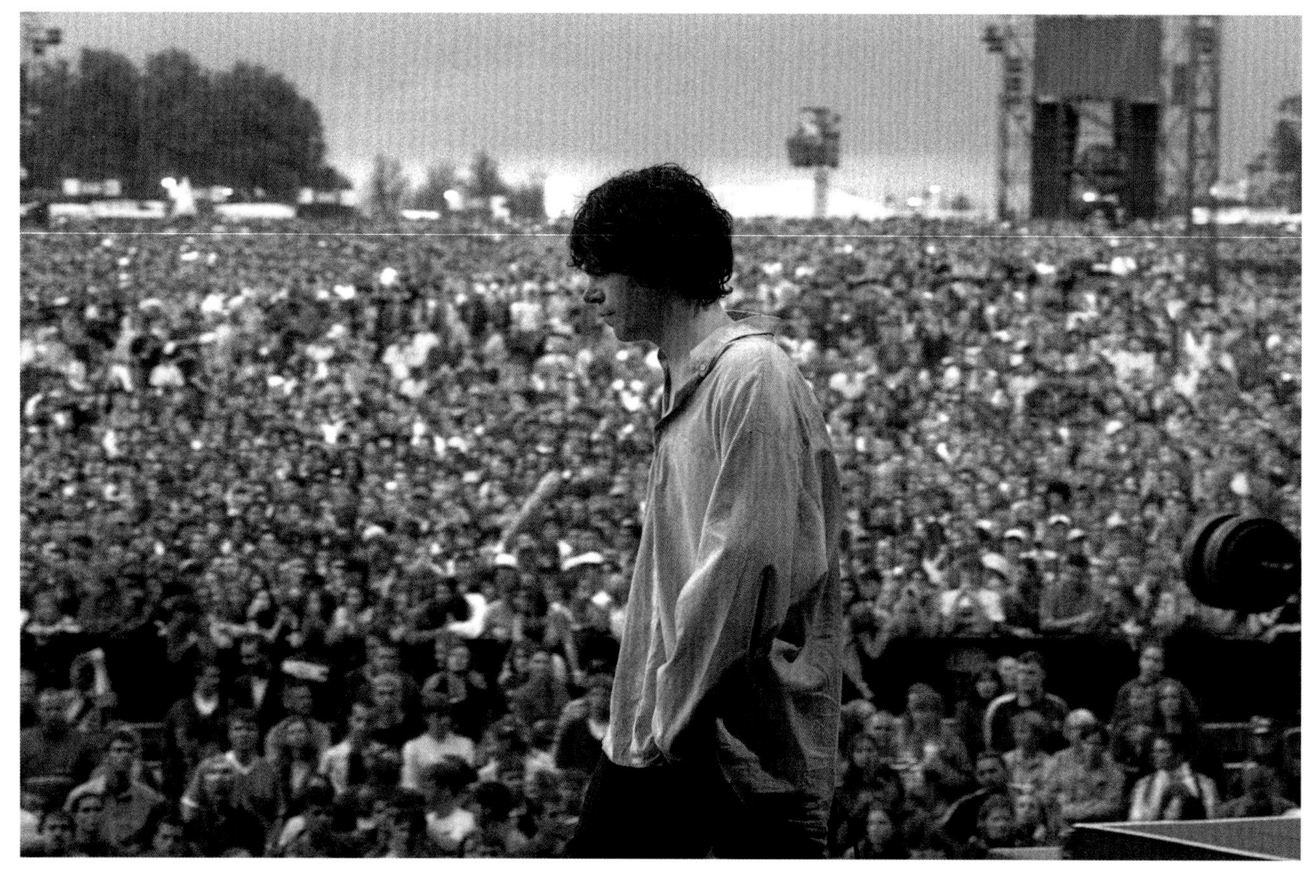

Growing up I'd seen photographs of Led Zeppelin and Elton John playing in US stadiums. The feel was just so different to UK gigs – vast openness and endless people. This reminds me of those. It felt like a huge rockstar moment, but everything was under the shadow of us having lost our friend. Maybe it was foolish, or just bravado, but we played two songs that we'd never played live before. Fortunately for us they were "North Country Boy" and "One To Another".

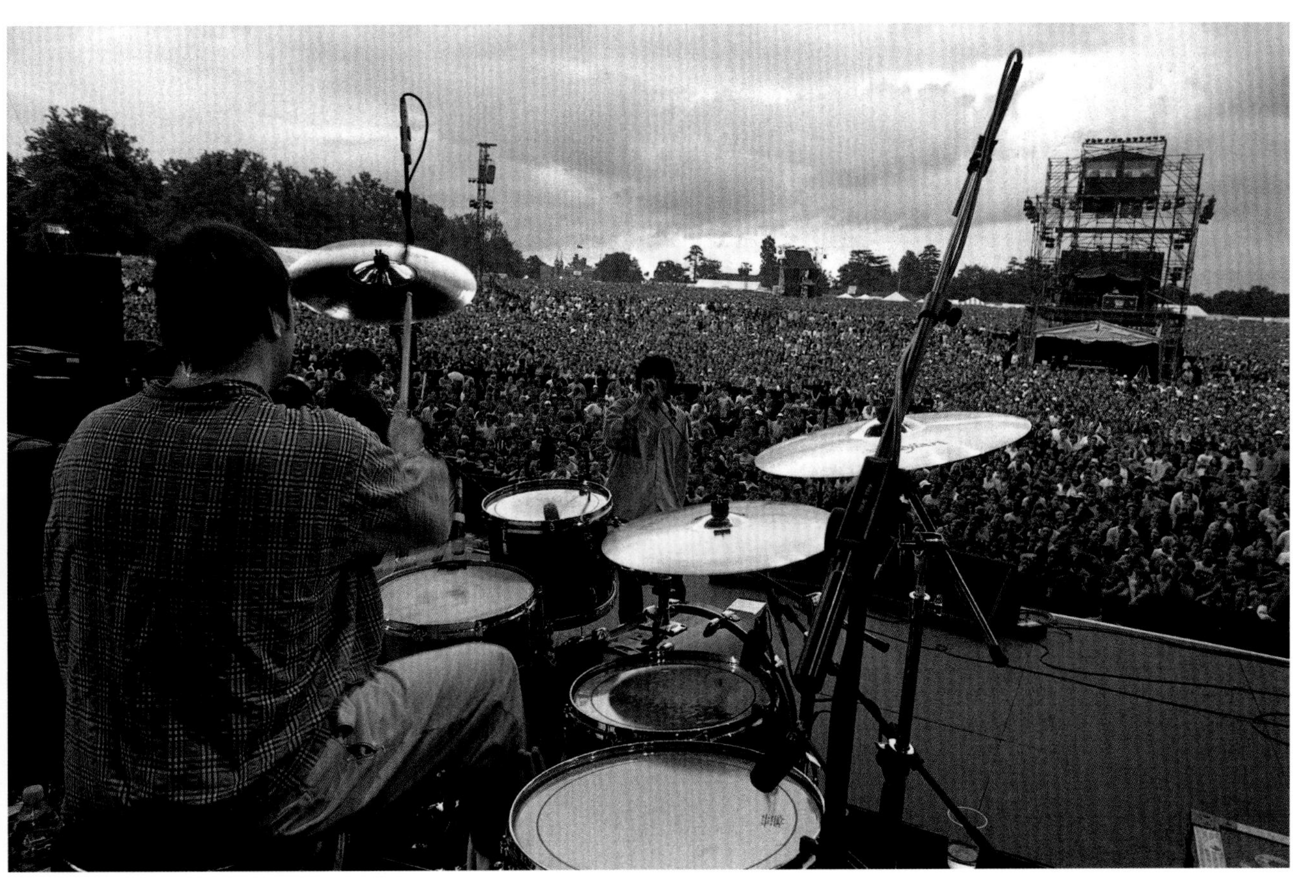

Tom:
The band were nervous. Rob was such a large, integral part of who they were, his presence on- and off-stage. He was brilliant, how could you replace his sound? But Duffy, the trooper that he was, God bless him, came in and fit the bill. But I could tell that for all their bravado the chaps were panicking, going out to that crowd. The great thing about Knebworth, though, was that everyone there was a Charlatans fan. The band had been around for years before Oasis and there was such love for them – for their records but also for Rob and for the fact that the band were enduring, carrying on. I remember Noel came to see the band before the show to say hello and good luck. After the gig we went to the bar backstage and all they wanted to do was let out a big, collective sigh. "We've done it."

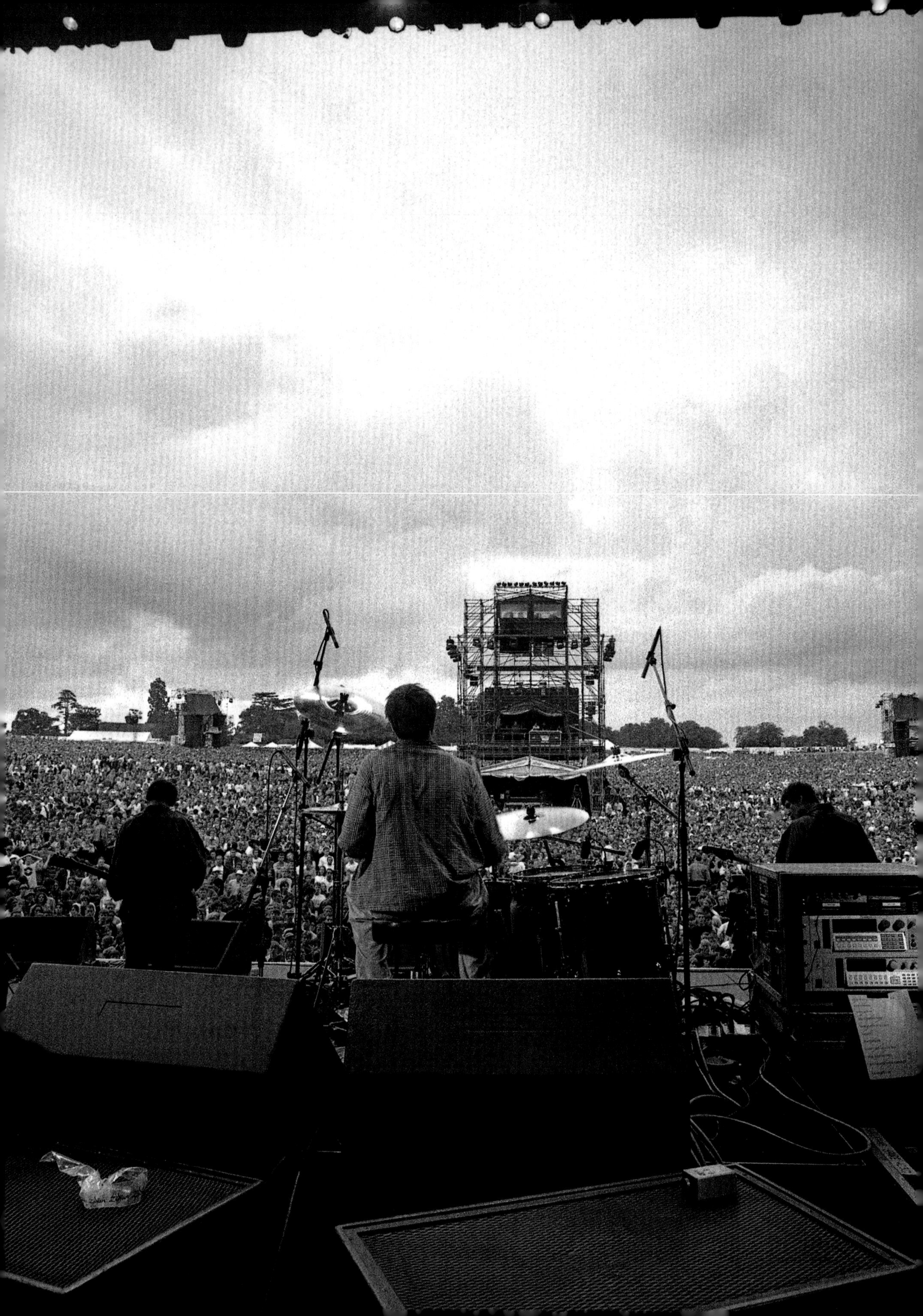

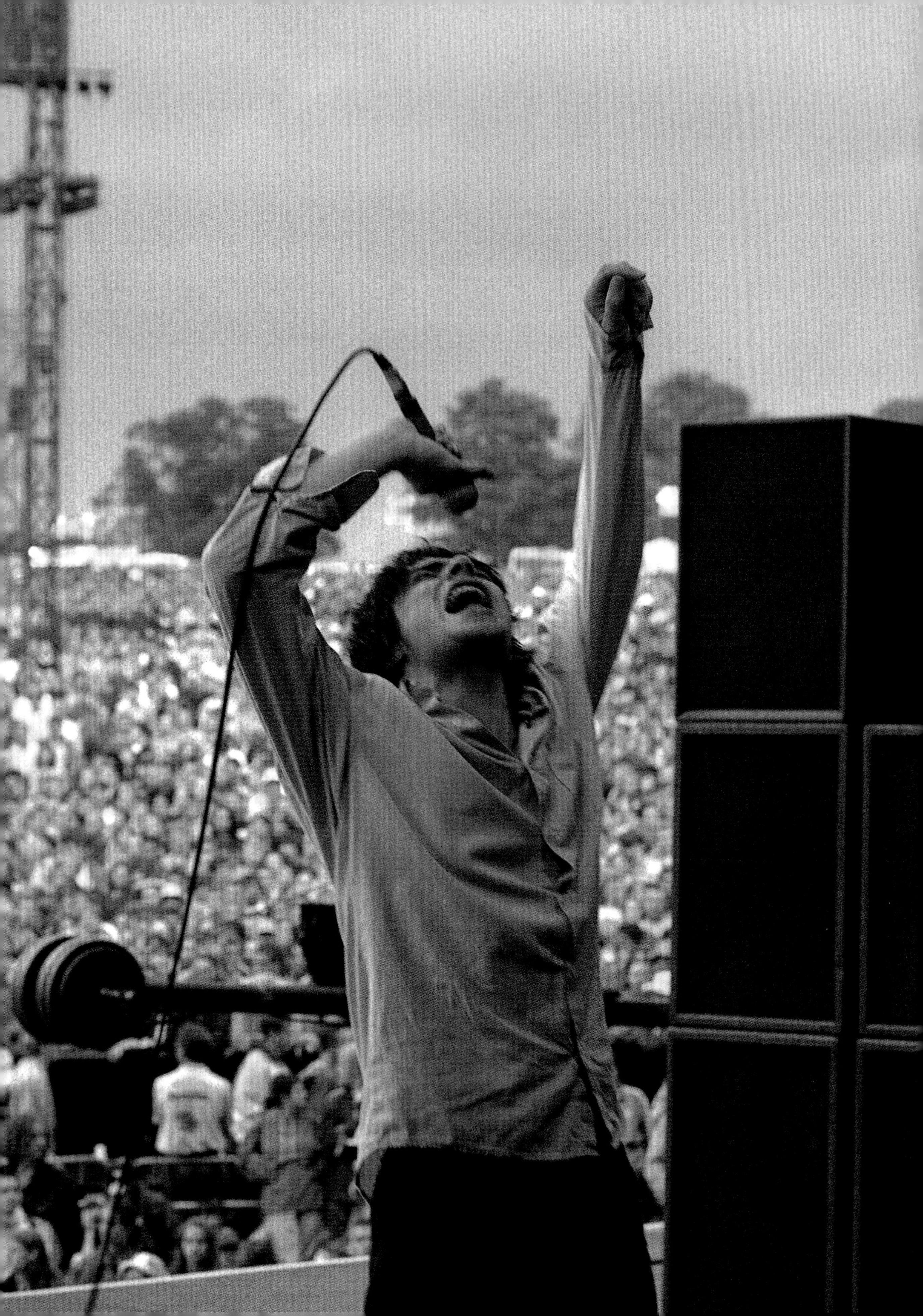

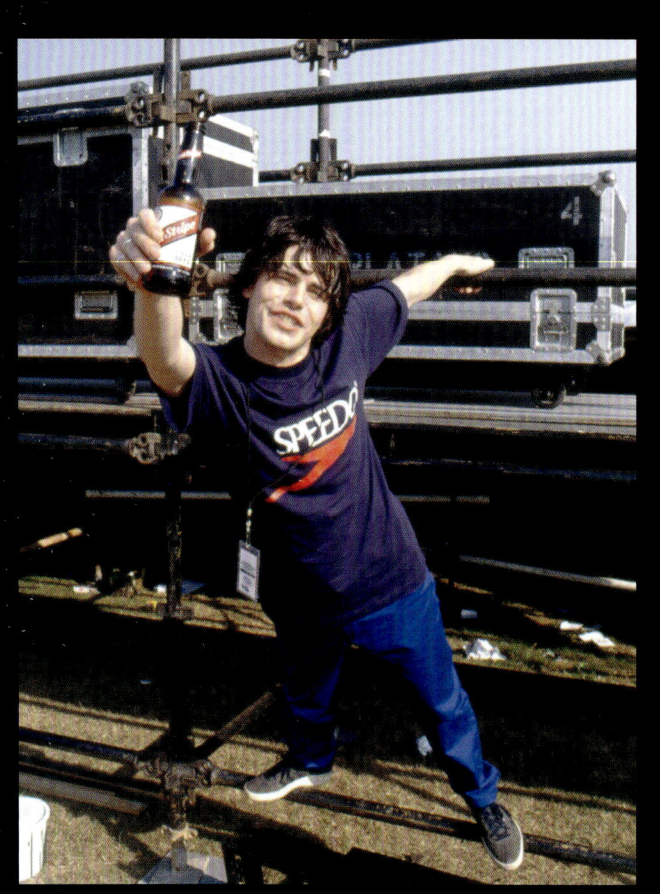
Stripe
SPEEDO

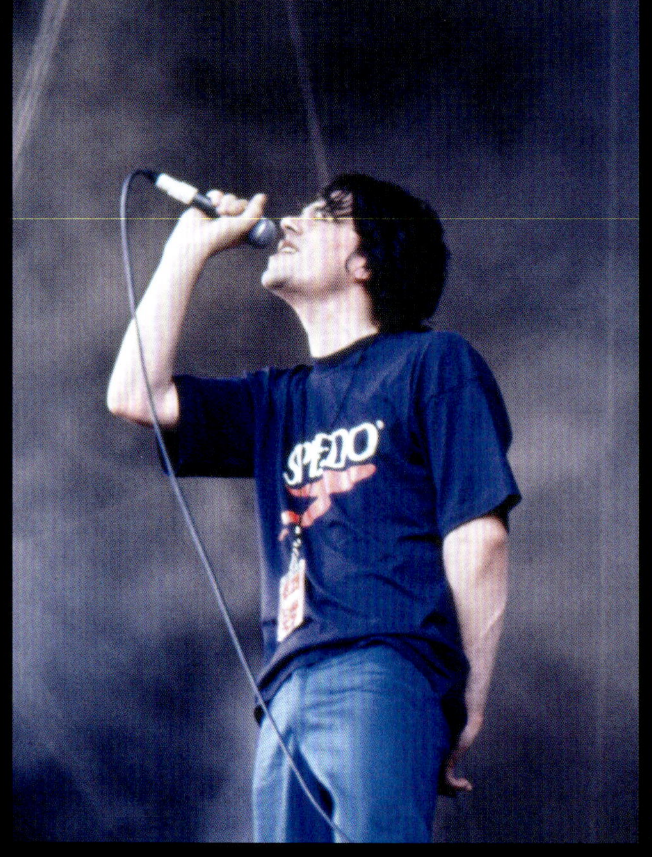
SPEEDO

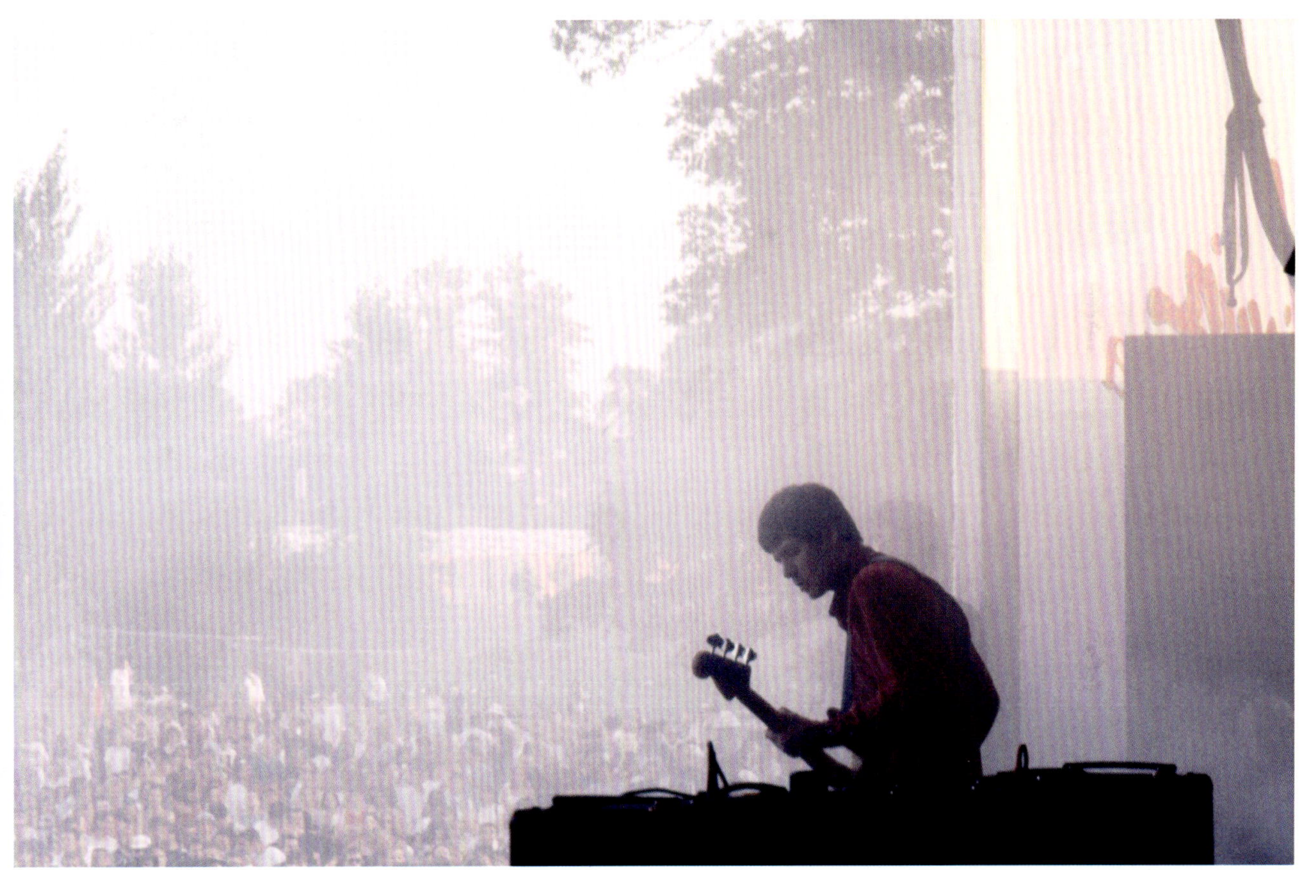

Everyone always concentrates on Knebworth, which was our first show back and obviously a real moment in time for Oasis and music in general. But the weekend after, we had chance to catch our breath and were playing before headliner Paul Weller and after The Lightning Seeds at the inaugural V Festival in Chelmsford. We felt so much love from everyone on the line up and the audience. It felt like we were doing the right thing by carrying on.

I love this picture of Martin.

If Knebworth was a statement of intent, this was the beginning of a new era.

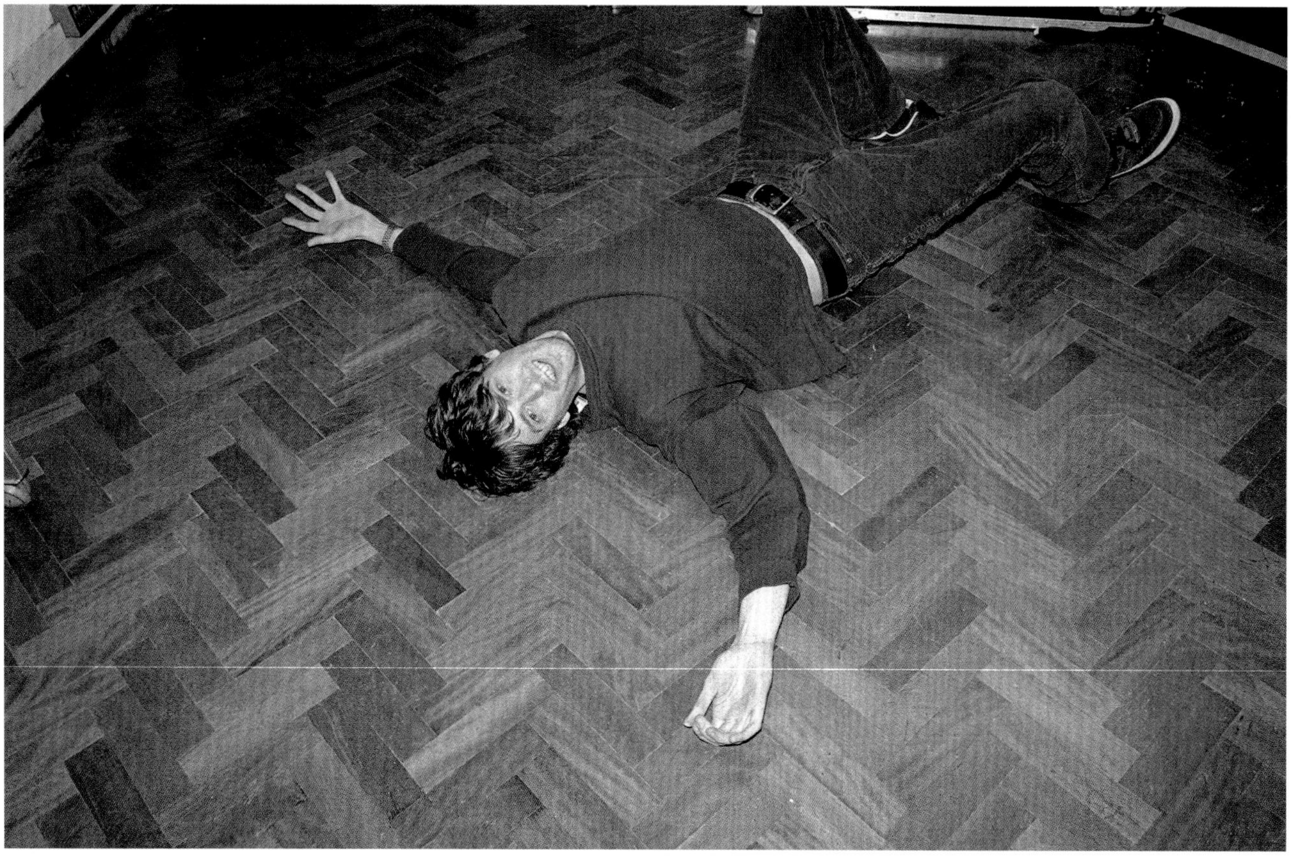

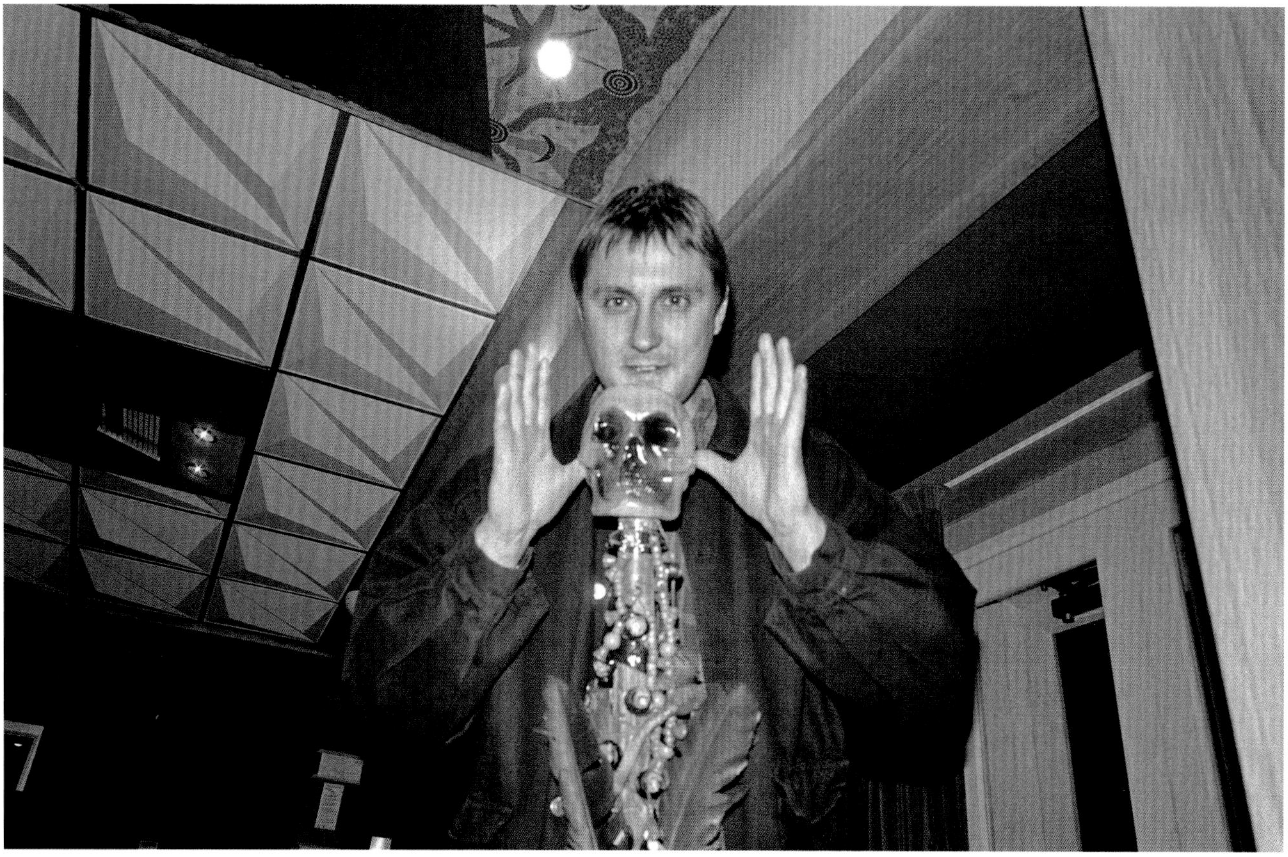

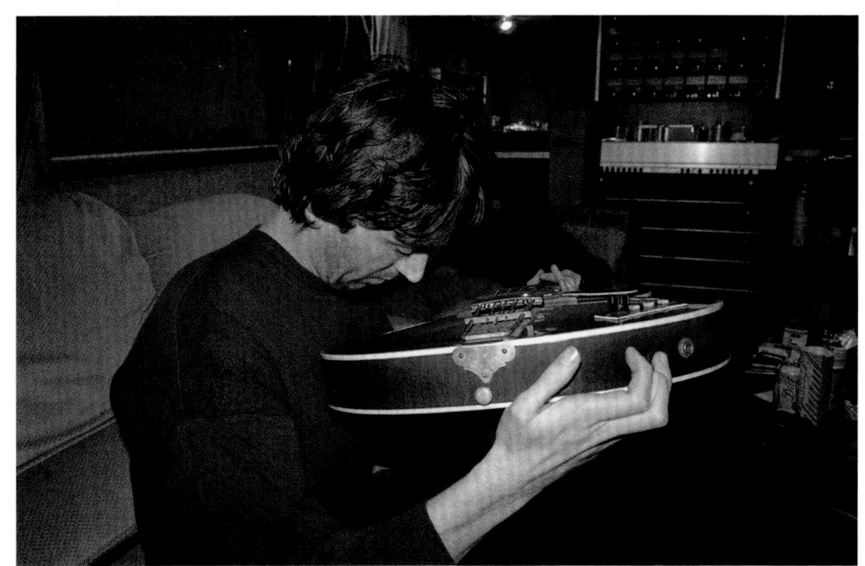

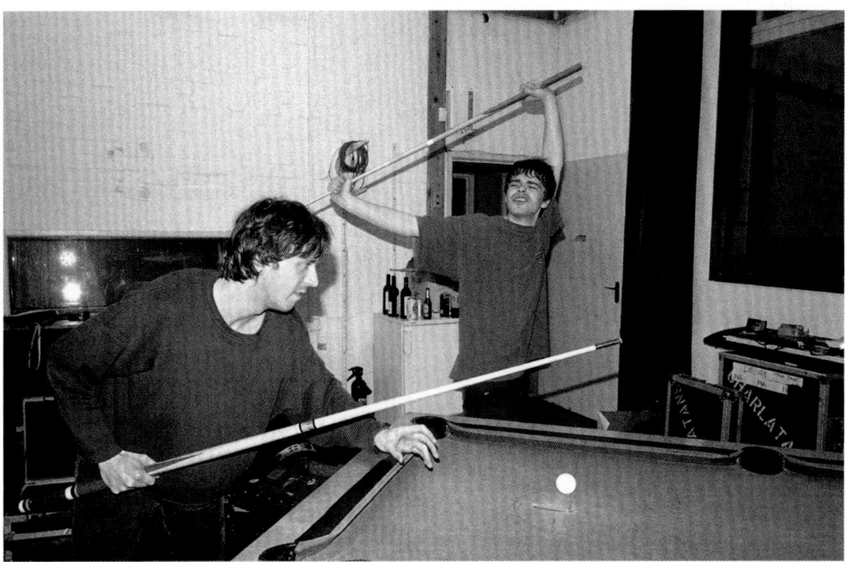

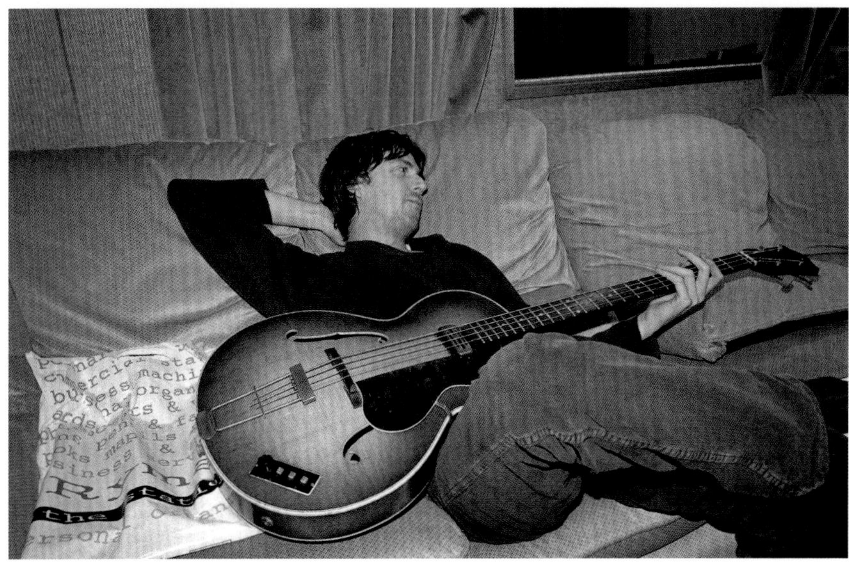

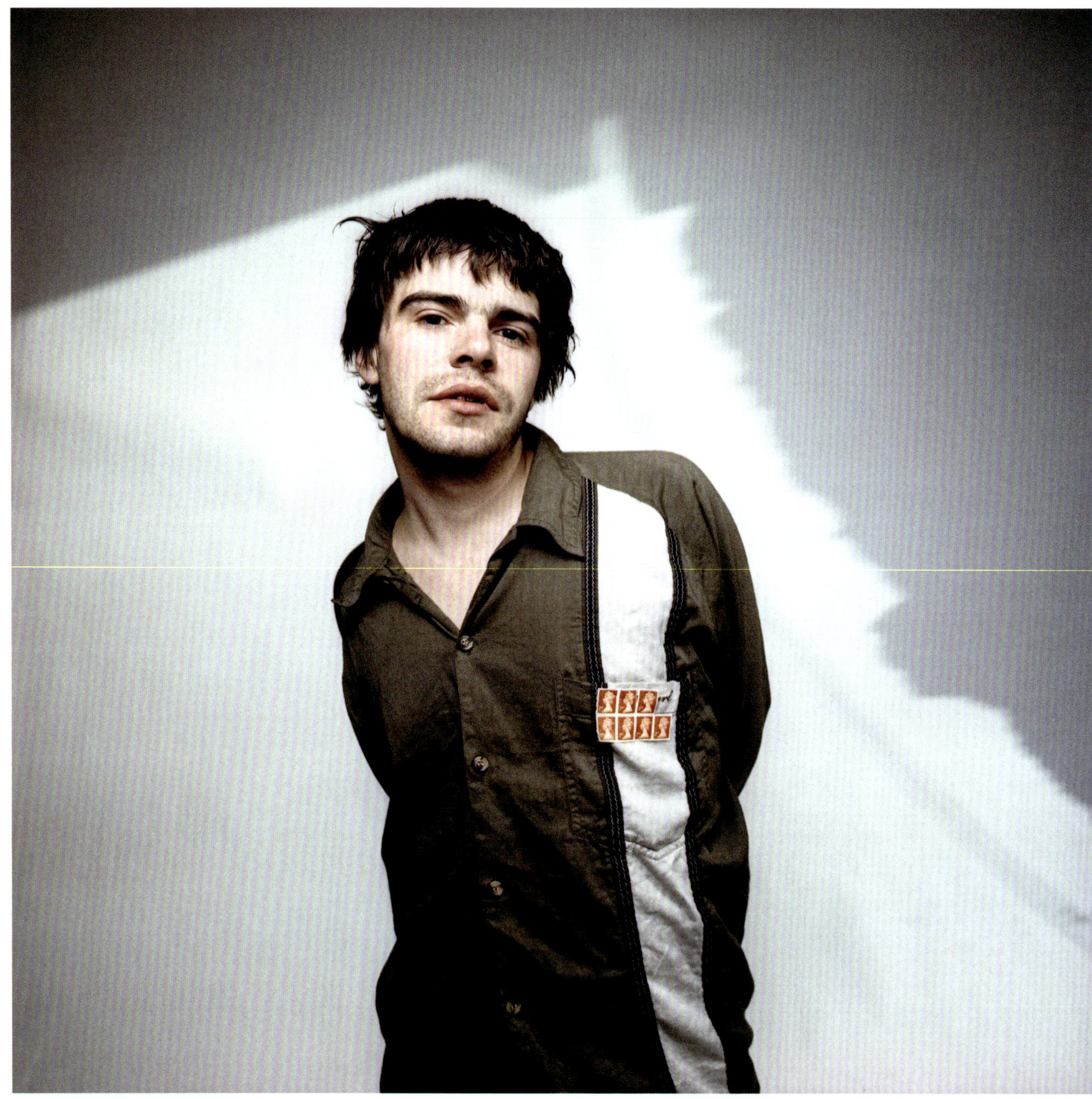

It was the final day of recording *Tellin' Stories*, a non-specific shoot that ended up as the sleeve for "How High". The final version was drenched in red, and in these original versions I am thinking I might be what they call "elegantly wasted".

Tom had given me a shout that I had ten minutes to get ready and for some reason I knew more than anything else that I had to have postage stamps stuck on me. First class, of course.

If you'd like an explanation of how or why I came up with this concept, I am no clearer now than I believe I was back then.

There is a small detail in the picture that, for me, places it back in those days. I was cutting my own hair so that dishevelled look is self-inflicted, but Photoshop would have zapped that pesky sprig on the left and brightened up my cheeks somewhat. But that was the thing back then, we didn't know which photoshoots would work and which wouldn't, so we dutifully jumped to it when Tom shouted. Some ended up as promo shots, some went on sleeves, some were put on ice until Tom sent them through to look at for this book.

While Martin Duffy stepped in to help us with live commitments, TV and even the final touches on *Tellin' Stories*, we missed everything about Rob, especially the more subtle elements he brought to the band – his leadership, his general demeanour on stage and his skill in the studio. As a lead vocalist I was at the front of the stage and the front of the mix shouting, "look at me". Rob would always choose the perfect moment and line to harmonize, bringing out the best in the songs. I felt so much

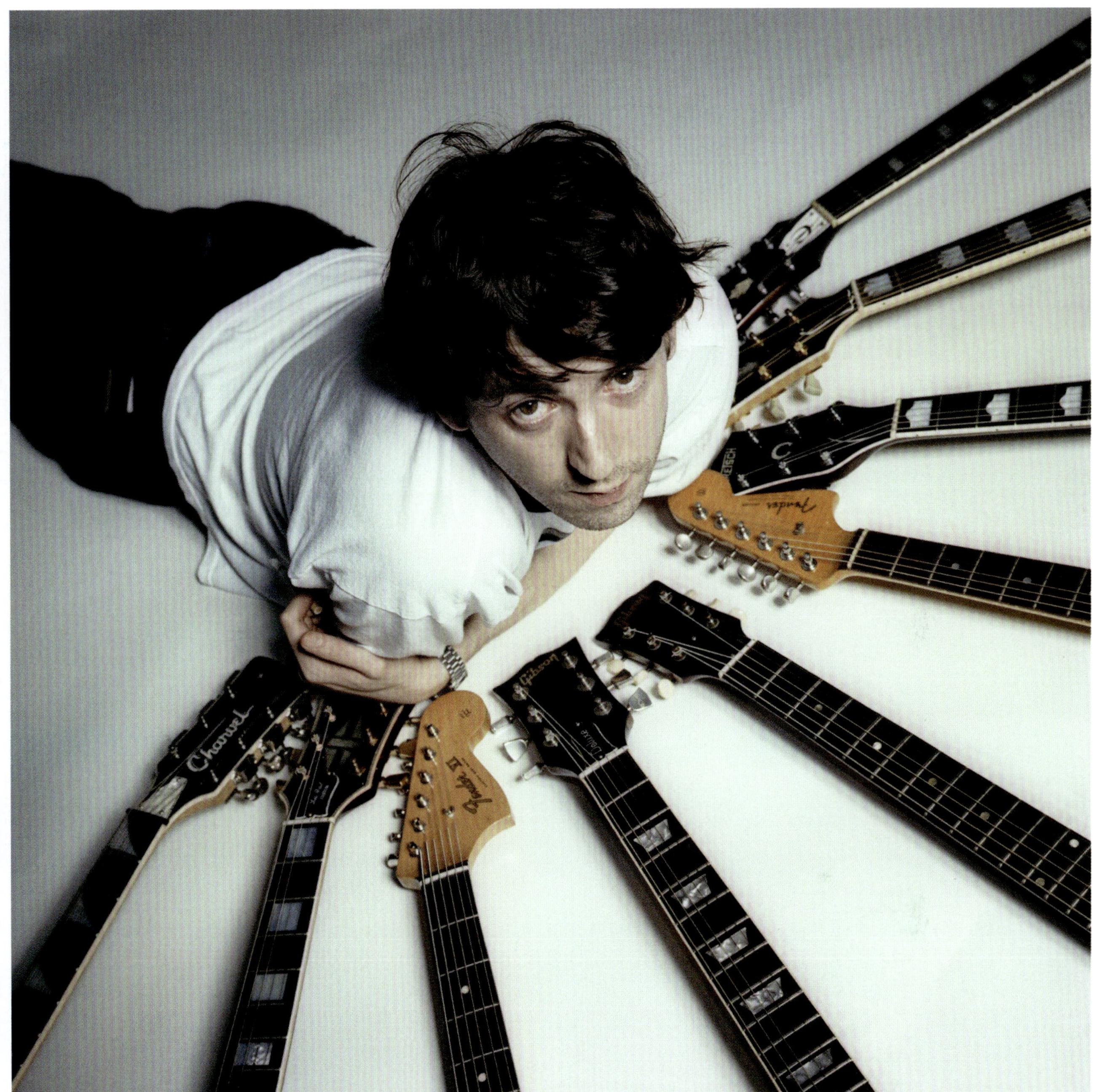

more weight on my shoulders, but it was a privilege to take on Rob's backing vocals, which gave me a feeling of being closer to him at the time I needed it most.

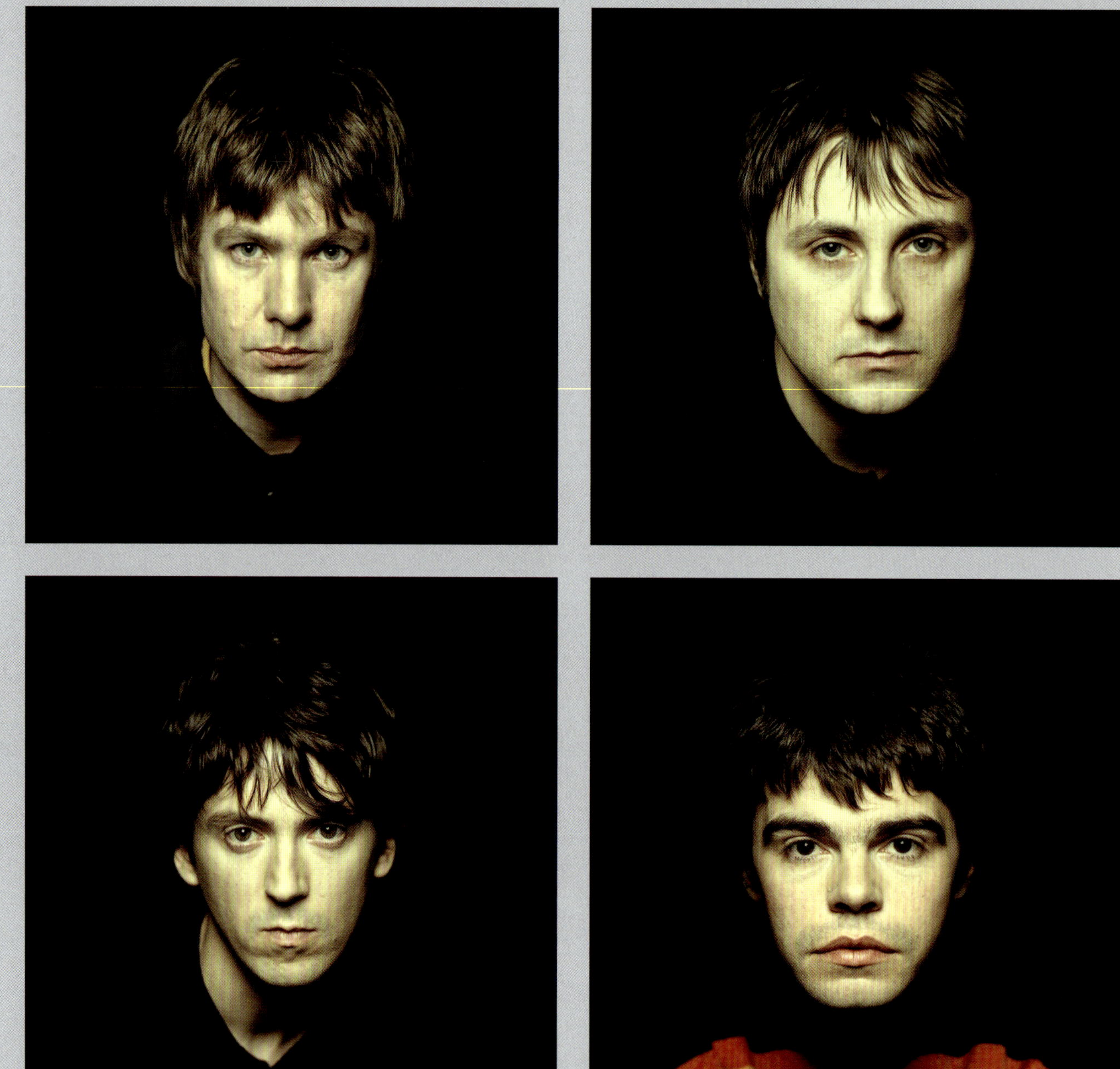

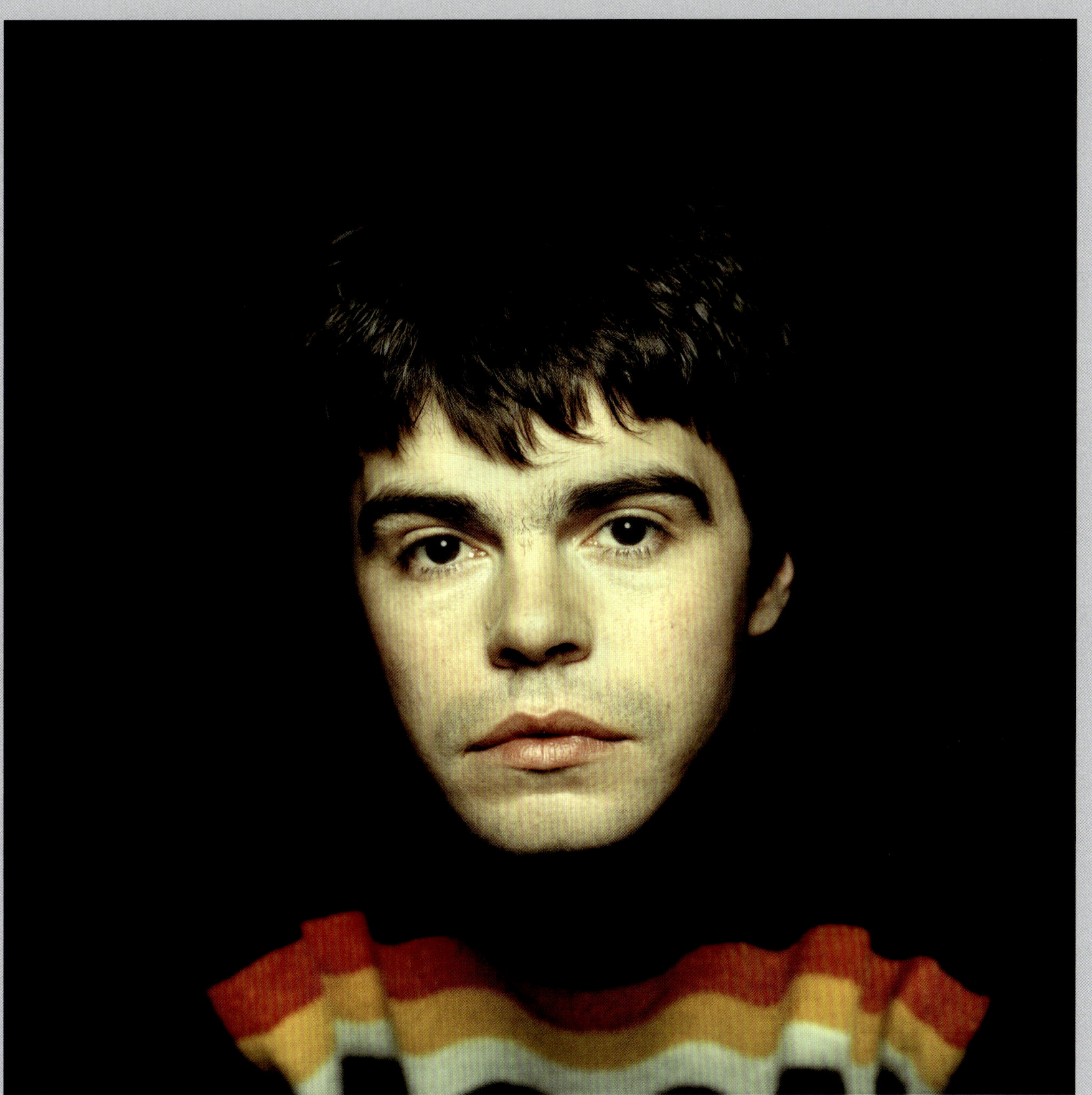

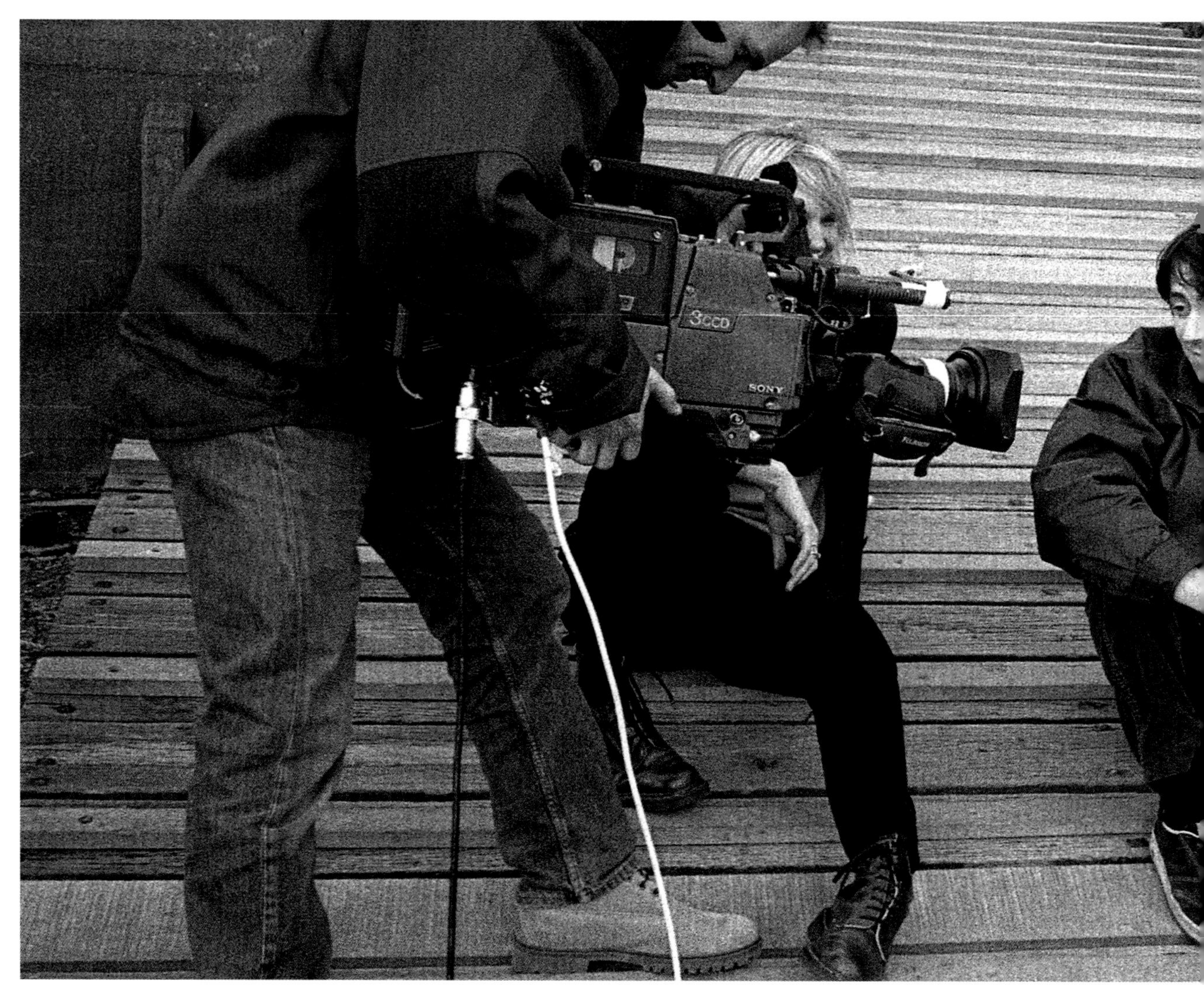
3CCD
SONY

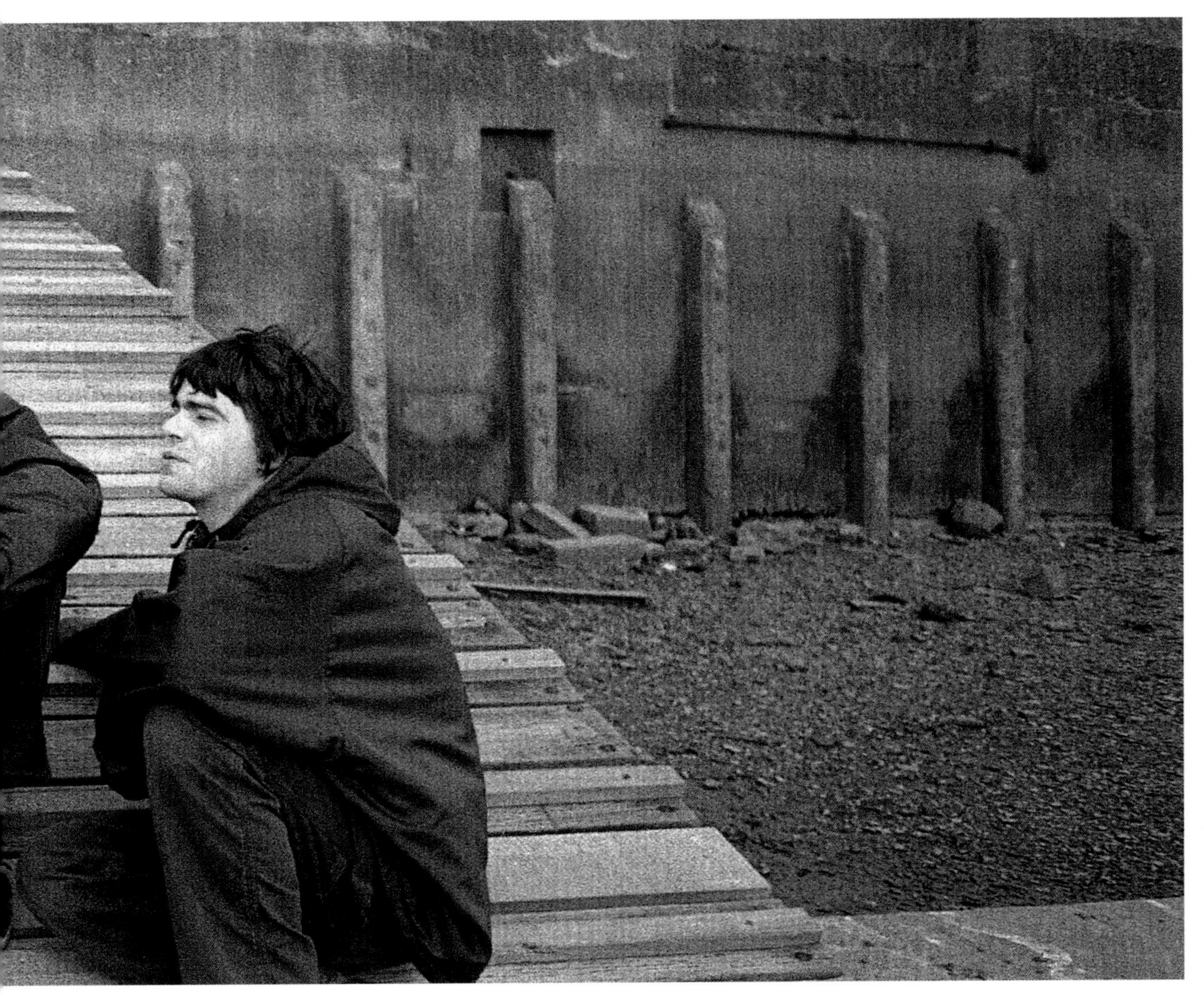

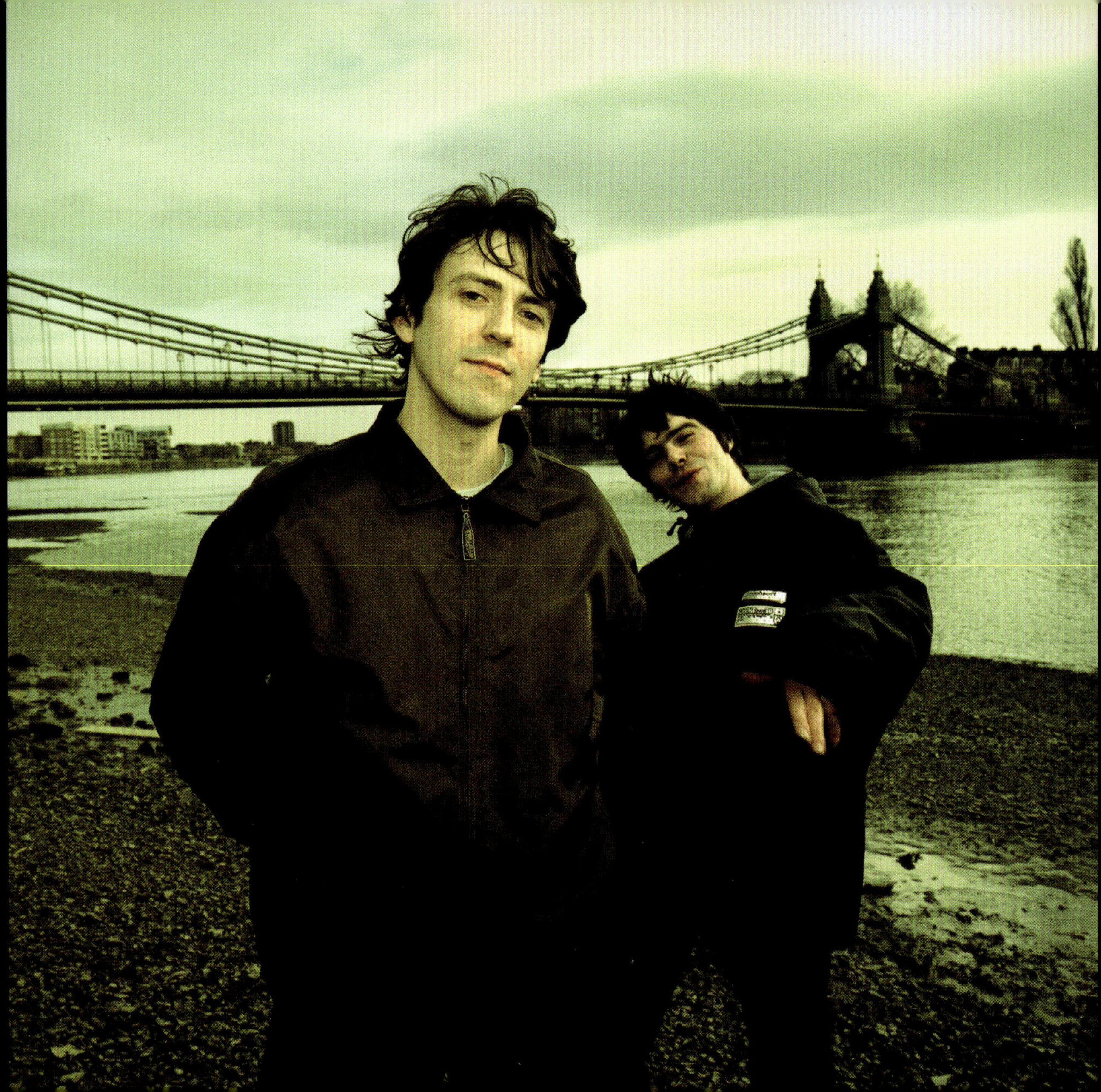

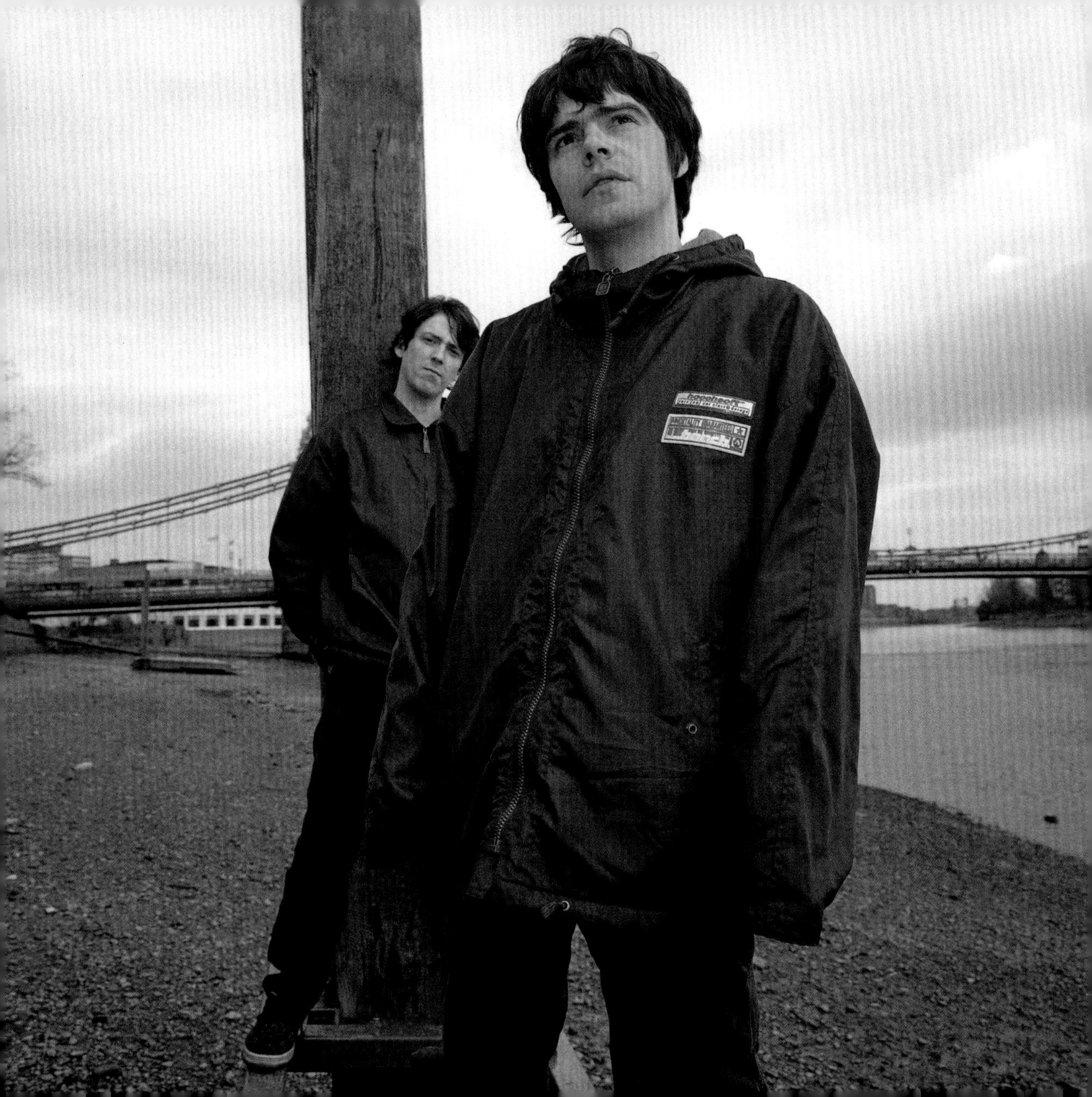

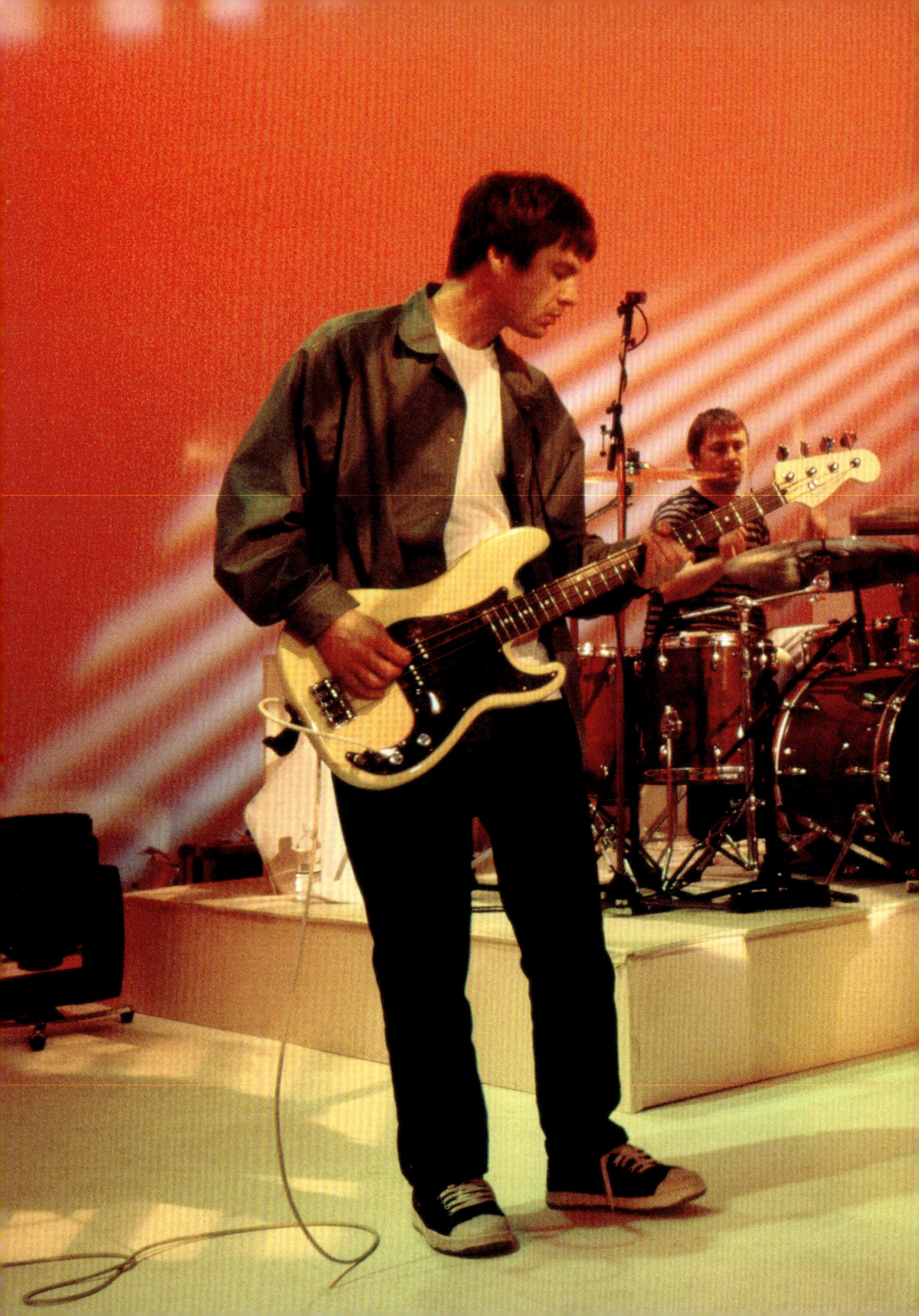

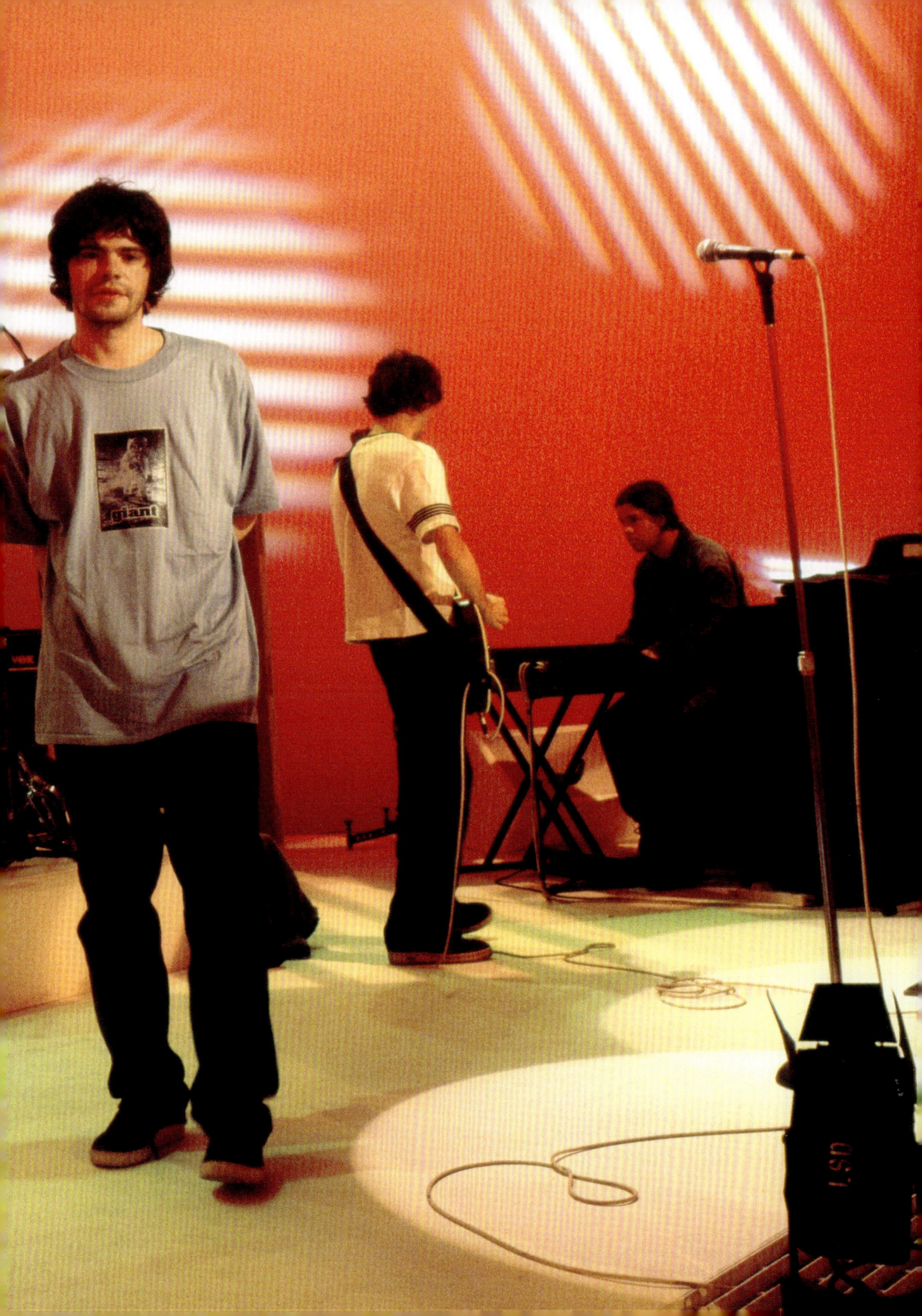
giant

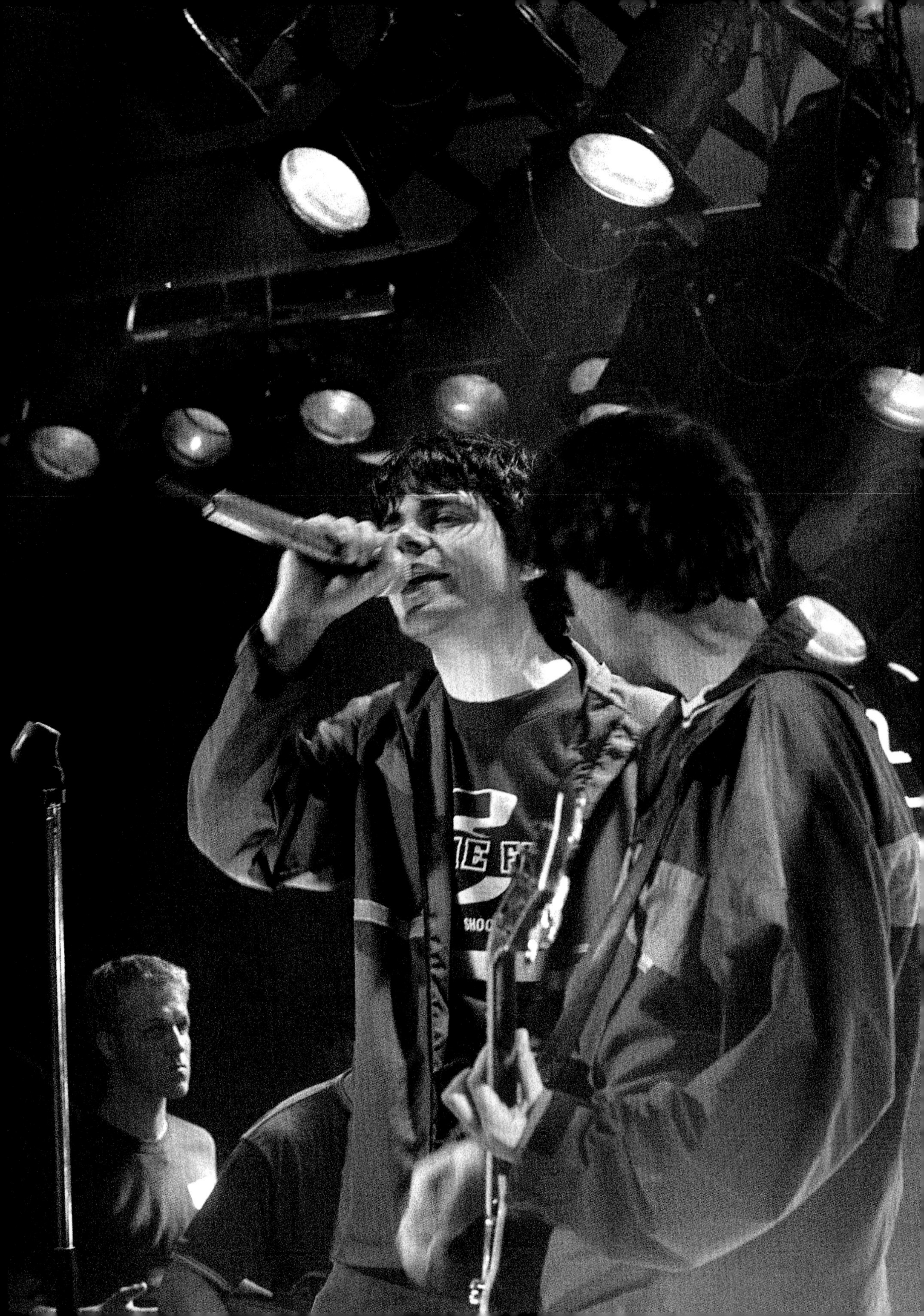

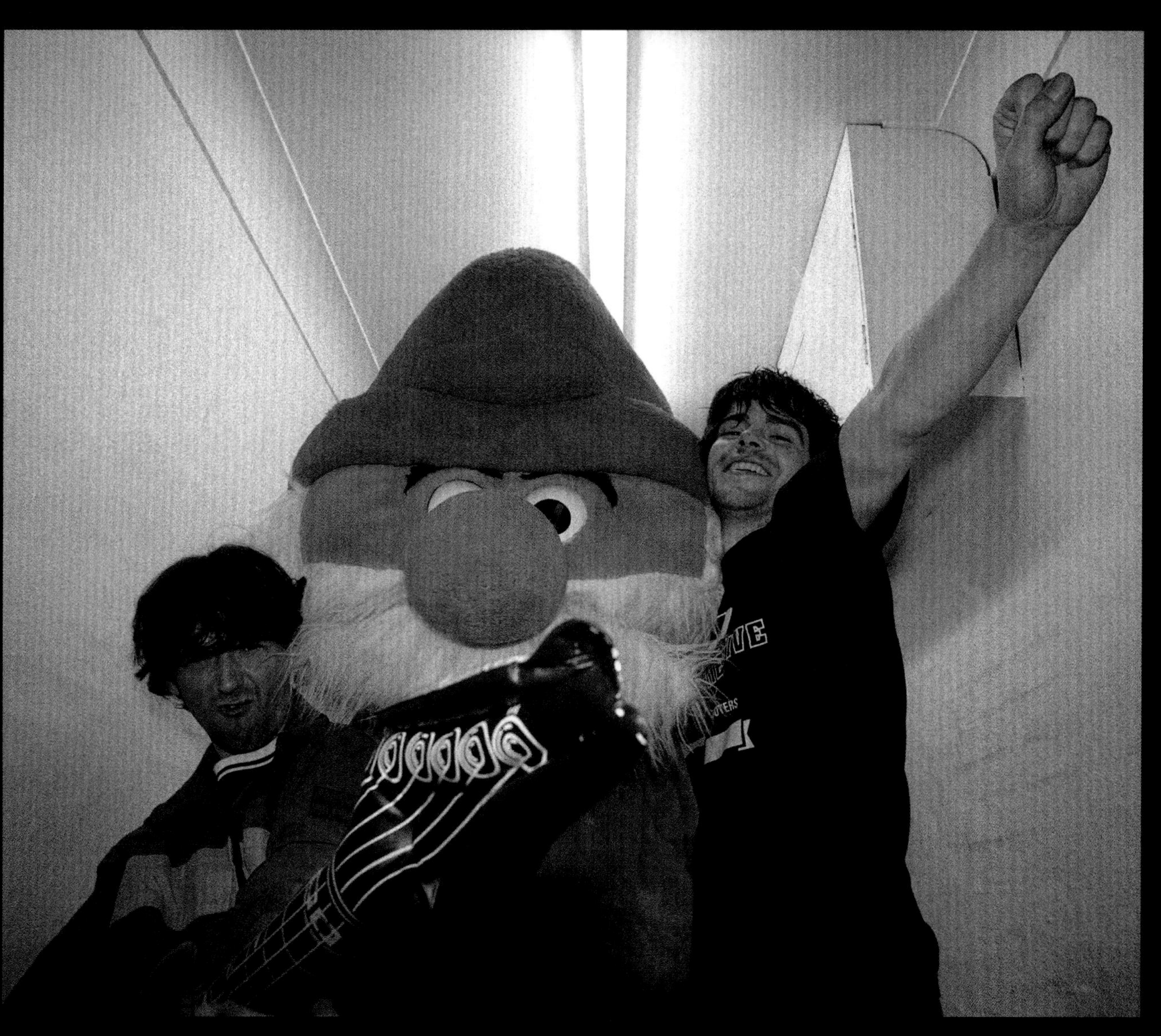

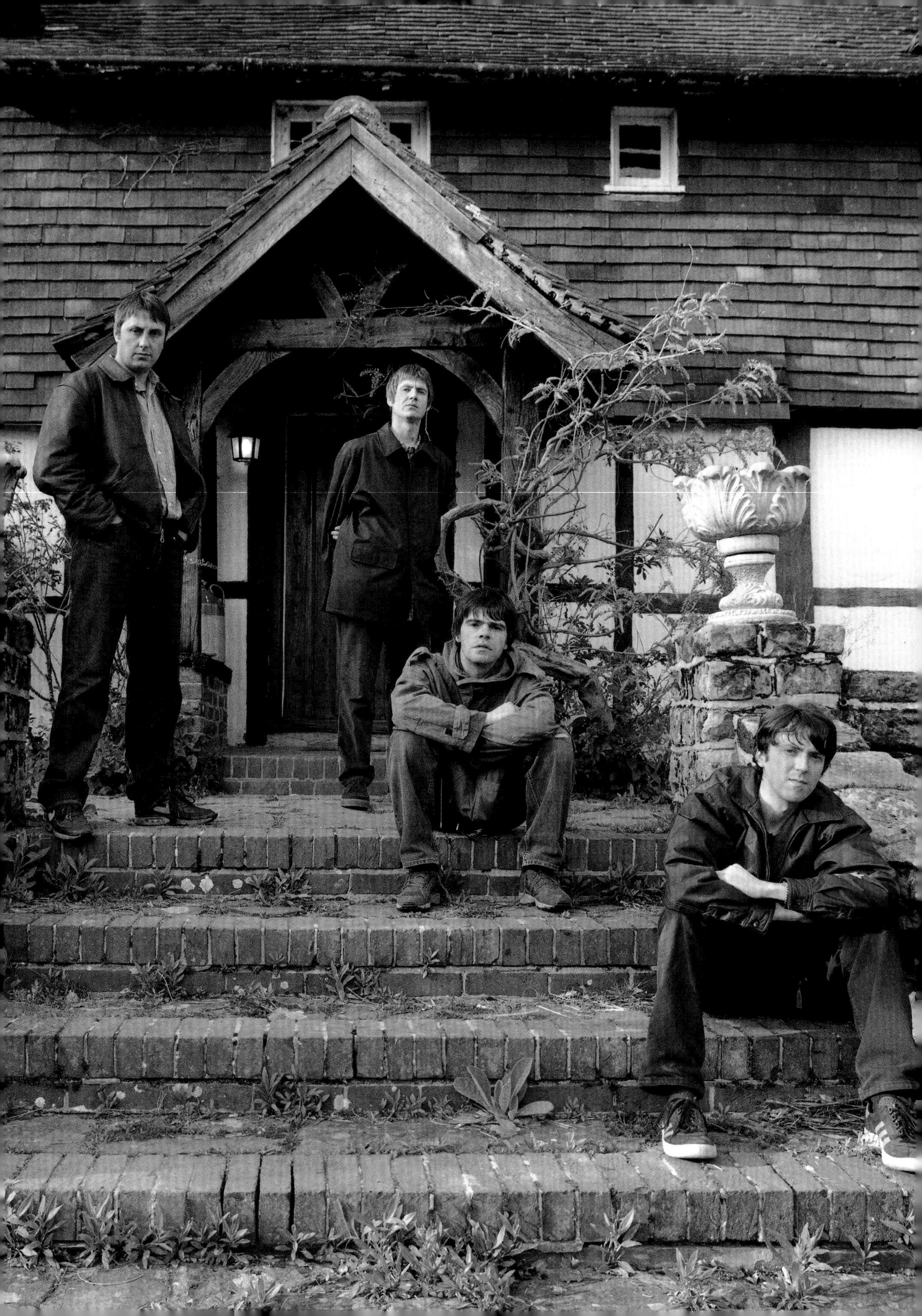

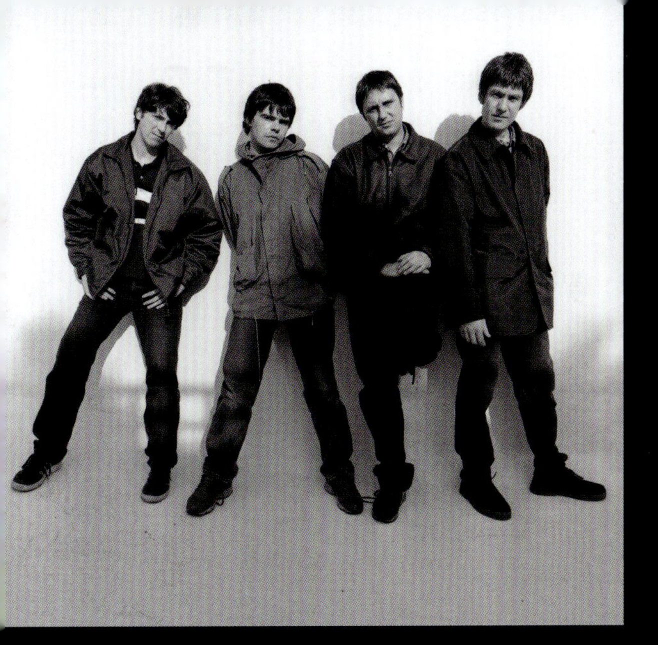

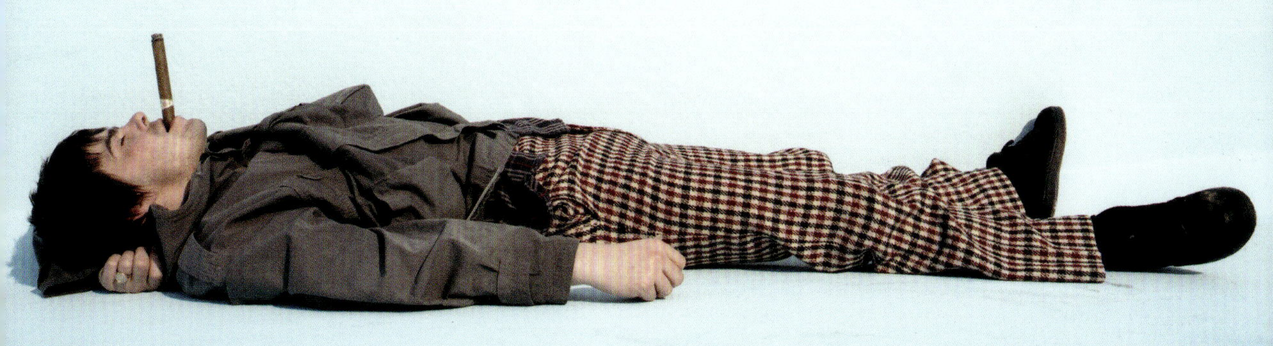

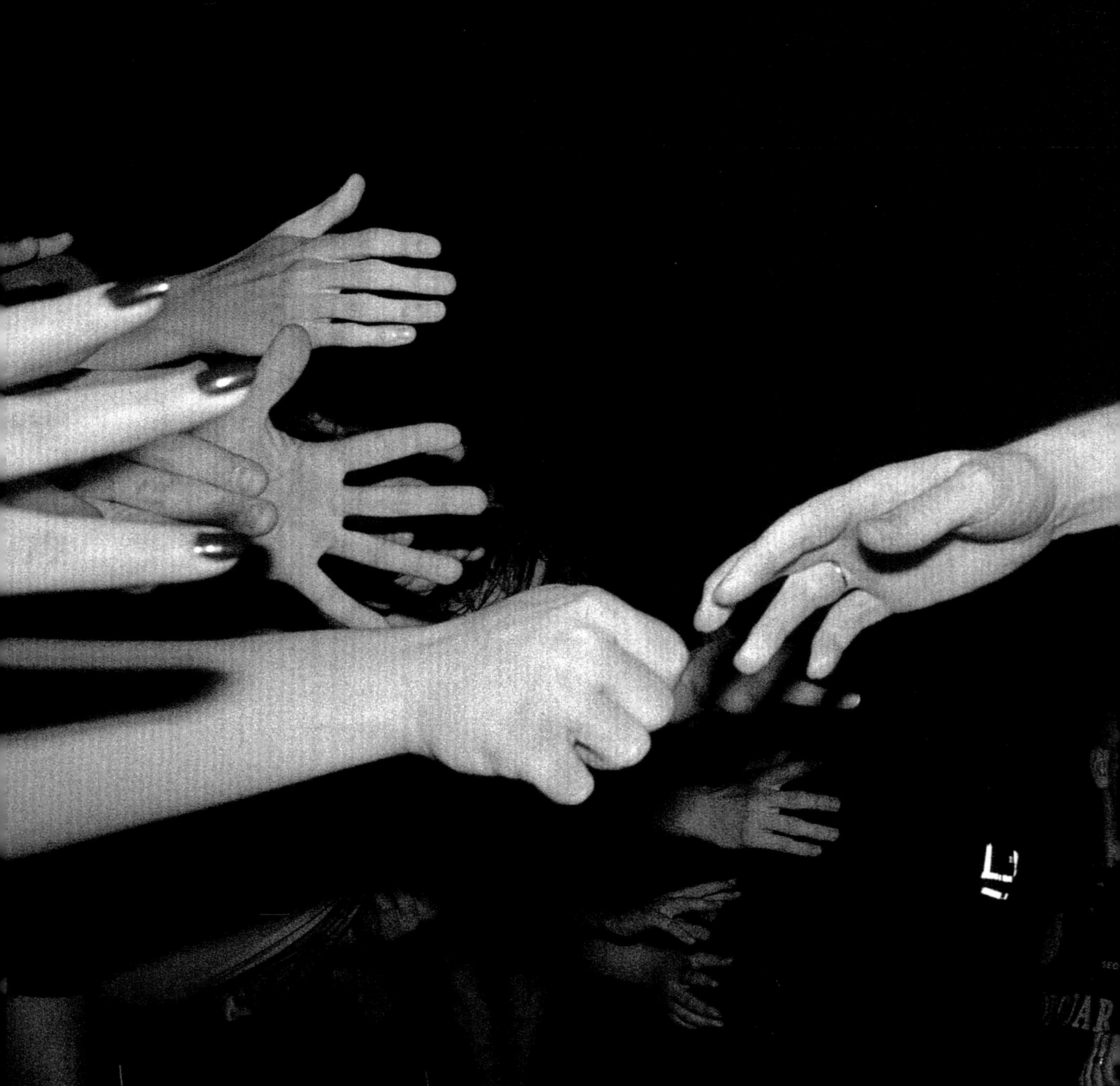

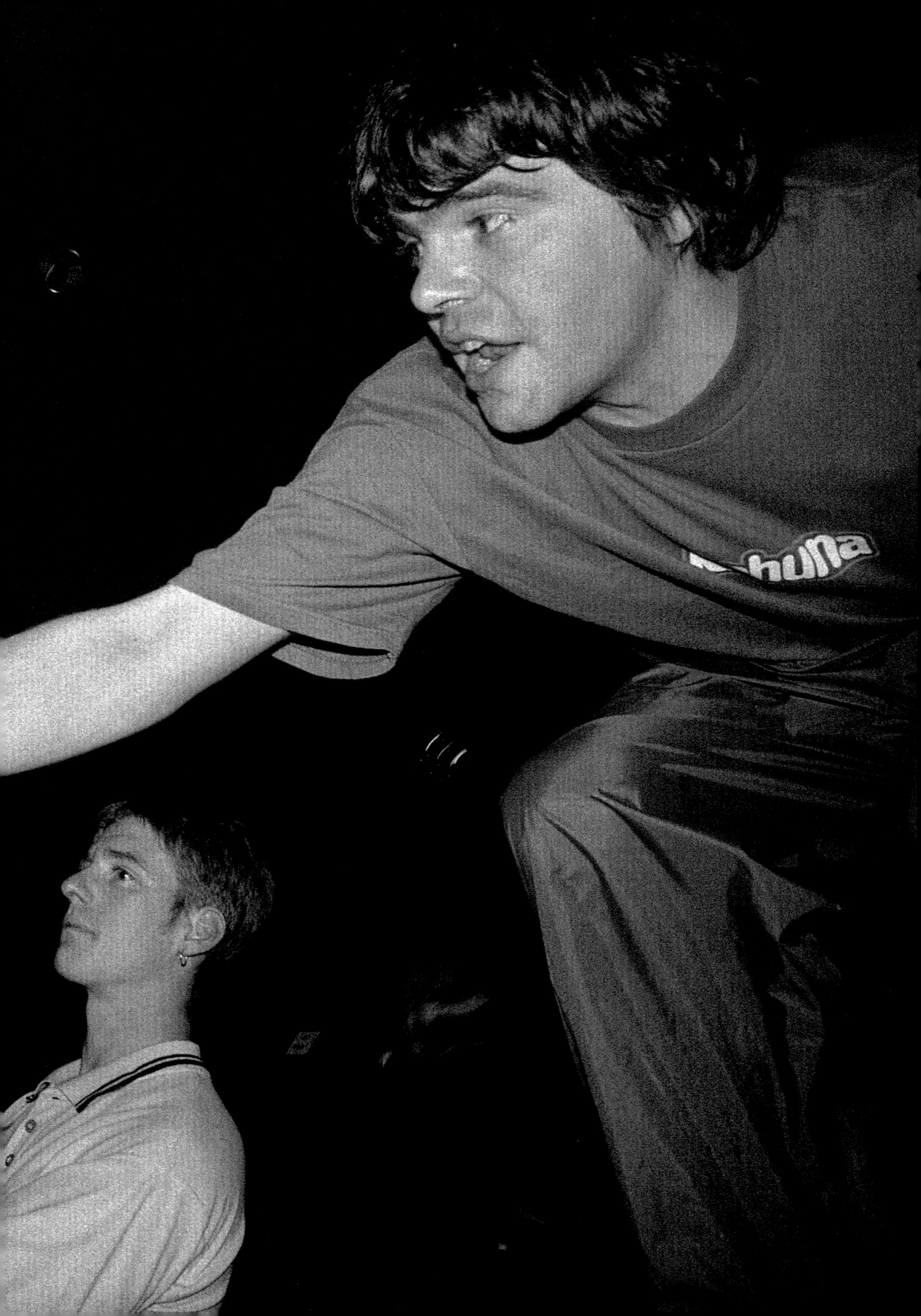

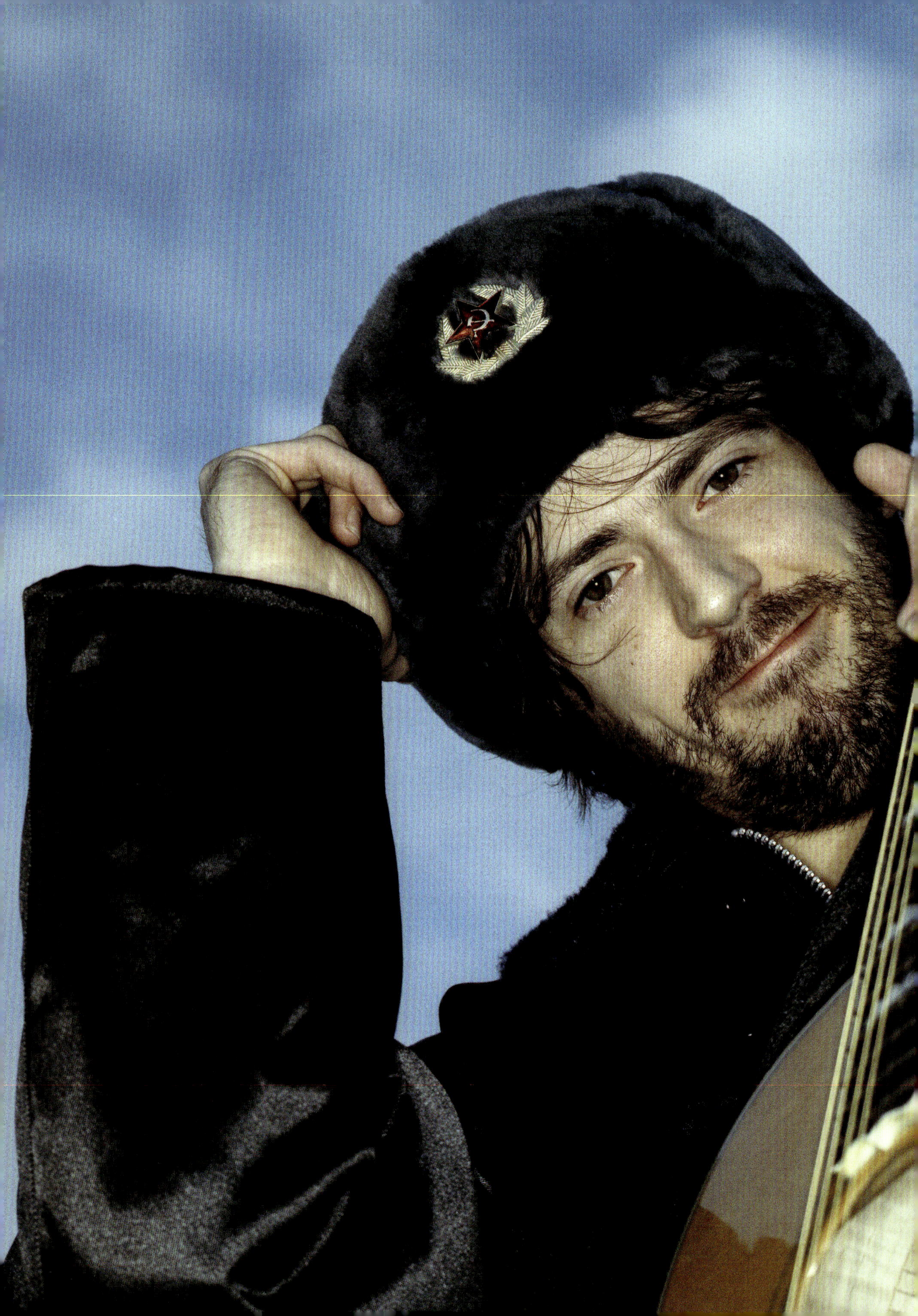

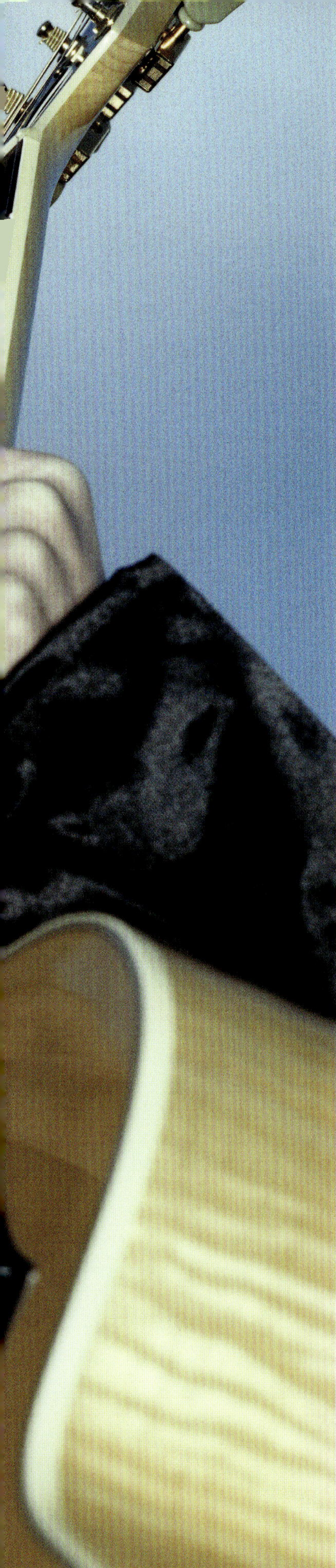

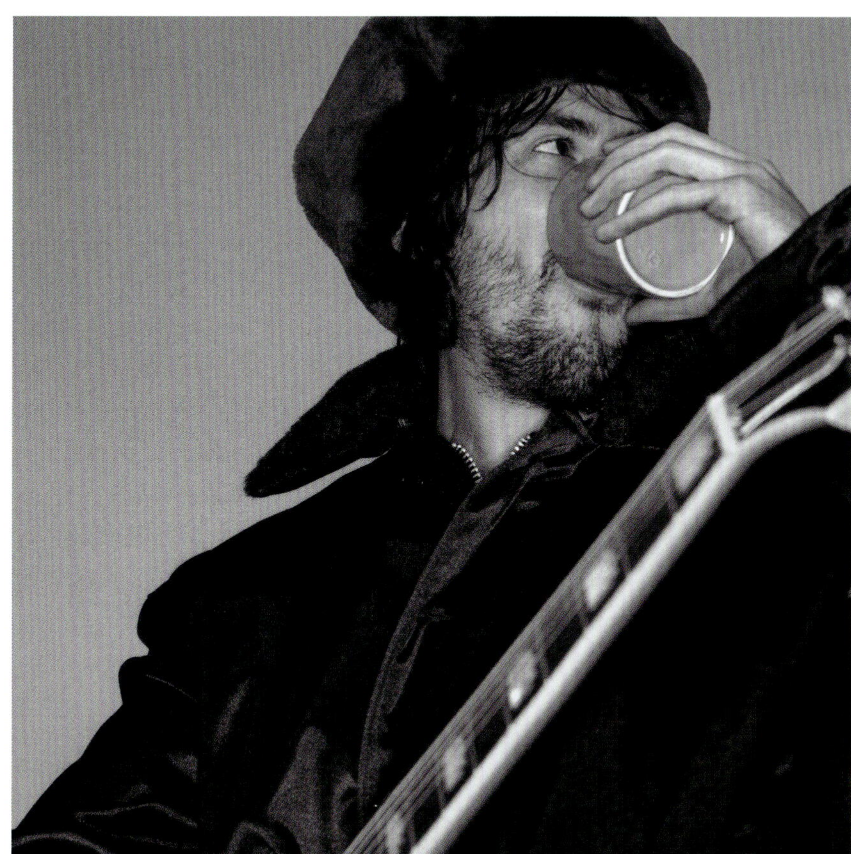

I was keen that the other band members featured on single sleeves on their own, if I was going to. Mark was the newest arrival. Jon had featured on "Indian Rope", Rob on "The Only One I Know", Jon Baker was on the sleeve of "Then", Martin on "Me. In Time".

Tom's idea was to do an homage to *Nashville Skyline*, with Mark's Russian winter hat replacing Bob Dylan's Stetson. Everything else remained pretty much the same, and we were all pleased with the results.

Tom:
Tim and I are Bob Dylan fans and this was our homage to *Nashville Skyline*. The back cover of the original had a photo of the actual Nashville skyline, so our idea – just a bit of fun – was to have a shot of the Manchester skyline instead. It never quite happened for one reason or another, so instead I ended up on a flyover in Croydon, and it's the Croydon skyline we used. It's just a little joke, we tried not to be too serious about these things. The music was the important thing, then came the covers. There's got to be humour in the process somewhere.

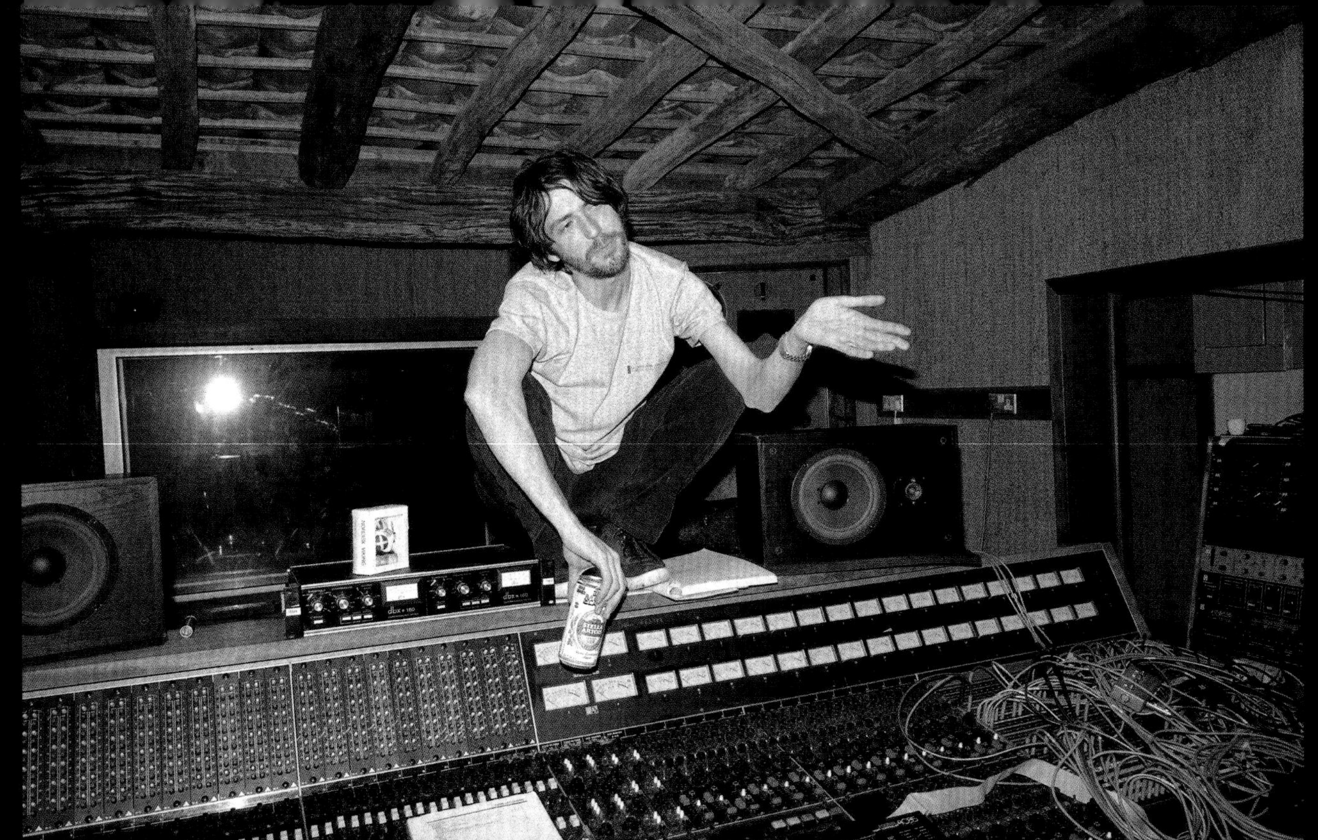

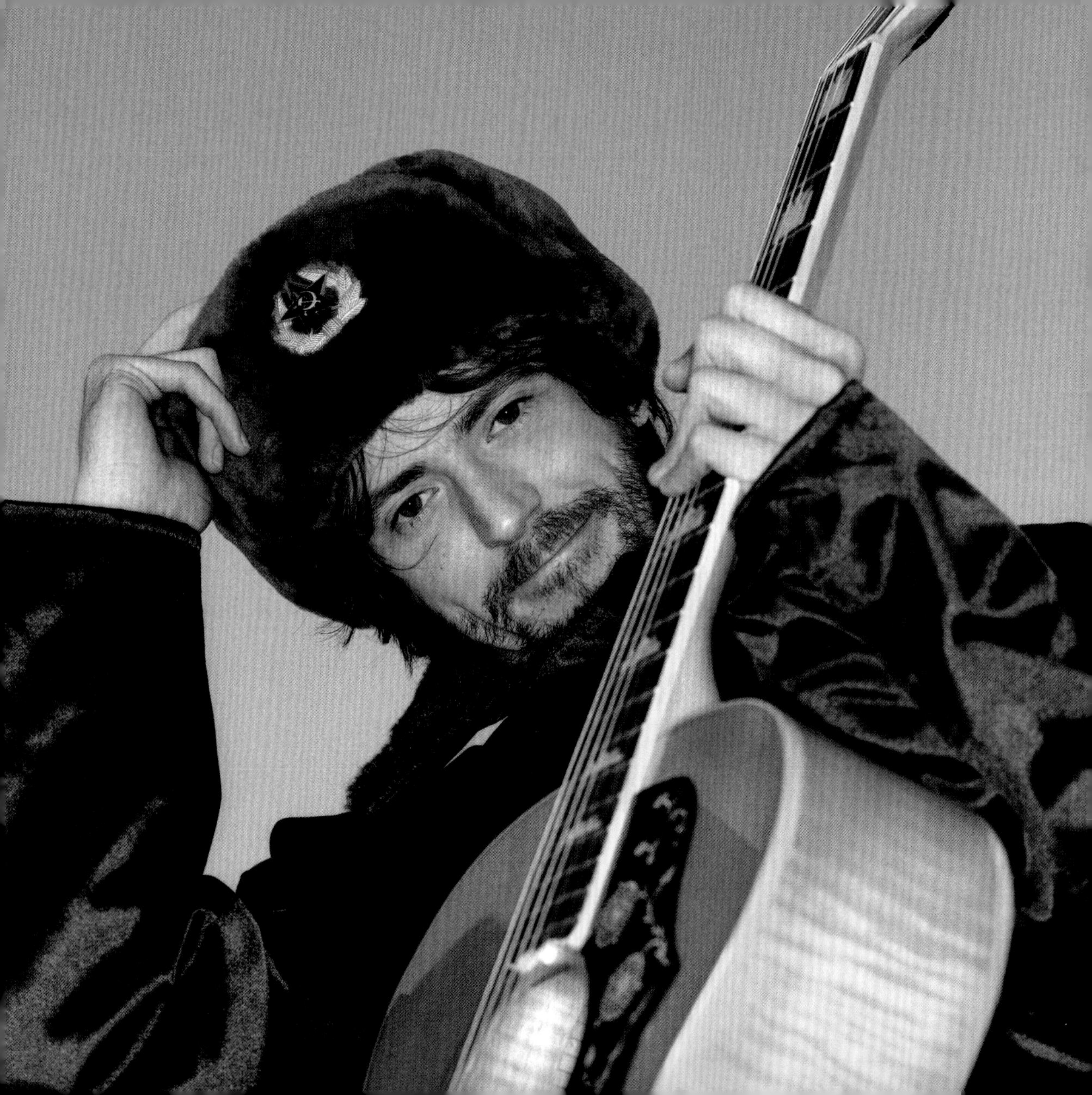

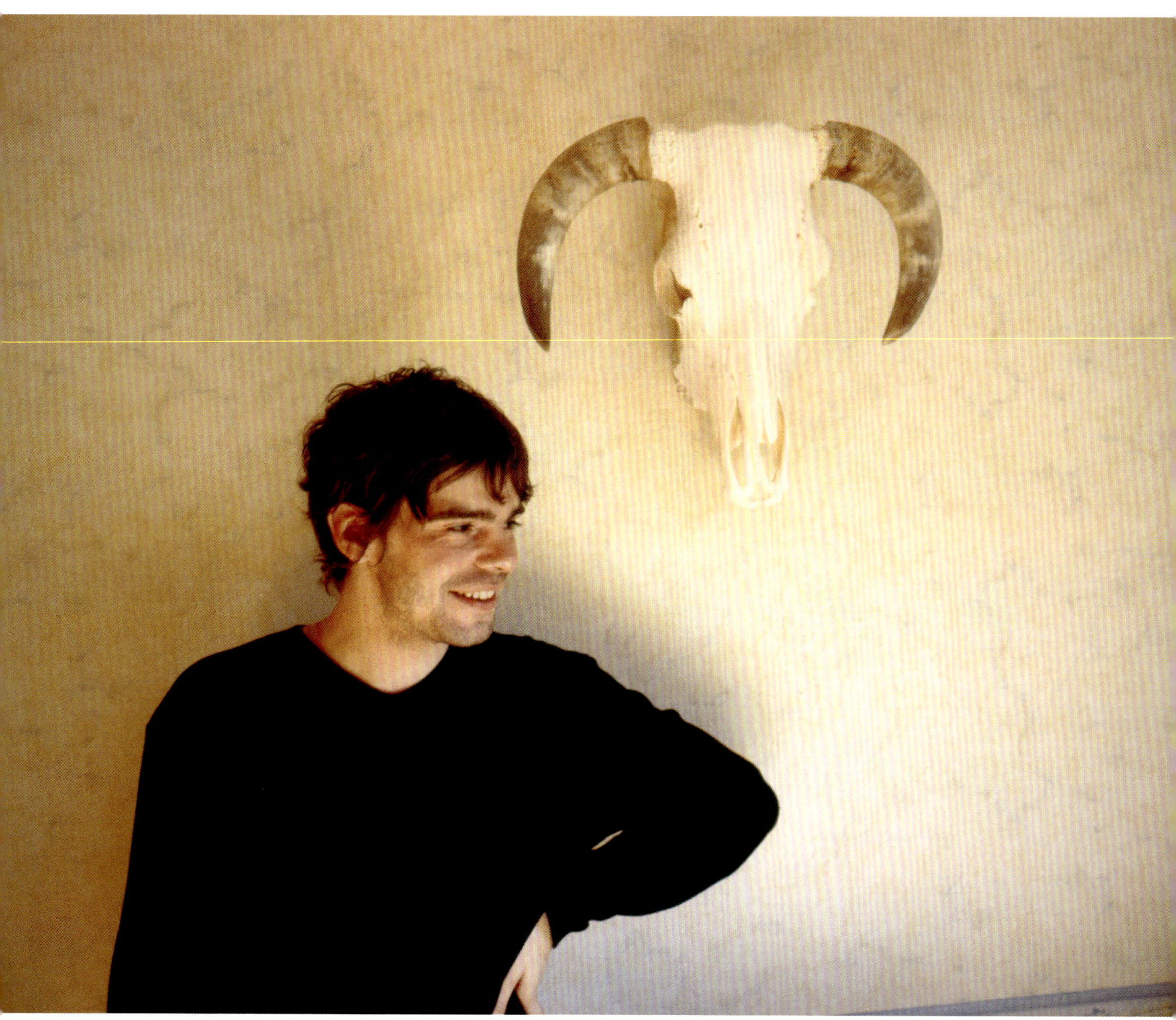

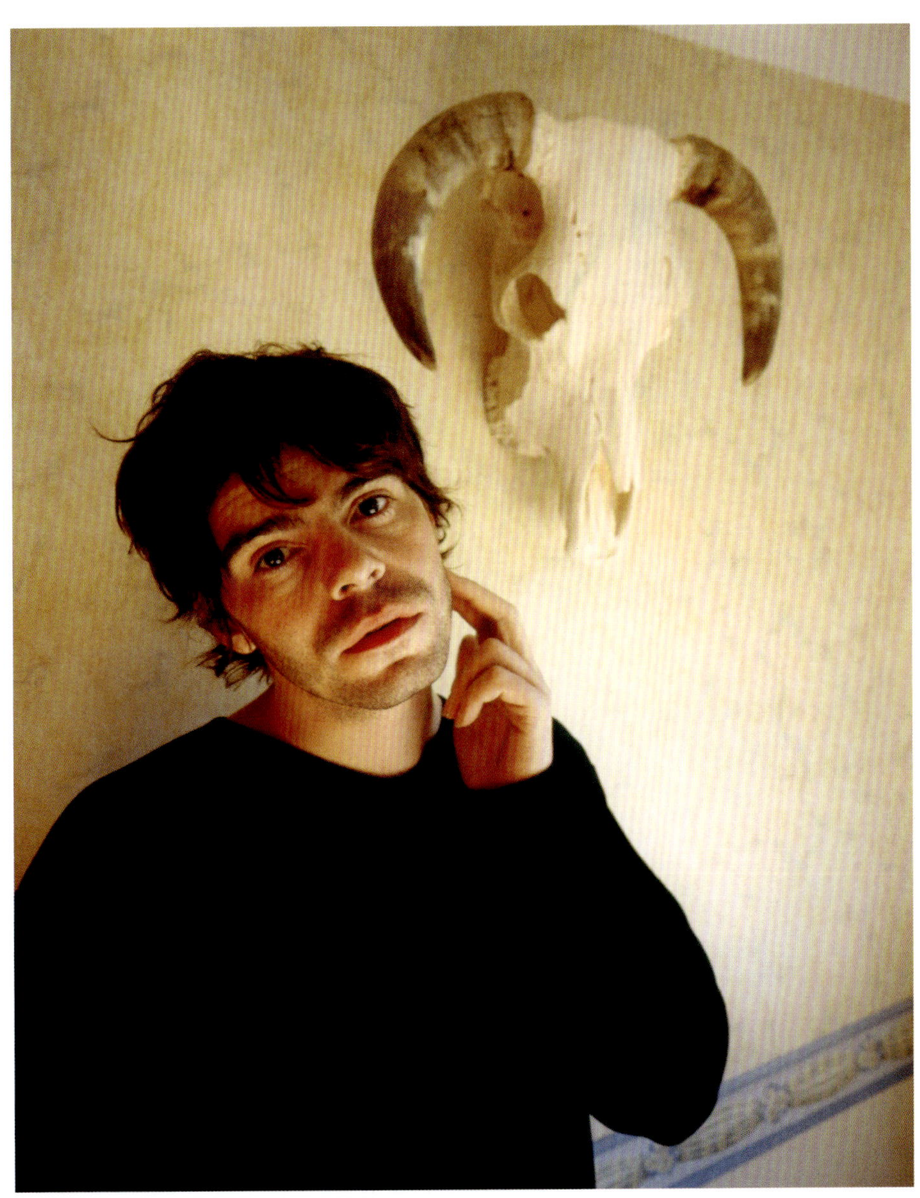

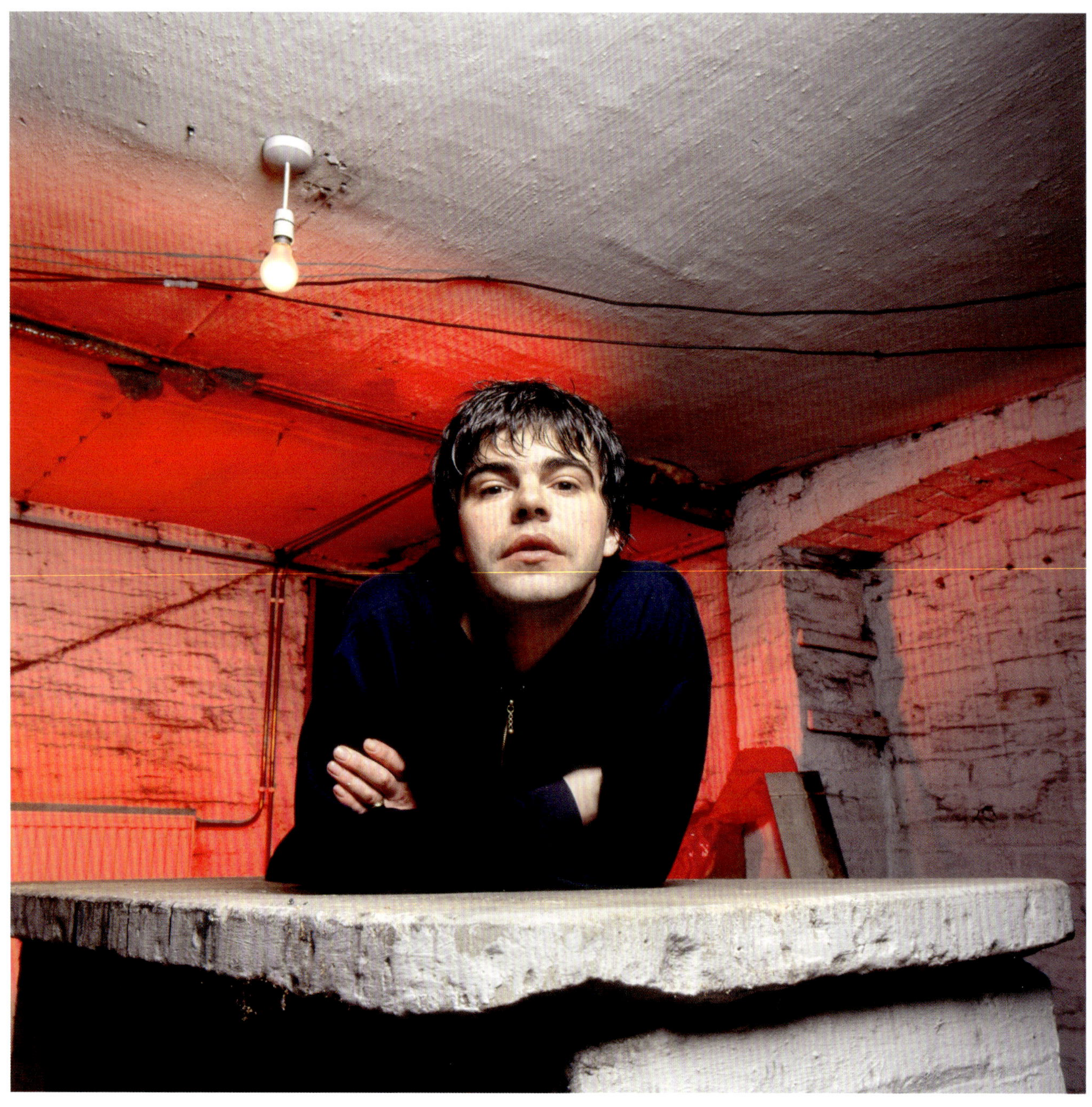

1998, in the basement of my old house on Victoria Avenue in Didsbury, Greater Manchester. Occasionally Tom would just pop round, and he always had a camera on him. That's how we would converse and communicate, and it was a form of therapy for both of us. That year was a strange time for us; we'd had our most successful album and a string of hit singles, but shortly after losing Rob we'd discovered that our accountant had been acting fraudulently, leaving a huge hole in our finances and a lot of unpaid taxes. It's a well-documented story that resulted in prison time for the accountant and for us a long period playing gigs to pay back what we owed – and to earn back what was missing.

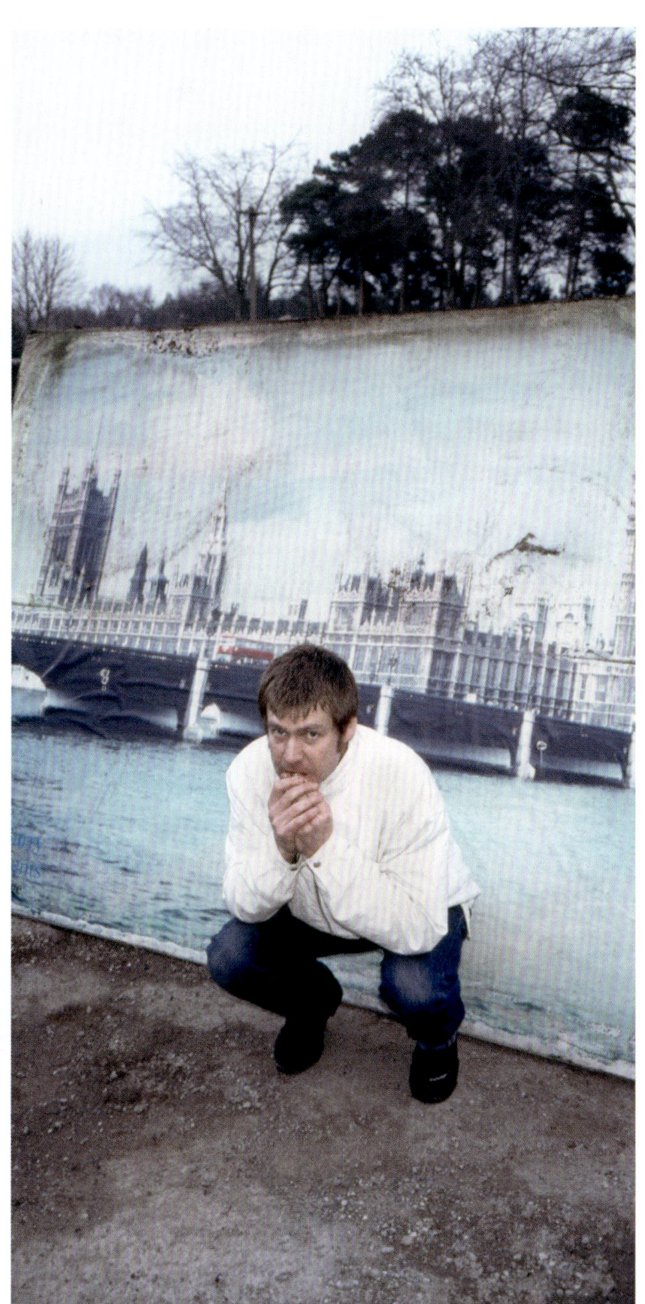

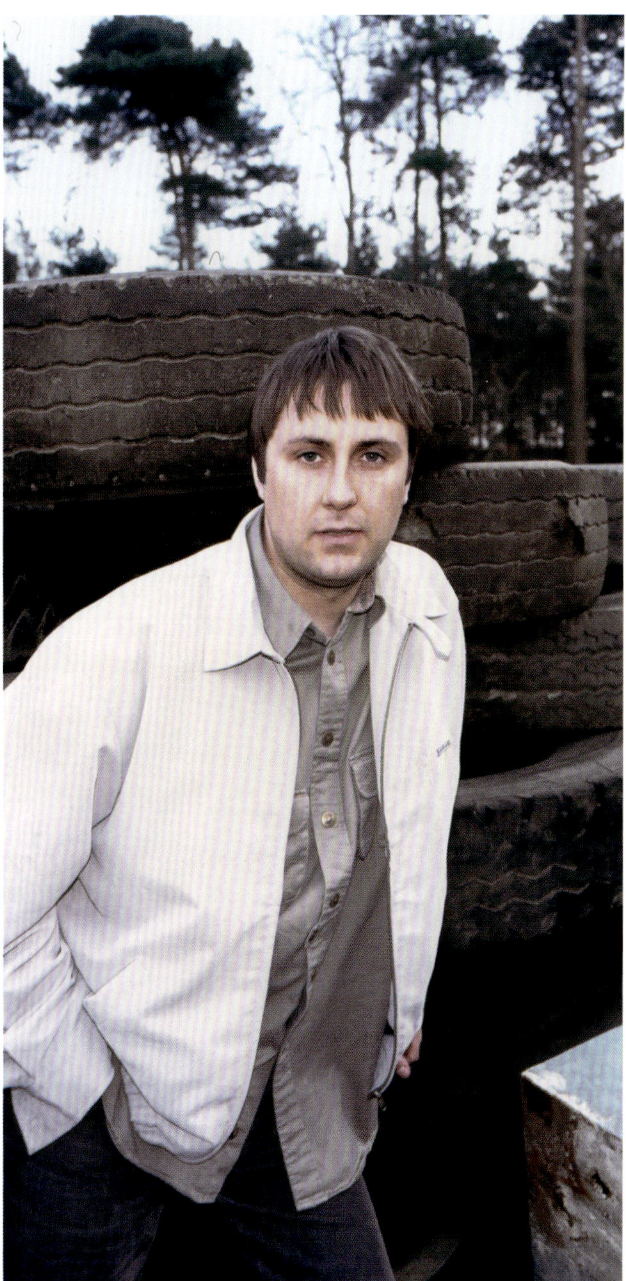

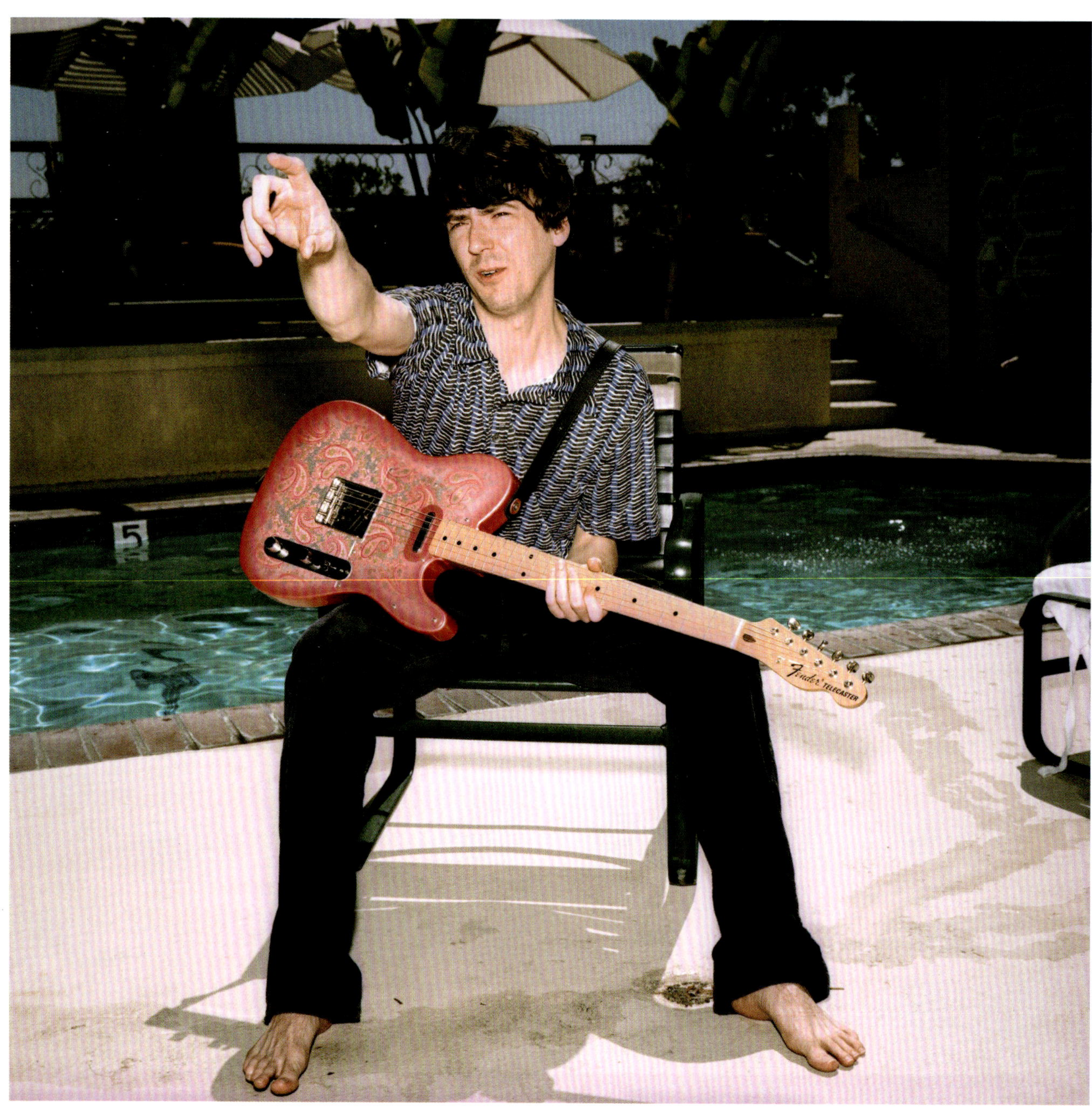

Swimming pool, check. Pink Telecaster, check.
Photo opportunity, check.

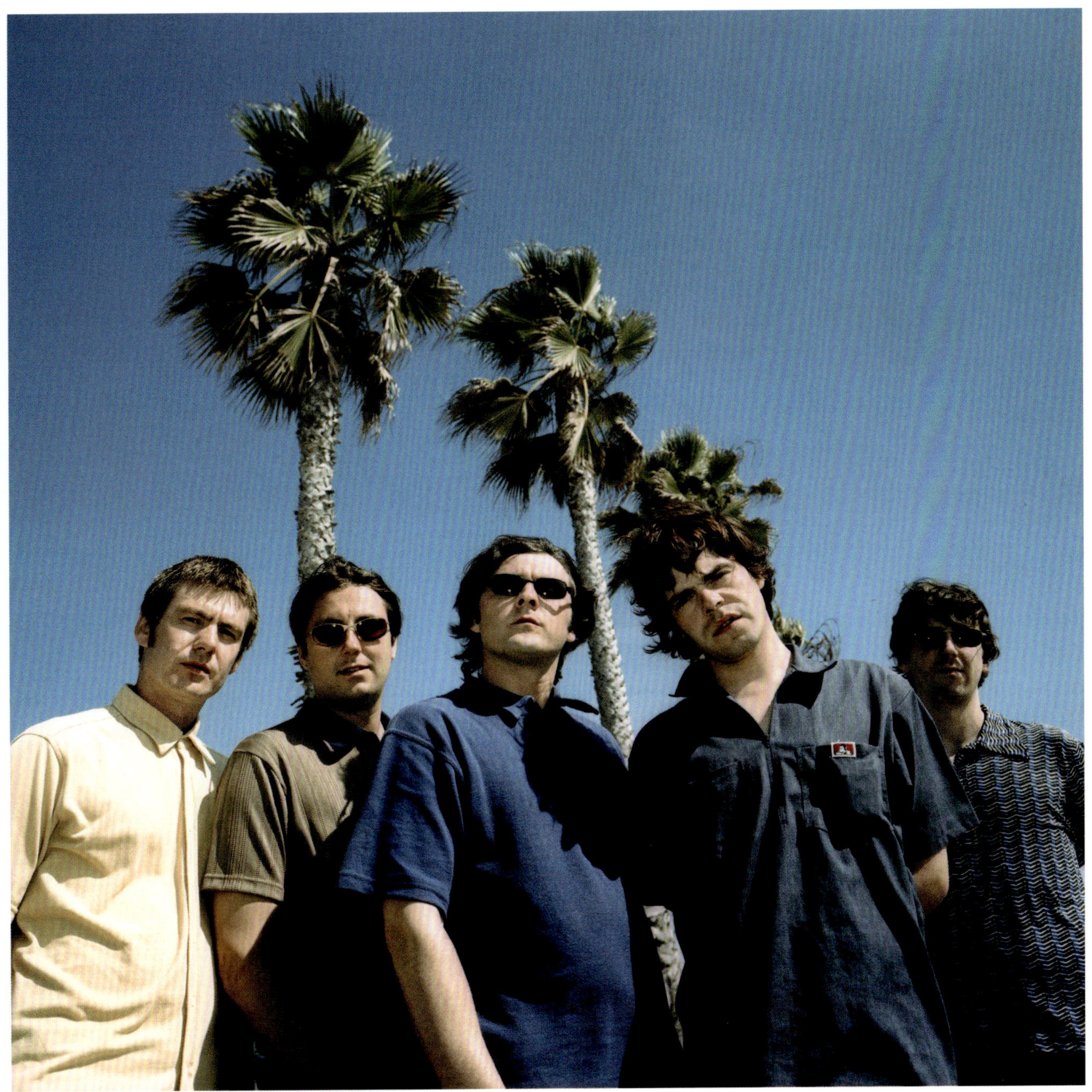

In 1998 we had a one-off show in Los Angeles, at the John Anson Ford Amphitheatre on a trip to play some dates in Japan. This was one of the first photoshoots with us back to being a five-piece, with Tony Rogers as our new keyboard player. Another huge part of Rob's role was his backing vocals, and as I've said many a time, he had a better singing voice than I have, so there was huge pressure on his replacement. But we knew we'd found the right person at Tony's first audition.

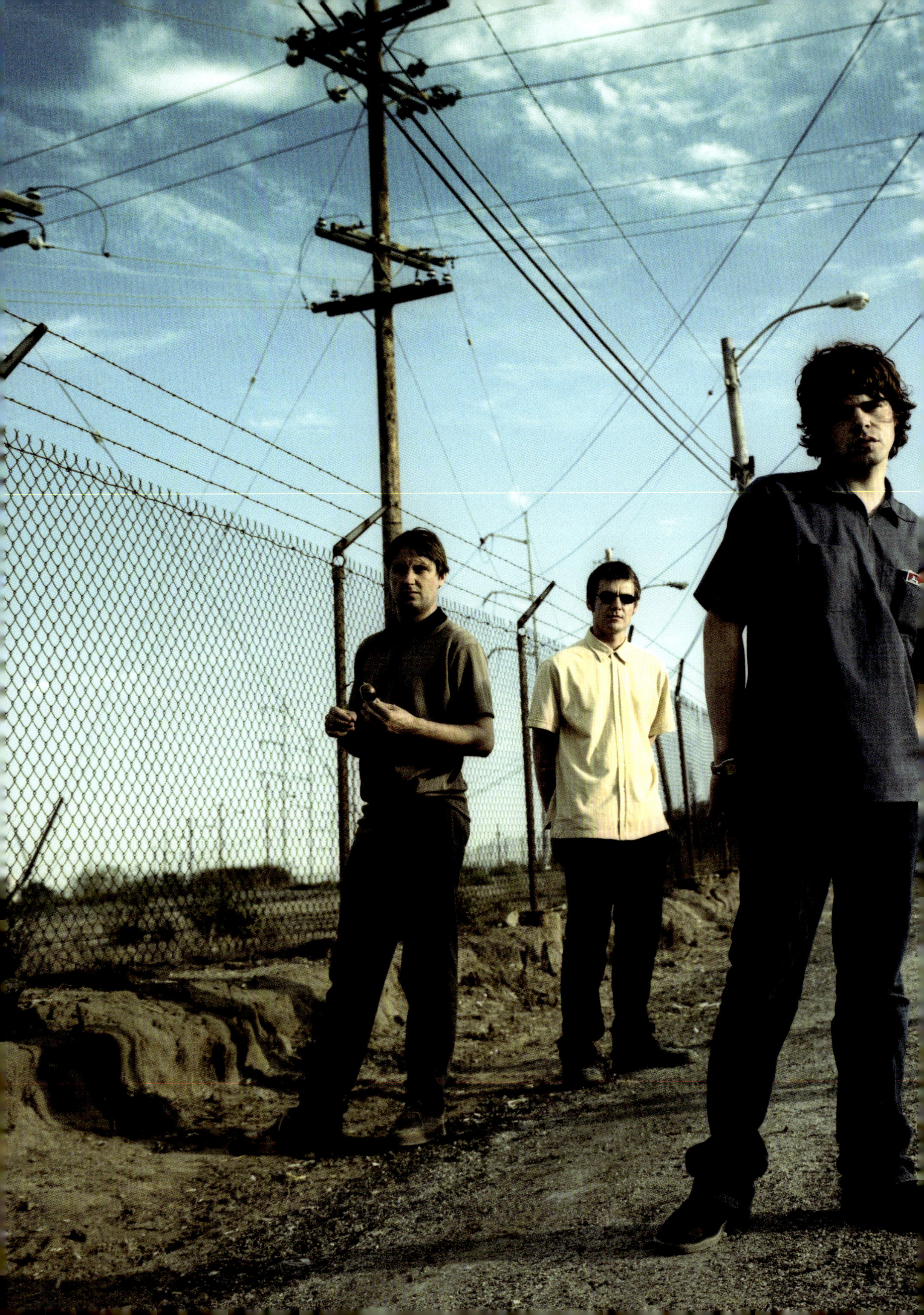

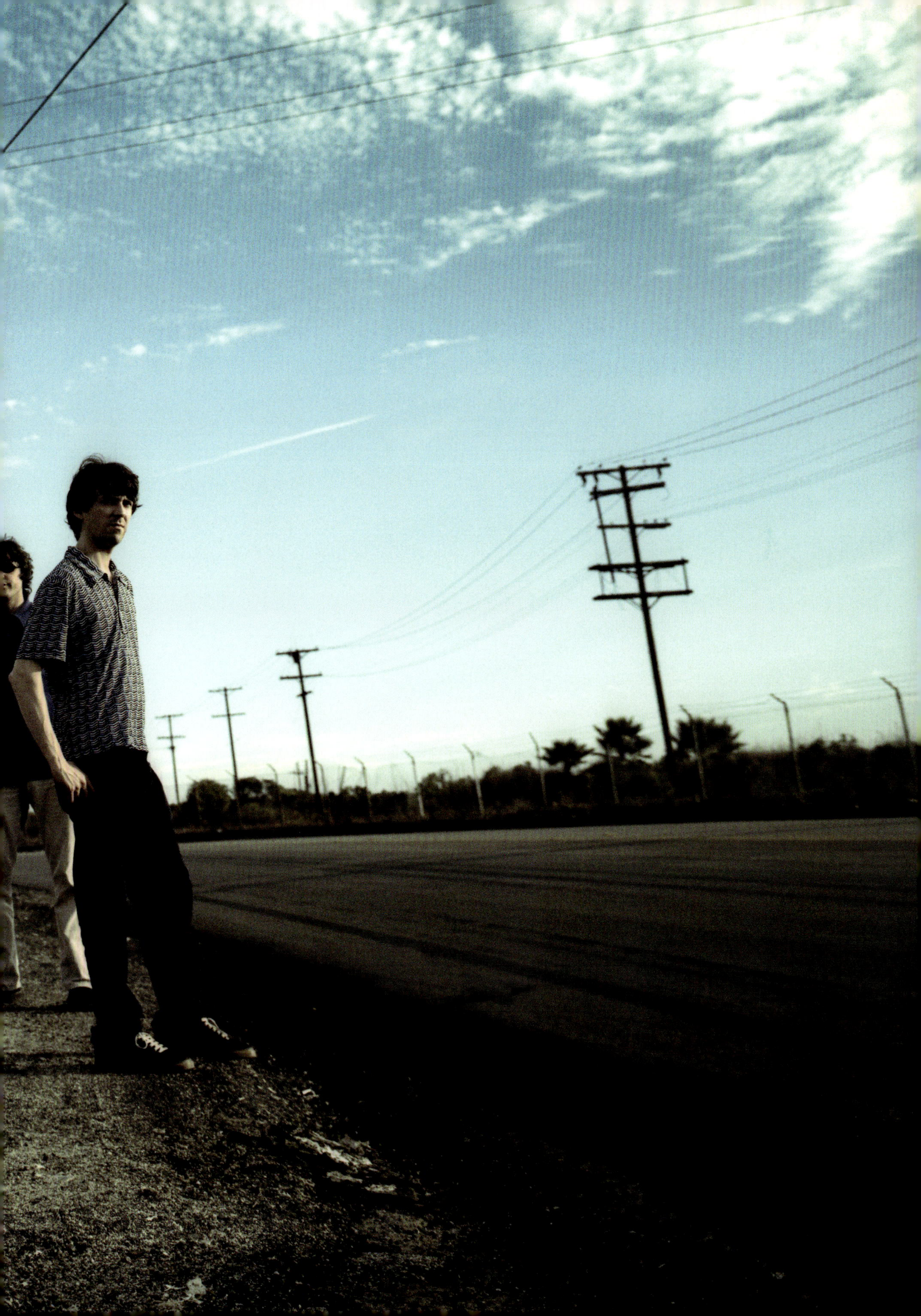

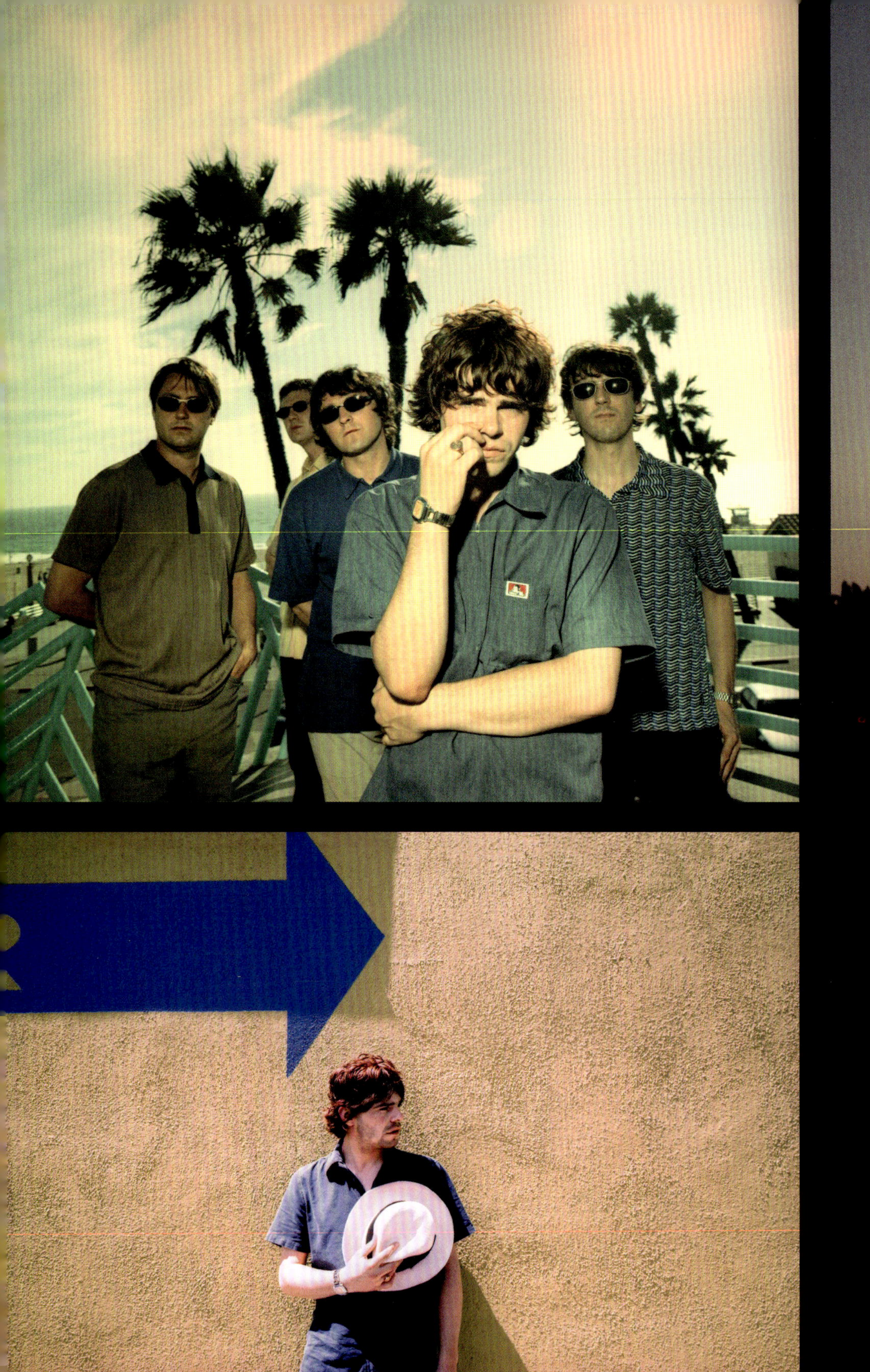

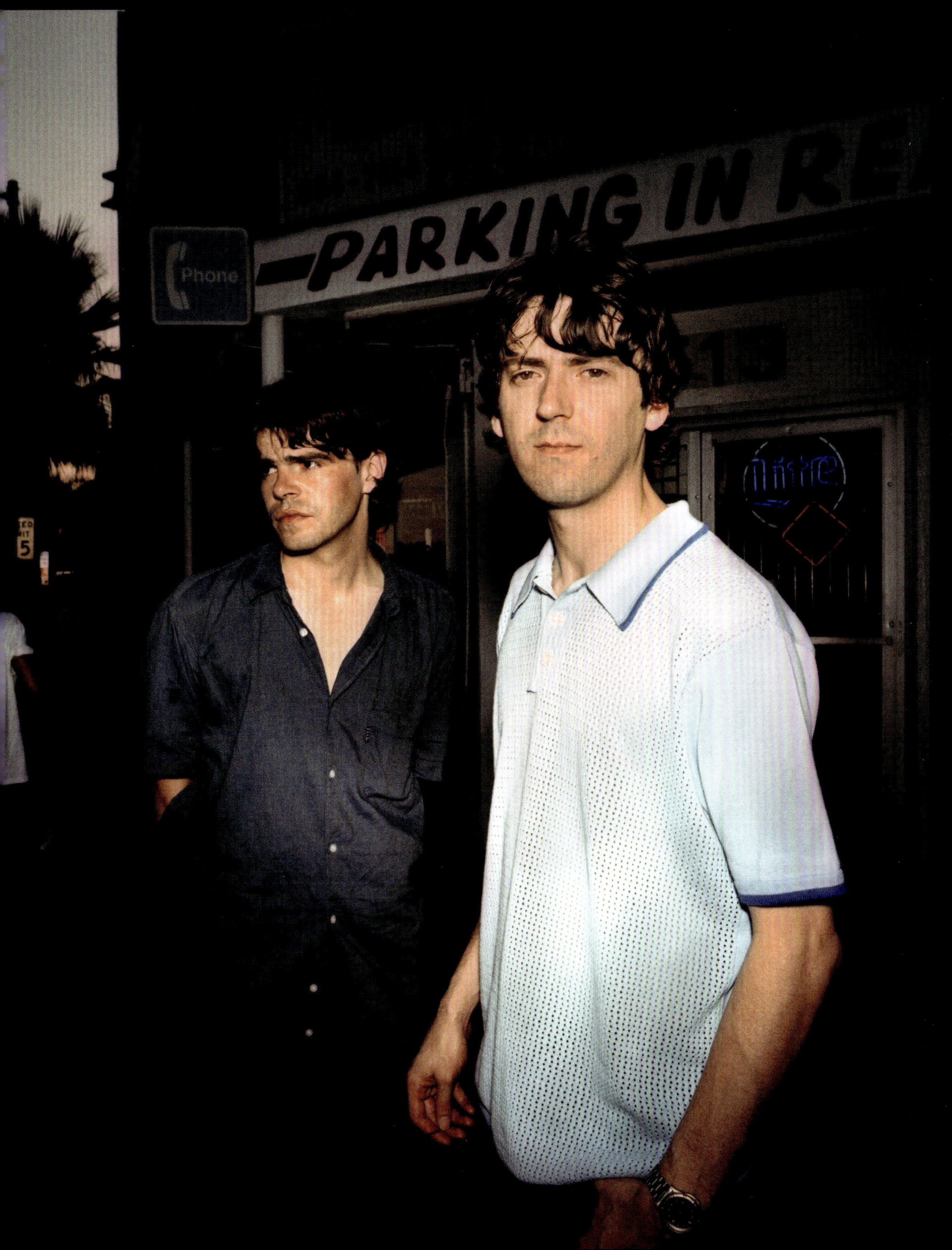
PARKING IN
Phone

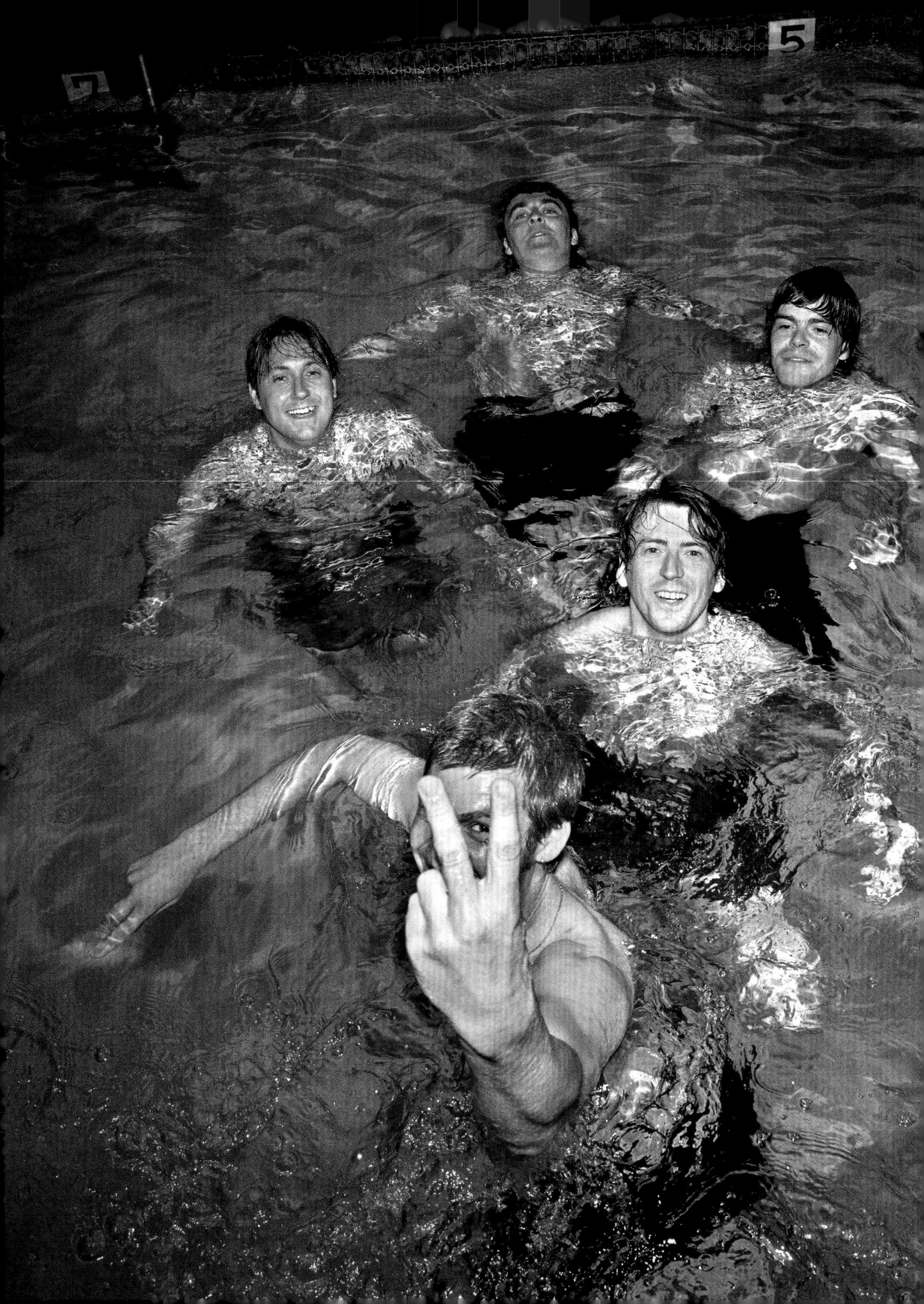
5

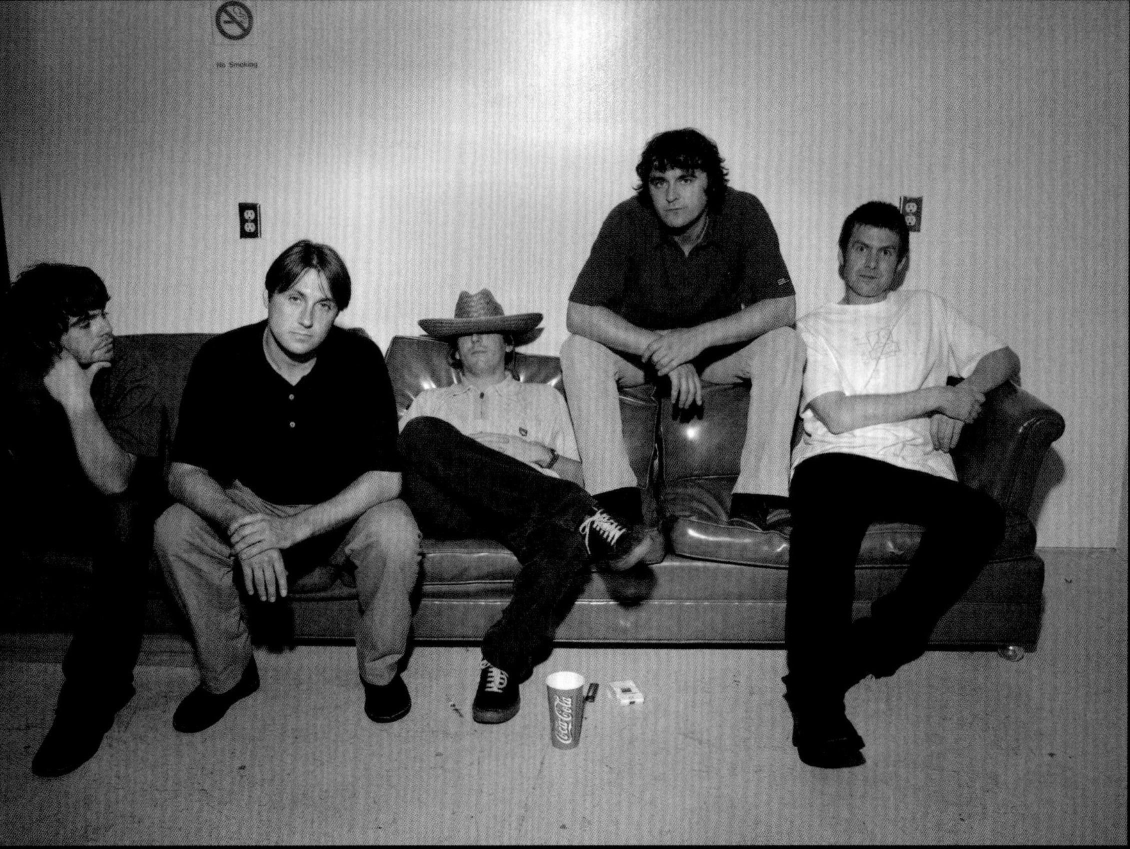

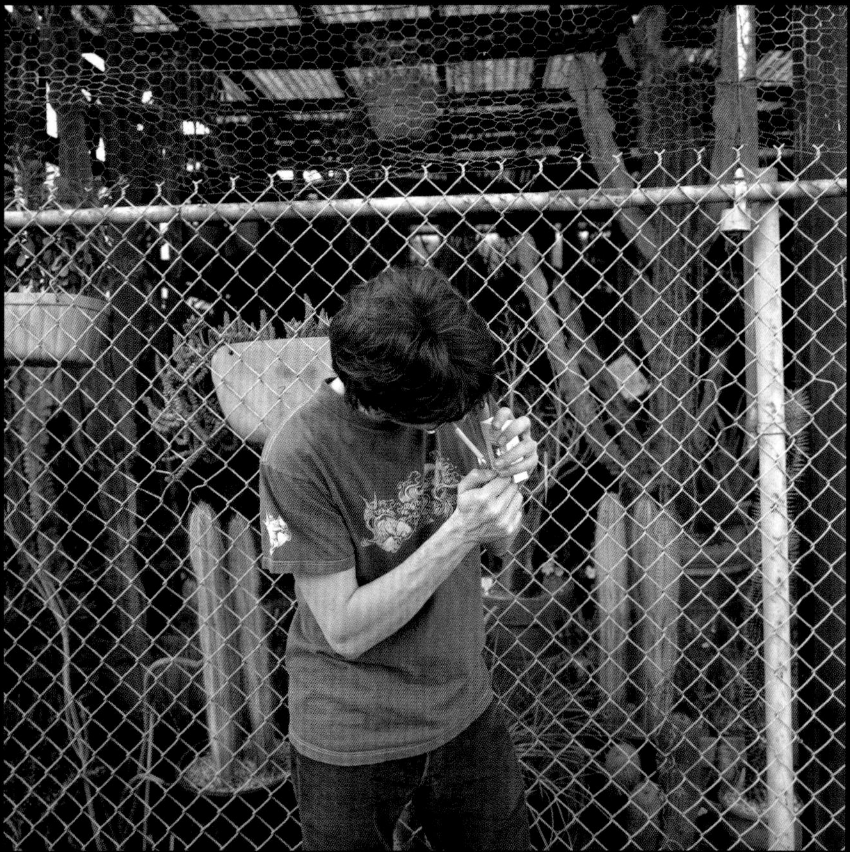

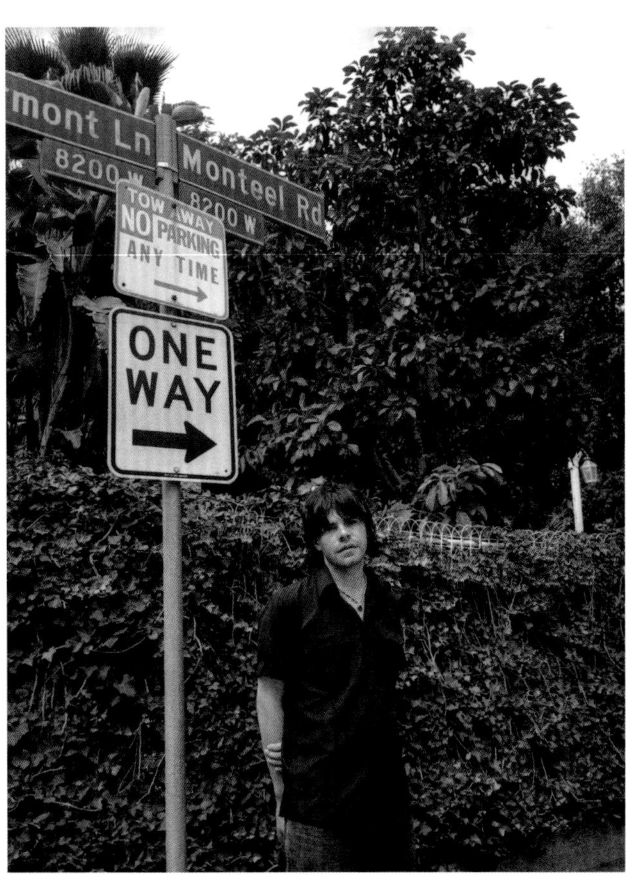
mont Ln
8200 W
Monteel Rd
8200 W
TOW AWAY
NO PARKING
ANY TIME
ONE
WAY

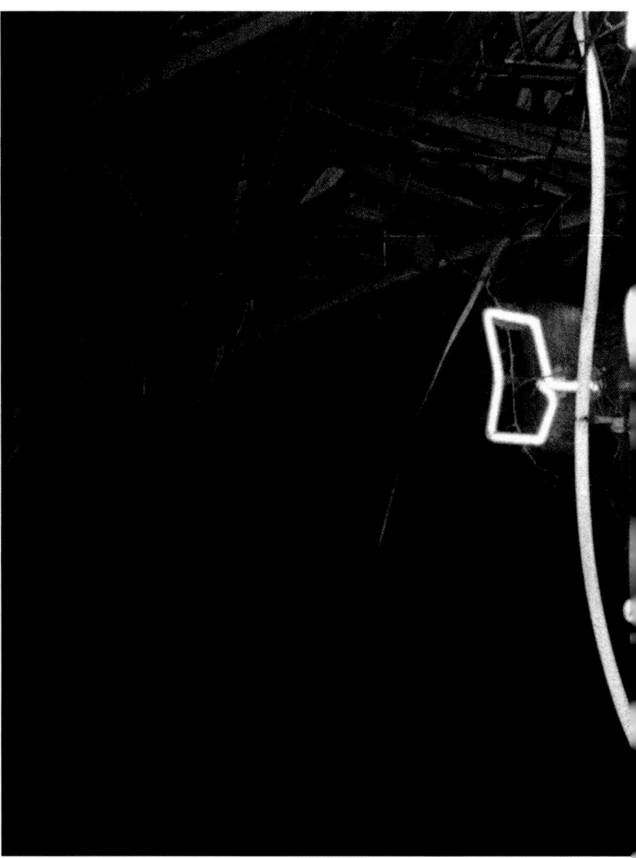

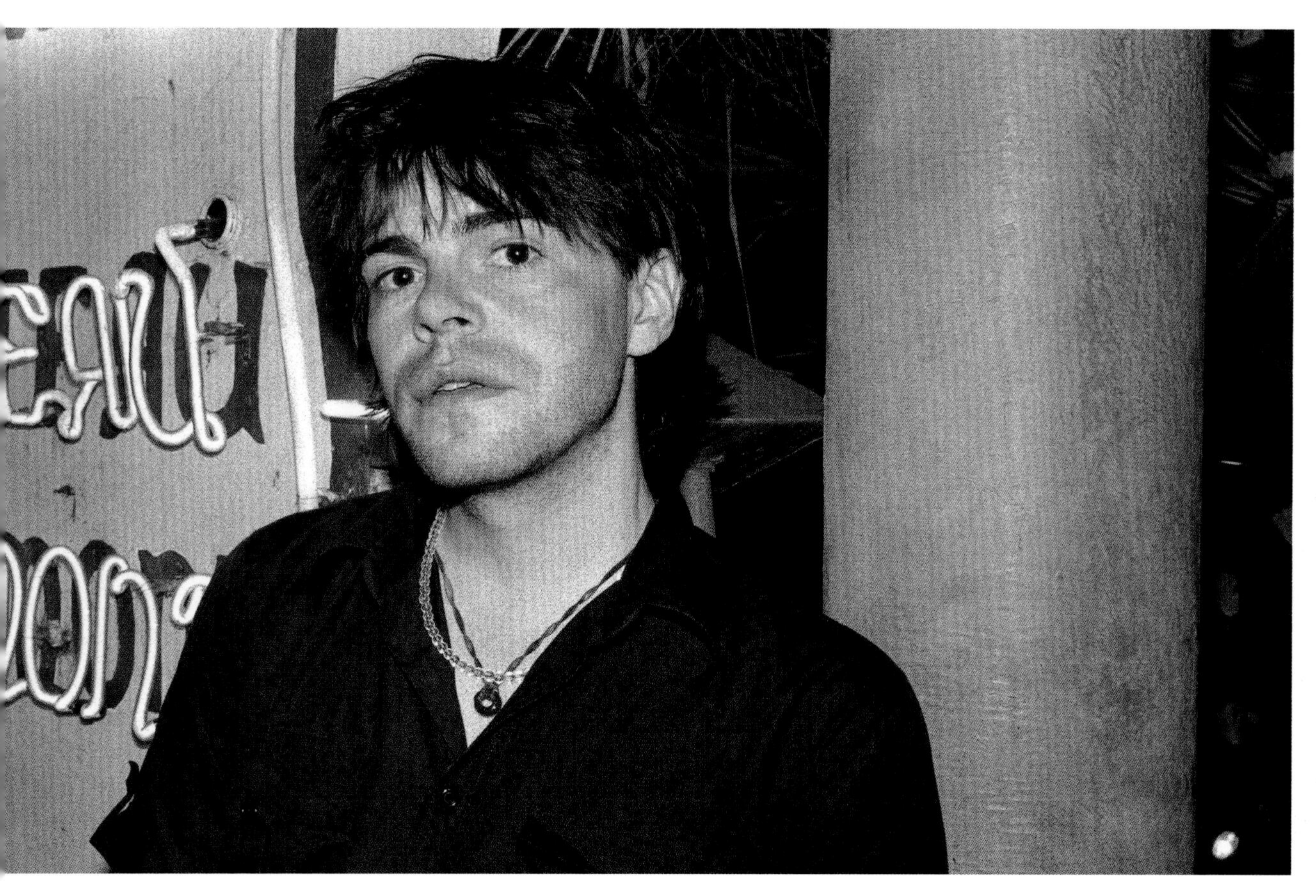

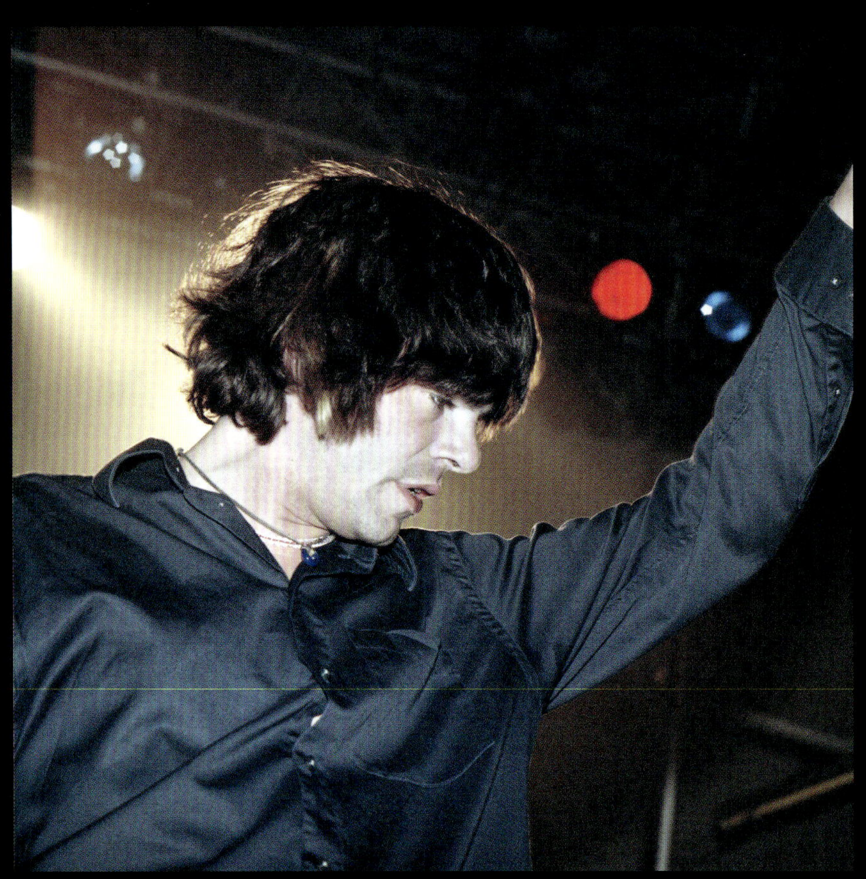

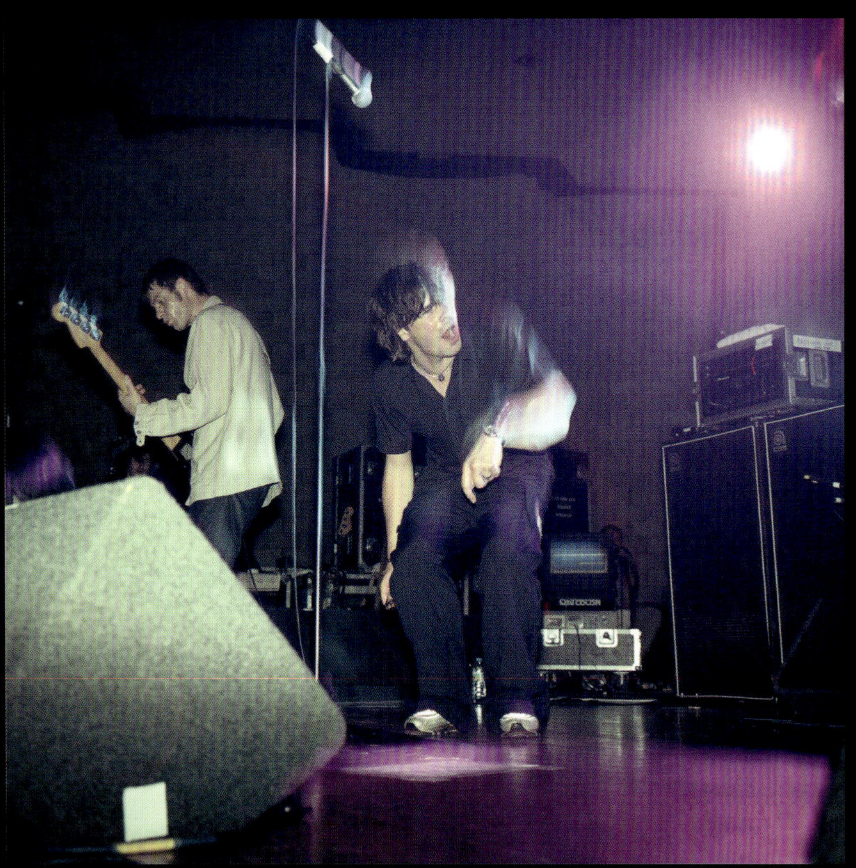

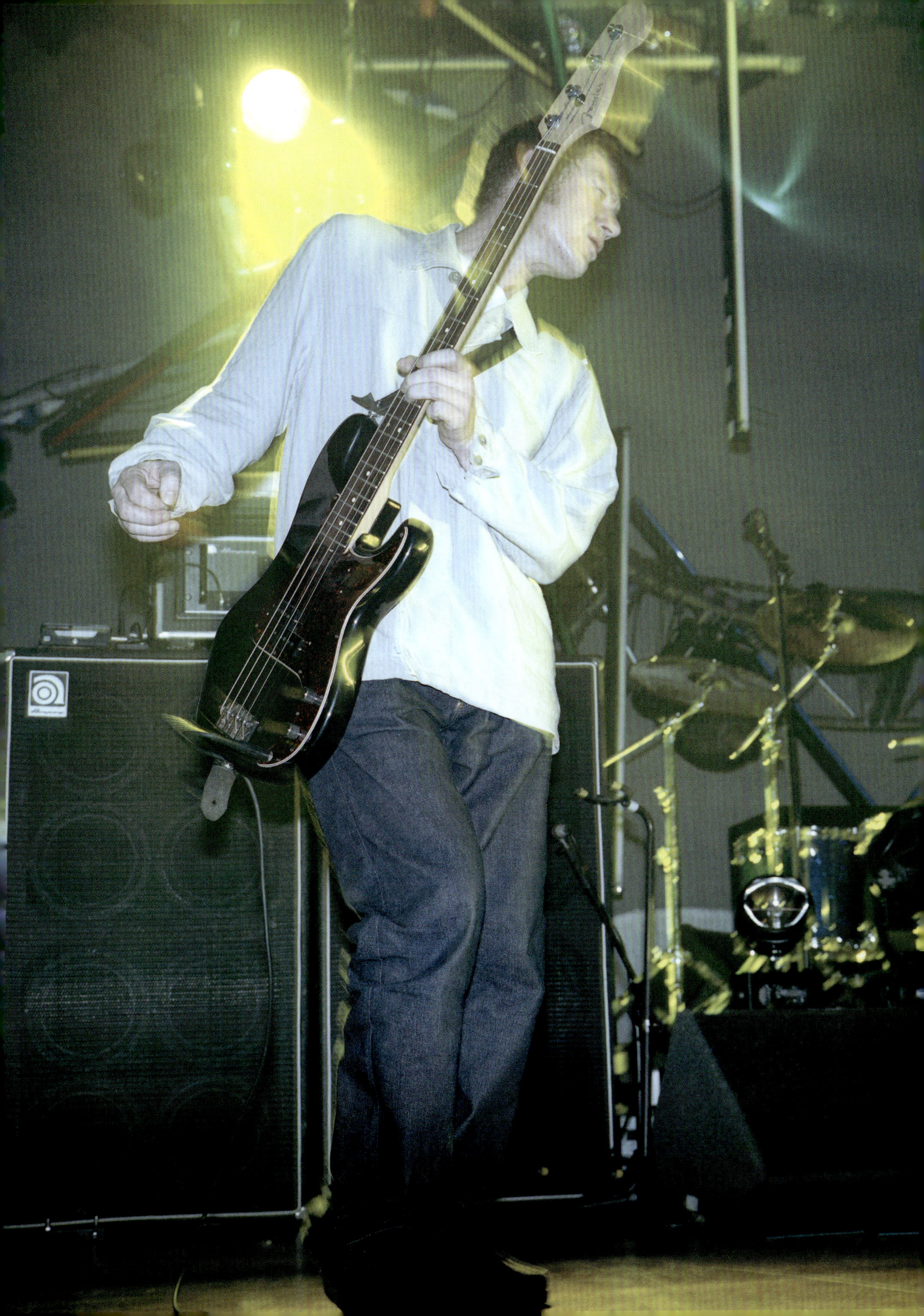

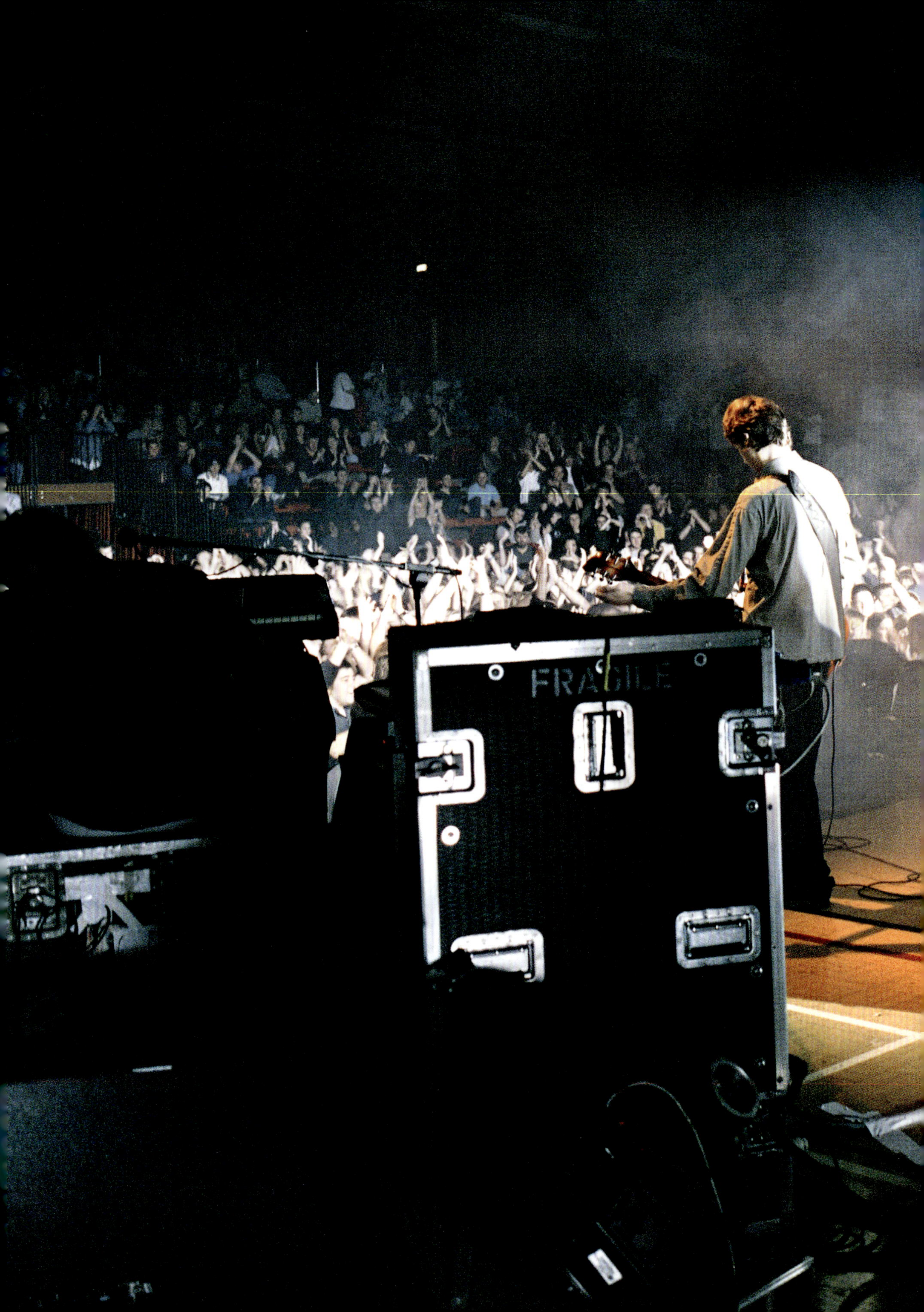
FRAGILE

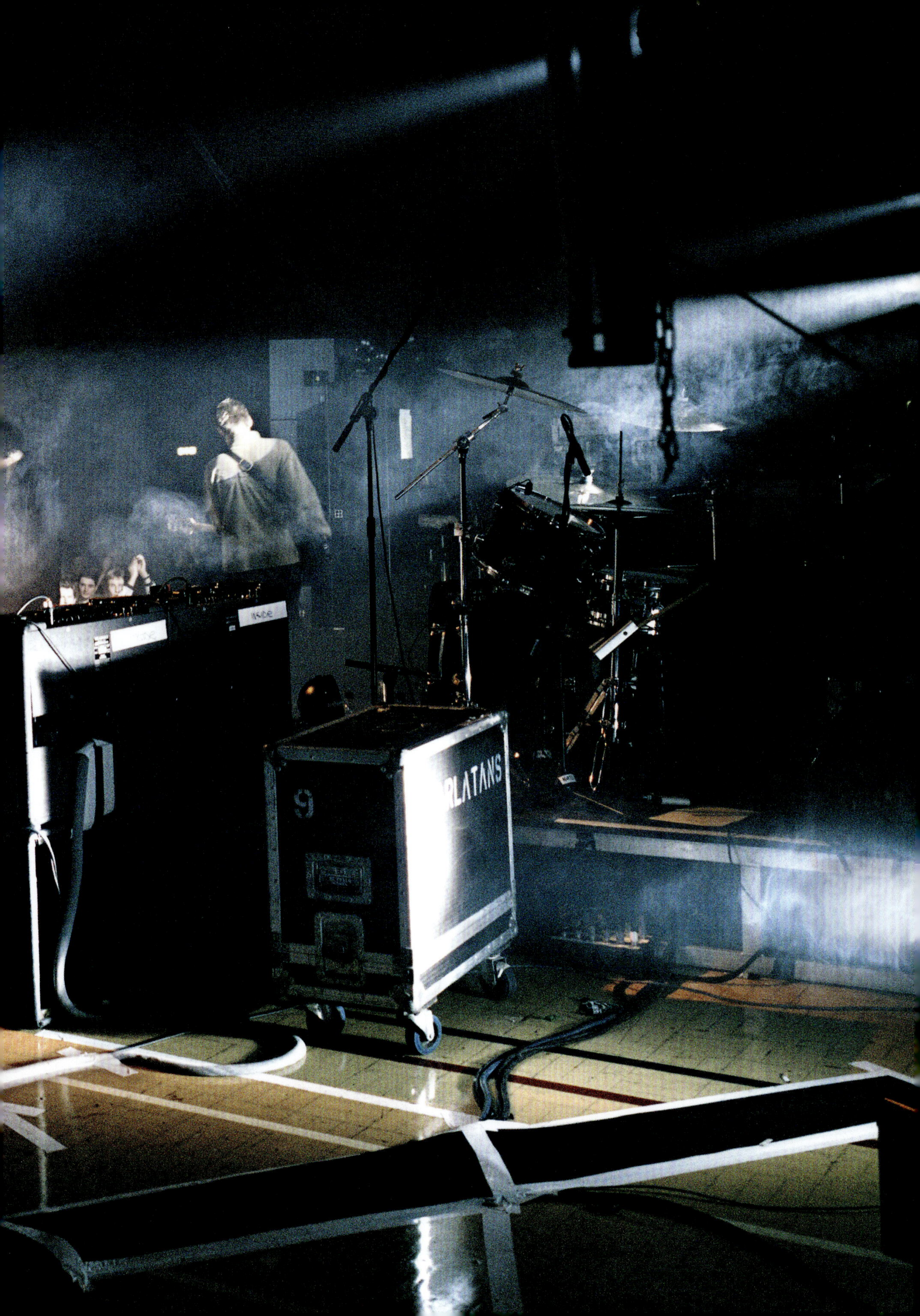

RLATANS
9

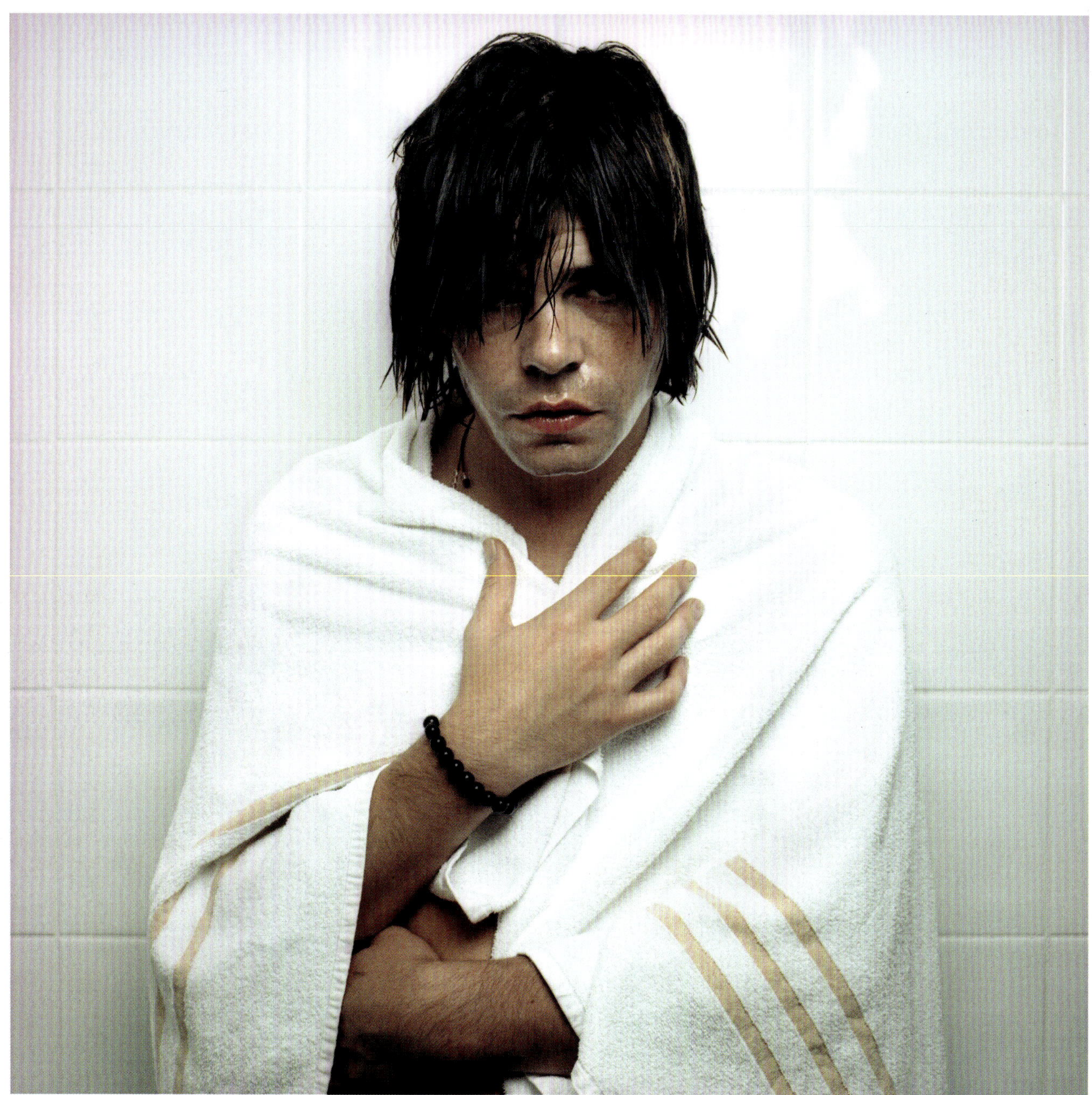

This was in Poole, Dorset, after a shower, after a show. It's one of Tom's favourites. This night was most notable for Jon's arrest, after he was caught trying to climb back into his hotel room through a window on the second floor.

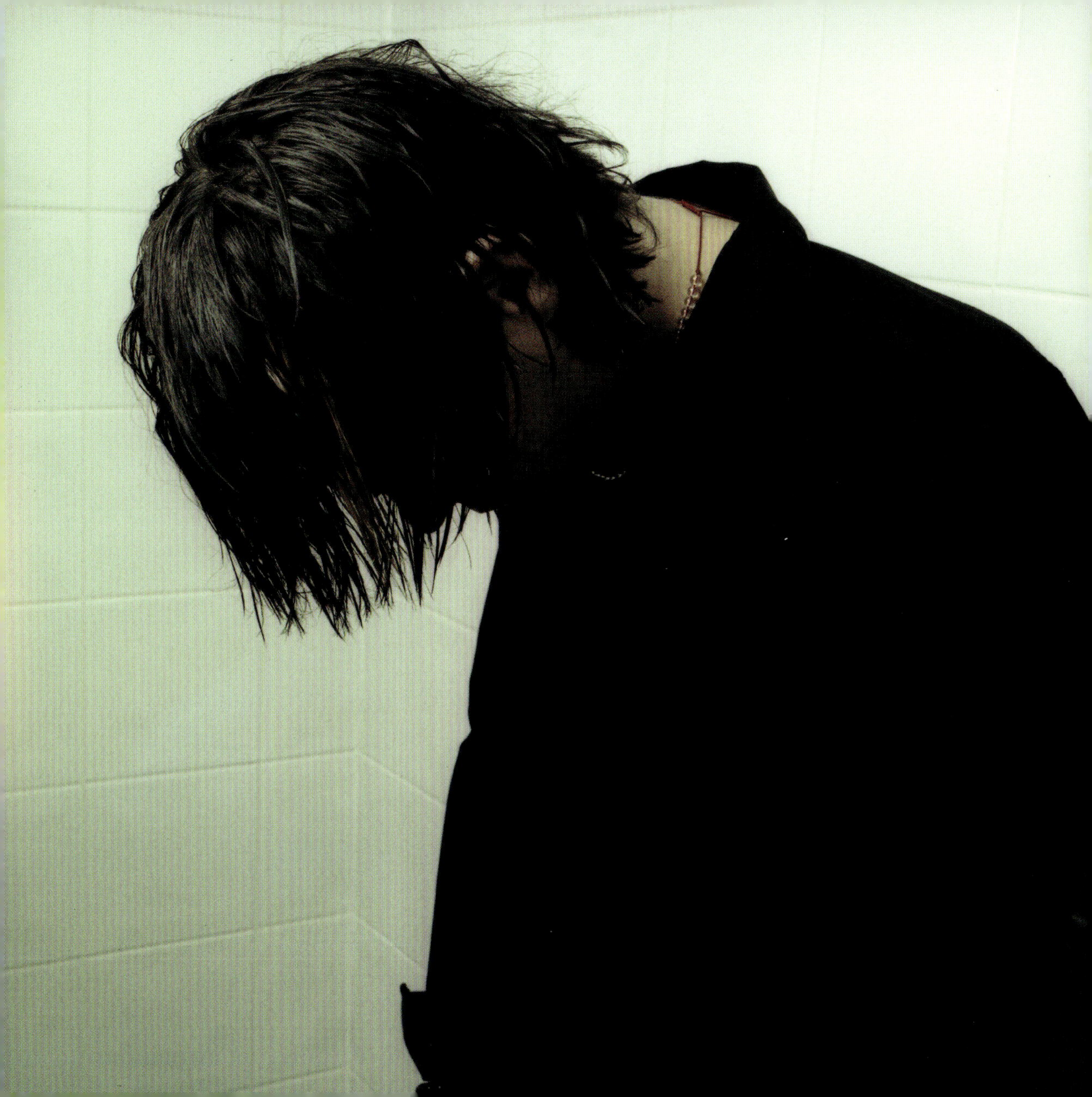

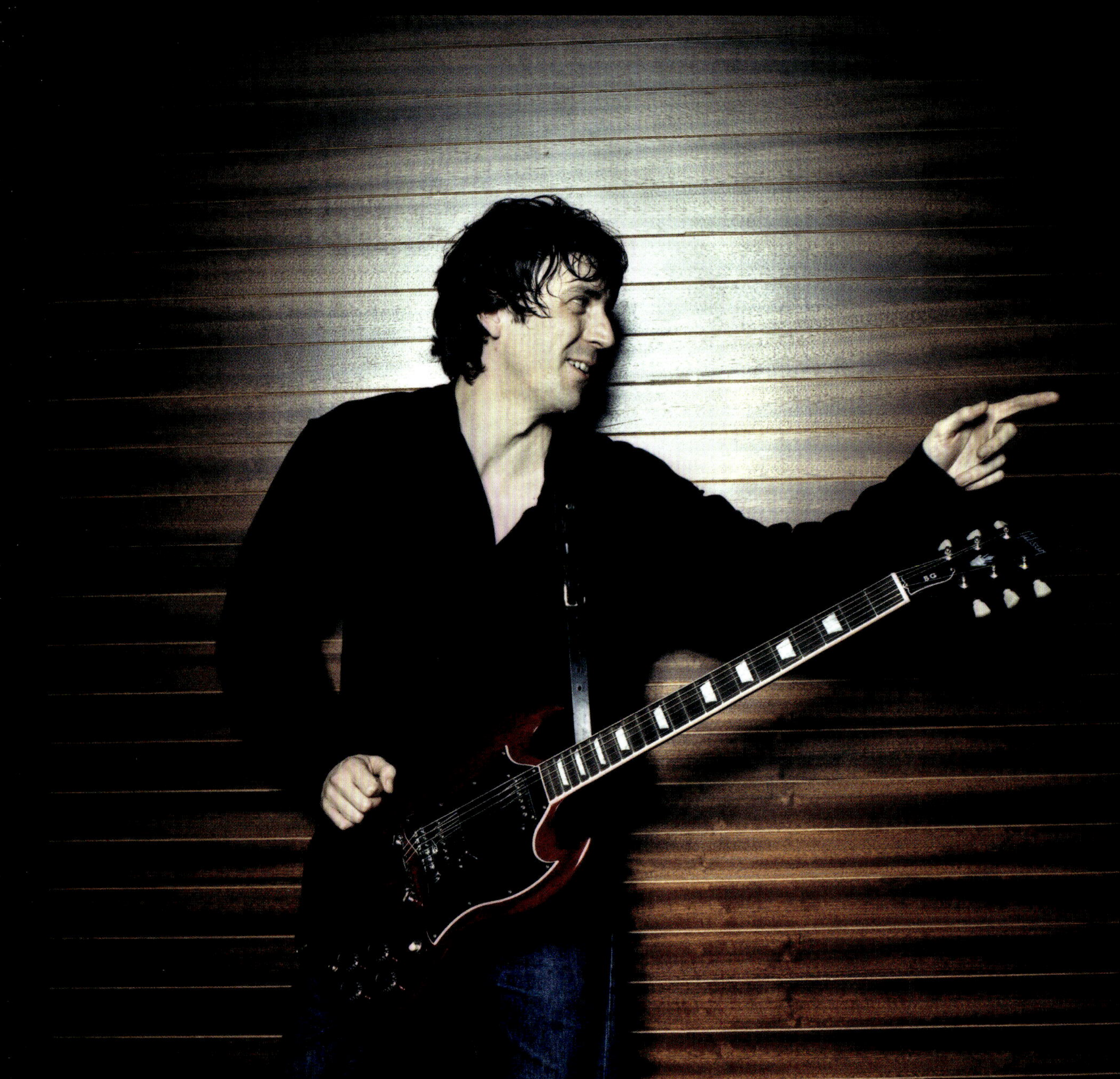
SG

Tom has a real good style of putting everyone at ease. For Mark, playing guitar is like second nature – even his foot looks like it's holding down an impressive chord.

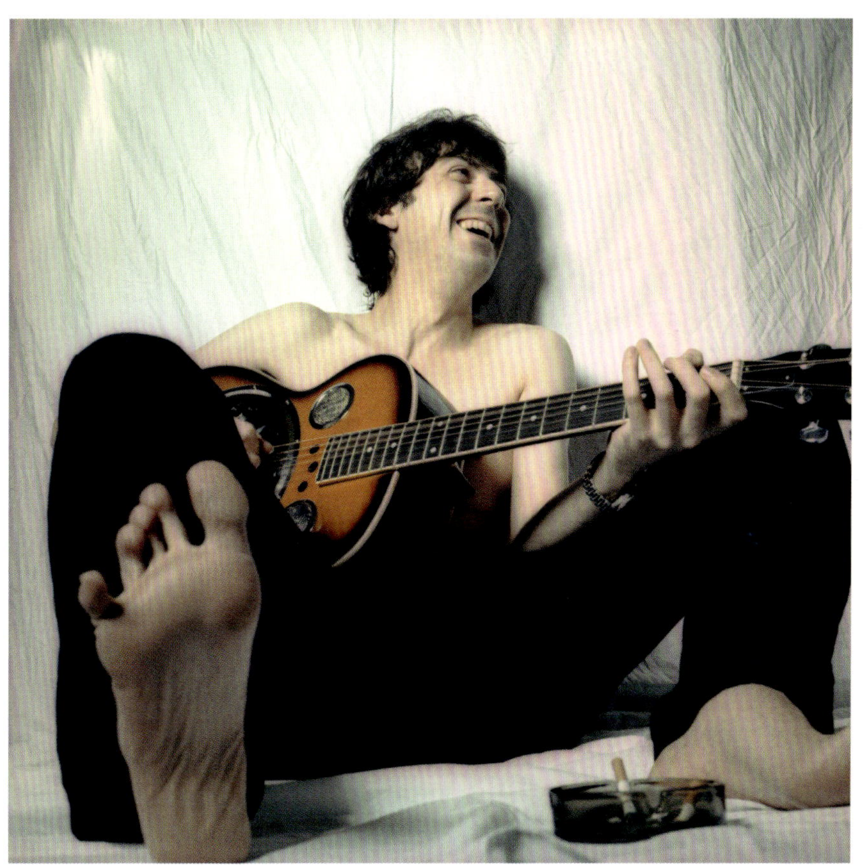

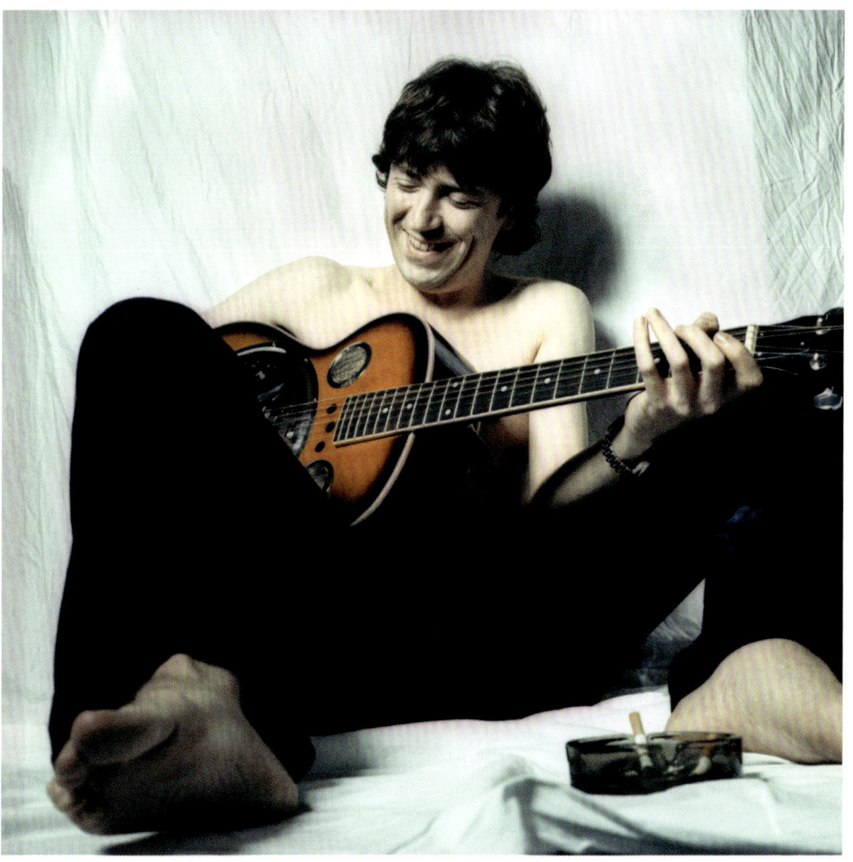

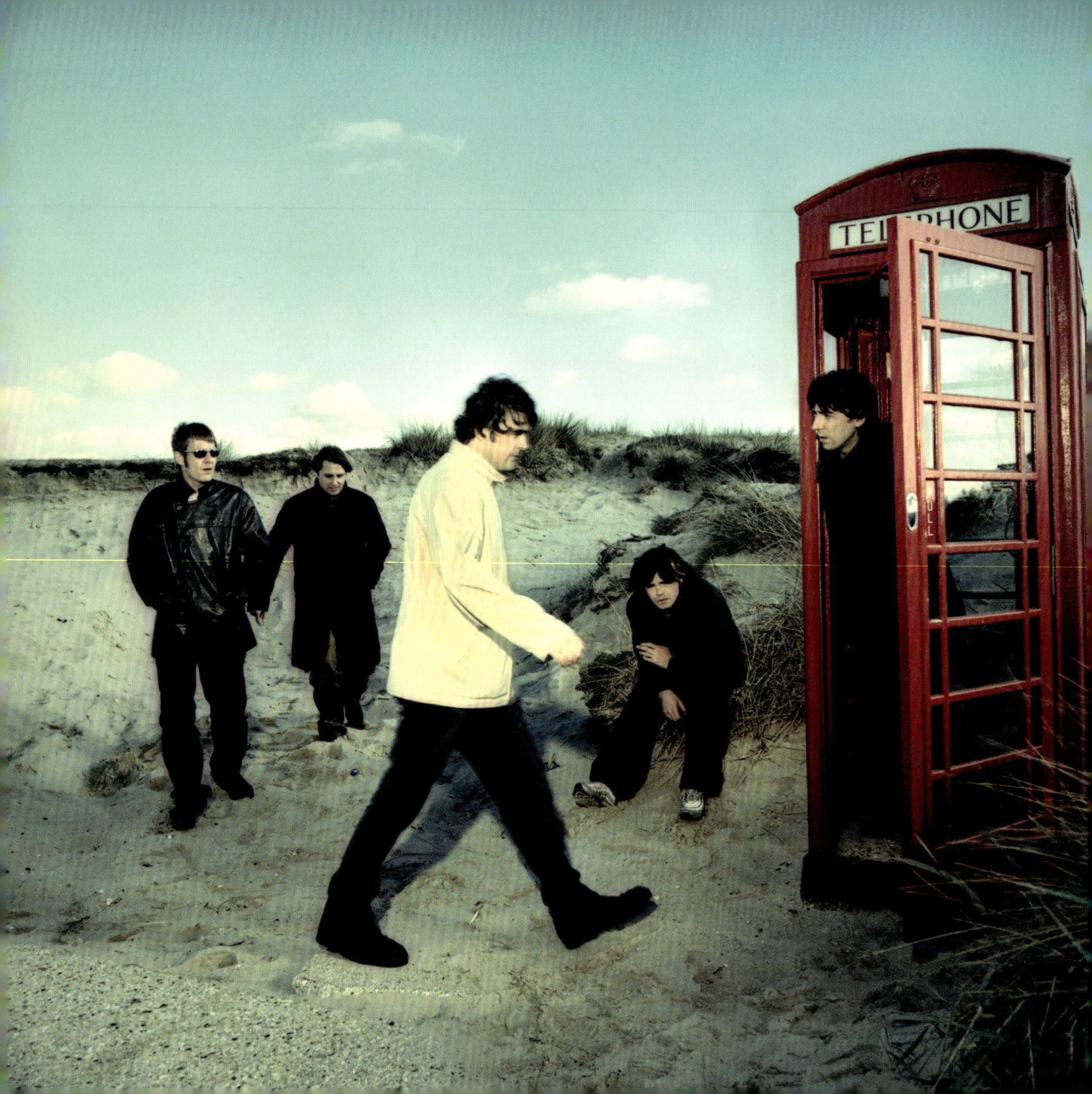
TEL
PHONE

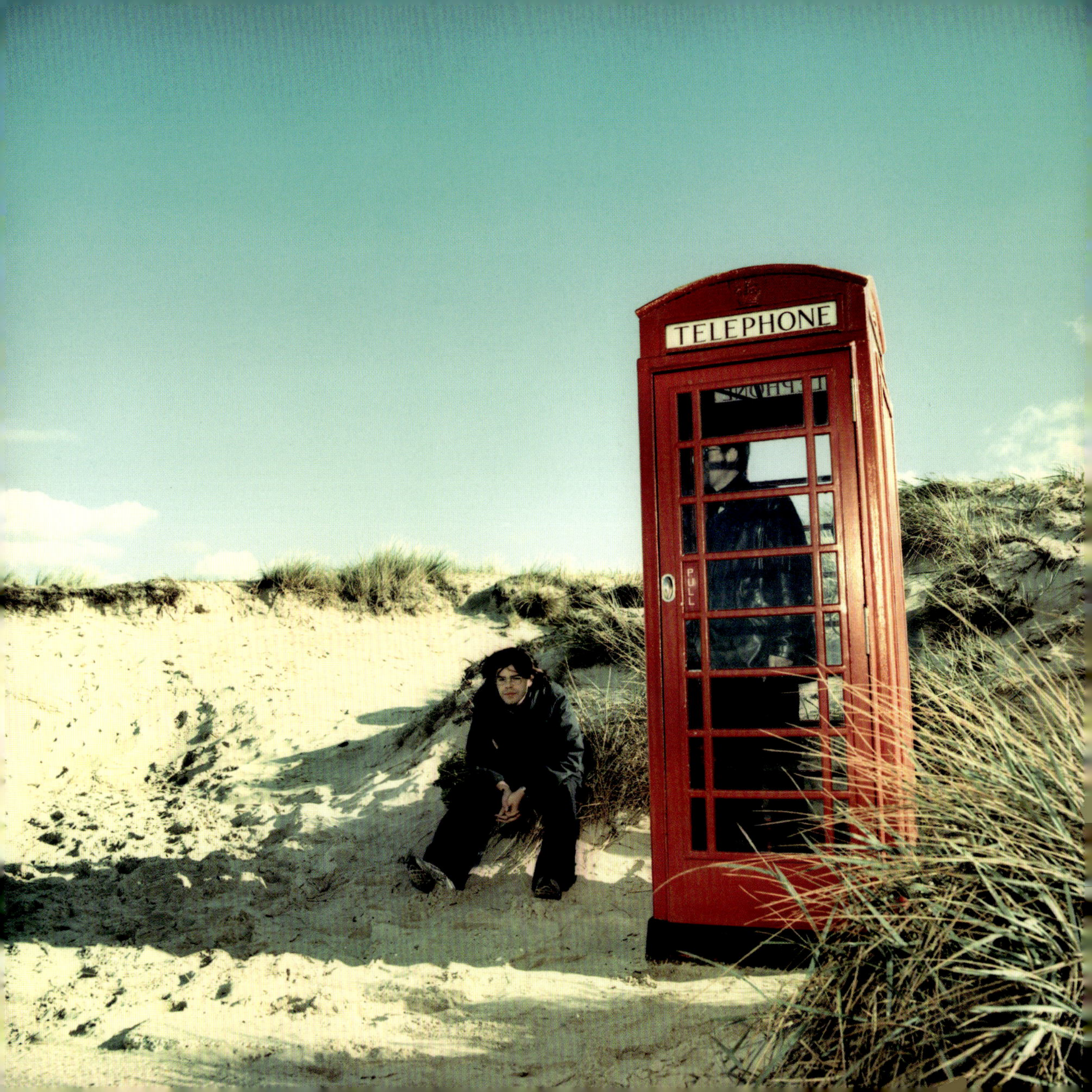
TELEPHONE
PULL

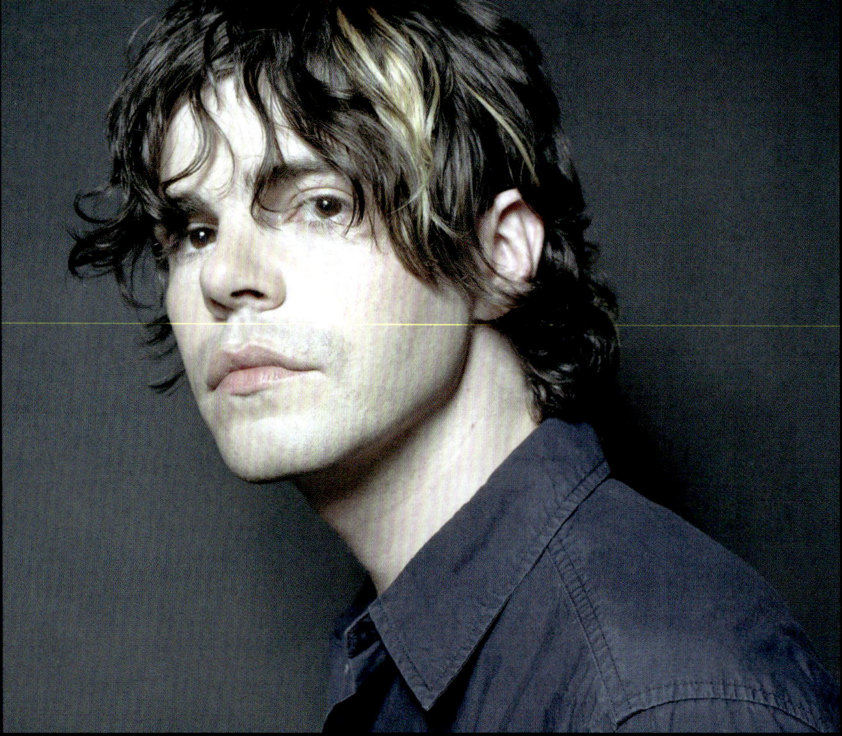

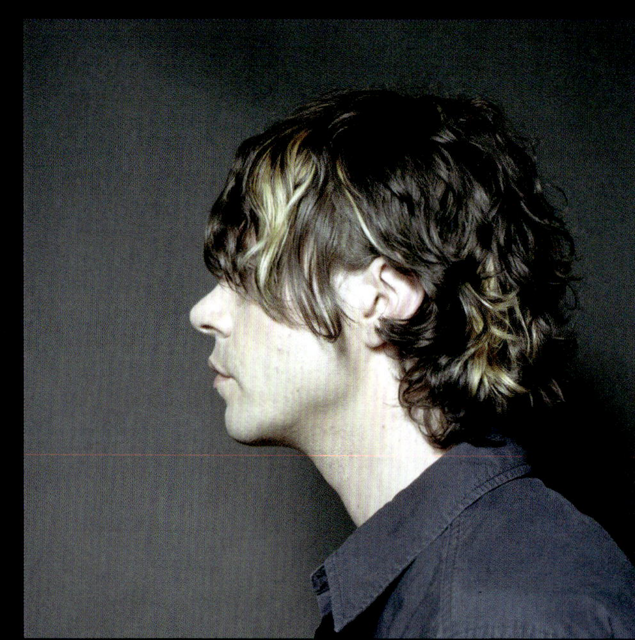

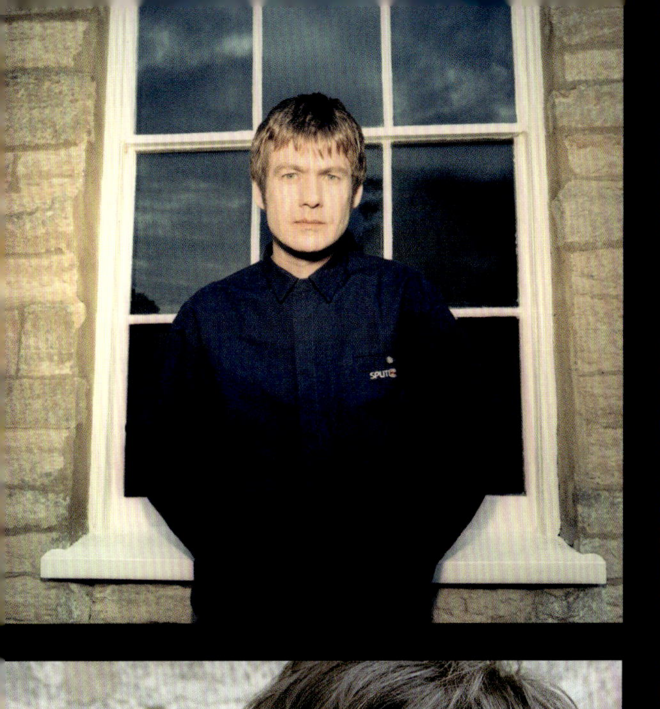
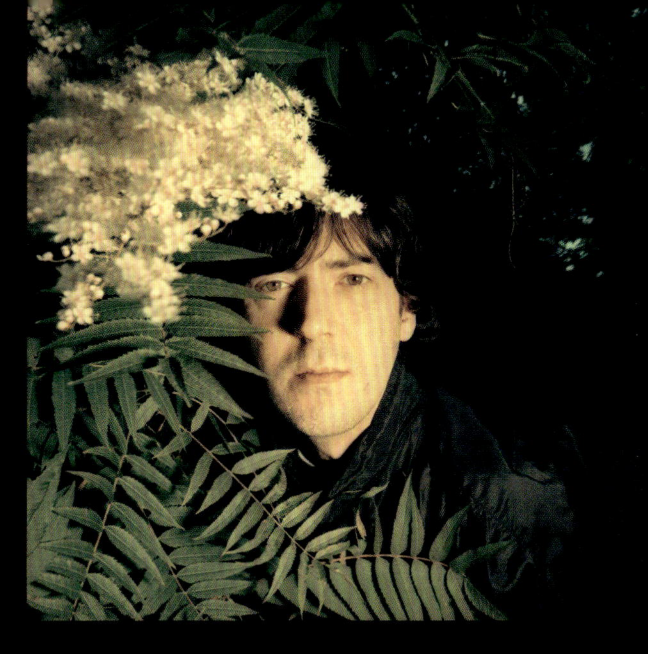
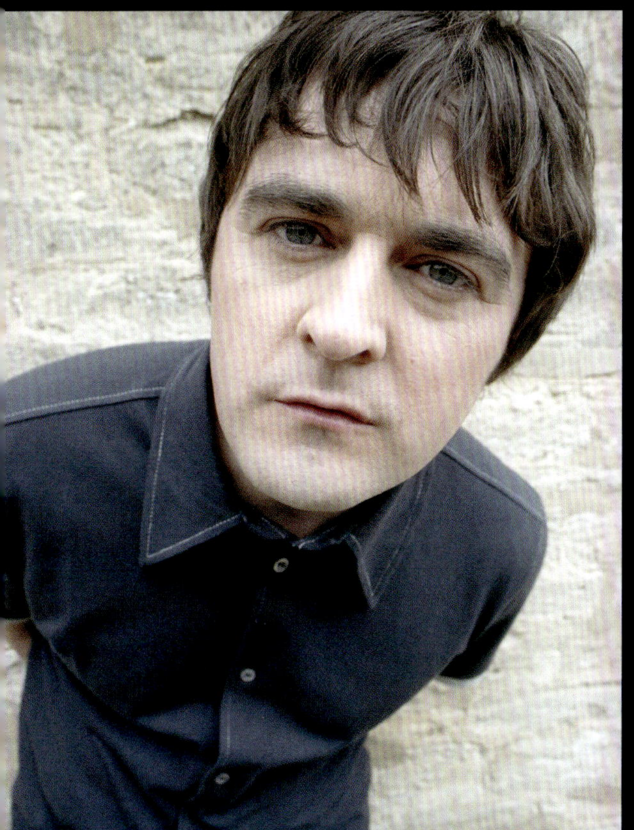
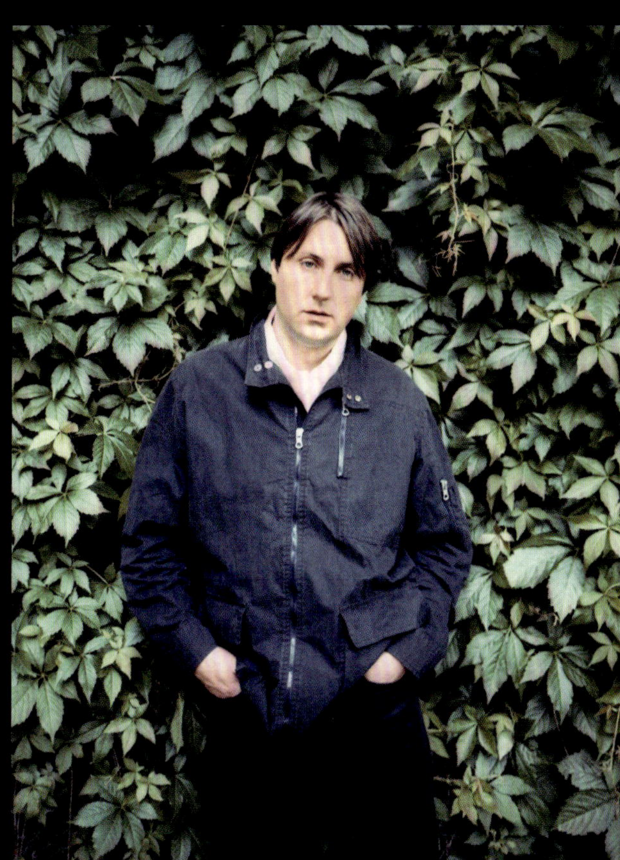

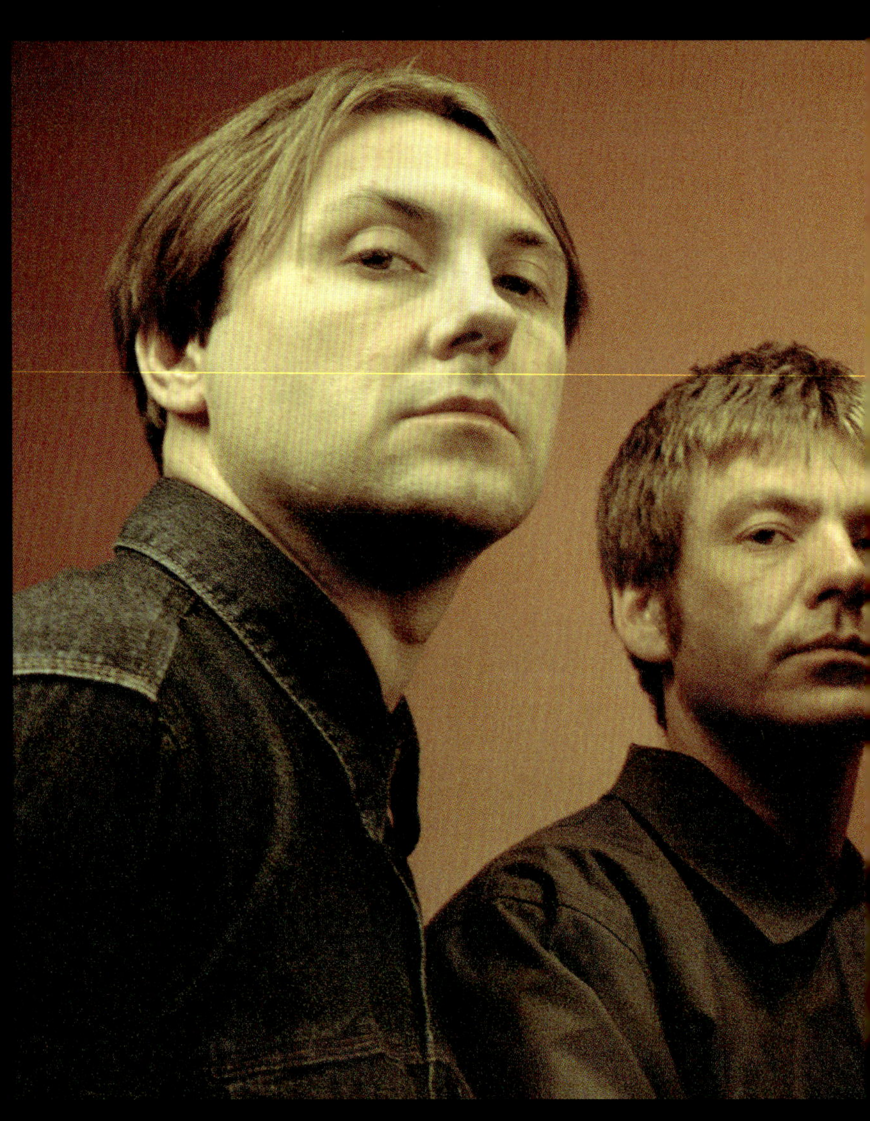

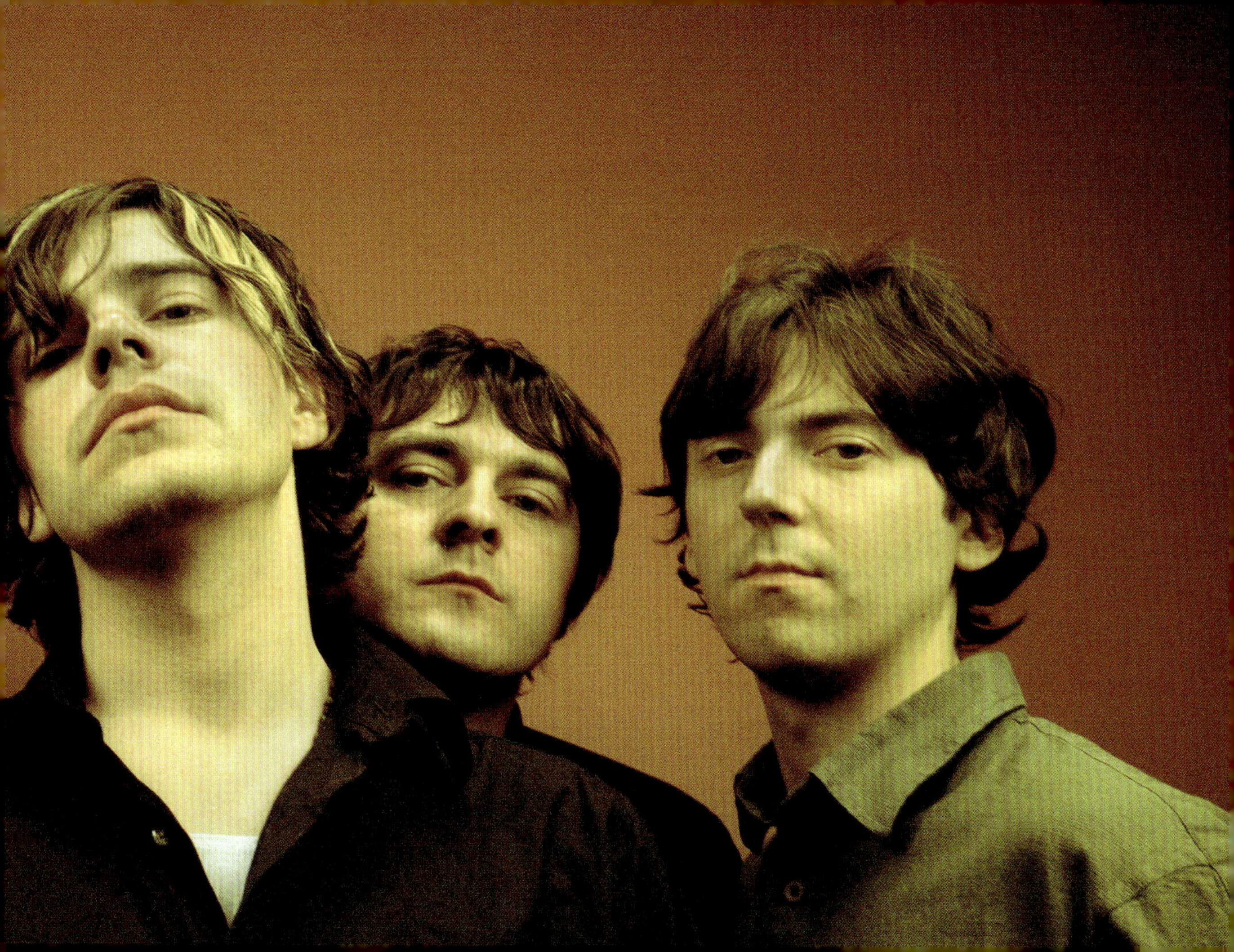

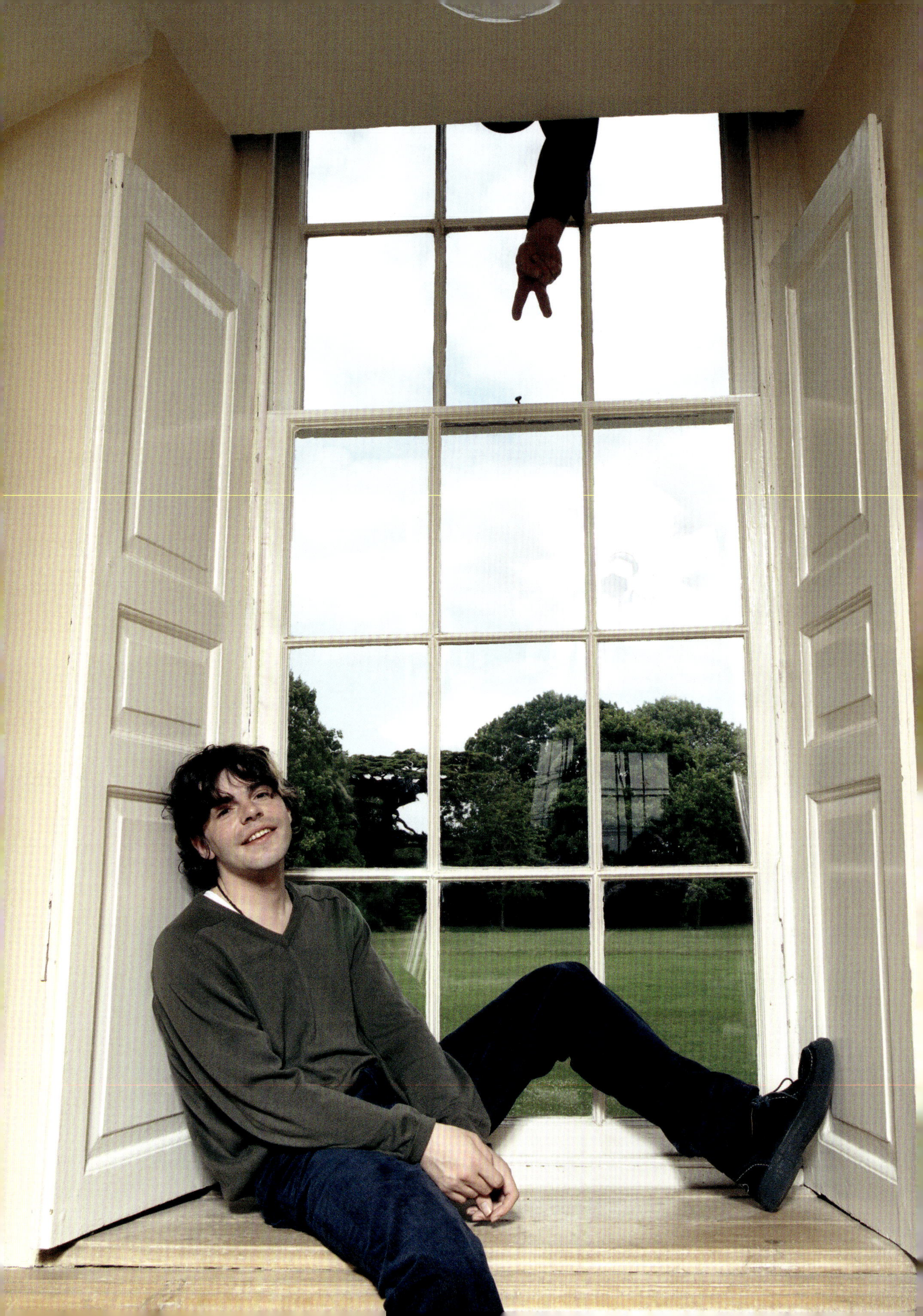

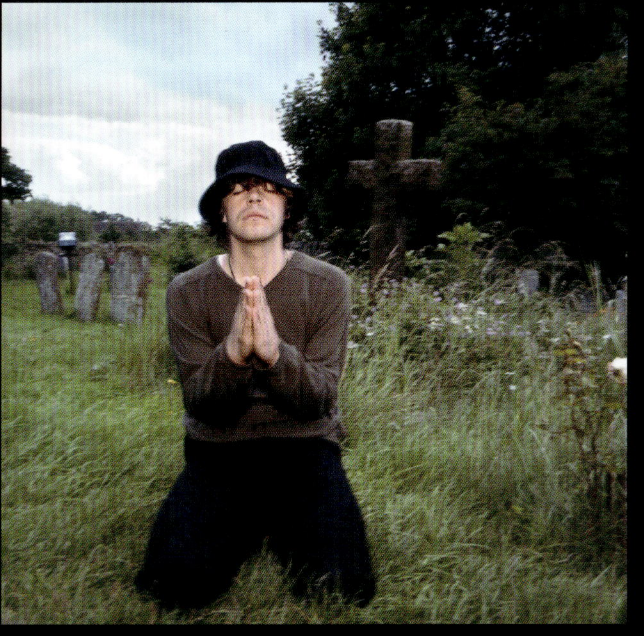

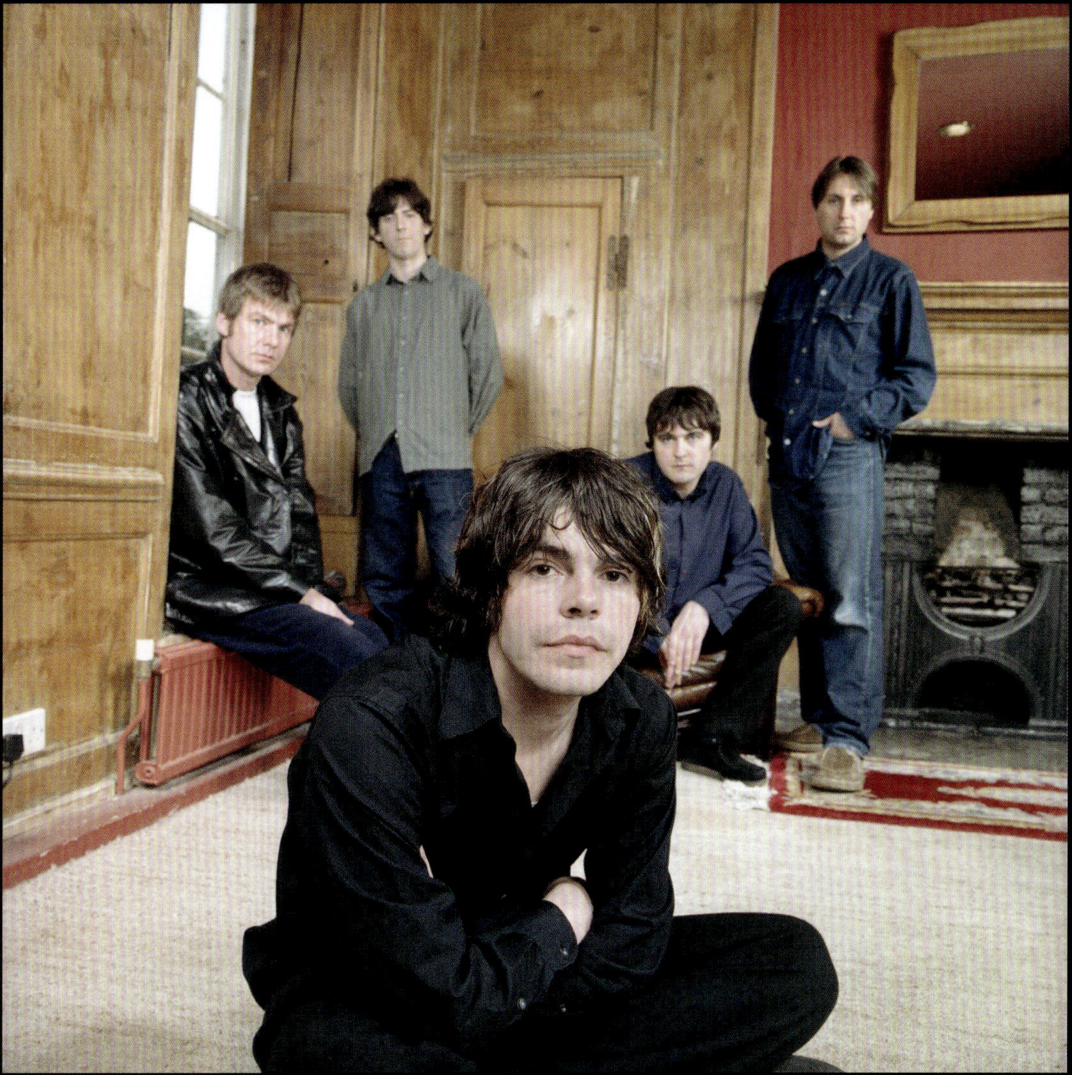

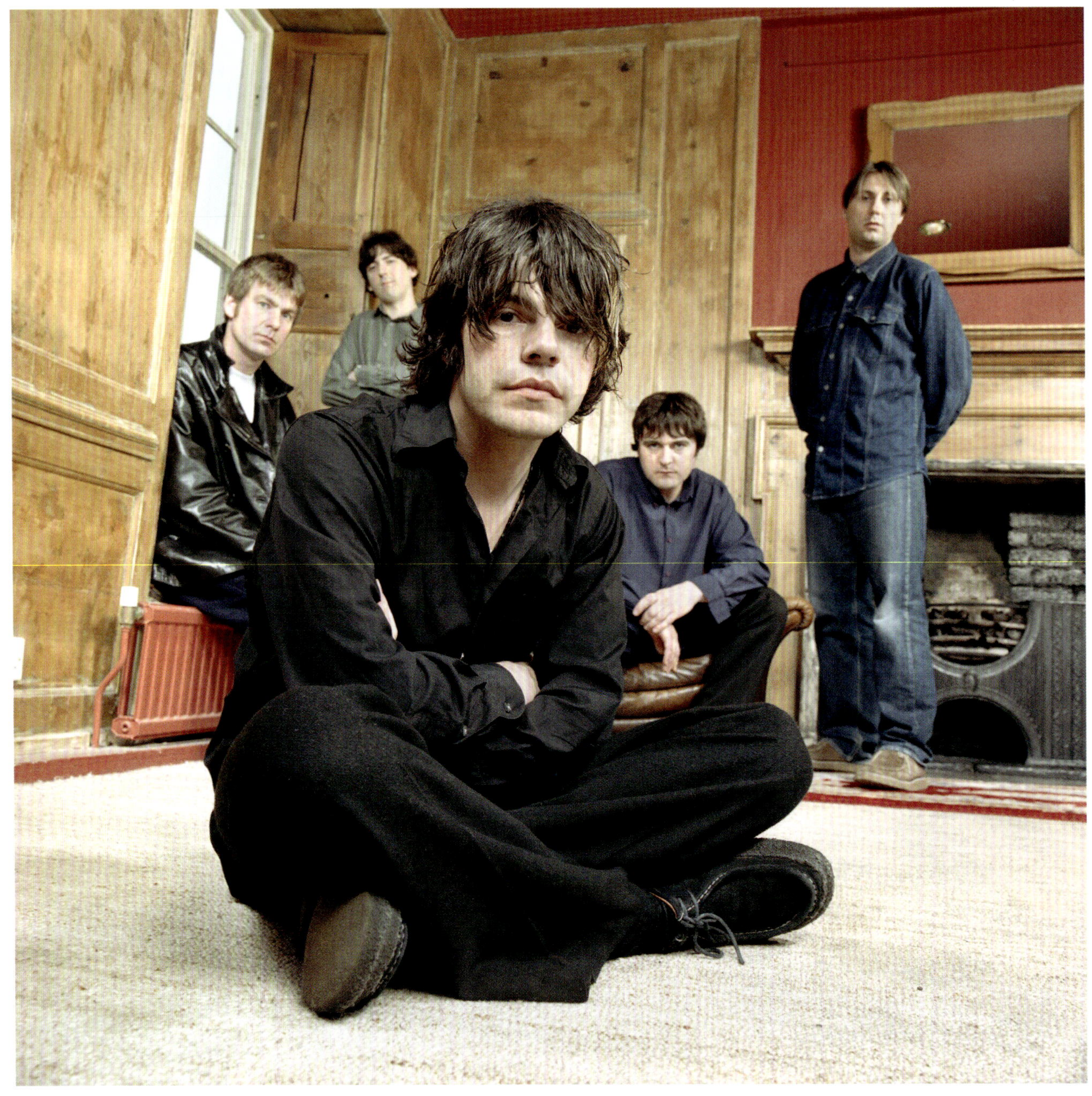

We were mixing *Us And Us Only* with Jim Spencer, working with him for the first time. Lots of elements were brand new to us. We had signed to Universal, I had moved to Los Angeles, Tony had settled in and was at the peak of his powers with songwriting and we had built ourselves a studio which we called The Big Mushroom, close to our spiritual home of Northwich.

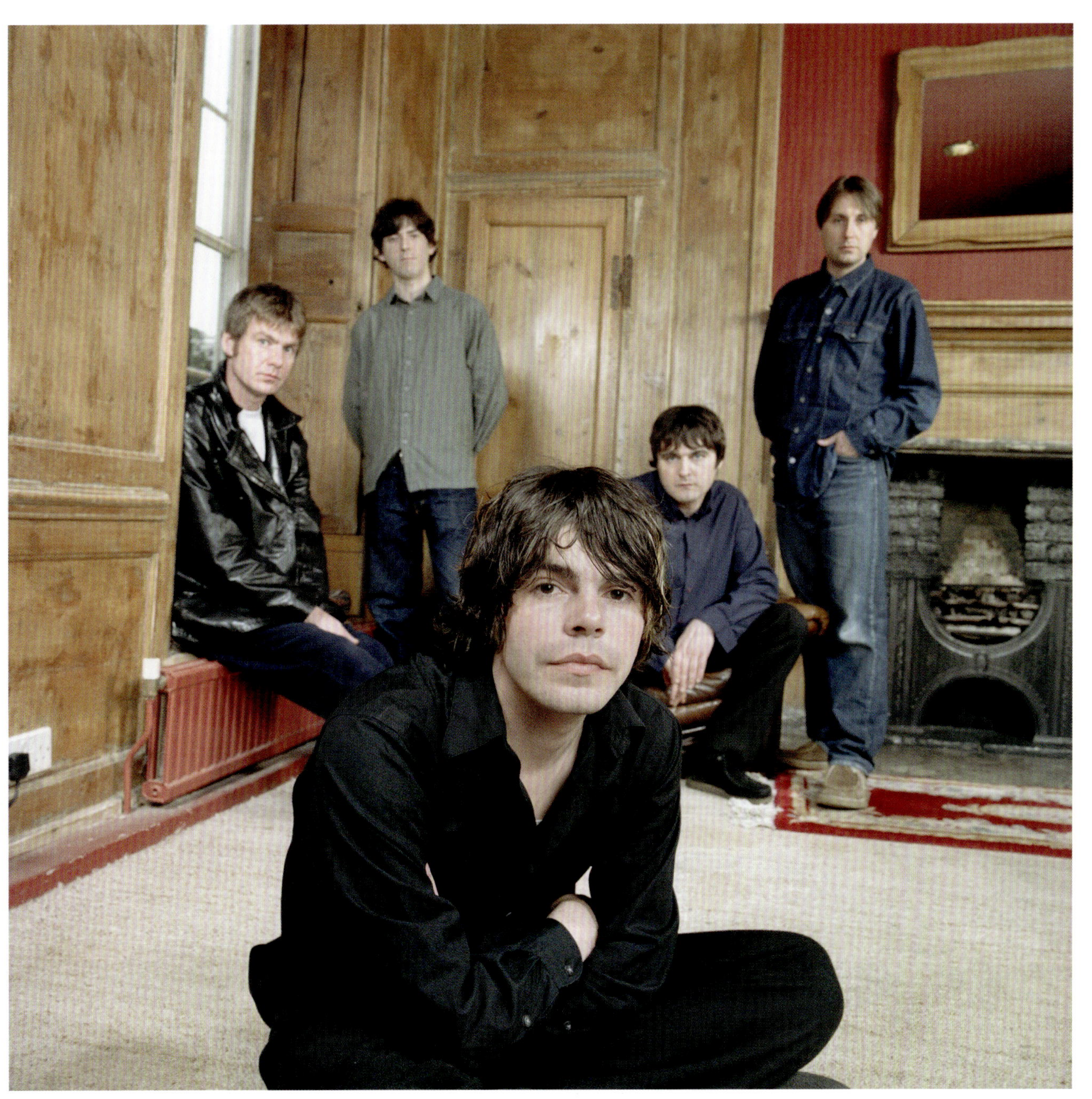

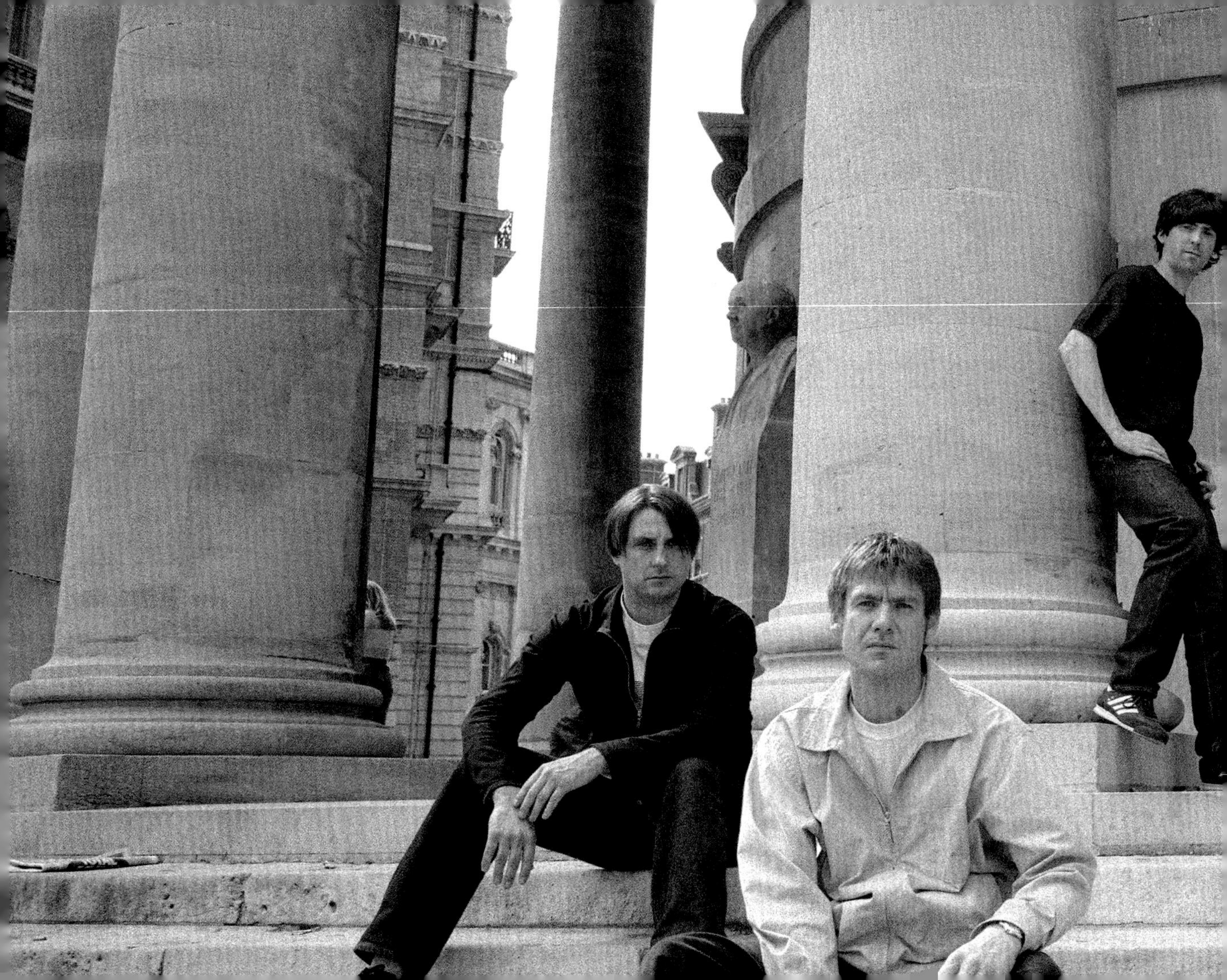

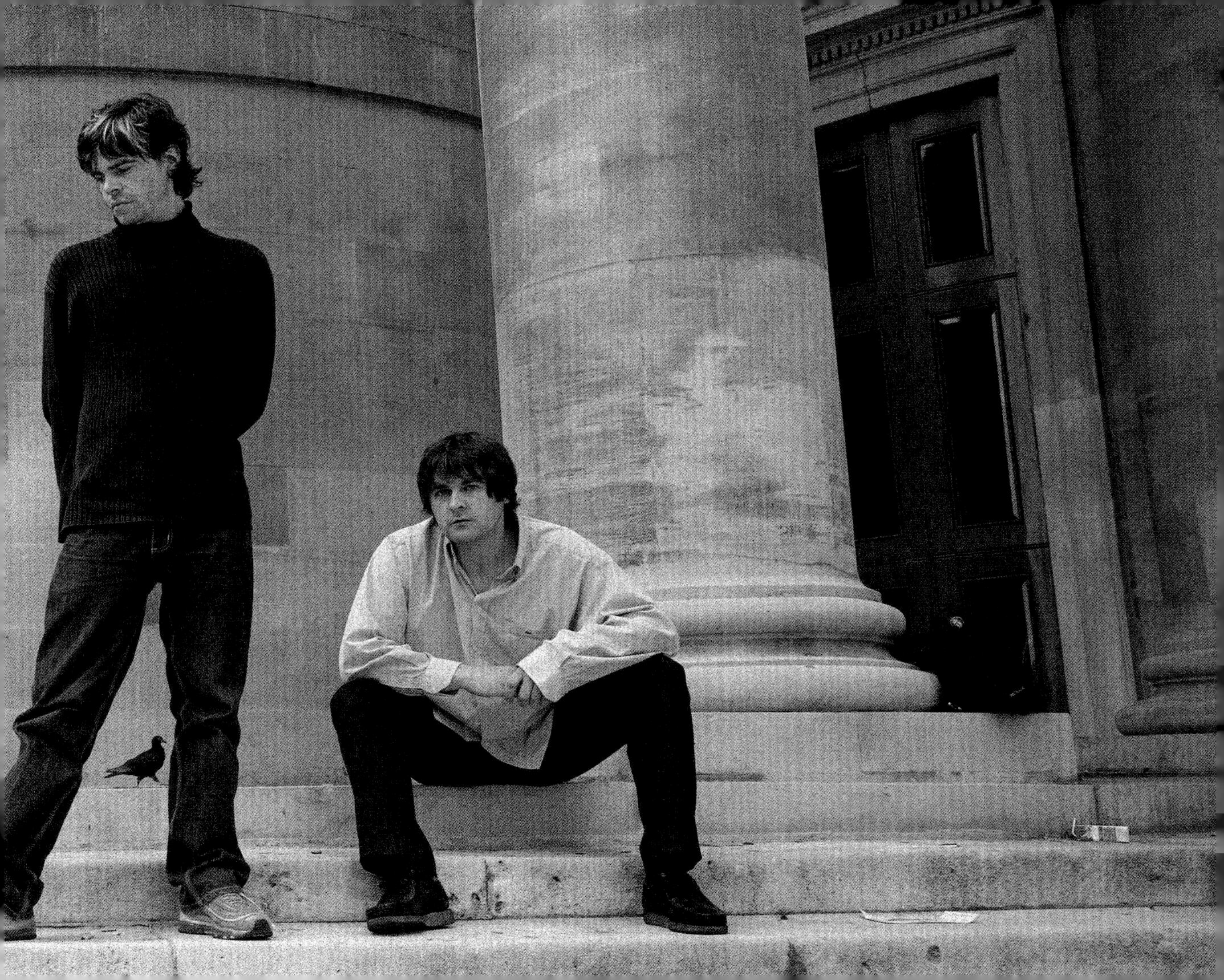

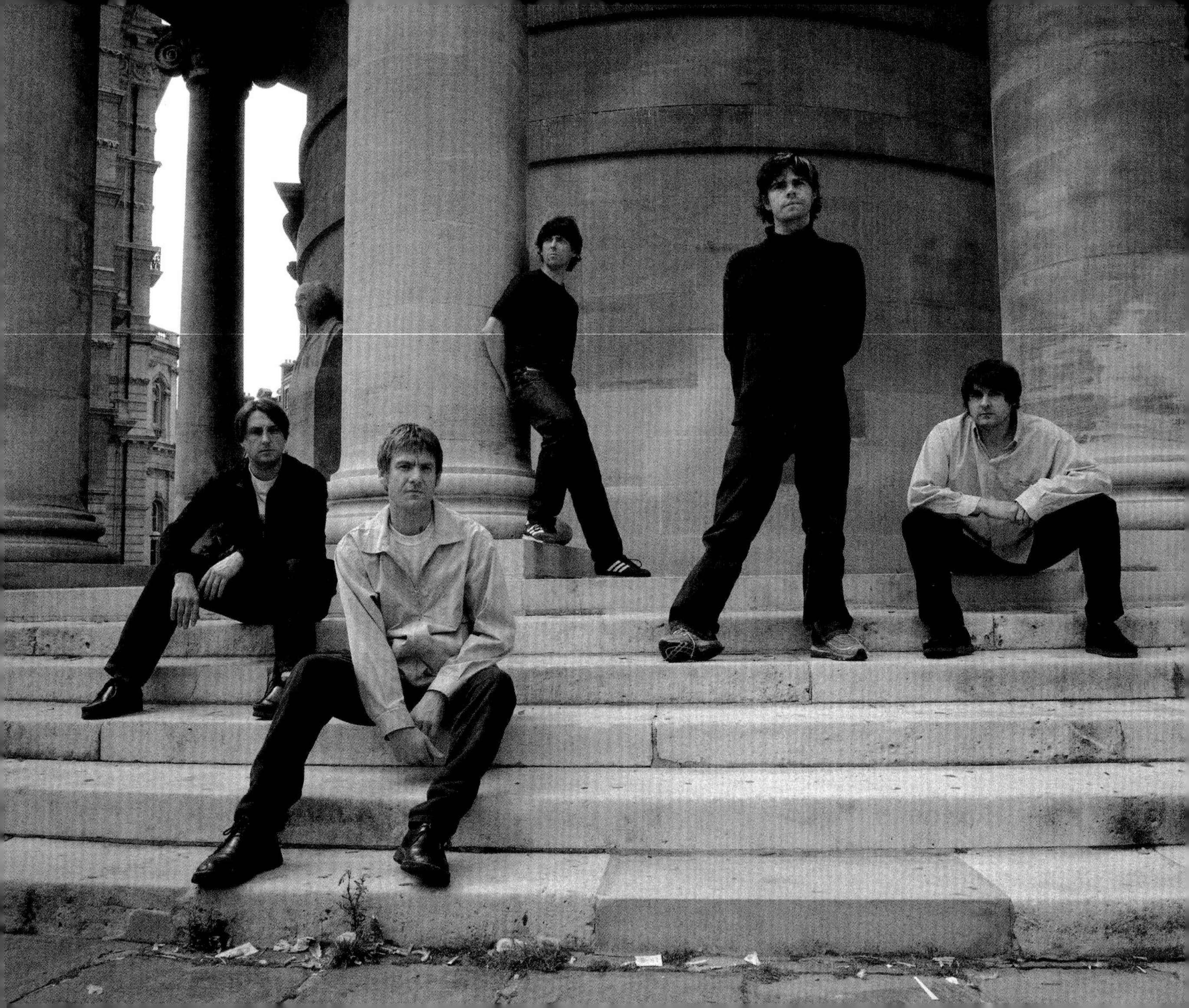

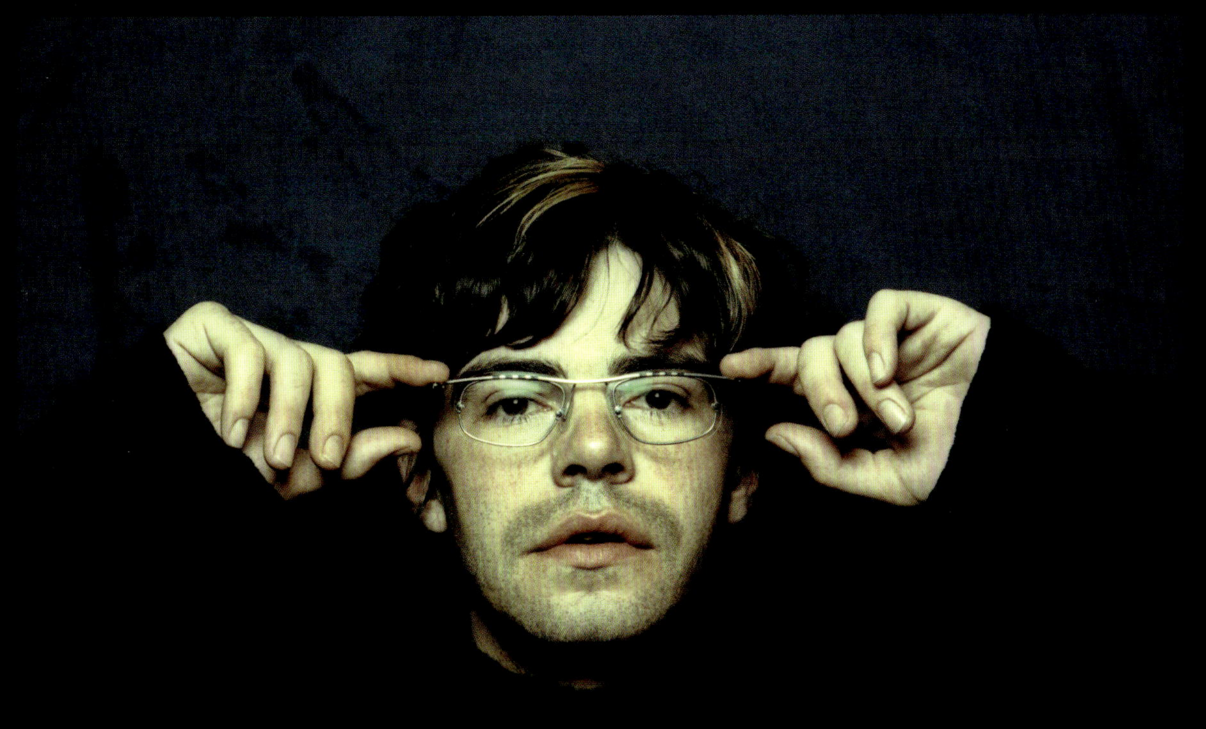

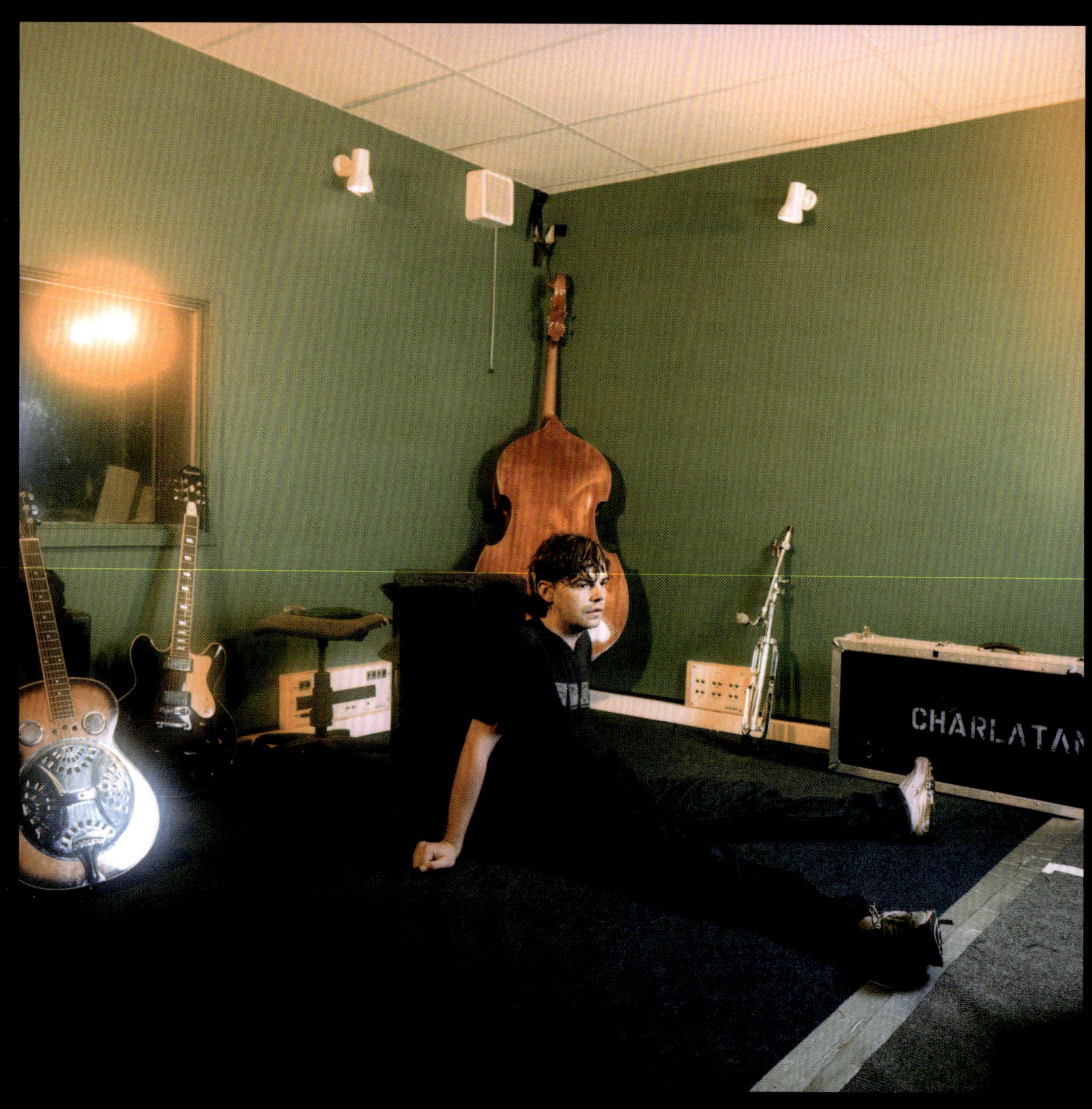
CHARLATAN

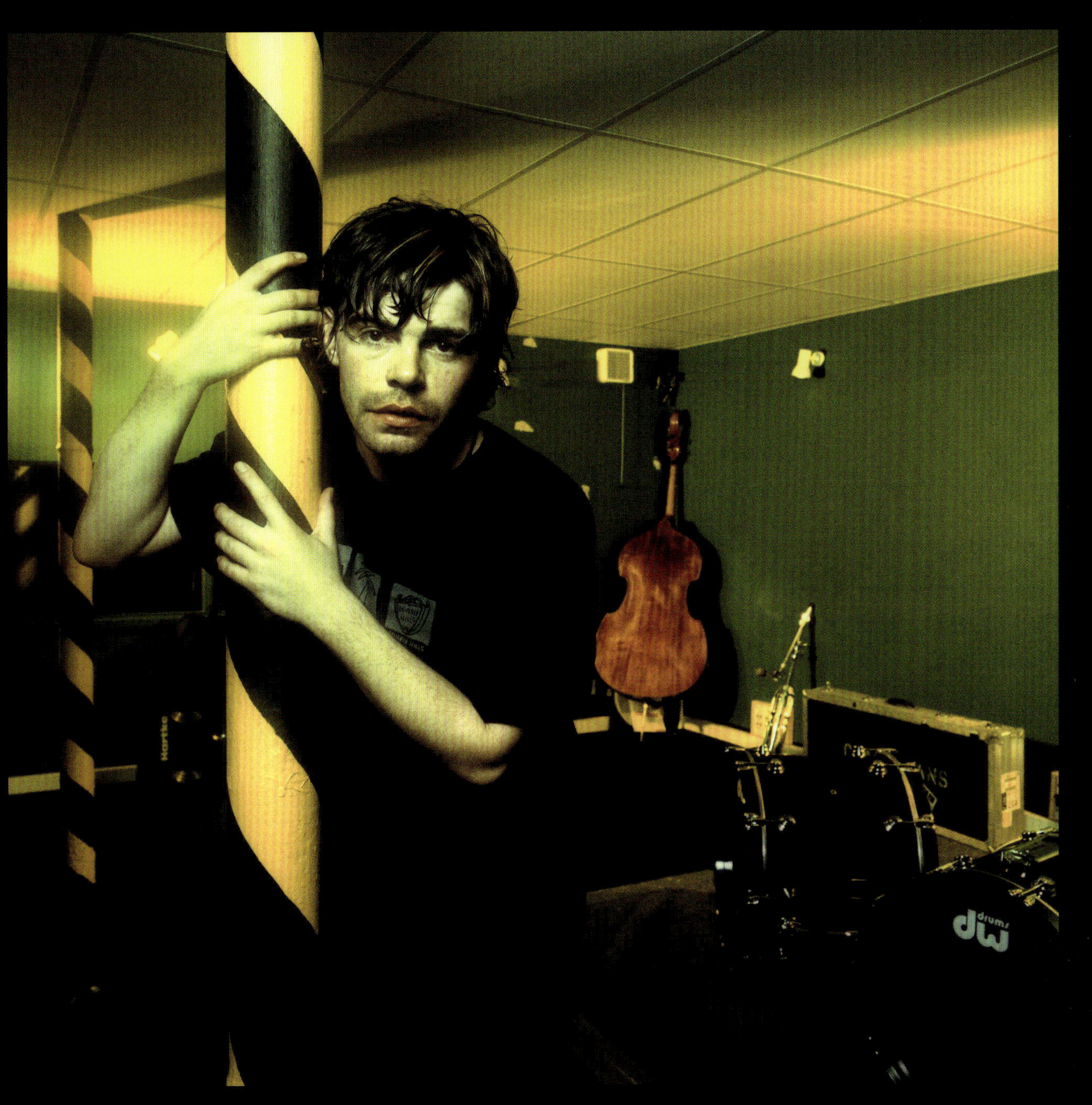

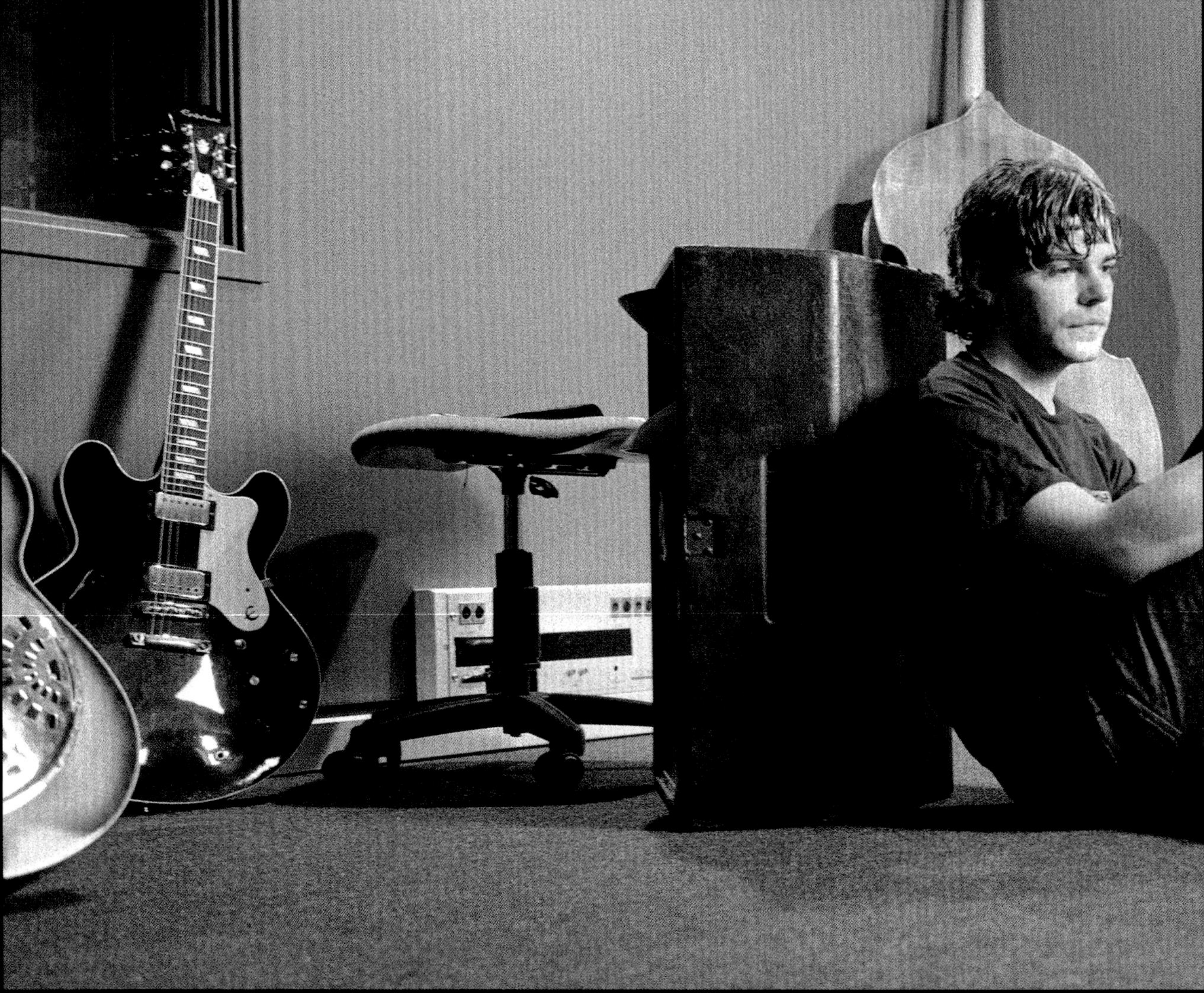

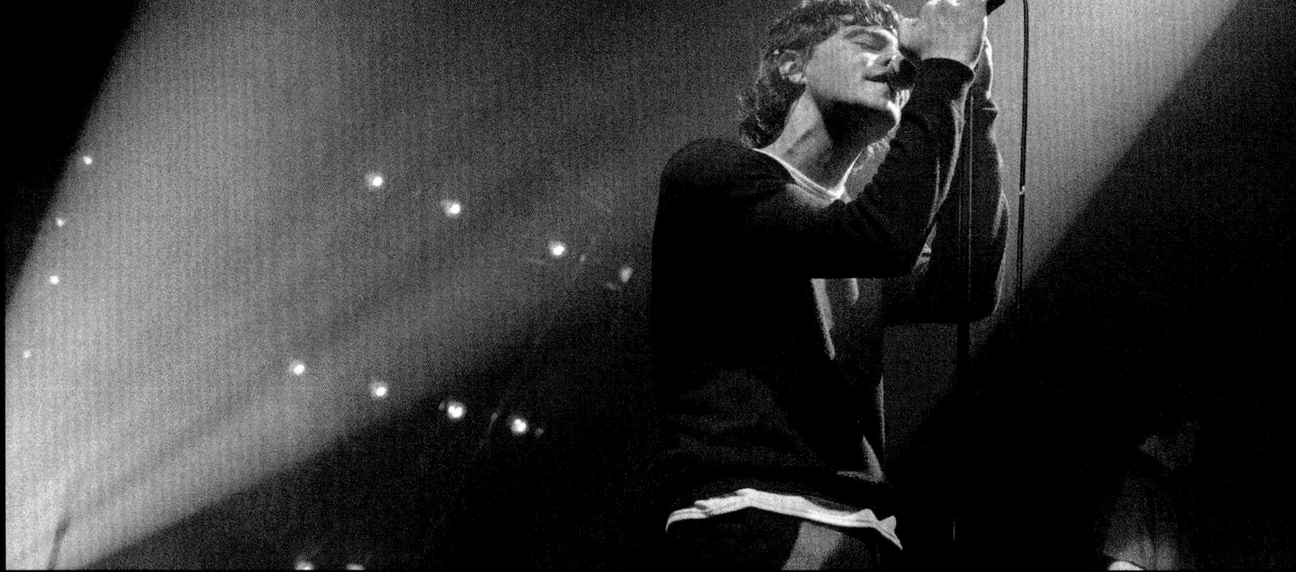

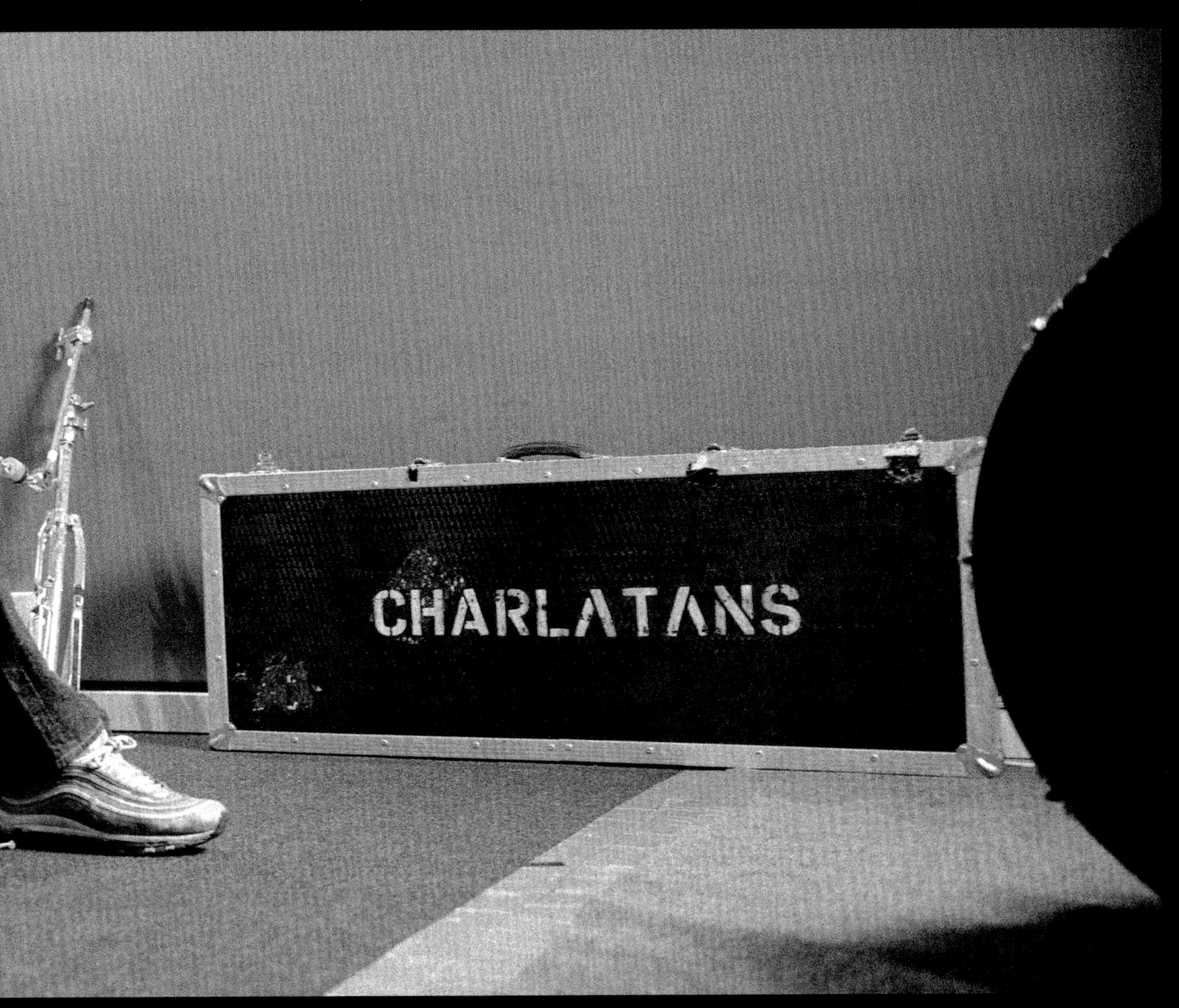
CHARLATANS

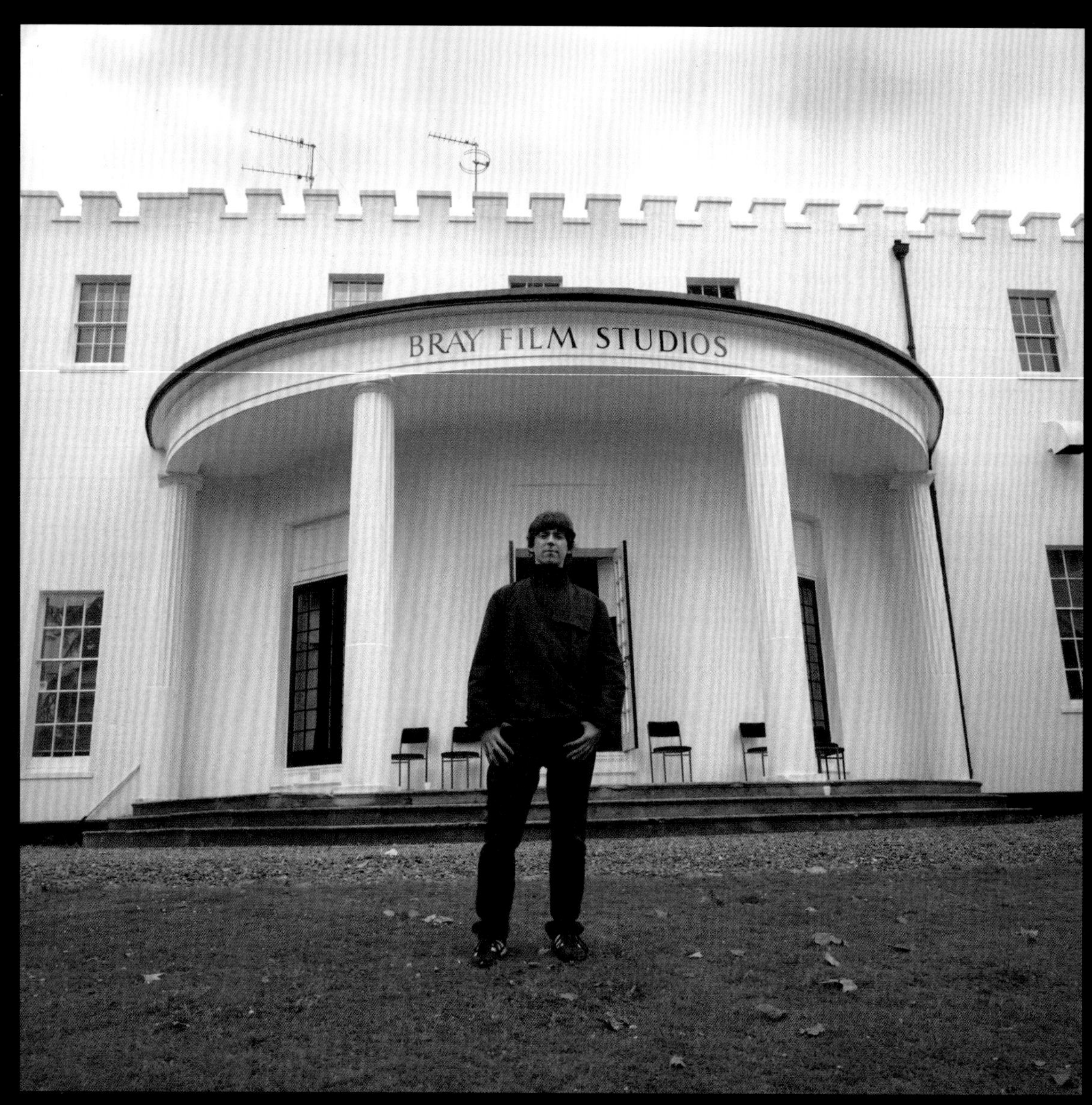
BRAY FILM STUDIOS

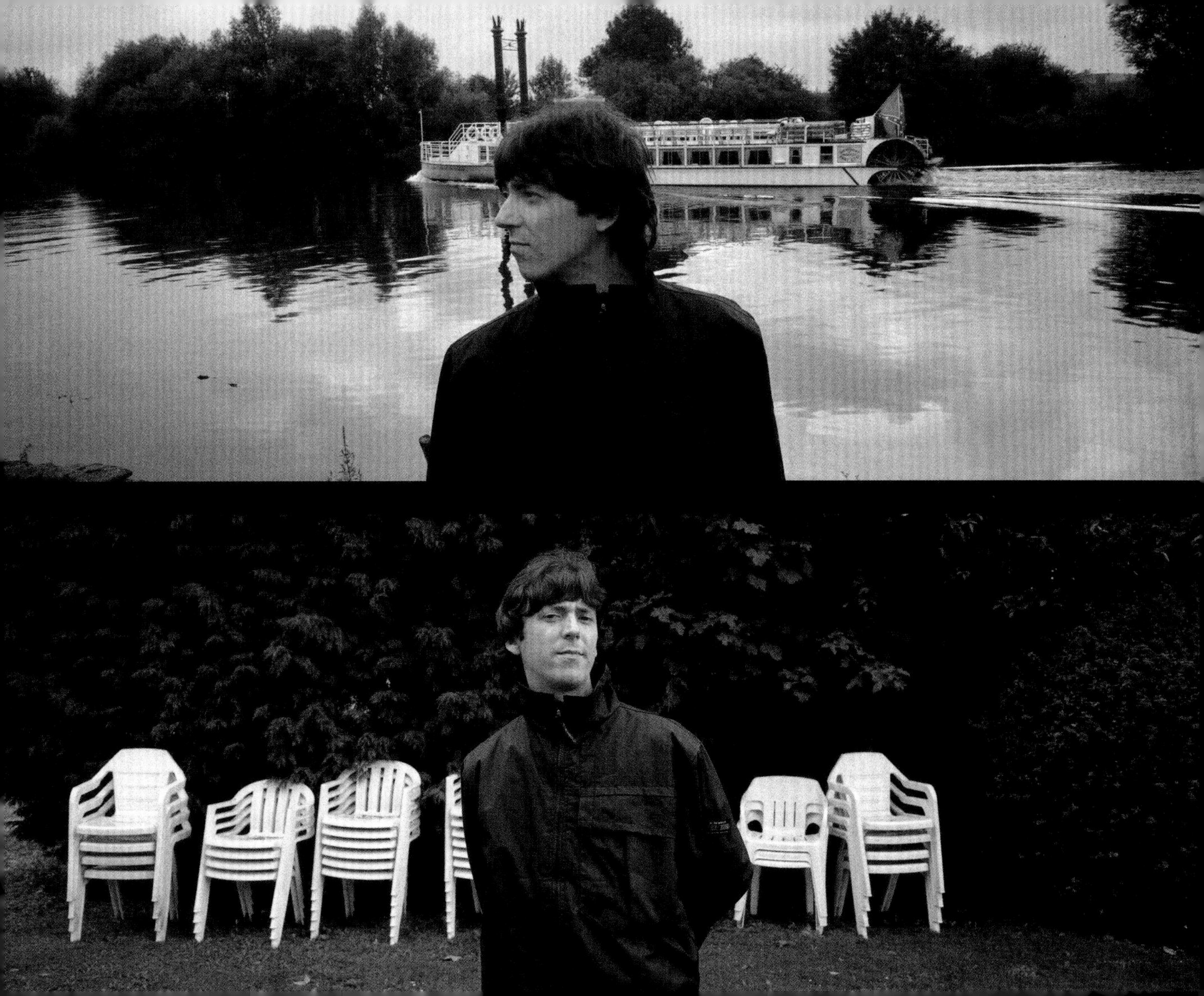

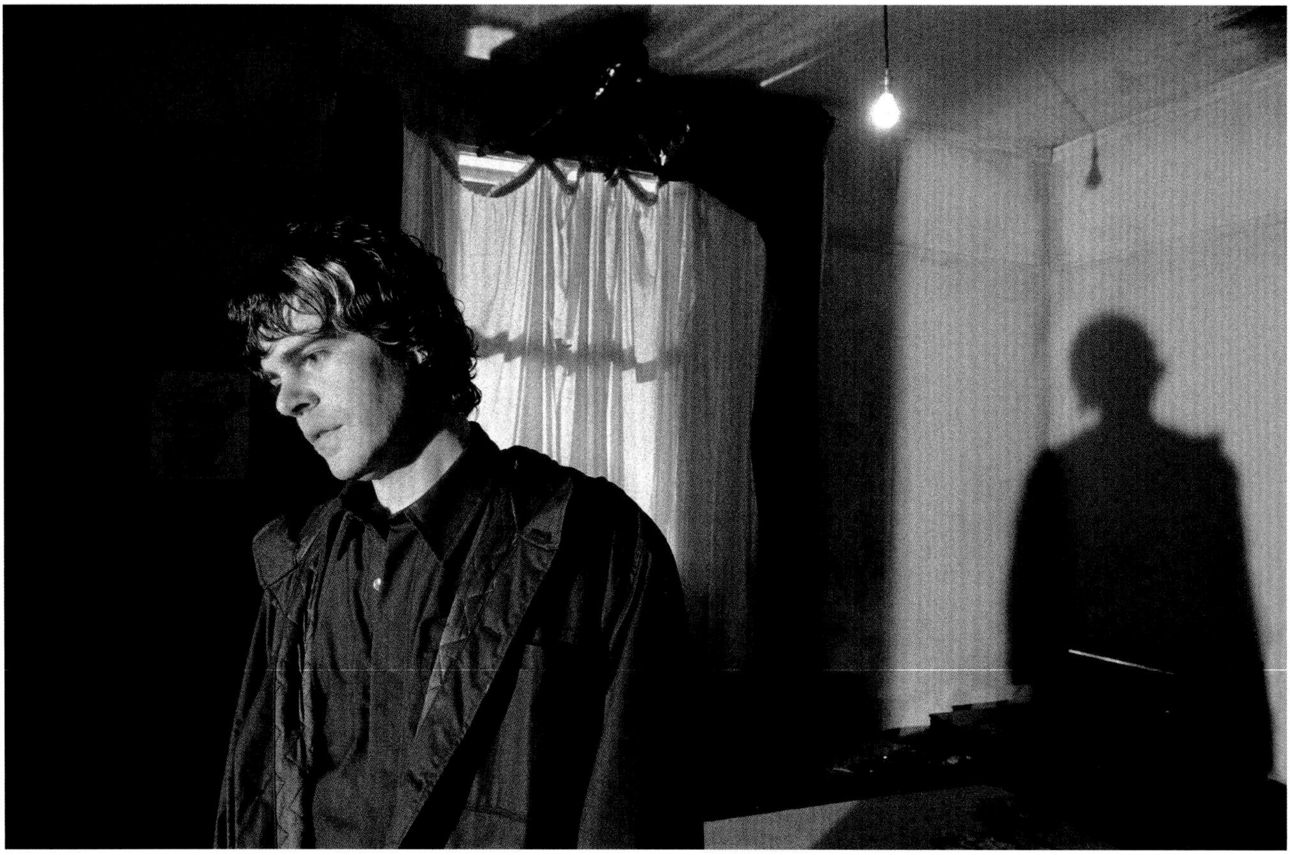

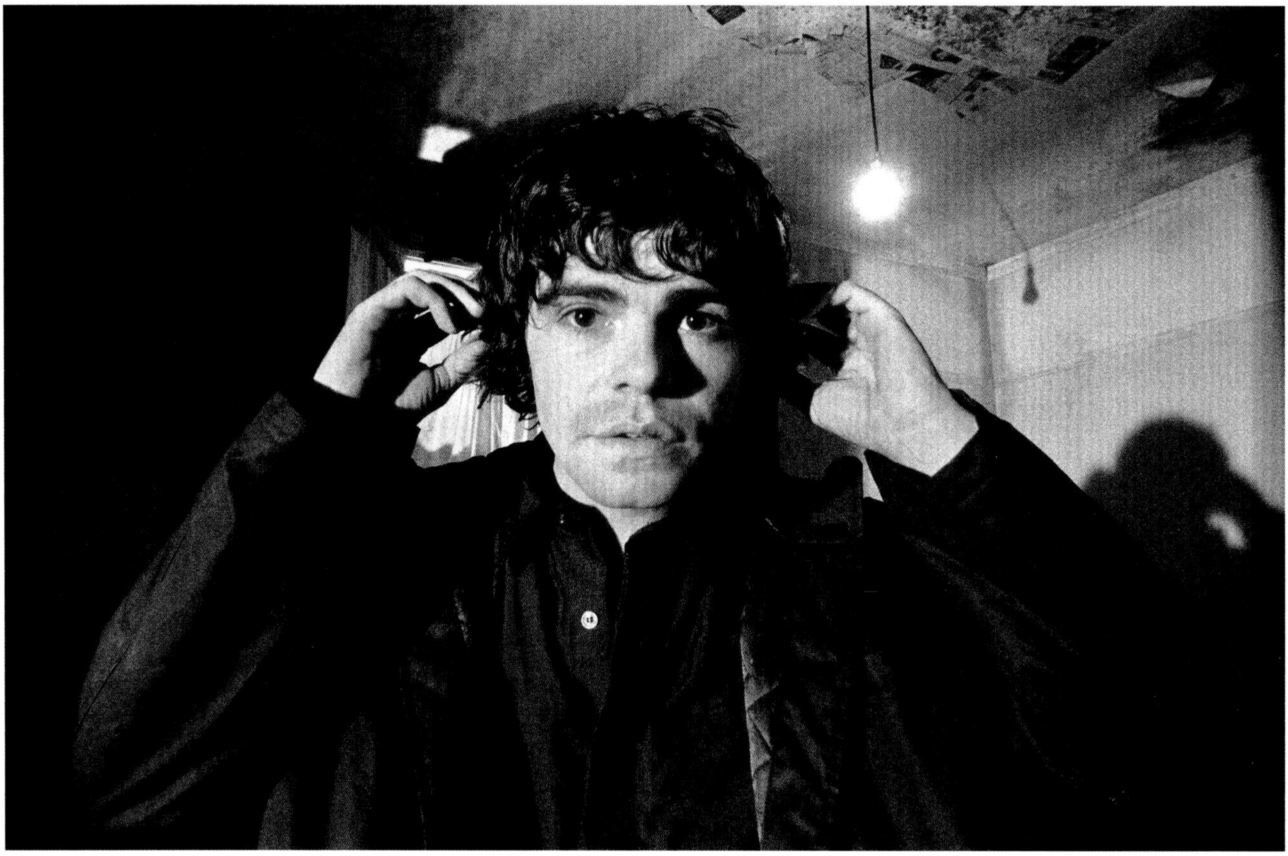

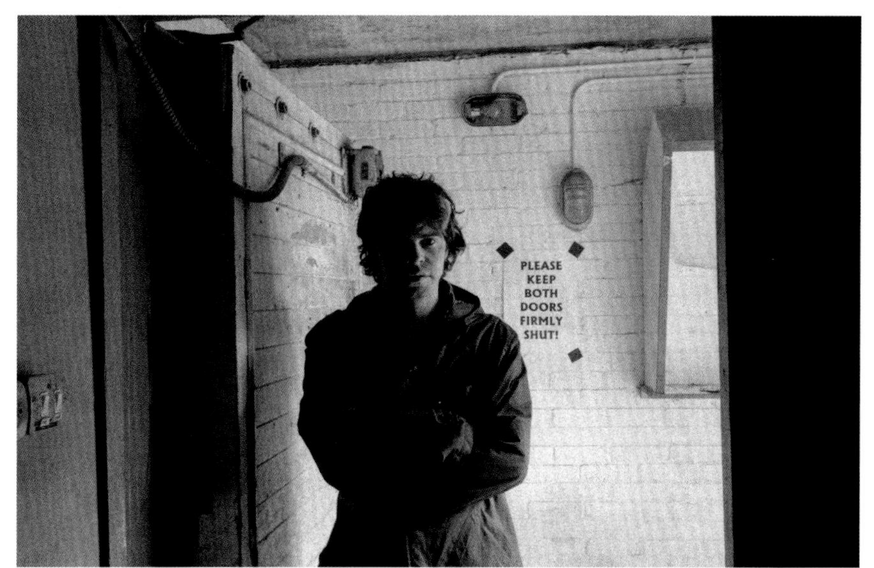
PLEASE
KEEP
BOTH
DOORS
FIRMLY
SHUT!

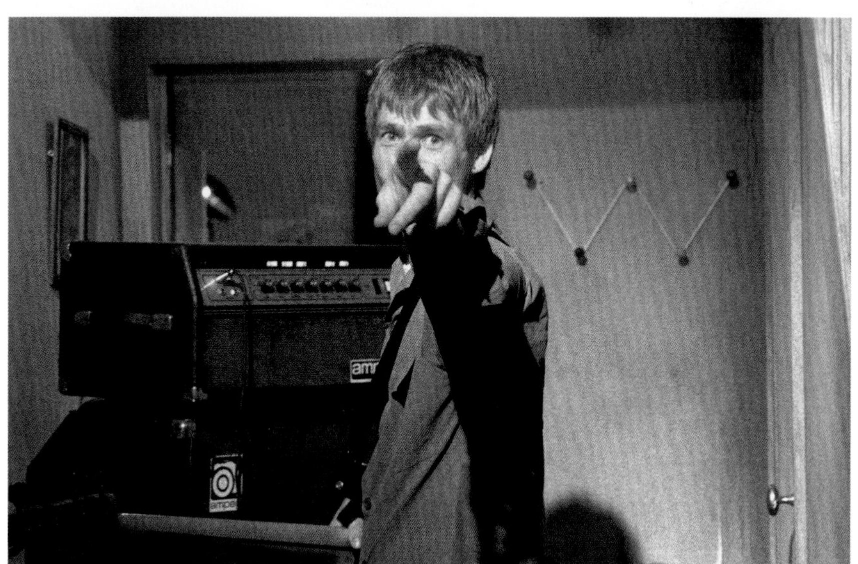

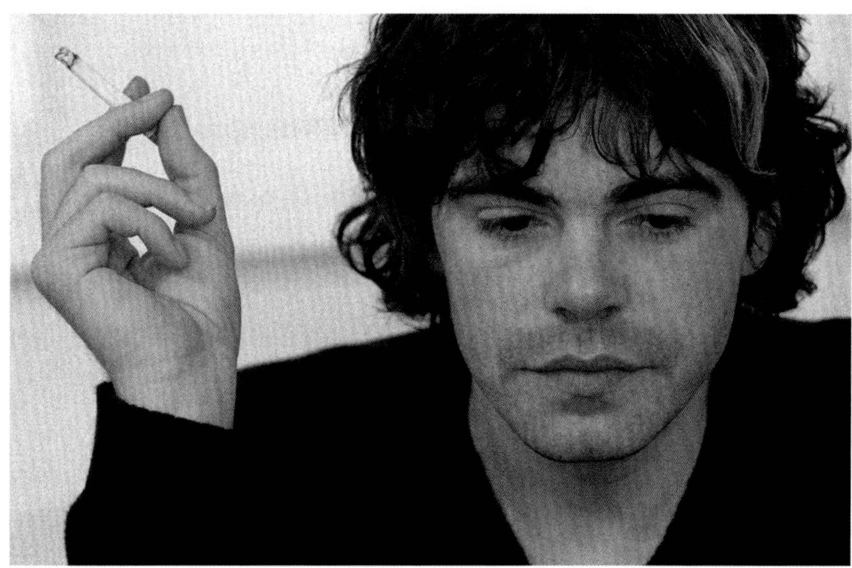

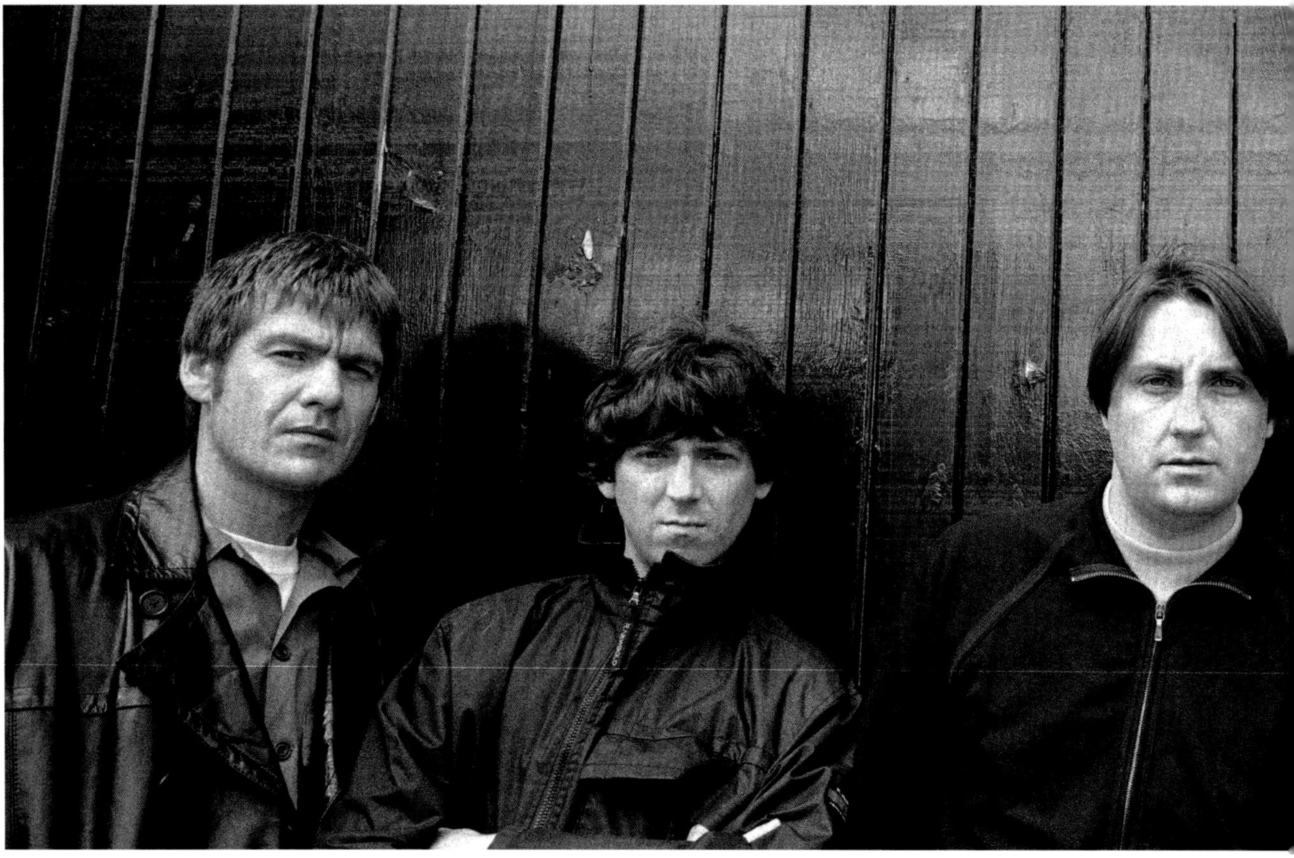

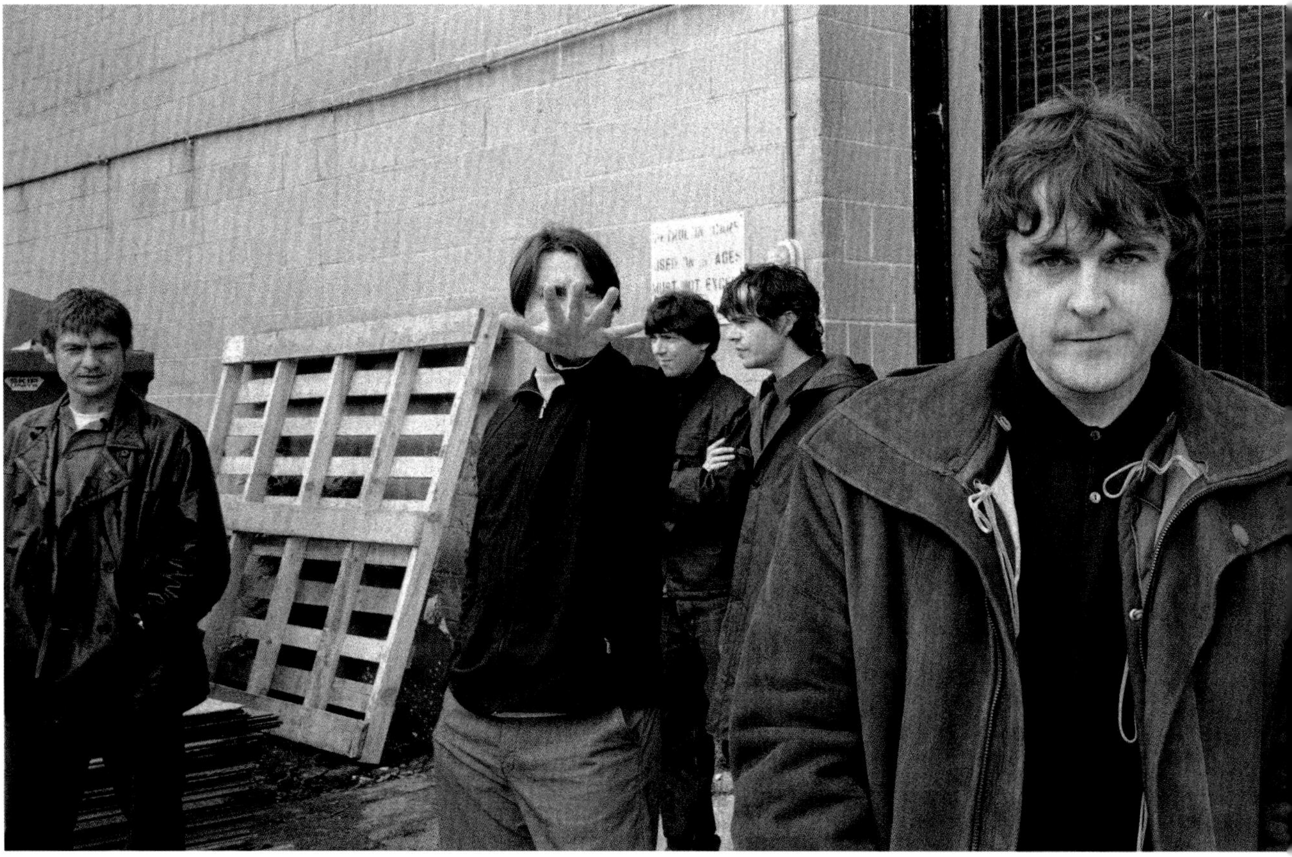

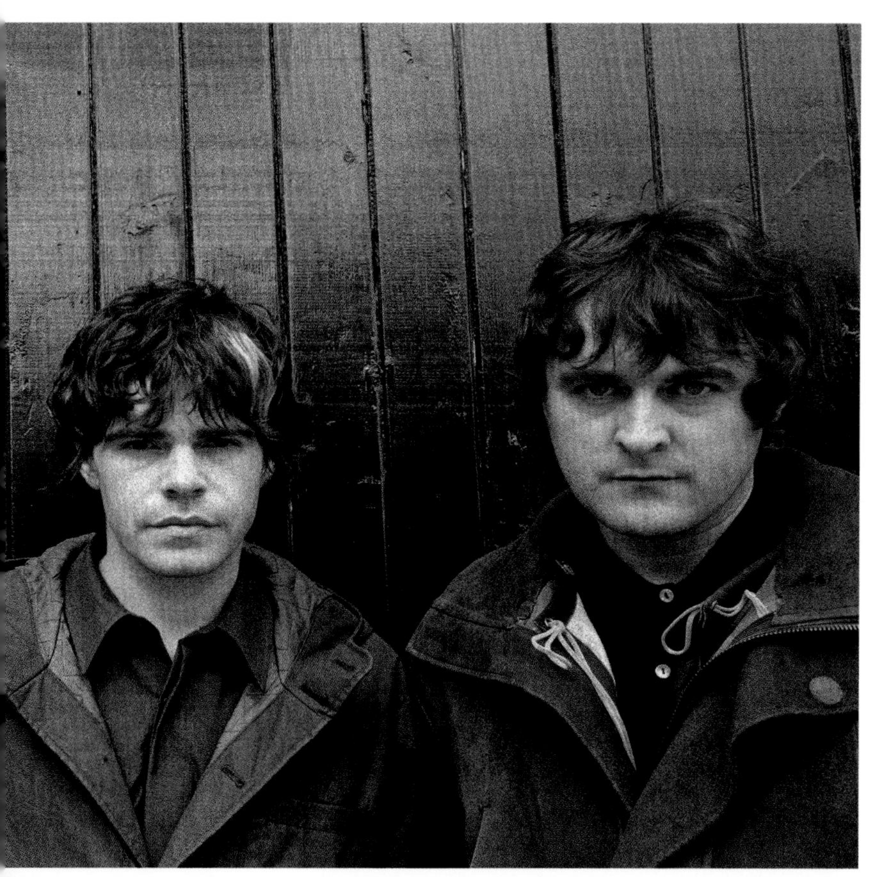

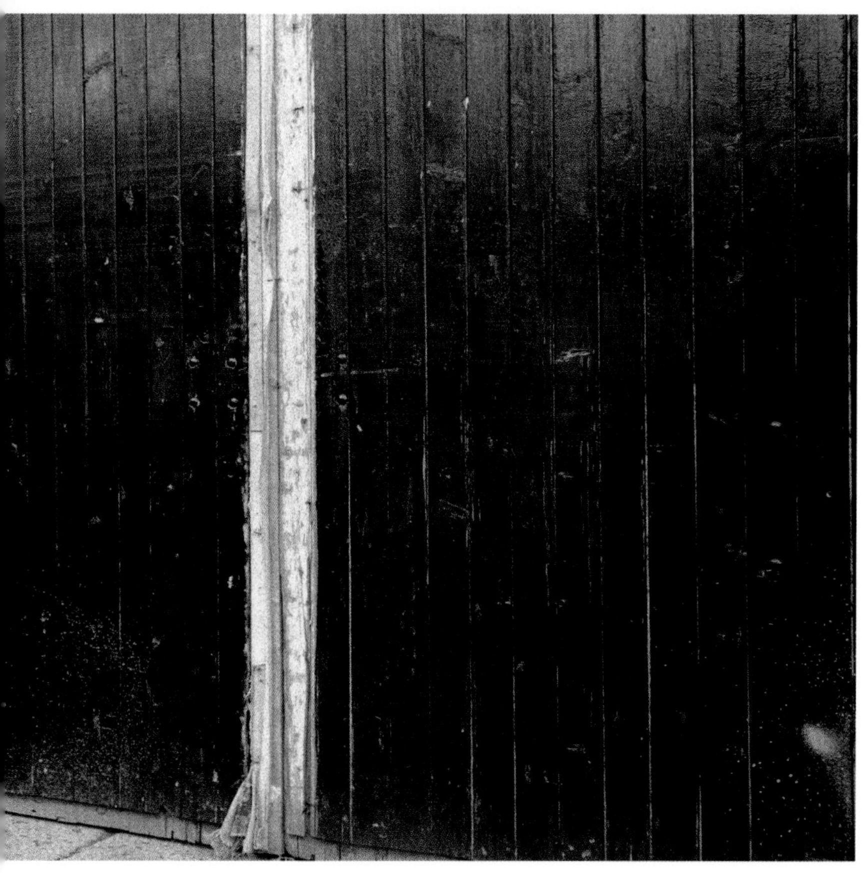

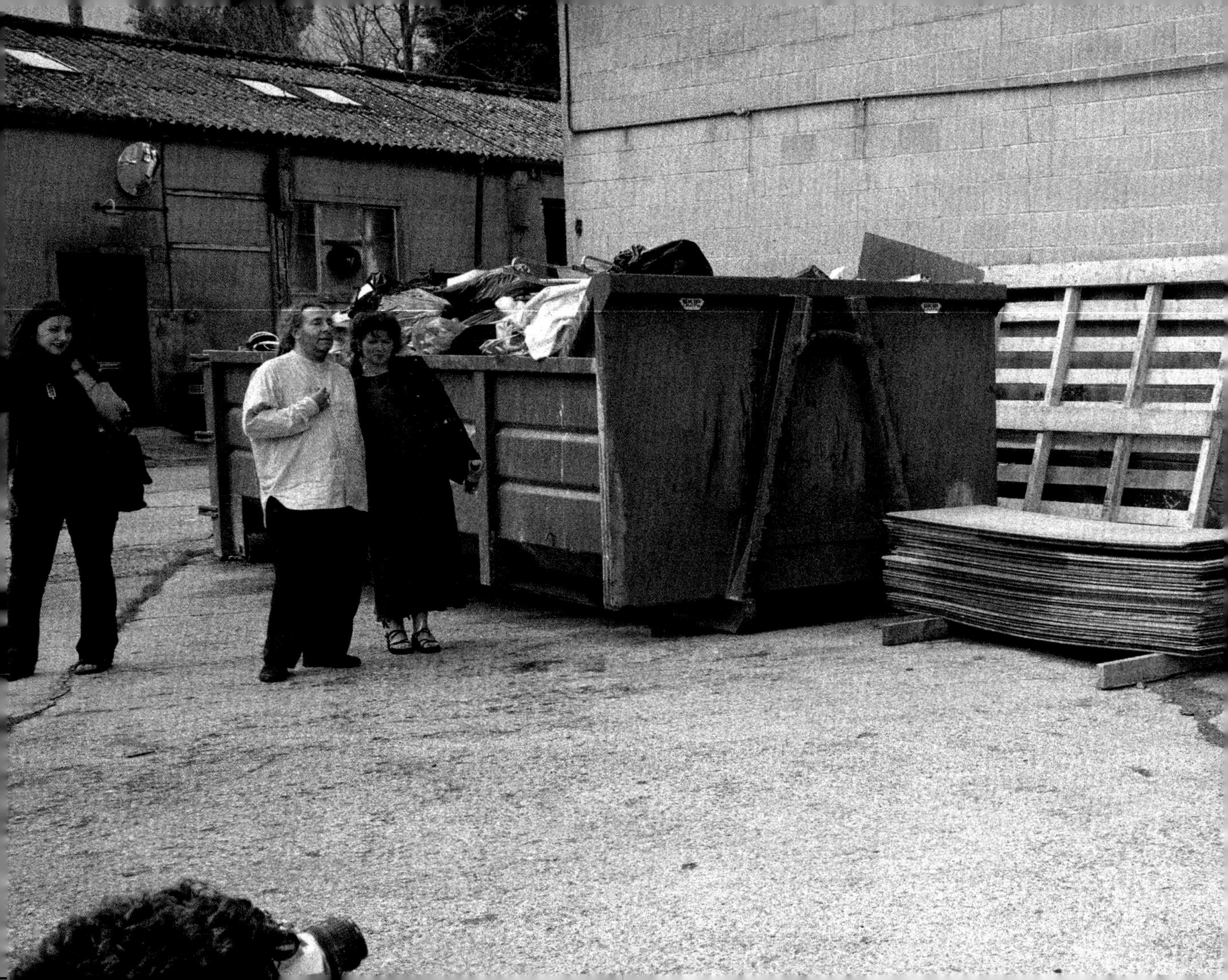

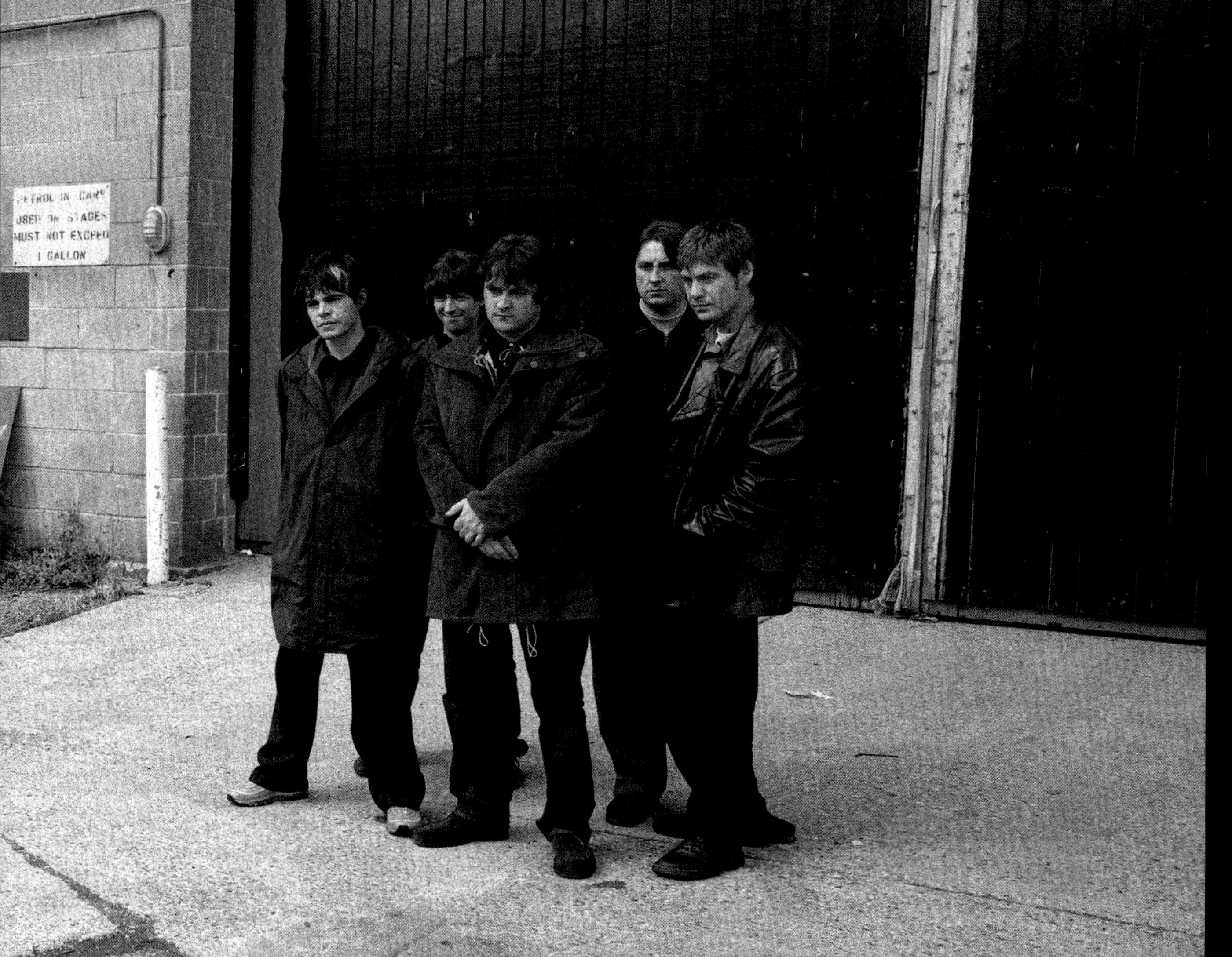
PETROL IN CARS
USED ON STAGES
MUST NOT EXCEED
1 GALLON

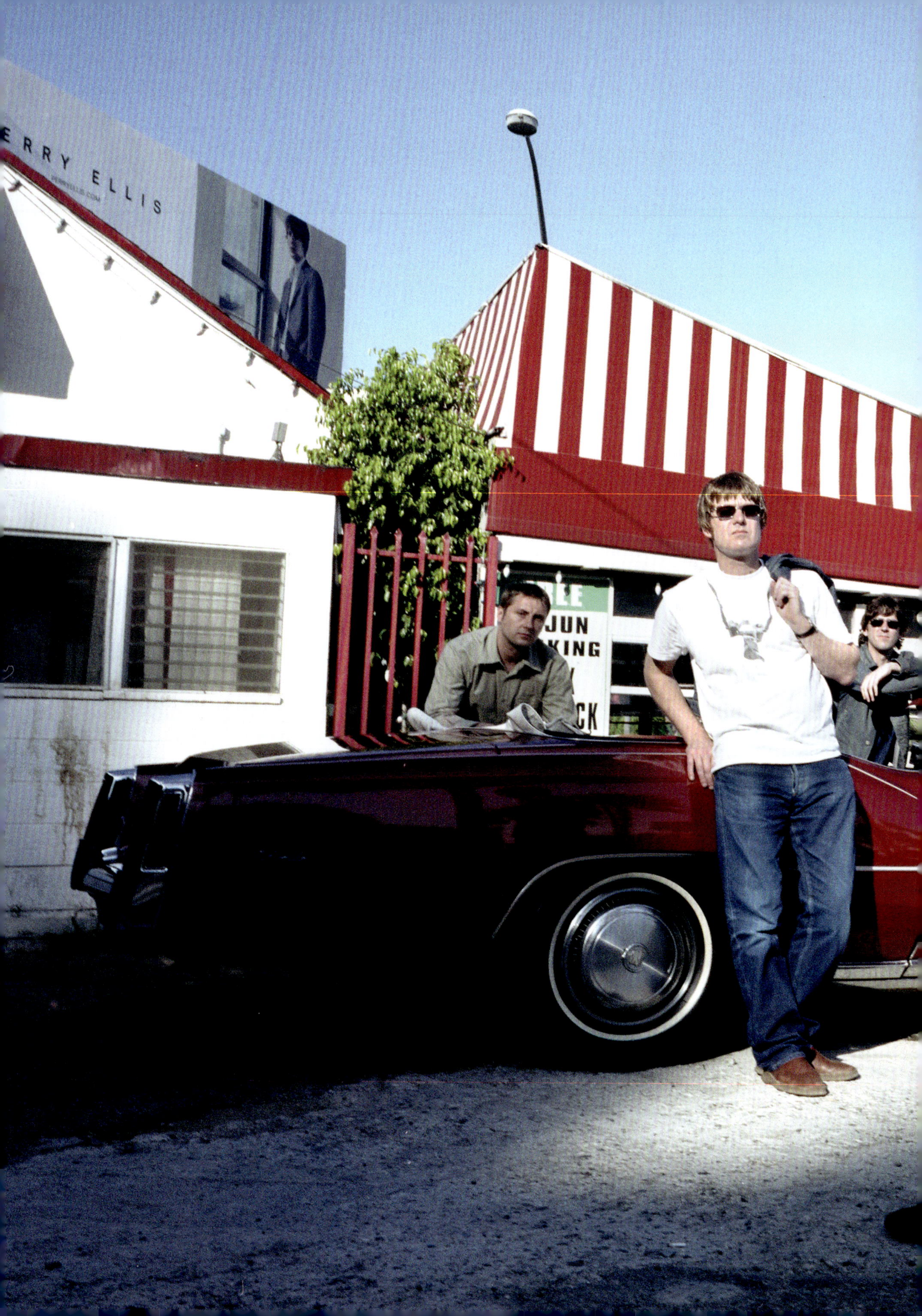
ERRY ELLIS

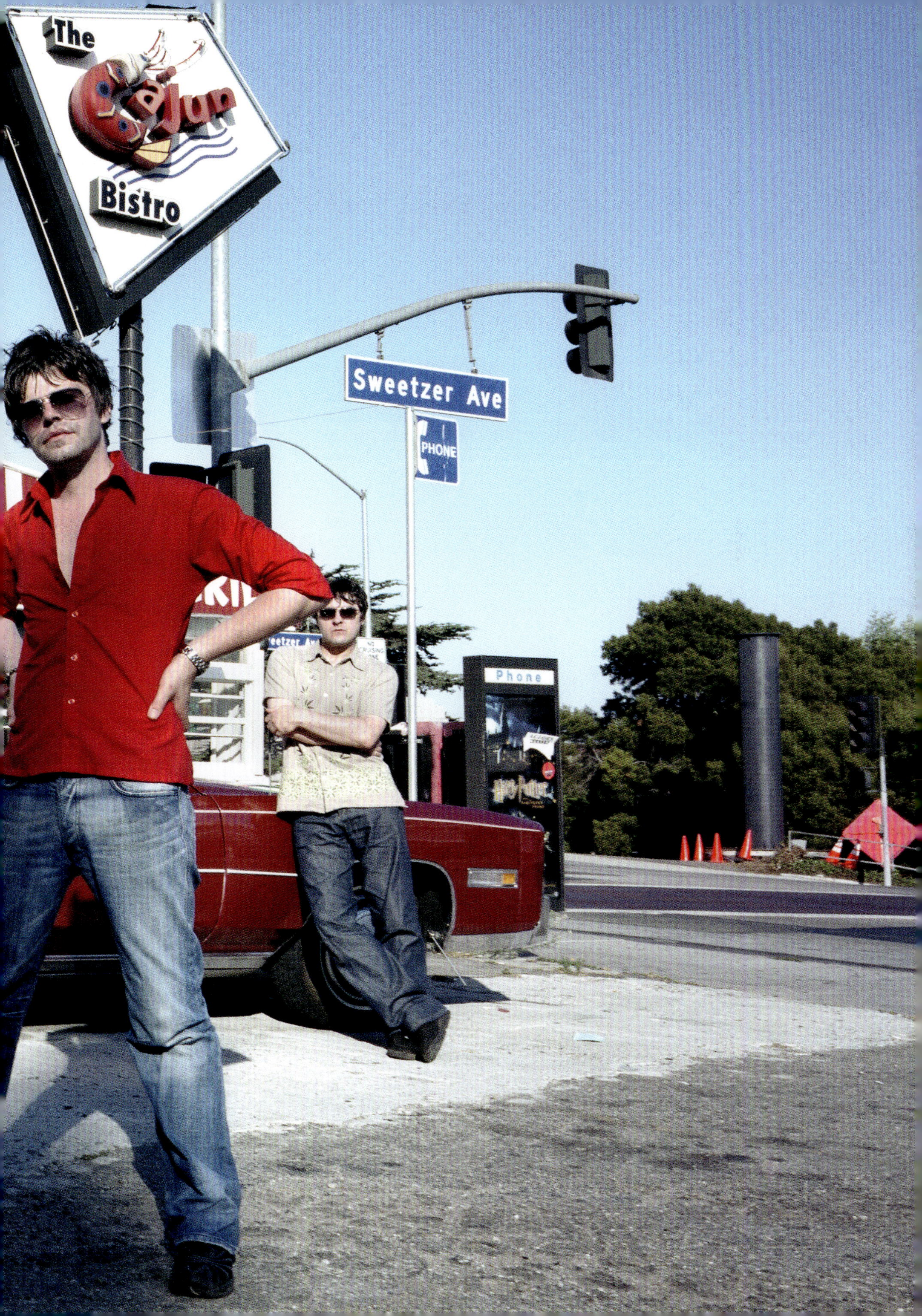
The
Cajun
Bistro
Sweetzer Ave
PHONE
Phone

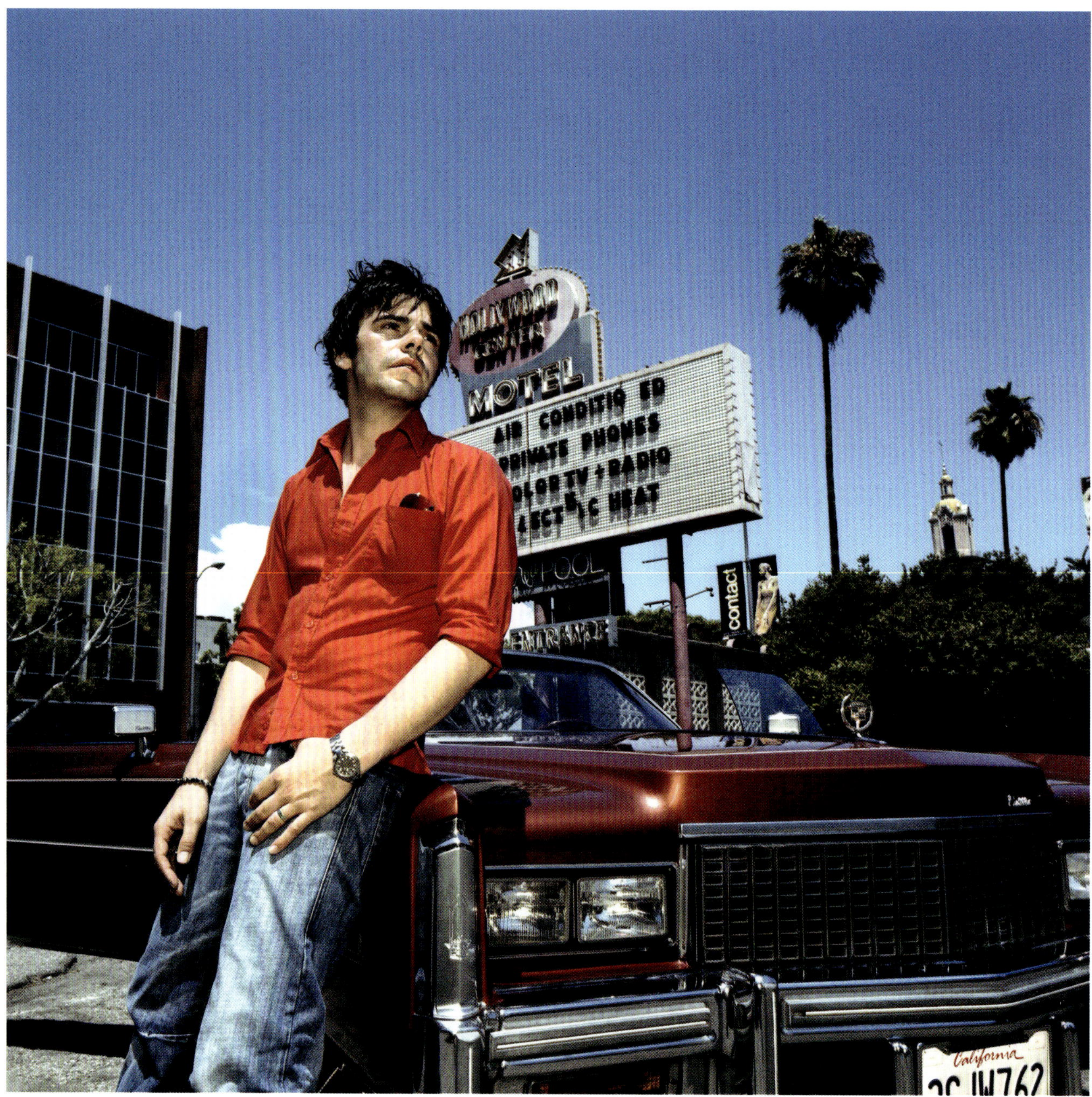

The sunlight in Los Angeles was like a new start for us. I took a different approach to my vocals on *Wonderland* and we were far from where we had started a decade before, both geographically and metaphorically. The 101 Freeway replaced the M6. Palm trees replaced Delamere Forest, and we had strategically placed sunglasses that covered up the damage from the early morning martinis. Having said that, life was good. These pictures are taken on Wonderland Avenue, which just in terms of its name was a playground. It had the bonus of being attached to Mulholland Drive – our neighbourhood was literally a film set. Tom arrived with a giant red Cadillac that was not only a prop but also our transport. As clichéd as it was, we were there for it. From roadside diners to Laurel Canyon, we'd hop out, grab drinks, take pics, jump back in. Rinse and repeat – documenting the upcoming release of *Wonderland*, pencilled in for 10 September 2001, but that's another story. We were absorbing all of the influences around us and if you poured these photographs into a mixing desk the resulting sound would definitely be the Sly Stone, Curtis Mayfield-esque recordings we'd been making.

Tom:
This shoot was done for the *NME*. It reminds me of how hard it was to get the "group shots only, we're a band" chaps together by this point, once they'd got used to Tim being the centre of attention. I had to drag them out of a hotel bar across the road to pose by this car for all of five minutes, with the promise they could go straight back after I'd got the shot.

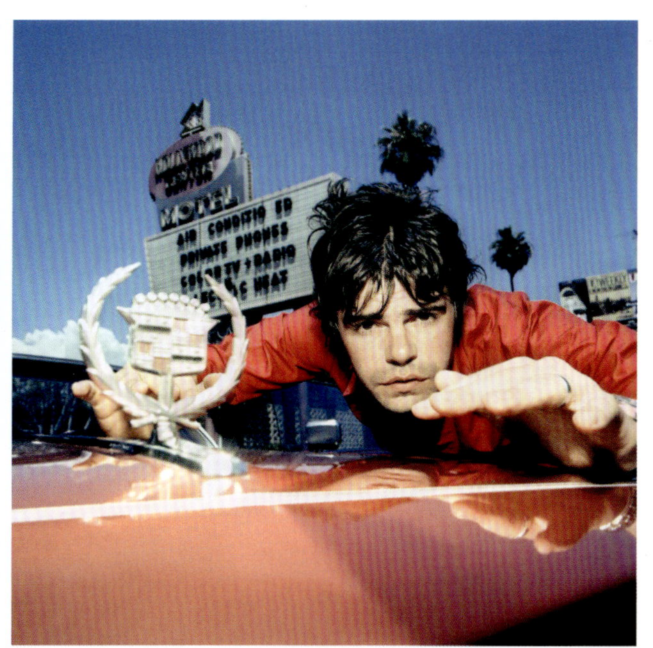
MOTEL
PRIVATE PHONES

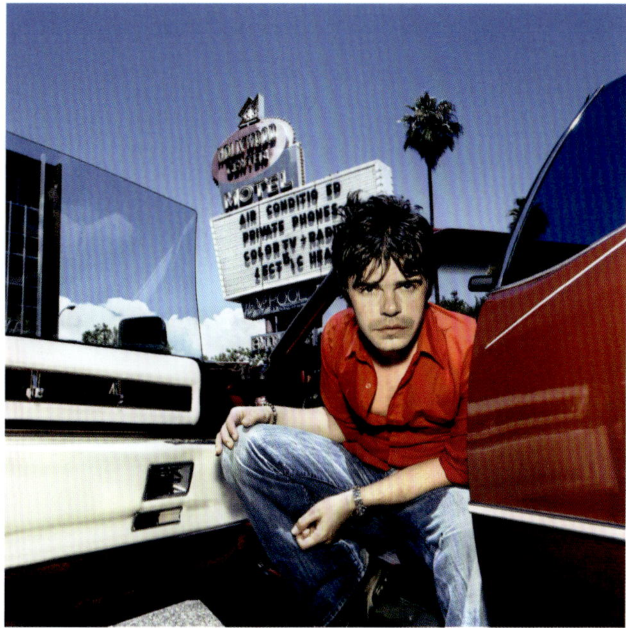
MOTEL

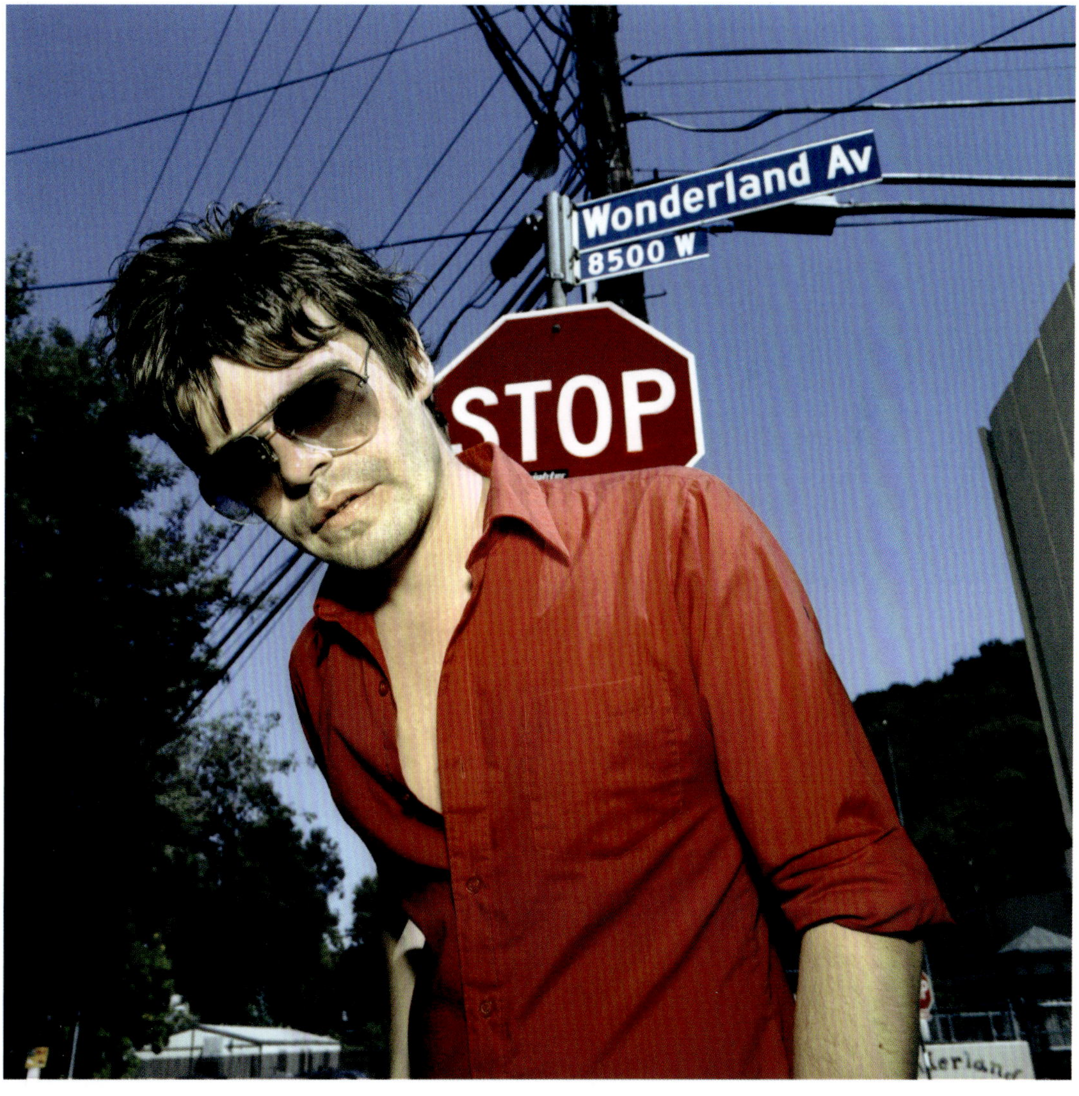

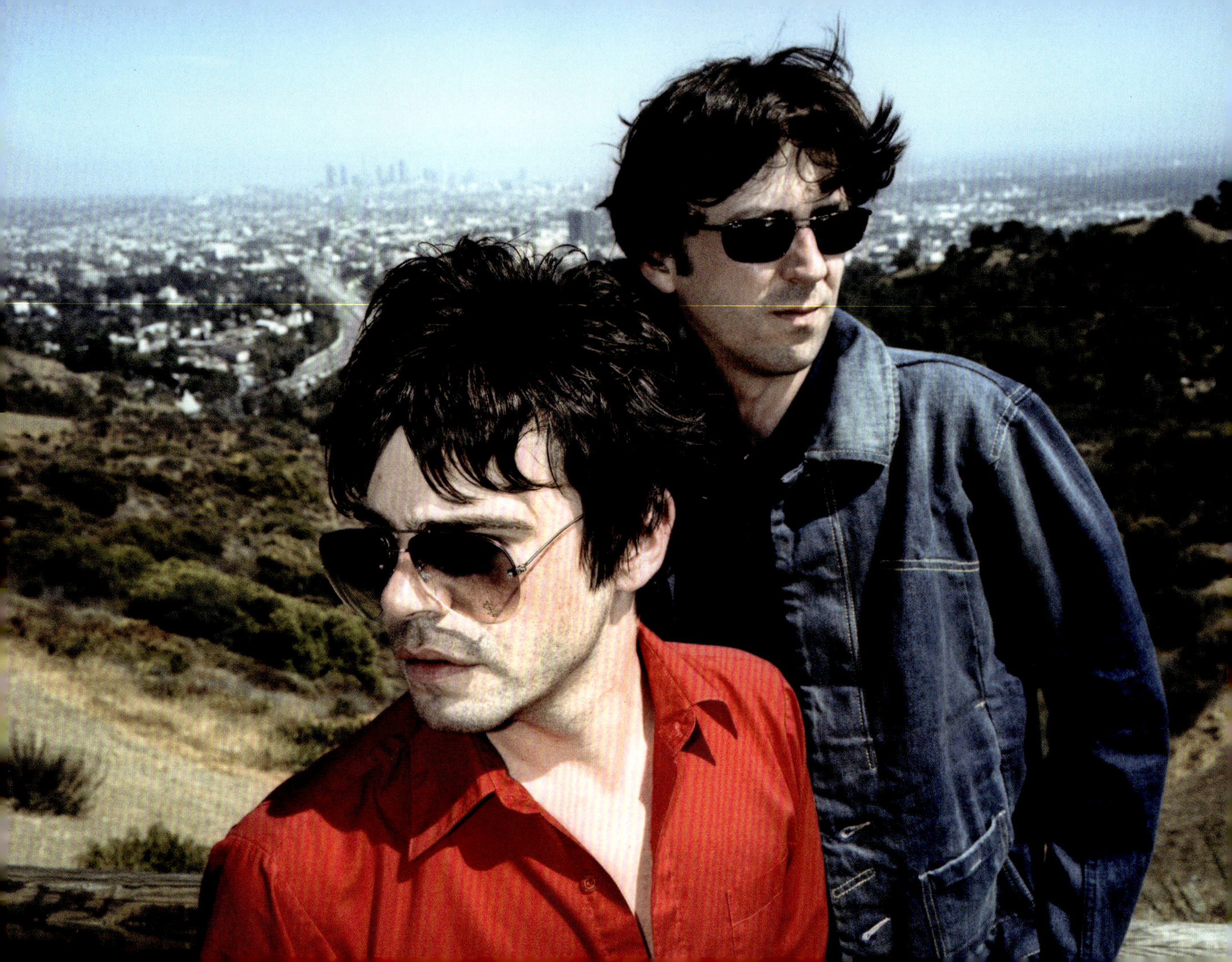

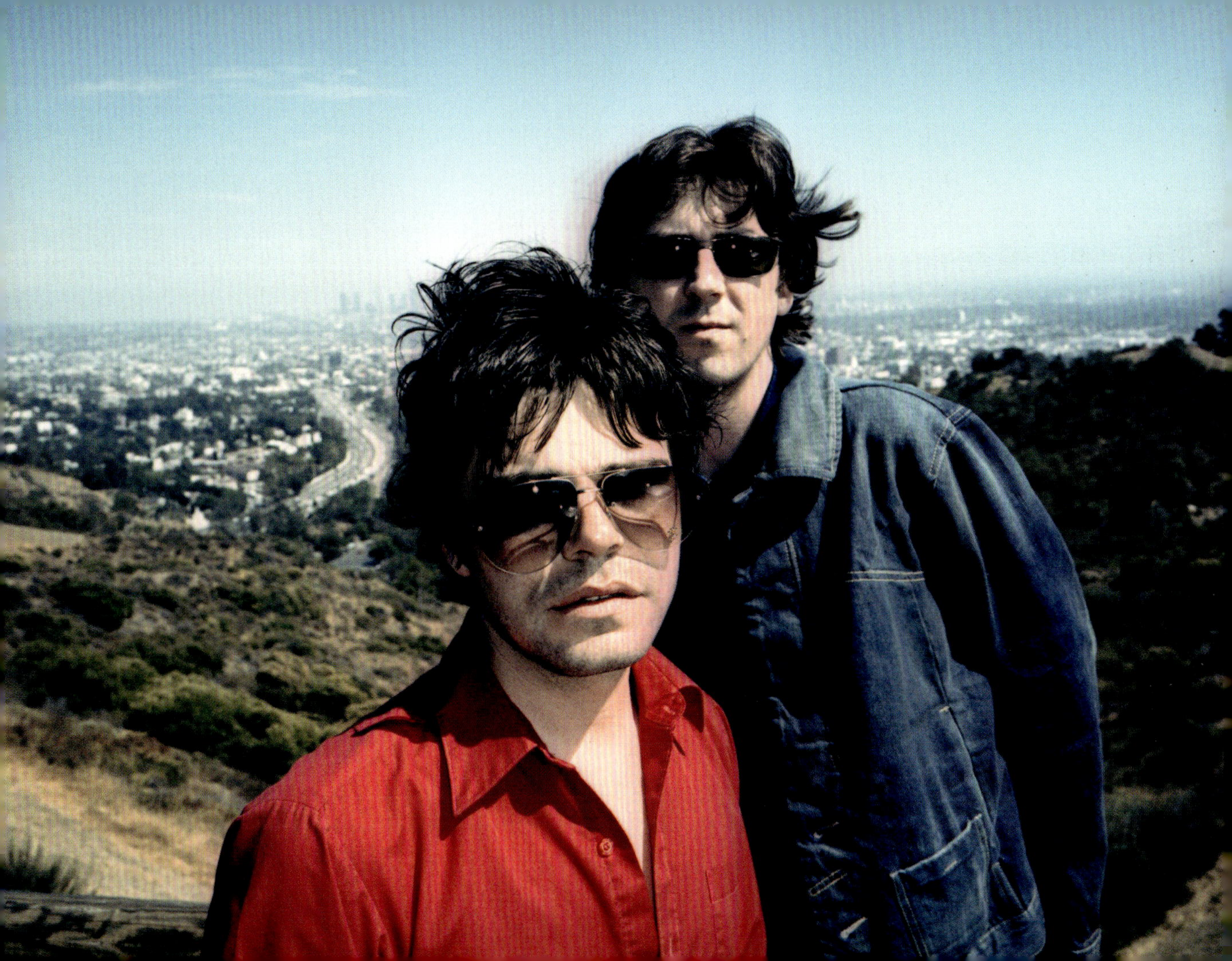

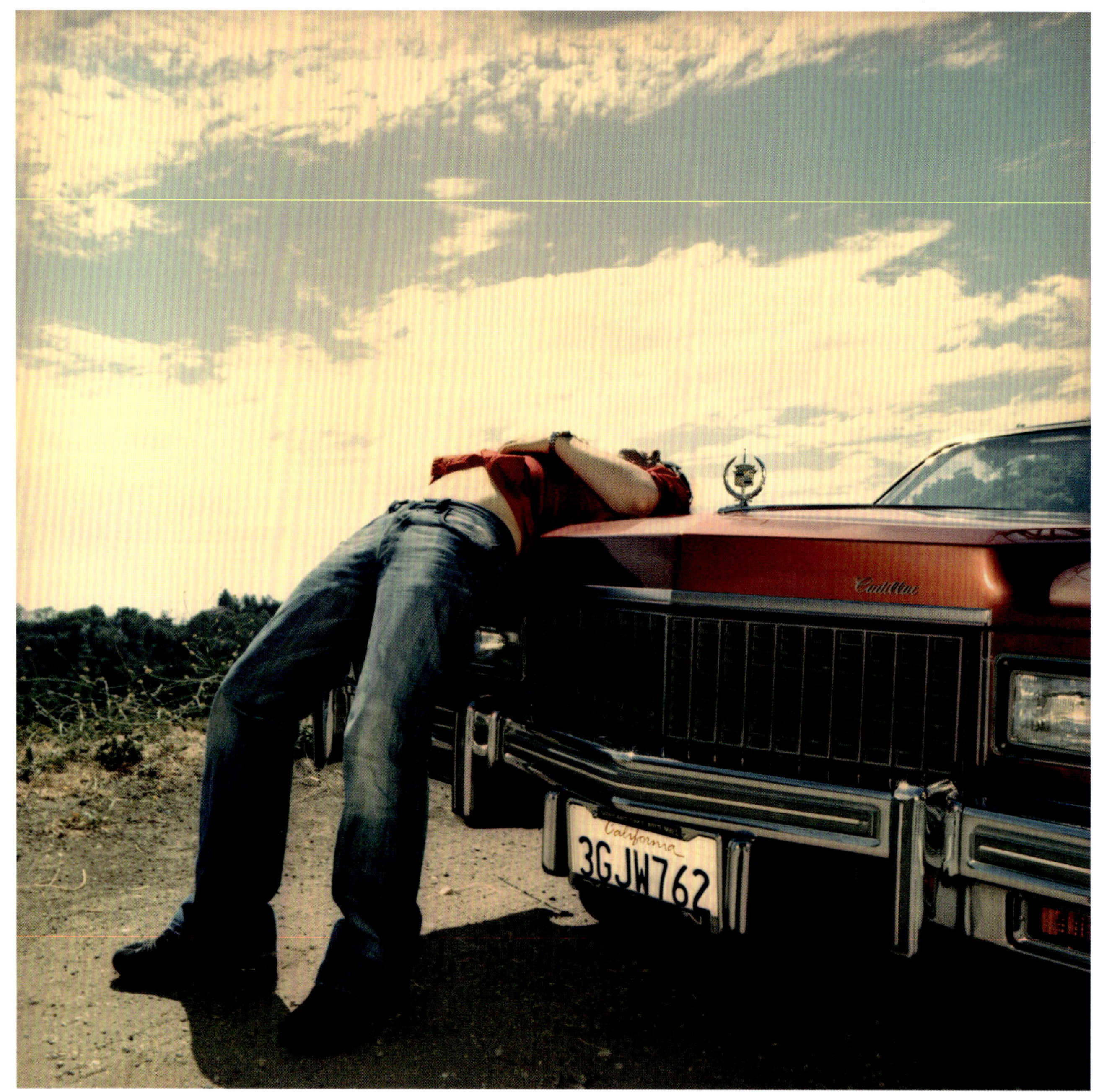
California
3GJW762

Epilogue

Reconnecting with Tom Sheehan for this book has been a fantastic experience for me. I don't spend a whole load of time listening to our old music or going through magazines and photos, but this has been a journey that I have loved. I could hear conversations with Rob. I could feel the heat of those early gigs and the power of Martin and Jon's bass and drums behind me. Inspirational writing sessions with Mark. The brief but beautiful times with Martin Duffy and how we thought we couldn't go on, but, how life changed when we met Tony.

I hope this book is as compelling to see as it was to read. Our times with Tom were some of the best we ever had.

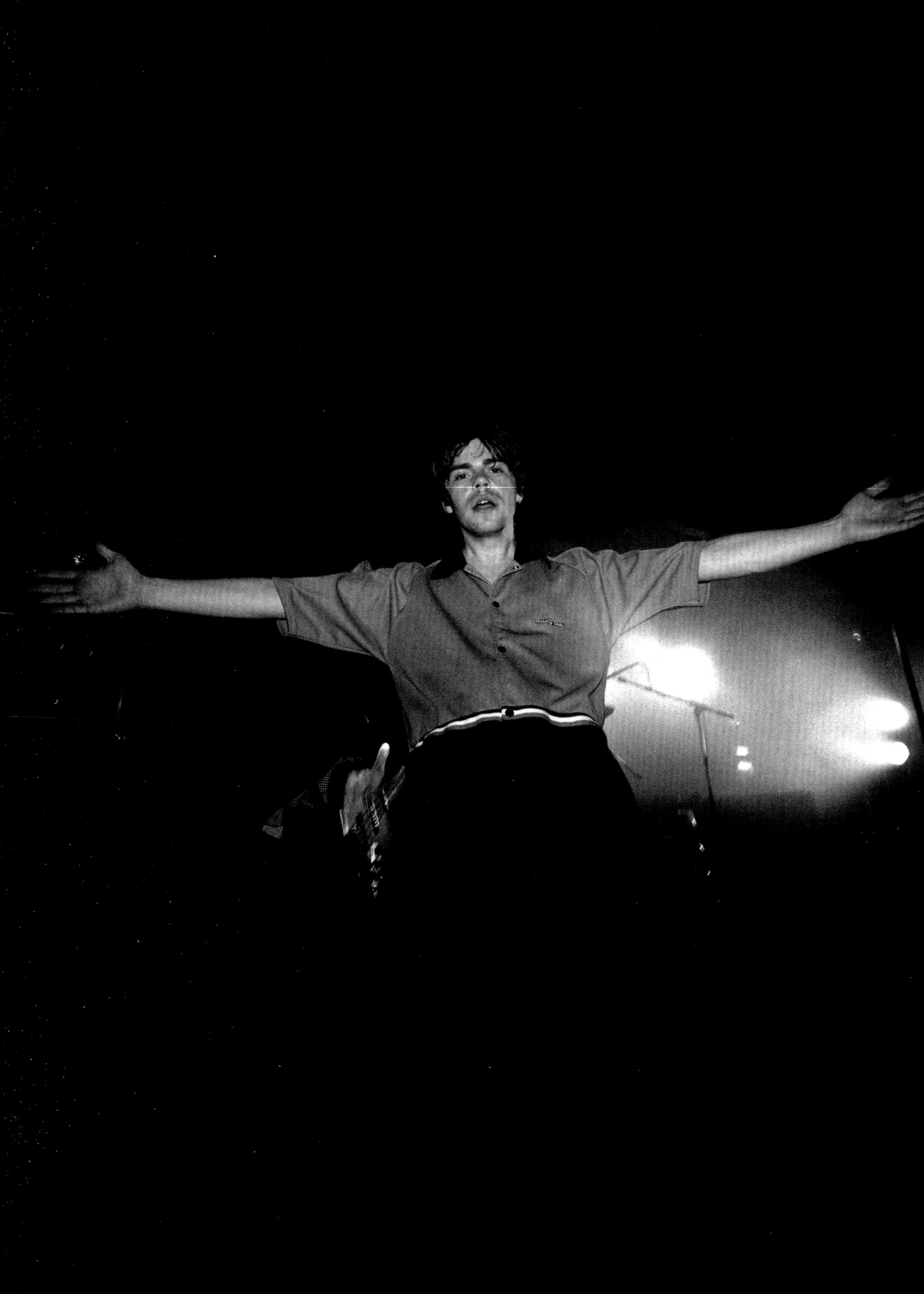

Design by Carl Glover at Aleph Studio
Scans by Adam Powell

First published in 2025 by Welbeck
An imprint of HEADLINE PUBLISHING GROUP

1

Cataloguing in Publication Data is available from the British Library

ISBN: 9781035424290

Printed and bound in China

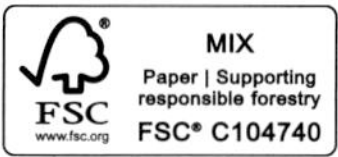

Headline's policy is to use papers that are natural, renewable and recyclable products and made from wood grown in well-managed forests and other controlled sources. The logging and manufacturing processes are expected to conform to the environmental regulations of the country of origin.

HEADLINE PUBLISHING GROUP
An Hachette UK Company
Carmelite House
50 Victoria Embankment
London EC4Y 0DZ

The authorised representative in the EEA is Hachette Ireland,
8 Castlecourt Centre, Dublin 15, D15 XTP3, Ireland (email: info@hbgi.ie)

www.headline.co.uk
www.hachette.co.uk

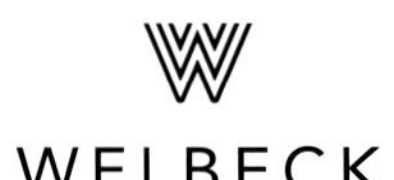
WELBECK

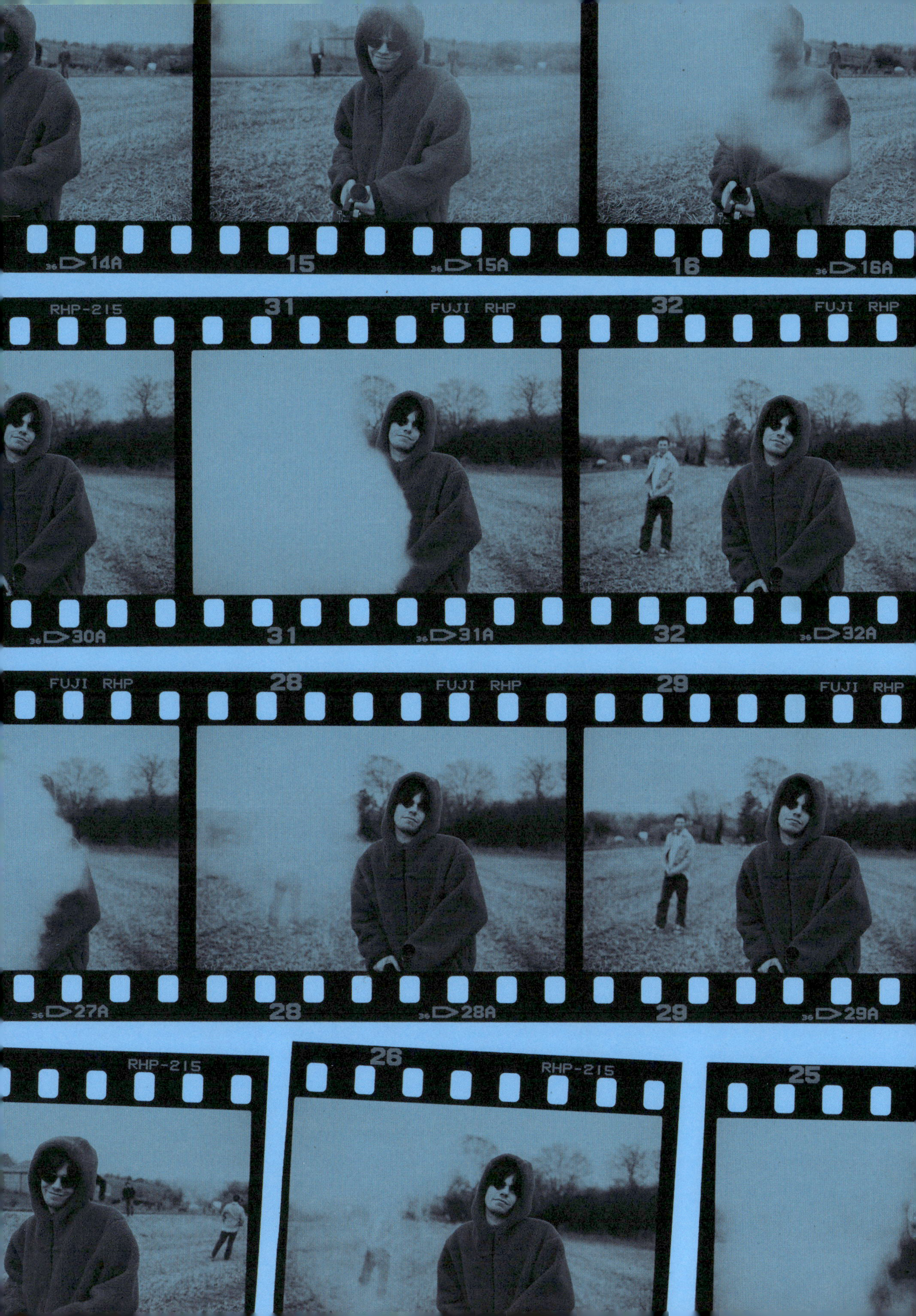

14A
15
15A
16
16A
RHP-215
31
FUJI RHP
32
FUJI RHP
30A
31
31A
32
32A
FUJI RHP
28
FUJI RHP
29
FUJI RHP
27A
28
28A
29
29A
RHP-215
26
RHP-215
25

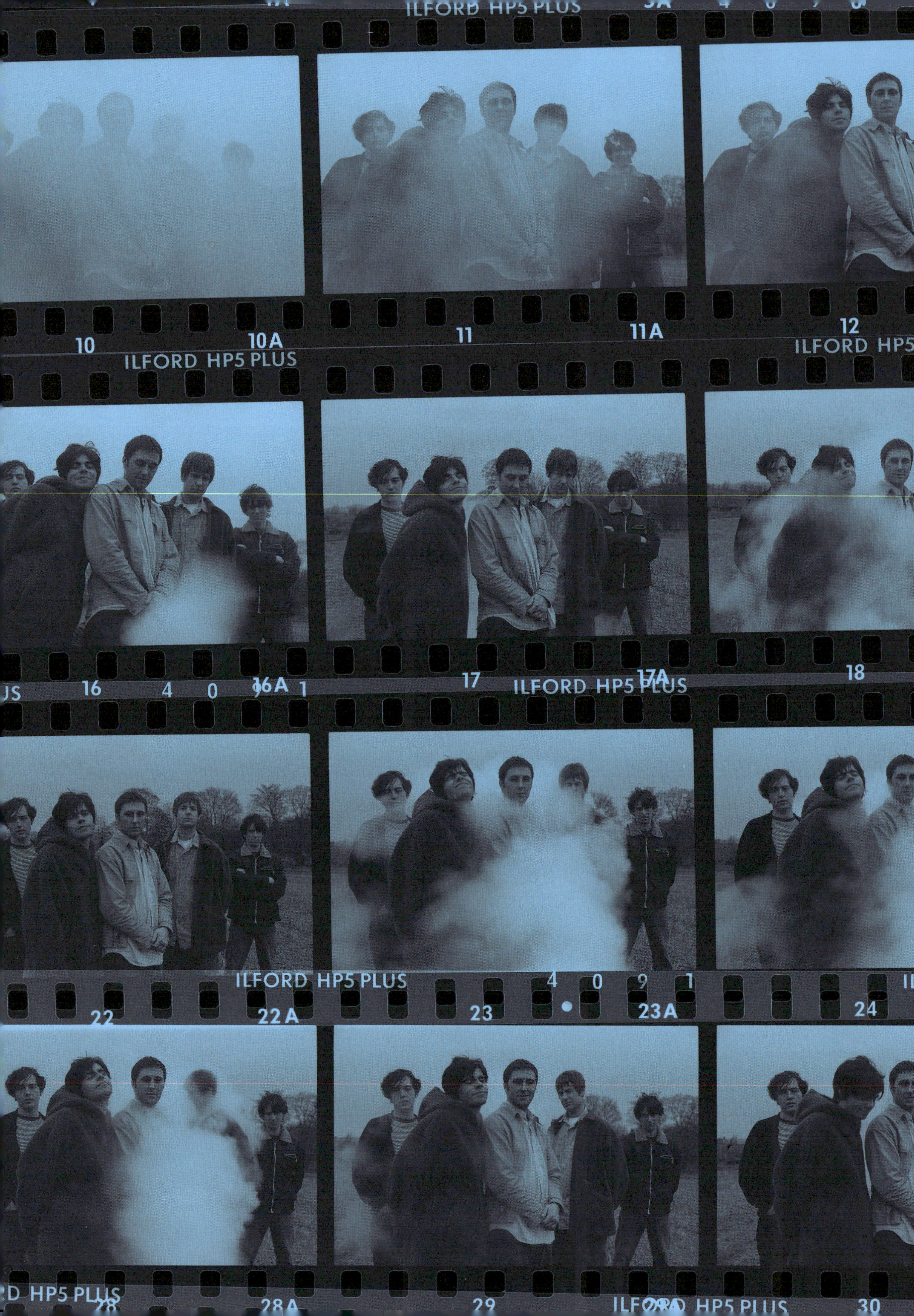
ILFORD HP5 PLUS
10
10A
11
11A
12
ILFORD HP5 PLUS
ILFORD HP5
16
16A
17
ILFORD HP5 PLUS
17A
18
ILFORD HP5 PLUS
22
22 A
23
23 A
24
D HP5 PLUS
28A
29
30